PENGUIN BOOKS

VANITY FAIR'S WRITERS ON WRITERS

GRAYDON CARTER has been the editor of *Vanity Fair* since 1992.

DAVID FRIEND is *Vanity Fair*'s editor of creative development.

ALSO FROM *VANITY FAIR*

Vanity Fair's *Hollywood*

Oscar Night: 75 Years of Hollywood Parties

Vanity Fair *The Portraits*

Vanity Fair's *Tales of Hollywood*

Vanity Fair's *Proust Questionnaire*

Vanity Fair's *Presidential Profiles*

The Great Hangover: 21 Tales of the New Recession

Vanity Fair *100 Years*

Bohemians, Bootleggers, Flappers, and Swells: The Best of Early Vanity Fair

Vanity Fair's Writers on Writers

Edited by

Graydon Carter

with an Introduction by

David Friend

PENGUIN BOOKS

PENGUIN BOOKS

An imprint of Penguin Random House LLC
375 Hudson Street
New York, New York 10014
penguin.com

ISBN 9780143111764

Printed in the United States of America
1   3   5   7   9   10   8   6   4   2

Set in Adobe Garamond with Vintage and Futura Display
Designed by Elke Sigal

CONTENTS

A Family Affair

Behind the Best-sellers

Memoir

A Final Tale

INK IN OUR VEINS

By David Friend

Literature runs in *Vanity Fair*'s veins.

"Vanity Fair," for starters, was the name of a fictional festival in John Bunyan's *The Pilgrim's Progress* (1678), a nonstop, year-round debauch that attracted hedonistic rascals and swells. (Bunyan took a dim view of all this.) One hundred and seventy years later, William Makepeace Thackeray adopted the term as the title of his most famous novel, which satirized social climbers in Victorian England. When *Vanity Fair*—the American magazine—came along in 1914 it was immediately a hothouse for literary talent, and among the first people hired by its fabled first editor, Frank Crowninshield, were writers destined for prominent careers. There was P. G. Wodehouse, *V.F.*'s theater critic and most prolific columnist. And Dorothy Parker (*page 3*), who wrote everything from poetry to famously scathing reviews of Broadway plays. And her pal Robert Benchley, who served as an editor while polishing his chops as a humorist.

For twenty-two years—until *Vanity Fair* suspended publication—many of the finest writers of the day walked the magazine's corridors (first on West 44th Street, and then in the Graybar Building, next to Grand Central Station). Frequent contributors included Alexander Woollcott and Sherwood Anderson, Aldous Huxley and Edna St. Vincent Millay, Colette and D. H. Lawrence, Paul Gallico and Janet Flanner. Noël Coward sold his first work in America (a short satire) to *V.F.*—at the age of twenty-one. A. A. Milne gained international renown when the magazine ran his first children's poem, "Vespers." Not a half-bad bunch.

In 1936, the magazine, a casualty of the Depression, went on a hiatus—for five decades. But when it was relaunched, in 1983, its founders—Condé Nast chairman S. I. Newhouse, Jr., and editorial director Alexander Liberman—set a high bar for serious prose. *Vanity Fair*'s inaugural editor, Richard Locke, was brought over from *The New York Times Book Review*. His successor, Leo Lerman, was a swami of high culture who had a Rolodex like a Ferris wheel. In succession, Locke and Lerman commissioned stories from writers of every ilk: Gore Vidal and Gloria Emerson, Carlos Fuentes and Paul Theroux, Jan Morris and Robert

Stone. Covers featured Philip Roth, Susan Sontag, and Italo Calvino. And as the decade progressed, editor Tina Brown brought on contributors such as Martin Amis (*pages 77 and 196*), Gail Sheehy, Norman Mailer (*page 104*), Walker Percy, and George Plimpton. Little wonder that *Vanity Fair* would take home its share of National Magazine Awards, including for powerful pieces by Francine du Plessix Gray (on Klaus Barbie, the Gestapo's "Butcher of Lyons") and William Styron (on his battles with depression, *page 371*).

. . .

Graydon Carter arrived as *Vanity Fair*'s editor in 1992, intent on broadening the magazine's literary and journalistic footprint. On his watch, *Vanity Fair* has continued to publish many of the most compelling voices in American letters. Sometimes we cover the back stories: "the making of" classic books. At other times we focus on the craft of writing or on the publishing trade in the digital age or on messy literary feuds and scandals. And with regularity, as this collection makes plain, we assign writers to explore the life and work of other word-smiths, from novelists to poets to correspondents to mandarins of the publishing world, knowing, in our bones, that the life of every storyteller brims with reve-latory tales—and guided by a common-sense rule often attributed to Mark Twain: "Write what you know."

Herein, then, are the best pieces *about* writers from the modern-era magazine—forty-three essays from the past thirty-three years. Taken together, they speak volumes about the wonder and richness of the Writer's Life: a life lived doubly, both *in* the world and *outside* of the world, as James Joyce described it when envisioning a creator above his handiwork, looking down and "paring his fingernails."

When our friend and colleague Christopher Hitchens (*pages 3 and 334*), a contributor to *Vanity Fair* for two decades, passed away in 2011, Salman Rushdie wrote about him in the magazine (*page 222*), describing a snapshot taken of the two of them standing on either side of a bust of Voltaire: "That photograph is now one of my most treasured possessions: me and the two Voltaires, one of stone and one still very much alive. Now they are both gone, and one can only try to believe, as the philosopher Pangloss insisted to Candide in the elder Vol-taire's masterpiece, that everything is for the best 'in this best of all possible worlds.'"

It's a great life, the writer's life. So, too, the life of the reader.

Please, have at it.

ONE *VANITY FAIR* CONTRARIAN FONDLY RECALLS ANOTHER

··

DOROTHY PARKER

REBEL IN EVENING CLOTHES

by Christopher Hitchens

OCTOBER 1999

In the fall of 1914, as Europe was marching over the precipice, Miss Dorothy Rothschild of New York wrote a poem entitled "Any Porch," and sent it off to *Vanity Fair* editor Frank Crowninshield. It was a nine-stanza lampoon, satirizing the hotel-porch babble of spoiled upper-crust ladies in Connecticut, and its acceptance, for an emolument of $12, marked the first time that the future Dorothy Parker got anything into print:

> "My husband says, often, 'Elise,
> You feel things too deeply, you do—'"
> "Yes, forty a month, if you please,
> Oh, servants impose on me, too."
> "I don't want the vote for myself,
> But women with property, dear—"
> "I think the poor girl's on the shelf,
> She's talking about her 'career.'"

Crowninshield—the granduncle of Benjamin Crowninshield Bradlee, late of *The Washington Post*—soon after hired Miss Rothschild for Condé Nast and thereby enabled her to quit her day job as a pianist at a Manhattan dance school. This was an odd alliance, between the cultivated and immaculate super-Wasp Crowninshield, who combined fashion-plate tastes with an interest in Picasso, and the daughter of an ambitious sweatshop artist in the New York Garment District. From then on, young Dorothy divided her time agreeably enough between writing suggestive fashion captions for *Vogue* and incendiary verses for *Vanity Fair*. The fashion lines had an edge to them—"Brevity is the soul of lingerie," she wrote, and also: "There was a little girl who had a little curl, right in the middle of her forehead. When she was good she was very very good, and when she was bad she wore this divine nightdress of rose-colored mousseline de soie, trimmed with frothy Valenciennes lace."

This sort of thing was a revenge for the detested convent school to which her upwardly mobile parents had insisted upon sending her. The poetry, though, was sometimes so subversive that Mr. Crowninshield had to publish it under the pseudonym "Henriette Rousseau." Composed in free verse rather than conventional stanzas, they included "Women: A Hate Song" ("I hate Women. They get on my Nerves"). There was also a pungent prose article, "Why I Haven't Married," in which it was the turn of the male sex to get the treatment. There was another poem with the "Hate Song" title, from 1919, subtitled "An Intimate Glimpse of *Vanity Fair*—En Famille." (You can read it here.) It began and ended with the italicized cry "*I hate the office; / It cuts in on my social life.*" Here one encountered such figures as:

> . . . the Boss;
> The Great White Chief.
> He made us what we are to-day,—
> I hope he's satisfied.
> He has some bizarre ideas
> About his employees getting to work
> At nine o'clock in the morning,—
> As if they were a lot of milkmen.
> He has never been known to see you
> When you arrive at 8:45,
> But try to come in at a quarter past ten
> And he will always go up in the elevator with you.
> He goes to Paris on the slightest provocation
> And nobody knows why he has to stay there so long.

(To this, one can only add, How different, how very different, is the style of our own dear *rédacteur en chef*.) Crowninshield was a stuffy man in some ways, but we owe him a debt of gratitude because it was he who kept Mrs. Parker—she married in 1917—in work, he who introduced her to Robert Benchley and Robert Sherwood and caused them to become friends and colleagues, and he who had the inspired idea of giving her P. G. Wodehouse's old job as *Vanity Fair*'s theater critic, when "Plum" took himself off to write musical comedies in collaboration with Jerome Kern and Guy Bolton. Mr. Benchley once observed that the joy of being a *Vanity Fair* contributor was this: you could write about any subject you liked, no matter how outrageous, as long as you said it in evening clothes. I have devoted my professional life to the emulation of this fine line.

· · ·

I never knew Mrs. Parker, but I did know Jessica Mitford, whose life in some ways reminds me of Parker's: refugee from a perfectly ghastly family; champion of the oppressed; implacable foe of the bores. Once, during Mitford's days in the Deep South as a partisan of civil rights, "Decca" was taken to an all-white garden party by her friend Virginia Durr. Introduced to the head of the local board of education, she sweetly confided that in Oakland, California, where she lived, the student honor roll was led by blacks. "It don't seem to make no sense, do it?" said the sturdy segregationist. "To me it do," retorted Decca, sweeping away as the education boss wilted like a salted snail. The crisp one-line comeback is among the least ephemeral things in the world.

People revere and remember Mrs. Parker's work to this day, for its epigrams and multiple entendres and for its terse, brittle approach to the long littleness of life. There's a tendency to forget, though, that the "edge" and the acuity came from an acidulated approach to stupidity and bigotry and cruelty. Much of this awareness originated in her family life; as the youngest of two brothers and two sisters she was the keenest in observing the difference between their uptown life and the dismal condition of those who toiled in the apparel industry. As, in 1939, she was to tell the readers of *New Masses*—arguably the least brittle and witty magazine ever to be published on American soil:

> I think I knew first what side I was on when I was about five years old, at which time nobody was safe from buffaloes. It was in a brownstone house in New York, and there was a blizzard, and my rich aunt—a horrible woman then and now—had come to visit. I remember going to the window and seeing the street with the men shovelling snow; their hands were purple on their shovels, and their feet were wrapped with burlap. And my aunt, looking over my shoulder, said, "Now isn't it nice there's this blizzard. All those men have work." And I knew then that it was not nice that men could work for their lives only in desperate weather, that there was no work for them when it was fair.

The word "fair" is beautifully deployed there, I think. Even when she was writing for *New Masses* (the Communist-dominated mutation of the old Greenwich Village *The Masses,* which had been associated with John Reed and Max Eastman), Mrs. Parker did not forsake her habit of stretching like a feline and then whipping out with a murderous paw. (Of some superior-minded socialists she used to know, she wrote: "Some of them are dead. And the rest are liberals, too.")

So that a life apparently consecrated to Broadway and the speakeasy and (oh God, not all that again) the Algonquin Hotel, with its celebrated Round Table and matching circle of wits—George S. Kaufman and Alexander Woollcott predominating—was also a life, as she phrased it, "wild with the knowledge of injustice and brutality and misrepresentation." And in 1927 she married her two styles—deadly perfect-pitch eavesdropping and cold contempt for prejudice—in a story entitled "Arrangement in Black and White." It opens like this: "The woman with the pink velvet poppies wreathed round the assisted gold of her hair traversed the crowded room at an interesting gait combining a skip with a sidle . . ."

Rather like her first poem, "Any Porch," much of Mrs. Parker's story is over-heard dialogue, made up of mingled inanity and condescension. The vapid woman of "assisted gold" hair is bent on meeting the "colored" singer who is the social lion of the evening. Yet she worries what her husband may think:

> But I must say for Burton, he's heaps broader-minded than lots of these Southerners. He's really awfully fond of colored people. Well, he says himself, he wouldn't have white servants. And you know, he had this old colored nurse, this regular old nigger mammy, and he just simply loves her. Why, every time he goes home, he goes out in the kitchen to see her. He does, really, to this day.

There are some moments of superb dryness to offset the electrifying embar-rassment, as when the woman gushingly asks her host, "Aren't I terrible?," and he replies, "Oh, no, no, no. No, no." Or when she asks:

"There are some bad white people, too, in this world. Aren't there?"

"I guess there are," said her host.

It's a fairly short story, but it seems longer—as moments of gross social bêtise always do—because the female character just cannot put a foot right. (When she eventually meets the black singer, she speaks "with great distinctness, moving her lips meticulously, as if in parlance with the deaf.") Viewed from more than seven decades later, it seems at moments a little obvious, until one remembers those seven decades and their passage, and the fact that Jim Crow—legally enforced segregation in everything from trains to the armed forces—was the unchallenged rule in 1927, and until one appreciates that Mrs. Parker had anticipated every agonized, patron-izing person who was ever to speak of the African-American and his divine sense of rhythm. Indeed, she was four decades ahead of *Guess Who's Coming to Dinner*.

She was also four decades away from her own death. "But I shall stay the way I am," she wrote in 1925. "Because I do not give a damn." In consequence, partly, of her non-damn donation policy, her end wasn't as sweet as it might have been. Lonely, except for her dog, Troy, and a bit sour, and a touch too fond of the pre-noon cocktail, she hung on in the Volney residential hotel in New York—within dog-walking dis-tance of Central Park and full of the sort of idle women she had always despised—and continued to make biting remarks to a diminishing audience. She was habitually hopeless about money, and her friends were surprised, after her demise, to find that she had bothered to make a will at all. But in 1965, feeling herself wasting away, she had summoned a lawyer named Oscar Bernstien and drawn up a very simple document. Her shares of common stock in *The New Yorker* (given to her by editor Harold Ross), her savings accounts, and her copyrights and royalties, she instructed him, were to go to the Reverend Martin Luther King. In the event of his death, they would be bequeathed to the National Association for the Advancement of Colored People (N.A.A.C.P.). Oscar Bernstien's widow, Rebecca, later said, "He understood completely what she had in mind. It seemed natural because she had no heirs, and racial injustice had always affected her very deeply." Having made these simple provisions—and meanwhile appointing Lillian Hellman as her literary executor—she told Zero Mostel that the least she could do now was die.

But this she didn't do until June 7, 1967. The Reverend Dr. King was chairing a meeting of the Southern Christian Leadership Conference, in an Atlanta restaurant called B. B. Beamon's, when he received the news of the bequest. It didn't amount to all that much—$20,448.39 after deductions—but at 1967 prices it caused him to tell his executive that it "verifies what I have always said, that the Lord will provide." At that moment, he had less than a year to live himself.

Mrs. Parker had stipulated that she be cremated, with no funeral service of any kind, and she nearly got her wish. Lillian Hellman organized a memorial at which she herself was the star attraction, and seems to have lost or destroyed all of her friend's remaining papers. The cremation, though, did take place.

"Excuse my dust" had been Mrs. Parker's jokey all-purpose epitaph. But the laugh was on her. Lillian Hellman sent her ashes to the law firm of Oscar Bernstien and Paul O'Dwyer, and Mr. O'Dwyer, one of New York's greatest people's attorneys and labor defenders, receiving no instructions about their disposal or their disposition, kept them in a filing cabinet in his office for two decades. There is only one plausible explanation for this amazingly unaesthetic outcome, and that is the vindictiveness of Lillian Hellman—surely one of the least attractive women produced by the American "progressive" culture in this century. Furious at not having been named owner of the estate, she contested the transfer of the rights from Dr. King to the N.A.A.C.P. A court ruled in favor of the organization, causing Ms. Hellman to explode with irritation and to speak with almost as much condescension as the frothy lady in "Arrangement in Black and White." "It's one thing to have real feeling for black people," she expostulated, "but to have the kind of blind sentimentality about the N.A.A.C.P., a group so conservative that even many blacks now don't have any respect for it, is something else." To her playwright friend Howard Teichmann, according to Marion Meade's surpassingly good Parker biography, *What Fresh Hell Is This?*, Hellman raged about Mrs. Parker's alleged promise that "when she died, she would leave me the rights to her writing. At my death, they would pass directly to the N.A.A.C.P. But what did she do? She left them to the N.A.A.C.P. Damn her!" (To the present day, those who want to reprint Mrs. Parker have to go to the N.A.A.C.P. and discuss royalties: a perfect posthumous revenge from two points of view.)

That period of spitefulness and neglect came to its close in October 1988, when Benjamin Hooks of the N.A.A.C.P. became aware that Mrs. Parker's remains had no resting-place except for a dank filing cabinet. A small memorial garden was prepared on the grounds of the organization's national headquarters in Baltimore, and a brief ceremony was held at which Mr. Hooks improved somewhat on the terse line about "excuse my dust." It might be better, he said, to recall her lines from "Epitaph for a Darling Lady":

> *Leave for her a red young rose*
> *Go your way, and save your pity.*
> *She is happy, for she knows*
> *That her dust is very pretty.*

Mrs. Parker had never been very affirmatively Jewish—she disliked her father's piety and always insisted that her hatred of Hitler and Fascism was, so to say, secular—but Mr. Hooks took the opportunity to stress the historic comradeship between blacks and Jews. The inscription at the little memorial reads:

> Here lie the ashes of Dorothy Parker (1893–1967) Humorist, writer, critic, defender of human and civil rights. For her epitaph she suggested "Excuse My Dust". This memorial garden is dedicated to her noble spirit which celebrated the oneness of humankind, and to the bonds of everlasting friendship between black and Jewish people.

This rather affecting gesture drew little publicity at the time. And black-Jewish relations were not exactly flourishing in the late 1980s. A few years ago, when I was in Baltimore to visit the H. L. Mencken Library, I heard about the Parker monument and made a brief detour-cum-pilgrimage. I was sad to find the garden slightly neglected, and some of the staff unaware that it was even there. But the N.A.A.C.P. was undergoing a dismal interlude then, with its executive director, the Reverend Ben Chavis, accused of diverting its hard-won funds to pay off his mistress. (He has since changed names and identities and sought relief in the "ministry" of Louis Farrakhan.)

On my most recent visit, in June of this year, things were already looking up. I was greeted by Ms. Chris Mencken, one of the N.A.A.C.P.'s staffers, whose grandfather's second cousin was the sage of Baltimore himself. (H. L. Mencken, indeed, published several of Mrs. Parker's early stories in *The Smart Set*, the middlebrow-baiting review that he edited with George Jean Nathan. But that didn't prevent her, when they met in Baltimore in 1924, from walking out when he took too many drinks and began to give off slurring jokes about black people.) Ms. Mencken, whose presence seemed like a sort of ideal recompense for that spoiled evening, had just finished sweeping up around the memorial. It stands in a small grove of pines, which could be mistaken for a circle of listeners. The plaque with the above inscription sits on a cylindrical urn which contains the ashes. The whole is set in three circular courses of brown brickwork. Harry G. Robinson, then dean of the School of Architecture at Howard University, was given the commission for the memorial and wrote that it was intended to symbolize the center of a Round Table.

With America's most venerable civil-rights organization until recently facing bankruptcy and other sorts of discredit, it has been a time for volunteers. Mrs. Myrlie Evers-Williams, widow of the civil-rights martyr Medgar Evers, first stepped forward to assume responsibility. So did former congressman Kweisi Mfume, and so did Julian Bond, the brilliant Georgian activist and orator who was a student of Dr. King's. As the N.A.A.C.P. itself "came back" from an interval of decline, and as Bond and others began to speak back boldly against the black separatist demagogues (and the mealymouthed senators and congressmen who would not disown the so-called Council of Conservative Citizens), I had a tiny idea. I wrote to Julian Bond, proposing that Mrs. Parker's memorial garden be refurbished and re-dedicated. (One hopes that she, who so despised the church, would "excuse" the fact that the N.A.A.C.P. building is a converted nunnery.) By this means, I thought we could do honor to one of *Vanity Fair*'s founding minxes, and also to the brave causes that she upheld so tenaciously. Julian Bond right away agreed it was a sound scheme, so we're going to have a little party to celebrate said scheme. I would modestly propose adding a line of Mrs. Parker's from 1939, about the misery and bigotry she saw around her: "I knew it need not be so; I think I knew even then that it would eventually not be so." These are only words, and this is only a gesture, but as Mrs. Parker proved somewhat to her own surprise, there is power in words, and in gestures too.

ON POETS

W. H. AUDEN

A PASSION OF POETS

by Joseph Brodsky

OCTOBER 1983

"Time . . . worships language and forgives
Everyone by whom it lives . . ."
—W. H. AUDEN

I

When a writer resorts to a language other than his mother tongue, he does so either out of necessity, like Conrad, or because of burning ambition, like Nabokov, or for the sake of greater estrangement, like Beckett. Belonging to a different league, in the summer of 1977, in New York, after living in this country for five years, I purchased in a small typewriter shop on Sixth Avenue a portable "Lettera 22" and set out to write (essays, translations, occasionally a poem) in English for a reason that had very little to do with the above. My sole purpose then, as it is now, was to find myself in closer proximity to the man whom I considered the greatest mind of the twentieth century: Wystan Auden.

I was, of course, perfectly aware of the futility of my undertaking, not so much because I was born in Russia and into its language (which I'll never abandon—and I hope vice versa) as because of this poet's intelligence, which in my view has no equal. I was aware of the futility of this effort, moreover, because Auden had been dead four years then. Yet to my mind, writing in English was the best way to get near him, to work on his terms, to be judged if not by his code of conscience, then by whatever it is in the English language that made this code of conscience possible.

These words, the very structure of these sentences, all show anyone who has read a single stanza or a single paragraph of Auden's how I fail. But, to me a failure by his standards is preferable to a success by others'. Besides, I knew from the threshold that I was bound to fail; whether this sort of sobriety is my own or has been borrowed from his writing, I can no longer tell. All I hope for while writing in his tongue is that I won't lower his level of mental operation, his plane of regard. This is as much as one can do for a better man: to continue in his vein; this, I think, is what civilizations are all about.

I knew that by temperament and otherwise, I was a different man, and that in the best case possible I'd be regarded as his imitator. Still, for me that would be a compliment. Also I had a second line of defense: I could always pull back to my writing in Russian, of which I was pretty confident and which even he, had he known the language, probably would have liked. My desire to write in English had nothing to do with any sense of confidence, contentment, or comfort; it was simply a desire to please a shadow. Of course, where he was by then, linguistic barriers hardly mattered, but somehow I thought that he might like it better if I made myself clear to him in English. (Although when I tried, on the green grass at Kirchstetten eleven years ago now, it didn't work; the English I had at that time was better for reading and listening than for speaking. Perhaps just as well.)

To put it differently, unable to return the full amount of what has been given, one tries to pay back at least in the same coin. After all, he did so himself, borrowing the "Don Juan" stanza for his "Letter to Lord Byron" or hexameters for his "Shield of Achilles." Courtship always requires a degree of self-sacrifice and assimilation, all the more so if one is courting a pure spirit. While in flesh, this man did so much that belief in the immortality of his soul becomes unavoidable. What he left us with amounts to a gospel which is both brought about by and filled with love that's anything but finite—with love, that is, which can in no way all be harbored by human flesh and which therefore needs words. If there were no churches, one could have easily built one upon this poet, and its main precept would run something like his

> *If equal affection cannot be,*
> *Let the more loving one be me.*

II

. . . .

If a poet has any obligation toward society, it is to write well. Being in the minority, he has no other choice. Failing this duty, he sinks into oblivion. Society, on the other hand, has no obligation toward the poet. A majority by definition, society thinks of itself as having other options than reading verses, no matter how well written. Its failure to do so results in its sinking to that level of locution by which society falls easy prey to a demagogue or a tyrant. This is society's equivalent of oblivion; a tyrant, of course, may try to save his society from it by some spectacular bloodbath.

I first read Auden some twenty years ago in Russia in rather limp and listless translations that I found in an anthology of contemporary English poetry sub-titled "From Browning to Our Days." "Our Days" were those of 1937, when the volume was published. Needless to say, almost the entire body of its translators along with its editor, M. Gutner, were arrested soon afterward, and many of them perished. Needless to say, for the next forty years no other anthology of contemporary English poetry was published in Russia, and the said volume became something of a collector's item.

One line of Auden in that anthology, however, caught my eye. It was, as I learned later, from the last stanza of his early poem "No Change of Place," which described a somewhat claustrophobic landscape where "no one goes / Further than railhead or the ends of piers, / Will neither go nor send his son . . ." This last bit, "Will neither go nor send his son . . ." struck me with its mixture of negative extension and common sense. Having been brought up on an essentially em-phatic and self-asserting diet of Russian verse, I was quick to register this recipe whose main component was self-restraint. Still, poetic lines have a knack of straying from the context into universal significance, and the threatening touch of absurdity contained in "Will neither go nor send his son" would start vi-brating in the back of my mind whenever I'd set out to do something on paper.

This is, I suppose, what they call an influence, except that the sense of the absurd is never an invention of the poet but is a reflection of reality; inventions are seldom recognizable. What one may owe here to the poet is not the sentiment itself but its treatment: quiet, unemphatic, without any pedal, almost *en passant*. This treatment was especially significant to me precisely because I came across this line in the early '60s, when the Theater of the Absurd was in full swing. Against that background, Auden's handling of the subject stood out not only because he had beaten a lot of people to the punch but because of a considerably different ethical message. The way he handled the line was telling, at least to me: something like "Don't cry wolf" even though the wolf's at the door. (Even though, I would add, it looks exactly like you. Especially because of that, don't cry wolf.)

Although for a writer to mention his penal experiences—or for that matter, any kind of hardship—is like dropping names for normal folk, it so happened that my next opportunity to pay a closer look at Auden occurred while I was doing my own time in the North, in a small village lost among swamps and forests, near the polar circle. This time the anthology that I had was in English, sent to me by a friend from Moscow. It had quite a lot of Yeats, whom I then found a bit too oratorical and sloppy with meters, and Eliot, who in those days reigned supreme in Eastern Europe. I was intending to read Eliot.

But by pure chance the book opened to Auden's "In Memory of W. B. Yeats." I was young then and therefore particularly keen on elegies as a genre, having nobody around dying to write one for. So I read them perhaps more avidly than anything else, and I frequently thought that the most interesting feature of the genre was the authors' unwitting attempts at self-portrayal with which nearly every poem "in memoriam" is strewn—or soiled. Understandable though this tendency is, it often turns such a poem into the author's ruminations on the subject of death from which we learn more about him than about the deceased. The Auden poem had none of this; what's more, I soon realized that even its structure was designed to pay tribute to the dead poet, imitating in a reverse order the great Irishman's own modes of stylistic development, all the way down to his earliest: the trimeters of the poem's third—last—part.

It's because of these trimeters, in particular because of eight lines from this third part, that I understood what kind of poet I was reading. These lines overshadowed for me that astonishing description of "the dark cold day," Yeats's last, with its shuddering

The mercury sank in the mouth of the dying day.

They overshadowed that unforgettable rendition of the stricken body as a city whose suburbs and squares are gradually emptying as if after a crushed rebellion. They overshadowed even that statement of the era

. . . poetry makes nothing happen . . .

They, those eight lines in trimeter that made this third part of the poem sound like a cross between a Salvation Army hymn, a funeral dirge, and a nursery rhyme, went like this:

> *Time that is intolerant*
> *Of the brave and innocent,*
> *And indifferent in a week*
> *To a beautiful physique,*
>
> *Worships language and forgives*
> *Everyone by whom it lives;*
> *Pardons cowardice, conceit,*
> *Lays its honours at their feet.*

I remember sitting there in the small wooden shack, peering through the square porthole-size window at the wet, muddy dirt road with a few stray chickens on it, half believing what I'd just read, half wondering whether my grasp of English wasn't playing tricks on me. I had there a veritable boulder of an English-Russian dictionary, and I went through its pages time and again, checking every word, every allusion, hoping that they might spare me the meaning that stared at me from the page. I guess I was simply refusing to believe that way back in 1939 an English poet had said, "Time . . . worships language," and yet the world around was still what it was.

But for once the dictionary didn't overrule me. Auden had indeed said that time (not *the* time) worships language, and the train of thought that statement set in motion in me is still trundling to this day. For "worship" is an attitude of the lesser toward the greater. If time worships language, it means that language is greater, or older, than time, which is, in its turn, older and greater than space. That was how I was taught, and I indeed felt that way. So if time—which is synonymous with, nay, even absorbs deity—worships language, where then does language come from? For the gift is always smaller than the giver. And then isn't language a repository of time? And isn't this why time worships it? And isn't a song, or a poem, or indeed a speech itself, with its caesuras, pauses, spondees, and so forth, a game language plays to restructure time? And aren't those by whom language "lives" those by whom time does too? And if time "forgives" them, does it do so out of generosity or out of necessity? And isn't generosity a necessity anyhow?

Short and horizontal as those lines were, they seemed to me incredibly vertical. They were also very much offhand, almost chatty: metaphysics disguised as common sense, common sense disguised as nursery rhyme couplets. These layers of disguise alone were telling me what language is, and I realized that I was reading a poet who spoke the truth—or through whom the truth made itself audible. At least it felt more like truth than anything else I managed to figure out in that anthology. And perhaps it felt that way precisely because of the touch of irrelevance that I sensed in the falling intonation of "forgives / Everyone by whom it lives; / Pardons cowardice, conceit, / Lays its honours at their feet." These words were there, I thought, simply to offset the upward gravity of "Time . . . worships language."

I could go on and on about these lines, but I could do so only now. Then and there I was simply stunned. Among other things, what became clear to me was that one should watch out when Auden makes his witty comments and observations, keeping an eye on civilization no matter what his immediate subject (or condition) is. I felt that I was dealing with a new kind of metaphysical poet, a man of terrific lyrical gifts, who disguised himself as an observer of public mores. And my suspicion was that this choice of mask, the choice of this idiom, had to do less with matters of style and tradition than with the personal humility imposed on him not so much by a particular creed as by his sense of the nature of language. Humility is never chosen.

I had yet to read my Auden. Still, after "In Memory of W.B. Yeats," I knew that I was facing an author more humble than Yeats or Eliot, with a soul less petulant than either, while, I was afraid, no less tragic. With the benefit of hindsight I may say now that I wasn't altogether wrong, and that if there was ever any drama in Auden's voice, it wasn't his own personal drama but a public or existential one. He'd never put himself in the center of the tragic picture; at best he'd acknowledge his presence at the scene. I had yet to hear from his very mouth that "J. S. Bach was terribly lucky. When he wanted to praise the Lord, he'd write a chorale or a cantata addressing the Almighty directly. Today, if a poet wishes to do the same thing, he has to employ indirect speech." The same, presumably, would apply to prayer.

III

················

As I write these notes, I notice the first person singular popping its ugly head up with alarming frequency. But man is what he reads; in other words, spotting this pronoun, I detect Auden more than anybody else: the aberration simply reflects the proportion of my reading of this poet. Old dogs, of course, won't learn new tricks, but dog owners end up resembling their dogs. Critics, and especially biographers, of writers with a distinctive style often adopt, however unconsciously, their subjects' mode of expression. To put it simply, one is changed by what one loves, sometimes to the point of losing one's entire identity. I am not trying to say that this is what happened to me; all I seek to suggest is that these otherwise tawdry I's and me's are, in their own turn, forms of indirect speech whose object is Auden.

For those of my generation who were interested in poetry in English—and I can't claim there were too many of them—the '60s was the era of anthologies. On the way home, foreign students and scholars who'd come to Russia on academic exchange programs would understandably try to rid themselves of extra weight, and books of poetry were first to go. They'd sell them, almost for nothing, to secondhand bookstores, which subsequently would charge extraordinary sums if you wanted to buy them. The rationale behind these prices was quite simple: to deter the locals from purchasing these Western items; as for the foreigner himself, he would obviously be gone and unable to see the disparity.

Still, if you knew a salesperson, as one who frequents a place inevitably does, you could strike the sort of deal every book-hunting person is familiar with: you'd trade one thing for another, or two or three books for one, or you'd buy a book, read it, and return it to the store and get your money back. Besides, by the time I was released and returned to my hometown, I'd gotten myself some sort of reputation, and in several bookstores they treated me rather nicely. Because of this reputation, students from the exchange programs would sometimes visit me, and as one is not supposed to cross a strange threshold empty-handed, they'd bring books. With some of these visitors I struck up close friendships, because of which my bookshelves gained considerably.

I liked them very much, these anthologies, and not for their contents only but also for the sweetish smell of their bindings and their pages edged in yellow.

They felt so American and were indeed pocket-size. You could pull them out of your pocket in a streetcar or in a public garden, and even though the text would be only a half or a third comprehensible, they'd instantly obliterate the local reality. My favorites, though, were Louis Untermeyer's and Oscar Williams's— because they had pictures of their contributors that filled one's imagination in no less a way than the lines themselves. For hours on end I would sit scrutinizing a smallish, black-and-white box with this or that poet's features, trying to figure out what kind of person he was, trying to animate him, to match the face with his half or a third understood lines. Later on, in the company of friends we would exchange our wild surmises and the snatches of gossip that occasionally came our way and, having developed a common denominator, pronounce our verdict. Again with the benefit of hindsight, I must say that frequently our divinations were not too far off.

That was how I first saw Auden's face. It was a terribly reduced photograph— a bit studied, with a too didactic handling of shadow: it said more about the photographer than about his model. From that picture, one would have to conclude either that the former was a naive aesthete or the latter's features were too neutral for his occupation. I preferred the second version, partly because neutrality of tone was very much a feature of Auden's poetry, partly because anti-heroic posture was the *idée fixe* of our generation. The idea was to look like everybody else: plain shoes, workman's cap, jacket and tie, preferably gray, no beards or mustaches. Wystan was recognizable.

Also recognizable to the point of giving one the shivers were the lines in "September 1, 1939," ostensibly explaining the origins of the war that had cradled my generation but in effect depicting our very selves as well, like a black-and-white snapshot in its own right.

> *I and the public know*
> *What all schoolchildren learn,*
> *Those to whom evil is done*
> *Do evil in return.*

This four-liner indeed was straying out of context, equating victors to victims, and I think it should be tattooed by the federal government on the chest of every newborn, not because of its message alone but because of its intonation. The only acceptable argument against such a procedure would be that there are better lines by Auden. What would you do with:

> *Faces along the bar*
> *Cling to their average day:*
> *The lights must never go out,*

The music must always play,
All the conventions conspire
To make this fort assume
The furniture of home;
Lest we should see where we are,
Lost in a haunted wood,
Children afraid of the night
Who have never been happy or good.

Or if you think this is too much New York, too American, then how about this couplet from "The Shield of Achilles," which, to me at least, sounds a bit like a Dantesque epitaph to a handful of East European nations:

. . . they lost their pride
And died as men before their bodies died.

Or if you are still against such a barbarity, if you want to spare the tender skin this hurt, there are seven other lines in the same poem that should be carved on the gates of every existing state, indeed on the gates of our whole world:

A ragged urchin, aimless and alone,
*   Loitered about that vacancy; a bird*
Flew up to safety from his well-aimed stone:
*   That girls are raped, that two boys knife a third,*
*   Were axioms to him, who'd never heard*
Of any world where promises were kept,
Or one could weep because another wept.

This way the new arrival won't be deceived as to this world's nature; this way the world's dweller won't take demagogues for demigods.

One doesn't have to be a gypsy or a Lombroso to believe in the relation between an individual's appearance and his deeds: this is what our sense of beauty is based on, after all. Yet how should a poet look who wrote:

Altogether elsewhere, vast
Herds of reindeer move across
Miles and miles of golden moss,
Silently and very fast.

How should a man look who was as fond of translating metaphysical verities into the pedestrian of common sense as of spotting the former in the latter? How should one look who, by going very thoroughly about creation, tells you more about the Creator than any impertinent agonist shortcutting through the spheres? Shouldn't a sensibility unique in its combination of honesty, clinical detachment, and controlled lyricism result if not in a unique arrangement of facial features then at least in a specific, uncommon expression? And could such features or such expression be captured by a brush? Registered by a camera?

I liked the process of extrapolating from that stamp-size picture very much. One always gropes for a face, one always wants an ideal to materialize, and Auden was very close at the time to amounting to an ideal. (Two others were Beckett and Frost, yet I knew the way they looked; however terrifying, the correspondence between their facades and their deeds was obvious.) Sooner or later, of course, I saw other photographs of Auden: in a smuggled magazine or in other anthologies. Still they added nothing; the man eluded lenses, or they lagged behind the man. I began to wonder whether one form of art was capable of depicting another, whether the visual could apprehend the semantic.

Then one day—I think it was in the winter of 1968 or 1969—in Moscow, Nadezhda Mandelstam, whom I was visiting there, handed me yet another anthology of modern poetry, a very handsome book generously illustrated with large black-and-white photographs done by, if I remember correctly, Rollie McKenna. I found what I was looking for. A couple of months later, somebody borrowed that book from me and I never saw the photograph again; still, I remember it rather clearly.

The picture was taken somewhere in New York, it seemed, on some overpass—either the one near Grand Central or the one at Columbia University that spans Amsterdam Avenue. Auden stood there looking as though he were caught unawares, in passage, eyebrows lifted in bewilderment. The eyes themselves, however, were terribly calm and keen. The time was, presumably, the late '40s or the beginning of the '50s, before the famous wrinkled—"unkempt bed"—stage took over his features. Everything, or almost everything, became clear to me.

The contrast or, better still, the degree of disparity between those eyebrows risen in formal bewilderment and the keenness of his gaze, to my mind, directly corresponded to the formal aspects of his lines (two lifted eyebrows = two rhymes) and to the blinding precision of their content. What stared at me from the page was the facial equivalent of a couplet, of truth that's better known by heart. The features were regular, even plain. There was nothing specifically poetic about this face, nothing Byronic, demonic, ironic, hawkish, aquiline, romantic, wounded, etc. Rather, it was the face of a physician who is interested in your story though he knows you are ill. A face well prepared for everything, a sum total of a face.

It was a result. Its blank stare was a direct product of that blinding proximity of face to object which produced expressions like "not an important failure," "necessary murder," "conservative dark," "apathetic grave," or "well-run desert." It felt like when a myopic person takes off his glasses, except that the keen-sightedness of this pair of eyes had to do with neither myopia nor the smallness of objects but with their deep-seated threats. It was the stare of a man who knew that he wouldn't be able to weed those threats out, yet who was bent on describing for you the symptoms as well as the malaise itself. That wasn't what's called "social criticism"—if only because the malaise wasn't social: it was existential.

In general, I think this man was terribly mistaken for a social commentator, or a diagnostician, or some such thing. The most frequent charge that's been leveled against him was that he didn't offer a cure. I guess in a way he asked for that by resorting to Freudian, then Marxist, then ecclesiastical terminology. The cure, though, lay precisely in his employing these terminologies, for they are simply different dialects in which one can speak about one and the same thing, which is love. It is the intonation with which one talks to the sick that cures. This poet went about the world's grave, often terminal cases not as a surgeon but as a nurse, and every patient knows that it's nurses and not incisions that eventually put one back on one's feet. It's the voice of a nurse, that is, of love, that one hears in the final speech of Alonso to Ferdinand in "The Sea and the Mirror":

> *But should you fail to keep your kingdom*
> *And, like your father before you, come*
> *Where thought accuses and feeling mocks,*
> *Believe your pain . . .*

Neither physician nor angel, nor—least of all—your beloved or relative will say this at the moment of your final defeat: only a nurse or a poet, out of experience as well as out of love.

And I marveled at that love. I knew nothing about Auden's life: neither about his being homosexual, nor about his marriage of convenience (for her) to Erika Mann, etc.—nothing. One thing I sensed quite clearly was that this love would overshoot its object. In my mind—better, in my imagination—it was love expanded or accelerated by language, by the necessity of expressing it; and language—that much I already knew—has its own dynamics and is prone, especially in poetry, to use its self-generating devices: meters and stanzas that take the poet far beyond his original destination. And the other truth about love in poetry that one gleans from reading it is that a writer's sentiments inevitably subordinate themselves to the linear and unrecoiling progression of art. This sort of thing secures, in art, a higher degree of lyricism; in life, an equivalent in isolation. If only because of his stylistic versatility, this man should have known an uncommon degree of despair, as many of his most delightful, most mesmerizing lyrics do demonstrate. For in art lightness of touch more often than not comes from the very darkness of its absence.

And yet it was love all the same, perpetuated by language, oblivious—because the language was English—to gender, furthered by the deepest agony, because agony, in the end, would have to be articulated. Language, after all, is self-conscious by definition, and it wants to get the hang of every new situation. As I looked at Rollie McKenna's picture, I felt pleased that the face there revealed neither neurotic nor any other sort of strain, that it was pale, ordinary, not expressing but instead absorbing whatever it was that was going on in front of his eyes. How marvelous it would be, I thought, to have those features, and I tried to ape the grimace in the mirror. I obviously failed, but I knew that I would fail, because such a face was bound to be one of a kind. There was no need to imitate it: it already existed in the world, and the world seemed somehow more palatable to me because this face was somewhere out there.

Strange things they are, faces of poets. In theory, authors' looks should be of no consequence to their readers: reading is not a narcissistic activity, neither is writing, yet the moment one likes a sufficient amount of a poet's verse one starts to wonder about the appearance of the writer. This, presumably, has to do with one's suspicion that to like a work of art is to recognize the truth, or the degree of it, that art expresses. Insecure by nature, we want to see the artist, whom we identify with his work, so that the next time around we might know what truth looks like in reality. Only the authors of antiquity escape this scrutiny, which is why, in part, they are regarded as classics, and their generalized marble features that dot niches in libraries are in direct relation to the absolute archetypal significance of their *oeuvre*. But when you read

> *. . . To visit*

> *The grave of a friend, to make an ugly scene,*
> *To count the loves one has grown out of,*
> *Is not nice, but to chirp like a tearless bird,*
> *As though no one dies in particular*

> *And gossip were never true, unthinkable . . .*

you begin to feel that behind these lines there stands not a blond, brunette, pale, swarthy, wrinkled, or smooth-faced concrete author but life itself; and *that* you would like to meet; that you would like to find yourself in human proximity to. Behind this wish lies not vanity but certain human physics that pull a small particle toward a big magnet, even though you may end up by echoing Auden's own: "I have known three great poets, each one a prize son of a bitch." I: Who? He: "Yeats, Frost, Bert Brecht." (Now about Brecht he was wrong: Brecht wasn't a great poet.)

IV
....

On June 6, 1972, some forty-eight hours after I had left Russia on very short notice, I stood with my friend Carl Proffer, a professor of Russian literature at the University of Michigan (who'd flown to Vienna to meet me), in front of Auden's summer house in the small village of Kirchstetten, explaining to its owner the reasons for our being there. This meeting almost didn't happen.

There are three Kirchstettens in northern Austria, and we had passed through all three and were about to turn back when the car rolled into a quiet, narrow country lane and we saw a wooden arrow saying "Audenstrasse." It was called previously (if I remember accurately) "Hinterholz" because behind the woods the lane led to the local cemetery. Renaming it had presumably as much to do with the villagers' readiness to get rid of this "memento mori" as with their respect for the great poet living in their midst. The poet regarded the situation with a mixture of pride and embarrassment. He had a clearer sentiment, though, toward the local priest, whose name was Schickelgruber: Auden couldn't resist the pleasure of addressing him as "Father Schicklgruber." [Maria Schicklgruber was the name of Hitler's grandmother.]

All that I would learn later. Meanwhile, Carl Proffer was trying to explain the reasons for our being here to a stocky, heavily perspiring man in a red shirt and broad suspenders, jacket over his arm, a pile of books underneath it. The man had just come by train from Vienna and, having climbed the hill, was short of breath and not disposed to conversation. We were about to give up when he suddenly grasped what Carl Proffer was saying, cried "Impossible!" and invited us into the house. It was Wystan Auden, and it was less than two years before he died.

Let me attempt to clarify how all this had come about. Back in 1969, George L. Kline, a professor of philosophy at Bryn Mawr, had visited me in Leningrad. Professor Kline was translating my poems into English for the Penguin edition and, as we were going over the content of the future book, he asked me whom I would ideally prefer to write the introduction. I suggested Auden—because England and Auden were then synonymous in my mind. But, then, the whole prospect of my book being published in England was quite unreal. The only thing that imparted a semblance of reality to this venture was its sheer illegality under Soviet law.

All the same, things were set in motion. Auden was given the manuscript to read and liked it enough to write an introduction. So when I reached Vienna, I was carrying with me Auden's address in Kirchstetten. Looking back and thinking about the conversations we had during the subsequent three weeks in Austria and later in London, I hear more his voice than mine, although, I must say, I grilled him quite extensively on the subject of contemporary poetry, especially about the poets themselves. Still, this was quite understandable because the only English phrase I knew I wasn't making a mistake in was "Mr. Auden, what do you think about . . ."—and the name would follow.

Perhaps it was just as well, for what could I tell him that he didn't already know one way or another? I could have told him, of course, how I had translated several poems of his into Russian and took them to a magazine in Moscow; but the year happened to be 1968, the Soviets invaded Czechoslovakia, and one night the BBC broadcast his "The Ogre does what ogres can . . ." and that was the end of this venture. (The story would perhaps have endeared me to him, but I didn't have a very high opinion of those translations anyway.) That I'd never read a successful translation of his work into any language I had some idea of? He knew that himself, perhaps all too well. That I was overjoyed to learn one day about his devotion to the Kierkegaardian triad, which for many of us too was the key to the human species? But I worried I wouldn't be able to articulate it.

It was better to listen. Because I was Russian, he'd go on about Russian writers. "I wouldn't like to live with Dostoyevsky under the same roof," he would declare. Or, "The best Russian writer is Chekhov"—"Why?" "He's the only one of your people who's got common sense." Or he would ask about the matter that seemed to perplex him most about my homeland: "I was told that the Russians always steal windshield wipers from parked cars. Why?" But my answer—because there were no spare parts—wouldn't satisfy him: he obviously had in mind a more inscrutable reason, and, having read him, I almost began to see one myself. Then he offered to translate some of my poems. This shook me considerably. Who was I to be translated by Auden? I knew that because of his translations some of my compatriots had profited more than their lines deserved; yet somehow I couldn't allow myself the thought of *him* working for *me*. So I said, "Mr. Auden, what do you think about . . . Robert Lowell?" "I don't like men," came the answer, "who leave behind them a smoking trail of weeping women."

During those weeks in Austria he looked after my affairs with the diligence of a good mother hen. To begin with, telegrams and other mail inexplicably began to arrive for me "c/o W. H. Auden." Then he wrote to the Academy of American Poets requesting that they provide me with some financial support. This was how I got my first American money—$1,000 to be precise—and it lasted me all the way to my first payday at the University of Michigan. He'd recommend me to his agent, instruct me on whom to meet and whom to avoid, introduce me to friends, shield me from journalists, and speak ruefully about having given up his flat on St. Mark's Place—as though I were planning to settle in his New York. "It would be good for you. If only because there is an Armenian church nearby, and the Mass is better when you don't understand the words. You don't know Armenian, do you?" I didn't.

Then from London came—c/o W. H. Auden—an invitation for me to participate in the Poetry International in Queen Elizabeth Hall, and we booked the same flight by British European Airways. At this point an opportunity arose for me to pay him back a little in kind. It so happened that during my stay in Vienna

I had been befriended by the Razumovsky family (descendants of the Count Razumovsky of Beethoven's Quartets). One member of that family, Olga Razumovsky, was working then for the Austrian Airlines. Having learned about W. H. Auden and myself taking the same flight to London, she called BEA and suggested they give these two passengers the royal treatment. Which we indeed received. Auden was pleased, and I was proud.

On several occasions during that time, he urged me to call him by his Christian name. Naturally I resisted—and not only because of how I felt about him as a poet but also because of the difference in our ages: Russians are terribly mindful of such things. Finally in London he said, "It won't do. Either you are going to call me Wystan, or I'll have to address you as Mr. Brodsky." This prospect sounded so grotesque to me that I gave up. "Yes, Wystan," I said. "Anything you say, Wystan." Afterward we went to the reading. He leaned on the lectern, and for a good half an hour he filled the room with the lines he knew by heart. If I ever wished for time to stop, it was then, inside that large dark room on the south bank of the Thames. Unfortunately, it didn't. Although a year later, three months before he died in an Austrian hotel, we did read together again. In the same room.

V

By that time he was almost sixty-six. "I *had* to move to Oxford. I am in good health, but I have to have somebody to look after me." As far as I could see, visiting him there in January 1973, he was looked after only by the four walls of the sixteenth-century cottage given him by the college, and by the maid. In the dining hall the members of the faculty jostled him away from the food board. I supposed that was just English school manners, boys being boys. Looking at them, however, I couldn't help recalling one more of those blinding approximations of Wystan's: "triviality of the sand."

This foolery was simply a variation on the theme of society having no obligation to a poet, especially to an old poet. That is, society would listen to a politician of comparable age, or even older, but not to a poet. There are a variety of reasons for this, ranging from anthropologic ones to the sycophantic. But the conclusion is plain and unavoidable: society has no right to complain if a politician does it in. For, as Auden once put it in his "Rimbaud,"

> But in that child the rhetorician's lie
> Burst like a pipe: the cold had made a poet.

If the lie explodes this way in "that child," what happens to it in the old man who feels the cold more acutely? Presumptuous as it may sound coming from a foreigner, the tragic achievement of Auden as a poet was precisely that he had dehydrated his verse of any sort of deception, be it a rhetorician's or a bardic one. This sort of thing alienates one not only from faculty members but also from one's fellows in the field, for in every one of us sits that red-pimpled youth thirsting for the incoherence of elevation.

Turning critic, this apotheosis of pimples would regard the absence of elevation as slackness, sloppiness, chatter, decay. It wouldn't occur to his sort that an aging poet has the right to write worse—if indeed he does—that there's nothing less palatable than unbecoming old age "discovering love" and monkey-gland transplants. Between boisterous and wise, the public will always choose the former (and not because such a choice reflects its demographic makeup or because of poets' own "romantic" habit of dying young, but because of the species' innate unwillingness to think about old age, let alone its consequences). The sad thing about this clinging to immaturity is that the condition itself is far from being permanent. Ah, if it only were! Then everything could be explained by the species' fear of death. Then all those "Selected Poems" of so many a poet would be as innocuous as the citizens of Kirchstetten rechristening their "Hinterholz." If it were only fear of death, readers and the appreciative critics especially should have been doing away with themselves nonstop, following the example of their beloved young authors. But that doesn't happen.

The real story behind our species' clinging to immaturity is much sadder. It has to do not with man's reluctance to know about death but with his not wanting to hear about life. Yet innocence is the last thing that can be sustained naturally. That's why poets—especially those who lasted long—must be read in their entirety, not in selections. The beginning makes sense only insofar as there is an end. For unlike fiction writers, poets tell us the whole story: not only in terms of their actual experiences and sentiments but—and that's what's most pertinent to us—in terms of language itself, in terms of the words they finally choose.

An aging man, if he still holds a pen, has a choice: to write memoirs or to keep a diary. By the very nature of their craft, poets are diarists. Often against their own will, they keep the most honest track of what's happening (a) to their souls, be it the expansion of a soul or—more frequently—its shrinkage, and (b) to their sense of language, for they are the first ones for whom words become compromised or devalued. Whether we like it or not, we are here to learn not just what time does to man but what language does to time. And poets, let us not forget, are the ones "by whom it [language] lives." It is this law that teaches a poet a greater rectitude than any creed is capable of.

That's why one can build a lot upon W. H. Auden. Not only because he died at twice the age of Christ or because of Kierkegaard's "principle of repetition." He simply served an infinity greater than we normally reckon with, and he bears good witness to its availability; what's more, he made it feel hospitable. To say the

least, every individual ought to know at least one poet from cover to cover: if not
as a guide through the world, then as a yardstick for the language. W. H. Auden
would do very well on both counts, if only because of their respective resem-
blances to Hell and Limbo.

He was a great poet (the only thing that's wrong with this sentence is its
tense, as the nature of language puts one's achievements within it invariably into
the present), and I consider myself immensely lucky to have met him. But had I
not met him at all, there would still be the reality of his work. One should feel
grateful to fate for having been exposed to this reality, for the lavishing of these
gifts, all the more priceless since they were not designated for anybody in particular. One may call this a generosity of the spirit, except that the spirit needs a
man to refract itself through. It's not the man who becomes sacred because of
this refraction: it's the spirit that becomes human and comprehensible. This—
and the fact that men are finite—is enough for one to worship this poet.

Whatever the reasons for which he crossed the Atlantic and became
American, the result was that he fused both idioms of English and became—to
paraphrase one of his own lines—our transatlantic Horace. One way or another,
all the journeys he took—through lands, caves of the psyche, doctrines, creeds—
served not so much to improve his argument as to expand his diction. If poetry
ever was for him a matter of ambition, he lived long enough for it to become
simply a means of existence. Hence his autonomy, sanity, equipoise, irony,
detachment—in short, wisdom. Whatever it is, reading him is one of the very
few ways (if not the only one) available for feeling decent. I wonder, though, if
that was his purpose.

I saw him last in July 1973, at a supper at Stephen Spender's place in London.
Wystan was sitting there at the table, a cigarette in his right hand, a goblet in his
left, holding forth on the subject of cold salmon. The chair being too low, two
disheveled volumes of the OED were put under him by the mistress of the house.
I thought then that I was seeing the only man who had the right to use those
volumes as his seat.

E. E. CUMMINGS

THE PRINCE OF PATCHIN PLACE

by Susan Cheever

FEBRUARY 2014

During the last years of his life E. E. Cummings made a modest living on the high-school lecture circuit. In the spring of 1958 his schedule took him to read his adventurous poems at the uptight girls' school in Westchester where I was a miserable 15-year-old sophomore with failing grades.

I vaguely knew that Cummings had been a friend of my father (the novelist John Cheever), who loved to tell stories about Cummings's gallantry and his ability to live elegantly on almost no money—an ability my father himself struggled to cultivate. When my father was a young writer in New York City, in the golden days before marriage and children pressured him to move to the suburbs, the older Cummings had been his beloved friend and adviser.

On that cold night in 1958, Cummings was near the end of his celebrated and controversial 40-year career as this country's first popular modernist poet. Primarily remembered these days for its funky punctuation, his work was in fact a wildly ambitious attempt at creating a new way of seeing the world through language—and this even applied to his signature. The progression from Cummings's official name (Edward Estlin Cummings) to his signature as a Harvard undergrad (E. Estlin Cummings) to the emblem for which he became famous (e. e. cummings) began with his use of a lowercase *i* in his poems in the 1920s, though he wouldn't adopt the style officially until the late 50s.

Cummings was part of a powerful group of writers and artists, which included James Joyce, Gertrude Stein, Hart Crane, Marianne Moore, Ezra Pound, Marcel Duchamp, Pablo Picasso, and Henri Matisse—some of whom were his friends—and he strained to reshape the triangle between the reader, the writer, and the subject of the poem, novel, or painting. As early as his 1915 Harvard College graduation speech, Cummings told his audience that "the New Art, maligned though it may be by fakirs and fanatics, will appear in its essential spirit . . . as a courageous and genuine exploration of untrodden ways."

Modernism as Cummings and his mid-20th-century colleagues embraced it had three parts. The first was the method of using sounds instead of meanings to connect words to the reader's feelings. The second was the idea of stripping away all unnecessary things to bring attention to form and structure: the formerly hidden skeleton of a work would now be exuberantly visible. The third facet of modernism was an embrace of adversity. In a world seduced by easy understanding, the modernists believed that difficulty enhanced the pleasures of reading. In a Cummings poem the reader must often pick his way toward comprehension, which comes, when it does, in a burst of delight and recognition. Like many of his fellow modernists—there were those who walked out of Stravinsky's *Rite of Spring* in 1913, and that same year viewers at New York's Armory Show were scandalized by Marcel Duchamp's *Nude Descending a Staircase (No. 2)*—Cummings was sometimes reviled by those he saw as the fakirs and fanatics of the critical establishment. Poetry arbiter Helen Vendler suggested that his poems were repellent and foolish: "What is wrong with a man who writes this?" she asked.

Nothing was wrong with Cummings—or Duchamp or Stravinsky or Joyce, for that matter. All were trying to slow down the seemingly inexorable rush of the world, to force people to notice their own lives. In the 21st century, that rush has now reached Force Five; we are all inundated with information and given no time to wonder what it means or where it came from. Access without understanding and facts without context have become our daily diet.

Although in the 1950s and 60s Cummings was one of the most popular poets in America, he sometimes didn't make enough money to pay the rent on the ramshackle apartment in Greenwich Village on Patchin Place where he lived with the incandescently beautiful model Marion Morehouse. This bothered Cummings not at all. He was delighted by almost everything in life except for the institutions and formal rules that he believed sought to deaden feelings. "Guilt is the cause of more disauders / Than history's most obscene marorders," Cummings wrote.

Cummings was an American aristocrat with two degrees from Harvard; my father had been headed for Harvard when he was expelled from high school, and he adored Cummings's combination of academic success and lighthearted lack of reverence for academic success. In spite of his Establishment background, Cummings treated the Establishment with an amused contempt.

At a time when *The New Yorker* annoyingly bowdlerized my father's mentions of kissing, Cummings got away with writing graphic erotic poetry, neatly stepping around the Mrs. Grundys of the magazine world. "may i feel said he / (i'll squeal said she / just once said he)," he wrote, in a famous poem that doesn't upset the applecart as much as give it a new team of wild horses. He also wrote some of the sweetest love poems of the century:

i carry your heart with me(i carry it in
my heart)i am never without it(anywhere
i go you go,my dear;and whatever is done
by only me is your doing,my darling)

My father drove me to school that night—the Masters School, in Dobbs Ferry, was 30 minutes from where we lived, in Scarborough, New York. As we stepped into the entrance hall, Cummings bellowed *"Joey!"*—my father's boyhood nickname. The two men heartily embraced as the school's sour founders and head-mistresses glared down from their gold-framed portraits on the paneled walls.

Cummings was taller than my father and 18 years older, but they both wore tattered Harris Tweed jackets. Cummings had developed an electrifying and acrobatic way to give poetry readings, sitting on a chair and at times moving around the stage instead of hiding behind a lectern, and timing his readings to the second. For this audience, he knew enough to skip his erotic masterpieces. His elegance and courtesy got him a standing ovation, especially for a powerful, moving evocation of his father: "my father moved through dooms of love / through sames of am through haves of give, / singing each morning out of each night . . . " After an encore, he appeared in his coat and scarf to let the audience know he had to go home.

My father and I drove him home to Patchin Place. "He was the most brilliant monologuist I have known," wrote Malcolm Cowley, the novelist and critic, and that night, leaning forward from the backseat of our secondhand Dodge, I was treated to one of Cummings's "virtuoso performances," as the poet Archibald MacLeish called them. Cummings was an unabashed and very funny rebel; he also had an astonishingly mobile face and a flexible dancer's body. He wasn't just an inspired mimic; he seemed to become the people he was imitating. To this day my 94-year-old mother fondly remembers his imitations, his collapsible top hat, and his willingness to stand on his head for a laugh.

As we turned out of the school's genteel and leafy driveway and down the hill to Route 9, headed for the vibrant city, Cummings let out a deep, comic sigh of relief. My father drove, and Cummings talked, mocking the teachers who were making my life miserable—he said the place was more like a prison than a school. It was a hatchery whose goal was to produce uniformity. I was unhappy there? No wonder! I was a spirited and wise young woman. Only a mindless moron (Cummings loved alliteration) could excel in a place like that. What living soul could even survive a week in that assembly line for obedient girls, that pedagogical factory whose only purpose was to turn out so-called educated wives for upper-class blow-hards with red faces and swollen bank balances? I had been told not to be so negative all the time. Cummings reminded me of his friend Marianne Moore's fondness for the admonition: you mustn't be so open-minded that your brains fall out.

When we stopped for burgers at a White Castle in the Bronx, heads turned at Cummings's uncanny, hilarious imitation of the head of the Masters School English Department. In that well-lighted place, late at night, my father produced a flask and spiked the coffee. I was already drunk on a different kind of substance—inspiration. It wasn't those in authority who were always right; it was the opposite. I saw that being right was a petty goal—being free was the thing to aim for. My father, who had always sided with the school, listened. Within a year he had consented to send me to a different kind of school, an alternative school in South Woodstock, Vermont, where I was very happy.

History has given us very few heretics who have not been burned at the stake. Cummings was our generation's beloved heretic, a Henry David Thoreau for the 20th century. He lived most of his life in Greenwich Village, during a time when experiments of all kinds, social, artistic, and literary, were being carried out. He knew everyone in the city's downtown hobohemia, from the iconic vagrant Harvard alumnus Joe Gould, whose oral history of his Beatnik contemporaries was more myth than reality, to the sculptor Gaston Lachaise. In the 1920s, Cummings was a prolific contributor to *Vanity Fair,* writing poems, short satire, and long profiles of personalities such as Jean Cocteau and Josephine Baker. "I can't get enough of you," the magazine's legendary editor Frank Crowninshield wrote Cummings, "because you have exactly the touch we need." In 1927 the two men, both passionate Francophiles, fought over a Cummings piece which Crowninshield thought was unfair to the French. The editor asked for a re-write; Cummings refused, and the two parted ways.

And in his almost 3,000 poems he sometimes furiously, sometimes lovingly, debunked anything or anyone in power—even death, in his famous poem about Buffalo Bill, with its spangled alliterations and intimate last lines: "and what i want to know is / how do you like your blueeyed boy / Mister Death."

Cummings despised fear, and his life was lived in defiance of all who ruled by it. If freeing himself of inhibition allowed him to write some of the most stirring lines in American poetry, it also allowed him to blot his legacy. After a miserable stint trying to write screenplays in Hollywood, he wrote some stupidly anti-Semitic poems and sentences. His feelings about Communism led him to become a fan of Senator Joseph McCarthy's. On the other hand, when it came to writing about love and sex, Cummings did for poetry what Henry Miller was doing for prose.

Even more shocking, he was no respecter of social mores. "but it's life said he / but your wife said she / now said he) / ow said she / (tiptop said he / don't stop said she / oh no said he) / go slow said she . . ." Instead of using dialect as novelists do today, he explored phonetics in a way that urges the reader to speak the dialect in question: "oil tel duh woil doi sez, / dooyuh unnurs tanmih." In a world where his antithesis Robert Frost was famously observing that writing free verse was like playing tennis with the net down, Cummings—who, unlike Frost, had a rigorous classical education—showed that traditions like the sonnet form could be re-invented.

Cummings and my father met in New York City in the 1930s, introduced by the biographer Morris Robert Werner; his wife, Hazel Hawthorne Werner; and Malcolm Cowley. (Malcolm was later my father-in-law, but that's another story.) "His hair was nearly gone," my father recalled of their first meeting, with the kind of exaggerated black humor both men loved; "his last book of poetry had been rejected by every estimable publisher, his wife was six months pregnant by her dentist and his Aunt Jane had purloined his income and had sent him, by way of compensation, a carton of Melba toast." Cummings's second wife was leaving him, and he was having trouble finding a publisher. Yet he urged my father to be proud. "A writer is a prince!" he insisted. He also, with more success, urged him to abandon Boston, "a city without springboards for people who can't dive."

By the time I heard him read at the Masters School, that night in 1958, I was steeped in Cummings stories that few people had heard. My father's credo was taken from a letter Cummings had written to cheer him when my father was an infantry sergeant in the Philippines in 1942. "I too have slept with someone's boot in the corner of my smile," my father often quoted, although he cleaned up Cummings's experimental language. "listen, moi aussi have slept in mmuudd with a kumrad's feet in the corners of my smile," Cummings actually wrote. The letter included an autumn leaf and a $10 bill. I have it on my wall today.

In another favorite story of my father's, Cummings and Marion, literally penniless, used their last two tokens to take the subway uptown from Patchin Place to a fabulous New Year's Eve party. They were dressed to the nines: she, long-legged in a spectacular evening gown, and he in a glamorous gentleman's top hat and tails. The night was freezing cold; how would they get home? Neither of them worried at all as they dazzled the party-goers and had the time of their lives.

In the elevator on their way home in the early morning, the airy, beautiful couple noticed a leaden banker and his stodgy wife. They were all a little drunk on champagne. The banker admired Cummings's beautiful hat. "Sir," asked Cummings in his educated accent, "what would you give for the privilege of stepping on it?" The banker paid $10, the hat collapsed on cue, and Cummings and Marion took a cab back to Patchin Place.

The way he died, in 1962, at Joy Farm, the Cummings-family place on Silver Lake, New Hampshire, was another one of my father's often told stories. Marion had called him in to dinner as day faded and the glorious sky lit up with the fires of sunset. "I'll be there in a moment," Cummings said. "I'm just going to sharpen the ax." A few minutes later he crumpled to the ground, felled by a massive cerebral hemorrhage. He was 67. That, my father let us all know, was the way to die—still manly and useful, still beloved, still strong. "'how do you like your blueeyed boy / Mister Death,'" my father growled, his eyes wet with tears.

Fortunately, almost miraculously, Patchin Place is a corner of New York City that has been virtually untouched by the last 50 years. Still a small mews of shabby houses tucked off a tree-lined street in the West Village, it is home to a bohemian group of writers, eccentrics, and people who have lived there for decades. In the summer, through the open windows, you can see a woman reading in a room piled high with books. A gray tabby snoozes in the sun on the pavement. In the spring there are homemade window boxes and piles of literary junk from spring cleanings, and in the winter the snow falls softly on the peeling paint of white fences and sagging iron gates between the mews and 10th Street. Two plaques are bolted to No. 4, where Cummings rented a studio in the back on the third floor and later a ground-floor apartment with Marion.

You step away from the traffic and trendiness of lattes and expensive baby clothes on Sixth Avenue and into a place where time stands still. When I wander there under the streetlights on warm evenings, it could be the night 50 years ago when my father and I drove Cummings home. When we got to Patchin Place that night, Cummings warmly invited us to come in for more conversation. We could talk awhile, have a coffee, and listen to some of his new poems, but it was late, and we had a long drive home.

MARIANNE MOORE

··

EFFORTS OF AFFECTION

by Elizabeth Bishop

JUNE 1983

Marianne Moore was a beloved poet and public figure. She once threw out the ball to open the season for the Yankees, was asked by the Ford Motor Company to suggest names for a new car line, was frequently photographed and quoted in the popular press, and seemed to enjoy the role of public eccentric very much. Moore's 1951 Collected Poems *won the National Book Award and the Bollingen and Pulitzer prizes. She was born in 1887 and lived in Manhattan and Brooklyn from 1918 till her death in 1972.*

Elizabeth Bishop, by contrast, traveled very far from home during the course of her life. Born in Worcester, Massachusetts, in 1911, she was reared in Nova Scotia and Boston by her maternal grandparents and her aunt. In 1953, she abandoned the literary world of the United States for Brazil, where she lived for more than fifteen years in quiet, self-imposed exile, sending only two or three poems a year to the States for publication. Although she too received a Pulitzer and a National Book Award, her reputation was almost entirely restricted to the literary community. Her style—in person, in her poems, and in this memoir—was deliberately self-effacing.

The essay that follows was found unfinished among Elizabeth Bishop's papers after her death in 1979—unfinished only in the sense that there was no final draft. In another sense it was more than finished, with numerous versions of various passages accompanied by the author's marginal notes. Fortunately, there was also a detailed outline showing her intentions exactly. The memoir has been put into this final form by Bishop's friend, editor, and publisher, Robert Giroux.

In the first edition of Marianne Moore's *Collected Poems* of 1951 there is a poem originally called "Efforts and Affection." In my copy of this book, Marianne crossed out the "and" and wrote "of" above it. I liked this change very much, and so I am giving the title "Efforts of Affection" to the whole piece.

I first met Marianne Moore in the spring of 1934 when I was a senior at Vassar College, through Miss Fanny Borden, the college librarian. A school friend and the friend's mother, both better read and more sophisticated in their literary tastes than I was, had told me about Marianne Moore's poetry several years earlier. I had already read every poem of Miss Moore's I could find, in back copies of *The Dial*, "little magazines," and anthologies in the college library. I hadn't known poetry could be like that; I took to it immediately, but although I knew there was a volume of hers called *Observations*, it was not in the library and I had never seen it.

Because Miss Borden seems like such an appropriate person to have introduced me to Marianne Moore, I want to say a little about her. She was the niece of the Fall River Lizzie Borden, and at college the rumor was that Lizzie Borden's lurid career had had a permanently subduing effect on Miss Fanny Borden's personality. She was extremely shy and reserved and spoke in such a soft voice it was hard to hear her at all. She was tall and thin; she always dressed in browns and grays, old-fashioned, muted, and distinguished-looking. She also rode a chainless bicycle. I remember watching her ride slowly up to the library, seated very high and straight on this curiosity, which somehow seemed more ladylike than a bicycle with a chain, and park it in the rack. (We didn't padlock bicycles then.) Once, after she had gone inside, I examined the bicycle, which was indeed chainless, to see if I could figure out how it worked. I couldn't. Contact with the librarian was rare; once in a long while, in search of a book, one would be sent into Miss Borden's office, shadowy and cavelike, with books piled everywhere. She weighed down the papers on her desk with smooth, round stones, quite big stones, brought from the seashore, and once when my roommate admired one of these, Miss Borden said in her almost inaudible voice, "Do you like it? You may *have* it" and handed it over, gray, round, and very heavy.

One day I was sent in to Miss Borden's office about a book, I no longer remember what. We continued talking a little, and I finally got up my courage to ask her why there was no copy of *Observations* by that wonderful poet Marianne Moore in the Vassar library. She looked ever so gently taken aback and inquired, "Do you *like* Marianne Moore's poems?" I said I certainly did, the few I'd been able to find. Miss Borden then said calmly, "I've known her since she was a little girl" and followed that with the question that was possibly to influence the whole course of my life: "Would you like to meet her?" I was painfully—no, excruciatingly—shy and I had run away many times rather than face being introduced to adults of much less distinction than Marianne Moore, but I immediately said, "Yes." Miss Borden said that she would write to Miss Moore, who lived in Brooklyn, and also that she would be glad to lend me *her* copy of *Observations*.

Miss Borden's copy of *Observations* was an eye-opener in more ways than one. Poems like "An Octopus," about a glacier, or "Peter," about a cat, or "Marriage," about marriage, struck me, as they still do, as miracles of language and construction. Why had no one ever written about things in this clear and dazzling way before? But at the same time I was astonished to discover that Miss Borden (whom I now knew to be an old family friend of the Moores) obviously didn't share my liking for these poems. Tucked in the back of the book were quite a few reviews that had appeared when *Observations* was published, in 1924, and most of these were highly unfavorable, some simply obtuse. There was even a parody Moore poem by Franklin P. Adams. Even more revealing, Miss Borden hadn't seen fit to place a copy of her friend's book in the college library. (Later that year I found a copy for myself, on a secondhand-book table at Macy's.)

The day came when Miss Borden told me that she had heard from Miss Moore and that Miss Moore was willing to meet me in New York, on a Saturday afternoon. Years later I discovered that Marianne had agreed to do this with reluctance; in the past, it seems, dear Miss Borden had sent several Vassar girls to meet Miss Moore and sometimes her mother as well, and every one had somehow failed to please. This probably accounted for the conditions laid down for our first rendezvous: I was to find Miss Moore seated on the bench at the right of the door leading to the reading room of the New York Public Library. They might have been even more strict. I learned later that if Miss Moore really expected *not* to like would-be acquaintances, she arranged to meet them at the Information Booth in Grand Central Station—no place to sit down, and, if necessary, an instant getaway was possible. In the meantime, I had been told a little more about her by Miss Borden, who described her as a child, a strange and appealing little creature with bright red hair—playful, and, as might have been expected, fond of calling her family and friends by the names of animals.

I was very frightened, but I put on my new spring suit and took the train to New York. I had never seen a picture of Miss Moore; all I knew was that she had red hair and usually wore a wide-brimmed hat. I expected the hair to be bright red and for her to be tall and intimidating. I was right on time, even a bit early, but she was there before me (no matter how early one arrived, Marianne was always there first) and, I saw at once, not very tall and not in the least intimidating. She was forty-seven, an age that seemed old to me then, and her hair was mixed with white to a faint rust pink, and her rust pink eyebrows were frosted with white. The large flat black hat was as I'd expected it to be. She wore a blue tweed suit that day and, as she usually did then, a man's "polo shirt," as they were called, with a black bow at the neck. The effect was quaint, vaguely Bryn Mawr 1909, but stylish at the same time. I sat down and she began to talk.

It seems to me that Marianne talked to me steadily for the next thirty-five years, but of course that is nonsensical. I was living far from New York many of those years and saw her at long intervals. She must have been one of the world's greatest talkers: entertaining, enlightening, fascinating and memorable; her talk, like her poetry, was quite different from anyone else's in the world. I don't know what she talked about at that first meeting; I wish I had kept a diary. Happily ignorant of the poor Vassar girls before me who hadn't passed muster, I began to feel less nervous and even spoke some myself. I had what may have been an inspiration, I don't know—at any rate, I attribute my great good fortune in having known Marianne as a friend in part to it. Ringling Bros. and Barnum & Bailey Circus was making its spring visit to New York and I asked Miss Moore (we called each other "Miss" for over two years) if she would care to go to the circus with me the Saturday after next. I didn't know that she *always* went to the circus, wouldn't have missed it for anything, and when she accepted, I went back to Poughkeepsie in the grimy day coach extremely happy.

THE CIRCUS

I got to Madison Square Garden very early—we had settled on the hour because we wanted to see the animals before the show began—but Marianne was there ahead of me. She was loaded down: two blue cloth bags and two huge brown paper bags, full of something, one on each arm. I was given one of these. They contained, she told me, stale brown bread for the elephants, because stale brown bread was one of the things they liked best to eat. (I later suspected that they might like stale white bread just as much but that Marianne had been thinking of their health.) As we went in and down to the lower level, where we could hear (and smell) the animals, she told me her preliminary plan for the circus. Her brother, Warner, had given her an elephant-hair bracelet, of which she was very fond, two or three strands of black hairs held together with gold clasps. One of the elephant hairs had fallen out and been lost. As I probably knew, elephant hairs grow only on the tops of the heads of very young elephants. In her bag, Marianne had a pair of strong nail scissors. I was to divert the adult elephants with the bread, and, if we were lucky, the guards wouldn't observe her at the end of the line where the babies were, and she could take out her scissors and snip a few hairs from a baby's head, to repair her bracelet.

She was quite right; the elephants adored stale brown bread and started trumpeting and pushing up against each other to get it. I stayed at one end of the line, putting slices of bread into the trunks of the older elephants, and Miss Moore went rapidly down to the other end, where the babies were. The large elephants were making such a to-do that a keeper did come up my way, and out of the corner of my eye, I saw Miss Moore leaning forward over the rope on tiptoes, scissors in hand. Elephant hairs are tough; I thought she would never finish her haircutting. But she did, and triumphantly we handed out the rest of the bread and set off to see the other animals. She opened her bag and showed me three or four coarse, grayish hairs in a piece of Kleenex.

I hate seeing animals in cages, especially small cages, and especially circus animals, but I think that Marianne, while probably feeling the same way, was so passionately interested in them, and knew so much about them, that she could put aside any pain or outrage for the time being. That day I remember that one handsomely patterned snake, writhing about in a glass-walled cage, seemed to raise his head on purpose to look at us. "See, he knows me!" said Miss Moore. "He remembers me from last year." This was a joke, I decided, but perhaps not altogether a joke. Then we went upstairs and the six-ring affair began. The blue bags held our refreshments: thermos jugs of orange juice, hard-boiled eggs (the yolks only), and more brown bread, but fresh this time, and buttered. I also remember of this first visit to the circus (there were to be others) that in front of us sat a father with three young children, two boys and a girl. A big circus goes on for a long time and the children began to grow restless. Marianne leaned over with the abruptness that characterized all her movements and said to the father that if the little girl wanted to go to the bathroom, she'd be glad to take her.

260 CUMBERLAND STREET

After graduating from Vassar I lived for a year in New York City; I returned to live there from time to time for thirty years or so, but it was during this first year that I got to know Miss Moore and her mother and became familiar with their small apartment in Brooklyn. It was in the fourth floor front of an ugly yellow brick building with a light granite stoop and a big white glass globe on a pillar at either side of the door. (Marianne told taxi drivers to stop at the apartment with the "two mothballs" in front.) The elevator was small and slow. After I had buzzed, I used to try to get up in it to the fourth floor before Marianne could get down in it to take me up personally, but I rarely managed to. A very narrow hall, made narrower by waist-high bookcases along one side, and with doors to two tiny bedrooms opening off it, led back to the living room. On the end of the bookcase nearest the front door sat the famous bowl of nickels for subway fare (nickels for years, then dimes, then nickels *and* dimes, and finally quarters). Every visitor was made to accept one of these upon leaving; it was absolutely *de rigueur*. After one or two attempts at refusing, I always simply helped myself to a nickel as I left, and eventually I was rewarded for this by Marianne's saying to a friend who was protesting, "Elizabeth is an *aristocrat*; she *takes* the money." (I should like to mention here the peculiar way Marianne had of pronouncing my Christian name. She came down very hard on the second syllable, El*iz*abeth. I liked this, especially as an exclamation, when she was pretending to be shocked by something I had said.)

The small living room and dining room were crowded with furniture that had obviously come from an older, larger home, and there were many pictures on the walls, a mixture of the old and the new, family possessions and presents from friends (these generally depicted birds or animals). One painting of trees and a stream had suffered an accident to its rather blurry tree passage, and Marianne herself had restored this—I felt, unkindly, not too successfully—with what she said was "Prussian blue." She was modestly vain of her manual skills. A set of carpenter's tools hung by the kitchen door, and Marianne had put up some of the bookshelves herself. In one doorway a trapeze on chains was looped up to the lintel. I never saw this in use, but it was Marianne's, and she said that when she exercised on it and her brother was there, he always said, "The ape is rattling her chains again." A chest stood in the bay window of the living room with a bronze head of Marianne on it by Lachaise. The chest was also always piled high with new books. When I first knew Marianne she did quite a bit of reviewing and later sold the review copies on West Fourth Street.

I was always seated in the same armchair, and an ashtray was placed on a little table beside me, but I tried to smoke no more than one or two cigarettes a visit, or none at all. I felt that Mrs. Moore disapproved. Once, as I was leaving and waiting for the slow elevator, I noticed a deep burn in the railing of the staircase and commented on it. Mrs. Moore gave a melancholy sigh and said, "*Ezra* did that. He came to call on Marianne and left his cigar burning out here because he knew I *don't like cigars . . .*" Many years later, in St. Elizabeths Hospital, I repeated this to Ezra Pound. He laughed loudly and said, "I haven't smoked a cigar since I was eighteen!" Beside the ashtray and even a new package of Lucky Strikes, I was sometimes given a glass of Dubonnet. I had a suspicion that I was possibly the only guest who drank this Dubonnet, because it looked very much like the same bottle, at the level it had been on my last visit, for many months. But usually we had tea and occasionally I was invited for dinner. Mrs. Moore was a very good cook.

Mrs. Moore was in her seventies when I first knew her, very serious—solemn, rather—although capable of irony, and very devout. Her face was pale and somewhat heavy, her eyes large and a pale gray, and her dark hair had almost no white in it. Her manner toward Marianne was that of a kindly, self-controlled parent who felt that she had to take a firm line, that her daughter might be given to flightiness or—an equal sin, in her eyes—mistakes in grammar. She had taught English at a girls' school and her sentences were Johnsonian in weight and balance. She spoke more slowly than I have ever heard anyone speak in my life. One example of her conversational style has stayed with me for over forty years. Marianne was in the kitchen making tea and I was alone with Mrs. Moore.

I said that I had just seen a new poem of Marianne's, "Nine Nectarines & Other Porcelain," and admired it very much. Mrs. Moore replied, "Yes. I am so *glad* that Marianne has *decided* to give the inhabitants of the *zoo . . . a rest.*" Waiting for the conclusions of her longer statements, I grew rather nervous; nevertheless, I found her extreme precision enviable and thought I could detect echoes of Marianne's own style in it: the use of double or triple negatives, the lighter and wittier ironies—Mrs. Moore had provided a sort of ground bass for them.

She wrote me one or two beautifully composed little notes on the subject of religion, and I know my failure to respond made her sad. At each of my leave-takings she followed me to the hall, where, beside "Ezra's" imagined cigar burn, she held my hands and said a short prayer. She said grace before dinner, and once, a little maliciously, I think, Marianne asked *me* to say grace. Mercifully, a childhood grace popped into my mind. After dinner Marianne wrote it down.

Of course Mrs. Moore and her daughter were what some people might call "prudish"; it would be kinder to say "overfastidious." This applied to Mrs. Moore more than to Marianne; Marianne, increasingly so with age, was capable of calling a spade a spade, or at least calling it by its archaic name. I remember her worrying about the fate of a mutual friend whose sexual tastes had always seemed quite obvious to me: "What are we going to do about X . . . ? Why, sometimes I think he may even be in the clutches of a *sodomite* . . . !" One could almost smell the brimstone. But several novels of the '30s and '40s, including Mary McCarthy's *The Company She Keeps*, were taken down to the cellar and burned in the furnace. I published a very bad short story a year or two after I first knew the Moores and I was reprimanded by both of them for having used the word "spit." (Two or three years later I was scolded for having used "water closet" in a poem, but by then I had turned obstinate.) Marianne once gave me her practical rules for the use of indecent language. She said, "Ordinarily, I would never use the word *rump*. But I can perfectly well say to Mother, 'Mother, there's a thread on your *rump*, because *she* knows that I'm referring to Cowper's pet hare, 'Old Tiney,' who liked to play on the carpet and 'swing his rump around!'"

I was shown many old photographs and snapshots and, once, a set of post-cards of their trip to England and Paris—at that time the only European traveling Marianne had done. The postcards were mostly of Oxford, and there was a handwritten menu, including the wines, of the luncheon George Saintsbury had given for her. I was also privileged to look into the notebooks, illustrated with Marianne's delicate sketches.

Besides exercising on the trapeze, Marianne was very fond of tennis. I never saw her play, but from the way she talked about it, it seemed as if she enjoyed the rules and conventions of the game as much as the sport. She engaged a young black boy to play with her, sometimes in Prospect Park and sometimes on the roof of the apartment house. He was finally dismissed because of his lack of tennis manners; his worst offense seemed to be that instead of "Serve!" he *would* say "Okay!"

The bathroom in the apartment was small, long and narrow, and as if I were still a child, I was advised to go there when Marianne thought it would be a good idea. (Also in subway stations: "I'll hold your bag and gloves, Elizabeth.") In their bathroom was an object I liked, an old-fashioned shoeshine box with an iron footrest. On one visit this had just been repainted by Marianne, with black enamel, and so had a cast-iron horse, laid out on a piece of newspaper on its side, running, with a streaming mane. It looked as if it might have originally been attached to a toy fire engine. I asked about this little horse, and Mrs. Moore told me that when Marianne was two-and-a-half years old, she had taken her to visit an aunt; the horse had had to go along too. Mrs. Moore had gone into the guest room and discovered that Marianne had taken a length of lace, perhaps a lace collar, from the bureau and dressed the horse up in it. "Marianne!" she had said—one could imagine the awful solemnity of the moment—"You wouldn't take Auntie Bee's lace to put on your horse, would you?" But the infant Marianne, the intrepid artist, replied, "Pretty looks, ma! Pretty looks!"

Mrs. Moore's sense of honesty, or honor, like her respect for the proprieties, was staggering. Marianne occasionally teased her mother about it, even in front of me. One story was about the time Mrs. Moore had decided that five empty milk bottles must be returned to the grocery store, and thence to the dairy. They were not STORE BOTTLES, as bottles then said right in the glass, nor the kind that were to be put out on the doorstep, but they all came from the same dairy. The grocer looked at them and pushed them back on the counter toward Mrs. Moore, saying, "You don't have to return these bottles, ma'am; just throw them away." Mrs. Moore pushed the bottles back again and told him quietly, "It *says* BORDEN on the bottles; they belong to the dairy." The grocer: "I know it does, ma'am, but it doesn't say STORE BOTTLES or RETURN. Just throw them away." Mrs. Moore spoke more slowly and more quietly, "But they don't belong to me. They are *their bottles*." "I know, ma'am, but they really don't want them back." The poor man had underestimated Mrs. Moore. She stood firm, clarifying for him yet again the only honorable line of action to be pursued in regard to the five bottles. Finally the grocer took them all in his arms and, saying weakly, "My *God*, ma'am!" carried them into the back of the store.

Clothes were of course an endless source of interest to Marianne, increasingly especially so as she grew older. As she has written herself (in a piece for the *Christian Science Monitor*), her clothes were almost always hand-me-downs, sometimes very elegant ones from richer friends. These would be let out or, most frequently, let down (Marianne preferred clothes on the loose side, like the four-sizes-too-large "polo shirts"). The hats would be stripped of decorations, and ribbons changed so all was black or navy blue, and somehow perhaps *flattened*. There was the Holbein/ Erasmus-type hat, and later the rather famous tricorne, but in the first years I knew her, only the large, flat, low-crowned hats of felt or summer straw.

Once when I arrived at the Brooklyn apartment, Marianne and her mother were occupied with the old-fashioned bit of sewing called "making over." They were making a pair of drawers that Marianne had worn at Bryn Mawr in 1908 into a petticoat or slip. The drawers were a beautiful garment, fine white batiste, with very full legs that must have come to below the knee, edged with lace and set with rows of "insertion." These I didn't see again in their metamorphosed state, but I did see and was sometimes consulted about other such projects. Several times over the years Marianne asked me abruptly, "Elizabeth, what do you have on under your dress? How much underwear do *you* wear?" I would enumerate my two or perhaps three undergarments, and Marianne would say, "Well, I know that I [or, mother and I] wear many too many." And sometimes when I arrived on a cold winter evening dressed in a conventional way, I would be greeted by "Elizabeth, silk stockings!" as if I were reckless or prone to suicide. My own clothes were subject to her careful consideration. The first time I ever met a publisher, I reported the next day by telephone and Marianne's first question was "What did you *wear*, Elizabeth?"

Marianne's hair was always done up in a braid around the crown of her head, a style dating from around 1900, I think, and never changed. Her skin was fair, translucent, although faded when I knew her. Her face paled and flushed so quickly she reminded me of Rima in W. H. Hudson's *Green Mansions*. Her eyes were bright, not "bright" as we often say about eyes when we really mean alert; they were that too, but also shiny bright and, like those of a small animal, often looked at one sidewise—quickly, at the conclusion of a sentence that had turned out unusually well, just to see if it had taken effect. Her face was small and pointed, but not really triangular because it was a little lopsided, with a delicately pugnacious-looking jaw. When one day I told her she looked like Mickey Rooney, then a very young actor (and she did), she seemed quite pleased.

She said her poem "Spenser's Ireland" was not about *loving* Ireland, as people seemed to think, but about *disapproving* of it. Yet she liked being of Irish descent; her great-great-grandfather had run away from a house in Merrion Square, Dublin (once, I went to look at it from the outside), and I remember her delight when the book in which the poem appeared was bound in Irish green.

She had a way of laughing at what she or someone else had just said if she meant to show outrage or mock disapproval—an *oh-ho* kind of sound, rough, that went with a backward and sidewise toss of the head toward the left shoulder. She accepted compliments with this laugh too, without words; it disparaged and made light of them, and implied that she and her audience were both far above such absurdities. I believe she was the only person I have ever known who "bridled" at praise, while turning pink with pleasure. These gestures of her head were more pronounced in the presence of gentlemen because Marianne was innately flirtatious.

The Moore *chinoiserie* of manners made giving presents complicated. All her friends seemed to share the desire of giving her presents, and it must sometimes have been, as she would have said, a "burden." One never knew what would succeed, but one learned that if a gift did not succeed it would be given back, unobtrusively, but somehow or other, a year or two later. My most successful gift was a pair of gloves. I don't know why they made such a hit, but they did; they weren't actually worn for a long time, but they appear in a few of her photographs, held in one hand. Marianne brought them to the photographer wrapped in the original tissue paper. Another very successful gift was a paper nautilus, which became the subject of her poem "The Paper Nautilus":

> . . . *its wasp-nest flaws*
> *of white on white, and close-*
>
> *laid Ionic chiton-folds*
> *like the lines in the mane of*
> *a Parthenon horse . . .*

Fruit or flowers were acclaimed and examined but never, I felt, really welcomed. But a very unbeautiful bracelet from Morocco, alternate round beads of amber and black ambergris on a soiled string, was very well received. I was flattered to see this worn at a poetry reading, and afterward learned that, as it was too loose for Marianne's wrist, mother had carefully sewn it onto the edge of her sleeve. But another friend's attempt to give her a good gramophone was a disaster, a drama that went on for months. Eventually (it was portable but very heavy) it was carried back by Marianne to the shop in New York.

She liked to show her collection of jewelry, which had a few beautiful and valuable pieces. I once gave her a modest brooch of the semiprecious stones of Brazil, red and green tourmalines and amethysts; this she seemed to like so much that I gave her a matching bracelet. A few years later I wrote her from Brazil asking what I could bring her on my return to New York, and she wrote back, "I like *jewels*."

Knowing her fondness for snakes, I got for her when I was in Florida a beautiful specimen of the deadly coral snake with inch-wide rose red and black stripes separated by narrow white stripes, a bright new snake coiled in liquid in a squat glass bottle. This bottle sat on her hall bookcase, at the other end from the bowl of nickels, for many years. The colors gradually faded, and the formaldehyde grew cloudy, and finally I said I thought she could dispense with the coral snake.

A mutual friend told me that Marianne was relieved; she had always hated it. Perhaps it had only been brought out for my visits.

Marianne once told me a story on herself about her aversion to reds. Her physician in Brooklyn for some years was a Turkish woman, Dr. Laf Loofy, whom she often quoted as a great authority on health. Dr. Loofy had prescribed for Marianne a large bottle of red pills, but before taking one, Marianne would wash it thoroughly until all the shiny red coating had disappeared. Something, perhaps digestive symptoms, made her confess this to Dr. Loofy, who was incredulous, then appalled. She explained that medical genius and years of research, expressly for Marianne's benefit, had gone into developing the red enamel-like coating that she had deliberately washed away. Marianne was completely stoical about herself; once, at a New York doctor's office, she proved to have a temperature of 104 degrees. The doctor wanted to call a cab for her for the long trip back to Brooklyn, but Marianne would have none of it. She insisted on returning by subway, and did.

Despite what I assumed to be her aversion to reds, she once showed me a round, light tan, rather piglike piece of luggage, bought especially for her first trip to give readings on the West Coast, saying, "You will think this too *showy*, Elizabeth." The long zipper on the top could be locked with a bright red padlock. I said no, I thought it a very nice bag. "Of course," Marianne said, "the red padlock is the very best thing about it."

One winter Mrs. Moore was sick for a long time with a severe case of shingles. She was just recovering from this long illness when she also had to go to the dentist, whose office was in Manhattan. A friend who had a car and I went to Brooklyn to take Marianne and her mother to the city. Mrs. Moore was still feeling poorly. She was wearing a round flat fur cap, a very 1890-ish hat, mink, I think, or possibly sable, and since she couldn't bear to put her hair up yet, the remarkably un-gray hair hung down in a heavy pigtail. The dentist's office was high up in a tall office building. There were a good many passengers in the elevator and an elevator boy; we shot upward. What I remember most is that at the proper floor, as the passengers stared, Marianne and her mother both bowed to the elevator boy pleasantly and thanked him, Mrs. Moore the more profusely, for the ride. He was unaccustomed to such civility, but he was very pleased and tried hard not to push his handle or close the doors as quickly as on the other floors. Elevator men, subway change-makers, ticket takers, taxi drivers—all were treated to these formalities, and, as a rule, they were pleasantly surprised and seemed to respond in kind.

A very well known and polished writer, who had known Marianne since he was a young man and felt great admiration for her, was never invited to Cumberland Street although his friends were. Once, I asked innocently why I never saw him there and Marianne gave me her serious, severe look and said, "He *contradicted* Mother."

The atmosphere of 260 Cumberland Street was of course "old-fashioned," but even more, otherworldly—as if one were living in a diving bell from a different world, let down through the crass atmosphere of the twentieth century. Leaving the diving bell with one's nickel, during the walk to the subway and the forty-five-minute ride back to Manhattan, one was apt to have a slight case of mental or moral bends—so many things to be remembered; stories, phrases, the unaccustomed deference, the exquisitely prolonged etiquette—these were hard to reconcile with the New Lots Avenue express and the awful, jolting ride facing a row of indifferent faces. Yet I never left Cumberland Street without feeling happier: uplifted, even inspired, determined to be good, to work harder, not to worry about what other people thought, never to try to publish anything until I thought I'd done my best with it, no matter how many years it took—or never to publish at all.

To change the image from air to water: somehow, under all the subaqueous pressure at 260 Cumberland Street—admonitions, reserves, principles, simple stoicism—Marianne rose triumphant, or rather her voice did, in a lively, unceasing jet of shining bubbles. I had "taken" chemistry at preparatory school; I also could imagine that in this water, or heavy water glass, I saw forming the elaborate, logical structures that became her poems.

WRITING AND A FEW WRITERS

On the floor of the kitchen at 260 Cumberland Street I once saw a bushel basket, the kind used for apples or tomatoes, filled to overflowing with crumpled papers, some typed, some covered with Marianne's handwriting. This basketful of papers held the discarded drafts of one review, not a long review, of a new book of poems by Wallace Stevens. When it was published I found the review very beautiful, as I still do. Nevertheless, Marianne chose to omit it from her collected essays; it didn't come up to her standards.

If she was willing to put in so much hard work on a review running to two or two-and-a-half pages, one can imagine the work that went into a poem such as "The Jerboa," or "He 'Digesteth Harde Yron'" (about the ostrich), with their elaborate rhyme schemes and syllable counting meters. When not at the desk, she used a clipboard with the poem under construction on it, carrying it about the apartment, "even when I'm dusting or washing the dishes, Elizabeth."

Her use of "light" rhymes has been written about by critics. On principle, she said, she disapproved of rhyme. Nevertheless, when she read poems to me, or recited them, she obviously enjoyed rhymes very much, and would glance up over her reading glasses and exclaim that *that* was "gusto"—her favorite word of praise. With great gusto of her own, she read:

Strong is the lion—like a coal
His eye-ball—like a bastion's mole
  His chest against the foes:
Strong, the gier-eagle on his sail,
Strong against tide, th'enormous
  whale
  Emerges as he goes.

She admired Ogden Nash and liked to quote his poem about the baby panda for the sake of its rhyme:

I love the Baby Giant Panda;
I'd welcome one to my veranda.

Once, I found her consulting a large rhyming dictionary and she said, yes, it was "indispensable"; and I myself was congratulated on having rhymed "antennae" with "many."

Besides "gusto" she admired the "courageous attack," and for this reason she said she thought it a good idea to start off a poem with a spondee.

In *Observations* she seems undecided between free verse and her own strict stanza forms with their variations on "light" rhyme. Although she still professed to despise it, rhyme then seemed to win out for some years. However, by the time *Collected Poems* was published, in 1951, she had already begun a ruthless cutting of some of her most beautiful poems, and what suffered chiefly from this ruthlessness were those very rhymes and stanza forms she had so painstakingly elaborated in the years just before.

A conflict between traditional rhymes and meters came during the seven years (1946–53) Marianne worked on translating La Fontaine's *Fables*. For my own amusement, I had already made up a completely unscientific theory that Marianne was possessed of a unique, involuntary sense of rhythm, therefore of meter, quite unlike anyone else's. She looked like no one else; she talked like no one else; her poems showed a mind not much like anyone else's; and her notions of meter and rhyme were unlike all the conventional notions—so why not believe that the old English meters that still seem natural to most of us (or *seemed* to, at any rate) were not natural to her at all? That Marianne from birth, physically, had been set going to a different rhythm? Or was the explanation simply that she had a more sensitive ear than most of us, and since she had started writing at a time when poetry was undergoing drastic changes, she had been free to make the most of it and experiment as she saw fit?

When I happened to be in New York during those seven years, I was usually shown the fable she was working on (or she'd read it on the phone) and would be asked to provide a rhyme, or to tell her if I thought the meter was right. Many other people must have had the same experience. These were strange requests, coming from someone who had made contemporary poets self-conscious about their crudities, afraid to rhyme "bone" with "stone," or to go *umpty-umpty-um*. Marianne was doing her best, one saw, to go *umpty-umpty-um* when she sensed that La Fontaine had gone that way, but it seemed to be almost—I use the word again—physically impossible for her to do so. If I'd suggest, say, that "flatter" rhymed with "matter," this to my embarrassment was hailed as a stroke of genius; or if I'd say, "If you leave out 'and' or 'the' [or put it in], it will go *umpty-umpty-um*," Marianne would exclaim, "Elizabeth, thank you, you have saved my life!" Although I too am mentioned in the introduction, I contributed next to nothing to the La Fontaine—a few rhymes and metrically smoothed-out or slicked-up lines. But they made me realize more than I ever had the rarity of true originality, and also the sort of alienation it might involve.

Her scrupulous and strict honesty could be carried to extremes of Protestant, Presbyterian, Scotch-Irish literalness that amazed me. We went together to see an exceptionally beautiful film, a documentary in color about Africa, with herds of gazelles and giraffes moving across the plains, and we loved it. Then a herd of elephants appeared, close up and clear, and the narrator commented on their feet and tread. I whispered to Marianne that they looked as if their feet were being lifted up off the ground by invisible threads. The next day she phoned and quoted my remark about the elephants' walk, and suddenly came out with, "Elizabeth, I'll give you ten dollars for that." There was often no telling how serious she was. I said something like "For heaven's sake, Marianne, please take it," but I don't believe it ever made an appearance in a poem. I confess to one very slight grudge: she *did* use a phrase of mine once without a note. This may be childish of me, but I want to reclaim it. I had been asked by a friend to bring her three glass buoy-balls in nets, sometimes called "witch balls," from Cape Cod. When I arrived at the old hotel where I lived, a very old porter took them with my bag, and as I watched him precede me down the corridor, I said to myself, "The bellboy with the buoy-balls." I liked the sound of this so much that in my vanity I repeated the phrase to Marianne a day or so later. You will find "The sea- / side burden should not embarrass / the bell-boy with the buoy-ball / endeavoring to pass / hotel patronesses" in the fifth stanza of "Four Quartz Crystal Clocks." It was so thoroughly out of character for her to do this that I have never understood it. I am sometimes appalled to think how much I may have unconsciously stolen from her. Perhaps we are all magpies.

*The deepest feeling always shows
itself in silence;
not in silence, but restraint.*

These lines from her early poem "Silence" are simply another one of Marianne's convictions. Like Auden, whom she admired, she believed that graceful behavior—and writing, as well—demands a certain reticence. She told me, "Ezra says all dedications are *dowdy*," but it was surely more than to avoid dowdiness that caused her to write this postscript in *Selected Poems* (1935): "Dedications imply giving, and we do not care to make a gift of what is insufficient; but in my immediate family there is one 'who thinks in a particular way' and I should like to add that where there is an effect of thought or pith in these pages, the thinking and often the actual phrases are hers." This postscript was obviously meant for Mrs. Moore, and after her mother's death in 1947, Marianne became more outspoken about dedications; however when she wrote an acrostic on the name of one of her oldest and closest friends, it too was semiconcealed, by being written upside down.

The first time I heard Marianne read poetry in public was at a joint reading with William Carlos Williams in Brooklyn. I am afraid I was a little late. There was a very small audience, mostly in the front rows, and I made my way as self-effacingly as I could down the steep red-carpeted steps of the aisle. As I approached the lower rows, she spotted me out of the corner of her eye and interrupted herself in the middle of a poem to bow and say, "Good evening!" She and Dr. Williams shared the rather small high stage and took turns reading. There were two high-backed chairs, far apart, and each poet sat down between readings. The decor seemed to be late-Victorian Gothic; I remember a good deal of red plush, dark wood, and Gothic points, knobs, and incised lines. Marianne, wearing a hat and a blue dress, looked quite small and seemed nervous. I had the impression that Williams, who was not nervous in the slightest, was generously trying to put her at her ease. As they changed places at the lectern, he would whisper to her and smile. I have no recollection of anything that was read, except for a sea-monster poem of Williams's, during which he gave some loud and realistic roars.

She seldom expressed opinions of other writers, and the few I remember were, to say the least, ambiguous or ambivalent. She developed the strategy of damning with faint praise to an almost supersonic degree. One writer whom I rather disliked, and I suspect she did too, was praised several times for her "beautifully laundered shirtwaist." One day when I was meeting her in New York, she said she had just run into Djuna Barnes again, after many years, on the steps of the Public Library. I was curious and asked her what Djuna Barnes was "like." There was rather a long pause before Marianne said, thoughtfully, "Well . . . she looked very smart, and her shoes were *beautifully* polished."

I do not remember her ever referring to Emily Dickinson, but on one occasion, when we were walking in Brooklyn on our way to a favored tea shop, I noticed we were on a street associated with the *Brooklyn Eagle*, and I said fatuously, "Marianne, isn't it odd to think of you and Walt Whitman walking this same street over and over?" She exclaimed in her mock-ferocious tone, "Elizabeth, don't speak to me about that man!" So I never did again. Another time, when she had been talking about her days on *The Dial*, I asked how she had liked Hart Crane when he had come into her office there. Her response was equally unexpected. "Oh, I *liked* Hart! I always liked him very much—he was so *erudite*." And although she admired Edmund Wilson very much and could speak with even more conviction of *his* erudition, she once asked me if I had read his early novel *I Thought of Daisy*, and when I said no, she almost extracted a promise from me that I would *never* read it. She was devoted to W. H. Auden, and the very cat he had patted in the Brooklyn tearoom was produced for me to admire and pat too.

Lately I have seen several references critical of her poetry by feminist writers, one of whom described her as a "poet who controlled panic by presenting it as whimsy." Whimsy is sometimes there, of course, and so is humor (a gift these critics sadly seem to lack). Surely there is an element of mortal panic and fear underlying all works of art? Even so, one wonders how much of Marianne's poetry the feminist critics have read. Have they really read "Marriage," a poem that says everything they are saying and everything Virginia Woolf has said? It is a poem which transforms a justified sense of injury into a work of art:

> *This institution . . .*
> *I wonder what Adam and Eve*
> *think of it by this time . . .*
>
> *Unhelpful Hymen!*
> *a kind of overgrown cupid*
> *reduced to insignificance*
> *by the mechanical advertising*
> *parading as involuntary comment,*
> *by that experiment of Adam's*
> *with ways out but no way in—*
> *the ritual of marriage . . .*

Do they know that Marianne Moore was a feminist in her day? Or that she paraded with the suffragettes, led by Inez Milholland on her white horse, down Fifth Avenue? Once, Marianne told me, she "climbed a lamppost" in a demonstration for votes for women. What she did up there, what speech she delivered, if any, I don't know, but climb she did in long skirt and petticoats and a large hat. Perhaps it was pride or vanity that kept her from complaints, and that put her sense of injustice through the prisms dissected by "those various scalpels" into poetry. She was not too proud for occasional complaints; she was humorously angry, but nevertheless angry, when her publisher twice postponed her book in order to bring out two young male poets, both now almost unheard of. Now that everything can be said, and done, have we anyone who can compare with Marianne Moore, who was at her best when she made up her own rules and when they were strictest—the reverse of "freedom"?

Soon after I met Marianne in 1934—although I concealed it for what seemed to me quite a long time—somehow or other it came out that I was trying to write poetry. For five or six years I occasionally sent her my poems. She would rarely say or write very much about them except that she liked such and such a phrase or, oddly, the alliteration, which I thought I tended to overdo. When I asked her what the poems she had written at Bryn Mawr were like, she said, "*Just like Swinburne, Elizabeth.*" Sometimes she suggested that I change a word or line, and sometimes I accepted her suggestions, but never did she even hint that such and such a line might have been influenced by or even unconsciously stolen from a poem of her own, as later on I could sometimes see that they were. Her notes to me were often signed "Your Dorothy Dix."

It was because of Marianne that in 1935 my poems first appeared in a book, an anthology called *Trial Balances*. Each of the poets in this anthology had an older mentor, who wrote a short preface or introduction to the poems, and Marianne, hearing of this project, had offered to be mine. I was much too shy to dream of asking her. I had two or three feeble pastiches of late seventeenth-century poetry called "Valentines," in one of which I had rhymed "even the English sparrows in the dust" with "lust." She did not like those English sparrows very much, and said so ("Miss Bishop's sparrows are not revolting, merely disaffecting"), but her sponsorship brought about this first appearance in a book.

One long poem, the most ambitious I had up to then attempted, apparently stirred both her and her mother to an immediate flurry of criticism. She telephoned the day after I had mailed it to her, and said that she and her mother had sat up late rewriting it for me. (This is the poem in which the expression "water closet" was censored.) Their version of it arrived in the next mail. I had had an English teacher at Vassar whom I liked very much, named Miss Rose Peebles, and for some reason this name fascinated Marianne. The revised poem had been typed out on very thin paper and folded into a small square, sealed with a gold star sticker and signed on the outside "Lovingly, Rose Peebles." My version had rhymed throughout, in rather strict stanzas, but Marianne and her mother's version broke up the stanzas irregularly. Some lines rhymed and some didn't; a few other colloquialisms besides "water closet" had been removed and a Bible reference or two corrected. I obstinately held on to my stanzas and rhymes, but I did make use of a few of the proffered new words. I am sorry to say I can't now remember which they were, and won't know unless this fascinating communication should turn up again.

Marianne in 1940 gave me a copy of the newly published *Last Poems and*

Two Plays, by William Butler Yeats, and though I dislike some of the emphasis on lechery in the poems, and so did she, I wrote her that I admired "The Circus Animals' Desertion" and the now famous lines "I must lie down where all the ladders start / In the foul rag-and-bone shop of the heart." She replied:

> I would be "much disappointed in you" if you *could* feel about Yeats as some of his acolytes seem to feel. An "effect," an exhaustively great sensibility (with insensibility?) and genius for word-sounds and sentences. But after all, what is this enviable apparatus for? if not to change our mortal psycho-structure. It makes me think of the Malay princes—the *horde* of eunuchs and entertainers and "bearers" of this and that; then suddenly the umbrella over the prince lowered, because a greater prince was passing. As you will suspect from my treachery to W. B. Yeats. I've been to a lecture on Java by Burton Holmes, and one on Malay . . .

One day she abruptly asked me, "Do you like the *nude*, Elizabeth?" I said yes I did on the whole. Marianne: "Well, so do I, Elizabeth, but *in moderation*," and she immediately pressed on me a copy of Sir Kenneth Clark's new book, *The Nude*, which had just been sent to her.

SOME EXPEDITIONS

This was a story told me by Mrs. Moore, of an outing that had taken place the summer before I met them. There had been a dreadful heat wave, and Marianne had been feeling "overburdened" (the word *burden* was an important one in the Brooklyn vocabulary) and "overtaxed." Her mother decided that Marianne "should take a course in the larger mammals" and said, "Marianne, I am going to take you to Coney Island to see Sheba," an unusually large and docile elephant then on view at a boardwalk sideshow. Coney Island is a long subway ride even from Brooklyn, but in spite of the heat and the crowds, the two ladies went. Sheba performed her acts majestically, and slowly played catch with her keeper with a shiny white ball. I asked about the elephant's appearance, and Marianne said, "She was very simply dressed. She was lightly powdered a matte rose all over, and wore ankle bracelets, large copper hollow balls, on her front legs. Her headdress consisted of three white ostrich plumes." Marianne was fond of roller coasters; a fearless rider, she preferred to sit in the front seat. Her mother told me how she waited below while the cars clicked agonizingly to the heights, and plunged horribly down. Marianne's long red braid had come undone and blew backward, and with it went all her cherished amber-colored "real tortoiseshell" hairpins, which fortunately landed in the laps of two sailors in the car behind her. At the end of the ride, they handed them to her "very politely."

Two friends of Marianne's, two elderly Boston ladies, shared an exquisitely neat white clapboard house in northern Maine. I once spent a day there, and they teased Marianne about her habit of secreting food. She laughed, blushed and tossed her head, and did not seem to mind when one of them told of going into Marianne's room for a book only to discover two boiled potatoes lying on the dresser. Some years later the older lady phoned Marianne from Boston and told her she was dying of cancer. She was perfectly stoical about it, and said she was in a hospital and knew she could not last very long. She asked Marianne to come and stay near her until she died, and Marianne went. At the hospital, she told Marianne that while she would be grateful to her if she came to see her every day, she knew that Marianne couldn't possibly spend all her time with her, so she had arranged for her to take driving lessons. Marianne, who must have been nearly seventy at the time, agreed that this was a good idea; she had always wanted to learn to drive, and she did, with a lesson at the driving school every day and a visit to the hospital. A day or so after her friend died, Marianne passed her driving test. She said she had a little trouble with the lights in Copley Square and confessed she thought the "policeman" giving her the test had been a little overlenient. I said I hoped she hadn't driven too fast, and she replied, "A steady forty-five, Elizabeth!" On her return she proudly showed her driving license to her brother, Warner, and he, sounding no doubt very much as her mother used to sound, said, "There must be some mistake. This must be sent back *immediately*."

Marianne was intensely interested in the techniques of things—how camellias are grown; how the quartz prisms work in crystal clocks; how the pangolin can close up his ear, nose and eye apertures and walk on the outside edges of his hands "and save the claws / for digging"; how to drive a car; how the best pitchers throw a baseball; how to make a figurehead for her nephew's sailboat. The exact way in which anything was done, or made, or functioned, was poetry to her.

She even learned to tango. Before she acquired a television set of her own, she was in the habit of going down to the basement apartment at 260 Cumberland Street to watch the baseball games with the janitor and his wife, who had a set. During one of the games there was a commercial that advertised a Brooklyn dancing school. Any viewer who telephoned in was guaranteed a private tango lesson at a Brooklyn academy. Marianne announced that she had always liked the tango, and hurried to the fourth floor to put in her call, and got an appointment. The young dancers, male and female, may have been a little surprised, but soon they were competing with each other to dance with her. She was given a whole short course of lessons. I asked about the tango itself, and she allowed that they had felt perhaps it was a little too strenuous and had taught her a "modified" version of it. She had also learned several other steps and dances in more current use, and insisted everyone had enjoyed himself and herself thoroughly.

In the late winter or early spring of 1963, when I was in New York, one evening around eight I emerged from a Lexington Avenue subway station on my way to a poetry reading at the YMHA. Suddenly I realized that Marianne was walking ahead of me over half a block away, alone, hurrying along with a bag of books and papers. She reached the YMHA before I did, but she was not present at the function I was attending; I wondered what she could be up to. Later she informed me that she was attending the YMHA Poetry Workshop, conducted that term by Louise Bogan. She said she was learning a great deal, things she had never known before; Miss Bogan was another of the people she considered "erudite." Shortly afterward I met Miss Bogan at a party and asked her about the workshop and her famous student. Poor Miss Bogan! I am sure Marianne never dreamed what suffering she was causing her. It seemed that Marianne took notes constantly, asked many questions, and entered into discussions with enthusiasm. But the other students were timid and often nonplussed, and so was Miss Bogan, besides feeling that she was sailing under false colors and never knowing what technical question she might be expected to answer next.

I attended very few literary events at which Marianne was present, but I did go with her to the party for Edith and Osbert Sitwell given at the Gotham Book Mart. I hadn't intended to go to this at all; in fact I really didn't want to, but Marianne, who was something of an Anglophile, was firm. "We must be *polite* to the Sitwells," she said.

The party was given by *Life* magazine and was rather awful. The photographers behaved as photographers do: strewing wires under our feet, calling to each other over our heads, and generally pushing us around. It took some time to separate the poets, who were the subjects of the picture, from the nonpoets, and this was done in a way that made me think of livestock being herded into cattle cars. Nonpoets and some real poets felt insulted; then the photographer announced that Miss Moore's hat was "too big." She refused to remove it. Auden was one of the few who seemed to be enjoying himself. He got into the picture by climbing on a ladder, where he sat making loud, cheerful comments over our heads. Finally the picture was taken with a sort of semicircular swoop of the camera. Marianne consented to let a friend and me take her to dinner and afterward back to Brooklyn in a cab. I had on a small velvet cap and Marianne said, "I wish I had worn a *minimal* hat, like yours." The taxi fare to Brooklyn at that time was something over five dollars, not counting the tip. That evening my friend was paying for dinner and the cab. Between comments on the Sitwell party, Marianne exclaimed at intervals, "Mr. W———, this is *highway robbery*!"

She told me about another, more elegant literary party she had been to in a "penthouse," to celebrate the publication of a deluxe edition of a book, I think by Wallace Stevens. The chairs were upholstered in "lemon-colored velvet," there was a Matisse drawing she didn't altogether like, and she had taken a glass of champagne and regretted it all evening; it had made her face burn. I asked for further details. She became scornful: "Well, we signed our names several times, and after *that* thrill was over, I came home."

Sometimes we went to movies together, to *Kon-Tiki* twice, I recall. I never attempted to lure her to any dramatic or "artistic" films. Since Dr. and Mrs. Sibley Watson were her dearest friends, she must have seen his early experimental films, such as *Lot in Sodom*. I heard the sad story of two young men, however, who when they discovered that she had never seen Eisenstein's *Potemkin*, insisted on taking her. There was a short before *Potemkin*, a Walt Disney film; this was when the Disney films still had charm and humor. After the movies they went to tea and Marianne talked at length and in detail about the ingenuity of the Disney film, and nothing more. Finally they asked her what she had thought of *Potemkin*. Her opinion was brief but conclusive: "Life," she said, "is not like that."

Twice we went together to the Saturday morning lectures for children at the Museum of Natural History—once, to see Meshie, the three-year-old chimpanzee who came onstage pedaling her tricycle and offered us bites of her banana. And once to see a young couple I had known in Mexico show their collection of pets, including Aguilla, the bald-headed American eagle they had trained to hunt like a falcon, who had ridden all the way to Mexico and back perched on a broomstick in their car. There were more lovable pets as well: Marianne held the kinkajou in her arms, an affectionate animal that clutched onto one tightly with his tail. In a home-made movie the couple also showed us, the young man himself was shown in his library taking a book from the shelf. As he did so, he unselfconsciously blew the dust off the top of its pages. Marianne gave one of her laughs. She loved that; it was an example of the "spontaneity" that she admired as much as she admired "gusto."

The next to last outing I went on with Marianne was in the summer of 1968. This was long after her mother's death, when she had moved from Brooklyn and was living at 35 West Ninth Street in Manhattan. I was staying nearby in the Village, and one day she telephoned and asked me if I would come over and walk with her to the election polls; she wanted to vote. It was the first time, I think, she had ever actually asked me for assistance. It was a very hot day. She was ready and waiting, with her hat on. It was the usual shape, of navy blue straw, and she wore a blue and white checked seersucker suit and blue sneakers. She had become a bit unsteady and was supposed to use a cane, which was leaning against the doorframe. She hated it, and I don't think I ever saw her use it. The voting booths were quite near, in the basement of a public school off Sixth Avenue; there were a good many people there, sitting around, mostly women, talking. Marianne made quite a stir; they seemed to know who she was and came up to talk to her and to ask me about her while she voted. They were Greenwich Village mothers, with intellectual or bluestocking types among them. I thought to myself that Marianne's was probably the only Republican vote cast there that day.

It was the originality and freshness of Marianne's diction, in the most casual conversation, as well as her polysyllabic virtuosity, that impressed many people. She once said of a well-known poet, "That man is freckled like a trout with impropriety." A friend has told me of attending a party for writers and artists at which she introduced a painter to Marianne by saying, "Miss Moore has the most interesting vocabulary of anyone I know." Marianne showed signs of pleasure at this, and within a minute offhandedly but accurately used in a sentence a word I no longer remember that means an addiction, in animals, to licking the luminous numbers off the dials of clocks and watches. At the same party this friend introduced the then comparatively young art critic Clement Greenberg; to her surprise and no doubt to Mr. Greenberg's, Marianne seemed to be familiar with his writing and said, on shaking hands, "Oh, the *fearless* Mr. Greenberg."

There was something about her good friend T. S. Eliot that seemed to amuse Marianne. On Eliot's first visit to Brooklyn after his marriage to Valerie, his young wife asked them to pose together for her for a snapshot. Valerie said, "Tom, put your arm around Marianne." I asked if he had. Marianne gave that short deprecatory laugh and said, "Yes, he did, but very *gingerly*." Toward the last, Marianne entrusted her Eliot letters for safekeeping to Robert Giroux, who told me that with each letter of the poet's she had preserved the envelope in which it had come. One envelope bore Marianne's Brooklyn address in Eliot's handwriting, but no return address or other identification. Within, there was a sheet of yellow pad paper on which was drawn a large heart pierced by an arrow, with the words "from an anonymous and grateful admirer."

LAST YEARS

The dictionary defines a memoir as "a record of events based on the writer's personal experience or knowledge." Almost everything I have recorded was observed or heard firsthand, mostly before 1951–52, the year—as Randall Jarrell put it—when "she won the Triple Crown" (National Book Award, Bollingen and Pulitzer prizes) and became really famous. She was now Marianne Moore, the beloved "character" of Brooklyn and Manhattan; the baseball fan; the friend of many showier celebrities; the faithful admirer of Presidents Hoover and Eisenhower and Mayor Lindsay; the recipient of sixteen honorary degrees (she once modeled her favorite academic hoods for me); the reader of poetry all over the country, in settings very unlike the Brooklyn auditorium where in the '30s I heard her read with William Carlos Williams. She enjoyed every bit of the attention she received, although it too could be a "burden." After those long years of modest living and incredibly hard work, she had—until the helplessness at the very last—thank heavens, an unusually fortunate old age.

She once remarked, after a visit to her brother and his family, that the state of being married and having children had one enormous advantage: "One never has to worry about whether one is doing the right thing or not. There isn't time. One is always having to go to market or drive the children somewhere. There isn't time to wonder, 'Is this *right* or isn't it?'"

Of course she did wonder, and constantly. But, as in the notes to her poems, Marianne never gave away the whole show. The volubility, the wit, the self-deprecating laugh, never really clarified those quick decisions of hers—or decisive intuitions, rather—as to good and bad, right and wrong; and her meticulous system of ethics could be baffling. One of the very few occasions on which we came close to having a falling out was when, in the '40s, I told her I had been seeing a psychoanalyst. She disapproved quite violently and said that psychoanalysts taught that "Evil is not *evil*. But we know it *is*." I hadn't noticed that my analyst, a doctor of almost saintly character, did this, but I didn't attempt to refute it, and we didn't speak of it again. We never talked about Presbyterianism, or religion in general, nor did I ever dare more than tease her a little when she occasionally said she believed there was something *in* astrology.

Ninety years or so ago, Gerard Manley Hopkins wrote a letter to Robert Bridges about the ideal of the "gentleman," or the "artist" versus the "gentleman." Today, his ideas may sound impossibly Victorian, but I find this letter still applicable and very moving: "As a fact poets and men of art are, I am sorry to say, by no means necessarily or commonly gentlemen. For gentlemen do not pander to lust or other basenesses nor . . . give themselves airs and affectations, nor do other things to be found in modern works. . . . If an artist or thinker feels that were he to become in those ways ever so great, he would still be essentially lower than a gentleman that was no artist and no thinker. And yet to be a gentleman is but on the brim of morals and rather a thing of manners than morals properly. Then how much more must art and philosophy and manners and breeding and everything else in the world be below the least degree of true virtue. This is that chastity of mind which seems to lie at the very heart and be the parent of all good, the seeing at once what is best, and holding to that, and not allowing anything else whatever to be even heard pleading to the contrary. . . . I agree then, and vehemently, that a gentleman . . . is in the position to despise the poet, were he Dante or Shakespeare, and the painter, were he Angelo or Apelles, for anything that showed him *not* to be a gentleman. He is in a position to do it, but if he is a gentleman perhaps this is what he will not do." The word "gentleman" makes us uncomfortable now, and its feminine counterparts, whether "lady" or "gentlewoman," embarrass us even more. But I am sure that Marianne would have "vehemently agreed" with Hopkins's strictures: to be a poet was not the be-all, end-all of existence.

I find it impossible to draw conclusions or even to summarize. When I try to, I become foolishly bemused: I have a sort of subliminal glimpse of the capital letter *M* multiplying. I am turning the pages of an illuminated manuscript and seeing that initial letter again and again: Marianne's monogram; mother; manners; morals; and I catch myself murmuring, "Manners and morals; manners *as* morals? Or is it morals *as* manners?" Since like Alice, "in a dreamy sort of way," I can't answer either question, it doesn't much matter which way I put it; it *seems* to be making sense.

ON LITERARY LIONS

EUDORA WELTY

······································

MISSISSIPPI QUEEN

by Willie Morris

MAY 1999

The night sky over my childhood Jackson was velvety black. I could see the full constellations in it and call their names; when I could read, I knew their myths. Though I was always waked for eclipses, and indeed carried to the window as an infant in arms and shown Halley's Comet in my sleep, and though I'd been taught at our dining room table about the solar system and knew the earth revolved around the sun, and our moon around us, I never found out the moon didn't come up in the west until I was a writer and Herschel Brickell, the literary critic, told me after I misplaced it in a story. He said valuable words to me about my new profession: "Always be sure you get your moon in the right part of the sky."
—EUDORA WELTY, *One Writer's Beginnings.*

One recent Sunday I drove Eudora Welty along the spooky, kudzu-enveloped dirt and gravel back roads of Yazoo County, Mississippi, some 40 miles north of Jackson. Dwarfed like a child by the stark bluffs outside the car window, she rode shotgun through the sunlight and misty shadows. "I haven't even seen another car yet," she noted at one point. "When *was* the last time we saw a human being?" Her voice, according to her friend the novelist Reynolds Price, remains "shy, but reliable as any iron beam."

She was game for anything, always peering around the next bend. At the crest of a bosky hill, a narrower and darker byway intersected with the one on which we were traveling. "Eudora, I'm going to make a left and drive down Paradise Road," I said. "We'd be fools if we didn't," she replied.

One of Eudora Welty's fictional characters had occasion to remark that against old mortality life "is nothing but the continuity of its love." Welty, often called the Jane Austen of American letters, has charted this continuity in 13 books, including: three novels (*The Optimist's Daughter*, published in 1972, won the Pulitzer Prize); five collections of short stories; two novellas; a volume of essays; an acclaimed memoir, *One Writer's Beginnings;* and a children's book. (She has also published two volumes of her photographs, taken in Mississippi and elsewhere.)

Her work, marked by what the critic Jonathan Yardley calls an "abiding tolerance . . . a refusal to pass judgment on the actors in the human comedy," has won every literary prize except the Nobel, for which she has frequently been mentioned. Says Price, "In all of American fiction, she stands for me with only her peers—Melville, James, Hemingway, and Faulkner—and among them she is, in some crucial respects, the most life-giving." She once wrote, "My wish, indeed my continuing passion, would be not to point the finger in judgment, but to part a curtain, that invisible shadow that falls between people; the veil of indifference to each other's presence, each other's wonder, each other's human plight."

Eudora Welty, whom many consider America's greatest living writer, was born in Jackson 90 years ago. On April 13 she enters her 91st year. She is abidingly revered in her hometown, where her birthdays are cause for celebration. In 1994, when Eudora and friends gathered at her favorite restaurant, Bill's Tavern (which she helped get started by supplying quotes of praise for the newspaper), a Greek belly dancer performed. Above her navel were written the words "Eudora Welty I love you." During another celebration, at Lemuria Bookstore, letters were read from comrades and admirers around the world, including President Clinton. John Ferrone, her Harcourt Brace editor, wrote:

> *Hail Eudora*
> *Staunch perennial*
> *I'm looking forward*
> *to your centennial*

Eudora, who is quite simply the funniest person I have ever known, could easily have become the grande dame of American letters, but clearly would have found herself tittering at such a self-important posture. She is wryly self-effacing with a gentle irony. Our connections go back considerably, for I was born in a house two blocks from hers in the Belhaven neighborhood of Jackson and christened in the church of her childhood, Galloway Memorial Methodist, where as a girl she took nickels to Sunday school in her glove. I met her when I was eight or nine and can pinpoint exactly where: Eudora always shopped for groceries at an erstwhile establishment called the Jitney Jungle, which had wooden floors and flypaper dangling from the ceiling. One afternoon during World War II, on one of my many sojourns into Jackson from my home in Yazoo City, I accompanied my great-aunt Maggie, who was wearing a flowing black dress, to fetch a head of lettuce, or a muskmelon perhaps. Eudora was at the vegetable counter when my great-aunt introduced us. I remember her as tall and slender, her eyes luminous blue. As we were leaving, my great-aunt whispered, "She writes those stories *her own self.*"

Through the years I have learned to expect certain kinds of reactions from Eudora. For example, when one telephones her for a meeting, she does not say, "Let's have lunch," but rather, "We *must* meet." Her conversation is laced with phrases such as "That smote me," and with solicitous interrogations, including "Don't you think?" or "Can't you imagine?" Josephine Haxton of Jackson, who writes under the nom de plume Ellen Douglas, first met her many years ago when Eudora went to Greenville, Mississippi, to sign copies of a book called *Music from Spain.* "Many years later, when my children were long since grown and had children of their own," Josephine tells me, "Eudora said to me, 'Oh, I remember so well that day I came to Greenville to sign books. Your children— those *beautiful* children.'" Others recall such instances of her magnanimous spirit. One of them, the historian and novelist Shelby Foote, tells me, "In Eudora's case, familiarity breeds affection."

Stories about her have always abounded in Jackson. In the 1930s there was not much to do in town and she and her comrades had to look hard for entertainment. They were especially intrigued when one Jackson lady announced in the paper that her night-blooming cereus was about to blossom. According to Eudora's friend Suzanne Marrs, "Eudora and her group would often gather to attend the bloomings, and they eventually formed the Night-Blooming Cereus Club, of which Eudora was elected president. Their motto was: 'Don't take it cereus; life's too mysterious.'"

Patti Carr Black, recently retired as director of the Mississippi State Historical Museum, is one of the best sources of Welty anecdotes. "My favorite hours," she says, "are spent with Eudora in the late afternoon sipping Powers Irish Whiskey and going back in her incredible memory to high times in our favorite spot, New York City. She quotes entire Bea Lillie lyrics, especially 'It's Better with Your Shoes Off'; delivers Bert Lahr punch lines; and describes the moves of the Marx Brothers and W. C. Fields, including Fields's wiggle of his little finger. She also does a great rendition of Mae West inspecting the troops up and down."

But it isn't just the locals who savor their memories of Eudora. William Maxwell, who was her editor at *The New Yorker* beginning in 1951, loves to recall her visits to New York, particularly one specific night. "When I first got to know her she was staying in the apartment of her friend and editor at *Harper's Bazaar* Mary Louise Aswell, and what I remember of the evening is Eudora's acting out of her mother telling her niece the story of Little Red Riding Hood while simultaneously reading *Time* magazine. It could have been transferred to the stage without a single change of any kind, and I didn't know anybody could be so hilarious. Some years later, when we were living on the fifth floor of a walk-up in Murray Hill, she came with the manuscript of a novella, *The Ponder Heart*, and after coffee we settled down to hear her read it. In no time I was wiping my eyes. Nothing has ever seemed so funny since. What the world must be like for a person with so exquisite a sense of humor, I don't dare think."

At dinners these days Eudora's stories move here and there like a gentle breeze that emanates from Greenwich Village in the Prohibition years, past the names of friends long dead, and on to her travels through Mississippi with her Kodak during the Depression, when she worked as a photographer. Questions provoke peregrinations. "Eudora," I asked during a recent gathering, "would you like a little kitten? I have one named Bubba." "Well," Eudora began, "mine has been a dog house all my life. My mother can't stand the thought of a cat. Of course, she's been dead a number of years. I like little kittens, but I don't think I can take one. I remember [novelist] Caroline Gordon. The first time I ever saw her, I was living in the Village, and I was going to meet her. I was walking along Eighth Avenue and she was carrying around a bunch of newborn kittens with her, and she'd go up to people on the street and say, 'You look like a cat person. Wouldn't you like a kitten?' It didn't work very well. She had a good many left. Whatever became of those kittens, I've wondered."

No one else answers questions in quite this way now, not even in Jackson.

Eudora has never married, and she lives alone in the house her father built in 1925 when she was 16 and the nearby streets were gravel and there were whispery pine forests all around. On the front lawn is a majestic oak tree. ("Never cut an oak," her mother advised her.) The kitchen of the old house looks out on a deep-green garden with its formal bench beneath another towering oak tree. Eudora loves what she still calls "my mother's garden" and says she was "my mother's yard boy."

Her Tudor-style house has a sturdy vestibule, a brown gabled roof on the second story, and a screened-in side porch long unused. Excluding the time she has spent traveling, she has lived and worked here for 74 years. "I like being in the house where nobody else has ever lived but my own family," she says, "even though it's lonely being the only person left."

She calls it "my unruly home." Books of all kinds are everywhere, stacked in corners, on tables and chairs. There are mountains of books, and on every flat surface one finds unanswered mail. Her correspondence is so voluminous, she says, that she is unable to handle it. In a box on a table is the Richard Wright Medal for Literary Excellence she received in 1994. "I'm proud to have it," she says.

These days Eudora does not dress up for visitors. On the morning of one of my calls she was wearing a blue sweat suit and white sneakers. Her short hair curls around the top of her ears. Her eyes are large, very blue, a little sad, yet still, at times, vibrant with mischief. She sits near a front window in an electric lift chair that makes it easy for her to stand up. She calls it her "ejection seat." If it is late afternoon and she feels up to it, she will press the button to raise herself to an upright position and suggest you join her in the pantry while she pours a couple of Maker's Marks. "This is what Katherine Anne Porter called 'swish likka,'" she says, quoting "swich licour" from Chaucer. "This is powerful stuff." Then, faithfully at six P.M., she turns on the television for her favorite program, *The NewsHour with Jim Lehrer*.

Every conversation is a procession of supple images. One day after a winter storm in Jackson—the first real one here in years—she recalled for her friend Hunter Cole the first time she saw snow, from her elementary-school windows on North Congress Street. It was not cold enough for it to stick, she recalled, so the teacher raised a window, took off her cape, and extended it outside. Then the woman walked hurriedly about the classroom with the garment, showing the young writer and her contemporaries the glistening snowflakes.

She is not, by birth, what is called here "Old Jackson." Her father, a northerner originally from Ohio, was the top man in a fledgling insurance company. Her southern mother had been born in West Virginia. "I was always aware," Eudora has written, "that there were two sides to most questions." Before they built the house in Belhaven the Weltys lived on North Congress Street, right down from her elementary school. (The writer Richard Ford later grew up directly across from the old Welty house.) The family was by no means rich but lived comfortably, and Eudora's parents were particularly attentive to her. In *One Writer's Beginnings*, Eudora wrote of mornings in the household of her childhood. "When I was young enough to still spend a long time buttoning my shoes in the morning," she began, "I'd listen toward the hall: Daddy upstairs was shaving in the bathroom and Mother downstairs was frying the bacon. They would begin whistling back and forth to each other up and down the stairwell. My father would whistle his phrase, my mother would try to whistle, then hum hers back. It was their duet. I drew my buttonhook in and out and listened to it—I knew it was 'The Merry Widow.' The difference was, their song almost floated with laughter: how different from the record, which growled from the beginning, as if the Victrola were only slowly being wound up."

Her father, Christian Webb Welty, had "an almost childlike love of the ingenious." Eudora believes he owned the first Dictaphone in town and he put the earphones over her ears to let her discover what she could hear. He also owned one of the early automobiles, in which the family made long journeys on perilous gravel roads to Ohio and West Virginia. Her father told Eudora and her two younger brothers, Walter and Edward, that if they were ever lost in a strange land to look for where the sky is brightest along the horizon. "That reflects the nearest river. Strike out for a river and you will find habitation." This helped provide her with what she terms "a strong meteorological sensibility." As for her mother, Chestina Welty, "valiance was in her very fibre."

The Weltys loved literature. They had an encyclopedia in the dining room, and if someone had a question at the table, someone else was always jumping up to prove the other right or wrong. As a girl, Eudora's mother had been given a complete set of Charles Dickens's novels as a reward for having her hair cut, and when the Welty home caught fire one night before Eudora was born, Mrs. Welty—on crutches at the time—returned to the house and threw all 24 volumes one by one out the window for Mr. Welty to catch.

It was a disappointment to the young Eudora to discover that storybooks had been written by people, "that books were not natural wonders, coming up of themselves like grass." She was in love with books, their words, their smell, their covers and bindings. The public library was on the other side of the state capitol from her home, and on her trips to get books she would glide along the marble floors of the capitol on roller skates. This produced "very desirable echoes."

At the library itself, Mrs. Calloway, a witchlike lady with a dragon eye, intimidated the children. But she could not inhibit Eudora's reading, for her mother had told the librarian: "Eudora is nine years old and has my permission to read any book she wants from the shelves, children or adult, with the exception of *Elsie Dinsmore*."

She was absorbed by the stories all around her, the eternal and ubiquitous Mississippi storytelling she heard from family, neighbors, maids. Preparing for a Sunday-afternoon ride, she would settle onto the backseat between her mother and a friend and command, "Now talk!"

At the time, Jackson girls took piano lessons as a matter of course. Eudora's own teacher, "Old Jackson" to the core, dipped her pen in ink and wrote "Practice!" on her sheet music with a *P* that resembled a cat's face with a long tail, and slapped her fingers with a flyswatter when she made a mistake.

Even as a child she was drawn to the bizarre, the grotesque, the phantasmagoric. "This being the state capital, we had all the state institutions in Jackson—blind, deaf and dumb, insane." she once observed to me. "Made for good characters." There was also the occasional society murder, which Eudora found singularly fascinating. She recalls the Mississippi matron whom I myself had heard about who was convicted for the murder of her mother; part of the corpse was found, but not all of it. She was sent to Whitfield, the asylum. Eudora and all of us heard the stories of the bridge games the murderess played with other proper ladies confined there for alcoholism. One afternoon one of the ladies abruptly tossed down her bridge hand and said, "Not another card will I play until you tell me what you did with the rest of your mother."

In Eudora's childhood years, the two Jackson newspapers published the honor rolls and individual grades of all the honor students. Also, the city fathers gave the honor children free season tickets to the baseball games of the noble Jackson Senators of the Class B Cotton States League. Eudora adored Red Mc-Dermott, the Senators' third-baseman, and offered him her documents attesting to her 100s in all her subjects, even attendance and deportment. At age 12 she won the Jackie Mackie Jingle contest, sponsored by the Mackie Pine Oil Company of Covington, Louisiana; the company president sent her a $25 check and said he hoped she would "improve American poetry to such an extent as to win fame."

Eudora spent two years in the little town of Columbus, Mississippi—Tennessee Williams's birthplace—at the Mississippi State College for Women. Although "the W," as it is called, was impoverished, neglected, and overcrowded, Eudora remembers it as a place of great intellectual stimulation, with a dedicated cadre of female teachers who taught without pay for months during the Depression when the state could not pay their salaries. The college brought together 1,200 girls from every corner of Mississippi. They all wore identical uniforms, but Eudora learned to tell where a girl had grown up from the way she talked, ate, or entered a classroom. She once told me that she could distinguish a girl from the Delta by the way she walked.

Eudora became a cartoonist for the school paper and was chosen fire chief of Hastings Hall. At night she frequently sneaked out of the dorm to go downtown, where the action was, and, on one such evening, won a Charleston contest at the Princess Theater. Elizabeth Spencer first met Eudora some years after this when the former was a college student. "I was in great awe of her talent," Elizabeth remembers, "but I was not aware of her high-flying sense of humor." Then one afternoon the two of them were at a post office and noticed a tacked-up poster proclaiming: NO LOITERING OR SOLICITING. "Eudora saw it," Elizabeth recalls, "and said, 'Let's loiter and solicit.'" When Elizabeth said O.K., Eudora declared, "Then you solicit while I loiter."

Eudora's father, the northerner, wanted his daughter to spend her last two college years at some distinguished university up North, and in 1927 she enrolled at the University of Wisconsin. Her mother was already encouraging her aspirations to become a writer, and Mr. Welty gave his daughter her first typewriter, a little red Royal Portable, which she took with her to Madison. To get her through the harsh winters he also bought her a possum coat at Marshall Field in Chicago.

Many of the students, she recalls, had raccoon coats, but her family could not afford such luxury.

At first, the Midwest frightened her. Years later she wrote her longtime agent, Diarmuid Russell, about her first months above the Mason-Dixon line: "I was very timid and shy, younger than the rest and those people up there seemed to me like sticks of flint that live in the icy world. I am afraid of flintiness—I had to penetrate that. . . . I used to be in a kind of wandering daze, I would wander down to Chicago and through the stores, I could feel such a heavy heart inside me. It was more than the pangs of growing up, much more. It was some kind of desire to be shown that the human spirit was not like that shivery winter in Wisconsin, that the opposite to all this existed in full."

Her father, concerned about his daughter's future, persuaded her to go to graduate school in business. She immediately chose Columbia University because she wanted to live in New York for a year. She studied typing for a while, "so I could be a secretary and make a living." When she had to pick a major subject she selected advertising, "which wasn't awfully good, because all at once, when the Depression hit, nobody had any money to advertise with. For that matter, nobody had any money to do anything with." During the Manhattan winter her mother sent her boxes of camellias to remind her of home.

In 1931, shortly after Eudora returned to Jackson from New York City, her father died of leukemia. Her mother was left with two sons in high school and college, so Eudora worked at whatever she could do. Her first job, at age 22, was at a local radio station headquartered in the clock tower of Jackson's first skyscraper: the Lamar Life building, which had been built by her father's company.

As part of her job she wrote the radio schedule to mail out to listeners and also sent fake letters to the station which were to be read on the air: "Dear WJDX, I love the opera on Saturday. Don't ever take it away!" She remembered the office as being "as big as a chicken coop," with just enough room for Mr. Wiley Harris, the announcer and manager, and herself. He would go up into the clock tower to clean out the canary's cage, and she would yell "Mr. Harris! Mr. Harris!" because it was time for him to announce the call letters of the station. The absentminded Mr. Harris would come down and say, "This is Station . . . uh, this . . . This is Station . . ." Eudora would write the call letters—WJDX—on a sheet of cardboard and hold it up for him.

Later, still during the Depression, she was hired as a publicity agent, junior grade, with the Works Progress Administration. She visited the farm-to-market roads in Mississippi and interviewed people living along them. She rode around on bookmobile routes and helped put up booths at county fairs. She visited landing fields being hacked out of cow pastures, juvenile courts, the scene of the devastating Tupelo tornado, and even a project teaching Braille to the blind. She went mostly by bus and stayed in the old small-town hotels. At night, under a squeaky electric fan, she wrote up the projects for the county weeklies. The Depression, she would remember, "was not a noticeable phenomenon in the poorest state in the Union."

For her own gratification, she began taking photographs, using an old-fashioned Kodak. The Standard Photo Company of Jackson developed her film, and she printed it at night in her kitchen at home. She says that her years of "snapshooting," as she calls it, helped her arrive at the perception that she must go beyond silent images to the slower voice of words.

"Mostly I remember things vividly," she says of the years she spent taking pictures. "I remember how people looked, just people standing against the sky sometimes, at the end of a day's work. Something like that is indelible to me. In taking all these pictures, I was attended, I know now, by an angel—a presence of trust. . . . It is a trust that dates the pictures, more than the vanished years."

Soon her stories started to come to her. Her very first, in 1936, was "Death of a Traveling Salesman," published in an obscure Ohio quarterly called *Manuscript*. When she was awarded a Guggenheim fellowship in 1942, she told a friend's aunt in Jackson her news. The aunt responded, "A Guggenheim what?" "I think she thought it was a hat," Eudora said.

By 1944 she had published *A Curtain of Green* and *The Robber Bridegroom*, and for six months of that year she lived again in New York City. Robert Van Gelder of *The New York Times Book Review* had interviewed her in 1942 and later offered her a job. "Can you imagine?" she remembers. "Of course, I immediately accepted and then phoned my mother in Mississippi. She was glad I'd found a job, because they weren't easy to come by during the war." But she was not entirely comfortable. "I didn't want to give a book a bad review. No matter what it is, it's a year out of somebody's life." She used the pseudonym of Michael Ravenna when reviewing war books, and when readers wrote to Michael Ravenna, she replied that he was away at the front line.

Always unabashedly stagestruck, Eudora could look outside her office window and see the performers she most admired arriving at rehearsals and performances. Mae West was rehearsing *Catherine Was Great* just next door and Eudora often slipped in the back to watch. "I'd watch during my lunch hour. Nobody seemed to mind. And I was in heaven."

In 1949, with a $5,000 advance on a new book and a second Guggenheim, she made her first trip to Europe and fell in love with Ireland, as southerners often do. She walked alone on its country roads and hid under hedges when it rained. One of her writing idols was Elizabeth Bowen, whom she visited in County Cork. Later, at Cambridge, she lunched with one of her own admirers, E. M. Forster, and became one of the few women to enter the hall of Peterhouse

College. Eudora recalls, "They were so dear the way they told me: they said, 'Miss Welty, you are invited to come to this, but we must tell you that we debated for a long time about whether or not we should ask you.'"

Years later Eudora—with 29 other women, including Helen Hayes, Lauren Bacall, and Toni Morrison—was invited to become a member of the Players Club on Gramercy Park, the prestigious establishment for theater people. They were the first female members. "Let's invade them, girls," Eudora announced to the assembled companions at cocktail hour.

By 1955 she had published four short-story collections, a novel, and two novellas. For the next 15 years, with the exception of three short stories in 1963, 1966, and 1969, until the novel *Losing Battles*, there was silence. She was virtually unpublished. These were difficult years personally. Her mother had serious eye surgery, and as her complaints multiplied, her condition gradually deteriorated. Eudora had to take care of her; there were no others to do this except salaried outsiders. Eudora's brother Walter, six years younger than she, also became very ill at the age of 40 with heart problems compounded by arthritis. "I'm so ashamed of not producing anything," Eudora wrote Diarmuid Russell. "I should think all of my friends would have given me up."

Walter died in 1959. Eventually, Eudora was forced to put her mother in a nursing home in Yazoo City, nearly 50 miles away. Eudora drove there and back every day of the week for more than a year to read to her and help look after her. On the long drives she sometimes made notes for *Losing Battles* in a notebook propped on the steering wheel. Her mother and her other brother, Edward, died four days apart in 1966.

To help pay for the nursing home, Eudora had to take a job teaching a writing workshop at Millsaps College in Jackson. She had 16 talented students screened by the English Department. When the now famous writer called the roll for the first time, the students realized she was more nervous than they were. "We hadn't expected that," says John Little, who was one of the students and later became director of the writing program at the University of North Dakota. "We didn't know this was the first college class she ever taught. We didn't know she was intensely shy." After the roll call, she read Dylan Thomas's "A Child's Christmas in Wales." After the story, the students sat in stone silence. Eudora looked at her watch; they looked at theirs. Finally, Tom Royals—now a lawyer in Jackson—rescued the day. "Miss Welty," he said, "since this is the first class, we don't have to stay the whole two hours." Her sigh of relief was audible.

After a few classes they tried a more casual setting—a Sunday-night social at someone's house. John Little got there late; he was carrying a case of cold Budweiser on his shoulder. The hostess frowned at the beer and sent the young man to the kitchen with it. The stifling silence from the living room matched that of the classroom. "Anybody want a Bud?," Little shouted. "Please," came one small voice from the silence. It was Eudora's. "The sight of Miss Welty drinking that beer had the sound of ice breaking," Little says.

Eudora's closest friend, in almost every way a sister, was Charlotte Capers, who died two years ago at age 83. Charlotte, author of an essay collection entitled *The Capers Papers*, and a friend of my own family's, was a descendant of Episcopal bishops and Sewanee College presidents, and one of the brightest, wackiest women on earth. To each other they were "Cha-Cha," pronounced with a soft *ch*, and "Dodo," like the note. Once not long before her death when she and another companion were helping Eudora into a four-door sedan, Capers said, "Let's get Dodo . . . into the fo'do'."

Up until fairly recently, Eudora drove an ancient Oldsmobile Cutlass, and the sight of her, barely able to see over the steering wheel, making her way to Parkin's Pharmacy to buy *The New York Times*, was as familiar as another picture we all have in our memories, Eudora's profile through the open windows of her second floor, as she sat at her writing desk. She always declared that her work made her happy and fulfilled. With short stories she always tried to get down a first draft spontaneously, often in a single day's work. "After that," she says, "I revised with scissors and pins. Pasting is too slow and you can't undo it, but with pins you can move things from anywhere to anywhere, and that's what I really love doing— putting things in their best and proper place, revealing things at the time when they matter most. Often I shift things from the very beginning to the very end. Small things—one fact, one word—but things important to me. It's possible I have a reverse mind, and do things backwards, being a broken left-hander."

Because of her health, Eudora has a hard time writing now. "My body doesn't help me anymore," she tells me, quoting a friend.

Eudora was a tall woman in her prime, but osteoporosis and a compression fracture in her back eight years ago have left their mark. She has arthritis in her hands and can no longer use a typewriter. Some years ago, the New Stage, a community theater group in Jackson, had a rummage sale. Eudora drove over in her old car and took a half-dozen handblown Czechoslovak Easter eggs and an old Royal typewriter in its original travel case. It was the typewriter her father had given her years before, the typewriter on which she had written her novels and stories since the 1930s. Jack Stevens, an actor, bought it for $10. Later he donated it to the State Archives.

She laments not having direct access to the written page as she once did, in the days when we all watched her working as we walked or drove past the house. Directly across the street from the Welty home was the music building of Belhaven College, and from the practice rooms the sounds of piano music would drift across Pinehurst Street, keeping her company through the long and solitary hours at the old Royal. "Though I was as constant in my work as the students were," she has written, "subconsciously I must have been listening to them, following them. . . . I realized that each practice session reached me as an outpouring. And those longings, so expressed, so insistent, called up my longings unexpressed. I began to hear, in what kept coming across the street into the room where I typed, the recurring dreams of youth, inescapable, never to be renounced, naming themselves over and over again."

REYNOLDS PRICE

DUKE OF WRITERS

by Anne Tyler

JULY 1986

He used to wear a long black cape with a scarlet lining. Or at least I always thought he did. Everybody thought so. Whenever we compared our freshman English instructors, someone was sure to say, "Reynolds Price? Isn't he the one with the cape?"

Turns out it wasn't a cape after all. It wasn't even black. It was a navy-blue coat that he wore tossed around his shoulders. That's what he tells me now, at any rate, and I suppose he knows best. But I prefer to have it my way: He wore a long black cape with a scarlet lining, and he dashed across the campus with his black curls bouncing on his forehead and his cape swirling out behind him. Ask any of the people who went to Duke in the fall of 1958; I bet they'll say I'm right.

He was twenty-five years old back then, he tells me now, but in 1958 he seemed older than God. (I was sixteen and a half.) Which made it all the more remarkable when he perched on his desk tailor-fashion to read us his newest story; or when he said, to a student analyzing a poem, "You're *good* at this, aren't you!" (He seemed genuinely pleased, and admitted straight out that he hadn't seen what she had seen. For me, that girl's face will always symbolize the moment I first understood that we students, too, had something to offer—that we weren't the blank slates we'd thought we were in high school.)

"Wouldn't it be something," he says now, "if we could locate a photograph taken of us together as children?" I'm puzzled. Together? As children? But then I realize that in fact he wasn't quite grown up himself when he started teaching— and that maybe, in the best sense, he never will be. And I remember a thought I had when I was a sophomore, listening to one of his funny, incisive discussions. *He must have been a very much loved child*, I thought. I believe that occurred to me because he seemed, sitting in our midst, a naturally happy man. Not to mention the fact that there was something childlike about his face, which was— and still is—round and serene and gravely trusting.

And the other thought that occurred to me—not then but years later, when I revisited Duke and found him gray-haired but otherwise unchanged, affectionately guiding a whole new generation of students—was that Reynolds has had the great good fortune to know his place, geographically speaking. More than any other writer I'm acquainted with, except perhaps for Eudora Welty, he has a feeling for the exact spot on earth that will properly contain him, and he has never let himself be lured away from it any longer than necessary.

As luck would have it, that spot is his family stomping grounds—semirural North Carolina, a country of scrubby woods and scrappy little towns. He was born in Macon, North Carolina, in 1933, the son of a door-to-door salesman and a woman who hadn't been educated past the eleven years of public schooling then available. The family moved from place to place within a narrow radius, incidentally exposing him to a nearly unbroken stream of those dedicated, selfless teachers who used to be so prevalent back when teaching was still recognized as a noble profession. ("They were mostly single women that seemed old and wise," says the heroine of *Kate Vaiden*, his latest novel, ". . . and the fact that I've made it this far upright is partly a tribute to their hard example that you get up each morning and *Take what comes*.")

It was his eighth-grade teacher in Warrenton who first encouraged his interest in writing and art—especially art. The two of them used to paint everything available; if they had nothing better to do, they'd decorate wine bottles and china dishes. Then in eleventh grade, at Broughton High School in Raleigh, Reynolds began to concentrate on writing under the direction of Phyllis Peacock, an English teacher whose name is legend to anyone who grew up in Raleigh during the fifties or sixties.

From Broughton he went on to Duke University, and there, during his senior year, he wrote his first two short stories, "Michael Egerton" and "A Chain of Love," for William Blackburn's creative-writing class. (Do you notice how his history—as told by Reynolds himself—is a progression from teacher to teacher? It may explain why he's so wholeheartedly poured his gifts back into his students.)

While he was at Duke, he met Eudora Welty, who came to give a lecture during his senior year and arranged for him to send his writing to her agent, Diarmuid Russell. Reynolds had heard she'd be arriving alone on a three A.M. train, so he showed up to escort her to her hotel; He wore a gray suit which Eudora, decades later, remembers as snow white. I don't know why everyone is so confused about Reynolds Price's wardrobe.

After graduating in 1955, he spent three years on a Rhodes Scholarship to Oxford, where he was encouraged by such people as Lord David Cecil, Stephen Spender, and W. H. Auden. But he felt he should settle near home—his father had died by then, leaving a widow and younger son—so he returned to Duke to teach and finish his first novel, *A Long and Happy Life*. And at Duke he has remained, except for one further year at Oxford and brief trips abroad. He is now James B. Duke Professor of English; he teaches one semester a year and writes during the other semester. Some of his students are the children of the students he taught when he first arrived.

What this stability has meant for his writing is that his fiction has roots— deep, tenacious roots to a part of the country that remains absolutely distinct from other parts. You may find shopping malls in North Carolina; you may come across those ubiquitous chocolate-chip-cookie boutiques and Olde English potpourri marts; but the people still have very much their own style of speaking, and Reynolds Price knows that style by heart. Any North Carolinian, reading one of his novels, must stop at least once per page to nod at the rightness of something a character says. It's not just the tone that's right; it's the startling, almost incongruous eloquence, for some of the state's least educated citizens can sling a metaphor pretty handily and know how to pack a punch into the homeliest remark. A bosomy girl in *A Long and Happy Life* has "God's own water wings inside her brassiere," according to one of the characters, while in *A Generous Man* a boy describes tobacco farming so vividly that the reader sags in sympathy: ". . . lose half my plants to frost and blue mold, then transplant the rest in early May and nurse it all summer like a millionaire's baby—losing half again to wet weather, dry weather, worms, blight."

It may be too that staying on home ground has helped Reynolds Price keep his fiction centered on the family he grew up in. He has remained intensely curious about his parents, alert to every story they passed on to him. *Kate Vaiden* began to take form after he wrote a poem, "A Heaven for Elizabeth Rodwell, My Mother" (*Poetry*, June 1984), in which he took the three hardest events his mother had to endure and gave them happy endings. Then he began remembering her tales of an orphaned childhood, and her stoicism when she faced death from an inoperable aneurysm. (She died in 1965.) Kate Vaiden is not literally Reynolds's mother, but she does have his mother's independence and strength of character. She's a bit more self-possessed, is all, Reynolds says; she was offered a bit more scope than Elizabeth Rodwell Price ever was.

In the summer of 1983 he started writing the novel, and he finished Part One at the end of May 1984. Then in June he learned that he had cancer of the spinal cord. He underwent immediate surgery, followed by an exhausting course of radiation and steroid therapy. The tumor was arrested, but he was no longer able to walk, and he entered a rehabilitation clinic to learn the practical strategies for life in a wheelchair. A mere three months after the original diagnosis (though it must have seemed an eternity), he was back at work—first not writing but drawing, as if retracing his career from childhood on; then two months later inching into the written word with a play, *August Snow*, commissioned by Hendrix College; and sailing off on an astonishing creative burst that produced two more plays, a volume of poetry, and a collection of essays. At that point he felt ready to continue with *Kate Vaiden*. He worried that the break might have altered his narrative voice, but he worried needlessly. Following his usual routine, working in longhand on legal pads, he picked up with Part Two and continued to the end of the book.

Kate Vaiden, too, develops cancer, and Reynolds says that that part of her story emerged from his recent experiences. But otherwise the novel remains untouched by his illness, and lacks any trace of bitterness. You could say the same for Reynolds himself. Whatever those first months must have cost him, he is now as high-spirited as ever. All that's new about him is a bigger set of biceps (he's changed shirt sizes since he started wheeling himself around) and a stock of funny stories about nurse's aides and wheelchair salesmen.

He lives where he has lived for the past twenty-eight years, next to a pond in the pines outside Durham; and when I visited him a younger writer, Daniel Voll, was sharing the house in order to help him navigate the stairs. (A single-floor addition that's now being built will soon allow him to be self-sufficient.) The rooms are stuffed with a mesmerizing collection of unrelated objects: fossils, cow skulls, death masks, and a personal letter from General Eisenhower dated 1943. Even the bathrooms are hung with photographs, and the kitchen windowsills are so densely lined with antique coins and pottery shards that for a moment I took an ordinary black metal window lock to be some kind of prehistoric artifact.

Around this labyrinth Reynolds wheels competently. He has returned to teaching after an eighteen-month sabbatical; even if he were a billionaire, he says, he would want to go on teaching. Teaching is his "serious hobby"; it keeps him in touch with the next generation. And he knows he has at least one thing of value to offer his students: practical, concrete advice for getting on with the job of writing. (I can bear witness to that, certainly; and so can at least a half-dozen other published writers he's taught, in addition to who knows how many more who will sooner or later hit print.) Really what he offers is *strategy*, he says. In fact he's a sort of rehab clinic. This notion makes him smile.

Dan Voll, who audited Reynolds's course during undergraduate days, tells how he spent his first session lurking apprehensively just outside the classroom doorway. Oh, Reynolds is thought to be pretty intimidating, if you ask the average Duke student. But that's only at the start, Reynolds argues. At the start he tells his class how he loves to root through Dempster Dumpsters in hopes of finding other people's mail to read, and then everybody relaxes. How can you be intimidated by someone who's confessed to that?

He smiles again. He does a little turn in his sporty tour-model wheelchair. The scarlet lining of his long black cape swirls out behind him.

SAUL BELLOW

....

BELLOW'S GIFT

by Martin Amis

MAY 2015

When Saul Bellow emerged and solidified as an intellectual presence—in Chicago and New York during the 1940s—he seemed formidably, enviably, indeed inexcusably well equipped to flourish in the spheres of literature and love. "Extremely handsome," according to one observer; "stunning," "beautiful," "irresistible," according to others. After his first novel appeared, in 1944, Bellow got a call from MGM: although he was too soulful-looking for a male lead, they explained, he could prosper as the type "who loses the girl to . . . George Raft or Errol Flynn." We may be sure that Bellow hardly listened. And it doesn't sound quite right for him, does it—aping a series of sexual inadequates (Ashley to Gable's Rhett?), in makeup and fancy dress, under the hot stare of the kliegs?

No, from the start Bellow radiated what Alfred Kazin called in his 1978 memoir, *New York Jew,* "a sense of his destiny as a novelist that excited everyone around him." Electrically sensitive to criticism, Bellow had a chip on his shoulder—but it was what one critic called "the chip of self-confidence." As Kazin wrote, "He expected the world to come to him." And it did. To quote from the opening sentence of Zachary Leader's magisterial biography *The Life of Saul Bellow: To Fame and Fortune, 1915–1964,* Bellow would go on to become "the most decorated writer in American history." He faced only one serious obstruction, and this vanished, as if at a snap of the fingers, on a certain day in 1949, when he was 33 and discovered "what I had been born for." As for women and love, on the other hand, he didn't get it right until 1986, when he was 71.

To round out the panoply of the young Bellow's attractions, he had about him the glamour and gravitas of turbulent exoticism. When his family crossed the Atlantic from Russia (St. Petersburg) to Canada (Lachine, then Montreal) in the early teens of the century, Saul was no more than a twinkle in his father's eye. Well, Abraham's eyes were capable of twinkling; far more typically, though, they blazed and seeped with frustration and rage. A versatile business flop, he struggled as a farmer, a wholesaler, a marriage broker, a junk dealer, and a bootlegger. "His talent," Saul would later write, "was for failure." Bellow Sr. eventually thrived (peddling fuel to bakeries), but he got angrier as he aged, and had fistfights in the street well into his 60s. The aggression was intelligible: Abraham knew what it was to wear the moral equivalent of the Star; Russian autocracy had condemned him to outlawry, imprisonment, ruin, and flight; later, too, he lost three sisters to the mechanized anti-Semitism of Nazi Germany.

In the end, Abraham was grateful to America (and even came to enjoy the novelty of paying his taxes), yet his assimilation was always fragmentary. "Wright me," he wrote to Saul, late in life: "A Ledder. Still I am The Head of all of U." And his wife, vague, frail, dreamy Liza, a figure of quiet pathos, simply didn't live long enough to adapt. As Leader records (and this is a typically luminous detail): "A great treat for Liza was a movie matinee on the weekend. Bellow sometimes accompanied her and remembered a low rumbling in the theater, that of dozens of child translators, himself included, whispering in Yiddish to their mothers."

Home life, then, was archaic, violent, loudmouthed, and "wholly Jewish." A mixed blessing, you might say, but that's the kind of blessing that all writers hold most dear.

At the start of 1924, Abraham made his way to Chicago, and six months later the rest of the family was "smuggled across the border by bootlegging associates," arriving on the Fourth of July in the capital of American "hard-boileddom" (Bellow's epithet). And of all the "reality instructors" who lined up to shape Saul's sensibility, the most dominant was that exemplary Chicagoan, Maury, the oldest of the brothers. Maury bestrides Bellow's fiction, making no fewer than five undisguised appearances—as Simon (*The Adventures of Augie March*), Shura (*Herzog*), Philip ("Him with His Foot in His Mouth"), Julius (*Humboldt's Gift*), and Albert ("Something to Remember Me By"). "You don't understand fuck-all," Albert characteristically informs his bookish kid brother. "You never will." Originally a bagman (and a skimmer), Maury married money and set about amassing a fortune in that hyperactively venal fringe between business and politics (one of the guests at his daughter's wedding was Jimmy Hoffa). As he saw it, all other concerns were mere snags in the engine of materialism.

"Enough of this old crap about being Jewish," Maury used to say. In *Herzog* (1964), when the hero weeps at his father's funeral, the senior brother, Shura, snarls at him, "Don't carry on like a goddamn immigrant." Brazen American plenitude was what Maury championed and embodied—with his "suburban dukedom," his 100 pairs of shoes and 300 suits. When Bellow won the Nobel, in 1976, Maury was at first affronted ("*I'm* really the smart one" was his attitude), then indifferent, despite a brief interest in the prize money—Was it tax-free? Could Saul stow it offshore? Yet Maury, a secret reader, harbored depth and convolution, and Bellow always believed that there was something tragic, something blind, headlong, and oblivion-seeking, in his drivenness. It was the revenge life takes on the man who knowingly chooses lucre over love.

And what about Bellow and love—the many affairs, the many marriages? Before we turn to them, we have to acknowledge a unique peculiarity of Bellow's art. When we say that this or that character is "based on" or "inspired by" this or that real-life original, we indulge in evasion. The characters are their originals, as we see from the family *froideurs,* the threatened lawsuits, the scandalized friends, and the embittered ex-wives. Leader deals with this crux immediately, in his introduction, and partly endorses the verdict of James Wood (one of Bellow's most sensitive critics), which invokes "an awkward but undeniable utilitarianism. . . . The number of people hurt by Bellow is probably no more than can be counted on two hands, yet he has delighted and consoled and altered the lives of thousands of readers." Bellow himself conceded that the question was "diabolically complex." But who in the end would wish things otherwise? That the characters come alive, or remain alive, on the page is not the result of artistic control so much as the sheer visionary affect of the prose. Bellow is *sui generis* and Promethean, a thief of the gods' fire: he is something like a supercharged plagiarist of Creation.

In his dealings with women he could be glacially passive, and he could be skittishly precipitate. "Somewhere in every intellectual," the brutal lawyer, Sandor, tells Herzog, "is a dumb prick." Bellow would have wholeheartedly agreed.

He got engaged to his first wife, Anita, in 1937; he was 21. And the only surprise is that the relationship took so long to wind down—after 15 years, 22 changes of address, and numberless infidelities. "I have no intention," he then wrote to his agent in 1955, "of bouncing from divorce into marriage." But that of course was exactly what he did, homing in, despite a fusillade of warning shots, on the naïve and volatile Sasha. Early on, a female friend noted that Bellow "was the kind of man who thought he could change women. . . . And he couldn't. I mean, who can? You don't." This is well said. But one surmises that the answer, if there is one, had more to do with literature than with life.

Happiness, noted Montherlant, writes white; it is invisible on the page. And the same is true of goodness. Anita was upstanding and altruistic, and is therefore a pallid presence in the novels; Sasha, by contrast, would be mythologized, demonized, and immortalized in *Herzog* as the terrifying emasculatrix, Mady. The terms of divorce No. 2 were settled in 1961, and within a month he was married to the equally glossy and unpromising Susan. It seems that his creative unconscious was attracted to difficulty—to make his fiction write black. This time he did at least manage an interlude of what Leader calls "strenuous womanizing": he returned from a tour of Europe "trailed by letters not only from Helen, Annie, Jara, and Alina" but also from Maryi, Hannah, Daniela, Maude, and Iline. As the first volume of *The Life* closes, Bellow is halfway through his matrimonial career; we know that there are two more divorces to go (Susan, Alexandra) before all is solved and salved with Janis, his true Platonic other. Hope triumphed over disappointment, and innocence triumphed over experience.

Something similar unfolded in the fiction. Again and again in his *Letters* (assembled in 2010), Bellow describes himself as a "comic" novelist, and this feels just. But there was little sign of such a cheerful self-assessment, and such an outcome, in his "prentice works" of the 1940s, *Dangling Man* and *The Victim*, which epitomize the sullen, cussed earnestness of the midcentury mood. His life-changing moment came with the conceptual birth of *The Adventures of Augie March* (1953) and took place, fittingly, in Paris—the world HQ of cerebral gloom. Bellow was in despair about his third novel, and with good reason: it was about two invalids in a hospital room. As he paced the streets one day Bellow watched the gutters being sluiced in "sunny iridescence." And it was a comprehensive epiphany: that was that. Marx, Trotsky, Sartre, *cafard, nausée*, alienation, existential woe, the Void, et cetera: all this he canceled and cursed. From here on he would commit himself to the free-flowing, and to the childhood perceptions of his "first heart" and his "original eyes." In short, he would trust his soul. And now the path was clear to the exuberantly meshuga glories of Augie March, Henderson, Herzog, and all the rest.

I knew Saul Bellow for two decades; I have known Professor Leader for three, and he is the author of a much-praised biography of my father, Kingsley Amis. So, full disclosure. It is, however, certain that I will not be alone in the expectation that *The Life of Saul Bellow* will prove definitive. Leader is respectful but unintimidated, balanced but never anodyne, and his literary criticism, like his prose, is unfailingly stylish and acute. The book is very learned and very long—the author happens to be a putter-in, not a leaver-out. But readers who enter into it will find a multitude of various fascinations: the gangland machine of Chicago, for instance; the tremors and prepercussions of the sexual revolution; Bellow's Romantic lineage (the affinities with Blake and Wordsworth); and the currents and commotions of the American cultural terrain, with its factions and rivalries, its questing energies, its fierce loyalties, and its fiercer hatreds.

The really fit biography should duplicate and dramatize a process familiar to us all. You lose, let us say, a parent or a beloved mentor. Once the primary reactions, both universal and personal, begin to fade, you no longer see the reduced and simplified figure, compromised by time—and in Bellow's case encrusted with secondhand "narratives," platitudes, and approximations. You begin to see the whole being, in all its freshness and quiddity. That is what happens here.

Right up to his death, in 1955, Abraham Bellow described Saul as a chronic worry to the family, the only son "not working only writing." Not working? He should tell that to Augie March (for Augie, it turns out, is the author of his *Adventures*):

> All the while you thought you were going around idle terribly hard work was taking place. Hard, hard work, excavation and digging, mining, moling through tunnels, heaving, pushing, moving rock, working, working, working, working, working, panting, hauling, hoisting. And none of this work is seen from the outside. It's internally done. It happens because you are powerless and unable to get anywhere, to obtain justice or have requital, and therefore in yourself you labor, you wage and combat, settle scores, remember insults, fight, reply, deny, blab, denounce, triumph, outwit, overcome, vindicate, cry, persist, absolve, die and rise again. All by yourself! Where is everybody? Inside your breast and skin, the entire cast.

JACK KEROUAC

KEROUAC'S LONESOME ROAD

by James Wolcott

OCTOBER 1999

Jack Kerouac, who died 30 years ago this October at the age of 47, committed suicide on the installment plan. He took his time on the checkout line, drinking himself numb. As a young man Kerouac was blessed with a handsome jaw, a dark, virile Superman forelock, an athletic build (he played football for Horace Mann), and a raft of life experience which set him apart from the baby owls in academe trying to emulate T. S. Eliot's dry-sherry manner. (Such as Allen Ginsberg, whom he met in 1944 at Columbia University, where Ginsberg was a student of the distinguished literary critic Lionel Trilling, the J. Alfred Prufrock of the English department. Kerouac met the other member of the Beat trinity, William Burroughs, later that year.) Kerouac's most famous achievement as a writer—*On the Road*, one version of which was typed on a 120-foot scroll of wire-service paper during a three-week Benzedrine-and-caffeine binge—was as much a physical feat as a creative splurge, the work of a powerful locomotive. Add to this a movie-star name (it even rhymed!) and a tough, wounded masculinity reminiscent of Marlon Brando, and it was no wonder fame found Kerouac a natural. But far more swiftly than Brando, Kerouac turned to bloat. As he wrote in a ditty called "Rose Pome," "I'd rather be thin than famous . . . / But I'm fat. Paste that in yr. Broadway Show."

When Kerouac died on October 21, 1969, of massive abdominal hemorrhaging in St. Petersburg, Florida, where he was visiting his mother, he was fat and mostly forgotten. "He was a very lonely man," his third wife, Stella, told the Associated Press. The portrait of Kerouac's last days was captured in an illustration for *Esquire* magazine (March 1970) which showed a beer-gut has-been slumped in an armchair surrounded by a stack of *National Review*s and a scatter of empty bottles: the king of the Beats on his crumb-bum throne. Once a charioteer hurtling toward the horizon, his car radio tuned in to the cosmos, Kerouac had degenerated into a test model for *All in the Family*'s Archie Bunker, grumbling about hippies, Commies, and Jews. The year 1969, remember, was also the year of *Easy Rider*, whose shock climax of bikers bushwhacked by rednecks spelled the end of the wind-whistling romance of freedom and acceptance celebrated in *On the Road*. At the time, it seemed plausible that his rebel yell would fade into a historical footnote, but 30 years after his death, Jack Kerouac still broods over the landscape, larger than ever. Kerouac lives.

Not only does he live in the minds of readers, he remains a wanted man, one of the few writers worth stealing. Like a saint's relics, his books attract thieves. At the St. Marks Bookstore and the Union Square Barnes & Noble in lower Manhattan, his paperbacks are so prey to shoplifting that they're kept behind the counter. Skyline Books, a secondhand store in Manhattan's photo district, offers a section of Beat memorabilia, a humble shrine which occasionally stocks back issues of *Holiday, Evergreen Review*, and *Escapade* containing articles by Kerouac. The Kerouac cult is part of the larger unquenchable fascination with all things Beat. For a group of writers who exalted and peddled drug highs, jazz sensations, spontaneous kicks, transient moods, Oriental-rug visions, and other wordless transports, it's ironic that they not only amassed mountains of their own pesky words but also inspired a beaver community of hangers-on, historians, critics, former lovers, and idolaters whose output threatens to dwarf the original peaks. Hundreds of titles have been published on the Beats from every personal-critical-psychosexual angle. A larger irony, given how heavily the Beats stressed the Zen Now, is the persistent backwash of nostalgia they left behind, a beckoning piano concerto of typewriter keys striking the page rivaled only by Hemingway's Paris in the 20s. The Beats have proved such an enduring beacon and monument on the pop-culture scene that even those who might be called children of the Beats, such as Patti Smith and Bob Dylan, have become sacred elders, presiding over their own flock of crows. The permanent Beat cult isn't strictly a literary phenomenon, even though the reading of *Howl, Naked Lunch*, and *On the Road* has become a classic rite of passage for every restless kid staring out the window at school. It's an initiation into a mythic tribe.

Kerouac was the heart and soul of the Beat operation. He coined the term "Beat"—beat as in worn, beat-down; beat as in beatific—and was its true apostle. William Burroughs, with his banker's suits and vampire demeanor, was the surrealist of the group, dishing up pristine cuts of rotting carcasses in *Naked Lunch*. Allen Ginsberg was the chief propagandist, a Jewish Buddhist huggy-bear devoted to good works and street theater (the attempt to levitate the Pentagon in the 1967 anti-war march, a quixotic magic act immortalized in Norman Mailer's *The Armies of the Night*, had Ginsberg written all over it). The great outlaw inspiration was Neal Cassady, Kerouac's model for Dean Moriarty in *On the Road* and the title character of *Visions of Cody*. An autodidact, pool shark, jail-bird, satyr, and roustabout,

Cassady bulleted through life with none of the inhibitions or Sorrows of Young Werther that plagued undergraduate bookworms like Kerouac and Ginsberg. (Burroughs, an old soul with no illusions to rend, always plotted his own pirate course.) Without the example of Cassady goosing them into action, the Beats might have remained a Romantic offshoot, a homegrown version of Rimbaud, Blake, and Shelley syncopated to the incantatory lines of Walt Whitman, never getting beyond the chatterbox stage.

Kerouac led the way out. He did what Cassady was unable to do—translate fugitive experience into what the critic and Beat-scene maker Seymour Krim dubbed Action Writing. In *On the Road* (1957), Kerouac piped the license and movement he found in Cassady through his own tenor-sax prose. It's become fashionable to say that *On the Road* doesn't "hold up," that it's dated and sentimental and backtracking. The issue of whether *On the Road* holds up is irrelevant to a kid cracking it open for the first time; to him (and it's usually a him, Kerouac's disciples being overwhelmingly male, in my experience), the novel isn't a literary artifact to be judged against the inner gold of other artifacts, but a personal saga and broadcast that bypass normal communication. To newbies, Kerouac's exploits aren't filtered through layers of critical analysis but come at them point-blank, just as Ginsberg's haranguing lines in *Howl* manage to hit new generations of readers full blast. Kerouac writes as if he's right there with you, a fellow passenger. (Kerouac himself seldom drove.)

> *"Everything in life is foreign territory. Kerouac—he's my teacher.*
> *The open road, my school."*
> —XANDER (NICHOLAS BRENDON),
> BRANDISHING A COPY OF *On the Road*
> IN AN EPISODE OF *Buffy the Vampire Slayer.*

It would be unfair to leave the patronizing impression that *On the Road* appeals only to untapped minds. I recently reread it, not having dipped into it since high school, and was bowled over by its superabundance of incidents, energy, open-pored passion, and canine devotion. Like his literary hero Thomas Wolfe, whose cathedral detailing and rhetorical swollen glands provided the model for Kerouac's first novel, *The Town and the City* (1950), Kerouac had America mapped in the palm of his hand. (Together, Wolfe and Kerouac helped father Bob Dylan, who rattles off place-names in his lyrics like a train conductor.) The lifeline in this palm is the Mississippi River, "the great brown father of waters rolling down from mid-America like the torrent of broken souls." As Kerouac's Sal Paradise caroms like a pinball from one bank of city lights to another ("with the radio on to a mystery program, and as I looked out the window and saw a sign that said USE COOPER'S

PAINT and I said, 'Okay, I will,' we rolled across the hoodwink night of the Louisiana plains . . ."), the novel flickers with snapshots of the poor and neglected in an ongoing montage which evokes not only Wolfe's night-watchman reveries but also the photographs of Robert Frank. (Kerouac did the foreword for Frank's *The Americans*, the most evocatively shrouded book of postwar photography.) Although *On the Road* was published in 1957, its action takes place 10 years earlier, tinged with a sepia-toned longing for a pre-TV America which retained vestiges of vagabond individuality. *On the Road* is a paradise-lost elegy but—here's its secret—a buoyant one, not some limp flag of commemoration.

The energy is rooted in misfit comedy. Often forgotten today is what a funny writer Kerouac was. The humor doesn't spout from dyspeptic one-liners (Burroughs's specialty) or facile absurdism, but finds release through the sheer collision force of all these human cannonballs smacking together. The section in *On the Road* where we're introduced to Bull Lee, the William Burroughs character, is a comic lithograph of Tristram Shandy—like eccentricity, from the pet ferret Lee used to keep in his "well-appointed rooms" to his drug tinkering ("He also experimented in boiling codeine cough syrup down to a black mash—that didn't work so well") to the following psychological checklist:

> He had a set of chains in his room that he said he used with his psycho-analyst; they were experimenting with narcoanalysis and found that Old Bull had seven separate personalities, each growing worse and worse on the way down, till finally he was a raving idiot and had to be restrained with chains. The top personality was an English lord, the bottom an idiot. Halfway he was an old Negro who stood in line, waiting with everyone else, and said, "Some's bastards, some's ain't, that's the score."

Driving fast and fighting sleep, Kerouac's road warriors are crying to outrace their own nervous breakdowns and demons as they gulp the scented night air. The novel eventually veers off to Mexico, as all salvation tours must, because that's where the madonna-whores are, tiny crosses dangling between the tawny bosoms on which our heroes can rest their mangy heads until it's tequila time.

Despite that legendary scroll, *On the Road* wasn't published hot out of the typewriter. The novel took years to gel; draft after draft was rejected by various houses, the standard edition trimmed and massaged into shape by the editor and critic Malcolm Cowley over Kerouac's foot-dragging objections. For years afterward, Kerouac and Ginsberg complained that Cowley's commonsensical Yankee approach took the snap out of the novel's serpentine spirit, taming its pulsating swing for a more straight-ahead story line. Instead, they should have shown some gratitude, for *On the Road* prospers and endures precisely because

Cowley found a way to bottle the lightning. It's the one Kerouac book that seems fully assembled and guided. In a letter to John Clellon Holmes, the author of the Beat novel *Go*, Kerouac championed "*wild form*, man, *wild form*"—but without an authorial design or editorial oversight Kerouac's writing tended to taper off into wispy formlessness. Even novels graced with epiphanies of pencil-sketch portraiture (*The Subterraneans*) or nature worship (*The Dharma Bums*) suffer from a noodling-doodling lack of dramatic emphasis. It's like listening to a musician tune up, only words are more than notes and sounds: they signify and convey meaning. Without somewhere useful to go, they lie there orphaned, mere jottings, providing evidence for Truman Capote's famous gibe, "It's not writing, it's typing." For all its hoots and yelps, *On the Road* is undeniably writing.

With the publication of *On the Road*, Kerouac awoke one morning to find he had won the literary lottery. After a rave review by Gilbert Millstein appeared in *The New York Times*, Kerouac's publisher arrived bearing champagne, and the phone began ringing with congratulations. Kerouac, however, wasn't ready for his screen test. Where Burroughs and Ginsberg knew how to joust with the press and were foxy enough to create brand-name personae (Burroughs was doing jeans commercials shortly before he died), Kerouac stumbled into traffic like a tourist, lost in the oncoming lights. His radio and television appearances took mumbling beyond Method acting (he sat and moped), his public readings were amateur hour (he never developed Ginsberg's bardic showmanship), and a famous panel discussion featuring Kingsley Amis, Ashley Montagu, and James Wechsler, among others, reduced him to clown antics. He seemed to regard tabloid ink as if it were his own spilled blood. The fame and all its goodies that most writers chase like an ice-cream truck sent Kerouac literally reeling in the other direction. His drinking intensified, turning Superman into Stuporman, his blackouts a foolhardy way of blotting out the world's now insatiable demands. At the height of the *On the Road* hullabaloo, Kerouac told Jerry Tallmer of *The Village Voice* that he was splitting this crazy scene. "I'm going down to my mother's in Orlando. Always go back to my mother. Always."

A grown man living with Mom, what could be squarer? Who did he think he was, Liberace? (Kerouac's mother was no sweetheart, either—Mémère read her son's mail like a prison snoop, refused to let Ginsberg into her house because he was a drug user and homosexual, and was so nasty that even the unflappable Burroughs considered her a minor form of evil.) Kerouac wasn't kidding, though. He unplugged himself like a neon sign. The drastic U-turn Kerouac made in his life—from gypsy preacher of Beat prophecy ("a White Storefront Church Built Like a Man, on wheels yet," in Seymour Krim's majestic estimation) to stay-at-home hermit—has a pathos and rotting integrity worthy of a Eugene O'Neill play set in a dim interior. One of the reasons Kerouac is such an unresolvable case three decades after his death is that by chucking it all he turned his hunched back not only on fame but on the entire notion of a literary career. Even writers who have shrouded themselves in secrecy (J. D. Salinger) or move among us like the Invisible Man (Thomas Pynchon) have produced a recognizable body of work which they zealously safeguard. Kerouac, however, seemed to tear up the books he had within him into many pigeon scraps. Alcohol may have so hollowed him out that all he could hear were echoes of what he had done before and of those he had left behind. Jack McClintock, a newspaper reporter who visited Kerouac in St. Petersburg in his last few months, speculated in *Esquire:* "It was almost as if Kerouac, in the last years, had burrowed farther and farther back into his personality, back into the dense-packed delights and detritus of a life, and then turned around, and was peering out at the thronged world through the tunnel he made going in. Perhaps being back there clarified his sight in some ways, focused it more clearly on the things he could see. Perhaps it just gave him tunnel vision. I don't know."

After Kerouac died, his body was shipped to Lowell, Massachusetts, for burial. Vivian Gornick covered the funeral in an affecting piece for *The Village Voice*, recording the dignity of Allen Ginsberg and his lover Peter Orlovsky, the generous heft of the townspeople, and the sight of Kerouac in his open casket, waxy and remote, "stripped of all his ravaging joy." Kerouac seemed roadkill from a bygone era when he was put to rest, but over the succeeding years he rose to the stature of Hank Williams and James Dean and other saints of the celestial highway. Ginsberg and Dylan made a pilgrimage to his grave site during the Rolling Thunder tour of 1975, providing one of the few grace notes to the film *Renaldo and Clara*.

In 1988 the city of Lowell erected an elaborate memorial for Kerouac, an event which had the neoconservative commentator Norman Podhoretz shaking his fist at the temerity of officials honoring this hooligan. As a climbing young critic, Podhoretz had written a much-reprinted essay 30 years before called "The Know-Nothing Bohemians," which accused the Beats of being storm troopers in sandals (their marching orders: "Kill the intellectuals who can talk coherently, kill the people who can sit still for five minutes at a time, kill those incomprehensible characters who are capable of getting seriously involved with a woman, a job, a cause"—kill, kill, kill!). So he at least had the virtue of being a consistent crab. To Podhoretz and other cultural declinists, the Beats were nihilists responsible for the hedonistic disarray of the 60s, never mind that Kerouac himself repudiated Abbie Hoffman and his Yippie followers. He once removed an American flag Allen Ginsberg had wrapped around his, Kerouac's, shoulders like a shawl, folding it properly, and explaining, "The flag is not a rag." Which didn't deter Podhoretz from fuming in the *New York Post,* "Dropping out, hitting the road, taking drugs, hopping from bed to bed with partners of either sex or both—all in the name of liberation from the death-dealing embrace of middle-class conventions. . . . This, then, is what the City of Lowell is inescapably honoring in building a monument to Kerouac," those heathens.

What really bothers Kerouac's killjoy detractors is that a memorial for the Beat King is a victory for reckless creativity over critical rigor. In Podhoretz's Manichaean mind, it's reason, coherence, tradition, Judeo-Christian ethics, and monogamous maturity versus risk, itchy impulses, immediacy, Eastern mysticism, and dirty feet on a bare mattress, and guess what?—*his side lost*. O, the inequity of it all, mastering the nuances of modernism only to be shunted aside by this bony army of hairy armpits! Deeper than the Culture War or an Alamo defense of literacy and even more vexing to those suffering from Beat antipathy is the knowledge that replenishing waves of readers love Kerouac—no other word will do—love him despite himself, despite his drunkenness, racist insults, and unreliability (he's the deadbeat dad everyone's decided to forgive). Kerouac is loved and mourned for the loneliness that penalized him most of his life and for the rugged reflection he left in the hard surface of American life. "America is where you're not even allowed to cry for yourself," Kerouac observed in *Visions of Cody*, and he may have been the last American writer without a trace of cynicism or protective guile. (Of those who came after, only Raymond Carver tiptoed around similar heartbreak.) It was a tragedy for him and for American fiction once he was no longer able to articulate the tempests he felt. He withdrew, suffered like a saint, and prematurely aged, yet some part of him stayed rockabilly to the end. "The only time I saw him with his hair combed," Jack McClintock wrote in *Esquire*, "was in his casket."

TRUMAN CAPOTE

CAPOTE'S SWAN DIVE

by Sam Kashner

DECEMBER 2012

"Have you seen *Esquire*?! Call me as soon as you're finished," New York society doyenne Babe Paley asked her friend Slim Keith over the telephone when the November 1975 issue hit the stands. Keith, then living at the Pierre hotel, sent the maid downstairs for a copy. "I read it, and I was absolutely horrified," she later confided to the writer George Plimpton. "The story about the sheets, the story about Ann Woodward. . . . There was no question in anybody's mind who it was."

The story they were reading in *Esquire* was "La Côte Basque 1965," but it wasn't so much a story as an atomic bomb that Truman Capote built all by himself in his U.N. Plaza apartment and at his beach house in Sagaponack, Long Island. It was the first installment of *Answered Prayers,* the novel that Truman believed would be his masterpiece.

He had boasted to his friend Marella Agnelli, wife of Gianni Agnelli, chairman of the board at Fiat, that *Answered Prayers* was "going to do to America what Proust did to France." He couldn't stop talking about his planned *roman à clef.* He told *People* magazine that he was constructing his book like a gun: "There's the handle, the trigger, the barrel, and, finally, the bullet. And when that bullet is fired from the gun, it's going to come out with a speed and power like you've never seen—*wham!*"

But he had unwittingly turned the gun on himself: exposing the secrets of Manhattan's rich and powerful was nothing short of social suicide.

He had been a literary darling since the age of 23, when his first novel, *Other Voices, Other Rooms,* was published. Seventeen years later, in 1965, *In Cold Blood,* his extraordinary "nonfiction novel" about the brutal murder of the Clutters, a Kansas farm family, brought him international fame, sudden wealth, and literary accolades beyond anything he'd experienced before.

But trying to write *Answered Prayers,* and its eventual fallout, destroyed him. By 1984, after several unsuccessful stays at dry-out centers such as Hazelden and

Smithers, Capote seemed to have given up not only on the book but on life. Abandoned by most of his society friends, locked in a brutal, self-destructive relationship with a middle-aged, married, former bank manager from Long Island, Truman was worn out. Or heartbroken.

After "La Côte Basque 1965," only two more of its chapters were published, both in *Esquire:* "Unspoiled Monsters" (May 1976) and "Kate McCloud" (December 1976). ("Mojave," which had appeared in *Esquire* in June 1975, was initially intended to be part of *Answered Prayers,* but Truman changed his mind about its inclusion.)

Truman had recorded in his journals the outline for the entire book, which would comprise seven chapters. The remaining four were titled "Yachts and Things," "And Audrey Wilder Sang," "A Severe Insult to the Brain" (which according to urban legend was the cause of death on Dylan Thomas's death certificate), and "Father Flanagan's All-Night Nigger Queen Kosher Café," the provocative title for the teeth-rattling concluding chapter. Truman claimed in his journals he had actually written it first.

But was the novel ever completed? A number of Truman's friends, including Joanne Carson (the second wife of television host Johnny Carson), say that he had read various unpublished chapters to them. "I saw them," Joanne recalls. "He had a writing room in my house—he spent a lot of time here because it was a safe place and nobody could get to him—and he had many, many pages of manuscript, and he started to read them. They were very, very good. He read one chapter, but then someone called, and when I went back he just put them aside and said, 'I'll read them after dinner.' But he never did—you know how that happens."

After Capote's death, on August 25, 1984, just a month shy of his 60th birthday, Alan Schwartz (his lawyer and literary executor), Gerald Clarke (his friend and biographer), and Joe Fox (his Random House editor) searched for the manuscript of the unfinished novel. Random House wanted to recoup something of the advances it had paid Truman—even if that involved publishing an incomplete manuscript. (In 1966, Truman and Random House had signed a contract for *Answered Prayers* for an advance of $25,000, with a delivery date of January 1, 1968. Three years later, they renegotiated to a three-book contract for an advance of $750,000, with delivery by September 1973. The contract was amended three more times, with a final agreement of $1 million for delivery by March 1, 1981. That deadline passed like all the others with no manuscript being delivered.)

Following Capote's death, Schwartz, Clarke, and Fox searched Truman's apartment, on the 22nd floor of the U.N. Plaza, with its panoramic view of Manhattan and the United Nations. It had been bought by Truman in 1965 for $62,000 with his royalties from *In Cold Blood.* (A friend, the set designer Oliver

Smith, noted that the U.N. Plaza building was "glamorous, *the* place to live in Manhattan" in the 1960s.) The three men looked among the stacks of art and fashion books in Capote's cluttered Victorian sitting room and pored over his bookshelf, which contained various translations and editions of his works. They poked among the Tiffany lamps, his collection of paperweights (including the white rose paperweight given to him by Colette in 1948), and the dying geraniums that lined one window ("bachelor's plants," as writer Edmund White described them). They looked through drawers and closets and desks, avoiding the three taxidermic snakes Truman kept in the apartment, one of them, a cobra, rearing to strike.

The men scoured the guest bedroom, at the end of the hallway—a tiny, peach-colored room with a daybed, a desk, a phone, and lavender taffeta curtains. Then they descended 15 floors to the former maid's studio, where Truman had often written by hand on yellow legal pads.

"We found nothing," Schwartz told *Vanity Fair.* Joanne Carson claims that Truman had confided to her that the manuscript was tucked away in a safe-deposit box in a bank in California—maybe Wells Fargo—and that he had handed her a key to it the morning before his death. But he declined to tell her which bank held the box. "The novel will be found when it wants to be found," he told her cryptically.

The three men then traveled to Truman's rustic beach house, tucked away behind scrub pine, privet hedges, and hydrangea, on six acres, in Sagaponack. They enlisted the help of two of Truman's closest friends in later years, Joe Petrocik and Myron Clement, who ran a small P.R. firm and had a house in nearby Sag Harbor.

"He was just a wonderful person to us, a great friend," Clement recalls. "Truman would talk to us about all these things that were going into *Answered Prayers,*" says Petrocik. "I remember I was at the other end of his couch, and he's reading all this from a manuscript. Then he'd take a break, get up, and pour himself a Stoli. But the thing is, at that time, I never saw the actual manuscript. And then it occurred to me, later, just before I nodded off to sleep, maybe he had made the whole thing up. He was such a wonderful, wonderful actor."

Later on, though, Petrocik remembers, he was traveling with Truman from Manhattan to Long Island when "Truman handed me the manuscript to read on the way. I actually had it in my hands."

But after a thorough search of the beach house, no manuscript was found. Now, nearly 30 years later, the questions remain: What happened to the rest of *Answered Prayers*? Had Truman destroyed it, simply lost it, or hidden it, or had he never written it at all? And why on earth did he publish "La Côte Basque 1965" so early, considering the inevitable backlash?

Gerald Clarke, author of the masterful *Capote: The Biography,* recalls

Truman telling him, in 1972, "I always planned this book as being my principal work . . . I'm going to call it a novel, but in actual fact it's a *roman à clef.* Almost everything in it is true, and it has . . . every sort of person I've ever had any dealings with. I have a cast of thousands."

He had begun thinking about it as early as 1958 and wrote a complete outline, and even an ending. He also wrote part of a screenplay that year with the title *Answered Prayers,* about a manipulative southern gigolo and his unhappy paramour. Though the screenplay was apparently abandoned, the idea took shape as a lengthy, Proustian novel. The title is taken from St. Teresa of Avila, the 16th-century Carmelite nun, who famously said, "More tears are shed over answered prayers than unanswered ones."

In a letter to Random House publisher and co-founder Bennett Cerf, written from Páros, Greece, in the summer of 1958, Truman promised that he was in fact working on "a large novel, my magnum opus, a book about which I must be very silent. . . . The novel is called, 'Answered Prayers'; and, if all goes well, I think it will answer mine." But before he could write it, another work took over Truman's life: *In Cold Blood.* Begun in 1959, it would consume six years of his life—most of it spent living in Kansas, a world away from the New York society he loved and from the city where he felt he belonged.

IN COLD INK

In "La Côte Basque 1965," Capote turned his diamond-brilliant, diamond-hard artistry on the haut monde of New York society fixtures: Gloria Vanderbilt, Babe Paley, Slim Keith, Lee Radziwill, Mona Williams—elegant, beautiful women he called his "swans." They were very soignée and very rich and also his best friends. In the story Capote revealed their gossip, the secrets, the betrayals—even a murder. "All literature is gossip," Truman told *Playboy* magazine after the controversy erupted. "What in God's green earth is *Anna Karenina* or *War and Peace* or *Madame Bovary,* if not gossip?"

The story was intended to be the fifth chapter of the book, its title referring to Henri Soulé's celebrated restaurant, on East 55th Street, across from the St. Regis hotel. It was where the swans gathered to lunch and to see and be seen. In the story a literary hustler and bisexual prostitute named P. B. Jones—"Jonesy"—runs into "Lady Ina Coolbirth" on the street. A much-married-and-divorced society matron, she has been stood up by the Duchess of Windsor, so she invites Jonesy to join her for lunch at one of the coveted tables at the front of the restaurant. Lady Coolbirth, in Truman's words, is "a big breezy peppy broad" from the American West, now married to an English aristocrat. If she had looked in the mirror, she would have seen Slim Keith, who had been well and often married, to film director Howard Hawks and film and theatrical producer Leland Hayward before wedding the English banker Sir Kenneth Keith.

The story unfolds as a long, gossipy conversation—a monologue, really—delivered by Lady Coolbirth over countless flutes of Roederer Cristal champagne. She observes the other ladies who lunch—Babe Paley and her sister Betsey Whitney; Lee Radziwill and her sister, Jacqueline Kennedy; and Gloria Vanderbilt and her friend Carol Matthau. Or, as Capote wrote, "Gloria Vanderbilt de Cicco Stokowski Lumet Cooper and her childhood chum, Carol Marcus Saroyan Saroyan (she married *him* twice) Matthau: women in their late thirties, but looking not much removed from those deb days when they were grabbing Lucky Balloons at the Stork Club." Other boldfaced names who appear undisguised include Cole Porter coming on to a handsome Italian waiter; Princess Margaret, who makes snide comments about "poufs"; and Joe Kennedy, jumping into bed with one of his daughter's 18-year-old school chums.

Lady Coolbirth grouses about having got stuck at a dinner next to Princess Margaret, who bored her into semi-unconsciousness. As for Gloria Vanderbilt, Capote presents her as empty-headed and vain, especially when she fails to recognize her first husband, who stops by her table to say hello. ("'Oh, darling. Let's not brood,' says Carol consolingly. 'After all, you haven't seen him in over twenty years.'") When Vanderbilt read the story, she supposedly said, "The next time I see Truman Capote, I'm going to spit in his face."

"I think Truman really hurt my mother," the CNN journalist and newscaster Anderson Cooper says today.

But the tale that spread like a prairie fire up Park Avenue was a thinly disguised account of a humiliating one-night stand endured by "Sidney Dillon," a stand-in for William "Bill" Paley, the head of the CBS television-and-radio network and one of the most powerful men in New York at that time. Bill and Truman were friends, but Truman worshipped his wife, Barbara "Babe" Paley—the tall, slim, elegant society doyenne widely considered to have been the most beautiful and chic woman in New York. Of Truman's haut monde swans, Babe Paley was the most glamorous. Truman once noted in his journals, "Mrs. P had only one fault: she was perfect; otherwise, she was perfect." The Paleys practically adopted Truman; photographs of the three of them at the Paleys' house in Jamaica show the tall, handsome couple with tiny Truman standing beside them, wearing swimming trunks and a cat-that-ate-the-canary smile, as if he were their pampered son.

The one-night stand in the story occurs between Dillon and the dowdy wife of a New York governor, possibly based on Nelson Rockefeller's second wife, Mary, known by her nickname "Happy." She was "a cretinous Protestant size forty who wears low-heeled shoes and lavender water," Truman cattily wrote, who "looked as if she wore tweed brassieres and played a lot of golf." Though married to "the most beautiful creature alive," Dillon desires the governor's wife because she represents the only thing that lies outside of Dillon's grasp—acceptance by old-money Wasp society, a plum denied Dillon because he is Jewish. Dillon sits next to the governor's wife at a dinner party, flirts with her, and invites her up to his New York pied-à-terre, at the Pierre, saying he "wanted her opinion of his new Bonnard." After they have sex, he discovers that her menstrual blood has left a stain "the size of Brazil" on his bedsheet. Worried that his wife will arrive at any moment, Dillon scrubs the sheet in the bathtub, on his hands and knees, and then attempts to dry it by baking it in the oven before replacing it on the bed.

Within hours of the story's publication in *Esquire,* frantic phone calls were made all over the Upper East Side. Slim called back Babe, who asked of the Sidney Dillon character, "You don't think that it's Bill, do you?"

"Of course not," Slim lied, but she had heard from Truman months earlier that indeed it was Bill Paley.

Babe was horrified and heartbroken. She was seriously ill at the time with terminal lung cancer, and, instead of blaming her husband for the infidelity, she blamed Truman for putting it into print. Sir John Richardson, the acclaimed Picasso biographer and *Vanity Fair* contributing editor, saw her often during the last months of her life. "Babe was appalled by 'La Côte Basque,'" he recalls. "People used to talk about Bill as a philanderer, but his affairs weren't the talk of the town until Truman's story came out."

Babe would never speak to Truman again.

But her response paled compared with the reaction of another one of Truman's subjects: Ann Woodward. She had achieved notoriety for having shot and killed her husband 20 years earlier, but the story had been largely forgotten before "La Côte Basque 1965" was published. Woodward—Ann Hopkins in Truman's story—enters the restaurant, creating an immediate stir; even the Bouvier sisters, Jacqueline and Lee, take note. In Truman's retelling of the saga, Ann is a beautiful redhead from the West Virginia hills whose Manhattan odyssey had taken her from call girl to "the favorite lay of one of [gangster] Frankie Costello's shysters," to—ultimately—the wife of David Hopkins (William Woodward Jr.), a handsome young scion of wealth and "one of the bluest of New York's blue bloods." Ann is another of the many Holly Golightly figures who make their appearances throughout Truman's oeuvre—beautiful, social-climbing waifs from the rural South who move to New York and re-invent themselves, not unlike Truman's own personal journey. But Ann continued to philander, and David—eager to divorce her—discovered that she had failed to dissolve a teenage marriage undertaken back in West Virginia, and thus they weren't legally married after all. Terrified that he will kick her out, Ann takes advantage of a rash of break-ins in the neighborhood and loads a shotgun, which she keeps beside her bed. She fatally shoots David, claiming that she mistook him for an intruder. Her mother-in-law, Hilda Hopkins (Elsie Woodward), desperate to avoid a scandal, pays off the police, and an inquest never brings charges against Ann for murder.

On October 10, 1975, just a few days before the November *Esquire* appeared, Ann Woodward was found dead. Many believed that someone had sent her an advance copy of Truman's story and she'd killed herself, by swallowing cyanide. "We'll never know, but it's possible that Truman's story pushed her over the edge," says Clarke. "Her two sons later committed suicide as well." Ann's mother-in-law grimly said, "Well, that's that. She shot my son, and Truman murdered her . . ."

LADIES WHO PUNCH

Luckily for Truman he was able to hightail it out of town when "La Côte Basque 1965" was published, to begin rehearsals for his first starring role in a film, Columbia Pictures' 1976 comedy *Murder by Death,* produced by Ray Stark. Accompanied by John O'Shea, his middle-aged bank-manager lover from Wantagh, Long Island, Truman rented a house at 9421 Lloydcrest Drive, in Beverly Hills. The murder-mystery spoof, written by Neil Simon and directed by Robert Moore, cast a number of great comic actors in roles parodying famous detectives—Peter Falk as Sam Diamond (Sam Spade), James Coco as Milo Perrier (Hercule Poirot), Peter Sellers as Sidney Wang (Charlie Chan), Elsa Lanchester as Miss Marbles (Miss Marple), and David Niven and Maggie Smith as Dick and Dora Charleston (Nick and Nora Charles). Alec Guinness played a blind butler (as in "the butler did it"), and Truman played Mr. Lionel Twain, an eccentric connoisseur of crime. It was supposed to be great fun, but Truman found working on *Murder by Death* to be grueling. O'Shea recalled that "he used to get up in the morning as if he were going to the gallows, instead of the studio."

Though his screen time was quite brief, he crowed to a visiting journalist on the set of *Murder by Death* in Burbank, "What Billie Holiday is to jazz, what Mae West is to tits . . . what Seconal is to sleeping pills, what King Kong is to penises, Truman Capote is to the great god Thespis!" In reality he was not much of an actor, and he looked bloated and unwell on-screen. The reviews were not kind.

While in Los Angeles, Truman spent much of his time at Joanne Carson's Malibu house. She stood by helplessly while he rattled around, still stunned by the reaction to "La Côte Basque 1965." He complained to Joanne, "But they know I'm a writer. I don't understand it."

To café society, his departure from New York looked like pure cowardice. He phoned Slim Keith, whom he often called "Big Mama," but she refused to talk to him. Unable to accept Slim's rejection, he boldly sent her a cable in Australia at the end of the year, where she was spending the holidays: "Merry Christmas, Big Mama. I've decided to forgive you. Love, Truman." Far from forgiving him, Slim had consulted a lawyer about suing Truman for libel. But what really broke his heart was the reaction from the Paleys.

Screwing up his courage, Truman phoned Bill Paley, who took the call. Paley was civil but distant, and Truman had to ask if he'd read the *Esquire* story. "I started, Truman," he said, "but I fell asleep. Then a terrible thing happened: the magazine was thrown away." Truman offered to send him another copy. "Don't bother, Truman. I'm preoccupied right now. My wife is very ill." Truman was devastated by those words—"my wife"—as if his wife weren't Babe Paley, a woman whom Truman idolized and whose friendship he had long treasured. Now she was mortally ill, and he wasn't even allowed to speak to her.

Babe died in the Paleys' Fifth Avenue apartment on July 6, 1978. Truman was not invited to the funeral. "The tragedy is that we never made up before she died," he told Gerald Clarke years after her death.

"Truman's 'Côte Basque' was all anybody was talking about," columnist Liz Smith remembers. She was asked by Clay Felker, the editor of *New York* magazine, to interview him. "Truman was thrilled that I was going to do it. I went to Hollywood to interview him. I'll never forget how distraught he was because the pressure was building. In the Padrino bar, in the Beverly Wilshire, he said, 'I'm going to call [former *Vogue* editor] Mrs. Vreeland, and you'll see that she's really on my side.' So he caused a big ruckus and they brought a phone [to the table]. He called her. He said, 'I'm sitting here with Liz Smith, and she tells me that everyone is against me, but I know you're not.' He went on and on, holding the phone out for me to hear." Vreeland spouted a series of inscrutable responses—"meaning everything and nothing—but Truman didn't get the vote of confidence he was hoping for."

Smith came away worried about Truman, "because it seemed as if he was going to go all to pieces. He was the most surprised and shocked person you can imagine, and he would call to ask me—torment me—about what people in New York had said about him. After 'La Côte Basque' he was never happy again."

Smith's ensuing article, "Truman Capote in Hot Water," ran in the February 9, 1976, issue of *New York*. "Society's sacred monsters at the top have been in a state of shock," Smith wrote. "Never have you heard such gnashing of teeth, such cries for revenge, such shouts of betrayal and screams of outrage." In her article Smith outed those swans Truman had bothered to thinly disguise: Lady Coolbirth was Slim Keith; Ann Hopkins was Ann Woodward; Sidney Dillon was Bill Paley. "It's one thing to tell the nastiest story in the world to all your fifty best friends," Smith wrote. "It's another to see it set down in cold, Century Expanded type."

And not only did the swans turn against him, their husbands did as well, even if they weren't mentioned in the story. Louise Grunwald, who had worked at *Vogue* before she married Henry Grunwald, the editor in chief of Time Inc. magazines, noticed that Truman's friendships with women would not have flourished had he not also charmed their husbands. "Most men of that era," she recalls, "were homophobic—very homophobic. But Truman was their exception, because he was so amusing. Nobody came into their houses that the husbands didn't approve of. In a way, Truman could be very seductive, and he was a good listener. He was sympathetic. He seduced both the men and the women."

But as the scandal unfolded, "Are you seeing Truman or are you not?" was whispered throughout New York's high society. Slim Keith would run into him occasionally at the restaurant Quo Vadis, on East 63rd Street between Madison and Park Avenues, but she "never looked up at his face again," Keith bragged to George Plimpton. Ostracizing Truman became the thing to do. "In the long run, the rich run together, no matter what," Truman said in a 1980 *Playboy*-magazine interview. "They will cling, until they feel it's safe to be disloyal, then no one can be more so."

At least Lee Radziwill and Carol Matthau, who did not come off badly in "La Côte Basque 1965," stood up for Truman. Radziwill felt that it was *Truman* who had been "taken advantage of by a lot of people he thought were his friends. After all, he was fun and interesting to talk to, and brilliant. Why wouldn't they want to have him around? He was absolutely in shock" about café society's re-action, she recalls. "He'd hear of another monument falling, and he'd say, 'But I'm a journalist—everybody knows that I'm a journalist!' I just don't think he realized what he was doing, because, God, did he pay for it. That's what put him back to serious drinking. And then, of course, the terrible fear that he could never write another word again. It was all downhill from then on."

"Unspoiled Monsters" appeared next. It's a mordantly funny, hair-raising, but deeply cynical account of a fictional writer named P. B. Jones (the P.B. standing for Paul Bunyan, Capote noted in his journals), who is the Jonesy in "La Côte Basque 1965." It's a far cry from the honeysuckle lyricism of Capote's earlier work, or the stark reportage of *In Cold Blood;* it tells the picaresque tale of young Jones, the gay hustler who beds men and women alike if they can further his literary career. Katherine Anne Porter makes a disguised appearance, as does Tennessee Williams, both in cruel caricatures. Like Truman, Jones is writing a novel called *Answered Prayers,* even using the same Blackwing pencils Truman favored. He's a charming but hard-bitten, male version of Holly Golightly, having escaped a Catholic orphanage to flourish in New York. His impoverished past, Truman later confided, was borrowed from the life story of Perry Smith, the dark-haired, dark-eyed murderer Truman came to know intimately while writing *In Cold Blood.* In a sense, P. B. Jones is both Truman *and* Perry, a figure who haunted Truman's last decade and whose execution by hanging—which Truman witnessed—would devastate him emotionally.

The title character of "Kate McCloud," which followed in *Esquire,* was modeled on Mona Williams, later Mona von Bismarck, another oft married socialite friend of Truman's whose cliff-top villa on Capri he'd visited. Of Mona's five husbands, one, James Irving Bush, was described as "the handsomest man in America" and another, Harrison Williams, as "the richest man in America." Also, like Holly Golightly, the red-haired, green-eyed beauty had begun life more modestly, the daughter of a groom on the Kentucky estate of Henry J. Schlesinger, who became her first husband. A generation older than Truman's other swans, she was not generally recognized as a model for Kate McCloud, except by John Richardson, who recalls, "I was convinced it was Mona—it was so obvious."

Why was Truman so surprised by the reaction of his swans? "I'd never seen anything like it," Clarke recalls. "I read 'La Côte Basque' one summer day in Gloria Vanderbilt's swimming pool in the Hamptons when Gloria and her husband, Wyatt Cooper, were away. I was reading it while Truman was floating in the pool on a raft. I said, 'People aren't going to be happy with this, Truman.' He said, 'Nah, they're too dumb. They won't know who they are.' He could not have been more wrong."

So, why did he do it?

"I wonder whether he wasn't testing the love of his friends, to see what he could get away with. We had Truman around because he paid for his supper," Richardson says, "by being the great storyteller in the marketplace of Marrakech. Truman was a brilliant raconteur. We'd say, 'Oh, do tell us what Mae West was really like,' or what did he know about Doris Duke? And he'd go on in that inimitable voice for 20 minutes, and it was absolutely marvelous, one story after another. And he loved doing it—he was a show-off."

Truman bristled at the idea that he was some sort of mascot or lapdog. "I was never that," he insisted. "I had a lot of rich friends. I don't particularly like rich people. In fact, I have a kind of contempt for most of them. . . . Rich people I know would be totally lost . . . if they didn't have their money. That's why . . . they hang together so closely like a bunch of bees in a beehive, because all they really have is their money." In what would become a mantra of Truman's, he often asked, "What did they expect? I'm a writer, and I use everything. Did all those people think I was there just to entertain them?"

BREAKFAST AT STUDIO 54

Truman's decline was unstoppable. In addition to his alcohol abuse, he was partaking heavily of cocaine. He fell in love with Studio 54, the quintessential 70s disco, which opened in April of 1977. Truman described it as "the nightclub of the future. It's very democratic. Boys with boys, girls with girls, girls with boys, blacks and whites, capitalists and Marxists, Chinese and everything else—all one big mix." He spent many nights watching from the D.J.'s crow's nest overlooking the dance floor—"the men running around in diapers, cocktail waiters in satin basketball shorts, often lured away by the customers"—or dancing madly by himself, laughing delightedly every time a giant man in the moon suspended over the dance floor brought a spoonful of white powder to its nose. Banished from café society, he embraced this louche, hedonistic world and was taken up by Andy Warhol and the Factory, where drugs flowed as freely as gossip had at La Côte Basque and Quo Vadis. The revelers at Studio 54 didn't care that Truman had spilled the beans—they didn't know or care who Babe Paley was.

V.F. special correspondent Bob Colacello, a former editor of Andy Warhol's *Interview* magazine, for which Truman was by this time writing a column called "Conversations with Capote," felt that "Truman enjoyed it all, but I think that deep down he wished that he could have just gone to lunch with Babe Paley."

The effect of his new lifestyle was devastating. His weight ballooned, drowning his once delicate features in alcoholic bloat. "Long before Truman died," John Richardson recalls, "I saw a sort of bag lady with two enormous bags wandering around the corner of Lexington and 73rd, where I lived then. And suddenly, I realized, Christ! It's Truman! I said, 'Come on by and have a cup of tea.'" At the apartment, Richardson went to the kitchen to make the tea, and by the time he got back, "half a bottle of vodka—or scotch or whatever it was—was gone. I had to take him outside and gently put him into a cab."

Lee Radziwill recalls she and Truman "drifted apart because of his drinking. We just forgot about one another. I mean, I never forgot about him, but we didn't see each other, because he wasn't making any sense whatsoever. It was pitiful. Heartbreaking, because there was nothing you could do. He really wanted to kill himself. It was a slow and painful suicide."

The last straw was when Truman and John O'Shea came to stay with Lee at Turville Grange, her and Prince Radziwill's country house in England. "They were not getting along well, to say the least. I didn't want them to come, because I knew, even before he arrived, that Truman was in terrible shape. Stas left me alone with them. I said, 'You can't!' Thank God we had a guesthouse in the courtyard because they were fighting the entire time, and they broke most of the furniture in the cottage. Finally, they left. That's the last time I remember seeing Truman."

But what really shattered their friendship was the lawsuit for libel brought against Truman by Gore Vidal. In an interview Truman had given to *Playgirl* magazine, he related a story about how Vidal "got drunk [and] insulted Jackie's mother" at a White House dinner party in November 1961 and was bodily removed from the White House by Bobby Kennedy and Arthur Schlesinger. The real incident was more benign—Gore and Bobby Kennedy had indeed gotten into an argument, when Bobby saw Gore's hand resting on Jackie's shoulder ("Fuck you"s were allegedly exchanged), but there was no physical heave-ho from the White House. Gore was incensed at Truman's story, the culmination of a feud that had smoldered between the two men for decades. Vidal demanded an apology and $1 million in damages.

Truman entreated Liz Smith to persuade Vidal to drop his lawsuit, which he refused to do. He then asked her to ask Lee Radziwill to give a deposition in his favor, as he said he had first gotten the story from Lee, but Lee was no longer returning Truman's calls. So the columnist called Radziwill and asked her to say at least that the incident had in fact occurred, "otherwise, Gore is going to win this lawsuit, and it's just going to crush Truman."

Radziwill told *Vanity Fair,* "I knew that Truman loathed Gore. [Vidal] was a very brilliant but very mean man. . . . When Truman asked me to do the deposition for him, I never knew anything about depositions. I was very upset that he lost. I felt it was my fault."

The lawsuit lingered for seven years, until Alan Schwartz made a direct appeal to Vidal himself. "Look," he said. "Truman is in terrible shape between the drugs and alcohol, and you may feel you've been libeled, but I'm sure you don't want to be part of a writer of Truman's gifts being destroyed." Gore eventually settled for a written apology.

In July 1978, Truman appeared in an inebriated state on *The Stanley Siegel Show,* a local morning talk show in New York. Taking note of Truman's incoherence during the interview, Siegel, the host, asked, "What's going to happen unless you lick this problem of drugs and alcohol?" Truman, through the fog of his own misery, replied, "The obvious answer is that eventually I'll kill myself." The appearance was such a disaster it made headlines: DRUNK & DOPED, CAPOTE VISITS TV TALK SHOW, the *New York Post* jeered later that day.

Truman had no recollection of what had occurred on *The Stanley Siegel Show,* but when he read the press accounts he was horrified. He nursed his wounds at a gay disco in SoHo that night, with Liza Minnelli and Steve Rubell, co-owner of Studio 54. The next day, one of his friends, Robert MacBride, a young writer Truman had befriended a few years earlier, removed a gun Truman kept in his apartment and delivered it to Alan Schwartz for safekeeping—a gun that had been given to Truman by Alvin "Al" Dewey Jr., the detective who had been in charge of the Clutter case. Truman was then bundled up and transported to Hazelden, the drug-and-alcohol rehabilitation center in Minnesota, accompanied by C. Z. and Winston Guest—the rare socialites who had remained loyal. Afraid he would back out, they flew with him to the clinic, where he spent the next month. He actually enjoyed his time there, but a few weeks after being discharged, he began drinking heavily again.

Exhausted and unwell, Truman foolishly agreed to a grueling, 30-college lecture tour in the fall of 1978. Gerald Clarke thought he had embarked upon such an ordeal because he needed to know that he was "still loved and admired," but the tour, too, was a disaster. He became so incoherent in Bozeman, Montana, that he had to be escorted offstage. Back on Long Island, Truman continued to slide. "I watch him when he's sleeping," observed Jack Dunphy, Truman's former partner and friend of more than 30 years, "and he looks tired, very, very tired. It's as if he's at a long party and wants to say good-bye—but he can't."

PUBLISH AND PERISH

"I did stop working on *Answered Prayers* in September 1977," Truman wrote in the preface to his 1980 story collection, *Music for Chameleons*. "The halt happened because I was in a helluva lot of trouble: I was suffering a creative crisis and a personal one at the same time." That personal crisis was John O'Shea.

O'Shea seemed an unlikely partner for Truman—married for 20 years, with four children—but he was "just the kind of man Truman liked," said Joe Petrocik, "a married, Irish, Catholic family man." O'Shea was an aspiring writer, and he loved the life Truman introduced him to, and the possibility that he, too, could have a viable writing career. But he lacked Truman's talent, charm, brilliance, and drive. "He was so ordinary that it was breathtaking," Carol Matthau told George Plimpton for his oral history of Capote, but she also felt that the relationship had "hastened Truman's death." Perhaps Truman was trying to capture his early childhood memories of his biological father, Arch Persons, a rascally, stout businessman and something of a con man. Curiously, O'Shea's wife and children adored Truman and didn't seem to resent the role he played in breaking up their family. Such was Truman's charm.

But if the arrangement suited Truman psychologically—and sexually—it had become disastrous, even dangerous. In late 1976, Truman was locked in a nasty battle with O'Shea, exacerbated when O'Shea became involved with a woman. Claiming that O'Shea had run off with the manuscript of the "Severe Insult to the Brain" chapter of *Answered Prayers,* he sued his former lover in Los Angeles Superior Court, eventually dropping the suit in 1981. The two men reconciled, then broke up, again and again. In an attempt at revenge, Truman hired an acquaintance to follow O'Shea and to rough him up. Instead, the person ended up setting O'Shea's car on fire.

Truman's decline is usually blamed on the debacle caused by "La Côte Basque 1965," but Gerald Clarke believes the seeds of his self-destruction were planted much earlier, when he was researching *In Cold Blood*. He'd gotten close to Perry Smith during those five long years of visiting him in a bleak Kansas prison and then waiting for him to be executed. In some ways, the two men were alike: short, compactly built, artistic, the products of deprived early childhoods—it would have been easy for Truman to look into Perry Smith's black eyes and think he was looking at his darker twin. "There was a psychological connection between the two of them," Clarke believes. "Perry's death took it out of him." But Truman knew that the value of *In Cold Blood* "required the execution to take place." He couldn't finish his book otherwise. "He wrote that he wanted them to die—that started the decline."

He wasn't prepared for the effect of watching Smith's execution by hanging. The man swung for more than 10 minutes before he was pronounced dead. After leaving the prison, Truman had to pull his car over to the side of the road, where he wept for two hours. It's possible that those events set the stage for the vitriol of *Answered Prayers,* originally conceived by Truman to be "a beautiful book with a happy ending"; instead it became a kind of *j'accuse* of the rich and socially prominent, revealing, if not reveling in, their treachery, deceit, vanity, and murderous impulses. Under their polished veneers, they are all users and hustlers, like P. B. Jones.

It was to his dear friend Joanne Carson that Truman turned when he was in desperate straits, sick and exhausted, buying a one-way plane ticket to Los Angeles on August 23, 1984. Two days later, Joanne entered the guest bedroom to find Truman struggling for breath, his pulse alarmingly weak. She said that Truman spoke of his mother and then uttered the phrases "Beautiful Babe" and "Answered Prayers." Against his wishes, she called the paramedics, but by the time they arrived Truman was dead.

As for what happened to the rest of the manuscript, no one really knows. If it was stowed away in a Greyhound bus depot, possibly in Nebraska, where he had stopped during his 1978 college tour, as Joe Petrocik believes, or in a safe-deposit box somewhere, as Joanne Carson believes, it has never surfaced. Alan Schwartz says that O'Shea "claimed Truman had written the book, claimed he had stashed it away, but we never found a clue that he did." Another theory is that Truman destroyed it himself, realizing, perhaps, that it didn't come up to his Proustian standard. Jack Dunphy, who died in 1992, believed that, after the publication of "Kate McCloud," in 1976, Truman never wrote another line of the book.

Gerald Clarke wrote in his biography, "All that the world will ever see of Truman's magnum opus is the one hundred and eighty pages that Random House published in 1987. . . . Like other unfinished novels—Dickens' *The Mystery of Edwin Drood,* for example, or Fitzgerald's *The Last Tycoon*—the abbreviated *Answered Prayers* [consisting of "Unspoiled Monsters," "Kate McCloud," and "La Côte Basque"] is tantalizingly incomplete. Yet, like them, it is substantial enough to be read, enjoyed and, to a limited degree, judged on its own merits." Clarke believes that Truman simply abandoned the novel.

As for Truman's posthumous reputation, John Richardson says, "I think that the gossipy part will fall away, and he'll be remembered as a very brilliant writer who, like so many other writers, died of drink. He joins a tradition. His name—it's such an unforgettable name—will be remembered."

Truman was "a giant talent, but after so much fame and fortune, he slid downhill," recalls Liz Smith. "He had loved all those beautiful women so much, but they never returned his love. I still miss him. New York doesn't seem to have epic characters like Truman Capote anymore. There are no major writers today that matter in the way that he mattered."

Louise Grunwald agrees. "There's no one like him anymore, not that there ever was anyone like him. Just as there are no places like La Côte Basque. It's all changed. Truman wouldn't recognize New York anymore. It's ghostly."

There was a memory that Truman liked to relate, about a husky boy from his childhood in Monroeville, Alabama, who spent an entire summer digging a hole in his backyard. "Why're you doing that?" Truman had asked. "To get to China. See, the other side of this hole, that's China." Truman would later write, "Well, he never got to China; and maybe I'll never finish *Answered Prayers;* but I keep on digging! All the best, T.C."

NORMAN MAILER

MAILER'S MOVIE MADNESS

by Patricia Bosworth

MARCH 2008

> *As Mailer had come to recognize over the years, the modest everyday fellow of his daily round was servant to a wild man in himself. . . . He would have been admirable, except that he was an absolute egomaniac, a Beast—no recognition existed of the existence of anything beyond the range of his reach.*
> —NORMAN MAILER DESCRIBING HIMSELF IN
> *The Armies of the Night.*

If you enter the search terms "Norman Mailer" and "hammer" on YouTube, you will be directed to a clip titled "Norman Mailer vs Rip Torn—on camera brawl." Click on the link and an amazing series of frames rolls across the computer screen: Torn, the accomplished and respected actor, bonks Mailer, the novelist and trailblazing New Journalist, over the head with a hammer, drawing blood. The two men tussle on the grass, grunting and cursing. Then Mailer bites Torn's ear half off in retaliation.

Four of Mailer's children (three of them under the age of 10) can be heard screaming and crying in terror as Mailer's fourth wife, Beverly Bentley, bursts into the frame, shouting obscenities at Torn and smacking him repeatedly in the head.

It's the horrifying climax of *Maidstone,* Mailer's third experimental film, which was released in 1971. He called it "a guerrilla raid on the nature of reality."

The film is well worth seeing, since it springs from the imagination of a singular artist whose failures were as big as his successes. Mailer, who died on November 10, 2007, is best known for his writings—the expansively macho attempts at the Great American Novel, the enormously influential fusion of fictional devices and nonfiction reporting that was a precursor to New Journalism. But he never limited his performances to the page. A publisher, politician, and combative regular on the talk-show circuit, he was also a filmmaker of grand—some would say grandiose—ambitions.

In 1968, the same year he published *The Armies of the Night,* for which he won his first Pulitzer Prize, Mailer released two experimental films and shot a third. In *Maidstone,* which was filmed that summer, his self-indulgence and excessiveness are on display, as are his egomania, voyeurism, and misogyny. But *Maidstone* also reflects the dreams and obsessions that fed into his finest work of the 60s and 70s. It was, in the words of *New York Times* film critic A. O. Scott, "the wildest, most productive and most contentious period in a career that has never been especially calm or easy to comprehend."

Mailer had loved movies from the time he was a little boy, growing up in a middle-class neighborhood in Brooklyn in the 1930s. He loved going to the double features on Saturday afternoon, especially if Jimmy Cagney and Humphrey Bogart were playing gangsters. His sister Barbara Wasserman says Norman began taking her to foreign films after he became an engineering student at Harvard, at the age of 16. "We saw stuff like [Jean Cocteau's] *The Blood of a Poet,*" she recalls.

By the time he turned 18, Mailer had read John Dos Passos's *U.S.A.* books, John Steinbeck's *The Grapes of Wrath,* and James Farrell's *Studs Lonigan* trilogy and had decided that he wanted to be a major writer. Shortly after he graduated from Harvard, in 1943, he was drafted into the army, serving in the Philippines and Japan. That experience was the basis of his critically acclaimed first novel, *The Naked and the Dead.* He wrote parts of it in Provincetown, Massachusetts, where he would spend summers for the next 50 years.

The Naked and the Dead was published in May 1948 and topped the *New York Times* best-seller list for 11 straight weeks. The Associated Press named him "Man of the Year" in literature. He was 25 years old.

Although he was hugely ambitious, he was completely unprepared for fame and fortune. Later he said, "Part of me thought [*The Naked and the Dead*] was possibly the greatest book written since *War and Peace.* On the other hand I also thought, 'I don't know anything about writing. I'm virtually an impostor.'"

He still had fantasies of becoming a filmmaker, and he used his first royalty check to buy a movie camera. In 1948 or '49, he used it to make a 10-minute silent film about a girl having an abortion.

In July 1948, Mailer went to Hollywood. He found the political climate there unsettling: it was the height of the Red scare, when actors and screenwriters who refused to name names of suspected Communists were being blacklisted. Mailer, already a committed left-winger, campaigned for the Progressive Party's presidential candidate, Henry Wallace, and even stage-managed a rally for Wallace at the Pan Pacific Auditorium. Before the curtain went up, Mailer broke up an argument between Katharine Hepburn and MGM head Louis B. Mayer, who threatened to ruin Hepburn's career if she spoke in support of Wallace. She gave her speech anyway.

Everybody in Hollywood had read *The Naked and the Dead,* and everybody wanted to meet its author. Mailer played tennis (badly) with Charlie Chaplin and had dinner at Gene Kelly's house with John Huston, Humphrey Bogart, and Shelley Winters.

People who knew him then remember Mailer as outspoken and excitable, with wild curly hair and big ears. He didn't care how he looked or how he dressed, and his socks hung over his shoes "until I pointed that out to him," says his friend the tough-talking actor Mickey Knox. The two became close during that first trip to Los Angeles. Knox introduced Mailer to Montgomery Clift and Burt Lancaster.

The following year, Knox and Mailer reconnected in New York, and they ended up driving back to California together. It was a wild ride, full of story-telling and arguing. On this visit, Mailer was determined to get *The Naked and the Dead* made into a movie. In 1950, Lancaster, with his partner Harold Hecht, decided to option the book, but he soon dropped it. ("The time just wasn't right for a novel about war and despair and the boredom of being a soldier," says Knox.) Eventually, Charles Laughton picked it up. Mailer kept busy trying to write screenplays for Samuel Goldwyn's studio. He and another friend, Jean Malaquais, worked on a script for Clift loosely based on Nathanael West's *Miss Lonelyhearts,* but the project fell apart. (A film version of *The Naked and the Dead* came out in 1958, starring Cliff Robertson and directed by Raoul Walsh. Mailer thought it was terrible.)

Mickey Knox observed mood changes in Mailer after the publication of his second novel, *Barbary Shore,* in 1951. A surreal parable about Cold War politics set in a Brooklyn rooming house, the book was panned by most critics. So was his third novel, *The Deer Park,* a dark satire of Hollywood during the blacklist era. It came out in 1955, but not before six publishers turned it down. The failures really shook up Mailer, who became depressed and irritable. He wouldn't write another novel for 10 years.

Instead, he built himself an "orgone accumulator"—a big box in which, ac-cording to the controversial psychoanalyst Wilhelm Reich, one could absorb energies that could cure neurosis or cancer. Mailer would go inside and scream his head off, but it didn't seem to help. His first marriage, to Beatrice Silverman, had broken up in 1952. Now he was living with the Peruvian-Spanish painter Adele Morales, whom he married in 1954.

He wanted to write, but his fame seemed to be cutting him off from expe-rience. He told Knox that he might become a psychiatrist, or go into business—anything to get some fresh material to write about.

He began smoking a great deal of marijuana and drinking heavily. He would continue to do both well into his 60s. Eventually he started keeping a journal, which would run to a couple hundred pages, noting down every idea, opinion, dream, and nightmare he experienced when he was stoned.

For a while he and Adele lived in a big, drafty loft near the East River, in Manhattan. Allen Ginsberg described it as "subterranean." Montgomery Clift used to get drunk there with Mailer. Clift and Marlon Brando were both at the loft the night a group of toughs stopped in looking for a girl and accosted Mailer. In a bit of unwitting foreshadowing, they hit him over the head with a hammer, but neither of the actors did anything. They just sat there. Brando had a girl on his lap.

Sometime in 1958, Mickey Knox took Mailer to the Actors Studio. The place bowled him over; there was so much creative energy, so much high-voltage talent. Paul Newman, Marilyn Monroe, Steve McQueen, Anne Bancroft, and Geraldine Page would all be there, working on scenes for the great acting teacher Lee Strasberg while Elia Kazan, the Oscar-winning director of *On the Waterfront,* prowled the halls. Kazan had co-founded the Studio, and his mantra was one that everybody practiced: the actor turns psychology into behavior because behavior illuminates character. The Studio was a place where actors weren't afraid to expose themselves, their traumas, their hang-ups.

Once, during a session, two actors went at it with knives until Strasberg stopped them from hurting each other. Another time, an actress doing a scene directed by Kazan had a "sense memory" of what it would be like if her hands were cut off. She let out a bloodcurdling scream and then passed out onstage.

Soon Mailer turned *The Deer Park* into a play, and he arranged for Anne Bancroft and Kevin McCarthy to perform it in a series of readings at the Studio. Mailer was critical of Bancroft's fiery, multi-level performance as the volatile Elena Esposito; the role had been inspired by Mailer's exotic wife. "Get Adele to play it. That's what you've wanted all along," Bancroft said one day after a particularly bad fight. "You'll never amount to anything," Mailer told the actress—who would soon win a Tony and an Oscar for her portrayal of Helen Keller's teacher in *The Miracle Worker.* The actor and director Andreas Voutsinas, who was Bancroft's close friend, remembers that Mailer was coming on to the actress. But she was dating the comedian Lenny Bruce and wasn't interested.

When a Playwrights Unit was formed at the Studio by Elia Kazan's wife, Molly, Mailer became one of its first members, together with William Inge and Tennessee Williams. That's when I met him. I'd just become a member of the Studio and was acting on Broadway in a show called *Mary, Mary,* but I spent all my free time doing scenes for Strasberg or attending sessions with the Playwrights Unit.

I remember Mailer's piercing blue eyes, his staccato way of speaking. He always seemed about to explode. Once he asked James Earl Jones and me to read a skit he had written about Adam and Eve. He wanted us to act in it in the nude. We refused, and the skit was ultimately read by other actors. After it was over, those in the room offered scathing critiques. Mailer glowered, then jumped to his feet and bellowed, "If Patti and Jimmy had read it naked, it woulda worked!"

Another afternoon, I was there when an unknown playwright named Edward Albee had a reading of a play called *The Zoo Story*. Many people spoke out against it, but not Mailer, who informed the group that it was probably one of the most important plays of the decade. "It's gonna be a classic and it's gonna change theater," he said.

He was right. He was amazingly prescient about so much. He never seemed able to stop talking, but it was such dazzling talk—about the rise of corporatization, and about how television was making everybody indifferent. He wrote dozens of counterculture essays during the late 50s. He wrote about sex and violence and drugs and racism in *The Village Voice*, the paper he'd co-founded in 1955. And he cultivated controversy with his essay "The White Negro," published in *Dissent*, which seemed to suggest that murdering a defenseless candy-store owner could be seen as a courageous act.

In 1959 he came out with *Advertisements for Myself*, which I devoured. It was a wild collection of short stories and essays, bits of discarded novels, and fascinating personal ramblings that sought to justify his failures and his obsessions, especially with violence. Mailer believed that the best lies close to the worst in people, that good intentions invariably produce ironic outcomes.

At the Studio he was swaggering a lot. He spoke in either an Irish accent or a Texas drawl. I was beginning to realize that his keen awareness of everything was making life unbearable and lonely, so he frequently acted the clown. He began to write about boxing, and I heard that he'd been butting heads with people and even provoking fights on the street.

Then, at a drunken party in November 1960, he stabbed Adele with a penknife, barely missing her heart. Mailer seemed to be testing the limits of evil in himself. Stabbing the woman he loved was as far as he could go.

Adele recovered and decided not to press charges. Meanwhile, Norman was held under psychiatric observation at Bellevue Hospital for 17 days. After his release, a subdued and much quieter Mailer dropped by the Studio. Nobody mentioned the stabbing, and he rarely spoke about it. Appearing on the PBS series *American Masters,* in 2000, he admitted, "It changed everything in my life. It is the one act I can look back on and regret for the rest of my life. And it happened out of the way I was living."

We all thought his career would be ruined, but instead the tragedy only enhanced his notoriety. Mailer's friend Rhoda Lazare Wolf told the biographer Peter Manso that she wasn't surprised at the public's reaction. She called it part of "the psychopathology of the time." People were fed up with safe, clean celebrities. They wanted a wild man, an outsider, someone who was reckless. Someone without a conscience.

The 1960s proved to be a hugely productive decade for Mailer. He became a reporter, covering the political conventions in Miami and Chicago and speaking out on a variety of causes. He even ran for mayor of New York City in a crazy, antic campaign.

He also divorced Adele, with whom he had two daughters, and, in 1962, married Lady Jeanne Campbell, the elegant daughter of the 11th Duke of Argyll. They had a daughter, Kate, and were divorced the following year. Mailer then married the actress Beverly Bentley, who was blonde, talented, and able to hold her own with Norman—at least for a while. Their tempestuous marriage produced two sons. In 1964 he wrote what would become one of his favorite novels, *An American Dream,* in installments for *Esquire.* It is described on the book jacket as "one part Nietzsche, one part de Sade, and one part Charlie Parker." Then, in 1967, he wrote an allegorical novel called *Why Are We in Vietnam?,* about a hunting trip in Alaska. The word "Vietnam" doesn't even appear until the last page.

From time to time he'd join the improvisation group at the Loft Theatre, in the West Village. This group of brainy, stage-hungry kids acted out spontaneous scenes populated by neurotic mothers, star-crossed lovers, double-talking politicians. Dustin Hoffman played parts there, and Andre Gregory began developing his avant-garde version of *Alice in Wonderland* on the Loft stage.

The producer of the group was the writer and actress Janet Coleman. She says Mailer used to arrive dressed like a gangster, in a trench coat with a hat pulled over one eye. "He loved to improvise," she remembers. "Unfortunately, he didn't come to enough classes to master the exercises that help you concentrate and relax in a stage space. He didn't really know how to create a character. He couldn't cooperate or share space with other actors very easily."

The Loft's work made an impression on him all the same. "Improvisation also orders chaos—gives its focus to random emotions," he wrote in his 1971 essay "A Course in Filmmaking." Improvisation "becomes a life which is not quite life."

Every so often he would invite some of us from the Studio to watch underground films with him at the Charles Theatre, on the Lower East Side. We saw Kenneth Anger's *Scorpio Rising,* Jack Smith's *Flaming Creatures,* and Andy Warhol's *Kitchen,* which, Mailer declared, "had the horror of the twentieth century in it."

He was fascinated by these new movies. He now realized that film, like sex, "is an experience you can never dominate." He was inspired by the idea that movies could be so mysterious, elusive, and unpredictable.

In January 1967 he finally got his stage adaptation of *The Deer Park* produced Off Broadway, at the Theatre de Lys. He'd been writing and re-writing the play for 10 years, and he would continue until his death.

Mailer was ruthlessly critical of everybody in the cast, which included Rip Torn, Mickey Knox, and Beverly Bentley. He couldn't figure out what actors *do*.

The reviews were mixed, with one critic calling *The Deer Park* "an uneasy gift from the mind of an uneasy man." Still, the play ran for 127 performances, and Torn won an Obie for his portrayal of Marion Faye, a leering, leather-clad pimp. By then Torn and Mailer had become close friends, and they would go on to collaborate often, including on a stage version of *Why Are We in Vietnam?* A charismatic, outspoken radical who was deeply involved in protesting the war, Torn says he was one of the few people who felt comfortable speaking freely to Mailer. Most people were afraid of him.

After each performance, everybody would end up at Casey's bar, in the Village. Mailer, Mickey Knox, and their friend Buzz Farbar, who had a role in the play, "would go off to the side of this bar. And we began playing this game," Mailer told the writer Joseph Gelmis. "We began improvising, to take on parts. I was like the head of a gang, very Mafia. These guys were like my hoods, and I was lecturing them all the time."

The three men thought these exchanges, which were loaded with obscenities and tough talk, were hilariously funny. "We had absolutely fantastic stuff," Mailer went on. "I said, 'Jesus, isn't it a shame that we can't film it? Instead of being ourselves, let's see what we're like as movie actors.'"

Eventually, Mailer persuaded the esteemed documentarian D. A. Pennebaker to work with him. Pennebaker had just finished his groundbreaking Bob Dylan tour film, *Don't Look Back,* and Mailer saw him as "not only a marvelously gifted photographer but . . . an innovator and a discoverer."

Mailer called his first film *Wild 90*. Shot over a period of four nights in a vacant, grungy loft on West 45th Street, the picture follows three "low-level thugs trapped in a room planning their next big heist," as film historian Michael Chaiken recently described it in *Film Comment*. At one point, Mickey Knox later wrote, Mailer's friend Jose Torres, the former light-heavyweight champion of the world, "brought a growling German shepherd. Norman bent down and matched it growl for growl."

Mailer and an editor spent close to six months cutting *Wild 90*. As soon as he was through, he started writing *The Armies of the Night,* about participating in the march on the Pentagon. As Chaiken points out, Mailer got the idea to write about himself in the third person after watching himself on-screen. The innovation, used throughout *The Armies of the Night,* helped inspire a new form of participatory journalism.

Wild 90 opened in early 1968 and was summarily dismissed by most critics.

For one thing, the sound was so bad that no one could understand it. *New York Times* critic Renata Adler wrote, "What the conversation turns into almost at once is a subsurface contest for the attention of the camera."

Mailer's second film, *Beyond the Law,* had already been shot by the time *Wild 90* opened. Speaking in an exaggerated Irish accent, Mailer plays a police lieutenant on the brink of divorce with his wife (Bentley). He spends his evening playing God to an array of sleazy suspects—and revealing his own demonic nature.

Beyond the Law premiered at the New York Film Festival in the fall of 1968. Mailer's idea was to use the techniques of cinéma vérité "to photograph feature-length movies which told imaginary stories."

But *Beyond the Law* was no more successful than *Wild 90.* Audience members booed at the opening, and many critics panned the film. Vincent Canby of *The New York Times,* however, wrote, "'Beyond the Law' is so good and tough and entertaining so much of the time that you simply have to forgive those moments when the actors suddenly smirk self-consciously—like the Gas House Gang caught in an amateur theatrical."

Maidstone was Mailer's third movie. It was filmed on Gardiners Island and at the East Hampton estates of Barney Rosset, who was the publisher of Grove Press, and the wealthy artist and art patron Alfonso Ossorio.

It was the summer of 1968, a little more than one month after the assassination of Robert Kennedy. Mailer later wrote that he never would have made *Maidstone* if he "had not sat in a room with Bobby Kennedy a month before his death and failed to realize danger; that the man was in mortal danger." Mailer sold part of his interest in *The Village Voice* to cover the production costs, which amounted to more than $200,000, but he didn't care. As far as he was concerned, this was the film that would finally erase the boundaries between fiction and truth, "the surface of reality and the less visible surface of psychological reality."

There was no script, just a bizarre scenario concocted by Mailer himself. He would direct and star as Norman Kingsley, an avant-garde director who is casting a film inspired by Luis Buñuel's *Belle de Jour.* In that critically acclaimed film, released in 1967, Catherine Deneuve played a demure wife who moonlights as a prostitute. In Kingsley's version, women go to a male brothel. Kingsley is also debating whether to run for president. He's scared, sensing the threat of more assassinations. As it turns out, his murder is being contemplated—by a secret-police force and even his own followers.

Two of Mailer's four wives to date—Beverly Bentley and Lady Jeanne Campbell—appeared in the film. So did his mistress, Carol Stevens, who can be heard warbling on the soundtrack. The cast also included Jose Torres and Buzz Farbar, the conservative commentator Noel Parmentel, the poet Michael McClure, the art patron John de Menil, and assorted wealthy socialites, militant black activists, and vacuous aspiring starlets. The actor Hervé Villechaize, best known for his role as Tattoo on TV's *Fantasy Island,* reportedly got so drunk that he almost drowned in Barney Rosset's swimming pool.

In addition to starring in the film as Norman Kingsley's half-brother, Rey, Rip Torn had the job of associate director. "I'd turned down *Easy Rider* to do this movie," he recalls. For the final fight scene, Torn says, Mailer told him to "let the conflict build and then take me out." Torn was surprised. He said, "*Really* take you out? Aren't we going to do some more films together?" Mailer told him, "Just make it look real."

The shoot took one week, during which most of the cast milled about aimlessly, getting drunk or stoned. A manic, bare-chested Mailer circulated among them, sparring on the grass, debating politics with the black activists, alternately flirting with and insulting the would-be starlets. He appeared to be trying to force confrontation, to create the atmosphere of dread and apprehension that he envisioned. Fueled by an angry, desperate energy, he grew increasingly exasperated. He knew the story, but the rest of the cast didn't.

Torn was frustrated, too. Nothing was coming together. At one point Lane Smith, one of the professional actors, told Mailer to "take your crew, your equipment, your camera and shove it up your ass!" Mailer responded by punching Smith and breaking his jaw.

The night before shooting ended, Torn met with Mailer and the other associate directors about how to do the final scene. Mailer and the others thought "they should do Mailer's character in with stoning," Torn says, but he "argued that you can't control a stoning, that Norman could get killed." Torn then came up with the idea of using a hammer.

The next morning dawned sunny and beautiful. At the start of the clip on YouTube, we see Torn and Mailer facing off on a sloping green hill on Gardiners Island.

From the screenplay, which was put together after the film was edited:

We see RIP-REY *stride toward him, raise the hammer, strike him on the head, raise the hammer again. A second blow! . . .*

NORMAN:
(Hand to his head—dodging back)
You crazy fool cocksucker!
RIP-REY:
(Holding the hammer, moving forward) You're supposed to die, Mr. Kingsley. You must die, not Mailer. I don't want to kill Mailer, but I must kill Kingsley in this picture.

NORMAN:
(Still backing up)
Let go of the hammer. Let go of the hammer. . . .

He rushes in to grapple with RIP-REY *who drops the hammer just before* NORMAN *gets a full bite of his ear. They go hurtling down the slope and through the air to land with* RIP-REY *on top.*

For the next couple of minutes they roll around slowly on the grass. Torn attempts to placate Mailer—"I'm sorry, Dad. I'm so sorry"—but it's no use. Apart from the physical pain, Mailer can't seem to stand the idea that someone else has taken control of his movie. Blood drips from the side of his head. They stop grappling for a minute, then begin again. Torn maneuvers into the upper position and puts his hands on Mailer's throat. Bentley soon arrives on the scene, shrieking and shouting curses. The children are wailing in terror. Two men run into the frame and eventually separate the antagonists.

The scene ends with Mailer saying, "You might as well turn off this tape." But Torn had already got his punch in: "You're just a fraud, aren't you?" he said to Mailer. The two friends didn't speak for many months, although Mailer phoned Torn in the hospital. His ear had become terribly infected. A few months later, I interviewed Torn's wife, Geraldine Page, for a story I was writing. She insisted that Torn had used a toy hammer.

This December, however, Torn, who remained close to Mailer until his death, told me in a quiet voice that it had been a real hammer. He had been careful to use the blunt end of the handle, he said, to minimize the damage: "Norman knew all along what I was going to do."

D. A. Pennebaker says the attack came as a surprise to him. "I had my camera full of film, but I didn't know exactly what was going to happen," he recalls. "I hadn't been told. Rip thinks he told me, but he didn't."

When he entered the editing room, Mailer was determined to leave the fight scene on the cutting-room floor. Then he watched all 45 hours of footage and realized that the scene was the only thing that could save his movie. Without it, he admitted, he would have "been left with the most embarrassing work of all, an ego trip."

He also realized that the scene accomplished the goal he'd set for the whole film: to be "both a fiction and a documentary at once" and to penetrate "the hard hide of the real."

The fight may have succeeded on an artistic level, but it had very real repercussions for the rest of the Mailer family. Friends say it hastened the ending of Mailer's already shaky marriage to Beverly Bentley. And their sons, Michael and

Stephen—both of whom now work in film, as a producer and an actor, respectively—acknowledge that the experience was traumatizing. Stephen, who was two at the time, says Mailer apologized shortly before he died. He had never wanted his children to be hurt.

Mailer took two years to edit *Maidstone*. It opened in 1971 at the Whitney Museum of American Art and played to packed houses. Its commercial release, however, was a bust. By then Mailer was broke, and he began paying off his debts by writing one big book after another: *The Prisoner of Sex, Marilyn, Portrait of Picasso as a Young Man*. In 1980, he won a second Pulitzer Prize, for *The Executioner's Song*, which portrayed the convicted murderer Gary Gilmore as an existential hero.

That November, Mailer divorced Bentley and married Carol Stevens, to legitimize their daughter. Then he divorced her and married his sixth wife, a gifted 31-year-old painter named Norris Church. They spent their honeymoon in London, where they both acted in Milos Forman's film *Ragtime*. Mailer continued to be obsessed with movies. He and Norris, a ravishing redhead, co-wrote a number of unproduced screenplays, and in 1986 he directed an adaptation of his novel *Tough Guys Don't Dance*, starring Ryan O'Neal as a hard-drinking, skirt-chasing writer. Mailer also continued to act. For one day, he worked with Jean-Luc Godard on *King Lear*. Mailer was cast as the Lear character, and his daughter Kate was set to play Cordelia, but he backed out, allegedly after Godard implied that their characters had incestuous feelings for each other.

Around that time, I saw Mailer and Kate collaborate on a play he had written called *Strawhead*, about Marilyn Monroe. A workshop was done at the Actors Studio, and Kate, wearing a tousled blond wig, was sensational as Monroe—sexy, vulnerable, funny. One night, during a kinky love scene between Marilyn and a biker, Shelley Winters jumped to her feet from the audience and yelled, "I was Marilyn's roommate and that didn't happen, Norman!" The audience roared, and so did Mailer. The following night he had his ex-wife Adele call out the same protest from the audience.

In 1993, Mailer directed and acted in a rollicking staged reading of George Bernard Shaw's *Don Juan in Hell*, starring Gay Talese as Don Juan, Gore Vidal as the Devil, and Susan Sontag as Doña Ana. It played at Carnegie Hall as a benefit for the Actors Studio.

In the early 90s, Mailer made Provincetown his home base and plunged into writing four enormous books: *Harlot's Ghost*, about the C.I.A.; *Oswald's Tale*, about Lee Harvey Oswald; *The Gospel According to the Son*, in which Jesus tells his own story; and *The Castle in the Forest*, a biography of Adolf Hitler narrated by a minion of Satan.

But every so often he would take a breather and act. He performed Eugene O'Neill's *Long Day's Journey into Night* in Provincetown with Norris, his daughter Kate, and two of his sons, Stephen and John Buffalo. "It was like a catharsis for me," Stephen says. "Got a lot of stuff worked out in my head."

In 2002, Mailer played Hemingway in a wonderful piece that George Plimpton and Terry Quinn had fashioned using F. Scott Fitzgerald's notes and letters. Plimpton played Fitzgerald, and Norris played Zelda. The three of them took the show to Moscow, Paris, and London. "Norman loved playing Hemingway," Norris recalls.

In the last years of his life, Mailer gave John Buffalo, his son with Norris, the rights to turn *The Naked and the Dead* into a screenplay. "I felt privileged to be able to work on it, and it was easy," John Buffalo says. "All I did was follow the book's narrative outline. Nobody else did when they tried to make it into a movie! My dad loved it." John Buffalo's version of *The Naked and the Dead* has a real chance of being made, and he says Alec Baldwin may do a reading of it.

In the spring of 2007, at the age of 84, Mailer decided that he was ready to direct again. After 52 years, the time had finally come to bring *The Deer Park* to the screen. I talked to him about it in New York after a staged reading of the play, directed by Stephan Morrow. "Finally somebody understood the language and what I was trying to say," Mailer said. His plan was to shoot the play on a stage in Provincetown.

We spoke about the project again at the *Paris Review* tribute to him, on April 23. He was frail, on two canes, but his blue eyes sparkled. Why, after all these years, are you still obsessed with this one book?, I asked.

"Because it's about the trouble men and women always have, dealing with each other," he replied. "It's a mystery. I still can't figure it out."

ERNEST HEMINGWAY

THE HUNT FOR HEMINGWAY

by A. Scott Berg

OCTOBER 2011

His earliest short story—five action-packed sentences—displayed several markings of his later works. "My First Sea Vouge" (1911) was a maritime adventure about two boys and their father voyaging from Martha's Vineyard to Sydney, Australia; its centerpiece was the spearing of a porpoise, excising its liver, and frying it for dinner. Beyond the virility of the 11-year-old author, the story also foreshadowed his budding nomadic nature. Fifteen years later, in his novel *The Sun Also Rises,* one of his characters would say, "You can't get away from yourself by moving from one place to another." But Ernest Hemingway spent his life trying.

Growing to disdain his father and despise his mother, Hemingway left Oak Park, Illinois, at 18 to begin his career as a journalist at *The Kansas City Star.* From that moment on, he was in perpetual motion, spinning tales of his travels into two dozen books and scores of stories. Along the way, he married four times, fathered three sons, caught marlin, fought bulls, bagged big game, reported wars, chased Nazi U-boats, skied, hunted, survived a plane crash only to read his own obituary, and became the fifth American to win the Nobel Prize for Literature.

Stories of his daring life intertwined with those he invented on paper, until he became as famous for his macho exploits as for his writing. Even more than his (sometimes two-dimensional) characters and his (sometimes creaky) plots, Hemingway's strength was in capturing locations, his remarkable ability to re-create settings, to bottle their ambience, to recall—as he said—"how the weather was." As a result, Hemingway put more places on the map than any writer of his time.

He wrote what he knew: the big Two-Hearted River country of his boyhood summers up in Michigan; Northern Italy, where he drove ambulances during the Great War; the Lost Generation's Paris of the early 20s, in which he was lucky enough to have lived as a young man with his first wife, Hadley; the Spanish town of Pamplona, where they ran the bulls through the streets; the green hills of Africa, over which loomed snowcapped Mount Kilimanjaro; a pine-needled forest floor in Spain's Guadarrama Mountains during the nation's Civil War;

Harry's Bar in Venice at the close of World War II; Sloppy Joe's in Key West; Bimini; the fishing waters where the Gulf of Mexico swirls into the Atlantic. His brisk style—suggestive, staccato, and deceptively simple—influenced much of the American writing that followed, transforming him into a national icon and an international celebrity, the most famous writer of his day. Ironically, few of his works are set in the United States, and the one house that remained his home longer than any other was in another country—the Finca Vigía, in Cuba.

Although he had stopped over on a few occasions, Hemingway didn't truly discover Havana until 1932, when he crossed the Straits of Florida from Key West. He went for the fishing and stayed for the quality of life there. He lodged at the charming Ambos Mundos Hotel, in La Habana Vieja, a particularly colorful part of the capital city, with its colonial architecture, plazas, and narrow streets leading to the Malecón, a great curving esplanade outlining the seafront. For those who could afford to get away from the United States at the start of the Depression and the end of Prohibition, Havana was a glamorous destination with drinking and gambling and plenty of sunshine.

In 1939, Hemingway left his house in Key West and his second wife, Pauline, for a striking writer named Martha Gellhorn. Thirty-one to his 40, she had looks and brains and deeper political convictions than he. At her urging, they had both covered the war in Spain and were moving in together in Cuba, where he would write his magnum opus about that war. Looking to share more than a hotel room, Martha found a tumbledown but private estate 15 kilometers to the southeast of Havana, up in San Francisco de Paula. Because of its hilltop view of the city and the sea, it was called Finca Vigía—generally translated as "Lookout Farm," though nothing about it felt especially agricultural. Hemingway didn't love the place at first sight, and so Martha returned on her own, paid to clean it up, and brought him back for a second look. They promptly moved in, and, upon their marriage in 1940, Hemingway purchased the Finca for $12,500.

But Martha was even more footloose than Ernest, and she would soon move on. (As she told me when I interviewed her in 1972 for a biography of the legendary Maxwell Perkins, who had edited each of them, "He was entering this great 'Papa' phase, and I wasn't looking for a Papa!") In the meantime, he had met in London another blonde reporter, one Mary Welsh. "Funny," he wrote Perkins, "how it should take one war to start a woman in your damn heart and another to finish her." Upon their respective divorces, they married; and Hemingway yearned for home. "We stayed in a lot of places," Mary told me, also in 1972, "but we lived at the Finca."

Hemingway's love for Cuba deepened. He presented his Nobel gold medal to the Cuban people, donating it to the country's patron saint, the Virgin of Charity, to be kept at her shrine in El Cobre Basilica, outside Santiago de Cuba; and he told a crowd of reporters that greeted him at the Havana airport in 1959 that he considered himself Cuban. Few Americans would have claimed as much at the time, as the United States government was already shunning the new Cuban leader, Fidel Castro. Then, during a prolonged Stateside visit in 1960, depression overcame a long-troubled Hemingway. After receiving electroshock treatments at the Mayo Clinic, conditions worsened. By the time he kept his appointment with a double-barreled shotgun in Ketchum, Idaho, on July 2, 1961, diplomatic ties between the two countries had been severed. Castro forces had repelled an American-backed invasion at the Bay of Pigs; Cuba had been expropriating foreign-owned properties on its soil; and the United States responded to the totalitarian Communist regime by imposing an embargo.

Cuba's Minister of Foreign Affairs telephoned Mary to announce that his government wished to acquire the Finca, intending to turn it into a Hemingway museum—*un monumento*. With that, either the Cuban government seized the house or the Hemingway Estate offered it to his adopted homeland, depending upon which side of the Straits one hears the story. In a respectful diplomatic gesture under hostile political circumstances, Cuba permitted Mary to revisit the house to retrieve some of the possessions there. She was able to empty a bank vault of her late husband's manuscripts and reclaim several works of art—including two Juan Gris paintings and a Paul Klee—as well as some personal papers and items. But the bulk of the Finca's contents—drawers and shelves and boxes with thousands of pages of accumulated correspondence and manuscripts—quietly became the property of the Republic of Cuba.

Forty years later, I received a call from Jenny Phillips, a psychotherapist from Massachusetts who is also a granddaughter of Max Perkins. She and her husband, Frank, the statehouse bureau chief for *The Boston Globe*—both of whom I had met years earlier—had recently visited the Finca Vigía. During their tour, Jenny explained to me on the phone in January 2001, an innocent query had turned into a quest. She had asked if the *museo* had any letters from her grandfather in its possession. So impressed were her hosts by this proximity to Hemingway's most trusted literary adviser, they surprisingly said yes, but they kept deflecting her requests to see them. They referred the Phillipses to the Ministry of Culture, a response that only added intrigue to their curiosity.

Upon their return to Boston, they visited the John F. Kennedy Library, which has long housed the bulk of the Hemingway Archives. Authorities there explained the situation to the Phillipses, how scholars had long presumed there was a wealth of Hemingway material in Cuban custody, but nobody there was willing to admit as much, for fear of American claims on his property. While Mary herself had spoken to me of all that she had left behind, and scholars had bemoaned the gaps that existed in his collected papers, nobody ever expected to get past the political blockade. Now the Phillipses were on a mission.

Putting her professional training to work, Jenny devised a shrewd approach to the Cuban government. Rather than suggest that she wanted something from the Hemingway Museum, she proposed giving them something. She was assembling a small team to rescue whatever Hemingway papers existed in Cuba—not to remove them but to preserve them, asking only that copies of everything be sent to the United States. The Phillipses would even raise enough money to pay for the operation. Good psychology, I thought.

They approached Congressman Jim McGovern, a Democrat from central Massachusetts, a human-rights advocate with a particular interest in re-establishing relations with Cuba. He secured a meeting with the Cuban Minister of Culture and found a receptive enough audience for Jenny to proceed with her plan. She recruited two conservators from the Northeast Document Conservation Center in Andover, and she enlisted Sandra Spanier from The Pennsylvania State University. A professor of American literature and the wife of Penn State's president, Spanier had recently been named general editor of the Hemingway Letters Project, an ambitious effort to publish all the author's extant letters—some six thousand of them, maybe more if they hit pay dirt in Cuba. Jenny Phillips hoped to add me to the team, knowing that I had mined a lot of Hemingway material for my biography of her grandfather—with whom the author had maintained the longest and most substantive correspondence of his life. She knew that if we were granted limited time with any papers, I could immediately help identify what they were.

In fact, my association with Hemingway's papers was greater than she knew. At Princeton, where my biography had begun as a senior thesis, I had been a disciple of Carlos Baker, Hemingway's official biographer, the first writer to have been granted access to his archives by Mary Hemingway herself. For many years—before the J.F.K. Library had been built and the Hemingway archives had a permanent home—much of the author's original correspondence had been stashed in Professor Baker's office in McCosh Hall. To incentivize my undergraduate research, he dangled these private letters, allowing me to borrow a folder at a time under the condition that I didn't tell anybody—"because if Miss Mary finds out, she'll kill you . . . if I don't get to you first." Several afternoons a week, I rapped on the door of McCosh 33 and swapped one folder for the next, sometimes without saying a word, as though we were trading nuclear secrets. I became proficient in deciphering Hemingway's handwriting, which for long periods at a time slanted heavily downhill.

Jenny's offer in 2001 was hardly irresistible, as she made this trip to Cuba sound like a steeplechase, full of hurdles and hazards. Obtaining permission to travel to Cuba had not been easy in the last four decades, and the new Bush administration was making it even harder; and if we should gain entry, there were no assurances that the Cubans would give us the necessary access to the Finca;

they still had not acknowledged that they had any significant archive in their possession; and if they did, there was still no permission to inspect it. Jenny suggested that we might very well find ourselves spending an entire week sitting in an office wooing government workers without ever seeing anything. Meanwhile, a travel agent informed me that, even with proper documents, one could fly all the way to Havana and still be refused admittance. After many phone conversations, extensive travel arrangements, and constant Congressional patience and prodding—one year later—Jenny and Frank Phillips, Sandy Spanier, and I (coming from Los Angeles via Cancún) converged upon Cuba. We would have four full days in which we hoped to meet our simple goal of seeing Papa's papers.

We were, of course, at the mercy of what I quickly gathered were suspicious hosts. Our first day—Tuesday, March 12, 2002—was heavily scheduled and largely ceremonial. We visited a journalism school and visited an English class; and we also met the vivacious Gladys Rodríguez Ferrero, the first curator of the Museo Hemingway and president of the Instituto José Martí, then conducting a Hemingway convocation. We listened to several writers and teachers, who spoke of different aspects of the author's life and work, and we met several people from Oak Park on a study tour. Gladys spoke repeatedly of *amistad,* and she expressed nothing but support for our mission. In the afternoon, she escorted us to the office of Marta Arjona Pérez, the president of the National Council of Cultural Heritage. Staring long and hard at each of us, she appeared to be a grim bureaucrat, especially alongside the animated Gladys. But at the end of our meeting—conducted in Spanish, with Gladys translating the bits we did not understand—she spoke of this "*momento histórico*" between our two nations and invited us to spend Wednesday at the Finca. Our team found a small outdoor restaurant for dinner in Old Havana, where music poured out of every other window. Moonlight bathed the dilapidated and overcrowded buildings enough to make us see how the city had once been "the Paris of the Caribbean."

It took 20 minutes to get to the Finca—as we drove up the gentle rise to San Francisco de Paula, and then farther up a long approach. Atop several large terraced steps perches the gracious cream-colored house, with its small, square-columned portico and its windows trimmed in white. Big palms across the property fanned an azure sky on what was already a hot morning, and dark-green areca fronds cascaded at the entrance. Each day the Finca receives 150 visitors, who are not allowed inside the house; but many of them were already walking its perimeter, getting a look into every room, as each featured a large window. Gladys and the museum staff welcomed us, letting us past the rope at the front door.

The Cubans obviously consider the house a shrine, and they have frozen it in time. The floors were polished, the windows were immaculate, and any sudden movements toward a piece of furniture excited guards into motion. The large, breezy living room was without pretense, with Papa's favorite reading chair and its mate dominating the salon. Between them sat a small table, with provisions for cocktails exactly as Hemingway had left them—bottles of Schweppes Indian Tonic, Gordon's gin, Old Forester bourbon, Campari, Bacardi rum, and El Copey Agua Mineral. A few other chairs and small tables filled the rest of the room; bookcases, paintings, bullfighting posters, and trophies from Africa and the American West covered the walls. The musical tastes of our absent host—as evidenced by the record collection—could not have been more mainstream: Benny Goodman, Tommy Dorsey, and Glenn Miller; Bach, Beethoven, and Brahms; Granados from Spain and Lecuona from Cuba.

All the other rooms in the house were barely adorned, and each provided insights. The workroom that was part of his bedroom suite, for example, showcased the Royal typewriter on which he had hammered out much of his work from 1939 on. The connecting bathroom had a doctor's scale, and on one of the walls, Hemingway had recorded his weight daily. It ranged from 242 pounds on February 21, 1955, to 190½ pounds five years later.

The most revealing items throughout the house were the books—almost 9,000 of them, many with marginalia. A copy of the *Oxford Book of English Prose* caught my eye, as I had suddenly remembered a letter Hemingway had sent Max Perkins in April 1940, when he was looking for a title for his nearly finished novel about Spain. He liked to leaf through anthologies of English literature, and upon reaching John Donne's "Meditation XVII"—the one that said, "Never send to know for whom the bell tolls"—he had written that he had found his title. Or, he asked Perkins, would people think of tolls as long-distance charges and Bell as the telephone company? I asked one of the guards if I might inspect the book. In an act of great trust, he removed it from its place and carefully handed it to me. I thumbed through the pages until I found the passage—circled.

After touring the house, we asked when and where we might see Hemingway's papers. Gladys Rodríguez suggested only that we explore the grounds. We visited the four-story tower Mary had built for her husband (hoping he might use the top floor as his workroom, which he did not); we ambled down the palm-lined paths among the nine acres to the shed that housed his cruiser, the *Pilar;* and we saw the emptied swimming pool, which in its splashier days had hosted a number of actors from film adaptations of his books—Spencer Tracy, Errol Flynn, Gary Cooper (who had brought Patricia Neal), and Ava Gardner, who had famously skinny-dipped there. Seeing the sights was informative and perfectly pleasant, but as we baked in the hot sun outside the unattached garage, Frank Phillips grumbled, "We still haven't seen any papers." He believed we were sitting but yards from our treasure trove—right there, he imagined, in the basement of the garage.

. . .

Another day had passed without any indication that we would be seeing any documents. We dined at El Floridita, "the cradle of the daiquiri" and a favorite haunt of Hemingway's. Gladys Rodríguez joined us, along with Enrique Cirules, a celebrated Cuban author, who had written about Hemingway. He spoke with a pronounced Cuban accent, which dropped a lot of consonants and made him difficult to understand. I thought at first that the problem was the rustiness of my Spanish after a few decades of disuse, but Sandy Spanier said she had trouble comprehending him as well. But after dinner, we all strolled toward the Malecón as Cirules held forth on Hemingway and Havana. And suddenly, Sandy—a few rum drinks for the better, I presumed—was not only gabbing away with him but also understanding every syllable, simultaneously translating for the rest of us.

The next day, I was separated from the pack and sent to meet administrators of the Instituto Cubano del Libro. Officials of the publishing industry asked if I would return to Cuba to attend some literary conferences, and did I want to speak to the press that day about America's policy toward Cuba? While I felt 40 years of malignant neglect had done nothing to bring Castro down and seemed only to make every Cuban I encountered even more patriotic, I thought it best to keep my opinions to myself. Later that morning, Enrique Cirules and I spent time interviewing each other about our respective lives and careers. ("We are a Third World country," he affirmed, "but the *best* in the Third World.") And as the authorities at the Hemingway Museum still had said nothing about our seeing any papers, I spent the afternoon visiting museums and walking through El Parque Central, where locals flock every day to argue about baseball. As the next day was our last opportunity to see any papers, our team strategized over dinner, deciding that I should bell the cat.

By morning, however, that seemed unnecessary. We were summoned to the Finca and told that we would be seeing documents. To our surprise, we were taken to a shed by the pool, where doors were opened, revealing stacks of papers. We were elated . . . until we realized they were not Hemingway's. They were, in fact, detailed inventories of the museum's holdings—handwritten by curators over the years. A description of each document was recorded on a separate sheet of cheap paper, many of which literally crumbled in our hands. Clearly, there had been some great misunderstanding. Sandy and I were grateful to see this much, startled by all that seemed to have been stored; but Jenny and Frank groused that we still did not know for a fact where the actual documents were and when we would see them. The clock was ticking, especially as we had a four-o'clock appointment with Marta Arjona that afternoon. Sometime around noon, I approached Gladys and thanked her for all the hospitality she had extended, but I explained that our trip really was a squandered opportunity unless we could see some papers immediately. I believe each of the others had similar conversations with her.

A little after one, Gladys escorted us back to the garage, but this time through the low gate marked ACCESO LIMITADO. There, at the rear of the building, a small door opened to steep stairs down into a basement. I guess the room was about 15 by 30 feet, and I'm sure it was a hair over six feet high, as my head brushed against the ceiling. Frank had to stoop the entire time we were there. Under the watchful eyes of two overseers, we four filed in.

It was a clean, badly lighted place. Five bulbs illuminated the space from above; a sixth had burned out. The curators took pride in having been good custodians, pointing out the dehumidifier in the room and two Samsung portable air conditioners, which ran 24 hours a day. But one couldn't help noticing an opening in a wall that had been boarded over, through which light passed. That meant insects and rain and dust could permeate as well; but the shortage of time kept us from dwelling on such problems. From the inventory, Sandy and I especially had compiled lists of must-see items, core samples that would indicate the breadth and depth of this collection.

The cellar was jammed with file cabinets as well as firearms and horned animal heads and photographs; and while the interests of my colleagues ranged from correspondence to curios, I used most of my time to comb through folders that pertained to Hemingway's writing career, anything that might illustrate the author's creative process. In an instant, I felt as though I had entered King Tut's tomb; literary riches abounded. There was a five-page fragment that ended up in *Death in the Afternoon* and a five-line exchange of dialogue intended for *Islands in the Stream* that had not seen the light of day; there was a snatch of World War II–vintage dialogue that Hemingway had hunt-and-pecked on his Royal typewriter—raw stuff which he had evidently meant to spin into fiction but which he ultimately judged "too frank"; galley No. 10 of *Across the River and into the Trees* bore author's revisions; pristine pages of *The Old Man and the Sea* did not.

I remembered from my research that Hemingway had had second thoughts about the ending of *For Whom the Bell Tolls,* how at the last minute he thought it should include an epilogue accounting for the supporting players. Perkins had read the proposed coda, and, knowing Hemingway's preference for minimalism, he had urged the author to drop the pages. He had backed his opinion by citing his daughter Peggy, with whom he had shared the manuscript. She had said the book had ended perfectly without it. Perkins had evidently returned those final pages to the author, because they did not exist among his papers Stateside. But there in an old file in the basement of the garage at the Finca Vigía remained a

12-page pencil draft of those very pages. As I quickly related that publishing anecdote, I handed the folder to Jenny Phillips, Peggy's daughter.

With an eye on the clock, because of our appointment with Marta Arjona, I frantically sprinted through a few folders of personal material, which proved to be as revealing as anything I had ever seen relating to the Hemingways' marriage. In my notebook, I scribbled some passages from love letters Ernest had sent to Mary during the war; and then, in another folder, I found a startling statement written less than 10 years later: "Right now the question is whether I should accept Mary as a scold and give up another illusion," it said. "Or whether I should ride along and learn not to give a damn." Oddly, Ernest had appended a note to Mary, saying he had jotted these thoughts to "clarify something in my head." Then, even more astonishing, he added, "Please return them."

Time was up—before I could study the folder of letters from Adriana Ivancich, the young Venetian aristocrat who had served as the model for the hero's inamorata in *Across the River and into the Trees* . . . or Hemingway's instructions for the cook on how to prepare his salads . . . or his letter to Ingrid Bergman, whom he hoped would play Maria in the film of *For Whom the Bell Tolls* . . .

We had come to Cuba hoping to find a few literary artifacts. Instead, we found ourselves amid a most significant literary dig, surrounded by "wonderful things." We had already identified enough significant pieces of quotidian life at the Finca to begin to understand Hemingway's 20 years there. As we drove back to Havana to report our findings and discuss the future of the documents, I could think only of the serious and solitary artist who lived there, not the swaggering figure of myth. "Writing at its best," Hemingway had confessed in his Nobel acceptance speech, "is a lonely life." I had never fully appreciated how that sentiment applied to him until I had processed all that I had seen at the Finca Vigía—from the tower top to the basement.

Now, 50 years after Hemingway's death, the Finca is being rehabilitated and its holdings are being protected. More than 3,000 pages of documents from the cellar have already been conserved, scanned, digitized, and made accessible to the public through the J.F.K. Library. And documents from that archive can now be included in the long-anticipated volumes of Hemingway's collected letters.

Their value cannot be overstated. Where Hemingway's published works had all been so deliberate and painstakingly chiseled, his letters were free-form and expansive—unsanded and unvarnished. "I would write one true sentence, and then go on from there," he famously said of the process he had applied to a lifetime of literary efforts. In the final analysis, however, his letters may prove to be the most honest log of Hemingway's fascinating life-voyage, the truest sentences he ever wrote.

TOM WOLFE

··

THE WHITE STUFF

by Michael Lewis

NOVEMBER 2015

I was 11 or maybe 12 years old when I discovered my parents' bookshelves. They'd been invisible right up to the moment someone or something told me that the books on them were stuffed with dirty words and shocking behavior—a rumor whose truth was eventually confirmed by *Portnoy's Complaint*. The book I still remember taking down from the shelf was *Radical Chic & Mau-Mauing the Flak Catchers*. The only word in the title I understood was "the." The cover showed a picture of a bored-looking blonde housewife nestled in the lap of a virile black man. It seemed just the sort of thing to answer some questions I had about the facts of life. It didn't. Instead, it described a cocktail party given in the late 1960s for the Black Panthers by Leonard Bernstein in his fancy New York City apartment. I'd never been to New York City, or heard of Leonard Bernstein, the conductor of the New York Philharmonic, and had only a vague notion of who or what a Black Panther revolutionary might be—and none of that turned out to matter. The book started out with this weird old guy, Leonard Bernstein, rising from his bed in the middle of the night and having a vision of himself delivering a speech to a packed concert hall while being heckled by a giant black man on-stage beside him. I remember thinking: How would anyone know about someone else's bizarre private vision? Was this one of those stories that really happened, like Bart Starr's quarterback sneak to beat the Dallas Cowboys, or was it made up, like *The Hardy Boys?* Then, suddenly, I felt as if I were standing in Leonard Bernstein's apartment watching his waiters serve appetizers to Black Panthers:

"MMMMMMMMMMMMMMMMMM. THESE ARE NICE. LITTLE Roquefort cheese morsels rolled in crushed nuts. Very tasty. Very subtle. It's the way the dry sackiness of the nuts tiptoes up against the dour savor of the cheese that is so nice, so subtle. Wonder what the Black Panthers eat out here on the hors d'oeuvre trail? Do the Panthers like little Roquefort cheese morsels rolled in crushed nuts this way, and asparagus tips in mayonnaise dabs, and *meatballs petites au Coq Hardi,* all of which are at this very moment being offered to them on ga-drooned silver platters by maids in black uniforms with hand-ironed white aprons?"

Were the books grown-ups read supposed to make you laugh? I had no idea but . . .

"But it's all right. They're *white* servants, not Claude and Maude, but white South Americans. Lenny and Felicia are geniuses. After a while, it all comes down to servants. They are the cutting edge in Radical Chic. Obviously, if you are giving a party for the Black Panthers, as Lenny and Felicia are this evening, or as Sidney and Gail Lumet did last week, or as John Simon of Random House and Richard Baron, the publisher did before that; or for the Chicago Eight, such as the party Jean vanden Heuvel gave; or for the grape workers or Bernadette Devlin, such as the parties Andrew Stein gave; or for the Young Lords, such as the party Ellie Guggenheimer is giving next week in *her* Park Avenue duplex; or for the Indians or the SDS or the G.I. coffee shops or even for the Friends of the Earth—well, then, obviously you can't have a Negro butler and maid, Claude and Maude, in uniform, circulating through the living room, the library, and the main hall serving drinks and canapés. Plenty of people have tried to think it out. They try to picture the Panthers or whoever walking in bristling with electric hair and Cuban shades and leather pieces and the rest of it, and they try to picture Claude and Maude with the black uniforms coming up and saying, 'Would you care for a drink, sir?' They close their eyes and try to picture it *some way,* but there *is* no way. One simply cannot see that moment. So the current wave of Radical Chic has touched off the most desperate search for white servants."

At some point came a thought that struck with the force of revelation: this book *had been written by someone.* Some human being must have sat down and scribbled the Hardy Boys series, along with the *Legends of the NFL*—how else would I have ever known that Dallas Cowboys defensive lineman Bob Lilly lifted a Volkswagen by himself? I'd never really stopped to ask who had written any of those books, because . . . well, because it didn't matter to me who had written them. Their creators were invisible. They had no particular identity. No voice. Now rolling around a living-room floor in New Orleans, Louisiana, howling with laughter, I asked a new question: Who wrote this book? Thinking it might offer a clue, I searched the cover. Right there on the front was a name!!! Tom Wolfe. Who was Tom Wolfe?

PARACHUTING IN
· ·

"Is he, like, really old?" Dixie asks. Dixie is my 13-year-old daughter, who, a few days earlier, had been told that her special trip with her father needed to be interrupted for the better part of a day so that he might pay a call on Tom Wolfe.

"Eighty-five," I say. "But he's a *very young* 85." As if that helps. To a 13-year-old, 85 might as well be 2,000. She doesn't like the idea of this trip at all. "Look," I say, or something like it. "I want at least one of my children to meet him. I think he's a big reason it ever occurred to me to do what I do for a living. Because the first time I ever thought 'writer,' I also thought 'delight.'"

She's not listening. She knows we're going to see Tom Wolfe for reasons that have nothing to do with her. She doesn't care what I do for a living. She doesn't care who Tom Wolfe is—it was all she could do to drag herself to click on his Wikipedia entry. What she cares about, intensely, are plane crashes. She hates flying, and, in this case, I can't say I blame her. So I try all over again to explain why, to travel quickly from Martha's Vineyard to Long Island, you can't fly in a normal plane, only a small one or a helicopter, and that the weather's too dicey for a helicopter. That's when our pilot finally appears. He's got a swagger about him, which might be reassuring, or the opposite, depending on your feelings about male confidence. He leads us onto the Martha's Vineyard airport runway and into a maze of Gulf-streams and Lears and Hawkers. The sight of the jets perks Dixie up—private planes aren't nearly as small as she imagined. They're sleek and indestructible, like the chariots of visiting gods. When our pilot stops, though, it is not beside a Hawker or a Lear or a Gulfstream. It's not clear what it is. When I first spotted it I thought it might be a drone. I half expected the pilot to pull out a remote control and show us how to play with it. Instead he produces a step stool and shows us how to climb up on the wing without breaking it. My child looks at me like, well, like a 13-year-old girl being taken on a suicide mission to visit a 2,000-year-old man—and then crawls on all fours across the wing, to squeeze into the doggy door on the side.

"Where's the other pilot?" I ask, before following.

"It's jes' me," the pilot says, with a chuckle. It's a reassuring chuckle. A faintly *southern* chuckle—though he's not from the South. "Something happens to me, here's what you do," he says as he straps himself in. "This lever here." He grabs a red knob beside his seat. "This shuts down the engine. Jes' pull that back and you shut it down. And this lever here . . ." He grabs a bright-red handle on the ceiling over his head. "Yank down on this with 45 pounds of pressure. That'll release the parachute."

"*The parachute?*"

"No sense having the engine running with the parachute open," he says, ignoring the 10 questions that naturally precede the one to which this is the answer.

"What did you say your name was?" I hadn't paid attention the first time. Now that I was going to be parachuting into the ocean with his inert body I needed to be able to explain to the authorities who he was.

"Jack Yeager," he says.

"Yeager?"

"Uh-huh."

"As in—"

"I get that all the time. People think we're related." He fires up his toy propellers.

"You know who Chuck Yeager is?"

"Everyone knows who Chuck Yeager is."

Dixie doesn't know who Chuck Yeager is, but her brain is on tilt. One day, perhaps, she'll want to know.

"You know why—right?" I holler.

"He broke the sound barrier."

"No, I mean, you know why anyone knows Chuck Yeager broke the sound barrier, or cares?"

He shakes his head. He's busy declaring to the airport authorities his improbable intention to take off from their runway in his toy plane.

"It's because of Tom Wolfe," I shout.

"Who's Tom Wolfe?"

There's a new answer to that question. Back in November 2013 the New York Public Library announced that it would pay $2.15 million to acquire Wolfe's papers. It wasn't until earlier this year that they became available for inspection. It's not hard to see why it took them so long. Wolfe saved what he touched—report cards, tailors' bills, to-do lists, reader letters, lecture notes, book blurbs, requests for book blurbs, drawings, ideas for drawings never executed ("Nude Skydiver Devoured in Midair by Ravenous Owls"), and dozens of sexually explicit and totally insane letters from a female stalker, including one consisting chiefly of 17 pages of red lip prints. He just tossed all this stuff in steamer trunks and hauled the trunks up to the attic, where some of them had sat undisturbed for 50 years. He kept postcards from friends with hardly anything written on them; he kept all the Christmas cards; he kept morning-after notes from New York society ladies:

> "Dear Tom, I wouldn't blame you for thinking I am a prevert [*sic*] or a sex fiend or something but actually, I have never tried to give anyone after dinner gropes before. Well not at the table anyway. . . .
>
> Don't be mad at me.
> Please." [Dated November 17, 1964.]

There's a thrill to be had in an old-fashioned archive—of poking around letters and papers and reporter notepads stuffed with random scribblings while the lady behind the library desk glances over to make sure you aren't doodling on the papers. It's the thrill of entering a private space, where the characters are unaware they are being watched. When some poor sucker's e-mails or texts wind up in public they offer everyone a thrill, but it isn't really the same—who writes an e-mail these days entirely free of the thought that he's being watched? The other pleasure of an old-fashioned archive is the pleasure of words on paper. Letters are different from e-mails and texts. They have stuff jotted in their margins; they reveal a bit more about the writer. And with nothing in them to click on, the words have to do a lot more work, to enable the reader to *see* what you mean:

I hate to say this but David McDaniel is the most devlish looking and the most devlish acting person I've ever seen. He looks like the typical "comic book" Jap. He is short—not over 4'2"—has a very, very, very, very short monkey's shave—high cheekbones—squinted eyes—wears glasses—a stubby nose—a toothy grin—and to top it all, he actually has pointed teeth!!!!!!!!!!!! He is as mean as he can be, he has no consideration for anyone, he acts spoiled to death. he is terribly babyish, <u>unhumanly</u> babyish for anyone 12 years old. This is what he looks like [see drawing on page 185, top right] . . .

The description and drawing seem terribly exaggerated I know, but every bit of it is true—and the picture is one of the most perfect likenesses I've ever drawn." [Tom Wolfe, aged 12, letter to his mother and father, 1943.]

The documents tell the story of the leading journalistic observer and describer of American life, in a time of radical cultural transformation, and of the sensational explosion in American literary journalism that occurred in the late 1960s and 1970s—on which the ashes and the dust are just now settling. But it's a bit different from the story Wolfe has long told. That story shifts the focus away from his particular self and stresses his techniques. The unaided imagination—Wolfe's story goes—is a poor substitute for reporting and experience. At some point in his checkered career The American Novelist forgot that he needed to venture into the world and learn how it worked before he wrote about it, and left the field wide open for The American Journalist.

In the late 1960s a bunch of writers leapt into the void: George Plimpton, Joan Didion, Truman Capote, Gay Talese, Norman Mailer, Hunter S. Thompson, and the rest. Wolfe shepherded them into an uneasy group and labeled them the New Journalists. The New Journalists—with Wolfe in the lead—changed the balance of power between writers of fiction and writers of nonfiction, and they did it chiefly because of their willingness to submerge themselves in their subjects, and to steal from the novelist's bag of tricks: scene-by-scene construction, use of dramatic dialogue, vivid characterization, shifting points of view, and so on.

I doubt I was ever alone in failing to find the whole New Journalism story entirely satisfying. (Hunter Thompson, for instance, wrote Wolfe, "You thieving pile of albino warts. . . . I'll have your goddamn femurs ground into bone splinters if you ever mention my name again in connexion [*sic*] with that horrible 'new journalism' shuck you're promoting.") For a start, there wasn't anything new about the techniques. Mark Twain used them to dramatize his experiences as a riverboat pilot and a gold miner. George Orwell set himself up as a destitute tramp and wrote up the experience as nonfiction. Virtually every British travel writer who has ever left an unpaid bill might be counted a New Journalist. When you look at that list of New Journalists, what pops to mind is not their common technique. It's their uncommon voices. They leapt off the page. They didn't sound like anyone else's.

OUT OF THE SOUTH

Thomas Kennerly Wolfe Jr. was born on March 2, 1930, and grew up in Richmond, Virginia, the son of a conservative, God-respectful southern editor of an agricultural trade magazine. Home was never something he was looking to get away from; it was never even something he was looking to pretend he was looking to get away from. He was accepted at Princeton but chose to attend Washington and Lee, to remain close to home. Every now and then one of his teachers would note that he had a way with words, and some artistic talent, but artistic ambition, for a conservative southern male in the 1950s or really any other time, was too vague and impractical to indulge. After college, he took the advice of his professor and went to Yale, for a doctorate in American studies— and right up to this point in his life there isn't a trace of institutional rebellion in him. He pitches for the baseball team, pleases his teachers, has an ordinary, not artistic, group of pals, and is devoted to his mother and father.

The moment he leaves the South, something comes over him. Whatever it is, the feeling seems to be heightened by the sight of a blank sheet of paper. For instance, he creates (while he's meant to be writing a Yale dissertation) an elaborate parody of a Beat poet, "Jocko Thor," complete with a small book of poems and a short biography. Jocko Thor has given birth to a "new poetic genre called Bonkism." In his preface he explains: "Most of these poems were composed beneath a Coca-Cola sign in the town of Accident, Maryland, in February of 1956. They are dedicated to my childe bride whom I first met on that very spot." There follows what is essentially a book of short poems written, it seems, purely for Wolfe's own amusement—he never mentions them to anyone.

> *"Regular Fellows*
> *We walk the sidewalk brick by brick*
> *We climb the brass-clapped stairs*
> *We spit into each other's faces*
> *And never put on airs."*

"*The Martyr*
. . . A Freudian Poem
In a moment I'll resume my martyrdom
In a moment, ready to trick myself,
Goad myself, to vex myself
With expert taunts,
I'll exhale and open my eyes.
Small designs will writhe
Behind my eyelids
Like bullwhips."

And so on. For the first time in his life, it appears, Tom Wolfe has been pro-
voked. He has left home and found, on the East Coast, the perpetual revolt of
High Culture against God, Country, and Tradition. He happens to have landed in
a time and place in which art—like the economy that supports it—is essentially
patricidal. It's all about tearing up and replacing what came before. The young
Tom Wolfe is intellectually equipped to join some fashionable creative movement
and set himself in opposition to God, Country, and Tradition; emotionally, not so
much. He doesn't use his new experience of East Coast sophisticates to distance
himself from his southern conservative upbringing; instead he uses his upbringing
to distance himself from the new experience. He picks for his Ph.D. dissertation
topic the Communist influences on American writers, 1928–1942. From their
response to it, the Yale professors, who would have approved the topic in advance,
had no idea of the spirit in which Wolfe intended to approach it:

"Dear Mr. Wolfe:
    I am personally acutely sorry to have to write you this letter but I
want to inform you in advance that all of your readers reports have
come in, and . . . I am sorry to say I anticipate that the thesis will not be
recommended for the degree. . . . The tone was not objective but was
consistently slanted to disparage the writers under consideration and to
present them in a bad light even when the evidence did not warrant
this." [Letter from Yale dean to T.W., May 19, 1956.]

To this comes appended the genuinely shocked reviews of three Yale professors. It's as if they can't quite believe this seemingly sweet-natured and well-
mannered southern boy has gone off half cocked and ridiculed some of the
biggest names in American literature. The Yale grad student had treated the
deeply held political conviction of these great American artists as—well, as a
ploy in a game of status seeking. This student seemed to have gone out of his way
to turn these serious American intellectuals into figures of fun. "The result is

more journalistically tendentious than scholarly. . . . Wolfe's polemical rhetoric is . . . a chief consideration of my decision to fail the dissertation." To top it all off . . . he'd taken some license with the details. One outraged reviewer compared Wolfe's text with his cited sources and attached the comparison. Sample Wolfe passage: "At one point 'the Cuban delegation' tramped in. It was led by a fierce young woman named Lola de la Torriente. With her bobbed hair, leather jacket, and flat-heeled shoes, she looked as though she had just left the barricades. Apparently she had. 'This is where our literature is being built,' exclaimed she, 'on the barricades!'" Huffed the reviewer: "There is no description of her in the source, and the quotations do not appear in the reference."

Which is to say that, as a 26-year-old graduate student, just as a 12-year-old letter writer, Tom Wolfe was already recognizably himself. He'd also found a lens through which he might view, freshly, all human behavior. He'd gone to Yale with the thought he would study his country by reading its literature and history and economics. He wound up discovering sociology—and especially Max Weber's writings about the power of status seeking. The lust for status, it seemed to him, explained why otherwise intelligent American writers lost their minds and competed with one another to see just how devoted to the Communist cause they could be. In a funny way, Yale served him extremely well: it gave him a chance to roam and read and bump into new ideas. But he didn't immediately see that:

"These stupid fucks have turned down namely my dissertation, meaning I will have to stay here about a month longer to delete all the offensive passages and retype the sumitch. They called my brilliant manuscript 'journalistic' and 'reactionary,' which means I must go through with a blue pencil and strike out all the laughs and anti-Red passages and slip in a little liberal merde, so to speak, just to sweeten it. I'll discuss with you how stupid all these stupid fucks are when I see you." [T.W., aged 26, letter to a friend, June 9, 1956.]

OFFBEAT REPORTER

He re-writes his thesis. He lards it up with academic jargon and creates a phony emotional distance from his material (he refers to "an American writer E. Hemingway"), and it is accepted. Then he flees Yale as fast as he can. He's entering his late 20s with only the faintest idea of what he might do to earn a living. But he's ambitious, eager to find his place in the world. His father introduces him to business associates. Wolfe writes to the head of a sales institute and sends "excerpts from work I have done on the subject of Communist activity among American writers and other 'intellectuals.'" He applies for jobs in public relations. He writes to American Airlines to inquire about a post. He even considers, briefly, a position teaching economics.

In short, he doesn't have any clear idea of what to do, although he has long liked the notion of being a writer or an artist. In May of 1955 he had written to the dean of Washington and Lee University, "I am thinking very seriously of going into journalism or a related field," but he was slow to pursue it, as he was sure it would disappoint his parents. He writes to one of his father's friends and confesses what he really wants to be is a *sportswriter*. Finally, he sends letters and curricula vitae to newspapers, offering his services as either a journalist or a graphic artist. (As a child he had enjoyed drawing and still seems at this point in his life as interested in drawing as in writing.) Only one newspaper writes back to express interest: the *Springfield Union,* in eastern Massachusetts. In 1956, at the age of 26, he takes the job.

A young man who had once assumed he'd become a professor now roams the streets of small-time America looking for car accidents or house fires or "color" stories—and he doesn't seem at all troubled about it. There's not a peep in his papers that suggests his parents are disappointed or that Wolfe is anxious about his career. Just the reverse: when he writes a story about the new fad of scuba diving and gets his picture in the paper in scuba gear, he is thrilled. He mails the clippings to his parents.

Still, he hasn't figured out who he is, at least on paper. When his byline is not merely "a staff reporter," it's "Thomas Wolfe," and the stuff that appears under it could have been written by anyone. He's a good daily journalist—first for the *Springfield Union* and then, two and a half years later, for *The Washington Post.* But there's nothing special about his work. The *Post* sends him to be the Latin America correspondent, and from Havana he sends dispatches that read just like the dispatches of the guy he replaced. But in Washington, when he's in his early 30s, come the first signs that he isn't entirely satisfied with the path he's on. He writes to his parents to complain of the *Post*'s "chronic mania for bleeding heart stories on the poor and downtrodden." He writes a 10-page single-spaced letter to interest the editor of *The Saturday Evening Post* in a piece for which there is no place in *The Washington Post,* on "status-seeking in Washington D.C." "I don't believe there is any subject, with the possible exception of the neighbors' finances, which people enjoy having lugged out into the open more," he writes. In his notebooks he catalogues his careful observations of the locals, in their hand-over-hand status climbs: the way the black Lincoln has replaced the Cadillac as the status car (because Jack Kennedy drove a black Lincoln); the way they used Cabinet members as cocktail-party status objects ("bagging a cabinet member"); right down to the way they had turned dog licenses into status symbols—by handing out low-number licenses to the dogs of high-ranking officials. Wolfe appears to have walked back and forth across Washington to determine which neighborhood said which things about which people. His notebooks list the addresses of all the important people and the high-status buildings. (The street with all the African embassies on it he labels "Cannibals Row.")

But he never writes the piece, maybe because his heart is only half in it: he is genuinely convinced that status concerns are at the heart of most human behavior. But the human behavior in Washington doesn't strike him as all that interesting. When people think about writers they notice the things they have chosen to write about. What writers choose *not* to write about is worth noticing, too. The man who would become the foremost chronicler of American life for a generation would decide, from his position inside *The Washington Post,* that Washington wasn't all that important. Decades later he writes a letter to a young friend in which he explains, in an aside, why:

"The Republican Party as now constituted is obviously too stupid to survive. . . . What is to be done? Of course, that was Lenin's line and the only lucid one he ever wrote. The answer is nothing. America's position is unassailable. We are the imperial Rome of the 3rd Millennium. Our government is a CSX train on a track. People on one side (the left) yell at it, and people on the other side (the right) yell at it, but the train's only going to go down the track. Thank God for that. That's why I find American politics too boring to write about. Nixon is forced from office. Does a military junta rise up? Do the tanks roll? Give me a break." [February 28, 2000.]

THE JOKER IS WILD

The Washington subject that catches Wolfe's fancy, at some deep level, is Hugh Troy. Hugh Troy is the first documented case in which Tom Wolfe set out into the world looking for one thing and found another, much more interesting thing. He'd been assigned to write a story about practical jokes in England and America. Someone told him there was a man living in Washington named Hugh Troy, who was "the most fabulous practical joker in the history of America." Wolfe had no interest in any of this—he was just doing his job—but he dutifully went off to meet Hugh Troy. The piece Wolfe wrote on practical jokes could have been written by anybody. The long obituary Wolfe foisted unbidden upon a New York newspaper after Troy's death three years later could have been written only by Tom Wolfe.

"Troy wasn't the fat little Shriner I had figured him for. He was huge, almost six feet six. . . . He must have weighed close to 240 pounds. He was in his mid-fifties. He dressed in soft white shirts, hard worsteds and boned leather shoes, like a lawyer in the financial district. He had the charm, voice, manners . . . the whole business . . . of the kind of individual who grew up in the right schools, clubs, fraternities, cotillions . . . they hadn't raised little Hugh to go around goosing the universe."

Troy didn't see himself as a practical joker: he didn't even really understand the impulse to think up practical jokes. He was, at heart, a social satirist. His jokes were responses to stuff that bothered him. During the Depression, for instance, he'd been bothered by the sight of New York City police officers harassing the homeless sleeping on benches in Central Park. He bought a bench, took it to the park, and lay on it until the cops came—whereupon Troy picked up the bench and ran. "This was just a buildup for the vignette he was waiting for . . . in court . . . the look on their faces as he whipped out his bill of sale and demanded the return of his bench." Or another time, in the early 1950s, Troy found himself bothered by the boom in "ghost writing."

"Dignitaries no longer even thought of writing their own speeches. The new president of a leading university had been caught delivering an inaugural address lifted by his lazy hulking ghost writer from an article in an educational journal by another university president.

"One night it just came to Troy: Ghost Artists Inc. He placed an ad in the Washington <u>Post & Times Herald</u> of February 5, 1952: 'Too busy to paint? Have the talent but not the time? Call on The Ghost Artists, 1426 33rd Street N.W. . . . We paint it—You Sign It! Any Style! Impressionist, Modern, Cubist, Primitive (Grandma Moses), Abstract, Sculpture . . . Also, Why Not Give an Exhibition?' Immediately orders began coming in, which Troy turned down, saying the firm was swamped with work. Then the newspaper and wire service reporters started calling up. In the most sincere and courtly tones he told each reporter that he would break down and tell the whole story if they would only please not use his name.

"The next day the story was going out all over the country: of how this ring of ghost artists had been operating for three years in New York and was now opening a branch in Washington to fill many orders from 'high in government circles.'"

Tom Wolfe had found his first kindred spirit. When he describes him he might as well be describing himself:

"I had the feeling Troy never wanted to explore himself that deeply, as if he weren't sure what he would find. . . . At every juncture there seemed to be two Hugh Troys—the one, well-brought-up, courtly, serious, concerned, sympathetic, and the other one riding off like hell, like Don Quijote in the Land of Logical Lunacy."

In the summer of 1962, Wolfe quits his job at *The Washington Post* and moves to New York City, where he takes a job as a daily reporter at the *Herald Tribune.*

There's a doubleness about Tom Wolfe, too. In person he is courteous and considerate and polite and teacher-pleasing: a nice boy of whom everyone would say, "His parents raised him right." He holds doors open for others, stands until the ladies are seated, and listens politely to the dullest conversation, and he always will—even when he's 85 years old and has earned the right to ignore idiots and take the first open seat. But something comes over him when he stares at a blank sheet of paper and is forced to contemplate other people, especially people convinced of their own brilliance or importance. Thoughts he'd never utter in public come bursting out of him. So long as he was a newspaper reporter, there was not much risk his private thoughts would get him into trouble. There are limits to what a reporter can say about people in a daily newspaper; there is the need to at least seem objective. And so Tom Wolfe, as he enters mid-career, finds himself wearing handcuffs: he's just good enough at writing for newspapers that he doesn't need to do anything else. And he doesn't have the money to stop writing for newspapers, even if the job keeps his inner dog on a leash.

THE MAN IN THE WHITE SUIT

Money is actually an important part of his story. When he moved to New York he owned two sports jackets. *Herald Tribune* reporters all wore suits, and so he went out and bought a suit: a white suit. The suit wasn't some kind of statement; it was what you wore in the summer in Richmond, Virginia. The first time he wore it, however, he realized the suit wasn't of summer weight. It was thick enough to wear in cold weather, too. That's how strapped for cash he is: he wears his white suit into the fall so he doesn't have to buy another.

Then comes a glorious accident. On December 8, 1962, every newspaperman in New York went on strike. Tom Wolfe is a newspaper journalist without a paper to write for. He would soon turn 33: he was no longer a young man. He had no real savings, and now he had no paycheck. He put out feelers to see if he could find work writing ads. He wrote to his father, seeking advice:

"I'm not terribly anxious to be writing ads, but they pay very well. . . . As yet, of course, no money has come rolling in from all this. Until it does I wonder if I should apply for state unemployment benefits? This perplexes me, and I would like your advice, because I have a great loathing of the idea of going on the dole. Perhaps it is only false pride." [T.W., letter to his father, January 13, 1963.]

His father wrote back to say he saw no shame in unemployment benefits. For some reason Wolfe didn't agree. Instead of going on the dole he went looking for work, and the work that naturally presented itself was magazine work. *Esquire* hired him to fly to California and explore the strange new world of custom-made cars. Wolfe wrote a letter to his parents to describe what he'd seen there:

"The trip was one of the most interesting I ever took. Los Angeles is incredible—like every new suburb in America all massed together in one plain. . . . Everyone drives, and drives and drives. Twenty-five miles for a hamburger is nothing. . . .

"The car-o-philes, or whatever they ought to be called, were an intriguing lot, especially the custom car designers. They starve for their art, such as it is, have many of the mannerisms and anti-social attitudes of artists, and, in general, are the Pentecostal version of High Culture's Episcopal, if I may make such a comparison." [April 1963.]

To his parents he has no trouble describing what he has seen. Putting the words onto paper for *Esquire* proves more problematic. He's written hundreds of thousands of words in newspapers. He has a subject that interests him intensely—it's not just about cars, it's about the sincere soul of American life. He sits down to write and . . . he can't do it. The words simply won't come. In the end he calls up his editor, Byron Dobell, and tells him he just can't get the piece out of himself. Dobell tells him that *Esquire* desperately needs something, and soon. They've spent $10,000 on a photo spread and they need the text to explain it. *Just write up your notes in a letter to me tonight,* says Dobell, *and I'll have someone hammer out the text for the piece.* And that's what Wolfe does. "Dear Byron," he writes—though he might just as easily have written "Dear Mother and Father:"

"The first good look I had at customized cars was at an event called a 'Teen Fair,' held in Burbank, a suburb of Los Angeles beyond Hollywood. This was a wild place to be taking a look at art objects—eventually, I should say, you have to reach the conclusion that these customized cars *are* art objects, at least if you use the standards applied in a civilized society."

A few pages in and he's not just relating what he's seen in a matter-of-fact way, the way you would if you were just trying to supply some poor editor with information to use in captions to some photos. He's letting it fly.

"Things have been going on in the development of the kids' formal attitude toward cars since 1945, things of great sophistication that adults have not been even remotely aware of, mainly because the kids are so inarticulate about it, especially the ones most hipped on the subject. They are not from the levels of society that produce children who write sensitive analytical prose at age seventeen, or if they do, they soon fall into the hands of English instructors who put them onto Hemingway or a lot of goddamn-and-hungry-breast writers. If they ever write about a highway again, it's a rain-slicked highway and the sound of the automobiles passing over it is like the sound of tearing silk, not that one household in ten thousand has heard the sound of tearing silk since 1945."

When he was done, his letter ran 49 pages. The exotic punctuation, the ellipses, the rococo mannerisms that sometimes enhance and sometimes detract from his later work aren't yet there, but his ability to see what others have missed, or found unworthy of attention, is sensational. The effect is of an opaque protective gauze being peeled back from the surface of the society to expose what's really under it. What really matters. In the morning, he walked his letter over to *Esquire.* "It was like he discovered it in the middle of the night," Dobell now recalls. "Wherever it came from, it seemed to me to tap a strain of pure American humor that wasn't being tapped. He didn't sound like Truman Capote or Lillian Ross . . . or anyone else." Dobell scratched out the *Dear Byron* salutation and ran the letter as the piece, called "There Goes (Varoom! Varoom!) That Kandy-Kolored (Thphhhhhhh!) Tangerine-Flake Streamline Baby Around the Bend (Brummmmmmmmmmmmmmmmmmm) . . . . . ."

In Wolfe's papers there is a copy of a letter from early 1965—less than 18 months after he first got his voice on the page, and after he'd published a dozen or so magazine pieces, mostly for the *New York Herald Tribune*'s new color supplement, *New York* magazine. The letter came from Rosser Reeves to the president of the *Herald Tribune.* Reeves was the splashiest adman in the 1960s; he's been fingered as a model for *Mad Men*'s Don Draper. He begins,

"There is a man named Tom Wolfe who is currently writing for the Herald Tribune. He is one of the sharpest and most perceptive talents that has appeared on the scene in many, many years. . . . I discover that he is becoming the object of a cult." [Rosser Reeves to Walter Thayer, March 30, 1965.]

STATUS UPDATE

Eighteen months! That's what it took for Wolfe, once he'd found his voice, to go from worrying about whether or not to go on the dole to a cult figure. By early 1965, literary agents are writing him, begging to let them sell a book; publishers are writing to him, begging him to write one. Hollywood people are writing to ask if they might turn his magazine pieces into movies—though really all they want is to rub up against him. Two years earlier his fan letters had come mainly from his mother. Soon they came from Cybill Shepherd. He's booked on *The*

Tonight Show with Johnny Carson. He's now as likely to use the margins of his notebooks to tally his lecture fees as to accommodate drawings of nude sky-divers. He has a stalker. He also has a strange new kindred spirit, and pen pal:

> "Dear Tom:
>
> I just got back from a quick shot in the East, and called from the airport but you weren't home again. Who are these old crones who answer your telephone? I have a picture of some gout-raddled old slattern on her knees in your hallway, waxing the floor when the phone rings and rising slowly, painfully, resentfully, to answer it and snarl 'He ain't here.' . . . What stage is the Kesey book in?" [To T.W. from Hunter Thompson, February 26, 1968.]

Wolfe's response to his new status—like Hunter Thompson's—is to create a public persona as particular and distinctive as the sounds he's making on the page. Once he becomes famous, people start to notice and remark upon his white suit, in a way they don't seem to have done before: they take it as one of those eccentricities that are a natural by-product of genius. He bought the thing because it was just what you wore in Richmond in the summer and kept on wearing it because it kept him warm in winter. Now it becomes this sensational affectation. He buys an entire wardrobe of white suits, and the hats and canes and shoes and gloves to accessorize them. His handwriting changes in a similar way—once a neat but workman-like script, it becomes spectacularly rococo, with great swoops and curlicues. In his reporter notebooks he tries out various new signatures and eventually settles on one with so many flourishes that the letters look as if they are under attack by a squadron of flying saucers. The tone of his correspondence becomes more courtly and mannered, and, well, like it is coming from someone who isn't like other people. Nine years after he bursts onto the scene he receives an honorary doctorate from Washington and Lee. "While a feature writer for *New York* magazine he, like Lord Byron before him, awoke one morning to find himself famous," said the college president. And, like Lord Byron before him, Wolfe had a pretty good sense of what the public wanted from its geniuses.

Yet the elaborate presentation of self never really interferes with the work or the effort he puts into it—at least not in the way it would do with Hunter Thompson. It doesn't even seem to interfere with his ability to report on the world. Wolfe gets himself on the psychedelic school bus Ken Kesey and his aco-lytes are taking cross-country to proselytize for LSD. There, in his white suit, he sits and watches Kesey and his groupies more or less invent the idea of sex, drugs, and rock 'n' roll. No one who reads Wolfe's take on it all, *The Electric Kool-Aid Acid Test*—at least no one whose letters or reviews are preserved—asks the obvious question: How the hell did he do that? How did he get them to let him in, almost as one of them? Why do all these people keep letting this oddly dressed man into their lives, to observe them as they have never before been observed?

And it's not just attention seekers, like Kesey, who throw open the doors to the man in the white suit. Wolfe writes a piece on the origins of this new sport called stock-car racing and its greatest legend, Junior Johnson. Junior Johnson doesn't talk to reporters. He's famously reticent: no one outside his close circle of family and friends has any idea who he really is. Without a word of explanation, Tom Wolfe is suddenly describing what it's like to be in Junior's backyard, pulling weeds with his two sisters and watching a red rooster cross the lawn, while Junior tells him everything . . . and the reader learns, from Junior himself, that NASCAR racing basically evolved out of the fine art, mastered by Junior, of outrunning the North Carolina federal agents with a car full of bootleg whiskey. Wolfe's *Esquire* piece about Junior Johnson, "The Last American Hero Is Junior Johnson. Yes!" is another sensation—and still no one writes to ask him: How did you do that? How did you get yourself invited into the home of a man who would sooner shoot a journalist than talk to him? (This fall, *50 years* after Wolfe introduced the world to Junior Johnson, NASCAR Productions and Fox Sports released a documentary about the piece. That's the effect Wolfe routinely has had: to fix people and events in readers' minds forever.)

New York City was—and still is—the only place on earth where a writer might set himself up as a professional tour guide and attract the interest of the entire planet. That's mainly what Wolfe was, at least in the beginning: his job was to observe the sophisticates in their nutty bubble for the pleasure of the rubes in the hinterlands, and then, from time to time, venture out into the hinterlands and explain *what is really going on out there* to the sophisticates inside the bubble. He moves back and forth like a bridge player, ruffing the city and the country against each other. He occupies a place in between. He dresses exotically and is talented and intellectually powerful, like the sophisticates in the bubble. But he isn't really one of them. To an extent that shocks the people inside the bubble, when they learn of it, he shares the values of the hinterland. He believes in God, Country, and even, up to a point, Republican Presidents. He even has his doubts about the reach of evolutionary theory.

None of this really matters. What matters is his X-ray vision. By the early 1970s it was as if there were, in the United States, two realities. There's the reality perceived by ordinary people and the reality perceived by Tom Wolfe—until Wolfe writes his piece or book and most people just forget their original perception and adopt his. He might be forgiven for believing that he is in the possession of some very weird special power. The entire planet might be fixated on some event and fail to see an essential truth about it—until he files his report on the matter.

Then, on July 20, 1969, Neil Armstrong stepped out of Apollo 11 onto the moon.

Like everyone else, Wolfe took an interest in the moon landing, but less in the mission than in the men. The early astronauts had some traits in common, he noticed. They tended to be born oldest sons, in the mid-1920s, named after their fathers, and raised in small towns, in intact Anglo-Saxon Protestant families. More than half of them had "Jr." after their names. In other words, they were just like him. What was it about this upbringing, he wondered, that produced these men? It was another way of asking: *What strange sociological process explains me?*

The more famous Wolfe became, the less often he wrote to his mother and father—at least to judge from his archives. His father still wrote to him, however, and it's clear that he still felt listened to, and consulted. At the end of a letter written after the moon landing he adds a note to his son:

> "Apropos . . . astronauts
> A hamlet breeds heroes
> a city breeds eunuchs.
> —Socrates"
> [To T.W. from his father, 1969.]

Chasing that idea, Wolfe spends the better part of a decade crisscrossing the country. He pays for his research by publishing several other books. Some of these are forgettable (*Mauve Gloves & Madmen, Clutter & Vine*); some are long essays that still hold up amazingly well (*The Painted Word*); all of them are less important to him than the astronauts. Reducing their story to a narrative proves to be incredibly difficult. The archives here tell the story of a writer working his ass off. Never mind what percentage of genius is talent; this feels like all perspiration. There's no main character. There are the seven astronauts scattered across the country, plus a lot of other people to track down. The reporting alone takes him seven years. His original idea of the story, he decides, is wrong. The astronauts were all drawn from the officer ranks in the U.S. military. They were indeed invariably Wasps; men born before the Great Depression; and often oldest sons. So of course they shared his basic background. But so did everyone else in the pool from which the astronauts were drawn. So, that alone was not interesting.

At great expense—and this is just about the best example a nonfiction writer could set for others—he abandons his first theory of the case. But because he is looking so hard, and so well, he finds another. The story Wolfe discovers isn't precisely about the forces that made him possible. On the other hand, it isn't precisely not:

. . .

"This is really a book not about the space program but about status battles be-tween pilots in the highly competitive world of military flying. To be successful the book should not expand our view of man into the dimensions of the cosmos—but draw the entire cosmos into the dimensions of man's love of himself or, rather, his ceaseless concern for his own standing in comparison to other men. This should not seem like a cynical discovery, but it should be amusing." [T.W. letter, Box 126.]

This from a long letter Wolfe writes, as much to himself as to his editor, to ex-plain what he thinks he's up to. *It's not really a book about the space program.* It turns out that it's not even, really, about flying. It's about the importance of status to men, and what happens when the rules of any status game change. There had been a status structure to the life of U.S. fighter jocks before the space program, and it was clear to everyone involved. At the top of the pyramid were combat pilots, and at the tippy top were the combat pilots who found their way to Edwards Air Force Base, in the California desert, to test new fighter planes. The courage and spirit required not just to get to Edwards but to survive the test flights, the pilots themselves never spoke of, but it's at the center of their exis-tence. That unspoken quality Wolfe calls *the right stuff.* The embodiment of the right stuff—everyone knows it and yet no one says it—is Chuck Yeager. Hardly anyone outside the small world of combat pilots has ever heard of him. Here is how Wolfe, in a single sentence, will change that:

"Anyone who travels very much on airlines in the United States soon gets to know the voice of *the airline pilot* . . . coming over the intercom . . . with a particular drawl, a particular folksiness, a particular down-home calmness that is so exag-gerated it begins to parody itself (nevertheless!—it's reassuring) . . . the voice that tells you, as the airliner is caught in thunderheads and goes bolting up and down a thousand feet at a single gulp, to check your seat belts because 'it might get a little choppy' . . . the voice that tells you (on a flight from Phoenix preparing for its final approach into Kennedy Airport, New York, just after dawn): 'Now, folks, uh . . . this is the captain . . . ummmm . . . We've got a little ol' red light up here on the control panel that's tryin' to tell us that the *land*in gears're not . . . uh . . . *lock*in into position when we lower 'em . . . Now . . . I don't believe that little ol' red light knows what it's *talk*in about—I believe it's that little ol' red light that iddn' workin' right' . . . faint chuckle, long pause, as if to say, *I'm not even sure all this is really worth going into—still, it may amuse you* . . . 'But . . . I guess to play it by the rules, we oughta *humor* that little ol' light . . . so we're gonna take her down to about, oh, two or three hundred feet over the runway at Kennedy, and the folks down there on the ground are gonna see if they caint give us a *vis*ual inspection of those ol' landin' gears'—with which he is obviously on intimate ol'-buddy terms, as with every other working part of this mighty ship—'and if I'm right . . . they're gonna tell us everything is copa*cet*ic all the way aroun' an' we'll jes take her on in' . . . and, after a couple of low passes over the field, the voice returns: 'Well, folks, those folks down there on the ground—it must be too early for 'em or somethin'—I 'spect they still got the *sleep*ers in their eyes . . . 'cause they say they caint tell if those ol' landin' gears are all the way down or not . . . But, you know, up here in the cockpit we're convinced they're all the way down, so we're jes gonna take her on in . . . And oh' . . . (*I almost forgot*) . . . 'while we take a little swing out over the ocean an' empty some of that surplus fuel we're not gonna be needin' anymore—that's what you might be seein' comin' out of the wings—our lovely little ladies . . . if they'll be so kind . . . they're gonna go up and down the aisles and show you how we do what we call "assumin' the position"' . . . another faint chuckle *(We do this so often, and it's so much fun, we even have a funny little name for it)* . . . and the stewardesses, a bit grimmer, by the looks of them, than *that voice,* start telling the passengers to take their glasses off and take the ball-point pens and other sharp objects out of their pockets, and they show them *the position,* with the head lowered . . . while down on the field at Kennedy the little yellow emergency trucks start roaring across the field—and even though in your pounding heart and your sweating palms and your broiling brainpan you *know* this is a critical moment in your life, you still can't quite bring yourself to be*lieve* it, because if it were . . . how could *the captain,* the man who knows the actual situation most intimately . . . how could he keep on drawlin' and chucklin' and driftin' and lollygaggin' in that particular voice of his—

Well!—who doesn't know that voice! And who can forget it!—even after he is proved right and the emergency is over.

That particular voice may sound vaguely Southern or Southwestern, but it is specifically Appalachian in origin. . . . In the late 1940's and early 1950's this up-hollow voice drifted down from on high, from over the high desert of California, down, down, down, from the upper reaches of the Brotherhood into all phases of American aviation. . . . Military pilots and then, soon, airline pilots, pilots from Maine and Massachusetts and the Dakotas and Oregon and everywhere else, began to talk in that poker-hollow West Virginia drawl, or as close to it as they could bend their native accents. It was the drawl of the most righteous of all the possessors of the right stuff: Chuck Yeager." [From Chapter 3, *The Right Stuff.*]

Such was the grip Chuck Yeager held on the imaginations of brave young men. Then came the Russians, and the seemingly existential need to beat them to the moon. NASA's rockets required none of Yeager's skill or nerve. The astronaut's job could be done—was done—by a monkey. By the old standards—the true standards—the astronauts weren't even flying. The job was to sit still and cooperate with technocrats—and not alert the wider public that whatever you were doing required any less of the right stuff than it had before. The space program vaulted the astronauts to the top of the heap and reduced Chuck Yeager to an afterthought. The world needed them to be heroic pilots, and so they played the part, but no one (except for one American writer) thought to look more deeply into the matter. No one noticed the best story. Process had replaced courage. Engineers had replaced warriors. A great romantic way of life, a chivalric code, had been trampled by modernity. Not for the first time! (As Wolfe might write.) It's the story of the American South in the 20th century—or at least the story a lot of white southern men told themselves.

Anyway, it resonated with Wolfe, to incredible effect. Never mind journalism, new or old. *The Right Stuff*, in my view, is a great work of American literature. It's also the last nonfiction story Wolfe ever tells. The book sells well enough that it provides him with the financial cushion to avoid jobs as difficult as this one. He'll use the cushion to prove a point he has always wanted to make, to High Culture but also to himself, that he can *report* a novel. That novel, *The Bonfire of the Vanities*, will sell nearly three-quarters of a million copies in hardcover and another two million in paper. The marketplace will encourage Wolfe to write nothing but novels. And a funny thing happens. The moment he abandons it, the movement he shaped will lose its head of steam. The New Journalism: Born 1963, Died 1979. R.I.P. What was that all about? It was mainly about Tom Wolfe, I think.

GOING TO THE SOURCE

"Long Island's jes' ahead," says our Yeager, with his faint, yet still detectable, drawl. The drone descends, and soon Dixie and I are back on the ground, in the Hamptons, and driving to the house in which Wolfe now spends a lot of his time.

We find the writer in his kitchen, with his wife, Sheila, whom he met when she worked as the art director at *Harper's*. The streets near his house are teeming with people in shorts and T-shirts, but he still wears his white suit and has it dressed out with a white fedora. Dixie meets him and sweetly hides her alarm ("When I saw him I was like, Whoa! That's a very outgoing fashion choice," she says later), then takes off for the beach with his dog. The next couple of hours Tom Wolfe supplies the answers to questions I've had since I was a child, along with some new ones.

Radical Chic was all *Legends of the NFL* and no Hardy Boys. Leonard Bernstein's weird private vision of the giant black man protesting the maestro's speech as he delivered it actually happened: Wolfe plucked it from an interview Bernstein had given. "Jocko Thor" was more Hardy Boys than *Legends of the NFL*. "I don't know what I was doing with Jocko," Wolfe says. "I never showed them [the poems] to anybody." He harbors no ill will toward the professors who failed his thesis, and thinks, in retrospect, that "Yale was really important for me." He recalls the epiphany of reading the sociologists—and especially Weber—on the subject of status. "I kept saying that's right. That's exactly the way it works. I honestly think that everyone—unless they are in danger of losing their lives—makes their decisions on status."

The idea that leaving Yale and becoming a beat reporter at a small-town paper should have created anxiety—well, he doesn't even understand my question. He had no student debt—no one did—and no sense that he had to make his way in the world immediately or be devoured by it. He seems to have been entirely free of pre-professional angst. The notion of roaming the earth and groping toward a purpose in life now seems ridiculous to 22-year-olds, but that's the notion Wolfe more or less embraced. By waiting until his late 40s to marry and have children he eluded his generation's tool for sacrificing the freedom of youth. He'd had time to figure out what he really loved to do. He'd written 20 letters to newspapers, and the *Springfield Union* was the only one to write back and offer him a job. "On the train to Springfield I was so happy that I just sang, over and over, "Oh, I am a member of the working press . . . Oh, I am a member of the working press." He did indeed worry that his parents would be disappointed with him, but they turned out, instead, to be relieved. "They just wanted me off the payroll." The memory of Hugh Troy brings a smile to his face, but he has no immediate memory of writing Troy's obituary. He doesn't recall his stalker either—or any of the many long letters she sent, along with her (surprisingly well done) pornographic drawings of him in various situations with her. He must have just tossed them into the steamer trunk along with everything else. He does recall, vividly, the dilemma of taking unemployment benefits. "If you wanted the benefits you had to march," he says. "I thought it was so demeaning to be out there picketing." He also recalls the night he spent writing his letter to Byron Dobell, and finding his voice. At that stage of his career he always kept the same books near at hand when he wrote: Céline's *Journey to the End of the Night* and *Death on the Installment Plan,* plus some of Henry Miller. "I thought they put me in the mood," he says, "but maybe I was fooling myself." Even after paging through Céline he couldn't get the words out of himself. "There are two kinds of writer's block. One is when you freeze up because you think you can't do it. The other is when you think it's not worth doing." His was not the second kind. The material, and what he had to say about it, caused him to freeze up. "I suppose I kind of feared doing something different," he says, "because I was doing this other thing perfectly well," meaning newspaper journalism. "But pretend you are writing a letter and you are all right."

Fame, to him, didn't come naturally. The world expected him to be a character he wasn't. "I was so used to interviewing other people," he says. "I had never been interviewed by anyone. People were expecting me to be a ball of fire. They felt so let down!" His gaze had been relentlessly outward-looking—one reason he saw so much, so well—and he didn't respond well when he was required to respond to the gaze of others. He wasn't like Hunter Thompson or even Norman Mailer or George Plimpton, all of whom seemed to enjoy playing themselves, maybe even more than they enjoyed writing about it. Hunter Thompson played his character so well and so relentlessly that he eventually *became* his character. Wolfe recalls a lunch he had with Thompson in New York. "He comes into the restaurant. He's got this bag. 'Hunter, what's in the bag?' Hunter says, 'I've got something in here that will clear out this restaurant.'" What's in the bag, it turns out, is a marine distress signal. "Hunter says, 'This thing can travel 20 miles across water.' He blows it and the restaurant clears out. Now, to Hunter, that was an event."

The Great White Males of that moment had decided that rather than be bus-tour guides they'd become *stops* on the bus tour. George Plimpton set himself up as New York City's fireworks commissioner, Norman Mailer ran for mayor, and Truman Capote hosted masked balls at the Plaza hotel. Wolfe now recalls a conference at which both he and Hunter Thompson were paid to speak. Hunter failed to show. He'd made it to the conference, but then had gone off on a bender and never made it to the podium, resulting in all manner of trouble. The organizer tracked down Wolfe, who he knew was Thompson's friend. "He was outraged. I said, 'Sir, you don't schedule Hunter for a talk. You schedule him for an event. And you just had yours!'"

Tom Wolfe wasn't like that. For years after he became famous for his writing he was unable to stand up and give a talk without writing it out first. He simply hadn't been raised for the job of being a famous American writer circa 1970. "I got by on the white suit for quite a while," he now says. The white suit reassured people that he was busy playing a character when he was in fact busy watching them. In truth he had no sense of himself as a character; he thought of himself as a normal guy in an abnormal world. That he had no great ability to attract attention to himself except through his pen proved to be a huge literary advantage. He wanted status and attention as much as anyone else, but to get them he had to write. His public persona he could buy from his tailor.

His career, he suspects, is no longer possible. I also think that is true, for all sorts of non-obvious reasons—the career turned on the distinctiveness of his voice, and he found that voice only because he was given lots of time to do it. The voice also came from a particular place, now dead and gone. Not New York in the 1960s and 70s but Richmond, Virginia, circa 1942, when he was a boy and figured out what he loved and admired. Wolfe thinks his career would no long-er be possible for a more obvious reason: the Internet. Electronic media aren't as able or as likely to pay for the sort of immersion reporting that he did. And the readers of it aren't looking—or at least don't think they are looking—for a writer to create their view of the world. "I wouldn't have the same pathway from the bottom to the top," he says. "At some point you get thrust into the digital media. God, I don't know what the hell I'd do."

Then he surprises me. Looking back on it, he says, *Radical Chic & Mau-Mauing the Flak Catchers* is his favorite book. His second novel, *A Man in Full*, published in 1998, sold the most copies, but *Radical Chic* was the one he wouldn't change a word of. In the same breath he says that he recalls his father's reaction to the book. "I remember him saying, 'God, you're really a writer.'"

Then there's this:

> MRS. LEONARD BERNSTEIN
> requests the pleasure of your company
> at 895 Park Avenue
> on Wednesday January 14 at 5 o'clock
> To meet and hear from the leaders of the
> Black Panther Party.

The invitation is right there, in one of the files stuffed with party invitations and thank-you notes and Christmas cards, without comment. Tom Wolfe is at this point the leading satirist of his age. That age appears intent on staging events for his benefit. He seems simply to stroll off Park Avenue in his white suit and into Leonard Bernstein's party for the Black Panthers, as if he belonged.

I now admit to him that I still wonder: How the hell did he get himself invited to Leonard Bernstein's cocktail party? He smiles and surprises me again.

He'd gone to *Harper's* magazine one day in late 1969, to pay a call on Sheila, then his girlfriend. Sheila was busy, and so he went looking around the offices, to see what he could see. He came upon the office of the Pulitzer Prize–winning journalist David Halberstam. Halberstam wasn't in it. The door was open; Wolfe walked in. On top of a great pile on Halberstam's desk he spotted an invitation—how could he not? It came from Mrs. Leonard Bernstein. He picked it up and read it . . . and had an idea . . . How could he not . . . These people . . . they had no idea . . . it was as if they were determined to insult the Gods . . . how could they not see themselves the way others would see them . . . all you would have to do is tell everyone in Richmond or anyplace else outside of a certain Manhattan zip code about this and the entire country would soon be collapsing in laughter . . . or outrage . . . but . . . really, when you think about it . . . laughing or screaming: does it even matter which?. . . . Oh God . . . This really is too good. . . . He called the number to R.S.V.P. "This is Tom Wolfe," he said, "and I accept." And they just take his name down, and he's on the guest list. He never tells Halberstam what he's done. He simply takes out a brand-new green steno notebook with the spirals on top and writes on the cover, in his new rococo script: *Panther Night at Leonard Bernstein's.* And then he's off, to see the world, anew.

DISTANT SHORES

PAUL BOWLE*S*

···

PAUL BOWLES IN EXILE

by Jay McInerney

SEPTEMBER 1985

Paul Bowles opened the world of Hip. He let in the murder, the drugs, the incest, the death of the Square . . . the call of the orgy, the end of civilization.
—NORMAN MAILER

As the faithful poured into the mosque for prayer, I searched for the door to a restaurant reputedly just across the street and tried to seem inconspicuous. It was my second night in Tangier. Men in dark robes huddled on the street corners, lowering their voices as I approached. The few women in evidence were upholstered in black from head to foot and looked like bandit nuns. I came upon an entrance gate at which two men in djellabas were either lounging or standing guard. I tentatively pronounced the name of my destination. They looked at each other, nodded, and ushered me inside. Even as I stepped forward I was thinking that they were too unkempt and uninviting to be doormen, and that the building before me was too dark and sinister for a public place. But I was committed. Advancing into the murky courtyard I heard the two men, both very large for Moroccans, hissing behind me. I recognized the situation immediately. It had all the ingredients of a Paul Bowles story.

I never found out what the hissing was about. The older of the two men caught up with me and led the way to the restaurant. I was relieved but vaguely disappointed, and later recalled something Bowles had said during the day: What can go wrong is always much more interesting than what goes right.

Paul Bowles's sense of what can go wrong is as acute as that of any American writer since Poe. In "A Distant Episode," one of his best-known stories, a professor of linguistics in search of new dialects ventures beyond the walls of a desert town one night and descends into a valley settlement—"an abyss"—realizing as he does that "he ought to ask himself why he was doing this irrational thing." He proceeds nonetheless, only to be set upon by nomadic

tribesmen who beat him, cut out his tongue, and dress him up in strings of flattened tin cans to serve as a jester, an object of amusement.

In his first and most famous novel, *The Sheltering Sky*, a husband and wife
travel deeper and deeper into the Sahara, their flirtation with danger and their
betrayals of each other finally consummated in madness and death. It's not
simply the subject matter but the pitiless clarity, the unblinking regard in the
face of human frailty and cruelty, that is so disquieting in Bowles's work.
Whereas the terror in Poe seems to arise from an overheated romantic imagination suffering the torments it bodies forth, Bowles's sensibility is classical in its
aloofness, his prose as hard-edged and dazzling as a desert landscape at noon.

If Paul Bowles, now seventy-four, were Japanese, he would probably be designated a Living National Treasure; if he were French, he would no doubt be
besieged by television crews from the literary talk show *Apostrophes*. Given that
he is American, we might expect him to be a part of the university curriculum,
but his name rarely appears in a course syllabus. Perhaps because he is not representative of a particular period or school of writing, he remains something of a
trade secret among writers. Of course, Bowles hasn't exerted himself in the
matter of greasing the machinery of celebrity. He has never been in this country
when a book of his was published, and much of his life has been spent several
days' travel beyond a poste restante address. More significantly, his dark view of
the species, as well as his rejection of the *Zeitgeist* of his age, may be too cate-
gorical and severe for most tastes. His estimation of human nature is like that of
Calvinism without the prospect of salvation.

This month [September 1985], Ecco Press is reissuing Bowles's autobiography, *Without Stopping*, which quietly disappeared shortly after its publication,
in 1972, and has long been out of print. Once again available, the book should
spark renewed interest in Bowles's work and a reappraisal of his career.

Lying just southwest of Gibraltar, within sight of Spain, across the famous strait,
Tangier was, when Bowles first saw it, in 1931, an internationally administered
city consisting of a crowded and labyrinthine native quarter—the medina—
surrounded by a European community. There were only a handful of taxicabs
then, Bowles recalls, and many more eucalyptus trees than there are now, but the
latter-day tourist who enters the medina will feel much like the protagonist in
Bowles's 1952 novel, *Let It Come Down*:

> The places through which he was passing were like the tortuous corridors
> in dreams. It was impossible to think of them as streets, or even as alleys.
> There were spaces here and there among the buildings, that was all, and
> some of them opened into other spaces and some did not. If he found the
> right series of connections he could get from one place to the next, but

only by going through the buildings themselves. And the buildings seem
to have come into existence like plants, chaotic, facing no way, topheavy,
one growing out of the other.

Outside the medina, however, the vistas open up: the sky is brilliant; the
Atlantic, mottled blue and green, about to encounter the Mediterranean, is suddenly visible as one turns the corner on a block of white stucco houses.

The day of my first visit to Bowles's apartment, a three-room flat on the top
floor of a concrete edifice across from the American Consulate, a flock of sheep
are grazing in the side yard. The living room has a permanent twilight aspect,
and a fire always burns in the grate, regardless of the temperature outside. The
sweet aroma of kif pervades the air. Although Bowles has inhabited the
apartment for more than twenty-five years, it has the provisional look of a temporary encampment—the foyer is crowded with a large stack of suitcases, and
framed paintings by Bowles's friend Brion Gysin lean against a wall. On a small
end table lies a shiny new volume of Kafka's collected stories, one of the few
objects that appear to belong exactly where they are.

"Would you like some tea?" Bowles asks after apologizing for the weather.

He rises to greet his visitors, of whom there is a steady influx, extending a
hand and addressing them in whatever language is appropriate—French,
Spanish, Arabic, or English. He is extremely polite and courtly in manner, giving
the impression of someone who does not take social occasions for granted. His
dress is rather formal for relaxing at home: a tie, a cardigan, and a tweed jacket.
The black cigarette holder seems quite natural and unaffected. My first impression, of extreme delicacy, is modified over the course of the afternoon by
evidence of a sinewy vigor. A friend of his wrote, "He has the beauty of a fallow
deer"; my feeling is that a predator who tried to make a meal of Bowles would
find his digestion unpleasantly disrupted. The craggy demeanor and laconic air
seem to betray his New Hampshire roots.

On the sofa are two Moroccans: Mohammed Mrabet, one of several illit-
erate storytellers whose oral tales and novels Bowles has translated into English,
and a young musician, who is oiling and polishing a wooden flute. "It's like
cleaning a shotgun," Bowles remarks of the process, a whistle in his *s*'s, as he
settles onto a cushion. The musician begins to play, filling the room with a
breathy, haunting sound. Bowles nods appreciatively. When the music ends,
Mrabet is eager to take center stage. He is a handsome man who appears to be in
his thirties, although he claims to be fifty-four; Bowles thinks he is in his late
forties. Mrabet has the sadsack aspect of Buster Keaton. He begins to complain
about the difficulties of his life, speaking of several of his children who have died.
"Paul, yo he sufrido más que tú. Tú no has sufrido. Yo, yo he sufrido." He has suffered, Paul has not. Bowles smiles. The litany is apparently familiar. But when I

express my sympathy, Mrabet becomes almost indignant. *"Todo es perfecto"*—everything is perfect—he says, expressing the Islamic belief that all is as Allah wills it. It is clear that Mrabet relishes attention, that he is a born performer, and that Bowles relishes the performances, not least perhaps because he finds in Mrabet something of an alter ego. Mrabet's tales of woe are in keeping with Bowles's somewhat morbid tastes.

The conversation—about Tangier, about music and writing—proceeds in English and Spanish. Rodrigo Rey Rosa, a young Guatemalan writer whose work Bowles is translating, arrives with his girlfriend. Cigarettes are emptied and refilled with kif. Bowles listens to the talk with an intensity that reminds me of a robin poised, head cocked, on a wet lawn; he dips forward suddenly to clarify a point or to dispute an opinion. Asked if he particularly admires any living American writers, Bowles taps his cigarette holder thoughtfully against the lip of an ashtray, then sits back and looks earnestly at the ceiling. Finally he asks, "Is Flannery O'Connor still alive?" When the field is expanded to include South America, he is able to endorse Jorge Luis Borges without hesitation.

When Bowles's friends wish to talk to him, they come to visit, for he has not had a phone in sixteen years. "Who can be bothered?" he says. "You'll be working, or else you're in the bathtub, and the phone rings. You answer and a voice says, *'Allo*, Mohammed?'" One quickly gets the sense that Bowles, having spent most of his life in undeveloped parts of the world—North Africa, Sri Lanka, Central America—does not have much use for high technology. He hates air travel, which is one of the reasons he has not been to the United States since 1968, when he taught college for a semester in California. The suitcases in the foyer bear the yellowing tags of dry-docked steamers.

"I don't particularly like mechanization, pollution, noise—all the things the twentieth century has brought and scattered over the world," he says, his voice soft, his accent patrician. "Who does, except those who have made money by it? I can't imagine anyone embracing it."

Bowles's fiction often presents Americans in flight from civilization, looking for escape from the bourgeois ideals of industrial progress and teleological rationality. This is not a unique theme in Western literature, but what makes Bowles's work so different is his tough-mindedness, his refusal to romanticize the exotic—something that the hippies who showed up at his door in the sixties failed to notice. "They would appear here," he remembers, "and say, 'Hey, man, can I crash with you?' I gather I was supposed to be a guru. But I never went in for acting."

Westerners who don djellabas and climb on camels in the hope of a quick spiritual boost are, in Bowles's view, as naïve as Arabs who borrow European customs wholesale. Bowles's protagonists, seeking the unknown, often discover the chaos that underlies the civilized mind. Ultimately his fiction is concerned not so much with the meeting of cultures as with the peeling away of layers of acculturation, the stripping of character and humanity to essential elements. He has more in common with Samuel Beckett than with T. E. Lawrence.

Bowles cautions against taking his fiction to represent the actual landscape of North Africa, and he sometimes speaks of his long residence in Morocco as if it were purely accidental, a matter of washing up on that shore rather than another. But one cannot help feeling the symbiosis between the writer and his adopted environment. Though *Without Stopping* is in general one of the most unrevealing American autobiographies since Benjamin Franklin's, Bowles writes frankly in it of his attachment to Tangier:

> If I am here now, it is only because I was still here when I realized to what an extent the world had worsened, and that I no longer wanted to travel. In defense of the city I can say that so far it has been touched by fewer of the negative aspects of contemporary civilization than most cities of its size. More important than that, I relish the idea that in the night, all around me in my sleep, sorcery is burrowing its invisible tunnels in every direction, from thousands of senders to thousands of unsuspecting recipients. Spells are being cast, poison is running its course; souls are being dispossessed of parasitic pseudo-consciousnesses that lurk in the unguarded recesses of the mind.
>
> There is drumming out there most nights. It never awakens me; I hear the drums and incorporate them into my dream, like the nightly cries of the muezzins. Even if in the dream I am in New York, the first *Allah akbar!* effaces the backdrop and carries whatever comes next to North Africa, and the dream goes on.

Bowles, a surrealist sympathizer, seems to have associated Morocco with the anarchic forces of the unconscious. As an artist, he discovered in North Africa a landscape and culture which are the objective correlatives of his vision of the psyche.

The population of Tangier represents several cultures and centuries: women in gray djellabas, only their eyes visible between wimple and kerchief; men in business suits; country Berbers driving donkeys along the sidewalk; cabdrivers in neo-Italian fashions piloting twenty-year-old Mercedes *grands taxis*. It is still possible to get lost in the medina for quite some time, and if one is obviously confused, obviously a tourist, he will soon be set upon by "guides," hustlers, hashish dealers, and predatory carpet sellers. For the visitor, the combination of the almost subterranean landscape and the alien culture of the place can be very menacing, although Bowles dismisses the likelihood of any real danger.

Paul Bowles makes his way around town in a bronze 1967 Mustang. The day after I arrived, he picked me up at my hotel for a trip into the hills outside of town. His driver, a tall Moroccan named Abdulwahaid, held the door for me. Life in Tangier, for an expatriate author living largely on modest royalties, is a blend of luxury and deprivation: the equivalent of a month's rent on a studio apartment in Manhattan pays the annual salary of a chauffeur or cook—or buys two months' supply of scarce firewood for heating, Bowles's biggest expense.

Abdulwahaid, whose name means "slave of the unique," stops at the post office and picks up several airmail letters and a small package. Bowles complains about the few stray clouds in the sky and then instructs Abdulwahaid to drive us up the Montaña Vieja, which winds along a ridge overlooking Tangier and the Atlantic. Cobbles from an old Roman highway are still visible in the roadbed. Bowles and Abdulwahaid converse in Spanish, both using the familiar form of address.

Most of the houses we pass are secluded behind white walls overhung with bougainvillea and other flowering vines. "This is my favorite part of town," Bowles says, leaning forward in his seat to take in the scenery and the memories, pointing out the villa Tennessee Williams once rented, and then the gate of the house where he and his wife, Jane, lived in '54, and then the place he stayed in '31, when he first arrived in Tangier.

The son of a Long Island dentist, Bowles is descended from old New England stock. Of his odd and isolated childhood he writes in his autobiography: "At the age of five I had never yet even spoken to another child or seen children playing together. My idea of the world was still that of a place inhabited exclusively by adults."

When he was eighteen and already a published poet, he went, like Poe, to the University of Virginia, but he left within a year and ran away briefly to Paris, where he sought out the community of artists and writers living abroad.

Bowles was twenty years old when he again traveled to Paris, this time as Aaron Copland's student. Having established a correspondence with Gertrude Stein, he one day appeared at her door with a sheaf of poems. Stein, never reticent with her opinions, told him he was no poet and suggested he stick to music. When she also suggested Tangier as a good place to spend the summer, he and Copland decided to go. Bowles contracted typhoid fever on his second visit, that winter, but North Africa continued to draw him back. He spent the following winter in the M'Zab region of the Sahara; almost fifteen years later this landscape was to become the setting, and ultimately the protagonist, of *The Sheltering Sky*.

Though he continued to travel in Europe and Latin America, Bowles resided mainly in New York during the thirties and forties, becoming a regular at Kirk and Constance Askew's legendary salon, and briefly joining the Communist Party. He supported himself as a composer of theater music, in which capacity he collaborated with Orson Welles, Elia Kazan, William Saroyan, and Tennessee Williams. Bowles was acclaimed by such peers as Virgil Thomson for his original compositions, including *The Wind Remains*, an opera that in 1943 was conducted by Leonard Bernstein and danced by Merce Cunningham at the Museum of Modern Art. In 1937 he met Jane Auer, a young aspiring writer. They barely knew each other when they decided to take a trip together to Mexico, and within a year they were married.

The marriage was an eccentric one, punctuated by long separations, dual residences, and other partners on both sides—at one point their mutual friend Libby Holman proposed to Paul—but those who knew them both agree that it was a remarkable romance. Bowles's stoicism flickers somewhat when he mentions his deceased wife, whom he usually refers to as Mrs. Bowles. As for Jane, an old friend of hers says, "She used to call him Fluffy and Bubbles. Can you imagine? Paul? That prickly man? It was the most extraordinary thing." That the austere Mr. Bowles would answer to these appellations says much about the intimacy of their relationship. "She was his muse," adds the friend. "You have to understand that."

Bowles had set writing aside when he discovered his talent for music. He credits his wife with inspiring him to return to the typewriter. "I never would have known that I wanted to start writing again if I hadn't been with her when she was writing her first novel," Bowles acknowledges of the time Jane was at work on *Two Serious Ladies*. "I got really interested in the whole process, and thought, I wish I had written this book. I started writing stories about two years after she published her novel."

The urge to write seemed inextricable from the urge to return to North Africa. On the strength of several short stories, Bowles found an agent. Doubleday gave him an advance against a novel, and in the summer of 1947 he sailed to Casablanca. He had only a vague outline in mind of the book he wanted to write, something about three Americans moving across the Sahara. "My idea was that the people would keep moving into the desert," he says, "that one would get ill and die, and at that point it would write itself."

Bowles traveled alone into the Algerian Sahara to work on the novel. "I wrote in bed in hotels in the desert," he says. When he reached the point where Port, the central character in the first half of the novel, becomes sick, Bowles realized that he had come to his crucial juncture. He wanted to describe Port's death from the interior of Port's mind, and to do so he decided to take *majoun*, a potent cannabis confection. "It gave me everything," he says. "Not that day. The day I took it I couldn't have written anything. I was lying flat on my back. I was lying on my back, dying. Not unhappy. Port's death became my death. That more or less broke the ice. I didn't need to take it after that."

The immense domed sky of the Sahara dominates the book. Early on, Port muses, "I often have the sensation when I look at it that it's a solid thing up there, protecting us from what's behind." As he is dying in the desert he sees the sky crack open, and in one of the most convincing and harrowing evocations of death since Tolstoy's *Ivan Ilyich* he looks into the void beyond. From there the novel follows Port's wife, Kit (who people in Tangier will assure you is a ringer for Jane), as she moves into the Sahara, fleeing the memory of her adultery with Port's friend Tunner, pursuing the primitive and the unknown, surrendering herself to a Bedouin who rapes her, finally leaving her reason behind. Bowles's desert becomes—like Conrad's jungle and Eliot's wasteland—a symbolic landscape, emblematic of a world in which individuals are radically isolated from one another.

Bowles finished *The Sheltering Sky* in nine months. "I sent it out to Doubleday," he says, "and they refused it. They said, 'We asked for a novel.' They didn't consider it a novel. I had to give back my advance. My agent told me later they called the editor on the carpet for having refused the book—only after they saw that it was selling fast. It only had to do with sales. They didn't bother to read it."

Eventually another house, New Directions, accepted the book; in the meantime Bowles sailed to New York to do the score for *Summer and Smoke*. Before he left again for Tangier, he persuaded Tennessee Williams to accompany him. "As always on a ship, I stayed in the cabin and generally in my berth, writing," he says of the journey. "It's a perfect place to write. I wrote this story and took it around to Tennessee's cabin, and he read it and said, 'Oh, I think it's wonderful, Paul, but you mustn't publish that story—people will think you're a monster.'" Bowles laughs and adds, "I was very flattered."

The piece he showed to Williams was to become "The Delicate Prey," the title story of his first collection. In it, a Moungari tribesman who commits an extremely gruesome murder is discovered by kinsmen of the victim, who take the murderer out into the desert and bury him up to his neck. The tale ends with one of the most striking images in contemporary fiction: "When they had gone the Moungari fell silent, to wait through the cold hours for the sun that would bring first warmth, then heat, thirst, fire, visions. The next night he did not know where he was, did not feel the cold. The wind blew dust along the ground into his mouth as he sang."

Bowles expresses sympathy for the surrealist notion of shocking the bourgeoisie out of its complacency by dredging up the raw material of the unconscious and exposing it to daylight. Norman Mailer's apocalyptic assessment of Bowles's work places it in this current of literary terrorism. But like one of his characters, Bowles claims that for him writing is merely a form of personal therapy. "I don't like the things I write about," he protests when asked why so much of his work deals with the dark side of human nature. "It's a kind of exorcism. It doesn't mean that I approve of what goes on in the pages of my book—God forbid."

After Tennessee Williams left Tangier, Truman Capote arrived and moved into the hotel in which Paul and Jane were staying. Of Capote, Bowles says dryly, "We did not lack for entertainment at mealtimes."

. . .

At this point, in the early fifties, Tangier was assuming the aspect of an international literary salon. The presence of Jane and Paul Bowles served as a magnetic force; then again, like the Americans who had moved to Paris in the twenties, the fashionable refugees landing in Tangier were attracted by cheap living and the atmosphere of duty-free morality. Male homosexuality was openly tolerated in Morocco. The second sons of English lords—and even first sons facing the burden of steep inheritance taxes—found that their pounds, if they could smuggle them into Tangier, went far. With life back in the States becoming increasingly puritan, Barbara Hutton, the Woolworth heiress, bought a palace in the Casbah and threw lavish parties. The Honorable David Herbert, son of the Earl of Pembroke, presided over the city's social life, as he still does today. A close friend of the Bowleses', Herbert once promised to marry Jane if anything ever happened to Paul.

Bowles, neither a joiner nor an avid partygoer, continued to travel, write, and compose. In 1955 he completed *The Spider's House*, which presciently depicted the Moroccan struggle for independence, and which remains invaluable, aside from its novelistic virtues, for its sympathetic insights into Islamic culture and postcolonial politics.

In the mid-fifties Bowles began to encounter members of the Beat movement. He first met William S. Burroughs in the spring of 1954. "He was living down in the medina, in a brothel," says Bowles. "He lay in bed all day, shot heroin, and practiced sharpshooting with a pistol against the wall of his room. I saw the wall, all pockmarked with bullet holes. I said to him, 'Why are you shooting your wall, Bill?' He said, 'It's good practice.' I didn't get to know him until '55, '56. He was writing *Naked Lunch*."

I ask Bowles about Burroughs's claim that he did not remember writing *Naked Lunch*, that he came out of a junk coma one day and it was simply there. "He ought to remember it," Bowles answers. "It was all over the floor. There were hundreds of pages of yellow foolscap all over the floor, month after month, with hcel prints on them, rat droppings, bits of old sandwiches, sardines. It was filthy. I said, 'What is all that, Bill?' He said, 'That's what I'm working on.' 'Do you have a copy of it?' I asked. 'No,' he said." Bowles manages a convincing imitation of Burroughs's harsh mid-western growl. "I couldn't help myself from saying, 'Why don't you pick it up?' Candy bar in hand, he said, 'Oh, it'll get picked up someday.' As he finished a page, he'd just throw it on the floor."

Jack Kerouac was in Tangier in 1956, but Bowles, who was in Portugal at the time, did not meet him. When Allen Ginsberg arrived, Bowles was again away, this time in Sri Lanka. "Jane wrote a wonderful letter," he remembers, "telling me that Ginsberg had called up. She'd never heard of him. He said, in his brash fashion, 'Hello, this is Allen Ginsberg, the bop poet.' She said, 'The what?' He said, 'The bop poet.' And she said, 'I got the poet, but the *what* poet?'

He said, '*Bop, bop, bop.*' And she said, 'All right.' Then he said, 'Do you believe in God, Jane?' And she said, 'I'm certainly not going to discuss it on the telephone. You'd better wait until Paul gets home.'"

Ginsberg was traveling with Alan Ansen and Peter Orlovsky. Soon after they arrived, Ginsberg and Ansen began sorting through the papers on Burroughs's floor. "I used to go over to Bill's apartment," says Bowles, "and they would all be sitting there, and Allen, who hasn't got a good reading voice, would be reading out loud. Bill wouldn't read it out loud. Hearing Allen Ginsberg read it, it wasn't very impressive. Have you heard him?" Bowles begins to drone a nasal Buddhist raga. "Anyway, Bill is wonderful reading his own stuff, but he wouldn't—I don't know why. He didn't think it existed yet. It was on the floor. So they put it together, and it spelled *mother*. Once it was published and I was able to read it cover to cover, I liked it. I read it three times. I think Bill's the greatest American humorist. I wish he'd concentrate on humor."

Bowles is frequently lumped in with the Beats in surveys of American literature, but his relation to the movement is a little like that of Manet to the Impressionists; Bowles stood between the European modernists and the Beats, an elder patron with an affinity for Beat ideals. "I was never part of a group," Bowles says, "but I felt sympathy for the Beats. I approved of their existence as a group. It seemed a new thing. I thought it was careless, though. There's a certain amount of carelessness in the writing of all those people." The fastidious craftsman shakes his head and smiles ruefully. "Jane said, 'I think they've all *just* read Céline.'"

When asked if he and others in the Tangier literary community ever discussed their work together, Bowles replies emphatically, "No. Bill and I talked about the dollar and what it was worth, or who had invaded whom with what justification. Nobody ever talks about his work except a few maniac writers, some that shouldn't even write. They're generally the ones who talk about their writing." Clearly, Bowles has not spent much time on campus recently, and I don't want to be the one to tell him that talking about writing is the growth industry of publishing and the humanities.

I ask Bowles if he and Jane ever talked about their work with each other. "When it was finished we did," he says. "Sometimes Jane discussed it in the middle of writing. It wasn't really a discussion—she would call me from the next room and say, 'What genus is the canary?' or 'Exactly how do you build a cantilever bridge?' I said, 'Does it matter how it was built? The word *cantilever* tells the whole story.' She said, 'I've got to know how it was made.' In the end she simply spoke of a bridge going across the gorge. She had to build the bridge before she could talk about it.

"We would work in hotels when we were traveling. We would have adjoining rooms. She'd be in her bed working, and I'd be in my bed working. She'd call out, 'Is it *i-e* or *e-i?*'" Bowles smiles at the memory.

In 1957 Jane Bowles suffered a stroke from which she was never to recover. Until her death, in 1973 at a clinic in Spain, she was afflicted with impaired vision, aphasia, seizures, and depression. In the sixties Paul Bowles turned increasingly to translation, virtually inventing a new genre when he began to transcribe and translate the tales of Moroccan storytellers, among them—in addition to Mrabet—Larbi Layachi and Ahmed Yacoubi. "The real reason I started translating," Bowles explains, "was that Mrs. Bowles was ill and I couldn't write, because I would only have twenty minutes and then I would be called downstairs. One needs solitude and privacy and more or less unlimited time to write novels."

Solitude seems an unlikely prospect for Bowles these days. In the morning he works on his translations, his correspondence, and his own short stories, but in the afternoon the visitors—a Danish architect, a French journalist, a British novelist, the semi-resident Mrabet—come and stay to chat, drink tea, and smoke kif. Though Bowles no longer goes out at night, he is a vivid presence in the English-speaking community, which gathers at Guita's, the restaurant across from the mosque. They argue about his work, which has for better or worse put a version of their experience on the map, and about his marriage, as if Jane and Paul had just left the room. But Bowles is a private man, with a reserved, almost impersonal interest in his neighbors. As the titles of his novels—*The Sheltering Sky, Let It Come Down, Up Above the World*—suggest, his is an aerial, cosmic point of view, that of an observer looking down from a great height.

When asked if there is a specific message in his fiction, Bowles snorts derisively and examines his cigarette holder as if reading an inscription. Three days later, on an expedition some thirty miles south of Tangier, he surveys the new cinder-block suburbs of a fishing village in which he once lived. "Here's my message," he says, then pauses and smiles. "Everything gets worse."

GABRIEL GARCÍA MÁRQUEZ

50 YEARS OF *SOLITUDE*

by Paul Elie

JANUARY 2016

The house, in a quiet part of Mexico City, had a study within, and in the study he found a solitude he had never known before and would never know again. Cigarettes (he smoked 60 a day) were on the worktable. LPs were on the record player: Debussy, Bartók, *A Hard Day's Night.* Stuck up on the wall were charts of the history of a Caribbean town he called Macondo and the genealogy of the family he named the Buendías. Outside, it was the 1960s; inside, it was the deep time of the pre-modern Americas, and the author at his typewriter was all-powerful.

He visited a plague of insomnia upon the people of Macondo; he made a priest levitate, powered by hot chocolate; he sent down a swarm of yellow butterflies. He led his people on the long march through civil war and colonialism and banana-republicanism; he trailed them into their bedrooms and witnessed sexual adventures obscene and incestuous. "In my dreams, I was inventing literature," he recalled. Month by month the typescript grew, presaging the weight that the great novel and the "solitude of fame," as he would later put it, would inflict on him.

Gabriel García Márquez began writing *Cien Años de Soledad—One Hundred Years of Solitude*—a half-century ago, finishing in late 1966. The novel came off the press in Buenos Aires on May 30, 1967, two days before *Sgt. Pepper's Lonely Hearts Club Band* was released, and the response among Spanish-language readers was akin to Beatlemania: crowds, cameras, exclamation points, a sense of a new era beginning. In 1970 the book appeared in English, followed by a paperback edition with a burning sun on its cover, which became a totem of the decade. By the time García Márquez was awarded the Nobel Prize, in 1982, the novel was considered the *Don Quixote* of the Global South, proof of Latin-American literary prowess, and the author was "Gabo," known all over the continent by a single name, like his Cuban friend Fidel.

Many years later, interest in Gabo and his great novel is surging. The Harry Ransom Center, at the University of Texas, recently paid $2.2 million to acquire his archives—including a Spanish typescript of *Cien Años de Soledad*—and in October a gathering of his family members and academics took a fresh look at his legacy, repeatedly invoking the book as his magnum opus.

Unofficially, it's everybody's favorite work of world literature and the novel that, more than any other since World War II, has inspired novelists of our time—from Toni Morrison to Salman Rushdie to Junot Díaz. A scene in the movie *Chinatown* takes place at a Hollywood hacienda dubbed El Macondo Apartments. Bill Clinton, during his first term as president, made it known that he would like to meet Gabo when they were both on Martha's Vineyard; they wound up swapping insights about Faulkner over dinner at Bill and Rose Styron's place. (Carlos Fuentes, Vernon Jordan, and Harvey Weinstein were at the table.) When García Márquez died, in April 2014, Barack Obama joined Clinton in mourning him, calling him "one of my favorites from the time I was young" and mentioning his cherished, inscribed copy of *One Hundred Years of Solitude*. "It's the book that redefined not just Latin-American literature but literature, period," insists Ilan Stavans, the pre-eminent scholar of Latino culture in the U.S., who says he has read the book 30 times.

How is it that this novel could be sexy, entertaining, experimental, politically radical, and wildly popular all at once? Its success was no sure thing, and the story of how it came about is a crucial and little-known chapter in the literary history of the last half-century.

LEAVING HOME

The creator of contemporary fiction's most famous village was a city man. Born in 1927 in the Colombian village of Aracataca, near the Caribbean coast, and schooled inland in a suburb of Bogotá, Gabriel García Márquez quit pre-law studies to become a journalist in the cities of Cartagena, Barranquilla (writing a column), and Bogotá (writing movie reviews). As the noose of dictatorship tightened, he went on assignment to Europe—and out of harm's way. He had hard times there. In Paris, he turned in deposit bottles for cash; in Rome, he took classes in experimental film-making; he shivered in London and sent back dispatches from East Germany, Czechoslovakia, and the Soviet Union. Returning south—to Venezuela—he was nearly arrested during a random sweep by military police. When Fidel Castro took power in Cuba, García Márquez signed on with Prensa Latina, a press agency funded by the new Communist government, and after a stint in Havana he moved to New York in 1961 with his wife, Mercedes, and their young son, Rodrigo.

The city, he later said, "was putrefying, but also was in the process of rebirth, like the jungle. It fascinated me." The family stayed in the Webster Hotel, at 45th and Fifth, and then with friends in Queens, but Gabo spent most of his time at the press office near Rockefeller Center, in a room with a lone window above a vacant lot overrun with rats. The phone rang and rang with calls from inflamed Cuban exiles who saw the agency as an outpost of the Castro regime they detested, and he kept an iron rod at the ready in case of attack.

He was writing fiction all the while: *Leaf Storm* in Bogotá; *In Evil Hour* and *No One Writes to the Colonel* in Paris; *Big Mama's Funeral* in Caracas. When hard-line Communists took over the press service and ousted its editor, García Márquez quit in solidarity. He would move to Mexico City; he would focus on fiction. But first he would see the South of William Faulkner, whose books he had read in translation since his early 20s. Traveling by Greyhound, the family was treated as "dirty Mexicans," he recounted—refused rooms and restaurant service. "The immaculate parthenons amidst the cotton fields, the farmers taking their siesta beneath the eaves of roadside inns, the black people's huts surviving in wretchedness. . . . The terrible world of Yoknapatawpha County had passed in front of our eyes from the window of a bus," he would remember, "and it was as true and as human as in the novels of the old master."

García Márquez struggled. He turned to screenwriting. He edited a glossy women's magazine, *La Familia,* and another specializing in scandal and crime. He wrote copy for J. Walter Thompson. In the Zona Rosa—Mexico City's Left Bank—he was known as surly and morose.

And then his life changed. A literary agent in Barcelona had taken an interest in his work, and after a week of meetings in New York in 1965 she headed south to meet him.

A SHEET OF PAPER

"This interview is a fraud," Carmen Balcells declared with conversation-ending finality. We were in her apartment above the offices of Agencia Carmen Balcells, in the center of Barcelona. In a wheelchair, she had rolled out to meet me at the elevator and then spun the wheelchair to a giant table laden with manuscripts and red file boxes. (VARGAS LLOSA, read the label on one; WYLIE AGENCY, another.) Eighty-five, with thick white hair, she had the formidable size and bearing that led her to be called La Mamá Grande. She wore a capacious white dress that suggested a resemblance to a female Pope.

"A fraud," she said in English, in a high, small voice. "When a celebrity, or an artist—when this person dies and is no [longer] there to answer many things, the first move is to interview the secretaries, the hairdresser, doctors, wives, children, tailor. I am not an artist. I am an agent. I am here as a person who really had an importance in Gabriel García Márquez's life. But this—it is not the real thing. The magnificent presence of the artist is missing."

Balcells was preparing for a future she would not be present to see. A deal to sell her business to the New York literary agent Andrew Wylie had recently come apart. (More on this later.) Now other suitors were making their entreaties, and Balcells was trying to decide who would look after her 300-plus clients, the estate of García Márquez chief among them. Our interview, she told me wearily, would be followed by a meeting with her lawyers—"a dirty business," she said.

That afternoon, grandiloquently alive, she pushed such matters aside and recalled the day she first felt "the magnificent presence of the artist" near at hand.

She and her husband, Luis, liked to read in bed. "I was reading García Márquez—one of the early books—and I said to Luis, 'This is so fantastic, Luis, that we have to read it at the same time.' So I made a copy of it. We both had enthusiasm for it: it was so fresh, so original, so exciting. Every reader says in his mind, of certain books, 'This is one of the best books I have ever read.' When that happens to a book again and again, all over the world, you have a masterpiece. That is what happened with Gabriel García Márquez."

When Balcells and Luis arrived in Mexico City, in July 1965, García Márquez met not just his new agent but two people who were intimate with his work. In the daytime, he showed them the city; nights, they all had supper together with local writers. They ate and drank, and ate and drank some more. And then García Márquez, having fully warmed to his guests, took out a sheet of paper, and with Luis as a witness he and Balcells drew up a contract declaring her his representative in all the world for the next 150 years.

"Not a hundred and fifty—I think a hundred and twenty," Balcells told me, smiling. "It was a joke, a spoof contract, you see."

But there was another contract, and it was no joke. In New York the week before, Balcells had found a U.S. publisher—Harper & Row—for García Márquez's work. She'd made a deal for the English-language rights to his four books. The payment? A thousand dollars. She had brought the contract, which she presented for him to sign.

The terms seemed onerous, even rapacious. And the contract also gave Harper & Row the first option to bid on his *next* work of fiction, whatever it was. "This contract is a piece of shit," he told her. He signed anyway.

Balcells left to return to Barcelona; García Márquez set out with his family for a beach vacation in Acapulco, a day's drive south. Partway there, he stopped the car—a white 1962 Opel with a red interior—and turned back. His next work of fiction had come to him all at once. For two decades he had been pulling and prodding at the tale of a large family in a small village. Now he could envision it with the clarity of a man who, standing before a firing squad, saw his whole life in a single moment. "It was so ripe in me," he would later recount, "that I could have dictated the first chapter, word by word, to a typist."

In the study, he settled himself at the typewriter. "I did not get up for eighteen months," he would recall. Like the book's protagonist, Colonel Aureliano Buendía—who hides out in his workshop in Macondo, fashioning tiny gold fish with jeweled eyes—the author worked obsessively. He marked the typed pages, then sent them to a typist who made a fresh copy. He called friends to read pages aloud. Mercedes maintained the family. She stocked the cupboard with scotch for when work was done. She kept bill collectors at bay. She hocked household items for cash: "telephone, fridge, radio, jewelry," as García Márquez's biographer Gerald Martin has it. He sold the Opel. When the novel was finished, and Gabo and Mercedes went to the post office to send the typescript to the publisher, Editorial Sudamericana, in Buenos Aires, they didn't have the 82 pesos for the postage. They sent the first half, and then the rest after a visit to the pawnshop.

He had smoked 30,000 cigarettes and run through 120,000 pesos (about $10,000). Mercedes asked, "And what if, after all this, it's a bad novel?"

MIND ON FIRE

"The past is never dead. It's not even past," Faulkner observed, and with *One Hundred Years of Solitude,* García Márquez made the presence of the past a condition of life in Macondo—like poverty, or injustice. Over seven generations José Arcadio Buendía and his descendants are relentlessly present to one another: in their inherited names, their fits of anger and jealousy, their feuds and wars, their nightmares, and in the current of incest that runs through them—a force that makes family resemblance a curse and sexual attraction a force to be resisted, lest you and your lover (who is also your cousin) produce a child with a pig's tail.

"Magic realism" became the term for García Márquez's violation of natural laws through art. And yet the magic of the novel, first and last, is in the power with which it makes the Buendías and their neighbors present to the reader. Reading it, you feel: They are alive; this happened.

Eight thousand copies sold in the first week in Argentina alone, unprecedented for a literary novel in South America. Laborers read it. So did housekeepers and professors—and prostitutes: the novelist Francisco Goldman recalls seeing the novel on the bedside table in a coastal bordello. García Márquez traveled to Argentina, to Peru, to Venezuela, on its behalf. In Caracas, he had his hosts stick up a handwritten sign: TALK OF ONE HUNDRED YEARS OF SOLITUDE FORBIDDEN. Women offered themselves to him—in person and in photographs.

To avoid distractions, he moved his family to Barcelona. Pablo Neruda, meeting him there, wrote a poem about him. At the University of Madrid, Mario Vargas Llosa, already acclaimed for his novel *The Green House,* wrote a doctoral dissertation about García Márquez's book, which was awarded top literary prizes in Italy and France. It was seen as the first book to unify the Spanish-language literary culture, long divided between Spain and Latin America, city and village, colonizers and colonized.

Gregory Rabassa bought the book in Manhattan and read it straight through, enthralled. A professor of Romance languages at Queens College, he had recently translated Julio Cortázar's *Hopscotch*—and had won a National Book Award for it. He'd served as a code breaker for the Office of Strategic Services during the war; he'd danced with Marlene Dietrich when she entertained the troops. He knew the real thing when he saw it.

"I read it without any thought of translating it," he explains, sitting in his apartment on East 72nd Street. Now 93, frail but mentally agile, he still attends reunions of surviving O.S.S. spies. "I was used to tried-and-true methods of storytelling. Oh . . . I'd done Cortázar. I knew [the work of] Borges. You put the two together and you got something else: you got Gabriel García Márquez."

Harper & Row's editor in chief, Cass Canfield Jr., having paid $1,000 for the previous four books, got an approval for $5,000 for the new novel, to be paid to the Balcells agency in installments. García Márquez asked his friend Julio Cortázar to recommend a translator. "Get Rabassa," Cortázar told him.

In 1969, at a house in Hampton Bays, on Long Island, Rabassa set to translating the novel, beginning with its unforgettable triple-time first sentence: "Many years later, as he faced the firing squad, Colonel Aureliano Buendía was to remember that distant afternoon when his father took him to discover ice." He established certain rules: "I had to make sure the patriarch was always José Arcadio Buendía, never any truncated version, much the way that Charlie Brown is never called anything but Charlie Brown in 'Peanuts.'"

Editor Richard Locke had first heard about the book in 1968 from novelist Thomas McGuane, while on a trip to visit him in Montana. "Tom was extremely well read," says Locke. "He said this was the guy everybody was talking about." By the time Harper & Row sent out advance proofs, in early 1970, Locke had become an assigning editor at *The New York Times Book Review*. "When the novel came in, I realized it was a very important book," Locke remembers, "by a very different kind of writer—and in a new form that we had never seen before. And I gave it an enthusiastic report."

Canfield, meanwhile, had sung its song to a *Times* reporter, and there appeared a preview of all the new Latin-American literature coming into English— El Boom—with García Márquez at the head of the line. "We are certain that García Márquez will cause the same sensation as some of the postwar French and German writers brought to the American literary scene," Canfield predicted.

One Hundred Years of Solitude was published in March 1970, its lush-green jacket and understated typography concealing the passion within. Then, as now, the key reviews for sales and prizes were those of the *Times*. The *Book Review* praised it as "a South American Genesis, an earthy piece of enchantment." John Leonard, in the daily *Times,* held nothing back: "You emerge from this marvelous novel as if from a dream, the mind on fire." He concluded, "With a single bound, Gabriel García Márquez leaps onto the stage with Günter Grass and Vladimir Nabokov, his appetite as enormous as his imagination, his fatalism greater than either. Dazzling."

Signed up for $5,000 on the basis of a "piece of shit" contract, the book would sell 50 million copies worldwide, becoming a year-in-year-out fixture on the backlist. Gregory Rabassa watched with mingled pride and unease as his work—paid for in a lump sum "of about a thousand dollars," like the work of a gardener "spreading manure on a suburban lawn"—became at once the most acclaimed novel in translation and the most popular. García Márquez himself read *One Hundred Years of Solitude* in the Harper & Row edition and pronounced it better than his Spanish original. He called Rabassa "the best Latin American writer in the English language."

THE ACCOLADES

Many have entertained the notion of making a movie of *One Hundred Years of Solitude.* None has come close. Sometimes author and agent named an astronomical sum for the rights. Other times García Márquez set fantastical terms. Gabo told Harvey Weinstein that he would grant him and Giuseppe Tornatore the rights, provided the movie was made his way. As Weinstein would recall: "We must film the entire book, but only release one chapter—two minutes long—each year, for one hundred years."

Instead of adaptations, then, there have been homages by other novelists—some explicit (Oscar Hijuelos's highly amplified novels of Cuban America), others indirect and furtive (William Kennedy's *Ironweed,* in which a dead child speaks to his father from the grave). Alice Walker bent the iron bars of plausibility in *The Color Purple,* where letters sent to God elicit real replies. Isabel Allende, a relative of the slain Chilean president (and herself a Balcells client), told the story of modern Chile through a family saga in *The House of the Spirits.*

"I was sitting in my office at Random House," says Toni Morrison, then an editor with two of her own novels published, "just turning the pages of *One Hundred Years of Solitude.* There was something so familiar about the novel, so recognizable to me. It was a certain kind of freedom, a structural freedom, a [different] notion of a beginning, middle, and end. Culturally, I felt intimate with him because he was happy to mix the living and the dead. His characters were on intimate terms with the supernatural world, and that's the way stories were told in my house."

Morrison's father had died, and she had in mind a new novel, whose protagonists would be men—a departure for her. "I had hesitated before writing about those guys. But now, because I had read *One Hundred Years of Solitude,* I did not hesitate. I got permission from García Márquez"—permission to write *Song of Solomon,* the first of a run of big, bold novels. (Many years later, Morrison and García Márquez taught a master class together at Princeton. It was 1998—"the year Viagra came out," Morrison recalls. "I would pick him up in the morning at the hotel where he and Mercedes were staying, and he said, 'The *peell:* the *peell* is not for us men. It is for you, for you women. We do not need it, but we want to please you!'")

John Irving was teaching literature and coaching wrestling at Windham College, in Vermont, an Iowa Writers' Workshop graduate in thrall to Günter Grass. Like *The Tin Drum,* García Márquez's book struck him with its old-fashioned breadth and confidence. "Here's a guy who's a 19th-century storyteller but who's working *now,*" says Irving. "He creates characters and makes you love them. When he writes about the supernatural, it's extraordinary, not ordinary. The incest and intermarriage . . . it's pre-destined, like in Hardy."

Junot Díaz, a generation younger, sees Gabo as a guide to current realities. Díaz read the novel in his first months at Rutgers, in 1988. "The world went from black-and-white to Technicolor," he says. "I was a young Latino-American-Caribbean writer desperately looking for models. This novel went through me like a lightning bolt: it entered through the crown of my head and went right down to my toes, redounding through me for the next several decades—up to right now." He was struck by the fact that *One Hundred Years of Solitude* had been written just after his own homeland, the Dominican Republic, was invaded by U.S. troops in 1965, and he came to see magic realism as a political tool—one "that enables Caribbean people to see things clearly in their world, a surreal world where there are more dead than living, more erasure and silence than things spoken." He explains: "There are seven generations of the Buendía family. We are the eighth generation. We are the children of Macondo."

Salman Rushdie was living in London and thinking about the country of his childhood when he first read the book. Many years later he wrote, "I knew García Márquez's colonels and generals, or at least their Indian and Pakistani counterparts; his bishops were my mullahs; his market streets were my bazaars. His world was mine, translated into Spanish. It's little wonder I fell in love with it—not for its magic . . . but for its realism." Reviewing García Márquez's novel *Chronicle of a Death Foretold,* Rushdie summarized the novelist's fame with the controlled hyperbole he and Gabo had in common: "The news of a new Márquez book takes over the front pages of the Spanish-American dailies. Barrow boys hawk copies in the streets. Critics commit suicide for lack of fresh superlatives." Rushdie called him "Angel Gabriel," an offhand gesture that suggests García

Márquez's influence on *The Satanic Verses,* whose protagonist is called the Angel Gibreel.

THE ALTERCATION

By then, Gabo was a Nobel laureate. He had a new U.S. publisher, Knopf. And in a rare stroke, *Chronicle of a Death Foretold* was published in full in the premiere issue of the revived *Vanity Fair,* in 1983, where Richard Locke had taken the editor's chair. Locke and Alexander Liberman, Condé Nast's editorial director, had commissioned accompanying artwork by Botero, the Colombian portraitist. The admiration for the author was universal. He was the laureate everyone could love.

Everyone, that is, except Mario Vargas Llosa. They'd been friends for years: Latin-American expats in Barcelona, prominent writers of El Boom, clients of Carmen Balcells'. Their wives—Mercedes and Patricia—socialized. Then they had a falling-out. In 1976, in Mexico City, García Márquez attended a screening of the film *La Odisea de los Andes,* for which Vargas Llosa had written the script. Spotting his friend, García Márquez went to embrace him. Vargas Llosa punched him in the face, knocking him down and giving him a black eye.

"And García Márquez said, 'Now that you've punched me to the ground, why don't you tell me why,'" Balcells told me, recalling the episode. Ever since, literary people in Latin America have wondered why. One story is that García Márquez had told a mutual friend that he found Patricia less than beautiful. A second is that Patricia, suspecting that Mario was having an affair, had asked Gabo what she should do about it, and Gabo had told her to leave him. Vargas Llosa has said only that it was "about a personal problem."

"Another writer said to Mario, 'Be careful,'" Balcells recalled. "'You don't want to be known as the man who clocked the author of *One Hundred Years of Solitude.*'"

For four decades, Vargas Llosa has categorically refused to discuss the episode, and he has said that he and Gabo made a "pact" to take the story to their graves. But in a recent conversation about his friend and rival, Vargas Llosa—himself a Nobel laureate—spoke affectionately and at length about what García Márquez has meant to him, from his first encounter with Gabo's fiction (in Paris, and in French translation) to their first meeting, at the Caracas airport, in 1967, to their years as boon companions in Barcelona, to their plan to write a novel together about the 1828 war between Peru and Colombia. And he spoke about *Cien Años de Soledad,* which he read and wrote about "immediately, immediately" when it reached him in Cricklewood, North London, a few weeks after publication. "This was the book that enlarged the Spanish-language reading public to include intellectuals and also ordinary readers because of its clear and transparent style. At the same time, it was a very representative book: Latin America's civil wars, Latin America's inequalities, Latin America's imagination, Latin America's love of music, its color—all this was in a novel in which realism and fantasy were mixed in a perfect way." About his falling-out with Gabo he kept his silence, saying, "That is a secret for a future biographer."

PERFECT MARRIAGE

Carmen Balcells will be known always as the agent who represented the author of *One Hundred Years of Solitude.* She met me in Barcelona, with the understanding that she would be speaking as the one who, in the title of Gabo's own memoir, was still "living to tell the tale."

Our encounter, as it turned out, would take a Márquezian twist. We were at the giant table in the sala, like a classic six on Park Avenue. A portrait made of Balcells many years earlier was hung on one wall—the same darting eyes, the same strong jaw—and it was as if the younger Balcells were present, too, witnessing the long story of the agent's relationship with her writer. It has been called "*un matrimonio perfecto.*"

I told her that I had worked as an editor with Farrar, Straus and Giroux. "Aha!," she exclaimed. "I have a photographic memory for faces, you see, and it must be that I saw your face when I was there to see Roger [Straus, the publisher]. You have the same face you had then!

"Because I met you, you can ask me anything you want," she went on, and we talked for an hour and a half. Ever the agent, she attached provisos to the conversation. She told me ("but not for your article") what it was that prompted Mario to slug Gabo that night in 1976. She explained ("but you must promise not to publish until I die") how she had leveraged *One Hundred Years of Solitude* again and again to "make a secret deal" with its publishers worldwide, granting them the rights to new books only on condition that they amended their individual contracts for Gabo's book—so that rights to it would revert back to the agency.

She spoke without proviso about the state of the agency. "I retired in the year 2000," she said. "The business was with three associates: my son, the man who does the contracts, [and another]. But I had to return because of the debts, the losses." She described her dealings with the most powerful agent in the English-speaking world: "Andrew Wylie is one of the persons who has wanted to buy my agency for 20 years. It should have been done six months ago. Andrew was here with Sarah [Chalfant, his deputy], and with a publisher who has become an agent . . ." She shook her head, unable to recall the name of Cristóbal Pera, who ran Penguin Random House Grupo Editorial in Mexico before joining Wylie in August [2015].

. . .

In May 2014, Agencia Carmen Balcells entered into a memorandum of understanding with the Wylie Agency about an eventual sale, and the *Times* reported the deal as all but done. Balcells clearly trusted Wylie enough to have taken things that far. So why wasn't the deal done? Because, Balcells said, she surmised that Wylie anticipated closing the office on the Diagonal in Barcelona and folding the Balcells agency into his operations in New York and London. This she was strongly against. So she began entertaining other offers: from the London-based literary agent Andrew Nurnberg, who represents authors ranging from Harper Lee to Tariq Ali (as well as the late Jackie Collins), and from Riccardo Cavallero, who previously ran Mondadori in Italy and Spain.

"Three offers, all very interesting," she told me. "But the process is frozen, because none of them was good enough." In a little while the lawyers would arrive and she and they would try to sort things out. She articulated her greatest fear: betraying her authors, should the needs of a new agency partner supersede the needs of individual writers. "To be a literary agent: it's a modest job," she said. "But it's a job that's important for the writer. It's a position that you take the right decision for your clients. And the problem is that the ego [of the agents] can get in the way. It's very important that the agency is a person, one person. It's not about money."

What *was* it about? Andrew Wylie won't talk about their discussions. So Balcells' word may be the last word. For her, it was also about something else— about the agent as a presence in the lives of her authors, and as a person who would be there when what she called "the magnificent presence of the author" was no more.

Rolling gracefully in her wheelchair, she showed me to the elevator. She kissed my hand in parting. Seven weeks later, she died of a heart attack, stricken in that Barcelona apartment. Despite her advanced years, her death took the publishing community by surprise. And with her passing she would become, like her magical author, altogether present, a specter that haunts the fight for her agency—and Gabo's legacy.

Who will represent *One Hundred Years of Solitude*? Right now, no one knows. But the Buendías and their village, Macondo, are ably represented: we are their descendants, and they are present to us, as vivid as a swarm of yellow butterflies in the pages of Gabriel García Márquez's magnificent novel.

PRIMO LEVI

....

THE SURVIVOR'S SUICIDE

by James Atlas

JANUARY 1988

In the spring of 1987, Primo Levi's literary reputation had never been higher. All over the world, translators were preparing his work for publication. There were even rumors that he might win a Nobel. "You'd better get ready to travel again," Levi's publisher teased him over the phone on Friday, April 10. "And this time you're going to Stockholm."

Around ten o'clock the next morning, Iolanda Gasperi, the concierge of Levi's building, at 75 Corso Re Umberto in Turin, rang the bell of his fourth-floor flat and handed him the mail. "Dr. Levi had a tired look," she recalled, "but that was nothing unusual. He was gentle. He took the mail, a few newspapers and some advertising brochures, and greeted me cordially."

A few minutes later, she heard a loud thud in the stairwell and rushed out of her lodge. "A poor man was lying crushed on the floor. The blood hid his face. I looked at him and—my God, that man!—I recognized him right away. It was Dr. Levi."

Lucia Morpurgo, Levi's wife of forty years, had been out shopping. Her arms were full of groceries as she pushed open the glass door. The concierge tried to hold her back, but she flung herself down beside her husband and tried to lift his head. Their son, Renzo, had also heard the commotion and hurried down the wide staircase. They were joined by Francesco Quaglia, a dentist who had known Levi since high school and had an office in the building. Levi's wife embraced him. "*Era demoralizato,*" she said tearfully. "He was demoralized. You knew it, too, didn't you?"

Turin is a beautiful, somewhat melancholy city in the northwest corner of Italy, not far from the French border. Once the residence of the royal family, it has a faded stateliness that reflects its history: grand piazzas with shuttered windows and cream-colored walls reminiscent of the Place des Vosges; elegant archways and arcades; wide boulevards where narrow orange trams clatter beneath the dusty trees. At night, the air is suffused with a gritty yellowish fog; the streets are clogged with traffic. In the distance, you can see the lovely hills of the Valle d'Aosta on the far side of the river Po, which divides the town. Since Fiat established its factories here, Turin has become an industrial city, poor in the suburbs and prosperous in the center, but it still possesses the sad, provincial character evoked in the poems of Cesare Pavese, the famous editor and writer who lived in Turin nearly all his life and committed suicide here in 1950. Looking out the window of my hotel room the night I arrived, watching the shop owners pull down their shutters, the waiters stacking chairs, I recalled Pavese's poem "A Mania for Solitude":

> *I can see the sky, but I know the lights already shine*
> *between the rusty roofs, and sounds are heard beneath them.*
> *A deep breath and my body savors the life*
> *of trees and rivers, and feels cut off from everything.*

Primo Levi was utterly rooted in Turin. The son of an educated middle-class Jewish family that could trace its arrival in the Piedmont region back to 1500, after the expulsion of the Jews from Spain, he died in the house where he had been born sixty-seven years before. "I live in my house as I live inside my skin," Levi observed toward the end of his life. It's a comfortable building, with iron balconies and ocher Tuscan walls, on a street that Philip Roth, who interviewed Levi for *The New York Times Book Review* the year before his death, likens to New York's residential West End Avenue.

Nowhere in Europe were the Jews more assimilated than in Italy. It was a small population—perhaps 50,000 before the war—but one that had been influential in the nation's life ever since the Risorgimento. Levi grew up in the comfortable neighborhood of Crocetta, near the center of town. Both his grandfather and his father were civil engineers; his mother's family were prosperous merchants. Levi's father was a great bibliophile who instructed his tailor to make the pockets of his suits large enough to hold books. "On the road, going to bed, getting up: he always had a book in his hand," Levi recalled. His family observed Rosh Hashanah, Passover, and Purim and knew a smattering of Yiddish, but, as Levi remarked wryly, "a Jew is somebody who at Christmas does not have a tree, who shouldn't eat salami but does, who has learned a little bit of Hebrew at thirteen and then has forgotten it."

Anti-Semitism scarcely existed. As a student at the prestigious Ginnasio-Liceo d'Azeglio, Levi was utterly at home, secure in the cloistered world of the library and the lab. He didn't smoke or drink or "go with girls." He studied: chemistry, Latin and Greek, Italian history, Dante. His high-school friend Livio

Norzi remembers his voracious reading: "*Point Counter Point, The Plumed Serpent,* and so on. He taught us all to read." Levi was an ambitious boy. "I hoped to go far," he confided in the autobiographical notes he was preparing for his Italian publisher, "to find the key to the universe, to understand the why of things."

It wasn't until the autumn of 1938, when Mussolini outlawed mixed marriages, banned Jews from universities, and prohibited them from owning certain property or holding jobs in government, that history intruded. "My Christian classmates were civil people," Levi wrote of his days as a chemistry student at the University of Turin. "None of them, nor any of the teachers, had directed at me a hostile word or gesture, but I could feel them withdraw and, following an ancient pattern, I withdrew as well." No professor would sponsor his studies, until he approached a young assistant who responded in the words of the Gospel: "Follow me." In the summer of 1941, a degree in chemistry (summa cum laude) was awarded to "Primo Levi, of the Jewish race."

Even with honors, Levi couldn't get a job. While his father lay dying of a tumor in the flat on Corso Re Umberto, he made a futile search for work and was finally hired by a nickel mine up in the mountains near Turin. In the summer of 1942, he transferred to a lab on the outskirts of Milan. Within a year, the Nazis had arrived, and he headed for the mountains to join the partisans.

Studious, shy around girls, insomniac, Levi was an unlikely revolutionary. Armed with a pearl-handled revolver that he didn't know how to use, he hoped to join forces with the Resistance; instead he found himself allied with "a deluge of outcasts." At dawn on December 13, 1943, Levi and his bedraggled crew woke to find themselves surrounded by the Fascist militia. Under interrogation, he weighed the dangers of identifying himself as a partisan and decided to confess that he was a Jew. He was interned at the notorious detention camp of Fossoli. A month later, the German SS arrived and mass deportations began. "Our destination? Nobody knew. We should be prepared for a fortnight of travel. For every person missing at the roll-call, ten would be shot."

Of the 650 men and women who departed in Levi's convoy for Auschwitz, only three returned. How did he survive? Levi insisted that it was largely a matter of luck. His training as a chemist enabled him to qualify for a job in the I. G. Farben laboratory; an Italian bricklayer who had been rounded up by the Nazis in France shared his meager ration with Levi for six months; and Levi happened to come down with scarlet fever just as the Red Army was advancing on the camp. In the forced evacuation that ensued, some 20,000 prisoners died.

To claim for himself special powers of intelligence or will would never have occurred to Levi; it wasn't in his nature. Yet reading *Survival in Auschwitz,* the story of his tenure in hell, I couldn't help feeling that his character must have contributed in some way to the miraculous defiance of statistics. One of the most notable things about this book is its magisterial equanimity. There is no self-pity, none of the lamentation characteristic of Elie Wiesel. "There is no why here," said one of Levi's guards; for Levi, inquiring into the "why of things" was simply what one did. His discourse on the social structure of the camp—the way clothes and rations were distributed, the work details, the insanely complicated rules and regulations—is amazingly precise. Auschwitz was an experiment, the most perverse and barbarous ever devised by man, but it could still yield knowledge, and it was in this scientific spirit that Levi observed "what is essential and what adventitious to the conduct of the human animal in the struggle for life."

For all the suffering it chronicles, *Survival in Auschwitz* is not a gloomy book. Time and again, Levi manages to find pleasure in the slightest things. On those rare nights when he doesn't have to share his bunk, he considers himself lucky. When the weather is warm, he rejoices because it isn't cold. When the ration of watery gruel is more plentiful than usual, he counts it "a happy day." Hope is the momentary absence of pain. In one memorable scene, struggling to carry a heavy soup pot, he begins to recite a passage from Dante's *Commedia* to a French comrade:

> *Think of your breed; for brutish ignorance*
> *Your mettle was not made; you were made men,*
> *To follow after knowledge and excellence.*

If *Survival in Auschwitz* is optimistic, its sequel, *The Reawakening*, a picaresque chronicle of the months Levi spent wandering the far reaches of Eastern Europe and Russia, is positively buoyant. Liberated from Auschwitz, he found himself shuttled off hundreds of miles in the wrong direction, transferred from camp to camp, an eternal refugee. Yet even as the dream of returning home receded, Levi reveled in his new freedom. The time adrift was "a parenthesis of unlimited availability," he declared, "a providential but unrepeatable gift of fate." Arriving in the ruined city of Katowice, he and his tattered compatriot are "as cheerful as schoolboys." Invigorated by a cup of tea as he's camping out on the floor of a train station in some distant province, he's "tense and alert, hilarious, lucid and sensitive." He had survived. He was alive.

In his interview with Levi, Philip Roth remarked on the "exuberance" manifest in *The Reawakening*, its atmosphere of celebration. "Family, home, factory are good things in themselves," Levi replied, "but they deprived me of something that I still miss: adventure." The experience of Auschwitz, catastrophic as it was, enlarged his character. "I remember having lived my Auschwitz year in a condition of exceptional spiritedness," he told Roth, comparing his absorption in camp routine to "the curiosity of the naturalist who finds himself transplanted into an environment that is monstrous, but new, monstrously new." For Levi, Auschwitz was "an education."

In October 1945, bearded and in rags, he arrived back in Turin. His mother had survived by hiding in the countryside; his sister, armed with false identity papers, had moved from house to house. No one expected him; Lorenzo, the Italian bricklayer who had done so much to preserve Levi's life in the camp, had reported him almost certainly dead. "I found a large clean bed, which in the evening (a moment of terror) yielded softly under my weight. But only after many months did I lose the habit of walking with my glance fixed to the ground, as if searching for something to eat or to pocket hastily or to sell for bread; and a dream full of horror has still not ceased to visit me, at sometimes frequent, sometimes longer, intervals."

Installed in the flat on Corso Re Umberto, Levi found work in a varnish factory, Duco Montecatini, near Turin, and embarked on the book that would become his masterpiece, typing at night in a freezing storeroom at the factory and scribbling on the tram. "I had a torrent of urgent things to tell the civilized world," he recalled in *The Reawakening*. "I felt the tattooed number on my arm burning like a sore." So intense was Levi's need to testify that he would approach strangers on buses or on the street and blurt out that he was a survivor. "Whether we like it or not," he wrote a fellow Auschwitz prisoner after the war, "we are the witnesses and we bear the weight of it."

Levi submitted his memoir to several publishers, including the illustrious house of Einaudi in Turin. It was turned down everywhere. Finally a small publisher, Franco Antonicelli, agreed to bring it out, and *Survival in Auschwitz* was published in 1947 under the title *Se Questo È un Uomo* (*If This Is a Man*), in a limited edition of 2,500 copies. It got favorable reviews but was largely ignored by the public. Newly married and out of a job—Duco Montecatini had let him go—Levi was hired as a lab chemist at SIVA, a family-owned varnish factory on the outskirts of Turin. His work of testimony, he decided, was done: "It was a forgotten book. I had dedicated myself to my work as a chemist, I had married, I had been catalogued among the authors 'unius libri' [of one book], and I hardly thought about this solitary little book any more, even if sometimes I burned to believe that the descent into hell had given me, as to Coleridge's Ancient Mariner, a 'strange power of speech.'"

Nine years later, inspired by the enthusiastic response to a talk he gave in Turin at an exhibition of photographs and documents about the deportation, Levi offered the book again to Einaudi, which reissued it in 1958. It hasn't been out of print since.

The tremendous success of *Survival in Auschwitz* gave Levi the confidence he needed to embark on *The Reawakening*. It was published in 1963, sixteen years after his literary debut. In his mid-forties, with two books to his credit, Levi "accepted the condition of being a writer," as he put it, but he was still primarily a chemist. By then he was manager of the plant, a job that entailed considerable responsibility. His company, which produced enamel coatings for copper wire, had prospered since the war, and Levi was often on the road, traveling to Germany and Russia. "At the peak of my career, I numbered among the 30 or 40 specialists in the world in this branch," he boasted to Roth.

For Levi, chemistry was inspirational, both an anchor in the world and a way of interpreting it. When he wrote about his profession in *La Stampa*, the Turin newspaper to which he contributed an occasional column over the years, it was in a spirit of adventure, and with a lucidity that verged on joy. The behavior of beetles, the challenge of astronomy, the physiology of pain: for Levi, the "two cultures" were one. Science enlivened his writing, made it precise; his job as a chemist got him out of the house. "My factory *militanza*—my compulsory and honorable service there—kept me in touch with the world of real things."

In 1977, Levi retired in order to devote himself to writing. By now he was a public figure of sorts in Italy, and a celebrity in Turin. When a German television crew showed up to make a documentary and followed him around the streets, people greeted him on the tram. He gave talks in the local schools, answered his ever increasing mail, made himself available to scholars and journalists in his study on the Corso Re Umberto. "He was a person of remarkable serenity, openness and good humor, with a striking absence of bitterness," wrote Alexander Stille, a young journalist who knew about Levi. To Roth, he was a vivid presence, voluble, shrewd, preternaturally attentive: "He seemed to me inwardly animated more in the manner of some little quicksilver woodland creature empowered by the forest's most astute intelligence. . . . His alertness is nearly palpable, keenness trembling within him like his pilot light."

His intellectual energy was prodigious. He studied Yiddish in order to write *If Not Now, When?*, his novel about a band of Jewish partisans fighting for survival at the end of World War II. He translated Heine, Kipling, Lévi-Strauss, and devoted long hours to playing chess with the Macintosh computer he'd installed in his study. Working with his British translator, Stuart Woolf, Levi was indefatigable. He would sit down after dinner, "beginning around nine o'clock, and go on until midnight or one in the morning, and he'd be up again the next day regularly," Woolf recalled in a television program dedicated to Levi. "Auschwitz had conditioned him to living with very little sleep."

Levi seemed happy in his fame; in a memoir called "Beyond Survival," published in 1982, he noted that *If Not Now, When?* had won "two of the three most coveted Italian literary awards" (the Campiello and the Viareggio) and was "meeting with great success in Italy among the public and the critics." On the wall of his study he put up a chart to help him keep track of the translations of his books in many languages. Levi was always dropping in at the Luxemburg, a bookstore near the Piazza Castello that stocked English and American periodicals, to read his reviews. "He was proud of his reputation," recalled Agnese Incisa, formerly of Einaudi. "He didn't have an agent. Everything we did, we had to call up Primo first."

Visitors to the Corso Re Umberto were struck by how close the family seemed. Both of Levi's children were unmarried: his son, Renzo, a physicist, lived next door, his daughter, Lisa, a biology teacher, had an apartment in the neighborhood. Levi's ninety-two-year-old mother, nearly blind and the victim of a paralytic stroke, was confined to her room in the fourth-floor flat. There were two nurses in attendance, and an Arab student, Amir, who helped around the house; but the Levis lived simply, and disapproved of servants. "It was a typical Turinese household," remembered Anna Vitale, of the Comunita Ebraica. "They were well-off, but they didn't live like wealthy people." Levi's book-lined study, furnished with an old flowered sofa and a comfortable easy chair, was his refuge. On the shelves were playful constructions made out of the enameled copper wire manufactured by Levi's factory: a wire butterfly, a wire owl, a bird, and one that Levi described to Roth as "a man playing with his nose." ("'A Jew,' I suggested. 'Yes, yes,' he said, laughing, 'a Jew, of course.'") The only emblem of his trauma was a sketch on the wall of a barbed-wire fence: Auschwitz.

As his mother's condition deteriorated, Levi traveled less and less, but in the spring of 1985 he was given the Kenneth B. Smilen award, sponsored by the Jewish Museum in New York, and his American publishers persuaded him to give a series of informal talks in the United States. *The Periodic Table* had appeared the year before, graced with a blurb from Saul Bellow, and been instantly recognized for the classic that it is. (Twenty publishers turned it down before Schocken Books picked up the rights.) Levi was a great hit in Boston and New York—though he was puzzled that his audiences were entirely Jewish. "I began to wonder if any goyim lived in America. I didn't come across a single one of them!" The press was charmed. "One trusts him instantly," reported Meredith Tax in the *Village Voice*. To Richard Higgins, writing in the Boston *Globe*, Levi was a paradox. "He is slight of build, softly-spoken, professorial and dapper in demeanor; but the inner man, say those who know him best, seems to be made of steel." AUSCHWITZ SURVIVOR PRIMO LEVI STRESSES HOPE, NOT THE DARKNESS, read the *Globe*'s headline.

It was a triumphant journey. "He loved his trip to America," recalled Agnese Incisa. "It gave him a chance to be away." Back in Turin, Levi resumed his tranquil routine. He made weekly visits to his publisher, Einaudi, whose offices were just around the corner. He was collecting material for a book in the form of love letters from a chemist to a young girl—"a sort of epistolary romance," according to Arthur Samuelson, who became Levi's editor when Summit Books acquired the rights to his work. Agnese Incisa remembers going to see him at Christmas 1986 and spending hours with him at his Macintosh computer. "It was the last time I saw him happy."

Suicide among Holocaust survivors is hardly uncommon. Levi addressed the issue himself in *The Drowned and the Saved*, out this month from Summit in a masterly translation by Raymond Rosenthal. He was haunted by the memory of his friend Jean Améry, a philosopher who had survived Auschwitz and committed suicide in 1978. Few suicides occurred in the camps, Levi noted: "The day was dense: one had to think about satisfying hunger, in some way elude fatigue and cold, avoid the blows; precisely because of the constant imminence of death there was no time to concentrate on the idea of death." Suicide, Levi argued, was a reflection of the victim's inward guilt, a punishment for suppressed, unspoken sins; but why punish yourself when you were being punished on a scale beyond what anyone had ever been called upon to endure? At Auschwitz, guilt was superfluous: "One was already expiating it by one's daily suffering."

The subject was clearly on Levi's mind. In one of his *La Stampa* essays, he examined the death of another survivor who eventually committed suicide, the Romanian-born poet Paul Celan. Celan was a "tragic and noble" figure, Levi conceded, but his inchoate, nearly indecipherable last poems constituted "the rattle of a dying man." They were devoid of hope. "I believe that Celan the poet should be meditated upon and pitied rather than imitated," Levi declared. Three years later, Levi was dead by his own hand.

Perhaps the most devastating aspect of Levi's suicide was its unexpectedness. Even among his closest friends, few were aware of his despair. "He was a happy man, *allegro*," says the eminent political scientist Norberto Bobbio, who had known Levi for decades. "Three days before his death, he was tranquil and serene." Roth, who visited him in Turin seven months before his death, insisted that "he was as filled with a sense of joy and well-being as a man can be."

But there were those who sensed a darkening in Levi's mood, and not only toward the end. "He was a deeply depressed person," Dr. Roberto Pattono, one of Levi's physicians, told me. "I thought he was suicidal the first time I met him. Years ago, I said to myself: It is only a matter of time." A close friend of the family showed me a poem Levi wrote in the mid-seventies. "It has gotten late, my dears" was the opening line.

"There were brief periods of depression," said Bruno Vasari, the former managing director of Italian public television. It was late at night, and we were sitting in the parlor of his apartment off the busy Via Roma. It was an old-world apartment, full of beautiful things: art books piled up on the coffee table, plush furniture, Impressionist prints on the walls. Vasari, a large, dignified, soft-spoken man with a mane of white hair, seemed weary. He had been in Mauthausen, he told me—"one of the most brutal camps." He opened one of Levi's books and showed me a poem entitled "The Survivor," dedicated to "B.V." In it Levi had quoted some lines from Coleridge:

Dopo di allora, ad ora incerta,

Since then, at an uncertain hour,
That agony returns:
And till my ghastly tale is told,
This heart within me burns.

"The most important thing for him was to write," Vasari stressed. "One had to live not only to write but to tell one's story, to testify." He left the room and returned with another book: the Bible. He opened it to Exodus 13:8. "And thou shalt shew thy son in that day, saying, This is done because of that which the Lord did unto me when I came forth out of Egypt." "To testify," Vasari said again with quiet emphasis, "in the religious sense." He referred me to the opening passage of *The Drowned and the Saved*, where Levi quotes the boast of an SS man who declares that even if a handful of Jews survive, the world will never believe their story. "Strangely enough," writes Levi, "this same thought ('even if we were to tell it, we would not be believed') arose in the form of nocturnal dreams produced by the prisoners' despair." That was Levi's great fear, said Vasari: that he wouldn't be believed.

Levi had devoted his life to bringing before the world the meticulous evidence of what had happened, what had been done by men to men. He had chaperoned children on trips to Auschwitz, lectured, and given interviews; he had written books. Yet he wondered if he had done enough. "How much of the concentration camp world is dead and will not return, like slavery and the dueling code?" he asked in *The Drowned and the Saved*. "How much . . . is coming back? What can each of us do, so that in this world pregnant with threats, at least this threat will be nullified?" To those who persisted in asking why the Jews hadn't fled, he replied: What are we doing about nuclear war? "Why aren't we gone, why aren't we leaving our country, why aren't we fleeing 'before'?"

The Drowned and the Saved, Levi's last testament, is very different from anything he wrote before. What comes through so powerfully in this anguished book is anger—a new emotion for Levi. "I'm not capable of acting like Jean Améry," he once told an interviewer, referring to an episode in which Améry had assaulted a Polish prisoner. Violence was alien to Levi. There's a moving passage in *The Periodic Table* where, confined in a cell at Aosta after his arrest by the

Fascists, he shares his crust of bread with a mouse: "I felt more like a mouse than he; I was thinking of the road in the woods, the snow outside, the indifferent mountains, the hundred splendid things which if I could go free I would be able to do, and a lump rose in my throat." That generosity was Levi's essence.

How long could he maintain his equanimity? *The Drowned and the Saved* is a cry of barely stifled rage against the Germans. Why did they do what they did? It was their nature. In the Third Reich, "the best choice, the choice imposed from above, was the one that entailed the greatest amount of affliction, the greatest amount of waste, of physical and moral suffering. The 'enemy' must not only die, but must die in torment."

It was this crime against the innocent that obsessed Levi. It was a crime beyond expiation, a wound that festered and would never heal. In his remarkable last chapter, Levi quoted at length from letters Germans had written him, remorselessly showing their evasions and lies, their feeble efforts to justify themselves in the face of what could never be justified. He would not grant the forgiveness they sought. The legacy of the camps was ineradicable. His dead friend Améry had written" "Anyone who has been tortured remains tortured. . . . Anyone who has suffered torture never again will be able to be at ease in the world."

For Levi, survival was a gift—perhaps undeserved. He was troubled by the thought that "this testifying of mine could by itself gain for me the privilege of surviving and living for many years without serious problems." Levi considered himself among the lucky few: not only had he lived, he had become a success. "We are those who by their prevarications or abilities or good luck did not touch bottom." The real victims were those who had suffered in silence.

But, in his own way, Levi himself was mute, enduring his life without complaint. Liberated from Auschwitz, he found himself four decades later a virtual prisoner in his own home. From her room down at the end of the hall, his mother, Ester, dominated his existence. She woke up at 6:30, demanded breakfast at 7, called out to Levi day and night. He pushed her around the neighborhood in her wheelchair, kept a vigil beside her bed. When he visited friends, he would rush off after an hour, explaining that he was needed at home. "He was the most dutiful Jewish son who ever lived," says Roth. "He and Lucia were like slaves to the family situation," according to Norberto Bobbio. Levi's mother-in-law, ninety-five, who lived down the block, required equally strenuous ministrations. "Primo had these two old ladies on his back," said one of his friends bluntly. "He was surrounded by sick old women." Why didn't he put his mother in a home? "Out of the question," declared Bobbio. "He was too good a son. He'd seen too much suffering to inflict any of his own."

Levi was on antidepressants, and briefly saw a psychiatrist, but when she tried to probe his feelings of aggression, he abruptly broke off treatment. In February

1987, he entered the hospital for a prostate operation, and was taken off his anti-depressant medicine. "Don't visit me," he told Giovanni Tesio, a scholar who had been interviewing him for months. "I'm very boring when I feel badly." The operation was a success, but it brought on a host of distressing urological problems.

Levi seldom ventured out. "He wasn't seeing anyone," said Agnese Incisa. "He would come in and sit in the office and stare." He refused invitations to speak and failed to attend meetings of his social club, the Famija Piemönteisa, or the weekly dinners with friends at the Cambio, Turin's most exclusive restaurant. "He was getting worse and worse," Ernesto Ferrero, an editor at Einaudi, told Valeria Gandus and Gian Paolo Rossetti, who interviewed many of Levi's friends and associates for the Italian magazine *Panorama* in the weeks after his death. "We cosseted him, telephoned him, urged him to take his mind off things, busy himself with concrete matters. . . . It was a bad period, but we were sure that it would pass." Toward the end of February, Levi broke off his conversations with Giovanni Tesio. "I don't feel like doing this anymore," he said tersely. "Let's stop."

One of Levi's most persistent complaints was that he couldn't write. *Non posso scrivere.* He had been a prolific author all his life; his last two novels, *If Not Now, When?* and *The Monkey's Wrench*, the garrulous monologue of an itinerant construction worker, had made his reputation as a novelist. But he was terrified that he had nothing more to say. Largely spared the negative reviews that few writers can avoid, he was perplexed by Fernanda Eberstadt's essay on him in the October 1985 issue of *Commentary,* which claimed that he was insufficiently Jewish, and argued that his later work suffered from "a certain inhibiting fastidiousness and insubstantiality." Levi was a writer who read his reviews.

In April, Levi seemed to improve. "He was eager to get back to work," recalled Dr. Pattono. Stuart Woolf thought Levi "seemed to be in much better spirits than I'd seen him in on the previous occasion." On April 8, Levi wrote a letter to the Venetian writer Ferdinando Camon. "Primo explained to me how much he would have liked to see his latest book translated and published in France," Camon told Gandus and Rossetti, the reporters from *Panorama.* "The thought that Gallimard, one of the most authoritative publishers on the other side of the Alps, should be interested in his work filled him with enthusiasm." The next day, Levi was offered the honorary post of president of Einaudi, then in the midst of a reorganization. He was flattered by the proposal, remembers Norberto Bobbio, and declined it with regret. On April 10, Giovanni Tesio called, and Levi answered in a happy voice. "*Ciao*, Giovanni," he said. "We should begin again."

That night, a friend concerned about Levi's state of mind called to see how he was doing. "Bad," Levi reported.

"At least you can play chess with your computer," said the friend.

"Yes, but it beats me."

The next morning, Levi's wife went out shopping and left him alone with his mother and a nurse. A few minutes later, after he'd gotten the mail, Levi rushed out to the landing and hurled himself over the railing of the wide staircase. Death was instantaneous.

That night, all of Italy watched the ghastly television footage of Levi, his face covered with blood, being carried off on a stretcher to the morgue in the Via Chiabrera. The next morning's papers carried the story beneath front-page headlines. In the weeks that followed, their pages were filled with tributes, reminiscences, appreciations of his work. Rita Levi Montalcini, a childhood friend of Levi's and a Nobel laureate in medicine, speculated in a lengthy interview that Levi hadn't committed suicide at all. Perhaps he had plunged over the railing by accident, while calling down to the concierge. More likely, Dr. Montalcini surmised, it had been what psychiatrists refer to as a raptus, a sudden fit of insanity that could have been precipitated by some irregularity in his reaction to the dosage of his antidepressant drugs. Whatever the cause, it was a frightening way to die, especially for a chemist, who could have found less violent ways to kill himself.

Every suicide, Levi had written, apropos the death of Améry, provokes "a nebula of explanations." Had there been financial problems? The year before, the house of Einaudi had gone into receivership, and Levi stayed on while most of the writers on its list jumped ship. Some people intimated that Levi's loyalty had cost him a lot of money, but Agnese Incisa told me that Einaudi had managed to pay "most of the royalties" from *If Not Now, When?*, despite its own financial difficulties.

Or was it heredity? In *The Periodic Table*, Levi had offered portraits of his eccentric relatives: the doctor uncle who neglected his practice and squandered his days on a cot in a filthy attic on the Borgo Vanchiglia reading old newspapers; his grandmother, who spent the last twenty years of her very long life mysteriously cloistered in her room; a remote ancestor, the uncle of his maternal grandmother, who took to his bed when his parents refused to let him marry a lowly peasant girl, and stayed there for twenty-two years; his grandfather, rumored to have killed himself over his wife's infidelities, the wife herself half mad. Levi's tone was ironic, but the history is significant.

Inevitably, there was speculation that the Holocaust had reached out to claim another victim. Levi "had built a public image for himself, but inside he was very corroded," testified Ferdinando Camon in *Panorama*. "The operation of memorizing, cataloguing, bearing witness to the Nazi horrors and barbarities took a tremendous psychic toll. This is a suicide that must be dated back to 1945. It did not take place then, because Primo wanted (and had) to write. Having finished his work (*The Drowned and the Saved* ends this cycle) he was free to kill himself. And he did."

Perhaps it did go that far back. As he was wheeled into the operating room last February, Levi rolled up his sleeve and pointed to the number tattooed on his arm: "That is my disease." Reading over *Survival in Auschwitz*, I was struck by the passage where Levi suggested that to come down with diphtheria in a concentration camp would be "more surely fatal than jumping off a fourth floor." That book was written in 1947, in Levi's fourth-floor flat on Corso Re Umberto.

NAGUIB MAHFOUZ

··

AT THE ALI BABA CAFÉ

by Christopher Dickey

NOVEMBER 1989

It is a year now since the old man won the Nobel. His face, half obscured by the dark glasses he wears, has appeared in countless newspapers and magazines, and his work, virtually unknown to Western audiences, has begun to receive similar attention: Jacqueline Kennedy Onassis is presiding over publication this winter of four of his novels. Yet as he sits in the Ali Baba Cafeteria just above Tahrir Square there is nothing, on the surface, that seems to have changed about the life of Naguib Mahfouz. He has not left Cairo except for the occasional summer week in Alexandria. He sent his two daughters to the Nobel award ceremony in Stockholm, and when they got back, he split the $390,000 prize four ways: a quarter to his wife and a quarter to each of the girls. The quarter for himself he gave to charity.

The Ali Baba is a dreary café advertised by a neon sign out front, at once garish and nondescript. Mahfouz comes here because it fits his routine. It is open twenty-four hours a day, and he likes to get his first coffee as early as seven in the morning. No one bothers him here, although he is only a couple of yards above the crowd as he sips his *masbout*. They are oblivious, running for the buses that never quite come to a stop, or winding their way through the traffic that crashes en masse through red lights. Mahfouz did not plan much work for the summer. "I will consider myself very fortunate if I can manage to write some short stories." He is alone with his newspapers, his memories, and, it is fair to say, the presence of death.

The threats began to come just a few days after the prize. And over the months they got worse, and became more public. It was at the height of the furor raised by the Ayatollah Ruhollah Khomeini against British author Salman Rushdie for his blasphemous best-seller, *The Satanic Verses*, that an "imam" in Egypt, who had been tried and acquitted in the plot against murdered president Anwar Sadat, told his followers it was time that Naguib Mahfouz, in the name of righteousness, should die.

This is serious business in Egypt. Presidents, Cabinet members, and newspaper editors have been lined up in the sights of revolutionaries over the last decade, and some have died. At the street level, Egypt is a police state that is never quite in control. The government offered Mahfouz round-the-clock guards, as if he were a politician, or, perhaps, a national treasure—one of the dusty relics in the Egyptian Museum. He refused.

"I never thought about asking for protection." His face creases, smiling. "It's like being under arrest. We would be sitting here now with somebody next to us. It would be worse than death." He shrugs at allegations of bravery. "Look, at my age, a threat of death is not really that frightening. I might receive a threat on Sunday and die of natural causes on Monday."

The Islamic grudge against Mahfouz goes back many years, to the late 1950s, when he started publishing his novels serially in the newspapers. The government of Gamal Abdel Nasser was looking for some liberal credentials by allowing writers a certain freedom of expression. But one of the first serials Mahfouz published was *Children of Gebelawi*, an allegory about the search for faith and eternal truths in a poor sector of Cairo. There were characters taken to be modeled on Moses, Christ, Muhammad himself. It seemed a blasphemous tale to the sheikhs beneath the minarets of Al Azhar. In a sense it was *The Satanic Verses* of its time, although Mahfouz says he intended no blasphemy, and in those days such issues were a matter of debate, not death sentences. The sheikhs denounced the book, and it has not been published in Arabic in Egypt since. Then, in the early 1970s, Mahfouz was one of the first Egyptian intellectuals to call publicly for an end to war with Israel, another strike against him in the eyes of Islam's self-appointed holy warriors.

But it's not Mahfouz's views on God or Zion that most offend the righteous. In the fundamentalist societies of young men with long beards and short robes, with the bright eyes of the faithful and the will to die for paradise, Naguib Mahfouz is known as "Sex Teacher."

Such a designation seems almost incomprehensible to a Western reader. The surprise award of the Nobel tore a hole in what John Fowles once called the "linguistic Iron Curtain" that keeps much of Arabic writing, and thus much of Arab culture, hidden from the West. Mahfouz is the greatest writer in one of the most widely understood languages in the world, a storyteller of the first order in any idiom. But new readers, even some of his recently acquired editors in New York, are often at a loss to understand what they encounter.

Especially for Americans, who are so curious and uncomfortable about the Old World, this oldest corner of the world is a disturbing place. There are few artistic reference points to guide our emotions. Egyptian culture, so dense and so old and so decayed, has a remarkable capacity to subsume the incursions of the foreigner. Outside influences come and stay and are absorbed, leaving only vague, disturbing allusions. And there remains behind a cultural tension between the expectations of modernity and the weight of the past, a constant disillusionment and confusion.

In his strongest works, Mahfouz uses this setting to play the traditions of family, love, and faith against social upheaval that is imposed, most often, from outside. The people in the streets don't change much. But the people in the palaces and the parliament do, courting or defying the British occupation, experimenting with revolution, trying to transform the immutable, fostering expectations difficult or impossible to attain—creating currents of politics that sweep over and through the masses like wind roiling the surface of the Nile. His characters are always searching for . . . what? For affection and respect and happiness, of course. But, above all, for some sense of order; and the search for order and reason, in the midst of chaos and blind faith, can be dangerous. "I had loved the village but could not bear to live there. I had educated myself," recalls the aged journalist in *Miramar*, one of Mahfouz's best novels, "and I had been wrongly accused and many people had said . . . that I should be killed. . . . I had been entranced by love, education, cleanliness, hope."

The life of Egypt, of the modern Egyptians themselves, was never interpreted in great works of English literature. (You will say Lawrence Durrell's *Alexandria Quartet*, and Mahfouz will reply, rightly, "It is very beautiful, but it is about foreigners.") The Orientalists who helped build the magnificent myth of the desert Arab loathed the sedentary effendi of Cairo. "Egypt, being so near Europe, is not a savage country," T. E. Lawrence wrote to Robert Graves. "The Egyptians are very bestial, very savage: but you need not dwell among them. Indeed it will be a miracle if an Englishman can get to know them." Those who extolled Egypt's glorious pharaonic past were disturbed by the seedy decay of its present. It was always a country for tourists and travel writers, not for artists. So this Egyptian novelist was dealing with sensibilities the West knew little or nothing about, in a society where men wear suits at the office, djellabas in the home.

I first went to see Mahfouz the day after the prize was announced. He lives across a little branch of the Nile from the island of Zamalek, in an apartment building haunted, as even new buildings in Cairo are, by an awkward air of remembered grandeurs. The Nubian janitor sat passively at the entrance watching cars careen by on Nile Street; he wore the traditional long Egyptian robe, a turban, and Ray-Ban knockoffs. Along the hallways Arabic graffiti were etched into the stucco. A black cat and a pair of rubber sandals sat outside the apartment door.

Mahfouz was just getting back home, a plastic bag full of newspapers in his hand, when he was surrounded by reporters. "No lights," he apologized in English as he arrived at the darkened door. Inside the apartment the sitting room was shaded from the sun by lace curtains, and the furniture, Egypt's own notion of Louis XIV, was swaddled against the dust by white slipcovers. The author, diabetic and frail, had come to appear like the octogenarian writer in *Miramar:* "I look at my hand and think of the mummies in the Egyptian museum. . . . There's nothing left for death to devour—a wrinkled face, sunken eyes and sharp bones." Mahfouz's wife is fifteen years younger than he—sturdy, protective, declining to talk to the strangers, constantly offering soft drinks, tea, coffee. Her hair was covered, in apparent deference to Islamic modesty. His daughters are both grown: Oum Kalthoum is thirty-two, Fatima is thirty, but they live at home, as good unmarried girls do in Egypt.

Long before the Nobel, Mahfouz and his family had settled into a quiet, well-regulated life. Mahfouz would spend part of each day in an office at the semi-official *Al-Ahram* newspaper, much of the rest in favorite coffeehouses in the center of the city—a world not without cares, but with little urgency. Word of the prize broke over the wires hours before anyone from Stockholm could reach Mahfouz to tell him about it. "I was having my daily siesta after lunch when my wife woke me up and said, 'Somebody wants to congratulate you on the phone. He said you won the Nobel Prize.' I told her, 'Enough of dreams.'"

Now, after all those years of obscurity in the West, Mahfouz has Jacqueline Kennedy Onassis as his editor. Within days of his winning the prize, she was poring through a French translation of *Palace Walk*, the first volume of Mahfouz's monumental trilogy about life in Cairo from 1911 to 1944. Along with Alberto Vitale, president and C.E.O. of Bantam Doubleday Dell Inc., she started calling around to see what pieces of Mahfouz she could buy. Vitale had grown up in Cairo during World War II, in an apartment on Zamalek, which in those days was a garden and a club. Mahfouz's most famous books were written about the Cairo of that era, although, Vitale says, "I didn't know that when I went after his works." What struck the fifty-five-year-old master of the massive publishing conglomerate was "a very interesting cultural event, an Egyptian author winning the Nobel." And this in a year when Graham Greene and V. S. Naipaul were in the running.

Elsewhere in Manhattan, Mark Chimsky, executive editor of the Quality Paperback Book Club, was quick to cut reprint deals with the American University of Cairo and Three Continents Press, both of which had been bringing out little editions of Mahfouz for years. Chimsky could see potential in Mahfouz, but he knew there would be a marketing challenge. "He came out of nowhere. All he had was the Nobel, as far as our readers knew."

In the United States "there's always a dilemma about how much information is needed for an American reader," says Roger Allen of the University of Pennsylvania, an Arabic scholar consulted by Chimsky. In the extant English versions of Mahfouz's shorter novels the original language, fraught with allusion and rhythm, has been rendered stiff and brittle. Much of the description is pedestrian; the dialogue reads like bad subtitles on a Mexican soap opera ("'Give me your lips so I can kiss them. I shall press so many kisses on them, a hundred or even a thousand kisses. I shall keep kissing them until I die,' he said, sobbing"). Allen, who translated *Autumn Quail* in 1972, wishes he had it to do over again. "All the people who've translated Mahfouz's novels into English are academics like myself. But there's nothing about a Ph.D. in Arabic studies that makes you able to write great literature."

As Mahfouz's several American editors read through his work in the wake of the prize, they groped painfully for ways to present it. Nobels apparently don't translate into sales the way Oscars do. Doubleday reprints of three of Mahfouz's books are due out this month: *The Beginning and the End, Wedding Song*, and *The Thief and the Dogs*. They have press runs on the order of an American writer's first novel: about 10,000 copies. A more graceful translation of *Palace Walk*, the first English-language edition ever, probably will run 15,000 in hardcover when it appears in January. Martha Levin at Anchor, which will bring out the softcover editions of Doubleday's acquisitions, says that is a respectable figure for a "literary novel."

Levin "started to look on these as English novels from the nineteenth century," while Chimsky, at Q.P.B., hit on a marketing approach tailor-made for New York. "Who is he like? Frankly, I said, reading *Midaq Alley* is like reading some of the *shtetl* stories of Isaac Bashevis Singer." The analogy certainly helped move books. By the end of the summer, a one-volume edition of *Midaq Alley, Miramar*, and *The Thief and the Dogs* was Q.P.B.'s biggest-selling first selection of the year. As in Singer there are quaint customs like the brokering of marriages; there is a pervasive sense of intimate family life and social ties; there are odd, unforgettable characters. The comic relief in *Midaq Alley* comes from a self-taught dentist who steals dentures from the dead assisted by a golemlike creature called "Zaita, the cripple-maker." But any visitor to Cairo quickly discovers that this grotesquerie is not the folksy stuff of legend; this is the stuff of the present. On a bridge that leads from Nile Street to the café in Tahrir Square where Mahfouz takes his morning coffee, there is often a beggar working his way among cars stuck in the city's perpetual traffic jam. One of his legs is missing, and he hops up to the windows of the Mercedeses and Fiats on his remaining, bare foot. The charitable must put their alms in the breast pocket of his djellaba. He has no arms at all. Taxi drivers call him the Venus de Milo.

Mahfouz has the authority of age as well as art. He has lived the experience of Egypt, its political frustrations, the personal privation. He was born into the warren of ancient alleys behind the Khan Khalili bazaar in December 1911. His father had worked for the government in a minor job, back when officials proudly donned the red fez as a badge of distinction; later he took work as the business manager of a copper merchant in the souk. Naguib was the baby in a family of seven children, the youngest by ten years, and his mother, Fatima, raised him almost as an only child. His first memories are of her songs as he fell asleep at night, and of her tales about genies. There are vague recollections, too, of feast days; of dervishes who twirled like tops in the streets, their long skirts becoming circular wings that seemed to lift them into the air; of wedding processions; and of what he thought were family celebrations in the ancient and enormous cemetery known as the City of the Dead.

As a young man, he knew the exaltation of a cause. His university years in Cairo in the 1930s he remembers as "the golden age of patriotism." The country had become a colony in 1882 because it couldn't pay its debts: the regime of the British creditors was called the Veiled Protectorate, but was in fact an outright occupation. After fifty years, the British wearied of their white man's burden, and began to loosen the political ropes. For boys at school, an end to colonialism seemed the beginning of all possibilities. "The university was a beehive of patriotic and intellectual movements. We were interested in what was going on around us more than we were interested in ourselves." In *The Thief and the Dogs* he recalls, "The times themselves were listening to you."

Mahfouz had always written. As a little boy, he would copy European detective stories he had read, putting in his own, Egyptian characters. In his first novels, when he was fresh out of the ferment of the university, he took pharaonic settings and tried to work modern political issues into them. But gradually, studying Proust, invoking Hemingway but evoking Dickens, he developed a style suited to the streets of his city. The novel, as a form, was something new in Arabic. It dates back less than a century in this language of poetry and prophecy. Even the idea of "naturalism" was alien. But slowly, slowly, Egyptians began to find themselves in Mahfouz's books, grabbing them up with the fascination of villagers seeing for the first time their image emerge in a Polaroid photograph. Here was a man who understood them, in a new form they could understand.

To wander through the streets of Cairo is to be surrounded by the creations and re-creations of Mahfouz. Go to the entrance of Midaq Alley in the Khan Khalili and the air is dense with the smell of herbs, the dust of spices. The narrow street runs thick with merchants, pushcarts, peasants in from the delta. The corridor of sky directly overhead darkens as the sun goes down somewhere behind the minarets of Al Azhar. The human traffic in the street thins quickly. "The noises of daytime life had quieted now and those of the evening began to be heard, a whisper here and a whisper there," just as he wrote they would more than forty years ago. The original of the coffee-house he called Kirsha's is still in business near the entrance to the alley, the elaborate Arabic calligraphy crumbling from the walls, "light streaming from its electric lamps, their wires covered with flies." The old proprietor speaks through strings of mucus, monosyllabic, suspicious, half shouting above the hiss of the gas jet boiling a thick mud of coffee in a little pot of black-encrusted brass.

Midaq Alley, the novel that immortalized Kirsha's, is one of Mahfouz's best-known in the Arab world. The film, made and remade many times since the 1950s, is one of his most popular—in theaters, on television, on video, anywhere within the realm of the language. The characters of the alley have been spread not only across the screen but across this city on crude watercolor movie posters, where all movie-star skin is the color of jaundice, all lips the color of blood, and raised knives, smoking "shisha," the faces of sullen, violent husbands and supplicant wives are the constant caricature of the streets teeming beneath them.

For most of his life Mahfouz made little money from his books. He was forced to find jobs with the government, sometimes in the Ministry of Religious Affairs, more often in the state's film-production business. "I was an employee for thirty years, despite myself. I lived like a student all that time. The job during the day, writing at night." He was thirty-nine before he married. "I didn't have time for marriage; there was no room for family life." He was not very different, in the pattern of his life or in the details, from the characters he created.

In 1952, when Mahfouz was forty-one, he finished "Trilogy." In the same year, the long-awaited revolution finally came. Nasser "embodied all the dreams of those who went before him," Mahfouz remembers. "The old society which I used to criticize disappeared from existence." Or so he thought. He left off writing novels, and concentrated instead on film scripts. But the promises of the revolution faded quickly, as revolutionary promises almost always do, and popular movies were not the place to say what Mahfouz now needed to say. When his novels started to appear again at the end of the 1950s they were sparer, the style more compressed and unleavened by hope. "Heaven is any place where you live in dignity and peace," says a character in *Miramar*. "Hell is simply the opposite."

These were no longer vast books for and about the masses. Increasingly they were hard-edged novellas about the rising despair among Egypt's political and intellectual classes. Mahfouz's reading had embraced the existentialists and the French "new novel." His notions of democracy, freedom, dignity, even of despair were influenced by the world of ideas far beyond the confines of the Egyptian desert.

Yet his frame of reference is a creation, purely, of intellect. Mahfouz has been out of the country only twice in his life: once to Yemen for three days, and once to Yugoslavia for three days. The world he knows he knows only from reading and talking to others who have read and who have traveled, meeting them in coffeehouses, in weekly talks on boats, or in tea gardens by the river. *Chitchats by the Nile* is one of his (badly translated) titles, one of his own favorite books, and was specifically cited by the Nobel committee: "an example of Mahfouz's impressive novellas. Here metaphysical conversations are carried on in the borderland between reality and illusion."

It is just this borderland between a dissonant present reality and a world outside that is dimly remembered from secondary sources, and mostly imagined, that Mahfouz evokes in all his greatest books. And his complete familiarity with this territory may help explain, in part, the empathy he feels for the women in his writing.

When she first read Mahfouz's work, Anchor's Martha Levin couldn't understand—couldn't stand—the pervasive atmosphere of sexual repression, the matter-of-fact subjugation of long-suffering wives, sisters, daughters, maids. "I consider myself as a modern woman," she says, "and at first there is a sense of revulsion almost."

American women may blanch at the stilted mores of the world he writes about, but it is the straightforward sensuality and the deep, painful, violent sexual frustration of his Egypt—of Egypt—that Mahfouz captures and conveys, and that cuts into the nerve of the fundamentalists. No society is so fraught with confusion about sex. Virginity was, in the 1930s and 1940s, and still is today, the badge of gentility among girls of the petite bourgeoisie. It was also the commandment of their God. Little girls are regularly mutilated by self-taught barbers in the alleys of Cairo, their clitoris removed and placed on a piece of cotton like a baby tooth, proudly displayed to the parents. Men dictate the terms of desire, then are thwarted by the system they have created: forced by the rules of their society to remain celibate until they marry; unable to marry until they can buy and furnish an apartment; unable to do that, in many cases, until they are in their thirties. Frustration and anger breed a still greater desire for control and domination.

The first paragraph of the new translation of *Palace Walk* is a metaphor for Egypt, but also the literal reality of daily life, still, for many Egyptian women:

She woke at midnight. She always woke up then without having to rely on an alarm clock. A wish that had taken root in her awoke her with great accuracy. For a few moments she was not sure she was awake. Images from her dreams and perceptions mixed together in her mind. She was troubled by anxiety before opening her eyes, afraid sleep had deceived her. Shaking her head gently, she gazed at the total darkness of the room. There was no clue by which to judge the time. The street noise outside her room would continue until dawn. She could hear the babble of voices from the coffeehouses and bars, whether it was early evening, midnight or just before daybreak. She had no evidence to rely on except her intuition, like a conscious clock hand, and the silence encompassing the house, which revealed

that her husband had not yet rapped at the door and that the tip of his
stick had not yet struck against the steps of the staircase.

The key event in *Palace Walk* is the wife's daring decision to leave her house
to visit a mosque after a lifetime of virtual imprisonment. Yet, for all this, Mahfouz's women still feel and love and want, and build their lives, for better or
worse, on something like their own terms. His narratives are often chronicles of
seduction and the sorry fate of fallen women, who are in turn his most sympathetic creations. In *Midaq Alley* and *The Beginning and the End*, the heroines
become whores.

For the fundamentalists, who seethe with repression and codify it into a
world where women would not go out into the street without cloth over every
inch of their flesh, from the gauze over their eyes to the wool gloves on their
hands, the sensuality of Mahfouz's work—the idea of sensuality itself—is the
threat. They can watch *Flamingo Road* and *Dynasty* on television. They can see
German backpackers, their asses hanging out of cotton shorts, hiking across the
Tahrir bridge. And sometimes they are revolted, and sometimes they are attracted. But they are distant from all that. To write about *Egyptian* women who
might have sexual desires—mere blasphemy pales by comparison. And Mahfouz
has, in the eyes of the intolerant, this damnable ability to understand.

Faith, ideologies—"love, education, cleanliness, hope"—have been found wanting
in the Egypt of today. There is little left but a kind of endemic fatalism that resides,
permanently entrenched, just this side of despair. In his most recent writing, and in
his many interviews, Mahfouz forgets, rather matter-of-factly, the myths that the
West has built up to try to understand his country. Europe and the United States
most often have seen Egypt in the image of a single name: the decadence of King
Farouk, the dashing, dangerous, demagogic Colonel Nasser. Sadat's was the
strongest image of all. But, for Mahfouz, he was "a very strange character." Few
Egyptians mourned his loss. "When you look at Sadat you would think he was
really very insignificant and nothing good would come from him. But you would
have been wrong." Mahfouz publicly advocated peace with Israel as early as 1972,
when Egypt was too weak and too humiliated to admit how desperately it wanted
to end twenty-five years of fighting. His books were banned in much of the militant
Arab world, like Coca-Cola and Hertz Rent A Cars, tainted by compromise with
Zionism. But then Sadat embraced peace. Won a Nobel Prize for it. And decorated
Mahfouz as the great writer he had long since been recognized to be.

Mahfouz has the medal, alongside other tokens of esteem, in a little display case
next to the front door of his apartment. But his feelings about Sadat are mixed. On
the one hand, "we owe him two things: a successful war, and peace. And also a
trend toward democracy." But Mahfouz loathed Sadat for creating an "open-door"

economic policy that made Egypt's rich filthy rich and the poor increasingly desperate, their envy tempered only by the preoccupations of survival. And still the economy is left like a humiliated beggar waiting for the largess of the U.S.—more than $2 billion a year—to be stuffed in the pocket of a djellaba.

If you mention President Hosni Mubarak, Mahfouz speaks of him pleasantly. The air-force pilot who inherited Sadat's mantle was long derided in the coffeehouses as "La Vache Qui Rit," for his bland joviality and his bovine public presence. But Egypt has gotten used to him after eight years; he has given intellectuals more freedom than they enjoyed, certainly, under Nasser's token nod to liberty. Mubarak may be learning from his mistakes, "but it's like somebody being thirty feet under water—he can bring you up ten feet, but there are still twenty feet to go." Maybe there is nothing to do. Mahfouz has been through so many phases of hope and despair: "This is not the first time we have had troubles. There have been famines and plagues before. Perhaps we will have to go through others."

So, with the kind of comprehension that infuriates the true believers, and the easy humor that turns their eyes to incandescent hate, Mahfouz can be perfectly philosophical about the men who want him dead. Who is this fundamentalist preacher, this Omar Abdel Rahman, who languished in jail for his affronts to the government, and, perhaps indirectly, for his threats against Mahfouz? "Ah," says Mahfouz, nodding as he bends toward each word of the question, "he represents the disillusioned youths, the unemployed who think religion will have an answer for their problems." Mahfouz sits back and thinks for a moment. "And within the groups themselves they do help each other, finding jobs, and getting married. It gives them a sense of belonging and productivity—which only they enjoy in Egypt now—compared with other young people. It's a rejection of the corruption that surrounds them." ("I had been wrongly accused, and many people said that I should be killed," comes the remembered voice from *Miramar*.)

But corruption has been around so long. There have been so many crusades, so many causes. "Weren't you the ones who proclaimed the holy war?" a young soldier screams plaintively at a government official at the beginning of *Autumn Quail*, set during the bloody riots of 1952. "Yes," the anguished official replies. "That's why I'm standing here in the middle of nowhere."

The buses careen by in the square below. People leap on, stumble off. They never quite stop. The old man barely watches now from the second floor of the Ali Baba. He goes back to reading his paper. "There's nothing left for death to devour."

SALMAN RUSHDIE

···

RENDEZVOUS WITH RUSHDIE

by Martin Amis

DECEMBER 1990

Salman Rushdie, the author of a much-discussed novel called *The Satanic Verses,* is still with us. One feels the need to emphasize this fact: that he is still around. He is caught up in a trap or a travesty; he is condemned to enact his own fictional themes of exile, ostracism, disjuncture, personal reinvention; he occupies a kind of shadowland; but he is formidably alive. The Rushdie Debate has reached a choke point where no one seems to be able to speak naturally. In that sense the forces of humorlessness have already triumphed. Rushdie's life has been permanently distorted. I hereby assert, then, that his humanity is unimpaired and entire.

Direct encounters with the man remain infrequent, and tortuous. If you want to meet up with the Minotaur, you have to enter the labyrinth of his security arrangements. Yet various glimpses and sightings are always current among his friends: Rushdie, at midnight, proposing to recite the Complete Works of Bob Dylan; or watching the World Cup on television last summer (with his remorseless parodies of the sportscasters); or falling over while demonstrating an ambitiously low-slung version of the twist; or eating pizza and earnestly listening to bootleg Jimi Hendrix. Rushdie's situation is truly Manichaean, but he is neither a god nor a devil; he is just *a writer*—comical and protean, ironical and ardent. To bear this out, Rushdie has now produced a defiantly high-spirited and chivalrous novel, a children's book for adults called *Haroun and the Sea of Stories.* There are times when Rushdie's predicament feels like a meaningless divagation, a chaotic accident; there are other times when it feels rivetingly central and exemplary. Rushdie's friends, I imagine, think about him every day. But his writer friends, I suspect, think about him every half an hour. He is still with us. And we are with him.

"When I first heard the news, I thought, I'm a dead man. You know: That's it. One day. Two days." This interview took place at a Mystery Location; we had joined up via something that *Haroun* would call a P2C2E: a Process Too

Complicated to Explain. "At such moments you think all the corny things. You think about not being able to watch your children growing up. Not being able to do the work you want to do. Oddly it's those things that hurt more than the physical idea of being dead. In a way you can't grasp that reality."

Reality seemed to be generally elusive on that day, February 14, 1989—the day of Khomeini's *fatwa*. Even the sky, I remember, was preternaturally radiant. Rushdie first heard the news when a radio station rang him up—to ask for his response to it. "How do you feel about being sentenced to death by the ayatollah? What about a quote?" He managed the quote ("God knows what I said"), and then ran around the house drawing the curtains and shutting the shutters. Next, he sleepwalked through an interview for the CBS morning show, and proceeded to what would be his last public appearance: the memorial service for his close friend Bruce Chatwin.

The church was Greek Orthodox, somber, dusty, big-domed, and full of writers. Rushdie entered promptly with his wife, the American novelist Marianne Wiggins. "I was in shock," he now says. He looked excitable. We were all excitable. Saul Bellow calls it "event glamour." "Salman," I said, as we hugged (he likes to hug his friends, and never routinely, always meaningly), "we're *worried* about you." And he said, "*I'm* worried about me." The Rushdies sat down beside me and my wife. I had a shameful impulse to recommend all those nice empty pews at the far end of the church. Rushdie kept glancing over his shoulder: representatives of the press were being kept at bay by his agent, Gillon Aitken. "Salman!" called out Paul Theroux, boyishly. "Next week we'll be back here for you!"

Appropriately, the service was a torment, a torment in its own right, with much incomprehensible yodeling and entreating. I found that my thoughts were all mildly but stubbornly blasphemous. The robed clerics waved their fuming caskets in the air, like Greek waiters removing incendiary ashtrays. This, I concluded, was Bruce Chatwin's last joke on his friends and loved ones: his heterodox theism had finally homed in on a religion that no one he knew could understand or respond to. We sat down and stood up, stood up and sat down, trying not to subvert with sigh or yawn the dull theater of an alien faith: an immortality system, in other words, and therefore inevitably dull, alien, theatrical. When it was over, Salman and Marianne ducked past the waiting journalists and were driven off in a friend's limousine. Rushdie would spend the day searching for his son, Zafar (who is now eleven)—searching too, I suppose, for a way to say good-bye to him, as he prepared to take up his new life.

I briefly attended the post-service reception. In normal circumstances we would have taken the chance to air our preoccupation with the mourned friend. But no one was thinking and talking about Bruce. Everyone was thinking and talking about Salman: his danger, his drastic elevation. As I went home I did about half a dozen things that Salman Rushdie was no longer free to do. I visited a bookshop, a toyshop, a snack bar; I went home. On the way I bought an evening paper. Its banner headline read: EXECUTE RUSHDIE ORDERS THE AYATOLLAH. Salman had disappeared into the world of block caps. He had vanished into the front page.

His case is of course unique. It is an embarrassment of uniquenesses. The terms of the *fatwa* (which was, at once, a death sentence and a life sentence); the size of the bounty (three times the reputed fee for perpetrating the Lockerbie crash); the nature of the exile, which removes the novelist both from his subject (society) and from his object (sober literary consideration): in his own phrase, Rushdie is firmly "handcuffed to history." His uniqueness is the measure of his isolation. Perhaps, too, it is the measure of his stoicism. Because no one else— certainly no other writer—could have survived so well.

I often tell him this. I often tell him that if the Rushdie Affair were, for instance, the Amis Affair, then I would, by now, be a tearful and tranquilized three-hundred-pounder, with no eyelashes or nostril hairs, and covered in blotches and burns from various misadventures with the syringe and the crack pipe. He has gained a little weight ("no exercise") and has resumed a very moderate cigarette habit; for a while he developed a kind of stress asthma. But Rushdie is unchanged: the rosy complexion, the lateral crinkle in his upper lip when he smiles (which gives an impression of babyishly short incisors), the eyes so exotically hooded that he has long foreseen minor surgery to prevent the lids from engulfing the irises. His urgently humorous presence is undiminished, undiluted. Sometimes, when you call him, his "Oh, I'm fine" lacks total conviction. Otherwise, he is a miracle of equanimity.

How is this? Unquestionably Rushdie has a great deal of natural ballast. He knows about exile, its deracinations, its surprising opportunities for expansion, how it can make you feel both naked and invisible, as in a dream. There has always been something Olympian about Salman Rushdie. His belief in his own powers, however (unlike other kinds of belief), is not monolithic and therefore precarious. It is agile, capricious, and droll. The first time I met him, seven years ago, he mentioned to me that he had recently played in a football match in Finland for a World Writers' Eleven.

"Really?" I said. "How did you do?" I expected the usual kind of comedy (sprained ankle, heart attack, incompetence, disgrace). But I was given another kind of comedy, out of left field.

He said, "I uh, scored a hat trick, actually."

"You're kidding. I suppose you just stuck your leg out. You scrambled them home."

"Goal number one was a first-time hip-high volley from twenty yards out.

For the second, I beat two men at the edge of the box and curled the ball into the top corner with the outside of my left foot."

"And the third goal, Salman? A tap-in. A fluke."

"No. The third goal was a *power header*."

Even if you don't know the game, you'll probably get the idea. This is Rushdie's style. He is always daring you to decide whether or not to take him literally.

Well, certain contemporary forces have made *their* decision, and they have duly arrived at a literalist's verdict: eternal remainderdom. Rushdie can take the weight of the anathema, and the vastly generalized animus, I think, because he has long been in training for it. He has skirmished with world leaders before, after all: in *Shame* with General Zia (the book was of course banned in Pakistan), and in *Midnight's Children* with Mrs. Gandhi (who sued him for libel). But then came the intensive training, which began on September 26, 1988, the day *The Satanic Verses* was published. Bannings and burnings, petitions and demonstrations, rioting in Islamabad (five killed), rioting in Kashmir (one killed, one hundred injured). Rushdie maintained at the time that these deaths were "not on [his] conscience"; but by this stage he was feeling, he says, "completely horrible. It was the most shocking thing—until the other most shocking thing." The riots took place on consecutive days. On the third day the *fatwa* was announced. Rushdie knew by then that his book had raised mortal questions. He had no choice; he was obliged to become world-historical.

"At first, I found it more or less impossible to switch off, to turn away. Before the ayatollah made his move, I saw myself as being part of a debate. Now the debate went on, but I was excluded from it."

Another dreamlike state: Rushdie was a spectator (not an advocate, not even a witness) at his own capital trial. And he found it was a full-time job keeping abreast of developments. His day began with *Breakfast News* at 6:30 and ended with *Newsnight* at 10:45. At that point the Rushdie story was at least three pages deep in every national newspaper; and for odd moments in between there was always the *Bradford Telegraph and Argus,* the South African *Weekly Mail,* the *Osservatore Romano,* the *Salzburg Kronen Zeitung, Al Ahram, Al-Noor,* the *Muslim Voice,* and *India Today.* Everywhere he looked he saw torched hardbacks and writhing mustaches.

Question: What's got long blond hair, big tits, and lives in an igloo in Iceland? Answer: Salman Rushdie . . . Such jokes, current in every pub and at every bus stop, were relayed to Rushdie by his Special Branch bodyguards; he also became a staple for TV comedians, as a type for the hunted, the marked, the evanescent. Rushdie found some Rushdie jokes funnier than others. But what disturbed him was the sudden promiscuity of his fame. "I kept thinking, What the hell am I *doing* here? What the hell am I doing in a TV sitcom? What the hell am I doing in the Jasper Carrot show?"

In a sense, though, the *fatwa* itself is a Rushdie joke. The blasphemy issue is at least debatable (and Rushdie wants to continue that debate); but what can you make of Khomeini's babblings, which portrayed Rushdie as a literary dog of war, hired by world Jewry to soften up Islam for a neo-imperialist blitzkrieg? Now that really *is* funny. When you write, when you try to instruct and entertain, you want the world to sit up and take notice. But not literally. And here on the evening news are the pulsing flash points on the color-coded world map, Bombay, Berkeley, Brussels, riot, fire, and murder. What's the story? You are the story. Your book is the story. And now another chapter of crossed lines, ungot ironies, atrocious misunderstandings.

To scrutinize him is to jeopardize him, but a little can be said about the way he lives now. He lives like a secret agent; he is both nomad and recluse. "An average day? I don't have average days, because there's always the possibility of having to move. I read a lot. I talk on the telephone a lot—two or three hours a day. I play computer games. Chess. Super Mario. I am a *master* of Super Marios I *and* II. Otherwise I do what I'd do anyway. I start work at 10:30, I never eat lunch, and I knock off around four." A writer is, on the whole, most alive when alone. You can then get on with the business of imagining other people. But there is normally a gregarious murmur behind the solitude—a murmur which Rushdie no longer hears. "The strange part is not being able to go out in the evening. Or indeed in the afternoon. Or in the morning. To clear your head out."

It comes as no surprise to learn that a death sentence *doesn't* concentrate the mind wonderfully. *Haroun and the Sea of Stories* is the result of unprecedented struggle. "The distractions were internal rather than external. When I write, I sink into the bit of myself where the novel comes from. But I had to fight my way past all this other stuff: the crisis. And by the time I got there I'd be wrecked." *Haroun* began as a series of bedtime stories which Rushdie told to his son, Zafar—"or bath-time stories. He would lie in the bath and listen, or sit wrapped in towels." When Rushdie was close to finishing *The Satanic Verses,* Zafar made his father promise to forget about grown-ups for a while and write a book for children. "I couldn't have written a grown-up novel. I didn't have the distance, the calm. I had to keep this promise to Zafar because it was the only thing I *could* keep to him. That was the whip I used to beat myself. It gave me the energy to do something as weird as write a fairy story in the middle of a nightmare. There's no more absolute thing than a promise to your child. You can't break it."

The new book can and will be read as a fantastical commentary on the author's situation. Such a reading is no doubt naïve, but purity of literary response is another privilege that Rushdie must resign himself to losing—for now. *All* his books suddenly seem to predict and explore his present situation, and parts of

The Satanic Verses are almost vulgarly prescient ("Your blasphemy, Salman, can't be forgiven. . . . To set your words against the Words of God . . ."). In any case *Haroun* is a minor classic of passionate invention. The change in genre is after all quite seamless: what is "magical realism" but the wishful laxity of a child's imagination? Here are the stories that Rushdie wanted to tell his child. More than that, though, you also see the child in Rushdie—his delight, his mischief, his innocence, his eager heart.

Asked if he has a *plan* for the future, Rushdie says, "A *plan*. Well, 'plan' would be a rather glorified word for it." His survival, like his capacity for hope, will continue to be a matter of daily improvisation. From time to time one hears a statement from Teheran along the following lines: that if Rushdie (a) admits he was wrong, (b) renounces the paperback, (c) recalls and pulps the hardback, (d) makes extensive reparations, and (e) becomes a devout Muslim, it *still* won't be enough. What will be enough? The tone of the challenge makes one think of the lovelorn, the wounded adolescent. It could almost be a less benign and forgiving Haroun. Fill the ocean with your tears. Cry me a river.

Once Rushdie got going on his fairy story, all the difficulties fell away. He wrote the first draft in two and a half months; he wrote the second in two weeks—"at enormous speed. A chapter a day." The breakthrough was unrelated to any change in circumstance. It had to do with the framing of the first sentence, "which seemed to contain a lot of energy. It was like a tuning fork." And Rushdie quotes it: "There was once, in the country of Alifbay, a sad city, the saddest of cities, a city so ruinously sad that it had forgotten its name."

But the reader is already sad, already moved and haunted, by the book's dedication (an acrostic), which refers to enforced distance, to a sense of thwarted homing, and to a lost time that no Happy Ending can redress:

> **Z** embla, Zenda, Xanadu:
> **A** ll our dream-worlds may come true.
> **F** airy lands are fearsome too.
> **A** s I wander far from view
> **R** ead, and bring me home to you.

SHORT TAKES

....

WILLA CATHER

WILLA, TRUMAN. TRUMAN, WILLA

by *Truman Capote*

NOVEMBER 2006

On August 24, 1984, the day before his death—at 59, from a probable overdose of pills—Truman Capote started this reminiscence as an early birthday gift for his friend Joanne Carson. The unfinished manuscript, reproduced here, [was] auctioned at Bonhams, in New York, on November 9, 2006.

REMEMBERING WILLA CATHER

All of my relatives are Southern, either from New Orleans or the rural regions of Alabama. At least 40 of the men, and possibly more, died during the Civil War, including my great-grandfather.

Long ago, when I was 10 or thereabouts, I became interested in these fallen soldiers because I read a large collection of their battlefield letters that our family had managed to keep. I was already interested in writing (in fact, had published small essays and stories in *Scholastic* magazine), and I decided to write an historical book based on the letters of these Confederate heroes.

Troubles interfered, and it was not until eight years later, when I was barely surviving as a very young journalist living in New York, that the subject of my Civil War kinfolk revived. Of course a great lot of research was necessary; the place I chose to do this research was the New York Society Library.

For several reasons. One being that it was winter, and this particular place, warm and clean and situated just off Park Avenue, provided a cozy haven the whole day long. Also, perhaps because of its location, the staff and clientele were a comfort in themselves: a bunch of upper-class, well-mannered literati. Some of the customers I saw frequently at the Library were more than that. Especially the blue-eyed lady.

Her eyes were the pale blue of a prairie dawn on a clear day. Also, there was something wholesome and countrified about her face, and it was not just an absence of cosmetics. She was of ordinary height and of a solid but not overly solid shape. Her clothing was composed of an unusual but somehow attractive combination of materials. She wore low-heeled shoes and thick stockings and a handsome turquoise necklace that went well with her soft tweed suits. Her hair was black and white and crisply, almost mannishly cut. The surprising, dominant factor was a beautiful sable coat which she almost never took off.

It was a good thing she had it on the day of the storm. When I left the library around four o'clock it looked as though the North Pole had moved to New York. Fist-sized snowballs pummeled the air.

The blue-eyed lady wearing the rich sable coat was standing at the curb. She was trying to hail a taxi. I decided to help her. But there were no taxis in view—indeed, very little traffic.

I said: "Maybe all the drivers have gone home."

"It doesn't matter. I live not too far from here." Her deep soft voice drifted toward me through the heavy snow.

So I asked: "Then may I walk you home?"

She smiled. We walked together along Madison Avenue until we reached a Longchamps restaurant. She said: "I could use a cup of tea. Could you?" I said yes. But once we were settled at a table, I ordered a double martini. She laughed and asked if I was old enough to drink.

Whereupon I told her all about myself. My age. The fact I was born in New Orleans, and that I was an aspiring writer.

Really? What writers did I admire? (Obviously she was not a New Yorker: she had a Western accent.)

"Flaubert. Turgenev. Proust. Charles Dickens. E. M. Forster. Conan Doyle. Maupassant—"

She laughed. "Well. You certainly are varied. Except. Aren't there any American writers you care for?"

"Like who?"

She didn't hesitate. "Sarah Orne Jewett. Edith Wharton—"

"Miss Jewett wrote one good book: *The Country of the Pointed Firs*. And Edith Wharton wrote one good book: *The House of Mirth*. But. I like Henry James. Mark Twain. Melville. And I love Willa Cather. *My Antonia. Death Comes for the Archbishop*. Have you ever read her two marvelous novellas—*A Lost Lady* and *My Mortal Enemy*?"

"Yes." She sipped her tea, and put the cup down with a slightly nervous gesture. She seemed to be turning something over in her mind. "I ought to tell you—" She paused; then, in a rushing voice, more or less whispered: "I wrote those books."

I was stunned. How could I have been so stupid? I had a photograph of her in my bedroom. Of course she was Willa Cather! Those flawless sky-like eyes. The bobbed hair; the square face with the firm chin. I hovered between laughter and tears. There was no living person I would rather have met; no one who could so have impressed me—not Garbo or Ghandi [*sic*] or Einstein or Churchill or Stalin. Nobody. She apparently realized that, and we were both left speechless. I swallowed my double martini in one gulp.

But soon we were on the street again. We trudged through the snow until we arrived at an expensive, old-fashioned address on Park Avenue. She said: "Well. Here is where I live"; then suddenly added: "If you're free for dinner on Thursday, I'll expect you at seven o'clock. And please bring some of your writing—I'd like to read it."

Yes, I was thrilled. I bought a new suit, and retyped three of my short stories. And, come Thursday, I was on her doorstep promptly at seven.

I was still amazed to think that Willa Cather wore sable coats and occupied a Park Avenue apartment. (I had always imagined her as living on a quiet street in Red Cloud, Nebraska.) The apartment did not have many rooms, but they were large rooms which she shared with a lifelong companion, someone her own size and age, a discreetly elegant woman named Edith Lewis.

Miss Cather and Miss Lewis were so alike one could be certain they had decorated the apartment together. There were flowers everywhere—masses of winter lilac, peonies, and lavender-colored roses. Beautifully bound books lined all walls of the living room.

The details of the dinner party are lost to posterity, but in 1967 Capote remembered Cather as "one of my first intellectual friends."

JAMEſ BALDWIN

....

WHY BALDWIN STILL MATTERS

by Jacqueline Woodson

MAY 2016

When James Baldwin died in December of 1987, I was 24 years old, living in a neighborhood jokingly referred to as Dyke Slope because of the high concentration of lesbians in one area. Although we were in the harrowing throes of Reaganism and the devastating H.I.V.-AIDS epidemic, gay men and their allies had come together to loudly fight the silence and shame surrounding the disease. And in our neighborhood, a struggling writer could still buy a dozen eggs for less than a dollar. It was in the energy of this moment that I reread *Giovanni's Room*, Baldwin's groundbreaking novel—published 60 years ago this fall—that explored both gay and bisexual relationships with subtlety and what I'd come to think of as Baldwin Brilliance. By 1987, I had known James Baldwin for 11 years, first meeting him in seventh grade when his novel *If Beale Street Could Talk* showed up in my classroom. The ordinary black lives he brought to the page were revelatory. My memory of this first meeting is one of awe, my mouth slightly opened, at once thrilled and terrified by the innocence and brutality of the love between two black teenagers in Harlem.

For many in the worlds I moved in—both that of my childhood and young adulthood—Baldwin was not yet a household name. We saw him at the edges of black-and-white videos of the civil-rights movement, heard his name lumped together with other "gay" writers—Lorde, Capote, Williams, Cather, Baldwin . . . And when the subject of Ebonics resurfaced nearly 10 years after his death, we turned back to his essays from the 60s and realized he had been talking about sexuality, language, race, and class long before many of us were born. Still, as a young writer what I had been most fascinated by were the "chances" Baldwin took—his ferocity, his fearlessness. (Decades later, these attributes still resonate as there seems to be a Baldwin revival happening right now. Carl Hancock Rux recently staged his mesmerizing *Stranger on Earth*, imagining a meeting between Baldwin and vocalist Dinah Washington. Educators are battling to get Baldwin back on school curricula. Scholars and writers are rallying around his legacy. His interviews and quotes are flooding social media.)

After Baldwin's death, I lay in bed rereading (by then I had lost count of how many times) *Giovanni's Room*, a tiny volume I'd move with me from my mother's house to college to my first apartment. We were years away from fighting for marriage equality, a struggle as foreign to me at the time as trans rights or Black Lives Matter. As Dyke Slope became Park Slope again and the price of rent skyrocketed, as thousands (including Liberace and Michael Bennett) died from H.I.V.-related illnesses, as members of ACT UP fought hard to get the F.D.A. to approve other drugs besides AZT, so many of us were simply trying to survive. In the midst of this, I lost a source of strength and light: Baldwin died from stomach cancer at the age of 63.

Having become intrigued by everything he wrote, I moved on to finding pictures and films about him. I knew well the gapped-toothed smile sometimes veiled over by cigarette smoke. I knew the eternal cigarette dangling almost absently between his fore and middle finger. I knew the head thrown back in laughter, the deeply furrowed brow, the rage behind the poetically nuanced answers he gave to deeply uninformed questions about race, economic class, sexuality. I believed I would one day meet him, that we would sit at a café in France (a place I had not yet traveled to) and discuss the politics of queerness, art, our shared Blackness.

When the radio announced Baldwin's death, I was standing in my kitchen in Brooklyn. I can lie and say I was making spaghetti but I don't remember much more than standing there in shock thinking, "But we were supposed to meet one day." My intimate relationship with Baldwin had been one-sided. I knew friends who had studied with him. Others who had shared meals with him. He was my six degrees of separation, my first celebrity crush. I wanted his candor, self-assuredness. I tried smoking but it didn't stick. Still, I, like so many writers of color I know, now believe that we're writing because Baldwin wrote, that history repeats itself and continues to need its witnesses.

ROGER ∫TRAU∫

··

ROGER AND ME

by Tom Wolfe

SEPTEMBER 1996

When I first met Roger Straus, in 1965, he and his wife, Dorothea, lived in a town house on Manhattan's town-house street of dreams, East 70th, from which he drove to his publishing house each morning in a tan Mercedes-Benz convertible. In the springtime he favored tan gabardine suits that went with the car, and Sea Island cotton shirts open at the throat to allow his silk ascots to debouch. His destination was the firm of Farrar, Straus & Giroux, which he had founded in 1946, when he was still in his 20s, at the unlikely address of 19 Union Square West, a small, cramped office building with two exhausted automatic elevators.

This was long before the reformation and restoration of Union Square in the 1980s, and Mr. Roger Straus's daily arrival was an event. As he pulled up to No. 19 in his Mercedes convertible, the top down, his chin up, his leonine hair swept back, his ascot debouching, the square's lurid carnival of ghetto blasters, angel-dust deals, methadone deprivation, and felonious assaults came to a momentary but deferential halt. I was there and can attest to it.

Roger speaks with what is known as a North Shore drawl. His accent sounds like a hybrid of Nelson Rockefeller's, Robert Dowling's, and Huntington Hartford's. His favorite word is maaahhhhhhhhhhhhhhhhhhhhhhhvelous, which he manages to make at least 31 letters long, and he is one of those people who can get away with calling grown men "dear boy" and women of any age "baby." Thanks to his voice, his high style, his flair, and his background—he is of the Macy's Strauses and the copper-and-newspaper Guggenheims—there were those who assumed that here was merely a rich young man dabbling in publishing. In fact, he proved to be not only the most seriously literary of all the industry's major publishers but also, in the long run, the most astute businessman. One of the things he found especially marvelous, as he never tired of reminding those dear boys, his competitors, was the fact that Farrar, Straus & Giroux was paying $2.75 a square foot on Union Square while they were paying 10 to 20 times that uptown in the East 40s, 50s, and 60s. Over the next two decades, as it turned out, many of them migrated downtown to join him in Low Rent land. Roger, meantime, was building Farrar, Straus up into the most durable of all the big independent publishing houses. It was the very last of the breed when he finally sold a controlling interest to the von Holtzbrinck publishing group in 1994. He remains as publisher.

Roger's sweetest victories, however, have been literary. His interests are worldwide, and his taste and his eye have been astonishing. Starting in 1978 with Isaac Bashevis Singer—who was signed up when he was still writing short stories in Yiddish for the *Jewish Daily Forward*—Farrar, Straus & Giroux authors have won 10 of the last 18 Nobel Prizes for literature. Writers so little known in the United States that publishing them here can only be described as an act of literary faith (such as Elias Canetti of Bulgaria, Wole Soyinka of Nigeria, and Camilo José Cela of Spain) had been Roger's authors for years when they won their Nobels. Stockholm's Grand Hôtel keeps two suites booked for Mr. Roger Straus the second week of every December, one for him and one for his Nobel perennial. This past December they were occupied by Roger and by Seamus Heaney, one of three Farrar, Straus poets (Joseph Brodsky and Derek Walcott are the others) who have been Nobel laureates over the past nine years. Roger Straus's is such a familiar face to Swedish television viewers that strangers greet him on the street believing him to be the American "minister of culture."

In fact, he has no title, unless there exists one for being the most illustrious and colorful American publisher of the past half-century. Believe me, Roger, dear boy, it's been marvelous. Happy 50th anniversary.

WARD JUST

....

BEAU JUST

by David Halberstam

MAY 1997

Ward Just is the bane of his better-behaved, allegedly healthier friends. He smokes cigarettes, Camels, a lot of them, and drinks hard liquor instead of white wine, and stays up late talking and arguing with his pals. The cigarettes seem particularly offensive. "Four packs a day?" I ask. "Only two," he answers. There is a pause. "Two?" I repeat in obvious disbelief. "Honestly," he says somewhat apologetically, "only two . . . it just seems like four." There has always been a touch of the Hemingway hero to him, and not only because Hemingway was his first literary role model; Just is one of those men, innately charming and charismatic, that other men want to be like. He may also be one of our best and yet least-appreciated novelists. No one, I think, writes better about the lives of modern politicians. "The best American novelist writing about politics since Henry James," notes Russell Baker. Just's books, among them now 11 novels and three collections of short stories, are consistently well reviewed, yet his audience is more a cult than a mass following—an irony, considering that his novels are, in both form and content, distinctly old-fashioned rather than postmodernist.

By working and reworking a specific piece of fictional territory, Just has created what might be called Just Country. He first surveyed it as a young journalist newly arrived in Washington with impeccable midwestern, Establishment lineage (if that is not a contradiction in terms) during the transition from the Eisenhower to the Kennedy years; then he was struck by the contrast between the Kennedy people, so coolly arrogant and eager to rule not just America but also the world, and the seemingly doddering Eisenhower people, most of them older businessmen, who could hardly wait to return to the bland comforts of the Midwest.

Just Country is located in mid-20th-century Washington. It has tended to be populated by extremely successful men, at once self-absorbed and coldhearted, whose personal lives exist in inverse proportion to their careers. Over the years the women in Just Country have become far more interesting—and significantly more likable—than the men. Bright, attractive, and usually wellborn, they are poorly loved, and they have become increasingly alienated, not just from their men but also from the norms and purposes of the government.

Just himself is one of those rare journalists who did exactly the right thing in leaving nonfiction for fiction. His decision to switch was greatly facilitated by a tour of Vietnam for *The Washington Post*. At the newspaper his stories were considered by his peers to be among the best-written dispatches of that war, but the longer he stayed in Vietnam the emptier he felt as a journalist. His transition to novelist was expedited by the events of June 6, 1966 (6/6/66: "Death numbers—four sixes"), when he went on a long-range patrol with a reinforced platoon of the 101st Airborne in the Central Highlands. It was mauled by a beefed-up company of N.V.A. regulars. About a dozen Americans were killed, and twice as many were wounded. A grenade landed a few feet from Just, literally lifting him off the ground. He was badly wounded, and 38 pieces of shrapnel were later taken out of his arm, legs, back, and head. Though as a civilian he had priority for any medevac, he gained the admiration of his colleagues both in the military and in the press corps by refusing to be airlifted out until all the wounded grunts had gone first.

After recovering at two hospitals, he soon found himself back in Washington at a dinner party at the house of Robert McNamara. That night, he had been warned in advance, his principal assignment was to tell everyone what Vietnam was *really* like. Besides the host, many of Washington's greats were there—journalist Joe Alsop and other Kennedy-era stars. "The only thing I remember about the night was that I did not say a single word," he notes. The dinner party confirmed his decision to leave reporting—this surreal world he was a part of could be described only in fiction, he felt. Since then he has lived a life of fierce commitment to his work. Zestful and gregarious, he is always up in the morning before anyone else and writing—no matter how late he was up the night before. He is now 13 years into his third marriage, to Sarah Catchpole; there are three children from the earlier marriages.

Just's writing seems year by year to derive less from Hemingway, and increasingly—because of the nuances it portrays in class, ambition, gender, and disappointment—to evoke memories of Fitzgerald, O'Hara, and even Marquand. His newest book, *Echo House*, is one of his most ambitious, telling of three generations of a Washington power-brokering family, from the pre-F.D.R. to the post-Reagan era. These are people who operate largely in the shadows, and inevitably their personal lives are a series of shipwrecks. An advance review in *Publishers Weekly* has called it "a political novel par excellence," noting that the writing has "weight, texture and subtlety, gravity, intelligence and wit." To me it is nothing less than vintage Just.

TONI MORRISON

....

LAUREATE OF DREAMS

by John Leonard

DECEMBER 2003

"Watch out for her," Denver told her ghostly sister about their mother in *Beloved:* "she can give you dreams." Giving us dreams has been Toni Morrison's business from the beginning, from Not Doctor Street and No Mercy Hospital and maple-syrup men with long-distance eyes to blind slaves, baby ghosts, black Medeas, and convent women shot like deer. *Love,* her new book from Knopf, is more such brilliant blues, in the echo chamber of a seashell. Mermaids sing of a beach resort on the Middle Atlantic coast where black people used to go to dance; of the glad-handed owner, "an ordinary man ripped, like the rest of us, by wrath and love," who traded favors with the local white pols to keep his hotel open from the Great Depression through the civil-rights era, even as he was enjoying too many women not at all wisely, including a child bride he married when she was only 11 years old; and of those antiphonal voices who were left behind in the haunted present to hate one another, dispute his will, and construe the meaning of his poisoned-foxglove passing. But like every other stealthy Morrison novel, *Love* has closets and cellars, bolt-holes and trapdoors and card tricks. More than "just another story to scare wicked females and correct unruly children," it is also a Greco-Freudian fairy tale about winged hands and webbed feet, bestiality and incest. Yet again, she gives us dreams.

ISHMAEL BEAH

THE WITNESS

by Dave Eggers

JULY 2007

It started, for a lot of readers, with that picture on the back cover of *A Long Way Gone.* That smile, good God! Has there ever been a more charming picture of anyone, let alone a young man who has seen the carnage and deprivation that Ishmael Beah has seen? But whatever brought readers to the book—the picture, the reviews, word of mouth, or even Starbucks [which sold thousands of copies of the memoir]—he finally brought the experiences of child soldiers to mainstream America. For years the world had known of the existence of child soldiers in Africa—in Uganda, the Congos, Liberia, Sudan—and around the world. But it took Beah's book, written while he was a student at Oberlin, to bring to readers the reality of the civil war in Sierra Leone, the absolutely wretched lives of child soldiers, and, most crucially, their humanity and capacity for recovery. The book is raw, run through with melancholy, but so honest and longing that hundreds of thousands have read it, and it's made Beah, now 26, arguably the most read African writer in contemporary literature. Beah's success, and that of other young and brilliant writers with close African ties—including Uzodinma Iweala, Dinaw Mengestu, Chris Abani, and Chimamanda Ngozi Adichie—means nothing less than a golden age of literature from the continent.

ROBERT HARRIS

....

by Nick Hornby

FEBRUARY 2012

The man who would one day become my sister's husband ticked all the right boxes, when I first met him. He was clearly smart. He looked as though he would prefer to spend the evening in an expensive but unpretentious London restaurant than in a crack house. He was warm, friendly, funny. If there was one tiny thing that might give a concerned brother pause for thought, it was the enormous bookshelf given over more or less entirely to books about the Third Reich: there were more swastikas in his one-bedroom Shepherd's Bush flat than in the whole of occupied France. But what was a brother supposed to do? It wasn't as though he was hiding them from my sister. She'd presumably seen them. I decided not to interfere. A few years later, in 1992, his first novel, *Fatherland*, was published, to enormous acclaim and grotesque international success, and it all started to make sense.

Before anyone becomes alarmed, it turned out that he had easily as many books about Churchill and the Allies, and Robert, 54, probably knows as much about World War II as anyone under the age of 80. His knowledge is so extensive that his analogies are a running joke in the family: a shortage of biscuits for his cheese may remind him inescapably of the Siege of Leningrad; a sunny day on the beach, of Montgomery's North African campaign. But then he started turning himself into an expert on other, equally vast subjects, and it became harder (although not, thankfully, impossible) to mock him for his eccentricities. Research for his 2003 novel, *Pompeii*, turned into an obsession with the Roman Empire and carried on into two novels of a planned trilogy about Cicero; for his terrific new thriller, *The Fear Index*, he has got to grips with the incomprehensible mechanics of the global market. There's no contradiction in the choice of subject matter, by the way. Both *The Fear Index* and the Cicero novels are about the world we live in now.

One of Harris's enormous strengths as a writer is that he makes the most unpromisingly complicated material accessible and compelling. Sooner or later, someone will recognize that he is quietly and quickly racking up a backlist that bears comparison to the work of, say, H. G. Wells, who also wrote a lot of genre fiction, and whose work also contained a political dimension. (Robert was the political editor of *The Observer* newspaper, and was with Tony Blair on the night he was elected in 1997. *The Ghost*—turned into the film *The Ghost Writer,* by Roman Polanski—will turn out to be one of the best and most astute books about the Blair years.)

How does one compete with a brother-in-law like this? I don't, and I don't have to, although I'm extremely glad that I don't write thrillers—our conversations about our work might be extremely painful if I did. I know, however, that despite his enormous success, and the benefits that have come from it, he writes because he's a writer and has no choice: he has a curiosity about the world and how it works, and that won't go away, no matter how many copies he sells.

JUDY BLUME

by Meg Wolitzer

JUNE 2015

Write what you know, novelists are often advised, and Judy Blume knew many things when she wrote the books that proved so influential and iconic that their author eventually became a question on *Jeopardy!*, and the inspiration for an episode of *South Park* and a *Saturday Night Live* skit, not to mention a hero and sentimental favorite of generations of readers. Among those things is that growing up is a time of powerful, dramatic occurrences. It's been more than 45 years since Blume's first book was published, but she is still writing what she knows, and still turning to the early years for that knowledge. Except this time, with *In the Unlikely Event,* instead of looking inward, examining the emotional upheaval evoked by bodily changes and new physical sensations, Judy Blume is looking outward. Or, more to the point, upward.

In the early 1950s, when Blume was a teenager in Elizabeth, New Jersey, three airplanes crashed in her town within 58 days, creating fear, anxiety, and bewilderment. But though Blume grew up amidst these events, it took her more than half a century to think about turning them into a book. It wasn't until 2009, while she was listening to the writer Rachel Kushner talk about stories her mother had told of growing up in Cuba in the 1950s, that Blume envisioned her own 1950s novel. It came to her in an instant, with various characters and plots. Blume spent five years on her story, which blends real-life facts with fiction. While the book is multigenerational, it's not at all surprising that the character at its heart is a 15-year-old girl.

Many of us, having long left behind girlhood and adolescence in a big, Love's Fresh Lemon–scented puddle of training bras and clogs, still remember with nostalgic pleasure and gratitude Blume's classic works, which mirrored and illuminated our own experiences. So, with this new book—her first adult novel in 17 years—is Blume, as we might hope, beginning a late-life fiction whirlwind? "I can't imagine writing another novel," she says. "Of course I said the same thing after *Summer Sisters.* I meant it then. But I think I mean it more now. I feel good about that," she adds. "I feel *elated* about that. And at 77 I think that's O.K."

WOLE ʃOYINKA

THE LITERARY LION

By Nadine Gordimer

JULY 2007

Albert Camus wrote, "One either serves the whole of man or one does not serve him at all. And if man needs bread and justice, and if what has to be done must be done to serve this need, he also needs pure beauty which is the bread of his heart," and so Camus called for "courage in one's life and talent in one's work." Wole Soyinka. This great Nigerian writer has in his writings and in the conduct of his life served the whole of humankind. He endured imprisonment in his dedication to the fight for bread and justice, and his works attain the pure beauty of imaginative power that fulfills that other hungry need, of the spirit. He has "courage in his life and talent in his work." In Soyinka's fearless searching of human values, which are the deep integument of even our most lyrical poetry, prose, and whatever modes of written-word-created expression we devise, he never takes the easy way, never shirks the lifetime commitment to write as well as he can. In every new work he zestfully masters the challenge that without writing as well as we can, without using the infinite and unique possibilities of the written word, we shall not deserve the great responsibility of our talent, the manifold sensibilities of the lives of our people which cannot be captured in flipped images and can't be heard in the hullabaloo of mobile-phone chatter. Bread, justice, and the bread of the heart—which is the beauty of literature, the written word—Wole Soyinka fulfills all these.

SONNY MEHTA

....

by Dave Eggers

OCTOBER 2015

His father was a diplomat, representing the newly independent nation of India, and Sonny Mehta grew up all over the world. When he was six, the family moved to Prague. When he was eight, they lived in New York. When he was nine, it was Nepal. A few years later, Geneva. For a peripatetic child, it would make sense that books became his most constant and reliable companions.

"It's really a cliché, isn't it?," Mehta says.

After Cambridge, he settled in London, eventually creating two small publishing houses, Paladin, then Picador, both focusing on paperbacks. When Robert Gottlieb, the editor of Knopf, the celebrated American publishing house, was leaving to edit *The New Yorker,* he recommended that Mehta succeed him.

"I was the least likely choice," Mehta says. "I was from somewhere else. Then all of a sudden I was here, in New York. With one suitcase."

The transition wasn't smooth. Gottlieb had had a brilliant run—he'd edited Toni Morrison and Joseph Heller and John Cheever, to name a few. Replacing him would have been difficult for anyone. "I was walking into a storm," Mehta says. "If you had taken bets on how long I'd survive, it wouldn't have been very long. To be here 28 years later—I'm as surprised as anyone."

He arrived shortly before Knopf's 75th anniversary. This year marks the company's 100th. Between then and now there have been a series of existential threats to the publishing business: radio, film, television, the Internet, the rise and fall of the big chains, Amazon. Knopf has survived them all and weathered an almost comical series of acquisitions and mergers: Random House bought the company in 1960; 20 years later, Random House was sold to Advance Publications (owner of Condé Nast, which publishes *Vanity Fair*), which, in 1998, sold it to Bertelsmann, which, in 2013, merged it with Pearson, creating Penguin Random House.

Through it all Knopf has seemed uniquely immune to the tumult. "We're part of something that is very large," Mehta says, "but we concentrate on our way of doing things. It may be illusory to insulate oneself from it all, but we try."

Mehta's Manhattan office is a manifestation of that sense of apartness. There are book-stuffed mahogany shelves, a pair of leather chairs, uncountable first editions, and the distinctly ahistorical smell of cigarette smoke. Situated in similarly paper-strewn offices all around him are Knopf's team of editors, to whom Mehta gives all credit, and who work much as editors did in 1915. They read proposals and manuscripts, advocate for them, and then hope the numbers work. If they do, and even if, occasionally, the economics require some suspension of disbelief—this is Knopf, after all—they go about bringing that book into the world.

"On a good day," Mehta says, "I am still convinced I have the best job in the world." Even after all these years, the unique delight in discovering a great unpublished work hasn't diminished. He recently read a submission, a novella by Graham Swift, that knocked him off his feet. "I opened it and didn't know what to expect, and I read it in one sitting right here in the office, utterly mesmerized. Sometimes you find something new and you just say *Wow*."

CHRISTOPHER HITCHENS

by Salman Rushdie

FEBRUARY 2012

On June 8, 2010, I was "in conversation" with Christopher Hitchens at the 92nd Street Y in New York in front of his customary sellout audience, to launch his memoir, *Hitch-22*. Christopher turned in a bravura performance that night, never sharper, never funnier, and afterward at a small, celebratory dinner the brilliance continued. A few days later he told me that it was on the morning of the Y event that he had been given the news about his cancer. It was hard to believe that he had been so publicly magnificent on such a privately dreadful day. He had shown more than stoicism. He had flung laughter and intelligence into the face of death.

Hitch-22 was a title born of the silly word games we played, one of which was Titles That Don't Quite Make It, among which were *A Farewell to Weapons, For Whom the Bell Rings, To Kill a Hummingbird, The Catcher in the Wheat, Mr. Zhivago,* and *Toby-Dick,* a.k.a. *Moby-Cock.* And, as the not-quite version of Joseph Heller's comic masterpiece, *Hitch-22.* Christopher rescued this last title from the slush pile of our catechism of failures and redeemed it by giving it to the text which now stands as his best memorial.

Laughter and Hitchens were inseparable companions, and comedy was one of the most powerful weapons in his arsenal. When we were both on *Real Time with Bill Maher* in 2009 along with Mos Def, and the rapper began to offer up a series of cockeyed animadversions about Iran's nuclear program and Osama bin Laden and al-Qaeda, Christopher became almost ferally polite, addressing Mos, as he tore into his ideas, by the faux-respectful moniker "Mr. Definitely," a name so belittlingly funny that it rendered even more risible the risible notions which Mr. D. was trying to advance.

Behind the laughter was what his friend Ian McEwan called "his Rolls-Royce mind," that organ of improbable erudition and frequently brilliant, though occasionally flawed, perception. The Hitch mind was indeed a sleek and purring machine trimmed with elegant fittings, but his was not a rarefied sensibility. He was an intellectual with the instincts of a street brawler, never happier than when engaged in moral or political fisticuffs. When I became involved in a public disagreement with the eminent spy novelist John le Carré, Hitchens leapt unbidden into the fray and ratcheted the insult level up many notches, comparing the great man's conduct to "that of a man who, having relieved himself in his own hat, makes haste to clamp the brimming chapeau on his head." The argument, I'm sorry to report, grew uglier after the Hitch's intervention.

The le Carré dispute took place during the long years of argument and danger that followed the 1988 publication of my novel *The Satanic Verses* and the attack upon its author, publishers, translators, and booksellers by the minions and successors of the theocratic tyrant of Iran, Ruhollah Khomeini. It was during these years that Christopher, a good but not intimate friend since the mid-1980s, drew closer to me, becoming the most indefatigable of allies and the most eloquent of defenders.

I have often been asked if Christopher defended me because he was my close friend. The truth is that he became my close friend because he wanted to defend me.

The spectacle of a despotic cleric with antiquated ideas issuing a death warrant for a writer living in another country, and then sending death squads to carry out the edict, changed something in Christopher. It made him understand that a new danger had been unleashed upon the earth, that a new totalizing ideology had stepped into the down-at-the-heels shoes of Soviet Communism. And when the brute hostility of American and British conservatives (Charles Krauthammer, Hugh Trevor-Roper, and Paul Johnson) joined forces with the appeasement politics of sections of the Western left, and both sides began to offer sympathetic analyses of the assault, his outrage grew. In the eyes of the right, I was a cultural "traitor" and, in Christopher's words, an "uppity wog," and in the opinion of the left, the People could never be wrong, and the cause of the Oppressed People, a category into which the Islamist opponents of my novel fell, was doubly justified. Voices as diverse as the Pope, the archbishop of New York, the British chief rabbi, John Berger, Jimmy Carter, and Germaine Greer "understood the insult" and failed to be outraged, and Christopher went to war.

He and I found ourselves describing our ideas, without conferring, in almost identical terms. I began to understand that while I had not chosen the battle it was at least the right battle, because in it everything that I loved and valued (literature, freedom, irreverence, freedom, irreligion, freedom) was ranged against everything I detested (fanaticism, violence, bigotry, humorlessness, philistinism, and the new offense culture of the age). Then I read Christopher using exactly the same everything-he-loved-versus-everything-he-hated trope, and felt . . . understood.

He, too, saw that the attack on *The Satanic Verses* was not an isolated occurrence, that, across the Muslim world, writers and journalists and artists were being accused of the same crimes—blasphemy, heresy, apostasy, and their modern-day associates, "insult" and "offense." And he intuited that beyond this intellectual assault lay the possibility of an attack on a broader front. He quoted Heine to me: Where they burn books they will afterward burn people. (And reminded me, with his profound sense of irony, that Heine's line, in his play *Almansor*, had referred to the burning of the Koran.) And on September 11, 2001, he, and all of us, understood that what had begun with a book burning in Bradford, Yorkshire, had now burst upon the whole world's consciousness in the form of those tragically burning buildings.

During the campaign against the fatwa, the British government and various human-rights groups pressed the case for a visit by me to the Clinton White House, to demonstrate the strength of the new administration's support for the cause. A visit was offered, then delayed, then offered again. It was unclear until the last minute if President Clinton himself would meet me, or if the encounter would be left to National-Security Adviser Anthony Lake and perhaps Warren Christopher, the secretary of state. Hitch worked tirelessly to impress on Clinton's people the importance of POTUS's greeting me in person. His friendship with George Stephanopoulos was perhaps the critical factor. Stephanopoulos's arguments prevailed and I was led into the presidential presence. Stephanopoulos called Christopher at once, telling him, triumphantly, "The Eagle has landed."

(On that visit to D.C., I stayed in the Hitchens apartment, and he was afterward warned by a State Department spook that my having been his houseguest may have drawn the danger toward him; maybe it would be a good idea if he moved house? He remained contemptuously unmoved.)

Christopher came to believe that the people who understood the dangers posed by radical Islam were on the right, that his erstwhile comrades on the left were arranging with one another to miss what seemed to him like a pretty obvious point, and so, never one to do things by halves, he did what looked to many people like a U-turn across the political highway to join forces with the war-makers of George W. Bush's administration. He became oddly enamored of Paul Wolfowitz. One night I happened to be at his apartment in D.C. when Wolfowitz, who had just left the administration, stopped by for a late-night drink and proceeded to deliver a critique of the Iraq war (all Rumsfeld's fault, apparently) which left me, at least, speechless. The Wolfowitz doctrine, Wolfowitz was saying, had not been Wolfowitz's idea. Indeed, Wolfowitz had been anti-Wolfowitz-doctrine from the beginning. This was an argument worthy of a character from *Catch-22*. I wondered how long Christopher would be able to tolerate such bedfellows.

Paradoxically, it was God who saved Christopher Hitchens from the right. Nobody who detested God as viscerally, intelligently, originally, and comically as C. Hitchens could stay in the pocket of god-bothered American conservatism for long. When he bared his fangs and went for God's jugular, just as he had previously fanged Henry Kissinger, Mother Teresa, and Bill Clinton, the resulting book, *God Is Not Great,* carried Hitch away from the American right and back toward his natural, liberal, ungodly constituency. He became an extraordinarily beloved figure in his last years, and it was his magnificent war upon God, and then his equally magnificent argument with his last enemy, Death, that brought him "home" at last from the misconceived war in Iraq.

Last things.

When I completed a draft of my memoir, I sent a copy to Christopher, who was by this time very unwell. I didn't expect him to do more than glance at it. Instead, I received a longish e-mail containing a full critique of the text, pointing out errors of fact and quotation I'd made about Rupert Brooke and P. G. Wodehouse.

There was a last dinner in New York, at which the poet James Fenton and I, by previous agreement, set out to make him laugh as much as possible. Distressingly, this unleashed, at least once, a terrifying coughing fit. But he enjoyed himself that evening. It was the only gift his friends could give him near the end: an hour or two of being himself as he had always wished to be, the Hitch mighty and ample amongst the ones he loved, and not the diminishing Hitch having the life slowly squeezed out of him by the Destroyer of Days.

On his 62nd birthday—his last birthday, a painful phrase to write—I had been with him and Carol and other comrades at the Houston home of his friend Michael Zilkha, and we had been photographed standing on either side of a bust of Voltaire. That photograph is now one of my most treasured possessions: me and the two Voltaires, one of stone and one still very much alive. Now they are both gone, and one can only try to believe, as the philosopher Pangloss insisted to Candide in the elder Voltaire's masterpiece, that everything is for the best "in this best of all possible worlds."

It doesn't feel like that today.

A Family Affair

JOAN DIDION

···

OUR LADY OF L.A.

by Lili Anolik

JANUARY 2016

In a 1969 column for *Life,* her first for the magazine, Joan Didion let drop that she and husband, John Gregory Dunne, were at the Royal Hawaiian hotel in Honolulu "in lieu of filing for divorce," surely the most famous subordinate clause in the history of New Journalism, an insubordinate clause if ever there was one. The poise of it, the violence, the cool-bitch chic—a writer who could be the heroine of a Godard movie!—takes the breath away, even after all these years. Didion goes on: "I tell you this not as aimless revelation but because I want you to know, as you read me, precisely who I am and where I am and what is on my mind. I want you to understand exactly what you are getting." I suppose I'm operating under a similar set of impulses—a mixture of candor, self-justification and self-dramatization, the dread of being misapprehended coupled with the certainty that misapprehension is inevitable (Didion's style is catching, but not so much as her habit of thought)— when I tell you I'm scared of her.

Before I get into why, I need to clarify something I said. Or, rather, some-thing I didn't say and won't say, but which I'm anxious you're going to think I said: that Didion isn't a brilliant writer. She *is* a brilliant writer—sentence for sentence, among the best this country's ever produced. And I'm not disputing her status as cultural icon either. As large as she looms now, she'll loom larger as time passes—I'd bet money on it. In fact, I don't want to diminish or assault her in any way. What I do want to do is get her right. And over the past 11 years, since 2005, when she published the first of her two loss memoirs, one about Dunne, the other about Quintana, her daughter, she's been gotten wrong. And not just wrong, egregiously wrong, wrong to the point of blasphemy. I'm talking about the canonization of Didion, Didion as St. Joan, Didion as Our Mother of Sorrows. Didion is not, let me repeat, not a holy figure, nor is she a maternal one. She's cool-eyed and cold-blooded, and that coolness and coldness—chilling, of course, but also bracing—is the source of her fascination as much as her artistry is; the source of her glamour too, and her seductiveness, because she *is* seductive, deeply. What she is is a femme fatale, and irresistible. She's our kiss of death, yet we open our mouths, kiss back.

The subject of this piece, though, is not just a who, Didion, but a what, Hollywood. So to bring them together, which is where they belong, a natural pairing, this: I think that Didion, along with Andy Warhol, her spiritual twin as well as her artistic, created L.A.—that is, modern L.A., contemporary L.A., the L.A. that is synonymous with Hollywood. And I think that Didion alone was the vehicle—or possibly the agent—of L.A.'s destruction. I think that for the city of Los Angeles, Didion is the Ángel de la Muerte.

There. I said it. Now you know why I'm scared. Who wants to get on the Ángel de la Muerte's bad side? Not that I believe I'm going to. Because I have one last thing to add, and I don't care how weird and screw-loose it sounds: I think she wanted me to say it.

AN INGÉNUE, DISINGENUOUS

The Joan Didion who moved from New York to L.A. in June of 1964 was no more Joan Didion than Norma Jeane Baker was Marilyn Monroe, or Marion Morrison was John Wayne, or, for that matter, Andrew Warhola was Andy Warhol. She was a native daughter, but only sort of. The California she grew up in—the Sacramento Valley—was closer in spirit to the Old West than to the sun-kissed, pleasure-mad movie colony. Just shy of 30, she'd recently married Dunne. Both had been working as journalists, she for *Vogue,* he for *Time.* Her first book, a novel, the traditional if not quite conventional *Run River,* had been published the year before. Critics hadn't taken much notice; neither had readers. Hurt, likely a little angry too, she was ready for a new scene. Dunne was equally itchy to blow town. Plus, he had a brother in the industry, Dominick—Nick.

In his memoir *Popism,* Warhol wrote, "The Hollywood we were driving to that fall of '63 was in limbo. The Old Hollywood was finished and the New Hollywood hadn't started yet." Old Hollywood, of course, didn't *know* it was finished. Was carrying on like it was show business as usual. And it still hadn't wised up the following spring when the Didion-Dunnes arrived.

Nick, young though he was, was Old Hollywood. Professionally he hadn't made it: a second-rate producer in a second-rate medium, TV. But socially he'd hit the heights. He and wife Lenny threw lavish, stylish parties, and lots of them. A month before the Didion-Dunnes showed, they'd thrown their most lavish and stylish, a black-and-white ball inspired by the Ascot scene in *My Fair Lady.* (That the ball—a ball!—wasn't in color is a detail almost too on the nose. Soon the whole town would turn psychedelic, and such evenings would seem so old-fashioned as to have been in black and white even if they weren't.) Among the splendidly monochromatic: Ronald and Nancy Reagan, David Selznick and Jennifer Jones, Billy Wilder, Loretta Young, Natalie Wood. Also present, Truman Capote, who, in a gesture either of rip-off or homage, would stage his own black-and-white ball in New York. Nick's invitation would get lost in the mail.

In later years, Didion and Dunne would play a double game with Hollywood: they were participants who were also onlookers; supported by the industry but not owned by it; in the thick of it and above the fray. They seemed much less ambivalent in their early years. In their early years, they wanted in. A line invoked by both so often you know they must have believed it gospel is from F. Scott Fitzgerald's *The Last Tycoon:* "We don't go for strangers in Hollywood." How lucky for them then that they were the brother and sister-in-law of Nick, and thus part of the Hollywood family, if poor relations. And, as poor relations, they were given castoffs: clothes, Natalie Wood's (for Didion); houses, too. They rented Sara Mankiewicz's, fully furnished, though Mankiewicz did pack up the Oscar won by her late husband, Herman, for writing *Citizen Kane.*

So Didion and Dunne wanted in and got in, but they wanted in deeper. Hollywood's appeal for writers isn't hard to figure: it's about the only place they can strike it rich. And doing it for the money seems to be how a writer stays respectable, at least in the eyes of fellow writers. Says writer Dan Wakefield, a friend of the couple's from New York, "They didn't give a shit about the movies except it was a way to make a lot of money. And I totally respect that." Only maybe the Didion-Dunnes weren't just tricking after all. Wrote Dunne, "The other night, after a screening, we went out to a party with Mike Nichols and Candice Bergen and Warren Beatty and Barbra Streisand. I never did that at *Time.*" They were doing it then for love, too, if not of the movies, of the glamour and celebrity that movies bring. Says writer Josh Greenfeld, a friend of the couple's from L.A., "Joan and John were star fuckers. They wouldn't miss a party. They could do four in a night—come, see what had to be seen, go." And Don Bachardy, the artist and longtime lover of Christopher Isherwood, then a reigning figure on the L.A. literary scene, recalls their ardent pursuit of Isherwood. "They were both highly ambitious, and Chris was a rung on the ladder they were climbing. I don't like to tell on Chris, but he wasn't very fond of either of them. I think he found her clammy." (Isherwood already told on himself. He makes numerous unflattering references to Didion and Dunne—"Mrs. Misery and Mr. Know-All"—in his diaries.)

The basic plan, careerwise, seems to have been that Nick would provide Didion and Dunne with introductions and they'd try their hands, collective—it would be a team effort—at scriptwriting. Their hands would remain idle for seven years, not counting an episode of *Kraft Suspense Theatre.* Well, idle and full. In 1964, Didion struck up a relationship with a magazine highly receptive to her sensibility and interests, *The Saturday Evening Post.* It would become the primary home for her work until its publisher filed for bankruptcy in 1969. And in 1966, she'd have a baby—or, have a baby without quite having had a baby. She and Dunne adopted, at birth, a girl, Quintana Roo. So Didion had plenty to keep her occupied.

Besides, she didn't need the movies to become a star.

A STAR IS BORN,
AN IMMACULATE CONCEPTION

In 1968, Didion published *Slouching Towards Bethlehem,* a collection of essays mostly and most strikingly about California, and, with a single exception, composed entirely while living in her new hometown. *Slouching* would become a touchstone for a decade and an era, its readers more than mere readers but followers, devotees, *fans.* The critics were just as beguiled. *The New York Times* called it "a rich display of some of the best prose written today in this country." And the writing *is* great: direct and matter-of-fact, yet lyrical and poetic and hypnotic, too—writing that casts a spell, though whether you've been enchanted or cursed isn't wholly clear. The true triumph of *Slouching,* however, is Joan Didion, or, rather, "Joan Didion," the central character in a book that famously denies that the center exists, or at least that it's capable of holding; also, as it happens, the most enduring creation of Joan Didion.

We're told at *Slouching's* outset that it was written in a state of acute emotional distress. From the preface: "I went to San Francisco [for the title piece, about the hippie scene in the Haight] because I had not been able to work in some months, had been paralyzed by the conviction that writing was an irrelevant act, that the world as I had understood it no longer existed." And many of the stories "Didion" tells are real-life horror stories: a suburban housewife who, one night when she was out of milk, set fire to her dumb lug of a husband; High Kindergarten, where children were given LSD; Howard Hughes. And yet the tone of the telling is noticeably, conspicuously not horrified; nor is it distressed, or even emotional; it's the opposite, is composed, affectless, flat. There are, I should note, two places in the book where the tone changes, becomes tender. The first is in "John Wayne: A Love Song." (Didion admirers like, I suspect, to believe that that "Love" is ironic—it's not; she's sweet on the Duke, who in his simplicity and stoicism represents to her a masculine ideal.) The second is in "Goodbye to All That," her profile of her young self.

Like Warhol, "Didion" presents herself as an observer—no, a witness—to unspeakable acts. In fact, "Death and Disaster," Warhol's early-60s series depicting all manner of grisliness—car accidents, riots, suicides—could have been the title of *Slouching,* and maybe a better one. (The Yeats reference, in retrospect, seems a little alarmist.) "Didion" is absorbed, intensely, in what's going on around her, but is not involved; her gaze fixed, even salivating, yet also vacant. Her motto might be: See everything, hear everything, do nothing. Still, her nothing *is* something, her extreme passivity a form of extreme aggression. She takes events, people, places that inspire violent and chaotic feelings—passion, hope, terror, despair—and subdues them, controls them, counteracting their awesome power simply by looking at them in a certain way. Her look, Warhol's look, too—it's aestheticizing, providing a psychic distance, a paradoxical kind of a cool. A burned-out cool. A cool that gives off heat.

THE STRANGE CASE OF EARL MCGRATH

So New York had missed Didion's star quality, its eye passing right over her. Not L.A., though. (Warhol, too, incidentally, would have to leave New York, go to L.A., to get discovered. It was the Ferus Gallery, on La Cienega, that gave him his big break, his first fine-arts show back in 1962, him and his soup cans.) L.A. knew how to talent-spot. But in 1968, it didn't know much else. It was in a state of flux, or maybe crisis. The culture had swung counter, and the movies hadn't swung along with it, not fully. Nineteen sixty-eight, remember, was the year of John Wayne's *The Green Berets,* about what a super-fantastic idea the Vietnam War was. Music, not movies, had captured the hearts and minds of the younger generation. Old Hollywood, though, now knew it was Old. Wrote Nick Dunne, "Everything was changing. . . . People were starting to smoke pot. . . . Hairdressers started to be invited to parties." And even if it wasn't clear what exactly the New was, it was clear that Didion was part of it. She and Dunne began to move in different circles, most notably Earl McGrath's.

Who is Earl McGrath? A mystery man I was never able to solve, is the short answer. Didion dedicated *The White Album,* her essay collection mainly about L.A. during the years she and Dunne and Quintana lived in a house on Franklin Avenue in Hollywood (1966–71), to him, which should give you some idea of his importance to her. He reminds me of Jay Gatsby, not for the obvious reason, though for that reason too—he threw killer parties—but because the claims made about him seem outlandish yet, somehow, plausible: "he ran Bobby Kennedy's career"; "he ran Rolling Stones Records"; "he ran an art gallery"; "he was head of production for Twentieth Century Fox"; "he married an Italian countess"; "he gave Steve Martin his I'm-a-Little-Teapot routine." All of that—some of that, none of that—though, was just a front, a cover. What he did really was get to know the ultra-hip and get them to know each other. Says artist Ron Cooper, "Earl is the Gertrude Stein of our era. He had a salon like Stein. I met Andy Warhol through him and Jack Nicholson and Dennis Hopper and Michelle

Phillips and Michael Crichton and Joan and John, of course—and, oh, just an amazing roster of people." Says singer-actress Michelle Phillips, "If you went to Earl's, you were going to a party that you knew was going to be staffed and stuffed with the most interesting, fuckable people, always, always."

Drugs were a big part of the scene. Says writer Eve Babitz, "Mostly pot and acid and speed—Dexedrine, Benzedrine. I thought Joan was more in control than we were, but I reread the *The White Album*. She didn't sound in control, did she?" So was Harrison Ford. Says Babitz, "Harrison was a carpenter then, a terrible one. He built a deck for John Dunne and John was outraged it took so long. John really expected him to build it! And Earl was in love with Harrison. He let Harrison basically get away with murder as far as his carpentry was concerned. But Fred Roos [famed casting director for Francis Ford Coppola] hired Harrison and made him finish his project, and then got him in *Star Wars*."

Didion's social life was now so vibrant, so vivid, so potent, her imaginative life became vulnerable to it. Says Babitz, "Michelle Phillips told the best stories in town. I remember her once lying down on the floor and telling that amazing story about Tamar Hodel. [Hodel, then 26, decided to kill herself after a love affair ended badly. She asked Phillips, then 17, to help. Phillips, believing it her duty as a friend, agreed. Hodel swallowed a bottle of Seconal. Phillips fell asleep beside her in bed. Fortunately, other friends came home in time to call an ambulance.] I guess Joan was listening."

THE AUTEUR THEORY

In 1969, Didion completed her third book, *Play It as It Lays*. "Joan Didion" was back, no matter that she was now called Maria Wyeth, and *Play It* a novel. Maria, a B actress fast sliding down the alphabet, has an estranged director-husband and a brain-damaged child, and is telling her story from a sanatorium. Things she does: has sex, listlessly, takes drugs, also listlessly, bleeds a lot—from a botched abortion—cries even more—from the abortion, but for other reasons, too. In the climactic scene, she cradles her friend, the homosexual producer, BZ, in bed as he overdoses on Seconal (sound familiar?).

Play It is a Hollywood book, not just because it's about Hollywood people, but because it's a book that's also a movie. Didion's the star. (I should mention here that "writer" was only ever her fallback plan; as a child she'd wanted to act.) The author photo on the jacket, taken by Julian Wasser, is an arresting one— Didion was always a shrewd subject, understood how the camera should see her, had an actress's sixth sense about lighting and mood—and shows a young woman, pretty and slight and troubled-looking. Between her fingers, a cigarette, rakishly angled, smolders. All decidedly Maria-ish. And if you'd caught the shots of Didion in *Time* in '68 (Wasser again), you'd know that, like Maria, who cruises the nerve pathways of the city to soothe hers—the San Diego Freeway to the Harbor to the Hollywood, and so on—she drives a Corvette. It's a snap to picture her cracking hard-boiled eggs on her steering wheel, drinking Coca-Colas at gas stations.

Stars, though, weren't really stars in Hollywood, directors were. And in *Play It,* Didion was that kind of star, too. If there's a prose equivalent to freeze-frames and jump cuts, this book is full of them; chapters are fractured, one just 28 words long; and the amount of white on the pages makes them look like miniature movie screens. Plus, her eye is eerily close to that of a camera's: all-seeing yet uncaring, a mode of perception both alienated and alienating.

And with *Play It,* Didion was able to return a favor. L.A. discovered Didion; now she was discovering it. Because if *Play It* actually were a movie, surely its opening credits would have read AND INTRODUCING L.A. The L.A. in *Play It* wasn't the L.A. that existed in the popular imagination of the time: a sunny land of innocent, adolescent pleasures, Surf-in' U.S.A., Eden before the fall. It's shadow L.A., jaded L.A., and it's hell on earth, or, L.A. being L.A., hell in paradise. It's the L.A. of plastic lemons and silver medallions and masseurs who want to be screenwriters. Didion intended, I think, to write a hate letter to L.A.; it's a love letter, though, in spite of itself. For Auden, L.A. was "The Great Wrong Place." It was for Didion, too, only her Wrong was so Wrong it was Right. She seduced even as she condemned. And there's also this: the fact that Didion, the girl New Journalist, the novelist who'd figured out how to be a female Hemingway (a contradiction in terms, yet she'd done it), chose the city as her subject was its own kind of validation and recommendation. Says Babitz, "Joan made it O.K. to be serious about L.A." Warhol made it O.K. before Didion, but only just. The profane assertion of his *Marilyn Diptych* (1962) was that movie stars had replaced religious icons as objects of worship; and, by extension, that L.A., home of Hollywood, was the country's new spiritual mecca. What's more, L.A., thanks to Warhol and Didion—maybe a handful of others—was becoming the country's new cultural mecca, too. New York? How about Old Hat.

PSYCHO KILLER, *QUI EST-CE QU'IL EST?*

The times were wild and weird, and getting ever wilder and weirder. Didion was almost uncannily in touch with them. Her health, mental and physical, began to break down. After an attack of vertigo and nausea, she checked herself into a psychiatric clinic. Later she'd write, "An attack of vertigo and nausea does not now seem to me an inappropriate response to the summer of 1968."

As bad as that summer was, though, it would get worse. Dark forces were gathering, gaining momentum. From *The White Album:* "I imagined that my own life was simple and sweet, and sometimes it was, but there were odd things going around town. . . . Everything was unmentionable but nothing was unimaginable." And then the disciples of an aspiring musician and ex-con named Charles Manson slaughtered Sharon Tate, eight months pregnant, and four others at the house Tate rented with husband Roman Polanski on Cielo Drive, and suddenly everything was both. Didion: "Many people I know in Los Angeles believe that the Sixties ended abruptly on August 9, 1969." Perhaps most unsettling of all: there was murder, but no murderer, not at first. Says Julian Wasser, "The cops didn't know shit, as usual. Roman took me and Tommy Thompson [a journalist] and a psychic to the house. He'd just gotten back from Europe. It was his first time on the scene. The carpet had a three-foot circle of jellied blood. Roman was crying. He wanted me to take pictures to give to the psychic so he could find out who did it." Says Michelle Phillips, "For a long time, nobody knew it was Manson. Everyone was a suspect. I started carrying a gun in my purse. To me, that was the end of the party."

Manson embodied so many counterculture clichés he was an almost allegorical figure: a singer-songwriter who'd come to L.A. with a guitar and hopes of stardom. You could find one of him on every corner, at least the corners by the Troubadour and the Whisky. Bogeyman as Everyman. And the Manson "Family" was like some grotesque parody of the era's peace-love-and-brotherhood ethos, the monster under the flower child's bed.

Didion and the Manson murders were linked, if only in Didion's mind. She sees occult significance in the fact that Polanski, at a party he attended with Tate, had spilled red wine on the dress she wore to her wedding, and that she and he were godparents to the same child, even if she can't figure out exactly what that significance is, even if her cool intelligence won't allow her to use the word "occult." Yet there's no question of the guilt in her tone. Is that because she felt somehow responsible for him? Did she believe he was a hallucination she'd conjured mid-migraine (her "vascular headache[s] of blinding severity")? A vision sprung to life during her psychic collapse the summer before (from the doctor's report: "In [the patient's] view she lives in a world of people moved by strange, conflicted, poorly comprehended, and, above all, devious motivations")? Her bad juju ("I remember a babysitter telling me that she saw death in my aura") made flesh?

Or maybe these are the wrong questions. Maybe this is the right one: Did Didion believe herself so harmonically—or, rather, disharmonically—in tune with the vibrations being struck around her, so imaginatively sympathetic a participant in her time and place, in the melancholy and despair lurking beneath hippiedom's blissed-out surface, in the hate that is the flip side of the Love Generation, that she became the medium of an evil spirit, the conduit through which it passed into the world, or did she believe she summoned it? In other words, was she Manson's instrument or was he hers?

WHO'S AFRAID OF JOHN GREGORY DUNNE?

John Gregory Dunne was Didion's husband, the father of her child, her first editor—that "in lieu of filing for divorce" clause, written, you'll recall, in 1969, went through his red pencil before *Life's*—and co-screenwriter. All of which gives you some idea of how essential to her he was. Not the whole idea, though. Here's how essential: without Dunne there would have been no Didion, not Didion as we know Didion. But before I talk about him, I want to talk about Didion's other mate, maybe her soulmate, if only in my imagination, Andy Warhol.

Didion is, and always has been, small, frail, quiet, recessive. As was Warhol. In so many ways, Didion was a Warhol who could pass, her smallness and frailness registering as pretty, gamine; her quietness and recessiveness as feminine, refined. She was, too, that least threatening figure—a wife. He, in contrast, was homely— blotchy-skinned and bulbous-nosed and bewigged—and obviously sexually Other. His weirdness was unconcealable, writ large. He had no choice but to turn it into personal style. In any case, these two mice became—not just against the odds, but seemingly against nature, certainly against *their* natures—social lions. How?

Entourages. The world's rawness was too much for Warhol. A protective layer was necessary. Says Ferus co-owner Irving Blum, "Andy needed to travel with people—he used them as shields." (It could easily be argued, by the way, that Warhol summoned his evil spirit. Valerie Solanas—a flamboyant oddball, just his type—was a member of his entourage. She'd written a play she thought he was going to produce. When she realized he wasn't, she shot him. In a physical sense, she failed. Not in a metaphysical, though. Once her bullets entered his body on June 3, 1968—the summer that had Didion's head spinning, stomach churning—it was the end of much of what was daring and original in his work.) Entourages, too, were good for the mystique.

Didion's entourage was an entourage of one: Dunne. "Joan was very soft-spoken and shrinking," says Don Bachardy. "John was very talky. He was her mouthpiece." Didion, no doubt, is genuinely introverted. But she's also somebody who, by her own admission, can spend "most of a week writing and rewriting and not writing a single paragraph." She's a control freak, basically. And conversation, as opposed to writing, is interactive, improvisatory. To engage in one you have to renounce a measure of control. Dunne's garrulousness allowed her to take some of that control back, to pick and choose her spots. Says writer David Freeman, "John was the talker. I'll tell you this, though. When she started talking, he knew to shut up."

This, too: while shyness can be a symptom of insecurity, it can also be a weapon in a power play. Says Josh Greenfeld, "Joan's weakness is her strength. It got John to run interference." And run it he did. To get to Didion you had to go through Dunne. This was true socially—at parties, and on the telephone (it was he who always answered). And professionally. He did the meetings and the memos, the pushing around. The last sentence in a fax he sent to the Writers Guild when a studio was slow on payment: "[O]ur position is fuck them, let's arbitrate." He was Didion's protector. And her caretaker. Says writer-actress Jennifer Salt, a one-time neighbor, "John was a very concerned and doting husband. A big part of their life was her migraines."

So, essentially, their marriage was an endless re-enactment of a classic scenario: a damsel in distress, a big strong man coming to her rescue. (Big strong men, we know from Didion's John Wayne profile, are very much her thing.) Or was it? Dot dot dot.

Dunne wasn't Didion's match artistically. Not so much a slight as it might sound. Dunne was a fine writer; Didion just happens to be more than that. And he seemed to have accepted his second-best status. Says Greenfeld, "John told Brian [Moore, the Irish novelist] he was walking on the beach one night and he ran into Jesus and Jesus said, 'I love your wife's work!'" Very smartly, too, Dunne carved out his own literary territory, his interests running to crooked cops and crooked crooks, gangsters and studio heads, i.e., gangsters by another name. Harder for Dunne to accept: that he wasn't Didion's match psychologically either. Greenfeld again: "What you see in John, you get in Joan. He came on blustering and tough, but he was softhearted."

That Didion could wipe the floor with Dunne anytime she chose must've been disturbing for him. And confusing. The girl he'd married, a slip of a thing, bookish and wallflowerish, turned out to be this spooky genius, a poet of paranoia or possibly a clairvoyant of paranoia fulfilled. And those were boozy days. From Isherwood's *Diaries:* "[Joan] drinks quite a lot. So does [John]." Dunne was a rager too. In that *Life* piece, Didion mentions "kicked-down doors." Says Babitz, "Joan had migraines because she was married to John. He'd give anyone a migraine. He was an alcoholic and he broke down doors." Often, though, when a man gets violent with a woman physically, it's because he feels beat-up emotionally. Scratch a bully find a victim.

There's a scene, very revealing, I think, in *Vegas* (1974), carefully described by Dunne as "a memoir" and "a fiction which recalls a time both real and imagined," though in a letter to writer Jane Howard he admitted that the "real and imagined" was a fakeout, an attempt to throw his mother—"the Mum"—off the autobiographical scent. *Vegas* is about a writer who leaves his wife—also a writer—and child—a little girl, adopted—to live in Las Vegas, precisely what Dunne did for six months in the early 70s. (In lieu of divorce coming perilously close to divorce divorce.) The scene is a phone call between the protagonist and his wife:

> "What's new with you?" she said.
> "Jackie's got me a date with a nineteen-year-old tonight. She's
> supposed to suck me and fuck me."
> "It's research . . . You're missing the story if you don't meet her."
> "But I don't *want* to fuck her."
> There was a long silence at the other end of the telephone. "Well,
> that can be part of the story, too," she said.
> There seemed nothing more to say. I was the one who was supposed
> to be detached.

This isn't a conversation. It's warfare. And the wife defeats the husband. A no-contest contest. How she does it: by not doing anything. She exhibits neither shock nor rage nor sadness at the prospect of his getting together with a teenager. In fact, she encourages him to, all but dares him. Which is the exact moment he turns meek and little-boy, backs down and off. Plainly, he's terrified of his wife. Well, why not? She's a dangerous character. (The answer to the section's opening question, by the way: Not Joan Didion.)

Interestingly, Quintana, at around this time, seems to have been driven to equal extremes to attract Didion's attention. In her memoir *Blue Nights,* Didion tells a story of a five-year-old Quintana calling Camarillo, the state mental hospital, to ask what she should do if she was going crazy. Didion tells another story of Quintana, at the same age, calling Twentieth Century Fox to ask what she should do to become a movie star. Quintana was clearly desperate to turn herself into one of her mother's characters—an insane person or a famous person, preferably both, like Maria Wyeth.

But back to Dunne: once this period—the publication of *Play It,* the book's major-cultural-eventness—passed, he mellowed or was tamed, depending on your viewpoint. Either way, the marriage settled down. And by the 80s, Didion would be telling *The New York Times* that she and Dunne were "terrifically, terribly dependent on one another," a statement that warms the heart or chills the blood, again depending on your viewpoint.

KISS ME DEADLY

In 1971, the Didion-Dunnes would move out of the house on Franklin Avenue to a house in Trancas, just north of Malibu. The couple's careers as screenwriters would begin in earnest, starting with that year's *The Panic in Needle Park,* and lasting until Dunne's death in 2003. The moment they leave Hollywood to go Hollywood, though, is the moment I lose interest in them as Hollywood figures.

There is one movie of theirs, however, I do want to discuss: *Play It as It Lays* (1972). As I already said, the book is both book and movie. Didion's temperament is a director's in that her controlling intelligence is so, well, controlling. The world Maria inhabits is a contrived one—an artifice. Not for an instant do you believe that the story can end other than in calamity, that life's random energies have a shot against tragedy's classic structure. If a character burped or cracked a joke, you feel the whole thing would collapse. Which is why *Play It*, taken on its own terms, is profound, high art; and, not taken on its own terms, profoundly silly, high camp. Pauline Kael's assessment of the book (she slammed it en route to slamming the movie) was so devastating because she laughed at it—"I found the . . . novel ridiculously swank, and I read it between bouts of disbelieving giggles"—and once you start laughing, you can't stop.

A movie, by definition, is not taking the book on its own terms, since a movie is made by many people, even if one of them is a "Didion freak" (Frank Perry, the director, a self-description) and two others are Didion and Dunne (they wrote the script). The movie exposed the book. Showed how weak the central concept was, how purest-corn and junk-Hollywood: the glamour of desolation, the romance of despair, how low-life are those living the high life, etc. Only, unlike the junk-Hollywood product, *Play It* took itself seriously. The movie also showed that for *Play It* to work—and the book, whether you like it or not, does work—it needed the magic of Didion's prose. Otherwise it's just a bummer version of *The Bad and the Beautiful*.

It didn't have to be. Didion's first pick for director was Sam Peckinpah. Didion in a letter to Peckinpah: "I want you to [do the movie]—you are the only person . . . I can see taking it beyond where it is and bringing back a picture of the very edge." Peckinpah seems, on the face of it, a counter-intuitive choice. The material was contemporary, urban, feminine. He was a director of Westerns, often set in the past, and extremely violent. Yet his violence was beautiful—sensuous and painterly—and he was a fatalist, and thus close to Didion in sensibility. Her hope, too, was that he would not just film the book—what Perry ended up doing—but reimagine it, and "[bring] back a picture of the very edge." Or, maybe, over the edge. It always struck me as false that Maria was so tranquil behind the wheel. How much more joy would she have gotten from her rides if she'd left devastation in her wake? Is there a better way for one of the most alienated characters in modern literature to connect than inside her metal shell, her barest touch resulting in blood and guts and severed limbs? (Didion: "Actually, I don't drive on the freeway. I'm afraid to.") Peckinpah, I think, would have said what Didion couldn't quite: that Maria—that Didion—was a victim who was also a victimizer. He'd have turned *Play It* into Warhol's *Orange Car Crash Fourteen Times* at 24 frames per second.

That version, of course, never happened. The studio balked at Peckinpah. Missed opportunities are always a shame. This one, though, was especially shameful because it was also Didion and Dunne's best opportunity to catch the American New Wave.

In 1969, the summer of Manson, *Easy Rider* roared onto screens trailing clouds of motorcycle exhaust and marijuana smoke. A new era in movies had begun. This new era, New Hollywood, was really an end-of-an-era era. Its decade was the 70s, and the 70s were less the 70s than the post-60s, the 60s once the light had been snuffed out. Its movies were, unsurprisingly, dark: innocence was lost or violated, promise unfulfilled, effort futile. Forget it, Jake, it's Chinatown. And while Didion and Dunne were in New Hollywood, literally (their house in Trancas was a stone's throw from New Hollywood Central, the houses of Julia and Michael Phillips, producers of *Taxi Driver,* and actresses Jennifer Salt and Margot Kidder, where every weekend people like Martin Scorsese, Steven Spielberg, and Paul Schrader—all unknowns then—could be found drinking wine, smoking grass, and talking movies), they were never of it, even if they'd occasionally attend its parties. I don't think they quite knew what "it" was.

"A few decades hence, these years may appear to be the closest our movies have come to the tangled, bitter flowering of American letters in the 1850s." Pauline Kael wrote those words in her introduction to *Reeling,* her collection of reviews, 1972–75, including that humdinger of *Play It.* In the 70s, movie culture would become central to American culture. Kael was its voice, which meant she was American culture's voice, which meant Didion no longer was. Didion didn't take the usurpation lying down. She went after Kael, writing in 1973, "The review of pictures has been . . . a traditional diversion for writers whose actual work is somewhere else." No serious writer takes movies seriously, is, essentially, what she's saying. And yet movies were, at that moment, it, *the* hot art form. So Didion, who missed nothing, had missed a major cultural shift. And just like that, the sharpest point on the cutting edge was dull, out of it, passé. That the movie she and Dunne are best known for is *A Star Is Born* (1976), a remake of a remake of a remake of a remake, tells, I think, the story of their Hollywood career.

So after 1969, Didion's special extra intuition was gone. (Kael, incidentally, wouldn't outlast her decade either. Her moment ended in 1979, when Warren Beatty, that skilled seducer, sweet-talked her into leaving *The New Yorker* for Paramount.) Didion would continue to be a great writer, but would cease to be a visionary one. While a number of her later books hit the best-seller list, they failed, with the exception of *The White Album*, published in 1979 though about the earlier period, to truly resonate. Her days as a cultural phenomenon were over.

Until the passing of Dunne and Quintana. In their deaths, Didion was resurrected professionally. *The Year of Magical Thinking* (2005) was a critical sensation—winner of the National Book Award—and a commercial one, selling a million-plus copies, far more than any other book in her career. And its sequel, *Blue Nights* (2011), was another smash. Why?

In this piece's opening I called Didion a femme fatale. I said it to startle and I said it because it's true. I suspect she's one in life. I know she's one in art. Her method, which is also her genius, has been to attenuate nature, strip it of its force and vitality. And then nature did that to her. Did it by aging her, taking away her youth and beauty. Did it again, and more violently, by taking away those she loved most. With just about anybody else, it would have ended there—heartbreak of that magnitude breaking the spirit and the will, as well. Not with Didion, though. She did it right back to nature. *Magical Thinking* and *Blue Nights* are loss and grief and pain transformed into meditations on loss and grief and pain; they're loss and grief and pain aestheticized. Death has always been Didion's great subject and theme, as it was Warhol's. And in these memoirs, she's confronting it directly, more than confronting it, besting it. Art won out over life, another way of saying the artist won out over the human being. It's her triumph. It's also her tragedy.

JOHN GREGORY DUNNE

A DEATH IN THE FAMILY

by Dominick Dunne

MARCH 2004

My brother the writer John Gregory Dunne, with whom I have had a complicated relationship over the years, as Irish Catholic brothers of our era often did, died unexpectedly on the night of December 30. I was at my house in Connecticut that night, sitting in front of the fire, reading John's provocative review in *The New York Review of Books* of Gavin Lambert's new biography, *Natalie Wood: A Life*. My brother and I both knew Natalie Wood, and our wives were among her friends. We were also both friends of Gavin Lambert's. I have always enjoyed my brother's writing, even when we weren't speaking. He knew his turf. He understood about getting at the essence of things. His first major work on Hollywood, *The Studio,* was an insider's unsparing, yearlong look at how Twentieth Century Fox was run. His best-selling novel *True Confessions,* about two Irish Catholic brothers, one a priest and the other a police lieutenant, was made into a film starring Robert De Niro and Robert Duvall. In his review of Lambert's fascinating book, John wrote about Natalie, "She was a movie star out of a post–Joan Crawford, pre–Julia Roberts age—promiscuous, insecure, talented, irrational, funny, generous, shrewd, occasionally unstable, and untrusting of anyone who would get too close to her—except for a Praetorian Guard of gay men." I was thinking to myself as I read it, He got her—that was Natalie.

Then the telephone rang, and I looked at the clock. It was 10 minutes before 11, late for a country call, especially the night before New Year's Eve. When I said hello, I heard, "Nick, it's Joan." Joan is Joan Didion, the writer, my brother's wife. It was rare for her to call. John was always the one who made the calls. I knew by the tone of her voice that something terrible had happened. In our immediate family there have been a murder, a suicide, and a fatal private-plane crash.

My brother and sister-in-law's daughter, Quintana Roo Dunne Michael, a recent bride, had been since Christmas night in an induced coma in the intensive-care unit of Beth Israel hospital, because of a case of flu that had turned into a virulent strain of pneumonia. There were tubes down her throat, and her hands were restrained so that she could not pull the tubes out. The night before, my brother had called me after a hospital visit and sobbed about his daughter. I had never heard him cry. He adored Quintana and she adored him, in that special father-daughter way. I don't think I have ever seen a prouder father than when he walked her to the altar at her wedding last summer. "It was like watching Dominique on life support," he told me on the phone. He was referring to my daughter, who had been strangled and then kept on life support for several days on police orders back in 1982. Hearing Joan's voice, I thought at first that she was calling to tell me of a setback in Quintana's condition, or worse. Instead she said, in her simple, direct manner, "John's dead." There were long seconds of silence as what she had said sank in. John's and my journey had been bumpy, sometimes extremely so, but in recent years we had experienced the joys of reconciliation. After the closeness we had managed to rebuild, the thought of his not being there anymore was incomprehensible.

Since Quintana's hospitalization, it had become their habit, that week between Christmas and New Year's, to visit her each evening and then have dinner in a restaurant before returning to their apartment on the Upper East Side. That night, after leaving the hospital, they didn't feel like going to a restaurant, so they went directly back to the apartment. Once inside, John sat down, had a massive heart attack, fell over, and died. "The minute I got to him, I knew he was dead," Joan said. She was crying. "The ambulance arrived. The medics worked on him for 15 minutes, but it was over." Joan went in the ambulance to the hospital, where he was pronounced dead. In recent years he had had a history of heart problems.

Joan Didion and John Dunne, or the Didion-Dunnes, as their friends referred to them, had a superb marriage that lasted 40 years. They were ideally matched. Once, years ago, they thought briefly about getting a divorce. They actually wrote about it in a weekly column they were then contributing to the *Saturday Evening Post*. But they didn't get a divorce. Instead they went to Hawaii, a favorite getaway place of theirs, and began a life of total togetherness that was nearly unparalleled in modern marriage. They were almost never out of each other's sight. They finished each other's sentences. They started each day with a walk in Central Park. They had breakfast at the Three Guys Restaurant on weekdays and at the Carlyle hotel on Sundays. Their offices were in adjoining rooms of their sprawling apartment. John always answered the telephone. When it was someone like me calling with an interesting bit of news, he could always be heard to say, "Joan, pick up," so that she could hear the same bit of news at the same time. They were one of those couples who did everything together, and they were always in accord on their opinions, whatever subject was under discussion.

They were very much a part of the New York literary scene. Major American writers such as David Halberstam, Calvin Trillin, and Elizabeth Hardwick, whom they called Lizzie, were their close friends. In John's obituary in *The New York Times* on January 1, Richard Severo wrote, "Mr. Dunne and Ms. Didion were probably America's best known writing couple, and were anointed as the First Family of Angst by *The Saturday Review* in 1982 for their unflinching explorations of the national soul, or often, the glaring lack of one." They dined out regularly, primarily at Elio's, a celebrity-oriented Italian restaurant on Second Avenue at 84th Street, where they always had the same table, next to framed jackets of two of their books. They wrote their books and their magazine articles separately, but they collaborated on their screenplays for movies.

I was the second and John was the fifth of six children in a well-to-do Irish Catholic family in West Hartford, Connecticut. Our father was an extremely successful heart surgeon and the president of a hospital. In Irish Catholic circles, my mother was considered a bit of an heiress. We lived in a big, gray stone house in the best part of town, and our parents belonged to the country club. We went to private schools and to Mrs. Godfrey's dancing classes. We were the big-deal Irish Catholic family in a Wasp city, but we were still outsiders in the swanky life our parents created for us. John once wrote that we'd gone from steerage to the suburbs in three generations. We were so Catholic that priests came to dinner. John was named after Archbishop John Gregory Murray of St. Paul, Minnesota, who had married my parents.

Our grandfather Dominick Burns was a potato-famine immigrant who came to this country at 14 and made good. He started in the grocery business and ended up a bank president. When we were kids, we stressed the bank-president part of his life rather than the grocery part. He was made a Knight of St. Gregory by Pope Pius XII for his philanthropic work for the poor of Hartford. A public school in a section of the city known as Frog Hollow—the old Irish section—is named after him. John kept a large photograph of him in the living room of his apartment. Papa, as we called him, was an extraordinary man, and he had an enormous influence on my brother and me. It was as if he spotted us for the writers we would one day be. He didn't go to school past the age of 14, but literature was an obsession with him. He was never without a book, and he read voraciously. Early on, he taught John and me the excitement of reading. On Friday nights we would often stay over at his house, and he would read the classics or poetry to us and give us each a 50-cent piece for listening—a lot of money to a kid back then. John and I had another thing in common: we both stuttered. We went to an elocution teacher named Alice J. Buckley, who must have been good, because we both stopped stuttering years ago.

In 1943, at the age of 18, I was drafted out of my senior year at the Canterbury School and sent overseas after six weeks of basic training. I was in combat and received a Bronze Star Medal for saving a wounded soldier's life in Felsberg,

Germany, on December 20, 1944. John was always fascinated by that period of my life. Several times in magazine articles he mentioned my wartime experience at such a young age. Just this past Christmas, a few days before he died, he gave me a book by Paul Fussell called *The Boys' Crusade: The American Infantry in Northwestern Europe, 1944–1945*. When it came time for college, my father was adamant that we go to the best schools in the East. My older brother, Richard, went to Harvard. I went to Williams, John went to Princeton, and my youngest brother, Stephen, went to Georgetown and Yale graduate school. After college, I went into television in 1950 and married Ellen Griffin, a ranching heiress known as Lenny, in 1954. Three years later we moved to Hollywood with our two sons, Griffin and Alex. I had known all my life that I was going to live in Hollywood one day, and Lenny and I were instant successes—knew everybody, went everywhere, gave parties, went to parties.

John graduated from Princeton in 1954, worked for *Time* magazine for five years, traveled to fascinating places, did an army stint, and married Joan Didion, who was not yet famous, in Pebble Beach, California. I photographed their wedding. In 1967, when they left New York and moved to California, Joan wrote her beautiful piece "Farewell to the Enchanted City" for the *Saturday Evening Post*. It later became the final essay, renamed "Goodbye to All That," in her widely heralded best-selling book *Slouching Towards Bethlehem*. While my wife and I were strictly Beverly Hills people, John and Joan lived in "interesting" places. Joan put an ad in the paper saying that a writing couple was looking for a house to rent. A woman replied, offering an attractive gatehouse on an estate on the sea at Palos Verdes and explaining that the main house had never been built, because the rich people who had commissioned it went bust. The lady wanted $800 a month. Joan said they were prepared to pay only $400. They settled at $500. As they got to know the movie and literary crowds, they started to move closer to town, at first renting a big, falling-apart mansion on Franklin Avenue in old Hollywood. Janis Joplin went to one of their parties in that house, as did other fabled figures of the 60s. Then they bought a wonderful house on the beach in Trancas and rebuilt it. They contracted Harrison Ford, who was not yet a movie star, to do the work. When Quintana was old enough to go to school, they moved to their last California house, in Brentwood.

Our worlds grew closer and closer. In the early 70s, John, Joan, and I formed a film company called Dunne-Didion-Dunne. They wrote, and I produced. Our first picture was *The Panic in Needle Park,* for Twentieth Century Fox, based on a *Life*-magazine article by James Mills about heroin junkies. I remember sitting in the projection room and watching the dailies for the first time. In the darkness, John and I looked at each other as if we couldn't believe that two Hartford boys were making a big Hollywood-studio movie on location in New York City. It was

Al Pacino's first starring role, and he was mesmerizing as the doomed Bobby. It was a marvelous period. We were in total harmony. The picture was picked as an American entry to the Cannes Film Festival, and we all went over and had our first red-carpet experience. The film won the best-actress award for a young beginner named Kitty Winn. There were cheers and huzzahs and popping flashbulbs. It was a thrilling experience for all three of us. The following year John and Joan wrote the screenplay for *Play It as It Lays,* which was based on Joan's best-selling novel of the same name. I produced it with Frank Perry, who also directed. The picture, made by Universal, starred Tuesday Weld and Anthony Perkins. It was an American entry at the Venice Film Festival, where Tuesday Weld won the award for best actress. That was our last film together. John and I came away from that picture not liking each other as much as we had after the first. Then Joan and John made a mint on the movie *A Star Is Born,* starring Barbra Streisand, which was an enormous success, and in which they had a share of the profits. I remember being at the star-studded premiere in Westwood, when Streisand made one of the great movie entrances. And there were John and Joan, up there, having arrived, being photographed, getting celebrity treatment. Was I jealous? Yes.

I had begun to fall apart. Drink and drugs. Lenny divorced me. I was arrested getting off a plane from Acapulco carrying grass and was put in jail. John and Joan bailed me out. As I was falling and failing, they were soaring and gaining renown. When I went broke, they lent me $10,000. A terrible resentment builds when you've borrowed money and can't pay it back, although they never once reminded me of my obligation. That was the first of the many estrangements that followed. Finally, in despair, I left Hollywood early one morning and lived for six months in a cabin in Camp Sherman, Oregon, with neither telephone nor television. I stopped drinking. I stopped doping. I started to write. At about three o'clock one morning, John contacted me through the telephone of the couple from whom I rented the cabin to tell me that our brother Stephen, who was particularly close to John, had committed suicide. We all gathered in New Canaan, Connecticut, a few days later to attend Stephen's funeral. There were misunderstandings and the kinds of complications that so often occur in large families. Stephen was the youngest of the six of us, but he was the first to go. After his funeral, I began to rethink my life. In 1980, I left Hollywood for good and moved to New York. Even when John and I weren't speaking, we would meet up at family funerals. Our sisters, Harriet and Virginia, both died of breast cancer. Our nephew Richard Dunne Jr. was killed when his plane crashed in the airport at Hyannis, Massachusetts. His two daughters survived.

The major experience of my life has been the murder of my daughter. I never truly understood the meaning of the word "devastation" until I lost her. Since I was still a failed figure at the time, an unforgivable sin in Hollywood, where the murder took place, I was deeply sensitive to the slights I met with when I returned there. In "Justice," an article about the trial of the man who killed my daughter, the first article I ever wrote for *Vanity Fair,* in the March 1984 issue, I said:

> At the time of the murder Dominique was consistently identified in the press as the niece of my brother and sister-in-law, John Gregory Dunne and Joan Didion, rather than as the daughter of Lenny and me. At first I was too stunned by the killing for this to matter, but as the days passed, it bothered me. I spoke to Lenny about it one morning in her bedroom. She said, "Oh, what difference does it make?" with such despair in her voice that I felt ashamed to be concerned with such a trivial matter at such a crucial time.
>
> In the room with us was my former mother-in-law, Beatriz Sandoval Griffin Goodwin, the widow of Lenny's father, Thomas Griffin, an Arizona cattle rancher, and of Lenny's stepfather, Ewart Goodwin, an insurance tycoon and rancher. She is a strong, uncompromising woman who has never not stated exactly what was on her mind in any given situation, a trait that has made her respected if not always endearing.
>
> "Listen to what he's saying to you," she said emphatically. "It sounds like Dominique was an orphan raised by her aunt and uncle. . . . *And,"* [she] added, to underscore the point, "she had two brothers as well."

When the trial of John Sweeney, my daughter's killer, was due to start, there were serious conflicts between my brother and me. John, who knew his way around the Santa Monica courthouse, thought that we should accept a plea bargain, and emissaries from the defense were sent to us to effect one. Lenny, Griffin, Alex, and I felt pushed, as if we didn't matter. The district attorney wanted a trial, and so did we. So we went to trial. John and Joan went to Paris. The trial was a disaster. I hated the defense attorney. I hated the judge. The killer got out of prison in two and a half years. The experience changed me as a person and changed the course of my life. Out of that disaster I began, at the age of 50, to write in earnest, developing a passion for it I had never felt before.

More problems arose between John and me when I changed careers. I was, after all, moving in on turf that had been his for 25 years. I was the upstart. He and Joan were the stars. But I wrote four best-sellers in a row, all of which were made into mini-series, and I wrote regular features for this magazine. Was John jealous? Yes. Our books came and went, but we never mentioned them to each other, acting as if they did not exist. There was no resemblance between our writing styles. His novels were tough and dealt with low-life criminals. My novels were more socially rarefied and dealt with high-life criminals. There were difficult periods. Sometimes we maintained civility, despite bad feelings on both sides. Sometimes we didn't. We were always competitive. If I called him with a hot piece of gossip I'd heard, rather than reacting to it, he'd top it with a story *he'd* heard.

The final break came over the defense attorney Leslie Abramson, who defended Erik Menendez, one of two rich Beverly Hills brothers who shot their parents to death in 1989. Abramson gained national attention during the Menendez trial, which I covered for this magazine. My brother and I both wrote about her. She was a character in his novel *Red, White, and Blue.* John admired her, and she doted on him. I despised her, and she despised me right back. It got ugly. The crux of our difficulties came when John dedicated one of his books to her at the very time she and I were in public conflict. After that my brother and I did not speak for more than six years. But our fight really wasn't about Leslie Abramson. She played no part in my life. I never once saw her outside of the courtroom. An eruption had long been building between John and me, and Abramson just lit the match. When a magazine wanted to photograph us together for an article it was doing on brothers, each of us declined without checking with the other.

Because we had overlapping friends on both coasts, our estrangement made for social difficulties from time to time. If we were at the same party, Joan and I always spoke and then moved away from each other. John and I never spoke and stayed in different rooms. Our brother Richard, a successful insurance broker in Hartford, managed to remain neutral, but he was troubled over the schism. The situation was particularly hard on my son Griffin. He had always been very close to John and Joan, and now he had to do a balancing act between his father and his uncle. I'm sure that, as the years passed, John grew as eager to end the conflict between us as I was. It had become too public. Everyone in the worlds in which we traveled knew that the Dunne brothers did not speak.

Then, three years ago, I was diagnosed with prostate cancer. It's a scary thing when they call to tell you that you have cancer. Mine has subsequently been licked, by the way. I told Griffin. He told John. Then, by happenstance, I ran into my brother at eight o'clock in the morning in the hematology department of New York–Presbyterian Hospital, where we were both giving blood samples, he for his heart, I for my P.S.A. number. We spoke. And then John called me on the phone to wish me well. It was such a nice call, so heartfelt. All the hostility that had built up simply vanished. Griffin has reminded me that John then called him and said, "Let's all go to Elio's and laugh our asses off." We did. The thing that made our reconciliation so successful was that we never tried to clear up what had gone so wrong. We just let it go. There was too much about each other to enjoy. During this time John was having problems with his heart. He had several overnight stays at New York–Presbyterian for what he always referred to as "procedures." He was dismissive about their seriousness, but Griffin has told me, "He always thought he was going to keel over in Central Park."

Let me tell you about reconciliation. It's a glorious thing. I hadn't realized how much I missed John's humor. I'm pretty good in that department myself. We called it our Mick humor. We quickly fell back into the habit of calling each other at least twice a day to pass on the latest news. We have always both been message centers. It was good to speak about family again. We talked about our grandfather, the great reader, and about our mother and father, our two dead sisters, and our dead brother. We talked about Dominique, who had been close to John and Joan and Quintana. We kept in touch with our brother Richard, who had retired and moved from Hartford to Harwich Port, on Cape Cod. We had our picture taken together by Annie Leibovitz for the April 2002 issue of *Vanity Fair*—something that would have been unheard of two years earlier. We even began to talk to each other about what we were writing. Last December he FedExed me an early edition of *The New York Review of Books* with his review of Gavin Lambert's book in it, which I was reading when Joan called to tell me he was dead. Last year, when I was sued for slander by former congressman Gary Condit, I was loath to go out in public, but John insisted we have a family meal at their regular table at Elio's. "Be seen," he said. "Don't hide." I took his advice.

It's hard to assess your own family, but I had the opportunity to watch my brother and sister-in-law quite closely last summer when Quintana, 38, was married to Jerry Michael, a widower in his 50s, at the Cathedral of St. John the Divine, on Amsterdam Avenue at 112th Street. It was the middle of July, desperately hot in New York, but their friends, mostly literary, came to the city from whatever watering holes they were vacationing in to watch John and Joan, in parental pride, beam with approval on their daughter and her choice. Joan, wearing a mother-of-the-bride flowered hat and her ever present dark glasses, was escorted up the aisle of the cathedral on the arm of Griffin. She gave little waves to her friends in the pews as she passed them. I had become used to Joan over the last 40 years, but that day I realized again what a truly significant person she is. She had, after all, helped define a generation.

Joan may be tiny. She may weigh less than 80 pounds. She may speak in such a soft voice that you have to lean forward to hear her. But this lady is a dominant presence. As a brand-new widow with a daughter in an induced coma who didn't yet know her father was dead, she made decisions and went back and forth to the hospital. She stood in her living room and received the friends who came to call. Joan is not a Catholic, and John was a lapsed Catholic. She said to me, "Do you know a priest who can handle all this?" I said I did.

Joan decided that there was to be no funeral until Quintana recovered. My nephew Anthony Dunne and his wife, Rosemary Breslin, the daughter of the writer Jimmy Breslin, went with Joan and me to identify John's body at the Frank E. Campbell funeral home, on Madison Avenue and 81st Street, before he was cremated. We walked silently into the chapel. He was in a plain wooden box with no satin lining. He was dressed in the uniform of our lives: a blue blazer, gray flannel trousers, a shirt with a button-down collar, a striped tie, and loafers. Tony, Rosemary, and I stood back while Joan went to look at him. She leaned over and kissed him. She put her hands over his. We could see her body shaking as she cried quietly. After she turned away, I stepped up and said good-bye, followed by Tony and Rosemary. Then we left.

DOMINICK DUNNE

OUR MAN DOMINICK

by Mike Hogan

NOVEMBER 2009

Nobody ever saw Dominick Dunne and wondered, "Is that who I think it is?" You knew right away. The Turnbull & Asser ensembles in Crayola hues, the circular tortoiseshell glasses, the aroma of talcum powder that preceded him by five paces. It was all by design. He wanted you to recognize him. He wanted you to introduce yourself. He wanted you to tell him what you knew.

"He always used to say that people told him things, and they did," says Betty Prashker, Dominick's longtime editor at Crown, "and not just the people he was sitting next to at a dinner party, but the waiters who were handing him the food and the butlers who were taking his coat and hat."

"When you were with him at a restaurant, he always seemed a little disappointed if no one came over," says his friend Cynthia McFadden, of ABC News, "but he didn't have to suffer that kind of disappointment often."

"People always responded to Nick," says his sister-in-law Joan Didion. "He was kind of magic."

"He was our pop star," says *Vanity Fair*'s Reinaldo Herrera. "I suppose it was his Hollywood training. He certainly knew how to become a star, and he did."

There is a reason it has become customary to compare Dominick Dunne to Truman Capote, whose career he consciously emulated. Both writers emerged from obscurity to play outsize roles in the social lives of America's upper classes. Both used their insecurities to their advantage, exposing the offhand ways in which social arbiters dispense with pretenders. And both were at their best when writing about crime, revealing, from very different angles, the visceral horror of murder and the mundane inhumanity of the criminal-justice system.

But Dominick had something Capote did not: a life-defining cause. Justice wasn't just a plot device to him; it was his passion. Again and again, he'd watched as wealthy, well-connected people got away with murder—sometimes literally—

and he never learned to accept it. "What drove Dominick was that sense of outrage," says *Vanity Fair*'s Marie Brenner. "He was furious."

"Nick kicked people who were on top," says the writer Jesse Kornbluth, "and to do that and have it published is not small. And then to be *celebrated* for it!"

What makes his accomplishments all the more astonishing is how low he was just three decades ago. Before he became one of the most instantly recognizable magazine writers in the world, Dominick Dunne's only claim to fame was his epic, humiliating failure. His charmed life as a Hollywood producer, party giver, and collector of A-list friends, from Gary Cooper and Jennifer Jones to Natalie Wood and Dennis Hopper, had been undone in spectacular fashion by his insecurity, addiction, and indiscretion. "He was really a mess," says his friend Brigid Berlin, the Andy Warhol insider. "If anybody was at the bottom, Dominick was."

How he climbed back to the top is one of the great turnaround stories of the celebrity age. "What got him in trouble in Hollywood was his big mouth, getting hammered and telling stories out of school," says his elder son, Griffin Dunne. "And what made him popular was telling the *same* stories and people *wanting* to have the stories told about them."

Even when he was nobody, Dominick knew everybody. The author Jane Stanton Hitchcock met him in New York in 1982, at a dinner party hosted by Bobo Legendre, whose family, the Sanfords, are said to have been the model for the aristocratic Setons in the 1938 movie *Holiday*, starring Katharine Hepburn and Cary Grant. Dominick had just arrived from Los Angeles, his wounds still fresh. "He did not have a dime," Hitchcock says. "He'd had this whole Hollywood life, but he was struggling."

According to Griffin Dunne, then a promising actor with a starring role in *An American Werewolf in London*, Dominick's vast social network extended all the way from the dinner-party circuit to the gutter. "I'd have lunch with him, and all these street hustlers and vagrants would go, 'Hey, Dominick,'" Griffin recalls. "This is a guy who based his life on Cecil Beaton. Now he's Damon Runyon. I said, 'How do you *know* these people?' And he goes, 'Oh, you know, they're from the rooms.' He'd become a star speaker at various A.A. rooms in the Village."

It's not hard to imagine Dominick honing his repertoire of self-lacerating stories at Alcoholics Anonymous meetings, but he wasn't afraid to tell them in polite company, either. Those who knew him eventually heard them all.

He was born into a well-to-do Irish-Catholic family in Hartford, Connecticut, at a time when being Irish was still a social handicap. His father, a prominent heart surgeon, called him a sissy, beat him with a wooden hanger, and never accepted him—until he came home from World War II with a Bronze Star for rescuing two fellow soldiers from behind enemy lines. After the war he married a beautiful Arizona ranching heiress named Lenny Griffin, moved to New York

City, and found work as the stage manager of the *Howdy Doody* show. But his lifelong fascination with movie stars soon propelled him to Los Angeles.

There he and Lenny became known for their extravagant parties, which were attended by the cream of Hollywood: Kirk Douglas, Jane Fonda, Billy Wilder, Merle Oberon, Roddy McDowall, Lauren Bacall, and so on. These affairs produced some world-class scrapbooks, but they took a toll on the Dunnes' marriage, not to mention on their children, Griffin, Alex, and Dominique. "If it was a particularly noisy or rowdy night," Griffin remembers, "we'd get bundled up in our pj's and checked into a hotel with our little schoolbags for school the next day."

Perhaps worse, from Dominick's perspective, he was never really accepted by these new friends. As a TV producer socializing with movie stars, he didn't rank. Frank Sinatra told him to his face that he was a no-talent hack. Others just said it behind his back.

Even the crowning triumph of the Dunnes' Hollywood life ended with a sour twist. In 1964, Dominick and Lenny celebrated their 10th anniversary with a lavish black-and-white ball at their home on Walden Drive, in Beverly Hills. "*Le tout* Hollywood was there, and my eyes were falling on the floor," says Mart Crowley, whose play *The Boys in the Band* was later adapted for the screen with Dominick as co-executive producer. Among the guests were Ronald and Nancy Reagan, Alfred and Betsy Bloomingdale, Billy and Audrey Wilder, David Niven, Angela Lansbury, Loretta Young, Natalie Wood, Vincente Minnelli, and Truman Capote, who was photographed for *Vogue* dancing with Tuesday Weld.

Two years later, Capote gave *his* famous black-and-white ball in New York and neglected to invite the Dunnes. The snub infuriated Dominick, but he had more in common with Capote than he realized. Not long after Dominick arrived in Hollywood, he attended a party thrown by the producer William Frye. "I had all the old movie people that were still alive," Frye recalls, including Joan Fontaine, Rosalind Russell, and Bette Davis. A week later, the Dunnes invited Russell and Davis to a party at their house, and they didn't invite Frye. As Dominick wrote in his memoir, *The Way We Lived Then*, "I used to say that I was good at writing assholes because I used to be one."

Lenny divorced Dominick in 1965. After that he went into a downward spiral. He was arrested for possession of marijuana following a flight back from Mexico and was paraded through the airport, handcuffed, past his brother John Gregory Dunne and sister-in-law Joan Didion, two of the literary celebrities of their day. He torpedoed his producing career, he always claimed, by making a tasteless joke—later printed word for word in *The Hollywood Reporter*—about the powerful and popular agent Sue Mengers and her husband. Mengers responds, "I was flattered that Nick Dunne would identify me as the person who ended his career in Hollywood because of my power. I wish it were true."

Realizing that his Hollywood life was over, Dominick left town, drove north, and wound up in a cabin in the Cascade Mountains of Oregon, where he stayed for six months. He contemplated suicide, but resolved instead to sober up. It occurred to him that he would be a writer. He was 50 years old.

Back in Los Angeles, he sold almost everything he owned, including his West Highland terrier. "I paid $400 for Alfie," remembers Connie Wald. Then he moved to New York, where he rented a tiny apartment on Ninth Street and focused on finishing his first novel, *The Winners*, which he'd sold as the sequel to the gossip columnist Joyce Haber's novel *The Users*. He must have thought the worst was behind him, but it was about to come.

George Hamilton still remembers what it was like in 1982 inside the intensive-care unit at Cedars-Sinai hospital, in Los Angeles. "There was no time or light," says the actor, whose 52-year-old half-brother, Bill, was terminally ill. "I would be there sometimes for 20 hours at a time." He was keeping vigil when an ambulance arrived carrying Dominick Dunne's daughter, Dominique, a 22-year-old actress who had just appeared in Steven Spielberg's *Poltergeist*.

Dominique had been strangled almost to death by her 26-year-old boyfriend, John Sweeney, a sous-chef at the L.A. hot spot Ma Maison. Dominick awoke in the middle of the night to a phone call from Lenny, and he boarded the next plane to Los Angeles. The family, re-united by tragedy, convened at Lenny's house, on Crescent Drive, then headed to the hospital. "At first I did not realize that the person on the bed was Dominique," Dominick later wrote. "Her neck was purpled and swollen; vividly visible on it were the marks of the massive hands of the man who had strangled her. It was nearly impossible to look at her, but also impossible to look away." Tests showed that Dominique was brain-dead, so the family, while still struggling to come to grips with this nightmare, gave consent for her to be taken off life support. Before his daughter was wheeled away for the last time, Dominick leaned over, gave her a kiss, and whispered, "Give me your talent."

Her killer's trial was a travesty. The judge was a preening attention seeker, Dominick later wrote, who wore "designer jeans, glossy white loafers, and no necktie beneath his judicial robes," and who seemed to go out of his way to accommodate the defendant, whose history of violence against women was not revealed to the jury. The Dunnes attended every session on the advice of victims'-rights activists, who told them, "It's the last business of your daughter's life." The judge, meanwhile, issued a Draconian set of restrictions at the defense attorney's request: "If any member of the Dunne family cries, cries out, rolls his eyes, exclaims in any way, he will be asked to leave the courtroom."

Dominick sat there and absorbed it all. Later, he would say he had never given "five seconds' thought" to the criminal-justice system until that trial. Now he found himself helpless to protect his family from a second tragedy. Only after the jury delivered its verdict—manslaughter, which meant that Sweeney would be back on the street within three years—did he finally erupt. After the judge thanked the jury on behalf of the attorneys and both families, Dominick shouted, "Not for our family!" Griffin remembers the moment: "He's being pulled out of the court by the bailiffs and met by the reporters, who had their cameras ready. *That's* when he found his voice." Dominick's article about John Sweeney's case was published in the March 1984 issue of *Vanity Fair* under the title "Justice." Even today, you can feel the rage pulsating behind his carefully chosen words.

By the time I met Dominick, in 1998, he had channeled that anger into a world-class writing career. He and his editor—my new boss at the time, Wayne Lawson—had been working together for 15 years, producing definitive coverage of the most notorious, and irresistible, criminal trials of the 80s and 90s. The world they introduced me to bore no relation to anything I had experienced before. My last big adventure had been a somewhat disappointing year abroad, studying Anglo-Irish literature at University College Dublin. There I decided that I wanted to work with real live writers, instead of spending my life figuring out what James Joyce had had for breakfast the day he wrote page 236 of *Finnegans Wake*. Wayne worked with some of the magazine's best, and my job, as his assistant, was to make the reporting and editing process as painless as possible for them.

I did what I could, though no one ever accused me of being the concierge type. Dominick inscribed a copy of his book *Justice* to me with the words "To Michael Hogan, who saves my life every day," but he wasn't always so charitable. I'll never forget how furious he was the day he called me from Wilmington, Delaware, where he was reporting a story about a drug-addicted DuPont heir whose prostitute girlfriend had wound up dead, stuffed inside an air-conditioning duct. I had been sloppy and booked him in a middlebrow hotel in the wrong part of town. "Do you know who I *am*?" he screamed. "I'm a *star* at this fucking magazine!"

But he was also capable of great kindness. His words of encouragement meant a lot to a 24-year-old scholarship kid who was struggling to get his bearings in the sophisticated atmosphere of *Vanity Fair*. And he could be funny. Once, Wayne took us to a fancy restaurant where on a previous visit I had spotted a tiny worm inching its way across my hamburger bun. When we arrived, the maître d' said it would be a few moments and motioned us to one side. Waiting for tables was not Dominick's thing, and after two or three minutes he could bear it no longer. Whipping out one of his signature green, leather-bound, personalized Smythson of Bond Street reporter's notebooks, he said in a very loud voice, "So, tell me about the *worm* you found on your *hamburger* the last time you ate here!" Within seconds we were seated.

Maybe Dominick was destined to become a star, and maybe *Vanity Fair* was destined to become the magazine it is today, but neither outcome seemed especially likely in the spring of 1985. The magazine had debuted just two years earlier and was still struggling to find its footing. Every week, it seemed, the papers ran another item predicting its demise. Being underestimated had its advantages, though, starting with the camaraderie it fostered among the small staff. "We were on a mission," Marie Brenner remembers. "And Dominick was the missionary. It was as if he was creating himself for the first time. He had the esprit of a kid, even though he was old enough to be everybody's uncle."

He wrote at a feverish clip, contributing to issue after issue—profiles of Diane Keaton, Gloria Vanderbilt, and Candy Spelling, as well as a dispatch from the trial of the man who killed Vicki Morgan, the ex-mistress of merchandising tycoon Alfred Bloomingdale.

Then came the sensational re-trial of Danish-born aristocrat Claus von Bülow. Two years in a row, in 1979 and 1980, his rich American wife, known as Sunny, had fallen into a coma during Christmas celebrations at the family mansion in Newport, Rhode Island. The first coma passed, but the second would hold her in its grip until her death 28 years later, in December 2008. In 1982, Claus was convicted of attempted murder and sentenced to 30 years, but the well-known defense attorney Alan Dershowitz won him his freedom on appeal.

Von Bülow's second trial began in Providence in April 1985, and Dominick was there, covering it in a way that would have appalled the hoary heads of journalism. He became a guardian figure to Sunny's children from her first marriage, Prince Alexander von Auersperg and Princess Annie-Laurie "Ala" von Auersperg, and never wasted a moment worrying about objectivity. "I took sides," he wrote on vanityfair.com after Sunny's death. "I believed Ala and Alex. I disbelieved Claus von Bülow."

But he was enough of a reporter to know exactly what to ask Claus and his girlfriend, Andrea Reynolds, when the opportunity presented itself. Reynolds, who later befriended Dominick and called him her "best enemy," says she and von Bülow had been warned not to speak to him, but an incident at the hotel in Providence where they were all staying softened her resistance.

"One evening I'm walking up the stairs to my apartment and what do I see? I see Dominick Dunne stuck between two floors in one of those old-fashioned metal elevators," Reynolds says. "Some people had gone to get help, so I lay down on the steps, and I took hold of his hand and tried to soothe him. My heart went out to him. So when he was saved, I said to Claus, 'You know, we're being unfair to this man. Let's give him the interview.' And Claus never really disagreed with me; he didn't dare."

On this occasion, at least, von Bülow would live to regret that policy. Dominick posed the two questions every other reporter had been too polite to ask: Did Claus ever really love Sunny ("Oh, yes"), and was it true that Andrea wore Sunny's jewelry? Andrea's reply—"Not true! I have far better jewels than Sunny von Bülow ever had"—wasn't likely to win her any fans in the cheap seats.

There was enough in Dominick's article to cause a stir, but what put it over the top were Helmut Newton's morbidly fascinating photographs of von Bülow and Reynolds in matching leather jackets that made them look, as Reynolds puts it, like "S&M people."

"That in itself was total trickery," says Reynolds, who claims that she and von Bülow had received the jackets as gag gifts from their respective children. (Hers had the words HELL'S GRANNY stitched on the back in silver lettering.) She also claims that the leather shots were done as a favor to Newton, who promised not to publish them.

Dominick phoned Marie Brenner, ecstatic with the news. "The phone call that I remember is: 'You're not going to believe this. We have gotten Claus to pose in a black leather jacket,'" she says. "That picture went around the world."

The August 1985 issue, with Claus von Bülow and Andrea Reynolds on the cover, set a new sales record for *Vanity Fair*. If the magazine had helped turn Dominick's life around, it was no less true that he had been instrumental in saving the life of the magazine.

There was just one problem with the von Bülow trial: Claus was found not guilty. The verdict came down on June 10. "The courtroom was strangely mute despite a few cheers from elderly Clausettes in the back of the room," Dominick deadpanned.

For the next few years, he mostly stayed out of court. At *Vanity Fair*, he flitted from topic to topic, as most magazine writers do: Imelda Marcos, the Duchess of Windsor, Robert Mapplethorpe. It was interesting and glamorous work, but some who knew Dominick doubt that he found it altogether fulfilling. "He could talk the society stuff very well, but I don't think that's what he was really dancing to," says George Hamilton. "I think his heart was wrapped around the loss of that child and that tragedy."

Then, in 1990, a story broke in Los Angeles that was almost too ghastly to believe. Two wealthy, handsome young brothers, Lyle and Erik Menendez, were arrested for murdering their parents at their home in Beverly Hills. They hadn't just murdered them, however. They had massacred them in the family living room, with shotguns, blasting their father in the head, their mother in the face, chest, arms, and legs, and then both in the kneecaps in a clumsy effort to cast suspicion on the Mafia.

Dominick took up residence at the Chateau Marmont and spent six months covering the trial. Rhode Island had been one thing, but now he was back in Los Angeles, where he had gone off the rails, suffered his disgrace, and watched John Sweeney win a slap on the wrist. How good it would feel to get even. He threw himself into covering the trial, bluffing his way into the Menendez home, which was for sale at a heavily discounted price, and trading insults with Erik's defense attorney Leslie Abramson, who happened to be a close friend of Dominick's brother John Gregory Dunne. (John later dedicated a book to Abramson, at which point Dominick stopped talking to him for more than six years.)

Simon Brennan, who fact-checked Dominick's dispatches from the trial for *Vanity Fair*, sensed that he was having a hard time finding a way into the story. There were no grieving family members to side with. Jose and Kitty were dead, and their children were the killers. Still, his coverage of the trial was notable in at least one respect: outraged by the defense's central claim, that Jose had sexually molested the boys, and that this somehow justified their actions, Dominick wrote for the first time about his own experience of abuse. "I was not abused sexually, but physically and psychologically. I was beaten with straps, hangers, and riding crops," he wrote. "But I never wanted to kill [my father]. The thought never once entered my mind."

On June 17, 1994, Orenthal James Simpson and his sidekick Al Cowlings hit the road in a white Bronco, sparking the highest-rated low-speed car chase in television history. Five days earlier, Simpson's ex-wife, Nicole Brown Simpson, and her friend Ron Goldman had been the fatal victims of an ultra-violent knife attack at her condominium in Brentwood. O.J., who had previously pleaded no contest to charges of spousal battery against Nicole, was the prime suspect.

The whole country paid attention, but Los Angeles was downright transfixed. O. J. Simpson wasn't just a retired football star—he was one of the nation's most charismatic African-American celebrities, as famous for his product endorsements and roles in films such as *Roots* and *The Naked Gun* as he was for his record-shattering 2,000-yard season as an N.F.L. running back with the Buffalo Bills.

The case painted a giant red stripe down the city's racial divide: white people, for the most part, thought O.J. was quite obviously guilty; African-Americans, remembering the Scottsboro Boys, Hurricane Carter, and countless other black men falsely convicted in crimes against whites, suspected the continuation of an old, sinister pattern. Jeffrey Toobin wrote extensively about the case's racial implications for *The New Yorker*, but he doesn't remember discussing them with

Dominick. "I think that was to him a case about a murder and victims," he says, "not a case about the racial climate in Los Angeles."

Dominick became obsessed with the ensuing murder trial. "He went almost insane," says Griffin Dunne. "It was like a disembowelment for him, with everything that happened with Dominique. It was just churning up every ugly memory."

"O.J. has taken over my life," Dominick wrote in a May 1995 article in *V.F.* titled "All O.J., All the Time," which began with a dizzying description of his daily routine, starting at six a.m., "when room service brings me my o.j. and coffee," continuing through a review of the day's O.J. news, culminating with a long session in court where "we all stare at O.J. to see what kind of mood he's in or to which lawyer he's talking," and ending at a dinner party where "they all wanted to talk about nothing but O. J. Simpson."

The trial represented everything Dominick had come to despise about the legal system as it applied to rich and famous defendants. One defense attorney dedicated to smearing the victim was bad enough, as he saw it, but O.J. shelled out millions of dollars on a "Dream Team," including F. Lee Bailey, Robert Shapiro, Alan Dershowitz, Robert Kardashian, and Johnnie Cochran, of whom Dominick wrote, "Personally, I have never liked brown, pale-blue, or mustard-colored suits, or ties with horizontal stripes, but when he wears them, they work."

Dominick was alive to the surreal glamour of what soon became known as "the trial of the century," but he was also dead serious about the outcome he desired. He befriended the victims' families, particularly Ron Goldman's father and sister, and wrote movingly of their ordeal. He wanted a guilty verdict as badly as they did.

As always, he met people who told him things. "At first there was some skepticism," remembers Cynthia McFadden, who covered the trial for ABC. "I mean, how could he possibly just *run into* all these people? But it was just simply the fact."

All his life he had been a repository of tips, information, and gossip, but never before had his morsels been so highly prized. "L.A. was obsessed with the O.J. case, and Dominick was their point person," says Dan Abrams, who was covering the trial for Court TV. "He wasn't writing just about the trial. He was writing about the spectacle. And part of the reason he could write about the spectacle is because he had this unique access."

Dominick's lifetime of aggressive, peripatetic socializing was paying off in a big way. "I sometimes thought he got unfair criticism about name-dropping," Toobin says, "because that was his life, and the information that came from that life was interesting and relevant. Dominick would have lunch with Nancy Reagan the way I would take my son to one of his soccer games. One of those things is journalistically relevant and the other is not."

Those who weren't privy to both sides of him—the party guest *and* the courtroom sleuth—might not have realized how hard he was working. "I don't know when he slept," says McFadden. "He literally was out every single night, and he was the first person in the courtroom every morning."

Vanity Fair published nine of his O. J. Simpson dispatches over the course of 1995. In that pre-Internet media landscape, Dominick's reports were the only ones that, in Toobin's words, "tore down the curtain between what journalists say to each other at lunch and what they put in their stories." If you cared about the O.J. case, and almost everybody did, you had to read them.

Dominick became a constant presence on television news programs, from *Nightline* to *Larry King Live*. It was the dawn of the 24-hour-news era, and America, with no wars to worry about, was endlessly fascinated by the courtroom travails of its domestic villains. He began to be invited out, every night, to some of the most exclusive parties in Hollywood. "Dominick would be the center of attention, because it was Dominick to whom everyone turned to tell what was really happening in the courtroom," Cynthia McFadden says.

"I said to him, 'But these are the very same fucking people who turned their backs on you and wouldn't give you the time of day. What are you *doing*?'" remembers Mart Crowley. "He said, 'Believe me, I'll never forget it, but that's not going to stop me.'"

McFadden remembers observing him at a party hosted by Tita Cahn surrounded by Jack Nicholson, Warren Beatty, and Frank Sinatra. "He had come back victorious to Los Angeles," she says.

As gratifying as it was for Dominick to reconquer the social world of Hollywood, it was nothing compared with the anguish he felt as one well-financed defendant after another wriggled off the hook. When Simpson's not-guilty verdict was announced, Dominick's mouth popped open in horror. His expression, captured by the courtroom cameras, became one of the indelible images of the trial.

"I was watching it live on television in a sublet apartment in the Village, and I saw the expression on my dad's face, and I started to cry," Griffin remembers. "Not long after that, he had a 70th-birthday party at Mortimer's, and I remember giving a toast and saying, 'I beg you, let this be your last murder trial.'" But there was no stopping him now. Dominick was already deeply involved in another murder case, one he would later be celebrated—and castigated—for single-handedly reopening.

The origins of his involvement in the Michael Skakel murder case stretched back to 1991, when William Kennedy Smith, the 30-year-old son of John F. Kennedy's sister Jean, was accused of raping a 29-year-old woman during an alcohol-fueled evening at his family's house in Palm Beach. But Dominick's complicated relationship with the Kennedys went back even further. "When I first met him," says Dominick's friend Fred Eberstadt, "he admired the Kennedys very much, and wanted to like them and be liked by them." Through a friend, Dominick attended Robert F. Kennedy's wedding to Ethel Skakel in 1950. And he later befriended Peter and Pat Kennedy Lawford, who were neighbors in Santa Monica.

Dominick was starstruck by Jack Kennedy when he saw him at the Lawfords', but he later became disenchanted by the family's treatment of Pat's husband. "Peter was ill-used by his famous and glamorous brothers-in-law," Dominick wrote in *The Way We Lived Then*. "Get the girls, Peter. Get the blow, Peter. Tell Sinatra we can't come, Peter, we're staying at Bing Crosby's instead. Having to give that message to Sinatra was the kiss of death for Peter. Sinatra hated him from then on." To Dominick, the Kennedys were just like his old tormentor, Frank Sinatra. They were the "careless people" F. Scott Fitzgerald had described, who "smashed up things and creatures and then retreated back into their money."

So it should have come as no surprise when Dominick, covering William Kennedy Smith's rape trial for *Vanity Fair*, sided with the accuser, Patricia Bowman. As he saw it, Bowman, being a "virtual nonentity," was no match for the amoral tactics of "America's most famous theatrical family."

In the end, Kennedy Smith too was acquitted. But the trial wasn't a total loss, from Dominick's perspective, because while he was covering it he heard a juicy piece of gossip: William Kennedy Smith, someone told him, had been at the Greenwich home of Ethel Kennedy's brother Rushton Skakel on the night a girl named Martha Moxley was murdered.

The rumor proved false, but it piqued Dominick's curiosity. What ever happened to the Moxley case? In 1975, Martha, a 15-year-old neighbor of Rushton Skakel and his seven children, had been found dead under a pine tree outside her house, with the broken shaft of a Toney Penna golf club protruding from her neck. Her body had been dragged from the driveway, and a set of Toney Penna clubs was found at the Skakel house, but no one was charged with the crime.

Through a local newspaper, Dominick contacted Martha's widowed mother, Dorthy, who had since moved to Annapolis, Maryland. "I was eager to have anybody help me who would, and he was eager for some information for his book," Moxley recalls.

"I told Mrs. Moxley that I thought I could write another [best-selling novel] based loosely on her daughter's murder," Dominick later wrote in *Vanity Fair*, "since no facts were known publicly at the time, and it might turn a spotlight on the long-dormant case."

Dominick wasn't just blowing smoke; he had a proven track record for provoking controversy with his books. His first successful novel, published in 1985, was based on the famous Woodward murder case of the mid-1950s. Dominick had toyed with the idea of writing a nonfiction account, but ultimately decided that his facts were "too good to check," as Jane Stanton Hitchcock put it. The resulting novel, *The Two Mrs. Grenvilles*, hit the best-seller lists and was soon adapted into a mini-series starring Claudette Colbert and Ann-Margret—to the dismay of the real-life Woodwards and their friends in high places.

Subsequent books would cause even more trouble. *People Like Us*, Dominick's thinly fictionalized study of New York society, earned him some very well-known enemies even before it was published. In January 1988, five months before the release date, the editors of *Women's Wear Daily* obtained a copy of the manuscript and printed a possible "who's who" of the characters. Among those mentioned were Elizabeth Taylor, real-estate agent Alice Mason, prominent walker Jerome Zipkin, and such power couples as Oscar and Annette de la Renta, Saul and Gayfryd Steinberg, Alfred and Judith Taubman, and John and Susan Gutfreund. "Nick felt that he got shut out of a certain group at that time," says Susan Magrino, who worked in the publicity department at Crown. "Some got over it, but some I don't think ever spoke to him again."

Two years later, *An Inconvenient Woman* arrived to offend a whole new set of drawing-room power brokers. The book was based on the tragic case of Vicki Morgan, who was murdered by her psychotic roommate in 1983. Betsy Bloomingdale, who had cut off Alfred's payments to Morgan after his death, did not enjoy seeing this painful history served up for general consumption, and stopped speaking to Dominick. They later reconciled, she says, at Swifty Lazar's Academy Awards party at Spago. "Everyone was looking because there he was and there I was and blah blah blah," Bloomingdale recalls. "But I said, 'Hello.' And he said, 'Hello.' And then we were all great friends after that. A 'hello' could do it."

But that was soft stuff compared with the trouble he invited with his 1993 book inspired by the murder of Martha Moxley. *A Season in Purgatory* was a fictional account of the killing, based on Dominick's informed speculation about what had happened. The killer in the novel had a good deal in common with John F. Kennedy Jr., though Dominick really suspected Tommy Skakel, the second son of Rushton Skakel. Tommy, who was 17 at the time of the murder, had been fooling around with Martha that night. "I was convinced that he had done it, and had said so on TV," Dominick later wrote.

A series of strange encounters followed, of the variety that could have happened only to Dominick. First, a mysterious woman gave him a sneak peek at the autopsy pictures of Martha Moxley's body, which police later informed him had been stolen. She also told him, "It wasn't Tommy." Then a young man slipped him a copy of a secret report prepared, at Rushton Skakel's request, by an investigative firm called Sutton Associates. The young man said the evidence pointed to Tommy's younger brother, Michael, who was the same age as Martha. Apparently the two boys had been rivals for her affection. Finally, Dominick's old friend Lucianne Goldberg, the literary agent, called and asked if he knew of any murder cases that her client Mark Fuhrman could investigate for his next book. Dominick didn't necessarily admire Fuhrman, the disgraced detective in the O. J. Simpson case whose past use of the word "nigger" had provided the defense with one of its most emotionally resonant victories, but he wasn't inclined to turn up his nose at Goldberg's suggestion. "It was a magic moment," Dominick later wrote. "'The Moxley case,' I said excitedly. 'I have some information that I will give him.'"

Assisted—and goaded—by Dominick and Fuhrman, the Greenwich police compiled a case against Michael Skakel, who was charged with murder on January 20, 2000. The trial began in the spring of 2002, and right away Skakel's attorney Mickey Sherman knew his client had a problem. "The jury isn't looking at me—they're looking at Dominick Dunne, they're looking at Dorthy Moxley," he remembers. "It was like arguing against apple pie."

Dominick and Dorthy may have held the moral high ground, but the evidence was worryingly thin. The murder had occurred a quarter of a century earlier, and even Dominick had to admit that "there were no fingerprints, no witnesses, no DNA—nothing, other than circumstantial evidence, on which to build a case." Skakel had made a series of confession-like statements over the years, but his confidants tended to be addicts and reform-school brats. Dominick was girding himself for another disappointment and enduring a bit of bullying from the Skakel and Kennedy clans. One day Michael's aunt Ann Skakel McCooey passed by, arm in arm with Robert Kennedy Jr., and loudly called out, "Jerk!"

Then the incredible happened: after deliberating for just three days, the jury found Michael Skakel guilty. Writing in the August 2002 issue, Dominick made plain what the outcome meant to him. "The verdict in the Moxley case is the one I wanted for John Sweeney, my daughter's killer," he wrote. "After covering celebrity trials for *Vanity Fair* over the years, I have become so cynical that I simply assumed Michael Skakel would walk, as people of his class and wealth so often do. But at the trial, justice prevailed. Here's to you, Martha Moxley and Dominique Dunne, who got gypped out of your lives. I send you both my love."

Robert Kennedy Jr., whose undisguised dislike of Dominick was decidedly mutual, struck back with a scathing, 16,000-word article in *The Atlantic*, in which he called Dominick "a driving force behind Michael Skakel's prosecution" and generally portrayed him as a loose cannon with a vendetta against the Kennedys. [In 2016, Robert Kennedy Jr. published a book on the case, *Framed: Why Michael Skakel Spent Over a Decade in Prison for a Murder He Didn't Commit.*]

But, for those who had known Dominick since the shattering ordeal of his daughter's murder, it was thrilling to see him vindicated at last. "Nick was at his best in the Moxley case," says Marie Brenner. "He made it his business to get this case avenged, and he did." At least one other journalist covering the case day in and day out thought Dominick had been in the right. "Robert F. Kennedy I think spent a total of about three hours in that courtroom and did not watch the trial," says Jeffrey Toobin, who covered it for CNN and *The New Yorker*. "I thought that was revealed in his silly piece about the case."

Dorthy Moxley, meanwhile, has nothing but gratitude for what Dominick did. "I have always said I had a team of angels helping me," she says, "and he was a very big angel on the team. Small in stature, but he was big."

Early in 2001, the syndicated columnist Liz Smith, one of Dominick's closest friends, ran into Graydon Carter at a party and asked why Dominick Dunne wasn't writing a monthly column. His life certainly was interesting enough, she said. Carter liked the idea, and in the March 2001 issue "Dominick Dunne's Diary" made its debut. "While I do go out entirely too much," Dominick wrote in that inaugural installment, "something always seems to happen which makes going out irresistible to me."

By that time, Dominick had long since become accustomed to trappings of success that would have seemed unthinkable when he washed up in New York in the early 80s. He had a penthouse on East 49th Street and a country house in Hadlyme, Connecticut, which Cynthia McFadden describes as "exactly the kind of house you wanted Dominick Dunne to live in, filled with books and beautiful chintzes."

He could have retired in comfort and style, but quitting wasn't in his DNA. It would be another year before the Moxley case wrapped up, and he'd since become embroiled in the controversy surrounding the mysterious death of Edmond Safra, an international financier who died in a fire at his apartment in Monaco. For some reason Safra's team of bodyguards had that night off, and Dominick was mistakenly convinced that the dead man's prominent wife, Lily, knew more than she was letting on.

Not much later, Dominick inserted himself into the case of Chandra Levy, a congressional intern whose disappearance raised questions about her relationship with Representative Gary Condit. After hearing a colorful—if far-fetched—theory about her disappearance from a man who claimed to be the inspiration for the movie *The Horse Whisperer*, Dominick made the mistake of repeating it on Laura Ingraham's radio show, on *Larry King Live*, and at dinner parties hosted by his friends Wendy Stark and Casey Ribicoff, widow of the Connecticut senator Abraham Ribicoff. In response, Gary Condit sued Dominick for defamation. "He just overreached," says Liz Smith. "He thought he was more powerful than he was." The $11 million suit, filed on December 16, 2002, did not name *Vanity Fair*, but Dominick nevertheless felt strongly that the magazine should finance his defense.

The fallout was unpleasant for all involved. The suit, which was later settled, "weighed heavily on him," says Dan Abrams. "He was embarrassed that he'd gotten it wrong, and I think that's reflective of the mentality of a real reporter." But the sting went deeper than that. Dominick felt betrayed by the magazine that had defined him, and that he had helped define. "He really almost couldn't bear it," says McFadden. "It was like breaking up with a lover."

Except the breakup never quite happened. Month after month, Dominick filed his dispatches. Month after month, his face appeared in the magazine's pages. He covered the Robert Blake, Phil Spector, and Martha Stewart trials, the Brooke Astor elder-abuse case, and O. J. Simpson's kidnapping trial in Las Vegas ("I don't really think he's guilty of this crime," he told Brigid Berlin), all the while keeping readers up-to-date on the latest developments in his starry universe. When he patched up the long-standing feud with his brother John, he wrote about that. When John died, followed nine months later by his adopted daughter, Dominick wrote, with heartbreaking candor, about that (*see page 243*). And when Dominick himself was diagnosed with two kinds of cancer—prostate, in 2000, and then bladder, in 2007—he wrote about that too. In all, he contributed no fewer than 67 monthly Diary entries to *Vanity Fair* in eight years— a remarkable feat for a man in his 70s and 80s writing for a magazine that comes out only 12 times a year.

Meanwhile, a new audience was discovering him on television. *Dominick Dunne's Power, Privilege and Justice*, an original series on Court TV (which has since been renamed TruTV), introduced viewers to the biggest trials of the past half-century—including several that had punctuated Dominick's career. The show premiered in 2002 and broadcast 57 episodes during his lifetime.

He also kept busy speaking to victims' organizations and finishing his long-gestating last novel. Crown is billing *Too Much Money* as a sequel to *People Like Us*, and its plot concerns a rich widow whose husband died in a suspicious fire and a congressman falsely implicated in the disappearance of an intern. As usual, Dominick's real-life inspirations are not hard to guess.

By the time work on the novel was completed, Dominick's cancer had taken a heavy toll. He declined to have his bladder removed after doctors discovered a potentially dangerous irregular heartbeat, and instead pursued a regimen of stem-cell treatment that took him to the Dominican Republic and Germany, where—not surprisingly, given his record for remarkable coincidences—he found himself one room away from Farrah Fawcett.

He seldom complained, and he bolstered his courage with gallows humor. Fred Eberstadt remembers a call from him that began, "Hi, am I dead yet?" And Mart Crowley still laughs at the response he got after complimenting Dominick on his svelte new figure: "Well, there's no diet like cancer!"

He spent his last days at home, welcoming a series of visitors, and Griffin took charge of making everything perfect for him. "I can't tell you how many vases of flowers were all around him," says Reinaldo Herrera. "He was the big star in the hospital in Hollywood in the 40s, like you saw in the movies."

Dominick died on August 26, 2009, but fate had prepared one last humbling joke for him. The night before, Ted Kennedy had beaten him to the punch. The man who, in Dominick's estimation, had "lived recklessly, performed brilliantly in Congress, and often failed miserably in life" was all anybody could talk about.

Even in death, Dominick was being tormented by the family he resented most. It was the kind of story that would have amused the hell out of him—if only it had happened to someone else.

BEHIND THE BEST-SELLERS

JOSEPHINE TEY

HER OWN BEST MYSTERY

by Francis Wheen

OCTOBER 2015

It begins with a body in the library. Two hundred pages later, when the police have exhausted all lines of inquiry and made hee-hawing jackasses of themselves, an amateur detective summons the dramatis personae to the same library—they may well include an actress, a tennis pro, an embittered widow, a disinherited younger son, and of course a butler—to reveal which of them is the killer.

That is the familiar template for crime fiction in the golden age, those years between the First and Second World Wars, when authors such as Agatha Christie, Ngaio Marsh, and Dorothy L. Sayers earned fortunes by satisfying an apparently limitless public appetite for corpses in English country houses. One of Agatha Christie's Miss Marple novels was actually titled *The Body in the Library*.

Christie and Sayers were founder-members of the Detection Club, a dining society formed in London in 1930. Recruits had to swear an initiation oath promising that their detectives "shall well and truly detect the crimes presented to them using those wits which it may please you to bestow upon them and not placing reliance on nor making use of Divine Revelation, Feminine Intuition, Mumbo Jumbo, Jiggery-Pokery, Coincidence, or Act of God." A joke, no doubt, but this was kidding on the level. Like any game, mystery writing had its rules, which were codified into "Ten Commandments" by the British author Ronald Knox—who, fittingly enough, was also a Catholic priest. His prohibitions included accidental discoveries and unaccountable hunches, undeclared clues and hitherto unknown poisons.

"The criminal must be someone mentioned in the early part of the story, but must not be anyone whose thoughts the reader has been allowed to follow," Knox decreed. "The 'stupid friend' of the detective, the Watson, must not conceal any thoughts which pass through his mind; his intelligence must be slightly, but very slightly, below that of the average reader. . . . Twin brothers, and doubles generally, must not appear unless we have been duly prepared for them."

. . .

No wonder Josephine Tey never belonged to the Detection Club. During her career as a crime novelist—from *The Man in the Queue* (1929) to *The Singing Sands* (published posthumously in 1952)—she broke almost all the commandments. As if willfully guying Monsignor Knox, the main character in her novel *Brat Farrar* (1949) was an impostor posing as a missing twin to grab an inheritance.

Her disdain for formulaic fiction is confirmed in the opening chapter of *The Daughter of Time* (1951). In a hospital recuperating from a broken leg, Detective Inspector Alan Grant despairs of the books on his bedside table, among them a writing-by-numbers mystery called *The Case of the Missing Tin-Opener*. "Did no one, any more, no one in all this wide world, change their record now and then?" he wonders despairingly.

> Was everyone nowadays thirled [enslaved] to a formula? Authors today wrote so much to a pattern that their public expected it. The public talked about "a new Silas Weekley" or "a new Lavinia Fitch" exactly as they talked about "a new brick" or "a new hairbrush." They never said "a new book by" whoever it might be. Their interest was not in the book but in its newness. They knew quite well what the book would be like.

Still true today (are you listening, James Patterson and Lee Child?), but this is not a charge that could ever be made against Josephine Tey. In *The Franchise Affair* (1948) she can't even be bothered to include the obligatory murder: all we have is a teenage girl who claims that two women kidnapped her for no apparent reason, and we know almost from the outset that she is lying.

The Daughter of Time exemplifies Tey's delight in subverting the conventions of the genre and defying expectations. Giving up on his bedside reading, Alan Grant decides to spend his convalescence solving one of the most notorious crimes in British history: did King Richard III really kill the princes in the Tower? Grant's interest is piqued when a visitor shows him a portrait of the 15th-century king. After staring at it for ages—"the slight fullness of the lower eyelid, like a child that has slept too heavily; the texture of the skin; the old-man look in a young face"—he reaches a preliminary verdict. "I can't remember any murderer, either in my own experience, or in case-histories, who resembled him." So the bed-ridden sleuthing begins.

It was William Shakespeare whose depiction of Richard III as a venomous hunchbacked monster damned him for centuries, and it was Shakespeare who, in *Macbeth,* had King Duncan say of the duplicitous Thane of Cawdor, "There's no art / To find the mind's construction in the face: / He was a gentleman on whom I built / An absolute trust"—by which he meant that no one can discern inner character from outward appearances.

Josephine Tey thought otherwise. "Lucy had long prided herself on her analysis of facial characteristics, and was beginning nowadays to bet rather heavily on them," she wrote in *Miss Pym Disposes* (1946). "She had never, for instance, come across eyebrows beginning low over the nose and ending high up at the outer end, without finding that their owner had a scheming, conniving, mind." Even chickens weren't safe from Tey's stern gaze: one of her characters mused on "the concentrated evil of a hen's face in a closeup."

This may seem a bit intense for a whodunit, and almost certainly falls foul of the ban on intuition, but it imbues Tey's novels with more honesty than you'll find in most of her contemporaries: which of us does not sometimes judge by appearances?

"I am a camera" might have been Josephine Tey's motto. "Oh, for one of those spy cameras that one wears as a tie pin!" she wrote in a letter to her friend Caroline Ramsden, a sculptor and racehorse owner, according to Ramsden's memoir, *A View from Primrose Hill.* "When I was in town this last time I thought that, apart from a well-fitting new suit, there was nothing in the world that I wanted. And then I thought that yes, there was. I wanted a camera that looked like a handbag, or a compact, or something. So that one could photograph a person standing two feet away and be looking in another direction altogether while one was doing it. . . . I am always seeing faces that I want to 'keep.'"

Tey herself had no desire to be "kept." Few photographs of her exist, and by dividing her life into discrete spheres she ensured that no one could know her too intimately. (One need hardly add that she never married.) To date, more than 60 years after her death—uniquely among the queens of the golden age—there is no biography (although one is due out in the fall). Oh, and her name wasn't Josephine Tey. Her literary friends called her Gordon, but that wasn't her name, either.

Before turning to crime she was the dramatist "Gordon Daviot," author of *Richard of Bordeaux,* which played to packed houses at the New Theatre, in London's West End. "I first met Gordon Daviot in 1932," the actor John Gielgud wrote in 1953, "when I played the title role in *Richard of Bordeaux.* We were friends until her death last year—1952—and yet I cannot claim ever to have known her very intimately. . . . She never spoke to me of her youth or her ambitions. It was hard to draw her out. . . . It was difficult to tell what she really felt, since she did not readily give her confidence, even to her few intimate friends."

This much we know. Elizabeth MacKintosh, pen name Josephine Tey, was born on July 25, 1896, in Inverness, capital of the Scottish Highlands. Her father was recorded on the birth certificate as a fruiterer. "Strange as it may seem, few of us had ever known the real person," recalled Mairi MacDonald, a contemporary at Inverness Royal Academy. "We had rubbed shoulders with her in our busy streets; admired her pretty home and picturesque garden—and some had even shared schooldays with her—yet no one enjoyed her companionship, for Gordon Daviot was, and wished to be what she herself termed herself, 'a lone wolf,' discouraging any attempts at fraternisation." A reluctant pupil, she preferred playing tic-tac-toe with a neighbor in class, or drawing mustaches and spectacles on portraits of the Kings of Scotland, or scampering off to a cloakroom "where, upon an old set of parallel bars—housed there for no apparent reason—she delighted herself and others by turning somersaults."

The next phase of her life, qualifying as a physical-training instructor, provided the backdrop for *Miss Pym Disposes,* set at a physical-training college in the English Midlands. According to most sources, including an obituary in the London *Times,* her teaching career was curtailed by family obligations. After teaching physical training at schools in England and Scotland, she returned to Inverness to care for her invalid father. It was there that she began her career as a writer.

Nicola Upson, who investigated Tey's life with the intention of writing a biography, finds the tale of the invalid father hard to credit, given that he was catching prizewinning salmon into his 80s. "A lot of myths and half-truths have been created and repeated over the years," she wrote to me. "Admittedly, she started one or two of them herself." Tey's description of a film actress in *A Shilling for Candles* may well have been a self-portrait:

> She wasn't fond of being interviewed. And she used to tell a different story each time. When someone pointed out that that wasn't what she had said last time, she said: "But that's so dull! I've thought of a much better one." No one ever knew where they were with her. Temperament, they called it, of course.

Nicola Upson eventually set aside her projected work, deciding that such an elusive figure was more suited to fiction. Her novel *An Expert in Murder,* published in 2008, was the first of a series in which Josephine Tey herself features as an amateur detective. Though the crimes are imaginary, the settings are accurate. We see her traveling to London to enjoy the success of *Richard of Bordeaux*—or, in another volume, meeting Alfred Hitchcock to discuss his film adaptation of her novel *A Shilling for Candles.* According to Upson, "Readers tell me that part of the fun of the books is guessing what's true and what isn't. . . . But the bigger picture of her that I've built up from her letters and from talking to people who knew her is reflected very truthfully throughout the series."

Tey's great genius, Upson says, is to create a story which can be read on many levels, and which differs according to its audience—a trick that Tey played with her life, too, and just as effectively. Elizabeth MacKintosh, Gordon Daviot, and Josephine Tey were distinct personae. Even her correspondence has that chameleon quality: a letter from "Gordon" is quite different in tone from a

"Mac" letter or a "Tey" letter. "She kept her life in compartments," says Upson, "and was different things to different people; private and insular in Inverness; carefree and more gregarious in London and on travels abroad."

Gregarious only within a small circle, however: Mairi MacDonald found Tey's unwillingness to meet strangers "almost pathological in its intensity." Having decided to model Brat Farrar's physical appearance on that of a well-known racehorse dealer, she asked her friend Caroline Ramsden to find out all she could about him. "It isn't a question of wanting to meet him—which I should actively dislike," she wrote to Ramsden. "It is a quite detached curiosity about him. . . . What he thinks, reads (I suppose he can?), says, eats; whether he likes his bacon frizzly or flaccid. . . . It always happens with someone I see casually, like that; and once my curiosity is satisfied my interest finishes. But until the picture is complete the curiosity is devouring."

The devotion to her craft was absolute. While writing a novel she could allow no distractions, and it shows. The prose is nimble, acute, witty. The texture of English interwar life is palpable. Tey's fictional worlds come fully furnished: even minor characters are never mere ciphers. Her regular detective, Alan Grant, has none of the eye-catching props—deerstalker hat, waxed mustache, monocle—that other authors append to fictional sleuths in lieu of a third dimension. He is dogged, diligent, ready to admit error. "By the time coffee had arrived he was no nearer a solution," Tey writes in *A Shilling for Candles*. "He wished he was one of these marvelous creatures of super-instinct and infallible judgment who adorned the pages of detective stories, and not just a hard-working, well-meaning, ordinarily intelligent Detective Inspector."

When Tey's work was finished, she displayed an equally absolute devotion to indolence. "Next to chocolates, the cinema and racing, her favourite pastime was a day in bed, lying flat on her back, wide awake," Caroline Ramsden wrote. After one of these epic lie-ins, Ramsden asked what she had been thinking about all day. "Nothing—absolutely *nothing*," Tey replied. "I've had a wonderful time."

Her death, in February 1952, could hardly have been better timed for such a shy and private person, a week after the demise of King George VI. "It was typical of her that she could slip out of her lives, and her own, at a moment when her passing was hardly noticed by the general public," Ramsden wrote. "The whole nation was much too busy mourning its king to pay much attention to the deaths of any of his subjects." John Gielgud read the news in his evening paper after coming offstage in a production of *The Winter's Tale*. He hadn't even known that she was ill.

A small party of mourners, including Gielgud and the actress Dame Edith Evans, gathered at Streatham crematorium in South London on a cold, dreary day to say their farewells. "We talked to Gordon's sister, whom we were all meeting for the first time," Caroline Ramsden recorded, "and she told us that Gordon had only come south from Scotland about a fortnight before, when she had stayed at her Club in Cavendish Square, on her way through London. What she did or thought about during that period was her own affair, never to be shared with anyone. . . . All her close friends were within easy reach, but she made no contacts—left no messages."

Ah, but she did. Read her novels and you'll find them.

GRACE METALIOUS

······································

PEYTON PLACE'S REAL VICTIM

by Michael Callahan

MARCH 2006

The summer of 1955 had not been good to Grace Metalious. A nine-week drought had left tiny Gilmanton, New Hampshire, bone dry, including the well in the back of the ramshackle cottage she'd sarcastically nicknamed "It'll Do." Her three children were living on lettuce-and-tomato sandwiches. She was three months behind on payments for her beat-up car. At the age of 30 she was broke, smelly, thirsty, exhausted, and desperate.

She had dreamed of a different life for herself, a life of romance and adventure, a life all little girls dream of. Escaping a troubled home to sneak off to her Aunt Georgie's bathroom, she would lock the door and sit in the tub for hours, putting those dreams to paper by scribbling tales of heroines and dashing princes.

She kept writing, even after her wedding at 18 to her high-school sweetheart, George Metalious; after giving birth to her third child and having her tubes tied when doctors told her she wouldn't survive a fourth pregnancy; after George went away during World War II and had an affair; after he came home and she had an affair of her own. Writing was neither hobby nor diversion, but lifeline. During those years when George was getting his teaching degree at the University of New Hampshire under the G.I. Bill, Grace often locked her children out of the apartment so she could write, leaving her runny-nosed charges to fend for themselves in the cold by knocking on neighbors' doors, asking to be let in.

In the end, she'd written a book. Actually, a polemic. She titled it *The Tree and the Blossom*—about the secrets, scandals, and hypocrisy in a fictional New Hampshire town not unlike her own.

Grace discovered literary agent Jacques Chambrun by browsing through a library directory, singling him out because his was the most French-sounding name. Born Marie Grace DeRepentigny (prone to embellish, she would later state that her birth name had been Grace Marie Antoinette Jeanne d'Arc de

Repentigny), she'd been brought up with an air of French snobbery that belied the modest apartment she'd shared with her mother, grandmother, and sister.

Chambrun, an unctuous dandy who favored long lunches and chauffeured cars, had an office facing the Plaza and a client roster that at one point included W. Somerset Maugham and Jack Schaefer, the author of *Shane*. He already knew Grace Metalious. The year before, she had sent him a passionate five-page plea outlining her dreams of becoming a published writer, along with a 312-page manuscript that focused on the travails of a pair of newlyweds—which had clear parallels to her life with George. The agent had circulated it among a few publishers; all of them declined.

So when Chambrun got *The Tree and the Blossom,* in April 1955, he wasn't optimistic. He perfunctorily sent it on its way through the publishing circuit, where it ended up on the desk of Leona Nevler, a manuscript reader at Lippincott. Most days, Nevler's job was to field the runoff from less discriminating agents, such as Chambrun, and sift through the mounds of unsolicited "slush," then pass along the rare jewel that might warrant an editor's attention. Nevler, it turned out, quite liked *The Tree and the Blossom,* but her bosses at Lippincott passed.

During a job interview at rival Julian Messner, Inc., Nevler told the firm's president, Kitty Messner, about the novel. Chic and thin, Kitty Messner was the Katharine Hepburn of the publishing world, known as much for her draping tailored suits and signature cigarette holder as for her sharp eye for commercial fiction. According to Emily Toth's 1981 biography *Inside Peyton Place*—the Rosetta Stone of Grace Me-talious arcana—on the night of August 16, Messner decided to stay in and read Grace's saucy, compelling, and surprisingly literary book.

The next day, Kitty called Chambrun. "I have to have it," she said. The title, however, would need to be changed to the name of the town where the novel was set: Peyton Place.

Grace had been at the market in nearby Laconia, buying frozen French fries because you don't have to wash them before you cook them. Then she had taken her kids to swim in Opeechee Park. When they got back to Gilmanton, Grace, carrying two bags of groceries, spotted the mail. Amid a pile of bills and past-due notices, a yellow telegram peeked out: PLEASE CALL ME AT YOUR EARLIEST CONVENIENCE. REGARDS. CHAMBRUN.

"He's sold it!" Grace screamed, waving around the wire. "He's sold it!"

Indeed he had, as she discovered when she placed the call to New York, a grocery bag still tucked under one arm. Two days later, Grace Metalious, the frowsy New Hampshire housewife whose bombshell would rock American publishing, slid into a booth at '21' with her dashing agent and toasted to her success with what she remembered as a daiquiri "all pale green and so cold it hurt my teeth."

Years later, her best friend, Laurose Wilkens, would remember the phone call she'd gotten from Grace that hot and humid August day, crying and laughing at her incredible news. "Grace Metalious," Wilkens said, "would never be really poor or really happy again."

Fifty years ago, *Peyton Place* helped create the contemporary notion of "buzz," indicted 1950s morality, and recast the concept of the soap opera, all in one big, purple-prosed book. It would spawn a sequel, a smash film nominated for nine Academy Awards, and television's first prime-time serial. A week before it hit bookstores, on September 24, 1956, it was already on the best-seller list, where it would remain for half a year. In its first month, it sold more than 100,000 copies, at a time when the average first novel sold 3,000, total. It would go on to sell 12 million more, becoming one of the most widely read novels ever published. During its heyday, it was estimated that one in 29 Americans had bought it—legions of them hiding it in drawers and closets due to its salacious content.

Peyton Place is the story of the denizens of a small New Hampshire town, ostensibly centered around pudgy adolescent Allison MacKenzie, who dreams of being a writer but finds herself stifled by the expectations and duplicity of her small-minded neighbors, and by her own mother, Constance MacKenzie, the original desperate housewife. What sold it was possibly the most clever marketing campaign ever launched for a novel of its era: a colorful author who made good copy, and a crafty, page-turning brew of illicit sex, secret lives, public drunkenness, abortion, incest, and murder.

But the story behind *Peyton Place*—a scandalous phenomenon that became a metaphor for scandal ever after ("Is this Watergate or Peyton Place?" U.S. congressman Lindsey Graham remarked at the Clinton impeachment hearings, in 1998)—is one almost as lurid as the original yarn. It is a saga of rags and riches, loves won and lost, and, in the end, betrayal, malefaction, and regret. It is the story of a restless, creative girl who never quite fit in and who found an outlet to express what that was like in 1950s America, only to be crushed by the people whose faux morality she had so scathingly critiqued. It is also a revelatory tale of an accidental and largely forgotten feminist pioneer.

Overnight, Grace Metalious became wealthy, spending lavishly on stays at the Plaza and flirting with Cary Grant, her name and face splashed in newspapers across the nation. Eight years, another husband, and more than a million pissed-away dollars later, at the age of 39, she lay dying in a Boston hospital, in the company of a mysterious British lover to whom she had left her entire estate—by changing her will on her deathbed. "Be careful what you wish for," she told him in the hours before she died. "You just might get it."

. . .

Grace DeRepentigny was born in 1924 in Manchester, New Hampshire, a heavily Franco-American working-class city known for its textile mills. Her father, Al, was a merchant seaman who left the family when Grace was 10; her mother, Laurette, was a bitter would-be socialite who, as Emily Toth has recounted in her book about Grace, dreamed of writing for *Harper's* and bought flea-market items, which she then passed off as French family heirlooms. Despite both families' objections, Grace, still a teenager, married George Metalious, a studious Greek whom she'd known since the age of nine. Almost instantly, the marriage hit the skids. "I did not like belonging to Friendly Clubs and bridge clubs," Grace wrote later. "I did not like being regarded as a freak because I spent time in front of a typewriter instead of a sink. And George did not like my not liking the things I was supposed to like."

With her ponytail, baggy flannel shirts, and jeans, Grace broke every mold of the prim New England country wife: she was outspoken, a terrible housekeeper (once, when some P.R. guys from New York came to It'll Do, she grabbed what looked like a Brillo pad, only to discover it was a dead mouse), and shockingly well read. "She was a totally unbridled, free, glorious spirit," says Lynne Snierson, the daughter of Grace's longtime attorney, Bernard Snierson. "I didn't know any other woman like her. Grace swore, a lot, and she drank, a lot, and she had lots of guys around her. She got married and divorced and had affairs. And she talked about sex and she talked about real life and she didn't filter it. I didn't know any other woman who was like that in the 50s."

As a result, she quickly became a lightning rod for gossip wherever she lived, particularly when she would hole up writing and ignore her kids. "We didn't bother her when she was writing," says her daughter, Marsha Metalious Duprey, now 62. "We wouldn't have gotten into trouble if we did, but we didn't *want* to bother her. When she was writing, basically everything else went to hell: no housework got done, no cooking got done, and my dad mostly took care of us. . . . I didn't know any better, so I didn't question it."

Grace struck up a friendship with Laurose Wilkens, who wrote part-time for *The Laconia Evening Citizen* and had tracked Grace down when rumors surfaced that the wife of George Metalious, the new school principal, was writing a novel about some of the townspeople. Grace confirmed that she was working on a book, but insisted it was pure fiction. Soon, she and Laurie were together almost every day in the kitchen of Shaky Acres, Laurie's farm in Gilmanton.

While George began his job as a teacher and principal, Grace wrote. Laurie told her the story of Barbara Roberts, a local 20-year-old who in 1947 shot and killed her father, then buried his body in a goat pen on their farm. She had pleaded guilty to second-degree homicide and was sentenced to 30 years to life. Then the truth came out: for years, Roberts and her sister had been raped regularly by their father, and at times chained to a bed for days. One night he flew into a rage, chasing Barbara and her young brother around the kitchen table and threatening to kill them. She reached into a drawer, extracted her father's gun, and shot him dead. Only after an exposé by some crusading journalists—including a cub reporter for the *New Hampshire Sunday News* by the name of Ben Bradlee—was Barbara Roberts freed.

Grace soaked up the details, and she used them in *Peyton Place* in the story of Selena Cross, the dark ingenue from the wrong side of the tracks who is brutally raped by her stepfather and kills him, burying his body in a sheep pen. (Saying that the American public wasn't ready for full-on incest, Kitty Messner insisted Grace change him from father to stepfather.) Grace frantically scribbled down additional tales of Gilmanton life, including some from Arlington "Chunky" Hartford, a Gilmanton cop and born storyteller who told Grace about "hard-cider parties" held in the basement of a local farmhouse. Men would supposedly pile in for up to a week at a time, getting sauced. The anecdotes also piled up—as did Gilmanton's wrath once they all appeared in print.

"A lot of people wouldn't read the book—or they said they wouldn't," says Esther Peters, who, as a radio host at WLNH, in Laconia, interviewed Grace shortly after *Peyton Place* was published, and who still lives in neighboring Guilford. "Of course what happened was that people in Gilmanton, they *had* the book. If you happened to go to their house and asked them to bring out a copy, they'd bring out a copy—and it generally fell open at one of the places where there was a rather torrid passage."

In retaliation, the town gossips spread Grace stories with brutal efficacy, from the outlandish (she had gone to the grocery store in a mink coat while naked underneath; she had greeted the milkman in the buff) to the valid (her house was filthy; she cheated on her husband). According to Emily Toth's biography, Grace had drifted into an affair with her neighbor Carl Newman and was often spotted carousing with him at the Rod and Gun Club, on Beacon Street. So people talked. And talked. Grace had, in effect, begun living *Peyton Place*.

The most damning rumor was also the most hurtful: that she hadn't actually written the book at all. "People would say, 'Oh, she couldn't have written that. Her husband went to college. I bet he wrote it,'" says John Chandler, Bernard Snierson's law partner. At one point Grace sat in Chandler's office, writing some background information for a legal matter. "After I read that," Chandler says, "there was no question in my mind about who wrote *Peyton Place*."

In public, Grace struck back at her neighbors. Her point wasn't that her life was perfect; it was that *their* lives weren't, either. The only difference was that she wasn't hiding it. "To a tourist these towns look as peaceful as a postcard picture," she said. "But if you go beneath that picture, it's like turning over a rock with your foot—all kinds of strange things crawl out. Everybody who lives in town knows what's going on—there are no secrets—but they don't want outsiders to know."

"Indian summer is like a woman. Ripe, hotly passionate, but fickle, she comes and goes as she pleases so that one is never sure whether she will come at all, nor for how long she will stay."

So begins *Peyton Place*, in an introduction that would become almost as famous as the work itself.

Peyton Place is a hybrid of the literary and the sordid, Upton Sinclair by way of *Forever Amber*. Although clearly influenced by Henry Bellamann's *Kings Row*, at its heart it is a manifesto, a blistering indictment of small-town values, classism, and racism—one that got lost in the titillating pages that Americans dog-eared and read behind closed blinds. John Waters, the flamboyant filmmaker who once left a bottle of liquor at Grace's grave, remembers the thrill of being 10 years old and reading his father's stashed-away copy. Indeed, he quotes "the V of her crotch" within the first two minutes of a phone call from Provincetown. "I thought, How filthy and great!" he says. "I just became obsessed with it."

"One of my earliest memories as a teenager is [of] sneaking off with friends and they grabbed their moms' copies of *Peyton Place* and we would go through 'the good parts,'" adds Barbara Delinsky, the best-selling romance novelist whose latest book, *Looking for Peyton Place*, is a tribute to Grace.

A "good part" meant sex, such as the famous scene where town harlot Betty Anderson, furious that bad boy Rodney Harrington has taken Allison MacKenzie to the school dance, gets him all riled up in his car.

> "Is it up, Rod?" she panted, undulating her body under his. "Is it up good and hard?"
>
> "Oh, yes," he whispered, almost unable to speak. "Oh, yes."
>
> Without another word, Betty jackknifed her knees, pushed Rodney away from her, clicked the lock on the door and was outside of the car.
>
> "Now go shove it into Allison MacKenzie," she screamed at him.

There were other steamy sections as well—most notably the scene where virile principal Tomas Makris, after a moonlit swim with the repressed Constance, commands her to "untie the top of your bathing suit. I want to feel your breasts against me when I kiss you." (It would turn out that Makris was the name of a co-worker of George's who matched his fictional counterpart's physical description; Makris sued Grace for libel, eventually settling out of court for $60,000. Years later, it was revealed that Grace had forged Makris's name on a release form. In the film and TV installments, the character's name was changed to Michael Rossi.) But it was through the nonsexual passages that Grace delivered her most withering social commentary, such as her description of the hidden, rancid shantytown, which the proper townsfolk pretended not to see.

In the end, reviews were largely negative. "Never before in my memory has a young mother published a book in language approximately that of longshoremen on a bellicose binge," bellowed the *New York World-Telegram*. Grace also took a hit in the editorial pages. In a scathing commentary under the headline THE FILTH THEY LIVE BY in the *Laconia Evening Citizen*, publisher William Loeb branded the book "literary sewage."

"If I'm a lousy writer," Grace shot back, "then a hell of a lot of people have lousy taste."

Grace, in fact, found an unlikely ally in *The New York Times Book Review*. Calling *Peyton Place* a "small town peep show," the paper applauded the book's stand "against the false fronts and bourgeois pretensions of allegedly respectable communities," recognizing the book for what Grace had intended it to be: a cultural bitch slap at the duplicitous notions of proper conduct in the age of Eisenhower.

"It was sort of like 'The Emperor's New Clothes.' She got herself into a lot of trouble because she had no idea that there was anything wrong with any of the things she was saying and doing," says screenwriter Naomi Foner Gyllenhaal, mother of actors Jake and Maggie, who has just completed a script based on Toth's biography. The author of *Peyton Place,* says Foner Gyllenhaal, "was doing something on a cultural level that was extremely important. She was telling women it was O.K. to be sexual beings . . . to have the aspirations that men had."

Kitty Messner suspected that she had a winner in *Peyton Place,* and not just because of its incendiary content. She also had the perfect selling tool: Grace Metalious, the plump, salty schoolteacher's wife. Messner hired publicist Alan Brandt to beat the media drums. Brandt dashed off a memo to Hal Boyle, the nationally syndicated columnist, including an irresistible hook: Grace's bookish husband was likely to be fired because of his wife's off-color novel.

Boyle took the bait. Calling the book "*Tobacco Road* with a Yankee accent," he reported on August 29, 1956, that "a young schoolteacher's wife who never took a writing lesson in her life may become a literary sensation of the year next month. 'I feel pretty sure of one thing—it'll probably cost my husband his job,' said Mrs. Grace Metalious cheerfully."

The column appeared in the *Boston Traveler* under a headline in massive type usually reserved for events such as the bombing of Hiroshima: TEACHER FIRED FOR WIFE'S BOOK. (George had, in fact, not had his contract renewed.)

Immediately, photographers and reporters in fedoras swamped tiny Gilmanton looking for Grace. She spent the day in Laurie Wilkens's bathroom, hiding.

The publicity did wonders for book sales but ravaged the Metalious marriage. George took a teaching job in Stow, Massachusetts, rented an apartment, and left Grace and the kids behind to weather the storm. Grace got threatening phone calls telling her to move, and her children suffered the fallout. "We had a lot of problems at school," Marsha Duprey recalls, "because parents didn't want their children playing with us." Her younger brother, nicknamed Mike, then nine, regularly beat up kids who taunted their sister, Cindy, six. "I felt sorry for all of them," says Esther Peters. "I wanted to make them happier, make them feel more accepted. What little I could do, I did."

If Grace was feeling blue, she hid it. She had bigger things facing her now. A publicity tour. A new man—a local D.J. who would change her life. And Hollywood, which had come calling.

In New York, Brandt arranged for Grace to be interviewed on a local news show called *Night Beat,* hosted by a young, rising journalist, Mike Wallace. Wallace had spent his boyhood summers in New Hampshire. "She was simply a surprise to all of us," he recalls. "Because of her background, because of the way she looked, because of 'Peyton Place,' New Hampshire. That kind of thing has been going on? Well, of course that kind of thing had been going on in small towns all over the world, forever. But suddenly here was this bland housewife."

Terrified at the thought of being on live television, Grace was a wreck, accidentally ripping her girdle right before the show aired. She was helped by an aspiring actress, Jacqueline Susann, who did commercial breaks for the station. (Ten years later, Susann would follow in Grace's footsteps by writing the steamy cult best-seller *Valley of the Dolls.*)

In her book on Grace, Toth relates how the author, just before the program started, begged Wallace's producer, Ted Yates, to promise that Wallace would not ask if *Peyton Place* was her autobiography. No sooner had the cameras begun rolling than Wallace, smoking a cigarette in his best *noir* fashion, turned to her and said, "So, Grace, tell me, is *Peyton Place* your autobiography?"

"Really," Wallace says with a chuckle when reminded of the incident. "Can you imagine that I would do a thing like that?"

Grace was more comfortable with the print media, where over the years she tossed out chewy bons mots feasted upon by reporters who were charmed by her self-effacing earthiness. "I have a feeling that Gilmanton got as angry with me as it did because secretly my neighbors agreed with me," she told the *St. Louis Post-Dispatch.* "That was where the shoe pinched. You get angrier about the truth than you do about lies."

In October 1956, Grace went to New York and checked into the Algonquin to sign a $250,000 deal with Twentieth Century Fox producer Jerry Wald for the movie and television rights to *Peyton Place*. Her attorney, Snierson—whom she'd met years earlier, after she'd passed a bad check—urged her to set up trusts for her children to protect her newfound wealth. He drafted all the paperwork. Even though Grace signed with Wald, she never got around to inking Snierson's documents.

She was distracted: she'd fallen in love with Thomas James Martin, "T.J. the D.J.," who spun discs at WLNH. Stocky and handsome, he was the anti-George, a throwback to the rugged princes Grace had written about in Aunt Georgie's bathtub. They quickly became fixtures at the Laconia Tavern, where Grace was soon as notorious for downing highballs as for her racy book.

One night, a car pulled up to the house in Gilmanton after midnight. Grace and T.J. awoke to a camera's blinding flash—and George standing at the foot of the bed, snapping pictures. He calmly told them to put on some clothes and meet him downstairs. Wrapped in a blanket, Grace tore into him. But George had the upper hand: adultery was illegal. "I've got you," he told T.J. "You're going to jail."

The next day, Grace went to Snierson to file for divorce. As part of the settlement, she agreed to pay George's tuition for his master's degree. In exchange, he turned over the undeveloped roll.

Grace and T.J.'s relationship was volatile at best, with T.J. assuming more and more control over Grace—including how she blew through her fledgling fortune. "He would say to her, 'Darling, you're Grace Metalious. You don't get a room at the Plaza. You get an entire *floor!*'" Snierson says. So Grace did—along with a new Cadillac, new clothes, dinners at '21,' cases of champagne, and chartered flights to the Caribbean. Grace poured thousands of dollars into renovating the country house she'd bought on Meadow Pond Road, which had once been owned by a Chicago gangster. Opportunistic "friends" began drifting in and out at all hours.

All the while, Grace wrestled with the notion of celebrity. Staying with T.J. and the kids at the Beverly Hilton, Grace played the part of the kid in the candy store. She glimpsed Elizabeth Taylor at a Screen Actors Guild dinner, and chitchatted with Cary Grant on the back lot. Producer Wald made sure the family was treated to limos and lavish dinners. Marsha even got whisked to a studio set to cop an autograph from Elvis Presley, who between takes was playing a pickup basketball game. But, for Grace, it was largely an act. "I regarded the men who made *Peyton Place* as workers in a gigantic flesh factory," she would write in a Sunday-newspaper supplement, the *American Weekly*, "and they looked upon me as a nut who should go back to the farm."

And as the press continued to play up *Peyton Place*'s more tawdry aspects,

Grace's insecurities ballooned. At lunch at Romanoff's, John Michael Hayes, who wrote the screenplay for the film, asked Grace the same question Mike Wallace had: Was it her autobiography? Grace asked him to repeat the question. Then she tossed her drink all over him.

The film adaptation of *Peyton Place,* released in 1957, was a sanitized sequence of slamming doors, wayward glances, and A-line skirts. The story line had no abortions, no moonlit swims, and certainly no Betty asking Rodney if it was up and hard. Despite the movie's almost picture-postcard tone of whimsy, it did manage to retain some of Grace's finger-pointing—most notably in a stunning montage of the duplicitous citizens filing into a myriad of churches, all dressed in their Sunday best.

It was, nonetheless, a roaring success, drawing nine Oscar nominations. The haunting score, by Franz Waxman, is instantly recognizable even today. The film earned generally positive reviews. (The *Chicago Sun-Times* crowed that it was "one of the best motion pictures ever made.") And it single-handedly revived the career of Lana Turner, then 36, who was coming off a string of box-office duds. Turner, in fact, received the only Academy Award nomination of her career for playing Constance MacKenzie—this, despite a performance that resembles that of a department-store mannequin that has somehow wandered away from its window. (A year later, Turner would find herself in her own, real-life Peyton Place, when her daughter, Cheryl Crane, said that in an act of self-defense she had wielded the knife that killed her mother's gangster lover, Johnny Stompanato, in the bedroom of Turner's Beverly Hills mansion.)

Peyton Place also made a sudden star of Diane Varsi, the wiry newcomer who anchored the narrative as Allison MacKenzie. Varsi got a best-supporting-actress nomination (as did Hope Lange, who played Selena), but, like Grace, Varsi was a bohemian who quickly grew to loathe the Hollywood machine. "Acting is destructive to me," she said later. "I don't see any reason to be made miserable because other people say I should go on with my career." Two years after her debut, she left motion pictures. And at the 1959 Academy Awards, M.C. Bob Hope closed the telecast by saying, "Goodnight, Diane Varsi . . . wherever you are."

The movie's premiere was held in Camden, Maine, where many of the exterior scenes had been filmed, but Grace stayed home, later insisting that she hadn't been invited. The studio, meanwhile, asked Gilmanton P.T.A. president and policeman's wife Olive Hartford to round up 25 people from the town to go on an all-expenses-paid junket for the New York opening. She could persuade only 13 to make the trip.

After the hullabaloo died down, Grace's violent relationship with T.J.—and her drinking—flared up. The pair would scream, drink, yell, drink, push and shove, then drink some more. As Toth describes it in her book, and as Marsha confirms, Grace, during one particularly vicious face-off in 1958, threatened to hurl a mink stole, a gift from T.J., out of a hotel window.

The next day, they got married; Grace wore the stole over a smart gray suit.

The pattern of highs and lows was set. Grace would throw raucous parties in Gilmanton, then call friends in the middle of the night after she and T.J. had fought. She once phoned Laurie Wilkens at one A.M. from the Plaza, telling her she had to come immediately. Laurie found Grace in the lobby, almost suicidal. "The phone would ring anytime, and it would be 'Bernie, I need you,'" Lynne Snierson recalls. Grace would come to the house, often drunk, and pass out in Lynne's bed.

After Grace and T.J. wed, George arrived in Gilmanton, packed up the kids, and took them to his home in Massachusetts. Mike and Cindy eventually returned to Grace, but Marsha, then 14, stayed behind with George to escape the madness. "At that point I decided, 'I need to do this for myself,'" she says. "I knew if I didn't do it, I wasn't going to make it."

Drowning in booze and running out of cash, Grace agreed to write a sequel, *Return to Peyton Place,* when Dell offered $165,000. She handed in 98 largely unintelligible pages that were re-written and fleshed out by a ghostwriter. The ensuing reviews, each more savage than the last, sent her spiraling further downward; a publicity tour was shelved. (Two later titles, *The Tight White Collar,* in 1960, and *No Adam in Eden,* in 1963, never caught on.)

One night Grace placed a call to Bernie Snierson, begging him to come over. After he arrived, he sat with her for a while.

"Bernie, I'm scared," Grace confided.

"What are you afraid of, Grace?" he asked.

Grace pointed to an empty fifth on the table. "I looked into the bottom of that empty bottle," she replied, "and I saw myself."

By 1960, T.J. was gone, fed up with the cycle of drinking and fighting. On the rebound, Grace reconciled with George, announcing to the world they'd re-married, even though they never had. They bought an inn and called it the Peyton Place Motel. Not surprisingly, no one wanted to stay there. They soon separated, this time for good.

Grace's highs grew more and more infrequent. One came in February 1961, when she received a letter from Jerry Wald that said, "We just ran a rough cut of *Return to Peyton Place* and I can certainly say that lightning does strike twice in the same place." Buoyed by the news, Grace convinced Wald that he should hold the premiere of the film—starring Carol Lynley, Mary Astor, Tuesday Weld, and Jeff Chandler (with Rosemary Clooney singing the theme song)—at the Colonial Theatre in Laconia.

The town crackled with excitement on the big night. Grace wore her hair in a stylish French twist; Marsha got to wear Grace's mink stole. Bernie and Muriel Snierson hosted a swanky post-premiere dinner party at their home, attended by co-star Chandler and actress Ina Balin.

But the reviews, with the exception of widespread praise for Mary Astor's deliciously evil appearance as Roberta Carter (in which she seems to be channeling Judith Anderson in *Rebecca*), were overwhelmingly grim. Even the promotional newsreel, featuring Lynley and Grace, was creepy. Onscreen, Grace appeared awkward, bloated, and tired; Lynley says she remembers her as being "a little discombobulated . . . and *verklempt*." Even so, the film did reasonably well at the box office: moviegoers, it seemed, couldn't get enough of the dirty denizens of *Peyton Place*.

In October 1963, John Rees, a tall, broad, bearded British journalist, arrived in Gilmanton looking to interview its most famous resident for a profile in the Boston *Daily Mirror*. Within weeks he had become her lover—and moved into her house.

One day Esther Peters came upon the couple in a Concord taproom. Grace "was still in command of herself, but she was way off somewhere in dreams that didn't correspond with reality," she says, adding that "by this time, I think her liver had gone to hell. . . . She was delusional."

Marsha had married and moved to Laconia; Rees and then 16-year-old Mike had a huge argument and Rees threw the boy out as Grace watched in an alcoholic stupor. Every time Marsha called, Rees would answer, offering an excuse as to why Grace couldn't come to the phone.

"I went to see her one day and he wasn't there," her daughter recalls tearfully. "So I got in the house, and it was pretty bad. It was just awful. She looked so bad." Grace was practically incoherent, shuffling around the premises. It was the last time Marsha saw her. "[Rees] came back and I left. I'll never forgive myself for that, just leaving her like that."

Rees and Grace went to Boston on a trip that winter. While there, Grace fell ill and was rushed via paddy wagon—they couldn't find an ambulance—to Beth Israel hospital. Three days later, lying in her hospital bed, she asked for a lawyer to change her will. She left everything to John Rees. Two hours after signing it, Grace suffered a hemorrhage and died. The attending physician, Dr. Herbert Saver, believed that Grace's cirrhosis was the result of her having consumed a fifth of liquor every day for five years.

That afternoon, in Laconia, young Cindy, then staying with Marsha, woke her elder sister up from a nap. "They said on TV that Ma's dead," she said. Mike found out from someone on the street.

The Metalious children retained John Chandler to contest the will, which had directed, among other things, that there be no funeral. During the subsequent media frenzy, it was revealed that Rees had a wife and five children back in England. He dropped any claim to the estate.

Not that there was anything to claim. Years of large living, extravagant gifts, bad loans to fair-weather friends, and pilfering by Jacques Chambrun—who, it turned out, had been stealing from her almost from the start, and had been fired by Maugham in 1948, reputedly for having done the same—had caused Grace Metalious to burn through about a million dollars. By the time her finances were untangled, she had $41,174 in the bank and debts of more than $200,000.

"What day is it," Grace once wrote, "when you wake up and realize that what you have is not what you want at all?" Clearly, that day had come. In the end, no one could dig her out of the hole she'd fallen into. "Maybe she just didn't know who to ask," Marsha Duprey says. "Or who she could trust."

Nate Abbott, a tall, avuncular man who today serves as the chairman of the Board of Selectmen in Gilmanton, New Hampshire, moved there in the summer of 1998, unaware that his new hometown had been the basis for the most scandalous book of its day—until the people who sold him his house whispered, "Did you know that this is 'Peyton Place'?"

Curious, he asked Geraldine Besse, whose family had lived in Gilmanton for generations, about the connection. She glared at him. "Don't ever mention that to me again," she said. He didn't.

"This is something that the town was dipped in a long time ago, and the odor lingers," he says. "For those who were related to the incidents and who were alive at the time or affected at the time, it's still something they're reluctant to talk about."

That's an understatement. Drive along the winding country roads of Gilmanton today and there is no clue that this is the box that Pandora opened with her Remington typewriter. There is no plaque commemorating the town's most famous author, no statue in the public square. While a new copy of the book sits on the shelf in the library—replacing the tattered paperback dedicated by Barbara Walters (who did a TV segment on the book in the 1970s)—the only real indication of Grace Metalious is the white headstone on her grave in the back of the Smith Meeting House Cemetery.

The center of Gilmanton, in fact, looks quite like it did some 50 years ago, when Grace, looking forlorn, posed for *Life* magazine standing in front of the town hall, steepled church, and tiny library. But while there is a sense of palpable disdain for *Peyton Place*—you get the feeling that right below the surface the town is still seething—Grace Metalious has found redemption in other ways.

Today, *Peyton Place* appears on women's-studies curricula at universities, including Louisiana State, where the book is required reading in a course taught by Professor Emily Toth, Grace's Boswell. "It's a breakthrough for freedom of expression," she says. "It set new parameters for what you could say in a book—especially about women. It was an exciting, dirty book." Ten years ago, Ardis Cameron, a professor at the University of Southern Maine, was astonished to discover the title was out of print, and mounted a one-woman campaign to resurrect it. She eventually persuaded Northeastern University Press to reissue the novel, and wrote a Camille Paglia–worthy introduction that casts Grace as a literary Joan of Arc, sword drawn, swinging at the oppressive social conventions of the 50s. The book, says Cameron, "spoke about things that were not discussed in polite society, and allowed people to talk about all sorts of issues—but particularly their own sense of being different in the 1950s."

Screenwriter Foner Gyllenhaal sees Grace less as feminist icon than as unwitting trailblazer, and has framed the script for the upcoming film version of her life in those terms. "I don't think she went out there to be a feminist," Foner Gyllenhaal says. "I think she went out there to be a human being who wanted to live in a world where people weren't hypocritical and told the truth and stood by their actions. And in that regard I think she was innocent as well as brave."

George Metalious is 80 now, and on the sunny day I knock on the door of his tidy blue Shaker saltbox, in Rye, New Hampshire, he is not glad to see me. I have written him and called several times, asking for an interview, but he has not responded.

He has been picking raspberries in his garden, and as he stands in the doorway, beads of sweat drip down, under the brim of his floppy straw hat. He still wears the big, square, dark-rimmed glasses that made him so recognizable in the endless publicity photos taken for *Peyton Place*.

He doesn't want to talk about Grace anymore, he says. There isn't anything left to say.

I beg him to answer one question. Why, I ask, did Grace have such a difficult time handling her success, after she'd fought so hard to get it?

He sighs the sigh of old men. "She cared deeply, and she loved deeply," he says quietly. "She was naïve, unfortunately. She put her trust in the wrong people, and she believed in the basic good of people. She had faith, and it worked against her."

In the fall of 1964, ABC premiered a half-hour *Peyton Place,* television's first-ever soap-opera-style serial in prime time, which introduced two new young actors, Ryan O'Neal and Mia Farrow; eventually Lee Grant won a supporting-actress Emmy for her role. Long before *Dallas, Dynasty,* and *Desperate Housewives, Peyton Place* pioneered sudsy appointment television, at one point airing three nights a week. The show ran for a staggering 524 episodes over five years and made $62 million for the network—not a dime of which went to the estate of Grace Metalious, who had signed away all the rights to her work during that stay at the Algonquin.

In the final episode, broadcast June 2, 1969, Dr. Michael Rossi, played by Ed Nelson, is charged with murder and thrown into the local jail. In the very last scene, he lies down on a cot as a guard slides closed his cell door—like his creator, a prisoner of Peyton Place.

MARY McCARTHY

....

VASSAR UNZIPPED

by Laura Jacobs

JULY 2013

Everyone loved Chapter Two. Straitlaced Dottie Renfrew—Vassar class of 1933 and a virgin—has gone home with the handsome but dissipated Dick Brown. He undresses her slowly, so that she "was hardly trembling when she stood there in front of him with nothing on but her pearls." Dick makes Dottie lie down on a towel, and after she experiences some "rubbing and stroking," and then some "pushing and stabbing," she starts to get the hang of things. "All of a sudden, she seemed to explode in a series of long, uncontrollable contractions that embarrassed her, like the hiccups . . ." No hearts and flowers here, simply a female orgasm described by a female writer who was as empirical and precise as the male writers of her day—perhaps more so—yet always attuned to the social niceties imprinted upon a certain class of female mind. Dick removes the towel, impressed by the minute stain, and in a remark that pulled the romantic veil from the usual novelistic pillow talk, says of his ex-wife, "Betty bled like a pig."

It was the first line of Chapter Three, however, that brought mythic status to Mary McCarthy's fifth novel, *The Group*. "Get yourself a pessary," Dick says the next morning, walking Dottie to the door. The chapter proceeds to offer a tutorial on the etiquette, economics, semiotics, and symbolism of this particular form of contraception, circa 1933. Diaphragm, ring, plug—call it what you will—when *The Group* was published, in 1963, the subject was still shocking. Sidney Lumet's movie of *The Group*—released three years later, smack in the middle of the sexual revolution—included Dottie's deflowering and subsequent trip to a gynecologist but substituted euphemisms for McCarthy's blunt language. Instead, Dick Brown says, "The right lady doctor could make us a lot happier."

Critics of *The Group* would call it Mary McCarthy's "lady-writer's novel" and "lady-book," insults meant to suggest it was a falling-off from her previous work. And it *was* different from what she'd done before. Up until *The Group*, McCarthy was feared and revered in the smart, tight, testy, and frequently backstabbing world of midcentury literary quarterlies and political reviews. Her critical assessments of theater and literature were scathing, and no one was too high to be brought low. Arthur Miller, J. D. Salinger, and Tennessee Williams—the greats of the day—all came in for vivisection, McCarthy's own Theater of Cruelty on the page. ("Torn animals," poet Randall Jarrell wrote of a character based on McCarthy, "were removed at sunset from that smile.") Her early novels read like moral chess matches where everyone is a pawn. And her memoirs, well, one thinks of brutal honesty dressed in beautiful scansion, Latinate sentences of classical balance and offhand wit in which nothing is sacred and no one is spared, not even the author herself. There was never anything "ladylike" about Mary McCarthy's writing. She struck fear in the hearts of male colleagues, many of whom she took to bed *without* trembling or pearls. For aspiring female writers, she remains totemic.

But *The Group*—a novel that followed eight Vassar roommates from commencement in 1933 to the brink of war in 1940—was her Mount Olympus and her Achilles' heel, a monster international success that brought world fame yet failed to impress the peers who mattered most.

"Women's secrets again," the poet Louise Bogan wrote to a friend, "told in clinical detail."

"No one in the know likes the book," poet Robert Lowell wrote to fellow poet Elizabeth Bishop, a Vassar classmate of McCarthy's.

"Mary tried for something very big," critic Dwight Macdonald wrote to historian Nicola Chiaromonte, "but didn't have the creative force to weld it all together."

All true, and all beside the point. Published on August 28, 1963, with a whopping first printing of 75,000, *The Group* was a sensation. By September 8 it was No. 9 on the *New York Times* best-seller list for adult fiction, with booksellers ordering 5,000 copies a day. By October 6 it had dethroned Morris L. West's *The Shoes of the Fisherman* to become No. 1, where it would stay for the next five months. By the end of 1964, nearly 300,000 copies had been sold, though now and then Harcourt Brace Jovanovich had to refund the price of a book. Women's secrets "told in clinical detail" were, for some, tantamount to pornography. The book was banned in Australia, Italy, and Ireland.

Countless novels have topped the best-seller list for months. Mention them now—*The Shoes of the Fisherman*, for instance—and people go blank. Not so with *The Group*. While its plot was almost nonexistent and its emotional hold next to nil, the secrets of these Vassar girls were chinked in stone and the racy one-liners etched in memory. As Helen Downes Light, a Vassar classmate of McCarthy's, told Frances Kiernan, the author of the biography *Seeing Mary Plain*, "I used to keep seventy-five dollars of mad money in a book. We had *The Group* on the shelf in our guest room and I thought, I'll remember where it is if I put it in there. Every guest we had would come down the next morning and say, 'Did you know you had money in that book?'"

Money in that book! Avon paid $100,000 for the paperback rights. Movie rights sold to producer-agent Charles Feldman for $162,500. *The Group* made Mary McCarthy a very rich intellectual, one of America's first highbrows to receive gargantuan sums, thus changing the financial expectations of serious writers and the scale on which their work could be judged.

By the time McCarthy began *The Group* she had been writing about groups for years. It was a fascination of hers, and you could say it was fated. When McCarthy was six, she and her three younger brothers lost both parents in the 1918 flu pandemic. Gone the beatific home created by an adored mother and charismatic father; gone the intimate group that is one's family. Her father, Roy McCarthy, was the son of J. H. McCarthy, a wealthy, self-made grain merchant in Minneapolis. Roy was charming and handsome, but he was a binge drinker, which made it difficult for him to hold a job. At 30, he went west to Oregon for a fresh start in a timber-brokerage business, and it was there that he met 21-year-old Tess Preston, dark-haired, beautiful, and accepting of Roy's alcoholism. They married in 1911, and when Mary was born, in 1912 in Seattle, Roy not only stopped drinking for good, he became a lawyer at 32. Unfortunately, the ill effects of childhood rheumatic fever left him increasingly bedridden. The decision to move the family back to Minneapolis, to be close to Roy's parents, proved fatal. Upon arrival, Roy and Tess died within a day of each other. The orphans would be shuttled between unsympathetic and sometimes sadistic relatives.

A little girl with a gimlet eye, Mary was acutely aware of her new status—the outsider looking in—and she became well acquainted with the power games played by those on the inside. Her coming-of-age brought more of the same. As a Seattle girl of uncertain class (not to mention—and she didn't—a Jewish grandmother), she was an outsider at East Coast, upper-crust Vassar. As an Irish Catholic of bourgeois upbringing, she was an outsider among *Partisan Review*'s gang of first-generation Jews, even as she ruled from within as the magazine's theater critic and queen cobra, entrancing male colleagues while living with *P.R.*'s editor Philip Rahv. In fact, being "inside" only brought ambivalence. "A princess among the trolls" is how she came to characterize her position at *P.R.*, rather nastily, in her astonishing short story of 1941, "The Man in the Brooks Brothers Shirt." This frank and often bawdy portrayal of a one-night stand on a cross-country train, its details drawn from McCarthy's own past tryst on a train, was a dropped bomb that brought career-making notoriety. "I was at Exeter at the time," the late George Plimpton told Frances Kiernan, "and it made almost as much of an impression as Pearl Harbor."

NOVEL IDEA

· ·

The Group is considered McCarthy's fifth novel, but, truth be told, it's hard to know exactly which of her books is the first. *The Company She Keeps,* published in 1942 and cited as the first, was actually a collection of previously published short stories, including "The Man in the Brooks Brothers Shirt," all sharing a protagonist, Margaret Sargent. Her piercing sensibility takes the place of a plot, sending waves of pitiless social insight and irony rippling through the book. McCarthy's "second" novel, *The Oasis,* was the winning entry in a 1949 fiction contest sponsored by the English literary monthly *Horizon.* A novelette in length, a political satire in tone, *The Oasis* was also a *roman à clef* that spoofed the *Partisan Review* intellectuals, presenting them as Realists or Purists and plopping them into a rural Utopia where they attempt to live outside society, without modern conveniences or class distinctions. Former lover Rahv, caricatured as the leader of the Realists, was so stung by the book he threatened to sue. In an interview with *The Paris Review,* McCarthy clarified: "*The Oasis* is not a novel. . . . It's a *conte,* a *conte philosophique.*"

An interesting choice of words on McCarthy's part, *conte* versus "story," for the French *conte* not only translates as "tale," it also connotes a narration, a story told orally. Setting aside the fact that McCarthy could be quite theatrical when reading her work before an audience, there *is* a distinctly narrated, documentary-voice-over quality to her fiction, as if her tales came straight from her head—eyes, ears, brain, mouth—without ever having traveled through her heart.

The Groves of Academe followed in 1951 and *A Charmed Life* in 1954. *Groves* is yet another chess match, an example of what the writer Elizabeth Hardwick, a lifelong friend of McCarthy's, termed her "ideological follies," this one between academics (recognizable to those in the know, naturally) at a small college modeled on Bard, where McCarthy had taught for a year. As for *A Charmed Life,* the plot, not ideological but still a kind of folly, zeroes in on the emotional dynamics of an iffy marriage dropped into a tiny community of bohemians, further complicated when the protagonist's former husband (based, in part, on McCarthy's second husband, the writer Edmund Wilson) lures her into a drunken roll on the couch. Booze and bad sex were never far apart in the world of Mary McCarthy, and *A Charmed Life* turns on what will be done with the pregnancy that follows.

In the year that brought forth *A Charmed Life,* the *Partisan Review* published yet another McCarthy tale, this one called "Dottie Makes an Honest Woman of Herself." Hard to believe Mary could go one better than "The Man in the Brooks Brothers Shirt," but she did. Sandwiched between an Irving Howe essay, "This Age of Conformity," and Hannah Arendt's "Tradition and the Modern Age" was the unabashed third chapter of *The Group*—"Get yourself a pessary." It was a scandalous sneak preview that made everyone want more.

PORTRAIT OF THE LADIES

. . . .

According to biographer Carol Gelderman (*Mary McCarthy: A Life*), the idea was articulated in 1951, when McCarthy applied for a John Simon Guggenheim Memorial Foundation grant. She wanted to write about "a group of newly married couples who emerge out of the Depression with a series of optimistic beliefs in science, engineering, rural electrification, the Aga stove, technocracy, psychoanalysis. . . . In a certain sense, the ideas are the villains and the people their hapless victims." It was a concept novel, with not so much a plot as a plan: the characters conned by progress with a capital *P*. The grant was denied, but McCarthy went ahead and began writing.

In 1959, five years after "Dottie Makes an Honest Woman of Herself" was published, McCarthy again applied for a Guggenheim, this time describing the book as a "history of the faith in progress of the nineteen-thirties and forties as reflected in the behavior and notions of young women—college graduates of the year 1933. . . . It is a crazy quilt of clichés, platitudes, and *idées reçues*. Yet the book is not meant to be a joke or even a satire, exactly, but a 'true history' of the times . . ."

The concept had been simplified and refined. In a way, it was the fictional flower of a nonfiction essay McCarthy had written in 1951, for *Holiday* magazine, in which she stated, "For different people . . . at different periods, Vassar can stand for whatever is felt to be wrong with the modern female: humanism, atheism, Communism, short skirts, cigarettes, psychiatry, votes for women, free love, intellectualism. Pre-eminently among American college women, the Vassar girl is thought of as carrying a banner." *The Group* was now the book McCarthy was destined to write. Her editor, William Jovanovich, of Harcourt Brace Jovanovich, thought it "might be one of the few important books that is about women without being actually *for* women." The jury at the Guggenheim must have thought so too, for the grant was given.

McCarthy would fulfill her proposal with *i*'s dotted (Dottied?) and *t*'s crossed. *The Group* isn't a joke, and though satirical it isn't a satire. The lives of McCarthy's eight graduates—nine if you count Norine, a classmate who envied the group from afar and is the novel's lone outsider—do indeed present a crazy quilt that captures the history of the time. Dottie proffers a peephole into the sexual mores of the 1930s and Priss into "enlightened" mothering. Literary Libby wants to be an editor but is steered toward agenting, while Polly's affairs shed light on the era's attitudes toward psychoanalysis and psychiatry. In Kay we have the consumer as climber, a woman in love with the intellectual cachet of modernism; for this she is mocked by her philandering husband, Harald Petersen (modeled on McCarthy's first husband, Harald Johnsrud). Androgynous Helena writes the class newsletter, and chubby heiress Pokey is present mostly through her butler, Hatton. Empress of them all is Lakey—Elinor

Eastlake, of Lake Forest, Illinois—the aloof aesthete who's studying art in Europe and spends most of the novel offstage. Most of the movie too. "Waiting for Lakey to reappear," the film critic Pauline Kael wrote in a 1966 essay on the making of Lumet's movie, "is about like waiting for Godot." But worth the wait, for she was played with sublime hauteur by a young Candice Bergen. It is upon Lakey's return from Europe that the group realizes she is a lesbian.

Getting the book written would take some doing. Late in 1959, the year McCarthy received her Guggenheim, she met the man who would become her fourth and last husband, the diplomat James West. McCarthy left her third husband, Bowden Broadwater, to wed West, who had to leave his second wife, Margaret. West was posted to Paris, where the couple bought a large apartment, and McCarthy took on extra writing assignments to help pay for its renovation. This annoyed Jovanovich, who'd drummed up huge advance interest in *The Group* and wanted to see it finished and in print pronto. Moreover, in early 1963, just as she should have been perfecting her final manuscript for its April deadline, McCarthy spent intellectual and emotional energy defending *Eichmann in Jerusalem,* an eyewitness report on the trial of Adolf Eichmann, a bureaucratic cog in the Holocaust machine and the man who would embody, in the report's infamous phrase, "the banality of evil." First serialized in *The New Yorker* and deeply controversial, the book was written by McCarthy's beloved friend and kindred spirit, the political theorist Hannah Arendt.

Yet even before the move to Paris and the Eichmann explosion McCarthy realized she couldn't manage *The Group*'s projected time frame—the Roosevelt 30s to the Eisenhower 50s. In 1960 she told *The Paris Review,* "These girls are all essentially comic figures, and it's awfully hard to make anything happen to them." She felt that comic figures, as if by Delphic decree, were not allowed to learn or grow. Reducing the time frame to seven years, she still had trouble wrapping it up. "I've lost all perspective," McCarthy told Arendt. "The main thing is to push on and deposit the burden. On Jovanovich's lap." That said, when McCarthy suddenly found herself on the verge of best-sellerdom, she was, she wrote, "very much excited by all the excitement about the book." The question of whether McCarthy had made the girls' fates feel like more than *faits accomplis* would be left for the critics to settle.

MCCARTHYISM

The year 1963 was a big one for what is now termed "second-wave feminism." McCarthy never rode *any* wave of feminism. Generously mentored by male editors and lovers, she scorned special pleading based on gender. Nevertheless, her Vassar girls burst upon the world in the same year that saw the publication of

Betty Friedan's *The Feminine Mystique,* a groundbreaking study of the nameless unhappiness that was plaguing postwar housewives. (Friedan's book was sparked by Smith girls, classmates she had surveyed at a 15th reunion.) Also in 1963, Radcliffe girl Adrienne Rich published her third collection of poetry, *Snapshots of a Daughter-in-Law,* a seismic shift into the terrain of gender politics. "All three of these books," says Katha Pollitt, essayist for *The Nation,* "were about the way very smart, educated women get trapped in the lesser life they are compelled to lead."

Unlike her sister-school sisters, McCarthy wasn't taking on the present in a way that was radically or even covertly subversive. She was looking at the past, specifically, she said, at a "vanishing class"—upper-middle, Protestant, educated. Her girls were bluestockings, not rebels. They graduate from Vassar embracing the social responsibilities required of their class and believing that America is inevitably improving. Almost all of them become less acute with the passing of time. One could and probably should read this diminuendo as an authorial statement on life. As W. H. Auden wrote in the poem *Lullaby,* "Time and fevers burn away / Individual beauty from / Thoughtful children . . ." But Pauline Kael also had a point when she said, "She beats up on those girls."

"I think she looked around at what happened to her classmates," says the novelist Mary Gordon. "Because she's really talking about what happened to women after the Second World War. They really got shut down. To give it a rosier coloration is something her honesty would never have allowed her to do."

It was honesty on another level that made the book controversial. McCarthy was matter-of-fact and often slapstick about subjects everyone else deemed sacred—sex, motherhood, one's relationship with one's shrink. And she was completely unfazed by physiology.

"'*Betty bled like a pig,*'" reiterates the writer Penelope Rowlands. "My mother had a whole circle of friends that were parents. We kids would play in Central Park and they would sit on the bench. I have a distinct memory of the mothers sitting there giggling. One of them had a book and she said, 'Read Chapter Two,' and handed it to someone else. I can see them all just savoring it."

Mary Gordon remembers "the pessary, that was such a major thing. I was in Catholic school at the time and I thought *The Group* was a dirty book. I read it under the covers, and it was very exciting among my friends. Even though it had taken place in the 30s, it still seemed like late-breaking news. Smart women able to be sexual—that just seemed, in 1963, very thrilling. And it had immense stylishness."

"There were scenes that were neat and snappy," recalls writer and critic Margo Jefferson. "Of course, everybody remembers Libby and her secret, what she called 'going over the top.' Written in that precise little way."

The reviews rolled in as expected, acknowledging McCarthy's reputation as a critic and trying, in the words of Jovanovich, "not to be wrong about the book." Some even went as far as to quote back McCarthy's own description of her objectives (progress, platitudes), a rare deference that attests to the fear factor attached to her name. In *The Saturday Review,* Granville Hicks lauded McCarthy's newfound sympathy for her characters yet suggested it was as "social history that the novel will chiefly be remembered." In *The New York Times,* Arthur Mizener detected no sympathy at all but decided that while *The Group* was not a conventional novel, "it is, in its own way, something pretty good." The *Chicago Daily News* called it a "whopper . . . one of the best novels of the decade."

PARTISAN POLITICS

Backlash arrived in October. Norman Podhoretz, writing in *Show,* went after the snobbery he perceived in McCarthy's novel: "Willfully blind to the spirit of moral ambition and the dream of self-transcendence that animated [the 30s], she can see nothing in it but foolishness and insincerity—despite the fact that she herself was produced by that spirit." Even worse was the broadside from a new publication—started up during the New York newspaper strike—*The New York Review of Books,* edited by Robert Silvers and Barbara Epstein. McCarthy considered *The New York Review* friendly, having written an essay on William Burroughs for its very first issue. Her good friends Robert Lowell and Elizabeth Hardwick, then husband and wife, were part of *The New York Review*'s inner circle. So she was stunned when the fortnightly slammed her not once but twice.

On September 26, 1963, a three-paragraph parody called "The Gang" was published under the pseudonym Xavier Prynne (a play on Xavier Rynne, the famous pseudonym of Francis X. Murphy, who wrote extensively on the Vatican). It zeroed in on Dottie's—now Maisie's—defloration, mocking the way McCarthy's avid, appraising omniscience doesn't shut off even during a shtup: "Gasping for breath, Maisie giggled and said, 'Remember Bernard Shaw? Something about brief and ridiculous.'"

McCarthy was not happy to be parodied so publicly and perfectly. And she was dumbfounded when she learned that Xavier Prynne was none other than her close friend Hardwick.

"Why did Lizzie do it?" asks Kiernan, who is now at work on a book about Robert Lowell and his wives. "Well, it was irresistible. And, to be fair, the one part she mocks is the best part of the book. She hasn't picked one of the weaknesses."

"Lizzie was a great friend of Mary's, so it was obviously complex," says someone who knew them both. "She felt it was a matter of justice—justice for literary judgment."

Worse would come three weeks later, when *The New York Review of Books* published Norman Mailer's strenuously virtuosic, outrageously sexist takedown. The razor sharpens on the strop in the opening paragraph, with Mailer hailing Mary as "our saint, our umpire, our lit arbiter, our broadsword, our Barrymore (Ethel), our Dame (dowager), our mistress (Head), our Joan of Arc . . ." et cetera. He gives *The Group* one compliment—"It has a conception of the novel which is Mary's own"—and then goes on (and on and on) to say in a thousand different ways that it is "good but not nearly good enough." In short, he gave her the Mary McCarthy treatment.

Negative reviews on such a grand scale are no fun, but they can bring positive publicity to a book, a greater sense of moment. And then there's the jealousy of friends. "The people at the *Partisan Review* were all very smart," explains cultural critic Midge Decter, who knew McCarthy in those days, "and very catty with one another because they were all living as literary figures in a shortage economy of fame and money. Mary had published some fiction, but not much attention was paid to it. Then *The Group* was a big success and nobody could stand it. Everybody was very mean about Mary and envious of her. It wasn't unheard of by then; Saul Bellow had had a big success. That was the first major trauma. But the idea that you could actually make money being a writer, that was new."

"High art and popular art were in very different worlds," says Pollitt. "You couldn't be in both. You might want your book made into a movie, but if you did, that was selling out."

"It was a best-seller and she was making all this money," Kiernan says. "You've got to realize, she had always been an intellectual—a New York intellectual. And so the people who had respected her, they look at her again. And she's now got Susan Sontag nipping at her heels, and Susan is suddenly *the* intellectual, and she looks a lot purer than Mary does at this point, and styles have changed. So did she sell out deliberately? I don't think she ever intended *The Group* to be a big best-seller."

THE PEN IS MIGHTIER THAN THE SWORD

Once critics and friends got their swipes in, Vassar classmates took their turn. For years McCarthy had been wounding friends and colleagues by liberally, transparently, and irreverently using them in her fiction. *The Group* was no different. But where her previous novels had highbrow readerships, vastly smaller, this one was titillating everybody. In her 1992 biography of the author, *Writing Dangerously,* Carol Brightman notes that among McCarthy's set "identifying the bodies in the 'blood-stained alley' behind *The Group* quickly became a favorite pastime." They knew that these girls were based on real people. It didn't help that McCarthy had hardly changed the names of the victims—for instance, Dottie Renfrew derived from Dottie Newton. Yet she insisted the book could not be called a *roman à clef* because the girls were "unknown to the public."

Whatever you call the book, the Vassar class of '33 viewed it as a betrayal. In a story titled "Miss McCarthy's Subjects Return the Compliments," which ran on the front page of the *Herald Tribune Book Review* in January of 1964, one of the affronted said, "It's all there—our parents, our habits, our prejudices, our classmates." Interviewed by the journalist Sheila Tobias, the "real-life" room-mates shot back, remembering McCarthy as narcissistic and unkempt. And they were withering about the bun she wore at the nape of her neck, a signature. "She may," one said, "be the only Vassar girl not to have changed her hairstyle in 30 years." Writing to Jovanovich in high dudgeon over the "horrible nasty piece," McCarthy protested that "The Group is an idea, not a study of the actual group disguised—a Platonic ideal." Sounds like the old *conte philosophique* defense. She did, however, finally cut her hair.

The provenance of the novel's most mysterious character, Elinor Eastlake, is to this day a fascinating question. The character is as self-contained as a cat, and in the novel's final scene—Lakey's verbal duel, behind the wheel of her car, with Kay's husband, Harald—she's mesmerizing, which is to say brilliantly written. Although McCarthy eventually said Lakey owed her "Indian eyes" to Margaret Miller and her "fathomless scorn" to Nathalie Swan, both Vassar classmates, a description that arrives late in the novel superimposes Mary upon Lakey: "They had all cut their hair and had permanents, but Lakey still wore hers in a black knot at the nape of her neck, which gave her a girlish air." Kiernan believes "she's many people. I think partly she's Mary, partly she was Margaret Miller, who had the physical beauty of Lakey. And Helen Dawes Watermulder, from Chicago, she thought she was Lakey." Others believe that Lakey was based on one person, a Vassar graduate of quiet renown, Elizabeth Bishop.

A distinguished poet, in literary stature right up there with Robert Lowell (and thus above Mary), Bishop happened to be a lesbian. When she first read *The Group*, she'd been amused. But, Kiernan writes, friends had persuaded her that "not only was she the model for Lakey . . . but Lota de Macedo Soares, her Brazilian lover, was the model for the baroness [Lakey's lover]." Bishop went cold on McCarthy, who as late as 1979 appealed to her in a letter: "I promise you that no thought of you, or of Lota, even grazed my mind when I was writing *The Group*."

"Mary thought that she had changed certain facts, and Elizabeth thought it was still too close," says an editor who knew both women. "This is what one thinks: Would there have been a Lakey if there hadn't been Elizabeth Bishop? The answer is probably no. Lakey is meant to be Mary-like in appearance and Elizabeth-like in superior sensibility. It's very important to the novel actually, because it's important to the novel's tone, which has this superiority, this sense of knowingness about different lives, different people. She clearly had followed these women. Vassar had been very important to Mary as the place where she formed her view of things, and you feel her attempt to locate people socially, where they stood, where their family stood. It's very much part of her writing and her sensibility, this question of who is superior in American social life."

Not until 1976, when *Esquire* published Truman Capote's "La Côte Basque," a short story that fouled the society dames he called his "swans," would another work of fiction upset so many women. [*Elsewhere in this collection: essays by Sam Kashner on Capote and Elizabeth Bishop on Marianne Moore.*]

GROUPTHINK

Novelists lift material from life because they must. First novels are invariably autobiographical, which is why second novels are so difficult: the writer needs to recede and let the characters create themselves. McCarthy never learned to back off and loosen her grip. Maybe she couldn't. She'd lost so much so young. She once said that the reason you write a novel is "to put something in the world that wasn't there before," so she had the artist's impulse for creation. But she did not have the artist's trust in stirrings that cannot quite be set to words. She couldn't leave characters to a fate that was out of her control. This is why the word "novel" keeps slipping off her fiction and why she herself was constantly coming up with other terms for her work.

McCarthy grew to dislike *The Group* and the best-seller treatment that accompanied it. "I hated the whole business of interviews and TV. I felt I'd been corrupted," she told the English newspaper *The Observer* in 1979, "that the world which I despised had somehow eaten its way into me." There were two more novels and reams of nonfiction. She continued hurling judgments like thunderbolts. One in particular, lightly tossed, wreaked havoc. In 1979, on *The Dick Cavett Show,* Cavett asked McCarthy which writers she thought were overrated. "The only one I can think of," she said, "is a holdover like Lillian Hellman." She then uttered the actionable sentence, "Every word she writes is a lie, including 'and' and 'the.'" Hellman was watching, and within weeks, citing defamation of character, she sued McCarthy, Cavett, and the Educational Broadcasting Corporation for $2.5 million. Hellman's lawyer said she would drop the suit if McCarthy issued a retraction, but McCarthy wouldn't, because she couldn't lie. It wasn't until 1984 that a first ruling came down, and it was in Hellman's favor. McCarthy planned to appear in court, but Hellman died a month later, and with her the lawsuit. In 1989, McCarthy died of lung cancer. She never had another book as big as *The Group.*

Until the end, admiring writers and journalists made pilgrimages to the apartment in Paris and to Castine, Maine, where the Wests summered in a 19th-century sea captain's house. While McCarthy remained politically left and in full support of reproductive rights, more than once she commented on her preference for doing things the old-fashioned way. "I like labor-intensive implements and practices. Cranking by hand an ice cream freezer . . . pushing a fruit or vegetable through a sieve . . . leaving some mark of the tools on the marble I think it has something to do with the truth." And again, "I love recipes that involve pushing things through sieves." In a way it describes her method as a novelist. McCarthy's plots, their ingredients measured out and mixed with an almost scientific objective in mind, *are* like recipes—usually for disaster. And instead of fruits or vegetables, it is her characters that get pushed and strained through a sieve.

The poet Robert Lowell, whom McCarthy adored and revered, said something similar but with more eloquence. In a letter to Mary dated August 7, 1963, he described her Vassar girls as "cloistered, pastoral souls breaking on the real rocks of the time." He went on to include himself in this group of cloistered souls, writing that in the late 30s "we were ignorant, dependable little machines made to mow the lawn, then suddenly turned out to clear the wilderness." Leave it to the poet to know an elegy when he sees it. Flowers of the culture, these young women, but shot from a gun.

JACQUELINE SUSANN

···

ONCE WAS NEVER ENOUGH

by Amy Fine Collins

JANUARY 2000

At 3:30 A.M. on December 25, 1962, Jacqueline Susann—a fading TV actress with an unemployed husband, an autistic son in a mental hospital, and a lump in her right breast—began to scribble in a notebook. "This is a bad Christmas," she wrote. "Irving has no job. . . . I am going to the hospital. . . . I don't think I have [cancer]. I have too much to accomplish. I can't die without leaving something—something big. . . . I'm Jackie—I have a dream. I think I can write. Let me live to make it!"

In her 12 remaining years—the tumor was malignant and a full mastectomy was performed the day after Christmas—Susann more than made good on her dream. Not only did she write *Valley of the Dolls* (1966)—registered in *The Guinness Book of World Records* in the 1970s as the best-selling novel of all time (30 million copies sold)—she also became, with her next two novels, *The Love Machine* (1969) and *Once Is Not Enough* (1973), the first author ever to have three consecutive books catapult to the No. 1 spot on *The New York Times's* best-seller list. No wonder she dared to proclaim to a Boston newspaper critic, who imagined he was hoisting her on her own petard, "Yeah, I think I'll be remembered . . . as the voice of the 60s. . . . Andy Warhol, the Beatles and me!"

It has taken longer than the apotheosis of the Beatles or the deification of Andy Warhol, but Susann's nervy prophecy has finally come to pass. The first to resurrect Jacqueline Susann as a pop-culture deity was Barbara Seaman, whose 1987 biography, the definitive *Lovely Me,* was reprinted in 1996. The following year Grove/Atlantic began reissuing the Susann trilogy of major novels, and, accelerating the momentum, the 1967 movie version of *Valley of the Dolls* was released on video in 1997. Michele Lee co-produced and starred in a 1998 USA Networks biopic, *Scandalous Me,* and in January, Universal opens a comedy feature entitled *Isn't She Great* (based on a *New Yorker* story by Michael Korda), with Bette Midler playing Susann opposite Nathan Lane as the writer's husband, Irving Mansfield. The manager of Susann's literary catalogue, filmmaker Lisa

Bishop, is in pre-production on a remake of *Valley of the Dolls* and is also co-authoring with poet and Susann archivist David Trinidad *The Jacqueline Susann Scrapbook: Dogs, Dames, and Dolls.* Writer Rae Lawrence is currently working on a *Valley of the Dolls* sequel, based on plot notes in Bishop's Susann files. And then there are the ritualized viewings of *Valley of the Dolls*—the 30th-anniversary screening in San Francisco's Castro Theatre attracted 1,550 zealots, some in *Doll* drag, who chanted every line, à la *The Rocky Horror Picture Show;* the inevitable Jackie-cult Web sites; and the Columbia University graduate school course in which *Valley of the Dolls* was required reading.

Feminist author Letty Cottin Pogrebin, the original publicist for *Valley of the Dolls,* reports, "This revival is the answer to Jacqueline Susann's prayers. She predicted the celebrity culture we live in now. Actually, she invented it: fame is as fame does." Impresario Anna Sosenko, whose friendship with Susann dated from the 40s, adds, "When Jackie was dying she'd call me—scared, sad, and crying. She worried that in a few years everything she'd done would be forgotten. And I told her, 'Darling, you have expressed your historical era—10 transitional years, from J.F.K.'s assassination to Watergate. Your time will return.'"

The exact historical era into which Jacqueline Susann was born, in Philadelphia on August 20, 1918, was that of the *fin de guerre* flu epidemic. Her mother, Rose, a fastidious schoolteacher, added a second *n* to the Sephardic Jewish family name, while her father, Robert, a philandering portrait artist, retained the original spelling. Perhaps because Bob liked to defy his wife by indulging their little girl's taste for films and theater, Jacqueline from a young age became obsessed with showbiz and its larger-than-life personalities. She papered her room with images of stage divas June Knight and Margalo Gillmore, and auditioned repeatedly for *The Children's Hour,* a Philadelphia radio program. One summer in Atlantic City, where the Susanns rented a beach house, Jackie, aged about 11, discovered that a celebrated actress had taken up residence in a nearby hotel. Anna Sosenko says, "So Jackie schlepped her poor little girlfriend over to this hotel and they knocked on the actress's door. . . . The actress shouted, 'Get lost!' and slammed the door in her face. Jackie was starstruck and that was the leitmotif of her world of thinking. Once Jackie wanted to know somebody, she pursued them relentlessly. Sometimes the door slammed, and sometimes it opened."

The exit door from Philadelphia opened when her father helped judge a local beauty contest. Deemed "Philadelphia's most beautiful girl" on April 16, 1936, the 17-year-old Jackie was awarded a silver loving cup and a Warner Bros. screen test in New York. The contest left her with the unshakable conviction that she was "a tearing beauty," Sosenko explains. "She always described herself exactly that way. Jackie was very sold on her looks."

· · ·

Having flunked her screen test, Jackie resided at Kenmore Hall, a ladies' hotel in New York, where she befriended a vaudeville waif named Elfie—the prototype for the young Neely in *Valley of the Dolls*. In the fall of 1936, Susann's father again intervened on her behalf, pulling strings to land her a part as a French maid in a show heading for rehearsals—Clare Boothe Luce's *The Women*, starring Susann's idol Margalo Gillmore. Despite the help she received from a fellow cast member, a patrician New England blonde named Beatrice Cole, Susann could not master the French accent required for her three lines, and was fired. But she felt so attached to the production, she watched every performance from the wings, nurturing what Irving Mansfield called her "fierce crush" on Gillmore. At last a part as a lingerie model opened up, and in acknowledgment of her devotion to the hit show, Susann was allowed to join the cast of *The Women* on June 2, 1937.

In the meantime, Susann demonstrated Lux toilet soap with Bea and hung out at Walgreen's, whose bank of phone booths functioned as a makeshift office for a motley assortment of Broadway types. It was in this humble setting that Susann and press agent Irving Mansfield "met cute," to use the parlance of old Hollywood. Dazzled by Mansfield's ability to get her picture in the paper, she married him at her parents' house in 1939. Mansfield admitted in his 1983 memoir, *Life with Jackie*, "I can't really claim that Jackie and I were propelled into each other's arms by an irresistible passion." Anna Sosenko observes, "The truth is she thought that Irving would make her a star."

Producer Armand Deutsch—who met Mansfield before the war when the press agent was publicizing *The Rudy Vallee Show* and Deutsch was the radio program's ad representative—calls the young Mr. and Mrs. Irving Mansfield "a Damon Runyon couple." The pair settled into the Essex House, and when Eddie Cantor, star of vaudeville, radio, screen, and stage, was in town, he stayed at the same residential hotel, usually in the company of his five daughters and his wife, Ida. Undeterred by this family entourage, Susann eagerly threw herself into an affair with Cantor. Actress Joan Castle Sitwell says, "When she told me about Cantor, I said, 'Are you kidding?' I suppose he was some kind of father figure for her." Actress Maxine Stewart adds, "Jackie was simply crazy for Jewish comics." Yet the liaison paid off in a way that mattered to Susann. Cantor gave her a small speaking part in his new vehicle, *Banjo Eyes*, which opened at Broadway's Hollywood Theatre in December 1941, just after America entered the war.

In the period when Mansfield was promoting CBS's *The Rudy Vallee Show*, the writers and Deutsch met regularly at the Essex House apartment of Vic Knight, their producer, to prepare the scripts. Partly because she lived in the same building where the radio men gathered, but mostly because she was "an odd girl, a different girl," Susann, Deutsch says, "hung around our working sessions, went to dinner with us. I always got the feeling she knew life could be better for her. She yearned for something more."

"Something more," at that moment, turned out to be an excellent part as Helen in the road version of the wartime drama *Cry Havoc,* which opened in Chicago on March 1, 1943. It so happened that the Jewish comic Joe E. Lewis— whose performances Susann had been following avidly since her first days in New York—was also in town doing a show. Consequently, when she dragged members of the all-female cast to see Lewis at the Chez Paree, she was by no means a total stranger to him. And neither was her husband—who, conveniently, had just been drafted into the army and was stationed at Fort Dix, New Jersey. Maxine Stewart, a *Cry Havoc* co-star, remembers, "Jackie was in love with Joe E. She had left Irving and she was staying at the Royalton. She said to me, 'I'm not going to live with a man who's making so little money'—he was on an army salary." The affair with Lewis ended when the U.S.O. shipped him to New Guinea. Yet even after she reconciled with Mansfield, around 1946, Susann still carried a torch for Joe E. She named her first poodle, Josephine, after him, and the title of her last book, *Once Is Not Enough,* came from the comic's 1971 deathbed words—an eleventh-hour variation on his signature line, that "if you play your cards right" in life, once is enough.

Susann's attitude toward the Jewish comics to whom she gave herself so freely surfaces in her portrait of *The Love Machine*'s TV host, Christie Lane, an uncouth tightwad given to leaving the bathroom door ajar as he lets rip "explosive bowel movement[s]." There is more than a little of her own sense of humiliation embodied in the same novel's awkward, promiscuous Ethel Evans, whose "cooze is like the Lincoln Tunnel." And her feelings about Irving at this juncture come through in her characterization of *Valley of the Dolls'* Mel Harris, a close replica of her own spouse: "Mel was kinda weakish," Neely says, but Jewish men like him "make marvelous husbands." Presumably the fact that Mansfield's career was, in his words, "leaping ahead" helped lure Susann back home, now at the Hotel Navarro on Central Park South. By the late 40s he had moved into radio production, and by 1949 he had maneuvered his way into the infant medium of television.

And Susann's own ambition to make herself a marquee name remained undiminished. She played in J. J. Shubert's fifth New York revival of *Blossom Time* and Cole Porter's *Let's Face It.* More satisfying was her role in Shubert's *A Lady Says Yes,* a 1945 vehicle for Hollywood pinup Carole Landis. (Barbara Seaman believes that Landis and Susann not only compared notes on their mutual conquest, George Jessel—yet another Jewish comic—but also were to some degree physically involved themselves.) During this time Susann began a scrapbook, reserving one cardboard page for a series of notations which amount to a fever chart of her search for fame. "Am I any nearer to success," she asks herself in August 1944. "Slightly," she answers in February 1945, a response followed by the addendum marked March 1946, "Oh yeah." At that date she was playing a stripper called Fudge Farrell in a bomb entitled *Between the Covers,* set in the publishing world.

Fed up, Susann hauled out of her closet comedian Goodman Ace's wedding gift, a portable typewriter. In a few weeks she and Bea Cole, whose acting career was also on the skids, co-wrote a bedroom farce called *The Temporary Mrs. Smith.* The play actually made it to the stage, retitled *Lovely Me* for its New York opening. Yet, foreshadowing her books' reception, the universal pans it received forced the play to close to standing-room-only audiences. Still steaming over bad reviews more than a year later, Susann "belted" *Daily News* critic Douglas Watt at Sardi's, Walter Winchell reported in April 1948.

Susann did not ditch her typewriter yet—she and Bea next tried writing an exposé about women in show business, a *Valley of the Dolls* precursor entitled *Underneath the Pancake.* Susann also availed herself of the wide-open opportunities of live television, frenetically pushing sponsors' products—Quest-Shon-Mark bras, Sunset appliances, Hazel Bishop cosmetics, and Vigorelli sewing machines—on a spate of ill-fated programs, some of which she hosted.

Though she was booted from one of these shows, WOR-TV's *Night Time, New York* (a one-to-seven-A.M. variety broadcast), for her confrontational, proto-shock-jock interview tactics, its sponsor, Schiffli Lace and Embroidery Institute, retained Susann as its spokeswoman. Never one to do things by halves, Susann not only acted in her Schiffli ads but produced and wrote them as well. From 1955 until 1962 she shilled on Schiffli's behalf on *The Ben Hecht Show* and then on *The Mike Wallace Interview.* Offscreen, the "Schiffli Troubadour" plugged her ware at shopping centers, synagogues, and department stores. "She loved the TV commercials," Joan Castle Sitwell says. "Anything to get her face in front of the public."

In January 1951, Mansfield took out a full-page *Variety* ad, in dubious taste and of unfathomable motivation. In banner typeface it declared, "This is Show Business—conceived by Irving Mansfield. The New Sam Levenson Show—conceived by Irving Mansfield. Arthur Godfrey's Talent Scouts—conceived by Irving Mansfield. The Stork Club—conceived by Irving Mansfield." And beneath this proud scroll of credits ran a photograph of a smiling little boy, accompanied by the caption "Guy Mansfield—conceived by Irving Mansfield.*" Farther below was the line "*in association with Jacqueline Susann." This was not the first press mention of the Mansfields' son. *New York Post* columnist Earl Wilson had run an item back on July 16, 1946: "Irving Mansfield and Jacqueline Susann will have a baby in December." Guy Hildy Mansfield was born on

December 6, 1946, under markedly inauspicious circumstances. Susann and Bea Cole's *Lovely Me* was in tryouts in Philadelphia, and "flop sweat" was in the air. Not far from her due date her water broke, and with a hotel towel wedged between her legs she took the train back to New York, where Guy was delivered with the aid of forceps.

"Guy seemed like a lovely little baby at first," Sitwell remembers. "But once he started to stand and walk he began screaming a lot." Penny Bigelow, a CBS producer for *Arthur Godfrey's Talent Scouts,* says, "Guy was standing up in his crib, hitting his head against the wall." When he started to speak, "Mama," "Dada," and "Goddamnit!" were the extent of a vocabulary that soon vanished entirely, Seaman says. Dr. Lauretta Bender, a pioneer in children's psychiatric disorders, diagnosed Guy's condition as autism, an illness just then being identified. In Dr. Bender's care the three-year-old underwent shock treatments. When that drastic measure failed, she advised the Mansfields to send Guy to the Emma Pendleton Bradley Home, a mental institution for children in Rhode Island. Sitwell says, "Jackie had a broken heart. That was the reason for all the pills. And I think it made her sick—what I mean is, I think it gave her the cancer."

The Mansfields said to the rest of the world that their son was attending school in Arizona due to severe asthma. Penny Bigelow explains, "They always hoped Guy might recover, and they didn't want him stigmatized once he got out." Says one ex-patient, Judy Raphael Kletter, who was at Bradley with Guy for three years, "The Mansfields were always there. They were very into Guy, but they couldn't help him." (Guy, now 53, is still institutionalized and visited regularly.)

Grieving, Susann began grasping at anything that would numb the pain or distract her. There were her pills, which she nicknamed her "dolls"—her favorite term of endearment. There was work—the manic forays into television and radio dated from this time, as did another playwriting attempt with Bea Cole. "Now, added to Jackie's innate drive to succeed," Mansfield wrote, "was this new sense of desperate need to earn money, big, big money, for Guy's sake and security."

There was also the considerable diversion provided by her female friends, loosely organized around her into a society known as the Hockey Club. The group took its name from a corruption of the Yiddish word for "banging," and the main topic of conversation was, Penny Bigelow says, "who was 'hocking' who." In addition to talking about their own romantic adventures, the women—many of them former actresses (Joyce Mathews, Joan Sitwell, Dorothy Strelsin) who had married well—spied on one another's errant men. "Billy Rose feared us—he said we were more efficient than the K.G.B.," says Bigelow. Their exploits were even chronicled in Leonard Lyons's *New York Post* column. Dorothy Strelsin (the inspiration for the character Cher played in Franco Zeffirelli's autobiographical *Tea with Mussolini*) says: "Jackie was our den mother. We all phoned her when we had nothing else to do and told her everything."

Under the spell of the glamorous chanteuse Hildegarde—whose popular performances at the Plaza Hotel in New York she attended with the fervor of a groupie—Susann also attempted to find solace in Catholicism. "Jackie was an impressionable woman," says Anna Sosenko, then Hildegarde's manager. "A hero-worshiper." Hildegarde became Guy's godmother, and Susann gave him the middle name Hildy after her. Sitwell says, "Jackie turned Catholic because of her huge crush on Hildegarde. She would go into Saint Patrick's and make deals with God for her son. She would quit smoking if Guy would get better." This unusual approach to religion led Mansfield to say his wife "was treating God like the William Morris office."

More complicated for Susann than her idolization of Hildegarde was her ill-fated friendship with Ethel Merman, which resembled an exceptionally hard case of puppy love. "She was absolutely loony, like a 12-year-old," says Sitwell. Yet, Sosenko elaborates, "Ethel was as intrigued by Jackie as Jackie was by Ethel. But all that baloney about them having an affair—they were just girlfriends. Then the two of them got into a fight over something. Ethel had a weird temper. Irving, I think, got mad and threw a drink at her in a restaurant, and Ethel was embarrassed and hurt. Jackie was mortified. That's how the fight started. Being rebuffed by Ethel stung Jackie deeply—she had really fallen for her. When Jackie wrote about her, as the character Helen Lawson in *Valley of the Dolls*, Ethel was very burnt up."

Susann, however, had found another female on whose constancy she could depend. Around 1954, "Jackie fell madly in love with my little Tinker Toy," Dorothy Strelsin says. "After that she simply had to have a poodle." Susann ended up adopting a black half-toy, half-miniature, whom she named Josephine, after Joe E. Lewis. Susann had Josephine's portrait painted on the side of her Cadillac Eldorado, appeared with her in Schiffli ads, and fed her foie gras, Bloody Marys, and coffee, some of it sent up courtesy of the Hotel Navarro's room service. Never mind that Josephine's teeth were coming out and her belly bulged to such proportions that her legs could barely support it. Susann now had a creature in the house to whom she could be "Mother." And with a Jewish mother's pride, Susann wrote letters detailing her beloved poodle's escapades, many sent to her friends Billy Rose and his wife, Joyce Mathews, then living in the South of France. When they returned to New York, the couple told Susann, "That dog of yours is a card." Susann objected, "It's not the dog that's a card, it's me." In that case, Rose advised, "put it in a book."

Once again, Susann dusted off her typewriter from Goodman Ace. "I decided to take a year off," Susann wrote in a long diary entry, recently rediscovered in Lisa Bishop's archive. "Neither TV or the theatre was about to fall apart with my temporary 'retirement.' I worked on the book for nine months. . . . Deep down I didn't expect it to be published. I figured after I'd get all the rejects, I'd type it neatly—paste in all her pictures—have it bound—and keep it as an album. But before I settled for this I was determined to try for the top. . . . To have it rejected would crush a very real belief I had nurtured all my life—that I could write."

Susann did begin at the top—with William Morris, which dealt with Mansfield's TV shows. But, Sosenko recalls, "when Irving would talk to them about Jackie, they turned a deaf ear." Sosenko agreed to have a look at the manuscript, entitled *Every Night, Josephine!* "It was adorable, delicious," she says. "I acted immediately." Sosenko sent it to her friend Annie Laurie Williams, an agent of John Steinbeck, who had just won the Nobel Prize in Literature, and Harper Lee, who had just won the Pulitzer Prize. Williams shared Sosenko's enthusiasm and invited the author to her office for a meeting. "I'll never forget that day," Susann wrote. "Before I went, I changed outfits ten times. First I tried a suit—I looked like a writer—but maybe I was too much 'on the nose'—perhaps a plain black dress." To Susann's relief, she noted in the diary, Williams spoke to her new client in exactly the language she understood. "As an actress when you're up for a part, if the producer says no—that's it. But with a book, if a publisher says no—you send it to another publisher. . . . It only takes one yes to make a hit."

In the early fall of 1962, Williams sent *Every Night, Josephine!* to Doubleday—which shortly thereafter stopped returning calls. To take her mind off Doubleday's maddening silence, Irving treated his wife and her mother, Rose, to a trip around the world. Susann recorded the monthlong odyssey in a journal with photographs, the kind of scrapbook that she feared would be *Josephine*'s fate. During the voyage, Susann happily discovered that Seconals were sold over the counter in Japan. She stockpiled them, intending to barter them with Joyce Mathews for "new outfits." But the revelation that would permanently alter Susann's life was made in Hong Kong. On November 9, 1962, she wrote an affectionate epistle to Mansfield: "Doll! . . . Any news from Annie Laurie Williams about *Every Night, Josephine!*? This waiting is a killer. . . . I love you. . . . Jackie. P.S. Call and make an appointment with Dr. Davids for me. I have a tiny lump. It's probably nothing, but we might as well make sure."

Like Jennifer in *Valley of the Dolls*, when Susann learned the truth about her tumor—infiltrating ductile carcinoma, Seaman states, was the diagnosis—her first instinct was to bolt from the hospital. Back at home, Susann made a diary entry for January 1, 1963: "I've looked at the ledger and it doesn't add up. God, Saint Andrew, the Chinese good luck charm and the whole mishpocheh owe me more than I owe them. I've got to leave something worthwhile on this earth before I go. I also don't want it discovered AFTER I go. I want to be around to get that Nobel Prize." And when she was strong enough, she went out to a rise in Central Park near the Navarro that she called her Wishing Hill and made a pact with God. If He would give her only 10 more years, she promised God, "she would prove she could make it as a writer," Mansfield said, "as the number-one writer."

Doubleday finally informed Susann that its editors liked *Every Night, Josephine!* But since the firm had already paid an advance to Beatrice Lillie for a book on her pet, Susann's poodle story would have to wait. Despairing, Susann began to see a psychoanalyst and ingest huge quantities of pills. Determined to help his wife, in February 1963 Mansfield sent a copy of the manuscript to Earl Wilson, their influential columnist friend. "Earl hadn't read [*Every Night, Josephine!*]," Susann recounted in her diary pages. "He was just being a good friend" when he rang up Bernard Geis, the head of the "flashy and prestigious" house that bore his name. Geis remembers, "When Earl Wilson called, he said, 'I've got a beautiful young woman in my office, in tears.'" After hearing Susann's tale, Geis told Wilson the distraught lady should "dry her tears." Intending to read only 20 pages as a courtesy, Geis instead "finished the manuscript" at seven A.M., Susann wrote in the diary. "He got dressed and took a walk. All the dogs and their masters or mistresses were emerging. He stared at them all. . . . When he came home, his wife was up and reading the MS. She looked up and said, 'you're publishing this, aren't you?' . . . *Josie* came out in November 1963. I always say I was 'born' on that day."

Bernard Geis Associates was "born" in 1958, and "five of our first six books were on the [best-seller] list," says Geis. These included books by Groucho Marx and Art Linkletter, who were also investors in Geis's new venture. By the time Susann came on board Geis had also published *Sex and the Single Girl*, by the unknown ad copywriter Helen Gurley Brown, and President Truman's *Mr. Citizen.* Thanks to what movie producer (and Helen's husband) David Brown calls Geis's "riverboat gambler's" instincts, his involvements with television personalities, and his clever publicity director, Letty Cottin Pogrebin, Geis at that time was, the publisher himself says, "the only one who knew how to promote books."

The Mansfields, who modeled their publicity tour on Helen Gurley Brown's for *Sex and the Single Girl*, also conjured up a few novel P.R. tricks of their own. "To remind people of the cover of the book," Susann wrote in her diary pages, on every TV show she and Josie dressed in matching leopard-patterned pillbox hats and coats. To her chagrin, however, some of Susann's "mother and dog" engagements were thwarted. "I was booked on a tour—first stop Los Angeles. And then a week later the whole world collapsed," Susann wrote, somewhat disingenuously, in the diary. "President Kennedy was assassinated." Pogrebin remembers clearly "how appalled she was that J.F.K. dared to be shot so close to her publication date! We were all watching the TV in my office, tears rolling down our eyes. And she was stomping around, demanding, 'What's going to happen to my bookings!'" *Josephine*, which had an initial printing of 7,500, sold 35,000 copies, made it to No. 9 on *Time* magazine's best-seller list, and went on to sell about a million copies when it was republished in the 70s. Susann earned a few thousand dollars, and Geis paid her $3,000 for the rights to whatever she wrote next.

The day that she put on her little black dress and introduced herself to Annie Laurie Williams, Susann "went home, put a piece of paper in the typewriter immediately—and wrote Chapter One of *VOD*. Because I figured," Susann told her diary, "in case, all the publishers said no, I wanted to be deeply involved in another book." The story had been gestating in Susann's mind all during the sojourn with her mother. In fact, in the letter from Hong Kong in which Susann had announced so offhandedly to her husband the presence of the lump in her right breast, she had also excitedly reported to him, "I think I have a great title— *Valley of the Dolls*—all based on our little red dolls in the medicine chest."

Susann labored on her manuscript for a year and a half, following a disciplined writing routine that would serve her for the rest of her career. Dressed in trousers, or, if it was warm, her nightgown (to which she would pin a Van Cleef poodle brooch, a gift from Irving to commemorate *Every Night, Josephine!*'s publication), and with her hair tied into pigtails, she sequestered herself daily from 10 until 5 in her Navarro office—Guy's former nursery. (When the Mansfields moved to 200 Central Park South in 1970, her office walls were upholstered in pink patent leather and the curtains made up from Pucci fabric.) "It's like giving up cigarettes or going on a diet," Susann said of her regime. "Only you have to do it every day." She pounded out five drafts, on as many different colors of paper stock, a practice appropriated from the theater. The first draft, typed on "inexpensive white paper," was where she would "spill it out," she explained in a 1968 WABC-TV documentary. On the yellow paper she worked out the characters, on the pink she focused on "story motivation," and on the blue she "cut, cut, cut." The final draft was written on "good white paper." Coordinating chalk colors to the paper colors, she would diagram the plot on a blackboard.

The origins of her system dated back to the summer of 1963, when producer Joe Cates, his wife, Lily, and the Mansfields were all staying together at the Beverly Hills Hotel. "I would see Jackie with her nose in a Harold Robbins book," says Lily Naify (the former Lily Cates). "She's smack her lips and say, 'I know exactly how he does it and I'm going to do it, too!' The two of us were having lunch at the Beverly Wilshire and we went to a nearby bookstore and bought three copies of whatever the latest Harold Robbins was. Then we proceeded to scissor it. What I mean is, we spent a week cutting these pieces out of the books, and then reorganizing the snipped pieces by character. Then each character was written up on a different-colored set of index cards. She decided that Harold Robbins had created a formula: give a set of different characters one common denominator. It could be the Beverly Hills Hotel pool, it could be the *Titanic*. In *Valley of the Dolls*, it was the pills."

In January 1965, Berney Geis heard from Annie Laurie Williams. "She told me, 'Don't laugh, but Jacqueline Susann is writing a novel,'" Geis says. "I suppressed a chuckle. Then along comes a huge manuscript, and I turned it over to my editorial staff. They marched into my office and begged, 'Please, don't publish this book. It's literary trash.'" The Geis editor who would take on *Valley of the Dolls*, Don Preston, recalls, "It was a big mess of a book. A cheap soap opera—not a book anyone with any brain cells could take seriously. Why did Berney go to such trouble for something so lousy? Well, when Jackie wanted a full-page ad for *Every Night, Josephine!* in *The New York Times Book Review*, and Berney said no, Irving pulled out his checkbook, wrote a check for about $6,000, and said, 'Let's just do it.' So Berney took the book home to do what we called 'Scarsdale Research.'" Geis, in other words, gave the manuscript to his wife, Darlene, to read. Halfway through it, Geis says, his wife "turned to me and said, 'I feel like I picked up the phone and I was listening in on a conversation of women talking about how their husbands are in bed. Who would hang up on a conversation like that?'"

What Darlene Geis was responding to was almost exactly that: a dialogue-heavy, highly fictionalized retelling of the checkered careers of the Hockey Club women and their far-flung friends. Anna Sosenko notes, "If you follow *Valley of the Dolls* closely, it's very autobiographical." Gossip columnist Cindy Adams, whom Sosenko once tried to pair with Susann for a radio show, says, "Jackie was the quintessential, the ultimate yenta—by which I mean 'storyteller.' Individually, the tales she'd tell over the phone would never have interested me. But she would extract the most delicious, wonderful parts, and with her incredible memory for detail she'd weave stories about the love lives, the chicaneries, the Machiavellian ways, the lies and limitations of the people she knew. You know, anyone could have done Schiffli. As an actress, she was no Meryl Streep. Her plays—anyone could have written them. But no one else could have taken all that dish and put it on the plate. So instead of the phone, it was the typewriter! Jackie was like the grass on the Wailing Wall. It's stone and six feet thick—but somehow grass finds a way to grow on it. Even if her career was fallow, Jackie would find a way. This woman had to be known, to be seen, to be heard. She would not be a nonentity."

As she wrote, Susann said, "It was like a Ouija board—characters would spring up." *Valley of the Dolls'* noble-hearted Anne Welles, whom many readers mistook for Grace Kelly (and who shares certain traits with the author), was in basic outline Bea Cole, whom Susann described in her diary as "the mother of the World." But Anne's selfless devotion to dashing agent Lyon Burke, even while he is sleeping with her friend Neely O'Hara, comes from the saga of Lee Reynolds, who remained loyal to her talent-agent husband, David Begelman, even after his entanglement with Judy Garland helped destroy their marriage. Lyon Burke's name was derived from Kenny Lyons, a man whom penny Bigelow loved when they worked together on Mansfield's *Arthur Godfrey's Talent Scouts*. The castle that Lyon Burke inherits refers to the family seat that Sitwell inhabited during her marriage to a British aristocrat. "Jackie," Mansfield noted, "didn't waste a thing."

Though the early Neely resembles Elfie, Susann's hapless ragamuffin friend from Kenmore Hall, the later Neely was based, a little too close for comfort, on Judy Garland, as readers suspected. Beautiful, vulnerable, pill-popping Jennifer was not Marilyn Monroe, as many supposed. Rather, she was a composite of Susann (the breast cancer), Carole Landis (the moneygrubbing mother, the extraordinary figure, the bisexuality, and the suicide), and Joyce Mathews, the creampuff showgirl twice married to both Milton Berle and Billy Rose. Mathews, whose raison d'être, Susann wrote in a diary entry, was striving "to be the prettiest girl in [EI] Morocco," was "the biggest pill taker of everybody," a friend says. "She hid pills all around the house, in chandeliers, in candy boxes. She even worked in a hospital as a nurse's aide. Everyone said, 'Oh, how noble.' But it was really just to get pills!" Mathews's ex-husband Milton Berle says, "Jackie milked that friendship for all it was worth." Tony Polar, the intellectually deficient crooner who performs anal sex on Jennifer, was Susann's revenge on one of her longtime infatuations, Dean Martin, Seaman says. When she finally met him, Martin barely looked up from the comic book he was reading. Tony's protective big sister Miriam's fears that his brain disorder could be genetic, and her worries that he would end up in a public institution if she didn't watch his money carefully, parallels Susann's concerns about Guy. It was hardly a secret that the aging, loudmouthed, ill-tempered, egomaniacal—but preternaturally talented—singer Helen Lawson was Ethel Merman. About the character, Susann said, "I loved Helen Lawson. . . . She could emasculate men with her strength." And about "the Merm," Susann said, "We didn't speak before the book came out. Let's just say that now we're not speaking louder."

Editor Don Preston says, "Berney sent me home with the manuscript and told me not to come back to the office until I was finished. I holed up in Rockland County with the thing, and I cut about a third out." Next, Preston had "a lot of meetings" with Susann to troubleshoot particular problems with the story. "I talked her into writing some scenes," he says. "For example, initially Neely and Helen Lawson didn't meet at any point during the book, which wasn't right. Both were flamboyant, spark-spitting characters. Readers would have wanted them to lock horns. So I said, 'Ladies are always going to the bathroom together. Why not have them meet in the ladies' room and get into an argument?'" Out of that grew the classic passage in which Neely yanks off Helen Lawson's wig and tries to flush it down the toilet. It's a camp catfight that echoes the climactic confrontation in the play that earned Susann her Equity card, *The Women*.

Preston continues, "Jackie didn't understand the emotional side of sex—which she always called 'humping.' All she understood was the physical act. When Anne loses her virginity to Lyon, I suggested that she set it in this tawdry hotel room with a naked lightbulb. She still loves him, but she's left wondering, How did it get kind of ugly when I thought it would be beautiful? But Jackie objected: 'Can't I just write, "and then they fucked," and leave it at that?' Jackie had far more sensitivity writing the sex scenes between women."

In February 1966, *Valley of the Dolls*—wrapped in a slick, spare jacket showing colored pills scattered against a white background—"exploded like a land mine in a placid landscape," says Letty Cottin Pogrebin. A primer for adults about pre-marital sex, adultery, lesbianism, drugs, abortion, and the domination of women by men, *Valley of the Dolls* "got at very lurid stuff that was then still subsurface," Liz Smith remembers. Geis Associates, which had already sold the paperback rights to Bantam for more than $200,000—enabling Mansfield to broker the movie rights to Twentieth Century Fox for ultimately around the same amount—cautiously ordered an initial printing of 20,000. Thanks to Bantam's money, the publicity campaign was budgeted at a hefty $50,000. Pogrebin kicked it off with the kind of splashy mailings, previously alien to book publishing, which had become a Geis trademark. The first, written on a prescription pad, advised, "Take 3 yellow 'dolls' before bedtime for a broken love affair; take 2 red dolls and a shot of scotch for a shattered career; take *Valley of the Dolls* in heavy doses for the truth about the glamour set on the pill kick." Fifteen hundred advance copies were dispatched to anyone who might help publicize it, including celebrities. Pasted in one of Susann's *Valley of the Dolls* scrapbooks are a charming thank-you letter, dated February 15, 1966, from Senator Robert Kennedy's press assistant, and a terse reply, dated February 20, from Norman Mailer's secretary, stating that Mailer "won't have time to read *Valley of the Dolls*." This was an admission Mailer may have come to regret, because Susann consigned him to the fate of becoming *Once Is Not Enough*'s Tom Colt—a hard-drinking, pugnacious writer with a child-size penis.

Mansfield by now had left television to manage his wife's career full-time. This gesture represented "Jackie's romantic ideal," says Lily Naify. "To her it was like the King of England giving up his throne for Wallis Simpson." And by hauling his showbiz know-how into a new arena, Mansfield could claim to *Life*, for once without exaggeration, "We've revolutionized book publishing."

. . .

Before embarking on her national tour—which never really stopped until she began hawking *The Love Machine* in 1969—Susann consulted a notebook she had kept while plugging *Every Night, Josephine!* Into it went minute notations about every reporter, bookshop clerk, and talk-show host she had encountered. Wives' and kids' names were recorded, as were birth dates, hobbies, and comments on their importance, personality, and physical appearance. "She studied it, memorized it, wrote the people on it letters," says *Love Machine* publicist Abby Hirsch. "She was a politician."

Advertisements for *Valley of the Dolls* were placed not just in the usual newspaper book pages but in entertainment sections as well. Cindy Adams says, "No effort was too humiliating, too horrifying, or too tough for Irving" if it meant helping them attain their "one goal—which was to make 'Jacqueline Susann' a household name."

Somehow, says talent manager Arnold Stiefel (then a Bantam P.R. assistant), Mansfield managed to obtain the names of the 125 bookstores that *The New York Times* polled when compiling its all-powerful best-seller list. Like a general spearheading a battle, Mansfield recruited friends for his strategic book-buying campaign. "Irving would say, 'You're going to San Francisco to visit your mother,'" Lily Naify recalls. "'Go to this bookstore on Post Street and buy every copy of the book you see. Then order five more.' In New York he'd want you to go into Doubleday or Coliseum and say, 'You only have four? I need 12 for Christmas.' And then we had to make sure the book was displayed up front. I had stacks of them in my closet." Twentieth Century Fox apparently also pitched in; it was in the studio's interest to be able to trumpet in its ads the exhilarating words "based on the best-seller."

Mansfield may have stirred up a lot of activity with his book-buying crusade, but the couple's real secret weapon was television, a medium each of them knew intimately. "All you had to do was point a TV camera at Jackie and she'd light up like a pinball machine," Don Preston says. Early in the game Mansfield had even borrowed CBS cameras and monitors to color-test *Valley of the Dolls'* cover. Television was a very different instrument in 1966—with just three networks, no cable, no channel-surfing, no competition from videos or computers, and no splinter demographics, America was one monolithic audience tuning in coast to coast to the same entertainment at the same time. And, Bernard Geis recalls, "Jackie knew how to manipulate every conversation right back to the book. It got to the point where you could not turn on a water faucet without getting Jacqueline Susann."

All told, Susann made about 250 appearances, visiting as many as 11 cities in 10 days and conducting up to 30 interviews a week. "I took amphetamine pills when I was on tour," she told *Pageant* magazine in February 1967. "I felt that I owed it to people to be bright. Rather than droop on television . . . I was suddenly awake, could give my best." Barbara Seaman says, "All Jackie's life she had been in training for this great, glorious explosion. Who else had spent 25 years learning to be a TV pitchwoman?—the soap, the bras, the sewing machines, Schiffli, and then the books."

On April 29, 1966, while she was in Florida, Susann left a note for Mansfield, who was out playing golf. "Our man in New York just called," she reported. "He said I'm Number One on the bestseller list in the *New York Times* next Sunday—WOW!!! Irv, it's finally happened! . . . I couldn't have done it without you. . . . I'll give up smoking and pills and never take more than two drinks. Anyway, tonight we'll bust out the Dom Perignon (see, I've already forgotten about the two drinks). . . . I love you. . . . Jackie." The book officially entered the top slot on May 8, its ninth week on the list, and stayed there for 28 consecutive weeks.

Though there was hardly a newspaper or magazine in the country that hadn't run a feature on Jacqueline Susann, there was a paucity of actual *Valley of the Dolls* reviews. One exception was a notice in the *New York Herald Tribune* by Gloria Steinem (who, David Brown says, sensibly turned down a Fox offer to write the novel's screenplay). In Steinem's opinion, compared with Jacqueline Susann, Harold Robbins wrote like Proust. But Susann had a ready defense for the "double-domed," "artsy-craftsy" critics. "So if I'm selling millions," she said, "I must be good." The results of the Mansfields' efforts on behalf of the Geis hardback were staggeringly impressive. *Valley of the Dolls* remained on the bestseller list for 65 weeks and sold close to 400,000 copies. And for each $5.95 book sold, Susann received about $1.35.

For Bantam's July 4, 1967, *Valley of the Dolls* paperback release, C.E.O. Oscar Dystel ordered a first printing of two million—with the goal of a Labor Day sellout. Unlike the staff at Geis, everyone at Bantam had immediately liked *Valley of the Dolls* and its author. "She had a sincerity, an almost naïve directness," Dystel says. "She wanted to know everything about how our business worked— the paper, the typography, the distribution mechanisms. Other publishers thought that was meddlesome. But we welcomed it—Jackie saw the big picture."

Thanks in no small part to Esther Margolis's endless P.R. ingenuity, her boss need not have worried. Not only did *Valley of the Dolls* in paperback become No. 1, it became the fastest-selling book in history, with a peak volume, *The Saturday Evening Post* reported, of 100,000 per day. "We sold between six and eight million copies in six months," Oscar Dystel states. "With a sale of that velocity, it had to be reaching men and younger people too, not just women." Margolis says the gargantuan sales of *Valley of the Dolls* even helped "bring suitors into Bantam," which had been put on the market by its owner, Grosset & Dunlap.

National General Corporation, the parent company of a chain of movie theaters, ended up making the purchase. "So Jackie definitely played a role in merging publishing with the entertainment industry and turning it into really big business," Margolis says.

Eddie Cantor had once advised Susann, "Never go to Hollywood; make them send for you." With a major motion picture of *Valley of the Dolls* in the works, Hollywood now beckoned. Hoping for the kind of control over the film that she had exercised over her book, she tried to muscle her way into Twentieth Century Fox's casting, writing and scoring decisions. The director, Mark Robson, was already on board, but Susann had assembled her wish list for the cast: Ursula Andress as Jennifer; Grace Kelly, "if she'd lose 10 to 15 pounds," as Anne; Shirley MacLaine as Neely; Bette Davis as Helen Lawson; and Elvis Presley as Tony Polar. She even wrote a theme song with Bob Gaudio and recorded it with the Arbors, a male quartet. "She was furious that they didn't use it," says Arnold Stiefel.

Though none of Susann's favorites made it into the picture, she became satisfied with some of the studio's choices. Barbara Parkins, already powerful at Fox because of her part in the TV show *Peyton Place*, was cast as Anne Welles. Sharon Tate was an ideal Jennifer; Patty Duke as Neely O'Hara was more problematic. But the most irksome casting dilemma concerned Helen Lawson. In a stunt-casting *coup de théâtre* the studio chose "a fast-fading Judy Garland," David Brown says. Susann and Garland teamed up for a press conference, at which reporters couldn't resist interrogating Garland about *Valley of the Dolls'* depiction of pill abuse among entertainers. "I find it prevalent among newspaper people," Garland snapped.

In April 1967, Parkins was called upon to do her first scene with Garland, in which she brings contracts to Helen Lawson backstage. "I was so scared I called Jackie," Parkins says. "She told me, 'Just go and enjoy her.' The first day Judy did fine, but as time passed she forgot her lines and smoked a lot. The director was not gentle with her." Finally, Garland locked herself in her trailer and refused to budge. She was given two weeks' respite to decide whether to stay or go. After the 14 days passed, the studio said, "We decided for you—you're fired," Parkins says. Susan Hayward was brought in to replace her, and, Parkins says, Garland "walked out of the studio with all the costumes." A few weeks later, Arnold Stiefel says, Garland performed at the Westbury Music Fair, glittering and twinkling in one of Fox designer Travilla's beaded pantsuits.

Fox held a sneak preview at San Francisco's Orpheum Theatre. The marquee, which could not give away the title, instead teased passersby with the come-on "the biggest book of the year." Those words alone attracted "a huge preview audience," David Brown recalls. "And the film was so campy, everyone roared with laughter. One patron was so irate he poured his Coke all over Fox president Dick Zanuck in the lobby. And we knew we had a hit. Why? Because of the size of the audience—the book would bring them in."

Susann's own reaction was not so different from the outraged cola tosser's. Fox publicity had orchestrated a snazzy, month-long floating premiere aboard the luxury liner M.V. *Princess Italia*. At each port of call there would be press screenings with the stars and the author. At the first screening, in Venice, Susann "was appalled," Barbara Parkins remembers. With its happy ending, lackluster male leads, incongruous casting, and $1,300 worth of false hair, the movie "had ruined her book. Jackie demanded to be flown off the boat."

When she had overcome her anger, Susann rejoined the junket in Miami—and kept quiet, for fear of damaging book sales. Despite the predictably nasty reviews, the movie, which opened in New York at the Criterion and Festival theaters on December 15, 1967, broke studio box-office records, grossing a total of around $70 million.

The picture was still playing in theaters in August 1969 when the Mansfields were at the Beverly Hills Hotel, this time hustling *The Love Machine*. On the eighth of the month, Sharon Tate invited Susann to her house for a small dinner party. But when critic Rex Reed dropped in for a surprise visit at the hotel, Susann and he decided to stay in for the evening. The next morning at the pool, where the Mansfields customarily held court at Cabana 8, "Jackie was crying her eyes out," recalls Svend Petersen, pool manager since 1963. "She had just found out that Sharon Tate was murdered the night before." Several years later when Susann was terminally ill, she said to Reed, "It could all have happened a lot sooner if we'd gone to Sharon's that night."

Why was *Valley of the Dolls*, movie and book, such an extraordinary success? Don Preston believes the answer lies in the Mansfields' peerless promotional skills. Clearly, it could not just have been the risqué subject matter; more prurient books were available, although maybe not ones a secretary could safely read on the subway. Without doubt Susann had an authentic, almost evangelical empathy for female emotional experience, at the exact moment when women's place in the world was about to undergo a seismic upheaval. Above all, she knew her audience. Before *People* or *Hollywood Babylon* had ripped the scales from the public's eyes, "*Valley of the Dolls* showed that a woman in a ranch house with three kids had a better life," Susann said, "than what happened up there at the top."

Just as Susann had begun *Valley of the Dolls* before *Every Night, Josephine!* was accepted by Geis, so *The Love Machine* was already germinating while she was peddling the first novel. In the August 19, 1966, issue of *Life*, Susann revealed that she had already finished the first draft of the new book. It would be called *The Love Machine*, she told reporter Jane Howard. And its hero would be "like the most exciting man in television. The title has a dual meaning, you see, the man is like a machine and so is the television box, a machine selling the love of the actors and love of the sponsors." Though he bore the initials of Susann's rogue father, *The Love Machine's* protagonist, Robin Stone, was in fact "like" the Mansfield's friend James Aubrey, the handsome, depraved head of CBS. Nicknamed "the smiling cobra," he abused women, drugs, animals, and his power until CBS chairman William Paley finally ejected him from the network in 1965. Liz Smith, who worked as an associate producer at CBS during Aubrey's reign of terror, recalls, "Aubrey was a mean, hateful, truly scary, bad, outré guy." Yet in 1969 he rebounded to become head of MGM studios. There he was known to refer to himself as "trisexual—I'll try anything," and to have at his disposal a dog trained to perform sex acts with women. Aubrey, fully aware of what Susann was up to, implored her to "make me mean, a real son of a bitch."

Rather than pills, the Beverly Hills Hotel pool, or the *Titanic*, the link this time among the heroines was hopeless love for Robin Stone; in her *Times* review, Nora Ephron called the female characters "the most willing group of masochists assembled outside the pages of de Sade." Model Amanda was based on the exquisitely elegant fashion journalist Carol Bjorkman. A muse of Halston's, a friend of Truman Capote's, and the mistress of Seventh Avenue mogul Seymour Fox, Bjorkman, like Amanda, died of leukemia at the height of her beauty, in July 1967. Susann, who worshiped Bjorkman's style, was a fixture in the dying woman's hospital room, and even dedicated *The Love Machine* to her. "Call it a crush if you want," says Anna Sosenko. "But don't put them in bed together."

Though legally Geis owned *The Love Machine*, the Mansfields maneuvered their way out of their contract with the little publishing house and into a much more lucrative arrangement with Simon & Schuster. "Essandess" (as Susann playfully called a publishing house in *The Love Machine*) plied the Mansfields with a $250,000 advance, a $200,000 promotional budget, and guarantees of suites and limousines. The Mansfields forged a completely separate agreement with Bantam, to whom they remained loyal, and from whom they extracted a 100-percent-royalties sweetheart deal.

Launched in May 1969, *The Love Machine* (to use one newsman's metaphor) was "a heat-seeking missile" headed "straight for first place on the bestseller list." It arrived at its intended destination on June 24, toppling Philip Roth's *Portnoy's Complaint* from the highest spot. About her rival Roth, Susann said, "He's a fine writer, but I wonldn't want to shake hands with him." Mansfield sold the movie rights to Columbia Pictures' Mike Frankovich for $1.5 million, a percentage of the gross, and a producer's credit. This embarrassment of riches was just a little more than some members of the literary establishment could bear.

On July 23, 1969, Mansfield's 61st birthday, Susann arrived at a studio to tape the David Frost show with a panel of friendly journalists: Rex Reed, Nora

Ephron, and Jimmy Breslin. At the last minute and without Susann's knowledge, critic John Simon was brought in to replace Breslin. Simon went for the jugular, lashing out at Susann for "writing trash" and smiling "through false teeth." Rex Reed recalls, "It was terrible. Simon was spitting all over Nora Ephron's arm and Nora was sitting there like a caged animal. It was the only time I ever saw Jackie lose her cool."

Later that evening at Danny's Hide-A-Way, Susann simmered down over Mansfield's birthday dinner. Back at home, the couple was drowsily viewing Johnny Carson's *Tonight Show* in bed. Susann suddenly jolted to attention at the sound of Truman Capote mentioning her name. He was calling her "a born transvestite" who "should have been cast in the title role of *Myra Breckinridge*" because, with her "sleazy wigs and gowns," she resembles "a truckdriver in drag." Susann dumped water on her dozing spouse, who, awakened, sprang into action. He called lawyer Louis Nizer, who advised against a suit. Instead, Mansfield extracted from NBC an agreement to place Susann on *The Tonight Show* and *Today*, as well as a daytime game show. And Susann took care of her vendetta by the usual means. Capote became an incidental figure in *Once Is Not Enough*, a pudgy "little capon" who "hadn't written anything" for years but had made "a whore" of himself "going on talk shows and attending celebrity parties." And he returned in *Dolores*, a 1974 novella Susann wrote for *Ladies' Home Journal*, this time as the viperish gossip Horatio Capon. As for Capote, he issued an apology— to the truckdrivers. [*See Sam Kashner's essay on Capote, page 89.*]

The Love Machine in paperback exceeded *Valley of the Dolls* in swiftness of sales; Susann's statistics moved David Frost to remark that the writer typed "on a cash register." From these first two novels, Barbara Seaman calculates, Susann earned $8 million between 1966 and 1972 (about $30 million today). Vigilant about Guy's future security, she cautiously invested the windfall in municipal bonds and bluechip stocks. And the frustrated thespian who only a decade before had longed to be identified at Sardi's as more than "just the Schiffli girl" now found herself seated ahead of Henry Fonda at Mateo's, the Beverly Hills restaurant. "No one ever said, 'Hey, you look familiar,'" publicist Abby Hirsch recalls. "It was always 'There goes Jacqueline Susann!'"

Susann, again, was at work on her third novel while still on tour with her second. If *The Love Machine* had been an "attempt to get inside of men's ids," then, Susann announced, *Once Is Not Enough* was all about "mental incest. I think it happens to every girl who has a great father." Bantam already owned the paperback rights to Susann's story of heiress January Wayne's efforts to find a man who measures up to her high-roller father, Mike Wayne. But, as before, Susann "felt she might be better off with another" hardback publisher, Mansfield wrote. Sherry Arden, whom Susann knew from the WABC *Valley of the Dolls* documentary, suggested Morrow, where Arden had become publicity director. Larry Hughes, then head of Morrow, says, "Jackie was a pretty shrewd person. She knew they laughed behind her back at Simon & Schuster. Jackie told a good story, and that's an art of its own. She's too easy a mark for derision."

Susann's editor at Morrow, Jim Landis, remembers, "Jackie would listen very carefully to your suggestions, and then revise. Other No. 1s stopped listening after a while, but never Jackie. Her books were driven by what happens to characters, and how they dealt with each other. The sex was just a part of that." One scurrilous episode that Landis asked Susann to rewrite made him wonder about the nature of Susann's own sexual experience. Linda Riggs, the raunchy nymphomaniac who edits *Gloss* magazine, at one point teaches the virginal January Wayne how to make a "facial mask" out of a lover's semen. "Linda originally told January that she had just collected 'a milkcartonful' of semen from a 'hand job,'" Landis recounts. "And I said, 'Jackie, what size milk carton is this?' And she asked me, 'Well, what size should it be, Jim—a gallon, a quart, a pint?' It was strange how naïve she was."

Susann, in turn, found Landis naïve. "Jackie wasn't a good speller. I came across an unrecognizable word one day and asked her what it was. She said, 'You poor darling, you don't know.'" She led Landis into the kitchen and opened the door to her refrigerator. It was empty except for a bottle of champagne, but when she opened the vegetable bin, inside there was also "something like an egg carton," Landis says. Angrily, she slammed the drawer shut and grabbed the kitchen phone, "a Touch-Tone, one of the first I'd ever seen," Landis recalls. After punching in the number of Mansfield's office, where her old friend Bea Cole now worked, she screamed into the receiver, "Bea! Where is he?!" And when Mansfield got on, she shouted, "Goddamnit, every night when you said you were getting out of bed for water, you were sneaking one of the Nembutal suppositories! You son of a bitch! There's only one left!" Susann banged the phone down and explained to her editor that Nembutal suppositories were what "rich people brought back for each other from Europe—they were sold over the counter there." And she said, "Do you know what you do with this? You get in your bed, shove it up your ass, and then you fall asleep—from your feet up." Landis concludes, "The word she couldn't spell was *suppositories!*"

Landis remembers that in the fall of 1972, while he was editing Susann, a former three-pack-a-day smoker, she had "a little cough. Irving kept telling me that I was working her too hard." And when Susann and Mansfield traveled to Paris in the summer of 1973 to spread the gospel about *The Love Machine*, which had just been published in France, Sylvie Messinger, Susann's subsidiary director at Éditions Belfond, paid a call at the Mansfields' Ritz suite. "I asked to use the bathroom," Messinger says. "There were bottles and bottles of pills everywhere.

I didn't understand, so I asked Jackie, 'How many pills do you take a day?' And she told me, 'Oh, they're all vitamins.' I thought that maybe this was a new American fashion." What Landis had noticed in the fall of 1972 and Messinger stumbled upon the next summer were both symptoms of a problem the Mansfields had at first dared not suspect. On January 18, 1973—just as Susann's 10-year pact with God was expiring—her internist informed her that she had developed "metastatic breast carcinoma." In other words, her breast cancer had spread to her lungs and was so advanced she probably had only a few months to live. In addition to cobalt treatments and daily chemotherapy injections, Seaman says, she was subjected to massive doses of a spectrum of powerful drugs, all with hideous side effects. Again, she kept her condition under wraps. She feared for her glamorous image—she could not bear "eyes of pity," she said—she feared for her book contracts, and, most of all, she feared for Guy.

Besides, Susann had a book to promote. "Grab every brass ring you can," Susann wrote in *Once Is Not Enough*, "because when you look back, it seems like a hell of a short ride." No longer just fashion statements, her Korean-hair wigs and theatrical makeup were now necessities. Even when she began sprouting a beard, she faced down the cameras. "She had hair all over her chin, and up the sides of her face," says Anna Sosenko, who was privy to her illness. "But her pride in her looks was so great that she went through this devastating procedure of electrolysis so that on the air she could still be 'a tearing beauty.'"

Not surprisingly, the reviews of *Once Is Not Enough* were cruel, and as always she toured incessantly, nationally and internationally, from April to October 1973, when she collapsed. Somehow, amid all these promotional efforts and harrowing medical treatments, she found time to write the novella *Dolores* for *Ladies' Home Journal* during the summer and fall of 1973. And the issue in which it appeared, February 1974, was the most successful in the magazine's history. But all that was just an upbeat footnote to the big news that had come months earlier. *Once Is Not Enough* had claimed top place on the *Times* bestseller list, pushing Frederick Forsyth's *The Odessa File* down to No. 2—making her the first author in publishing history to hit No. 1 three times in a row.

In the late spring and early summer of 1974 the Mansfields were back in L.A., where Howard Koch's Paramount movie version of *Once Is Not Enough* was wrapping. From the West Coast, Mansfield kept stalling Esther Margolis and Oscar Dystel, who were gearing up for the traditional July Fourth Bantam paperback launch. Finally, Mansfield told them they had better fly out for a meeting. Margolis says, "Irving made an early dinner reservation, six o'clock at the Beverly Hills Hotel. Jackie came in, looking thin, and joined us at the booth. And she told Oscar and me about her cancer. She was fabulous, matter-of-fact, and optimistic. She was deciding which book she should write next. Jackie went back to their room, Suite 135-136, and Irving stayed with us. He told us that her cancer had spread all over her body and it was unlikely she'd be able to do any of the books she talked about."

On her 56th birthday, August 20, 1974, Susann was admitted to Doctors Hospital for the last of her 18 stays there. In her final days Susann said to her husband, "Maybe we've had too many secrets. Guy, my illness earlier, my illness now." Mansfield told Oscar Dystel that shortly before she died, Susann, in the throes of a delusion, ripped off her turban and commanded her husband, "Let's blow this joint!"—which she finally did at 9:02 P.M. on September 21, 1974. The secret of Susann's terminal illness had been so rigorously guarded, the press—wary of yet another publicity stunt—called 200 Central Park South repeatedly for confirmation.

After a service at Frank E. Campbell's, Mansfield had Susann's body cremated and her ashes deposited in a bronze vessel the size and shape of a book. He placed it on a shelf, among the many rows of editions of his wife's books. The metallic volume, like all the No. 1 books into which Susann poured the substance of her being, was a work of fiction. Its cover was inscribed, not with the actual year of her birth, 1918, but with 1921, "the birthdate Jackie had chosen for herself," Mansfield said.

Susann died with several unwritten books in her. At the dinner three months before she expired during which she confessed her condition to Esther Margolis and Oscar Dystel, the author had spoken of her plans for a sequel to *Every Night, Josephine!* She had also mentioned the possibility of a *roman à clef* about a Cantor-like comedian—possibly a reworking of *Cock of the Walk*, the play she and Bea Cole had co-authored in 1950 right after Guy was taken to Bradley. But Susann's greatest aspiration, Oscar Dystel intimated in his eulogy, was to write what she called the "Real Book." In the rediscovered journal pages in Lisa Bishop's possession (Mansfield burned virtually all his wife's diaries immediately after her death), Susann resolved, "I am writing my autobiography first," rather than the "three more novels" for which she had ideas, "because I don't know how much time I've got. I don't know whether I'll live to finish the book. But it's important to me to set the facts straight." Her deathbed remarks to Mansfield about Guy and her fatal disease suggest some of the "facts" festering in her mind. New Millennium Entertainment's Michael Viner, who with his wife, Deborah Raffin (who played January in *Once Is Not Enough*), remained close to Mansfield until his 1988 death, says, "She definitely would have matured into writing a serious book about her experiences with autism and cancer." Sosenko is also convinced that "her plan was to become a really fine writer. She was already studying Dostoyevsky, all the Russians." Joan Castle Sitwell recollects, "Jackie would say, 'I don't want the Pulitzer Prize. I want the Nobel Prize. I'm not going to settle!' Was that dream any more unlikely than what had already happened to her?"

Columnist Jack Martin, who passed countless days with the Mansfields at Cabana 8 at the Beverly Hills Hotel pool, says, "I never met anyone who enjoyed fame more than Jackie. When she finally got it, she appreciated it, was grateful for it, loved everything about it. And Irving basked in her glory. They were two pigs in shit." Sosenko, a fellow insomniac who routinely received nocturnal calls from Susann, says that "one night shortly before she died Jackie became tragically philosophical. 'Jackie,' I said, 'you've been going through so much with your sickness. Do you think the whole thing was worth it?' And she said, 'Porky'—that's what she called me— 'I want to tell you something. These last 10 years were the 10 most meaningful of my life. I've been everywhere, met everyone, done it all. I've been successful beyond my fondest hopes.'" David Brown concludes, "Jackie had started out a starfucker, starved for love. But she was saved by a talent she never knew she had." The choice she presented to Neely O'Hara, "between mass love and a private life," was, for Susann, no contest. If Jacqueline Susann was not precisely the "voice of the 60s," then she was its aching female heart.

CORMAC McCARTHY

CORMAC COUNTRY

by Richard B. Woodward

AUGUST 2005

The parking lot at the Santa Fe Institute, in New Mexico, features rows of vehicles typical of American academia—S.U.V.'s and minivans, a few older-model BMWs and Mercedeses, a Toyota Prius, and an inordinate number of Subarus and Hondas. At this unique think tank, where an elite caste of scientists from around the world converge for days or months to analyze interdisciplinary problems in physics, biology, computer science, archaeology, linguistics, and economics, many of the cars also carry wilted bumper stickers (DEFOLIATE THE BUSHES) left over from the last election.

Standing out from the crowd is a red Ford F-350 diesel pickup with Texas plates. Equipped with a Banks PowerPack that boosts the 7.3-liter engine to more than 300 hp, it has a stripped-down profile in back, like a wrecker's, with no winch. Should everyone else be left floundering in two feet of snow, a common winter event in the hills above Santa Fe, it's a good bet this rugged conveyance could bull its way through and, if need be, haul other cars down the hill to safety.

The owner of the truck, the novelist Cormac McCarthy, would also seem not to belong here. He is the lone fiction writer at the institute, and his books, although they constitute one of the towering achievements in recent American literature, are often horrifically violent. *Blood Meridian,* ranked by Harold Bloom with the greatest novels of the 20th century, is a philosophic Western about a band of maniacal killers. At once brutally spare in terms of motivation and operatic in its soaring language, the book is based on documented events from southwestern history and is calmly realistic about the centrality of war, suffering, risk, and bloodshed in human existence. Even McCarthy's "Border Trilogy," begun in 1992 with *All the Pretty Horses,* the cause of his status as a best-selling author after decades as a cult figure, is not without graphic scenes of torture and sanguinary gunplay.

His grisly, male-dominated literary universe can hardly be said to overlap much with the hygienic concerns of scientists, especially not this international, predominantly liberal group, with whom the novelist, a quiet 72-year-old southern conservative, shares little in either background or education. (He never finished the University of Tennessee, whereas virtually all the academics here have at least one Ph.D.)

But at a place that prides itself on fostering brainy, unconventional thinkers—the S.F.I. is perhaps best known as the hub for complex-systems theory—McCarthy is actually right at home. He has been a mainstay among the rotating researchers for more than four years, and during that time if you strolled through the terraced-style headquarters, past the glass atrium and computer terminals, you were likely to hear him tapping away in his office on a blue Olivetti Lettera 32 portable typewriter. Indeed, his presence here, along with his anachronistic machine, makes him perhaps the maverick among mavericks.

"There isn't any place like the Santa Fe Institute, and there isn't any writer like Cormac, so the two fit quite well together," says his friend Murray Gell-Mann, a Nobel Prize winner in physics and one of the founding eminences of S.F.I.

Geoffrey West, a British high-energy physicist turned biologist who is also the institute's interim president, believes strongly that "people define the success of projects here. Cormac is the kind of extraordinary character we like to encourage. Even though we have no formal artist-in-residence program, he functions in this way. He interacts with everyone."

On any given day—and he comes to S.F.I. most days, even on weekends—the unsalaried McCarthy can be seen engaged in discussions with researchers about their specialties. If asked, he often looks over their texts before publication. But he has no official duties. "I have only two responsibilities," he says. "To eat lunch and attend afternoon tea."

Dressed in western attire (cowboy boots and jeans and a crisply pressed shirt), McCarthy is a courtly, soft-spoken man and a good listener. His is the unhurried manner of one who has never found reason to doubt his own worth or abilities. He regularly attends the workshops at S.F.I., where the topic may be the evolution of prion proteins or mammalian muscle adaptations or lying and deception or bounded inferences for decision-making in games. As a result, he often serves as a clearinghouse for those who want to know what everyone else is up to.

"I find it easier to talk to Cormac about what J. Doyne Farmer is doing"— Farmer is the economist-physicist-gambler celebrated in Thomas A. Bass's bestselling book *The Eudaemonic Pie*—"than to talk to Doyne himself," says the Russian linguist Sergei Starostin.

During informal get-togethers in the dining areas, McCarthy joins in by drawing on his extensive reading in 20th-century physics, the philosophy of mathematics, and animal behavior. In his office are manuscripts or galleys from friends in various arcane fields, such as Harvard's Lisa Randall, a leading string theorist. They send him their latest papers because they're curious to know what he thinks, and they know he likes to keep up on their research.

"He has a long-standing interest in a great many things and he knows an immense amount about them," says Gell-Mann. "I'm sure during some of the workshops, when the language becomes technical, he is at sea. But even then, if he weren't so shy, he could probably ask penetrating questions."

What McCarthy gains from immersion in this rarefied environment is unclear to some at S.F.I. His books show no sign of being shaped by high-flown scientific thought. Most of his characters can barely read. But when pressed about this puzzle, he returns the compliments of his colleagues.

"I like being around smart, interesting people, and the people who come here are among the smartest, most interesting people on the planet," he says, sitting with a coffee in an S.F.I. lounge. "It's sobering how investigations into physical phenomenon are done. It makes you more responsible about the way you think. You come to have a lot less tolerance for things that are not rigorous."

Dining with McCarthy can be rigorous and a pleasure. He likes punctuality ("If you can't know where a man is going to be when he says he's going to be there, how can you trust him about anything else?") but will linger over a meal for hours if the conversation suits him. This is usually best supplied by him. His knowledge of the natural world is vast and includes many of the Latin names of birds and animals. He can discourse on Harris's hawks ("the only raptor that hunts communally") or on poker (Betty Carey, the former high-stakes player, is an old friend) or on how gun manufacturers rifled their barrels before the invention of metal lathes. Only in his disdain for contemporary architecture, or for the modern world in general, can he sound off-key and crankish.

One of the few topics about which he will not willingly articulate an opinion is his own fiction. He is far from being an antisocial recluse on the order of Salinger or Pynchon. But it is impossible to imagine him chatting with Oprah or Charlie Rose. He doesn't do book tours, readings, signings, or blurbs. Just once before in his life, in 1992, prior to the release of *All the Pretty Horses,* has he granted an interview. Only because he has a new book coming out this summer from Knopf has he reluctantly consented to a second.

No Country for Old Men—his first novel since *Cities of the Plain,* the final volume of "The Border Trilogy"—is likely to further confound McCarthy's critics, as well as his friends at S.F.I. In some ways it doubles back to the carnage of *Blood Meridian* and to the relentless dread of his two earlier masterpieces,

Outer Dark and *Child of God.* Punctuated minimally, as is his style—don't get him started on the "idiocy" of semico-lons—the book rockets along, with the bodies piling up, until there are probably more corpses than commas.

More present-day than any of his other books, the novel concerns a character named Llewelyn Moss, who when out hunting antelope in the desert comes upon a drug deal gone awry: a pile of money and dead Mexicans in a truck. By deciding to take the cash for himself, Moss sets off a chase across Texas and the Southwest as the drug dealers, their hired guns, and their "legitimate" business overseers seek to retrieve their property. Following the trail of blood and acting at times as narrator is one Sheriff Bell.

But the character most readers won't soon forget is the drug dealer and killer Anton Chigurh, pronounced "sugar." He is, says McCarthy, "pretty much pure evil." We are introduced to this phantom-like psychopath upon his escape from prison. Cruising the interstate in a stolen highway-patrol car, he stops an unsuspecting civilian. As always in McCarthy's books, quotation marks are unnecessary.

> What's the problem, officer? he said.
> Sir would you mind stepping out of the vehicle?
> The man opened the door and stepped out. What's this about? he said.
> Would you step away from the vehicle please.
> The man stepped away from the vehicle. Chigurh could see the doubt come into his eyes at this bloodstained figure before him but it came too late. He placed his hand on the man's head like a faith healer. The pneumatic hiss and click of the plunger sounded like a door closing. The man slid soundlessly to the ground, a round hole in his forehead from which the blood bubbled and ran down into his eyes carrying with it his slowly uncoupling world visible to see. Chigurh wiped his hand with his handkerchief. I just didnt want you to get blood on the car, he said.

Some of McCarthy's fans may be surprised by the flat-out speed of the plot; his novels commonly unwind at a far more wayward and leisurely pace. *No Country for Old Men* has the structure of genre fiction and film; the late Don Siegel or the young Quentin Tarantino might have directed. But the book's streamlined screenplay qualities—it was written in a burst, in about six months—did not hurt it in the eyes of Hollywood. Rights were snapped up with a pre-emptive bid by producer Scott Rudin in what McCarthy's literary agent, Amanda Urban, calls "a substantial deal." (*Blood Meridian* is also a Rudin property, now being developed with Ridley Scott.) [The film *No Country for Old Men*, released in 2007, would win four Oscars, including Best Picture honors.]

The novel allows McCarthy to write again about violence and the people who choose to live in a state of constant peril. He has known more than a few drug dealers ("some of them lovely, gracious people, very well educated") who are no longer among the living.

"If you're in the drug business, you know when you get up that morning that there's some chance somebody's going to get killed," he says. "Maybe it'll be you. Maybe by you. People who are not prepared to face that are not going to be in that business. Being a drug dealer is like operating a machine gun in wartime. You're in a line of work where you're not going to live long."

He isn't sure what attracts him to the theme of violence, although he regards as "not serious" writers who don't address the issue of death. His backwoods or frontier characters experience it in various abrupt, painful ways that most of his readers know little about.

"Most people don't ever see anyone die. It used to be if you grew up in a family you saw everybody die. They died in their bed at home with everyone gathered around. Death is the major issue in the world. For you, for me, for all of us. It just is. To not be able to talk about it is very odd."

No Country for Old Men, one of four or five McCarthy novels that exist in various drafts, was simply the first that he was ready to part with. "He asked me, 'Which one do you want first?'" says Gary Fisketjon, his editor at Knopf for the last 14 years. "I said, 'Whichever you want us to publish first.' It would be foolish to express a preference." Fisketjon sees his role at this stage as one of "looking for small inconsistencies. If it is as Cormac wants it, that's how it stays."

Success has allowed McCarthy to live comfortably, a condition he seldom enjoyed during his early career. Born in Providence, Rhode Island, he grew up as the son of a well-off attorney in Knoxville, Tennessee, but has spent his life avoiding long-term stability of any kind. Before he dropped out of the University of Tennessee for the second time, his writing had been praised by his teachers, and he had even won an award or two. But he does not talk much about his early efforts. His favorite answer when asked why he became a writer is to quote Flannery O'Connor's response: "Because I am good at it."

His first novel, *The Orchard Keeper,* published in 1965, proved he was more than good. He had submitted it blindly to Random House's legendary Albert Erskine, editor of William Faulkner and Ralph Ellison, and Erskine was impressed enough to edit McCarthy's first five novels. But none sold more than 3,000 copies in hardcover, and he barely scratched out a living during his 30s and early 40s, when he wrote his books in a series of hovels in New Orleans, on the island of Ibiza, and in and around Knoxville. However vexing his devotion to a penurious writer's life may have been for his first two wives, McCarthy seems never to have lost heart.

"Something would always turn up," he says, recalling blithely the months he spent without electricity in a house in Tennessee. "I had no money, I mean none.

I had run out of toothpaste and I was wondering what to do when I went to the mailbox and there was a free sample."

Fortune smiled on McCarthy again, in 1981, when Saul Bellow, Shelby Foote, and others recommended him for a MacArthur Fellowship, the so-called genius grant. He calls winning the award "the most profound experience of my life." It wasn't so much that the $236,000 allowed him to leave Tennessee (and his second wife) for the Southwest, where he spent the next five years researching and writing *Blood Meridian*. More crucial, from his perspective, were the annual meetings of the MacArthur fellows ("They've been discontinued, but I think I'm the only one who went to every one"), where he hung out with mathematicians, biologists, and world-class physicists such as Gell-Mann.

"What physicists did in the 20th century was one of the extraordinary flowerings ever in the human enterprise," says a reverent McCarthy, who would much prefer to befriend a scientist than another writer. "They changed reality. And most of them were just kids."

The discipline of science, where rank depends on brains rather than money or fashion, appeals to McCarthy's own aristocratic temperament. Fame and security seem never to have been uppermost in his mind. Until *All the Pretty Horses* became a best-seller, and it and several of his other books suddenly turned into hot film properties, the author lived behind a shopping center in El Paso, in a tiny stone cottage on Coffin Street (the perfect address for this lover of *Moby Dick*). His thousands of books were in storage, and his backyard contained pickup trucks in various states of health. Twice divorced, he had a large circle of friends but was on his own.

McCarthy is now married to a woman several decades younger than himself named Jennifer Winkley. They have a six-year-old son, John, whom his father describes as "the best person I know, far better than I am." Home is a large two-story adobe in the chic Tesuque section of Santa Fe, where their neighbors include Ali MacGraw and other movie stars. The front yard has a gigantic nest woven out of branches and twigs, an art project of Jennifer's; the backyard has S.U.V.'s and pickups as well as John's scattered toys. The living room and basement are dominated by McCarthy's library of books, most of them finally out of boxes.

He seems settled here and yet not. He dotes on his son, whose bedroom is stuffed with books, maps, and models. One has the sense that he wants to atone for his shortcomings as a parent earlier in life. He seldom saw his first son, Cullen, after his first marriage dissolved. One night he brings John (and his plastic dinosaurs) to dinner after they have spent the day skiing. A traditionalist, McCarthy worries how well reading and writing are taught in this easygoing New Age enclave. He likes to complain about Santa Fe ("a theme park") and the people who have gathered here from the coasts. "If you don't agree with them politically, you can't just agree to disagree—they think you're crazy," he exclaims. He talks of moving back to Texas, where Jennifer's parents can help with child raising in a more congenial city.

S.F.I. seems to be his home as much as the house in Tesuque. Some days he enjoys the atmosphere so much he does little typing. When he is absent for long, it is often because he has left in one of his trucks for another part of the Southwest or for Mexico to research a novel. Last summer he flew to Ireland by himself to write for six weeks. "It's amazing what you can get done when there's nothing else to do but write," he says.

"Writing comes first for Cormac, before anything else," says the artist James Drake, another ex-Texan—they met in El Paso—who now lives in Santa Fe. "He's on a mission to continue the tradition of great literature."

S.F.I. is happy to grant McCarthy space so that he can continue this effort, and he is thankful to be offered camouflage. By holing up here he can be removed from the literary world, breathing more exalted air, honored for his novels and yet not nagged by questions about them. Describing a local dinner party where he met the artist Bruce Nauman, another Santa Fe celebrity, he says, "It was a very pleasant evening. We talked mostly about horses. I don't think the subject of writing or art ever came up."

This strategy of anonymity isn't always successful. One afternoon as we walk into his office, where his name and face are on a plaque by the door, he is recognized by a biophysicist visiting from the Weizmann Institute of Science, in Israel.

"You wrote that trilogy," says the man, in what could have been a question or a statement. Invited to Santa Fe to give a workshop on the use of DNA chips to analyze DNA sequences, he seems excited but perplexed by the context of this encounter.

"Well, there are a lot of trilogies by a lot of writers," says McCarthy.

"About the boys and the horses," the man persists, the titles not yet clarifying in his brain.

"Yes, I've written about horses. And I've written a trilogy," says McCarthy, still hoping to wriggle away. Finally, I can't stand the suspense and blurt out, "He wrote *All the Pretty Horses*."

The man brightens and sticks out his hand. "It's a tremendous honor to meet you. Wonderful books. I read all three." Then he laughs. "They allow writers in here?"

"Well," says McCarthy, "one, anyway."

STIEG LARSSON

THE AUTHOR
WHO PLAYED WITH FIRE

by Christopher Hitchens

DECEMBER 2009

I suppose it's justifiable to describe "best-selling" in quasi-tsunami terms because when it happens it's partly a wall and partly a tide: first you see a towering, glistening rampart of books in Costco and the nation's airports and then you are hit by a series of succeeding waves that deposit individual copies in the hands of people sitting right next to you. I was slightly wondering what might come crashing in after Hurricane Khaled. I didn't guess that the next great inundation would originate not in the exotic kite-running spaces at the roof of the world but from an epicenter made almost banal for us by Volvo, Absolut, Saab, and IKEA.

Yet it is from this society, of reassuring brand names and womb-to-tomb national health care, that Stieg Larsson conjured a detective double act so incongruous that it makes Holmes and Watson seem like siblings. I say "conjured" because Mr. Larsson also drew upon the bloody, haunted old Sweden of trolls and elves and ogres, and I put it in the past tense because, just as the first book in his *"Millennium"* trilogy, *The Girl with the Dragon Tattoo,* was about to make his fortune, he very suddenly became a dead person. In the Larsson universe the nasty trolls and hulking ogres are bent Swedish capitalists, cold-faced Baltic sex traffickers, blue-eyed Viking Aryan Nazis, and other Nordic riffraff who might have had their reasons to whack him. But if he now dwells in that Valhalla of the hack writer who posthumously beat all the odds, it's surely because of his elf. Picture a feral waif. All right, picture a four-foot-eleven-inch "doll" with Asperger's syndrome and generous breast implants. This is not Pippi Longstocking (to whom a few gestures are made in the narrative). This is Miss Goth, intermittently disguised as *la gamine.*

Forget Miss Smilla's sense of the snow and check out Lisbeth Salander's taste in pussy rings, tattoos, girls, boys, motorcycles, and, above all, computer keyboards. (Once you accept that George MacDonald Fraser's Flashman can pick up any known language in a few days, you have suspended enough disbelief to settle down and enjoy his adventures.) Miss Salander is so well accoutred with special features that she's almost over-equipped. She is awarded a photographic memory, a chess mind to rival Bobby Fischer's, a mathematical capacity that toys with Fermat's last theorem as a cat bats a mouse, and the ability to "hack"—I apologize for the repetition of that word—into the deep intestinal computers of all banks and police departments. At the end of *The Girl Who Played with Fire*, she is for good measure granted the ability to return from the grave.

With all these superheroine advantages, one wonders why she and her on-and-off sidekick, the lumbering but unstoppable reporter Mikael Blomkvist, don't defeat the forces of Swedish Fascism and imperialism more effortlessly. But the other reason that Lisbeth Salander is such a source of fascination is this: the pint-size minxoid with the dragon tattoo is also a traumatized victim and doesn't work or play well with others. She has been raped and tortured and otherwise abused ever since she could think, and her private phrase for her coming-of-age is "All the Evil": words that go unelucidated until near the end of *The Girl Who Played with Fire*. The actress Noomi Rapace has already played Salander in a Swedish film of the first novel, which enjoyed a worldwide release. (When Hollywood gets to the casting stage, I suppose Philip Seymour Hoffman will be offered the ursine Blomkvist role, and though the coloring is wrong I keep thinking of Winona Ryder for Lisbeth. [Daniel Crarg and Rooney Mara would take on the roles.]) According to Larsson's father, the sympathy with which "the girl" is evoked is derived partly from the author's own beloved niece, Therese, who is tattooed and has suffered from anorexia and dyslexia but can fix your computer problems.

In life, Stieg Larsson described himself as, among other things, "a feminist," and his character surrogate, Mikael Blomkvist, takes an ostentatiously severe line against the male domination of society and indeed of his own profession. (The original grim and Swedish title of *The Girl with the Dragon Tattoo* is *Men Who Hate Women,* while the trilogy's third book bore the more fairy-tale-like name *The Castle in the Air That Blew Up:* the clever rebranding of the series with the word "girl" on every cover was obviously critical.) Blomkvist's moral righteousness comes in very useful for the action of the novels, because it allows the depiction of a great deal of cruelty to women, smuggled through customs under the disguise of a strong disapproval. Sweden used to be notorious, in the late 1960s, as the homeland of the film *I Am Curious (Yellow),* which went all the way to the Supreme Court when distributed in the United States and gave Sweden a world reputation as a place of smiling nudity and guilt-free sex. What a world of nursery innocence that was, compared with the child slavery and exploitation that are evoked with perhaps slightly too much relish by the crusading Blomkvist.

His best excuse for his own prurience is that these serial killers and torture fanciers are practicing a form of capitalism and that their racket is protected by a pornographic alliance with a form of Fascism, its lower ranks made up of hideous bikers and meth runners. This is not just sex or crime—it's politics! Most of the time, Larsson hauls himself along with writing such as this:

> The murder investigation was like a broken mosaic in which he could make out some pieces while others were simply missing. Somewhere there was a pattern. He could sense it, but he could not figure it out. Too many pieces were missing.

No doubt they were, or there would be no book. (The plot of the first story is so heavily convoluted that it requires a page reproducing the Vanger dynasty's family tree—the first time I can remember encountering such a dramatis personae since I read *War and Peace*.) But when he comes to the villain of *The Girl with the Dragon Tattoo,* a many-tentacled tycoon named Wennerström, Larsson's prose is suddenly much more spirited. Wennerström had consecrated himself to "fraud that was so extensive it was no longer merely criminal—it was business." That's actually one of the best-turned lines in the whole thousand pages. If it sounds a bit like Bertolt Brecht on an average day, it's because Larsson's own views were old-shoe Communist.

His background involved the unique bonding that comes from tough Red families and solid class loyalties. The hard-labor and factory and mining sector of Sweden is in the far and arduous North—this is also the home territory of most of the country's storytellers—and Grandpa was a proletarian Communist up toward the Arctic. This during the Second World War, when quite a few Swedes were volunteering to serve Hitler's New Order and join the SS. In a note the 23-year-old Larsson wrote before setting out for Africa, he bequeathed everything to the Communist party of his hometown, Umeå. The ownership of the immense later fortune that he never saw went by law to his father and brother, leaving his partner of 30 years, Eva Gabrielsson, with no legal claim, only a moral one that asserts she alone is fit to manage Larsson's very lucrative legacy. And this is not the only murk that hangs around his death, at the age of 50, in 2004.

To be exact, Stieg Larsson died on November 9, 2004, which I can't help noticing was the anniversary of Kristallnacht. Is it plausible that Sweden's most public anti-Nazi just chanced to expire from natural causes on such a date? Larsson's magazine, *Expo,* which has a fairly clear fictional cousinhood with "Millennium," was an unceasing annoyance to the extreme right. He himself was the public figure most identified with the unmasking of white-supremacist and neo-Nazi organizations, many of them with a hard-earned reputation for homicidal violence. The Swedes are not the pacific herbivores that many people imagine: in the footnotes to his second novel Larsson reminds us that Prime Minister Olof

Palme was gunned down in the street in 1986 and that the foreign minister Anna Lindh was stabbed to death (in a Stockholm department store) in 2003. The first crime is still unsolved, and the verdict in the second case has by no means satisfied everybody.

A report in the mainstream newspaper *Aftonbladet* describes the findings of another anti-Nazi researcher, named Bosse Schön, who unraveled a plot to murder Stieg Larsson that included a Swedish SS veteran. Another scheme misfired because on the night in question, 20 years ago, he saw skinheads with bats waiting outside his office and left by the rear exit. Web sites are devoted to further speculation: one blog is preoccupied with the theory that Prime Minister Palme's uncaught assassin was behind the death of Larsson too. Larsson's name and other details were found when the Swedish police searched the apartment of a Fascist arrested for a political murder. Larsson's address, telephone number, and photograph, along with threats to people identified as "enemies of the white race," were published in a neo-Nazi magazine: the authorities took it seriously enough to prosecute the editor.

But Larsson died of an apparent coronary thrombosis, not from any mayhem. So he would have had to be poisoned, say, or somehow medically murdered. Such a hypothesis would point to some involvement "high up," and anyone who has read the novels will know that in Larsson's world the forces of law and order in Sweden are fetidly complicit with organized crime. So did he wind up, in effect, a character in one of his own tales? The people who might have the most interest in keeping the speculation alive—his publishers and publicists—choose not to believe it. "Sixty cigarettes a day, plus tremendous amounts of junk food and coffee and an enormous workload," said Christopher MacLehose, Larsson's literary discoverer in English and by a nice coincidence a publisher of *Flashman,* "would be the culprit. I gather he'd even had a warning heart murmur. Still, I have attended demonstrations by these Swedish right-wing thugs, and they are truly frightening. I also know someone with excellent contacts in the Swedish police and security world who assures me that everything described in the 'Millennium' novels *actually took place.* And, apparently, Larsson planned to write as many as 10 in all. So you can see how people could think that he might not have died but been 'stopped.'"

He left behind him enough manuscript pages for three books, the last of which—due out in the U.S. next summer—is entitled *The Girl Who Kicked the Hornet's Nest,* and the outlines and initial scribblings of a fourth. The market and appetite for them seems to be unappeasable, as does the demand for Henning Mankell's "Detective Wallander" thrillers, the work of Peter (*Smilla's Sense of Snow*) Høeg, and the stories of Arnaldur Indridason. These writers come from countries as diverse as Denmark and Iceland, but in Germany the genre already has a name: *Schwedenkrimi,* or "Swedish crime writing." Christopher MacLehose told me that he knows of bookstores that now have special sections for the Scandinavian phenomenon. "When Roger Straus and I first published Peter Høeg," he said, "we thought we were doing something of a favor for Danish literature, and then 'Miss Smilla' abruptly sold a million copies in both England and America. Look, in almost everyone there is a memory of the sagas and the Norse myths. A lot of our storytelling got started in those long, cold, dark nights."

Perhaps. But Larsson is very much of our own time, setting himself to confront questions such as immigration, "gender," white-collar crime, and, above all, the Internet. The plot of his first volume does involve a sort of excursion into antiquity—into the book of Leviticus, to be exact—but this is only for the purpose of encrypting a "Bible code." And he is quite deliberately unromantic, giving us shopping lists, street directions, menus, and other details—often with their Swedish names—in full. The villains are evil, all right, but very stupid and self-thwartingly prone to spend more time (this always irritates me) telling their victims what they will do to them than actually doing it. There is much sex but absolutely no love, a great deal of violence but zero heroism. Reciprocal gestures are generally indicated by cliché: if a Larsson character wants to show assent he or she will "nod"; if he or she wants to manifest distress, then it will usually be by biting the lower lip. The passionate world of the sagas and the myths is a very long way away. Bleakness is all. That could even be the secret—the emotionless efficiency of Swedish technology, paradoxically combined with the wicked allure of the pitiless elfin avenger, plus a dash of paranoia surrounding the author's demise. If Larsson had died as a brave martyr to a cause, it would have been strangely out of keeping; it's actually more satisfying that he succumbed to the natural causes that are symptoms of modern life.

JAMEſ PATTERſON

· ·

THE HENRY FORD OF BOOKS

by Todd S. Purdum

JANUARY 2015

It seems somehow fitting that James Patterson, the advertising Mad Man turned impresario of the global thriller industry, spends his summers perched high above the Hudson River in Westchester County, halfway between Don Draper's Ossining and Washington Irving's Sleepy Hollow, where the Headless Horseman once roamed the roads by night. Perhaps no author in literary history has more seamlessly melded commerce and creepiness to create an international brand, one that has transformed a wide swath of the publishing industry and given Patterson not only a Rockefeller's river view but a Rockefeller's bank account to boot.

With 305 million copies of his books in print worldwide, Patterson is the great white shark of novelists, a relentless writing machine who has to keep swimming forward in order to feed, and who, together with his army of about two dozen credited co-writers, has been the planet's best-selling author since 2001 (ahead of J. K. Rowling, Nora Roberts, Dr. Seuss, and John Grisham). Of all the hardcover fiction sold in the U.S. in 2013, books by Patterson accounted for one out of every 26. Altogether, he has produced more than 130 separate works—the "books by" page in his latest novels actually takes up three full pages. *Forbes* estimates his income for the year ending last June at $90 million. When I had a chance to ask Patterson about that figure, he at first said, "I don't know," and then followed up with "Yeah, probably."

The first 25 years of Patterson's career were spent in advertising, culminating with his tenure as C.E.O. of the North American branch of J. Walter Thompson, the giant international agency, where he was also creative director and led the "Aren't You Hungry?" campaign for Burger King, while writing fiction on the side. His first novel, *The Thomas Berryman Number,* about a Nashville newspaperman on a murderer's trail, was rejected by 31 publishers before Little, Brown published it, in 1976. It won the Edgar Award for best first novel from the Mystery Writers of America, but sold only about 10,000 copies. Since then—and especially since 1996, when he quit advertising to write full-time—Patterson has proved that his readers have insatiable appetites. He has produced a slew of books—detective series, stand-alone romances, illustrated novels for young adults and for middle-school readers—across a sea of genres, accounting, by his own estimate, for about 30 percent of Little, Brown's total revenues. He is intimately involved in designing his books and devising their marketing and advertising campaigns, with the help of a special in-house unit of half a dozen staffers at Little, Brown dedicated solely to serving the Patterson empire.

"I'm sure there's no publishing relationship like it," Michael Pietsch—Patterson's former editor who is now C.E.O. of Hachette Book Group (Little, Brown's parent company)—told me recently. "Jim is the smartest person I've ever worked with, across a vast landscape of things you can be brilliant about—suspense, emotions, and readers' expectations and how to work them." Pietsch said Patterson had built "a kind of studio system in which he can imagine these stories into being, then work with co-authors so that these stories come into the world."

Indeed, Patterson is to publishing what Thomas Kinkade was to painting, or the television producer John Wells was to a series like *E.R.* He is not a tortured artist in a garret but rather presides over an atelier that produces mass popular entertainment on an astonishing scale. He once said of his work, in a profile a decade ago, "I look at it the way Henry Ford would look at it." The remark has gained currency. Patterson today is busier than ever, in the midst of his current 24-book contract, preparing to launch a TV series based on his thriller *Zoo,* and campaigning with personal appearances and his deep pockets in support of young-adult literacy and independent bookstores. He has also been outspoken, loudly and prominently, on the subject of the long dispute—settled in November [2014]—between Amazon and Hachette Book Group, in the course of which the online retailer had penalized Hachette writers. Because Patterson is a Little, Brown author, many of his own books felt the pinch—they were often not in stock, or were unavailable for pre-order. (Books of Patterson's on Amazon's Top 100 list, like anyone else's on that list, tended not to be affected.) Speaking to BookExpo America last spring, Patterson told the audience of publishers and booksellers, "If Amazon is the new American way, then maybe it has to be changed."

Not surprisingly, his published output has drawn its share of detractors. Stephen King once dismissed Patterson as a "terrible writer" who is "very, very successful." The head of one rival publishing house said to me of Patterson's method, "It's a little disrespectful to say it's paint by numbers, but it *is* a little bit paint by numbers. Does that make him bad? No, I think it makes him smart."

There have been blockbuster authors for years, from a smashing one-off such as Margaret Mitchell to perennial favorites such as Dean Koontz and Dan Brown. The Stratemeyer Syndicate deployed a battalion of ghostwriters to produce Nancy

Drew, Hardy Boys, and Bobbsey Twins stories for generations of readers. But even his detractors agree that Patterson is in a class by himself. One secret to his success: outlines of up to 80 pages for each book, in which Patterson alone sketches virtually all the action in detail, in a brisk and breezy tone that mirrors the finished books. For the novels on which he works with co-authors (some recruited from his days at J. Walter Thompson, some recommended by other writers, one a former New York City doorman), Patterson sends his collaborator an outline, then revises the resulting manuscript multiple times. Here is an excerpt from the first-chapter outline for *Honeymoon,* a 2005 thriller about a black-widow killer, which Patterson co-wrote with Howard Roughan: "Nora and Gordon continue their quick banter, funny and loving. We like them. They're good together—and not just when they're standing up. A minute later the two engage in some terrific, earth-moving sex. It makes us feel great, horny, and envious."

I caught up with Patterson as he was about to make his annual fall migration from his summer place in Briarcliff Manor, New York—a roomy fieldstone house done in tasteful blue-and-white shades with a pool and terrace straight off the cover of a Frontgate catalogue—to his primary residence, a 20,000-square-foot oceanfront home in Palm Beach that he was quick to say is "pretty fucking . . . kind of obnoxious." Chipper and cheery at 67, with a ruddy face, twinkling blue eyes, and sandy hair gone to gray, and dressed in the soft lamb's-wool sweater, polo shirt, and moccasins of the retired executive he is, Patterson received me in a light-filled workspace whose dominant feature is a big sleigh bed, where he writes longhand on old-fashioned yellow pads, with the silver ribbon of the Hudson below him and framed *New York Times* best-seller lists and posters from the movie versions of his books filling the walls. All around us are thick stacks of manuscripts in progress, each topped by a light-blue cover page. A folder is emblazoned in bold type: IDEAS. Glittering honors dot the shelves. "I honestly don't know," Patterson said when I asked him to identify one statuette. "I think this is a Clio"—advertising's highest award. The decorating is the work of his wife, Sue, a former J. Walter Thompson art director, whom he met at work and married 17 years ago.

Patterson is the undisputed king of the digital publishing age, but he remains an analog kind of guy. A small Lucite frame on his office table holds this instruction: "How to Google: Press Safari icon at bottom of your iPad." He speaks in stop-and-start sentences, as if racing to keep pace with his own thoughts. And he can be touchy about his reputation for mass production. When an interviewer for the Catholic-themed Eternal Word Television Network asked him last spring about his process of "churning out" books, he interrupted with a steely glint in his eye, saying, "You mean *crafting?*" His work is akin to that of a TV "show-runner," who sets a series in motion and guides its tone and pace, no matter who else might write individual episodes. "And they don't take shit like I do," he says of someone such as Vince Gilligan, creator of *Breaking Bad*. "They go, 'Gilligan! This guy's great!'"

"MY WAY OR THE HIGHWAY"

For someone who says he "never cared for" the ad game, Patterson was awfully good at it. He insists today that his first profession has limited relevance to his second, but the record strongly suggests otherwise.

In the 1930s, J. Walter Thompson wrote the ads that made the grilled-cheese sandwich into a national staple, all to boost the sales of its client, Kraft Foods, a maker of processed cheese. Patterson has done something similar: he has built a powerhouse brand, then spread it wider and wider. The story behind *Along Came a Spider,* the tale of Alex Cross, a widowed, jazz-playing, African-American detective with a degree in forensic psychology, which became his first blockbuster success, in 1993, is by now the stuff of publishing-industry lore. Patterson believed the surest path to success was to use television advertising, a strategy then all but unheard of in publishing because of the high cost. Little, Brown balked, but Patterson knew the tricks of his trade: he created and shot his own commercial. After seeing the finished product, the publisher agreed to share the cost of broadcasting it in three markets—New York, Chicago, and Washington—cities where (Patterson had determined) thrillers sold briskly. The book started out at No. 9 on the *New York Times* best-seller list, eventually climbing to No. 2 in paperback. With more than five million copies in print, it is still Patterson's single most successful work.

Patterson built the Cross franchise into a successful series, then branched out into stand-alone books. In 1996, he proposed trying something more radical: publishing multiple titles a year. Little, Brown objected, fearing that Patterson would diminish his overall sales, but he prevailed: sales soared.

When Patterson's only son, Jack, now 16 and a student at Hotchkiss, was in grade school and proving to be a reluctant reader, Patterson decided to take aim at a new demographic. As he put it when we spoke, "I can write for these little creeps." Patterson launched a multi-series line of young-adult and children's novels—"Maximum Ride," "Witch & Wizard," "Treasure Hunters," and "I Funny"—that fill not only the shelves of every Barnes & Noble but those of your local grocery store too. Now Patterson produces a dozen titles a year, and there seems to be no upward limit to his overall sales.

Over time, Patterson has built a reputation for not suffering fools, and for demanding from Little, Brown's marketing team more rigorous research and analysis of the sort he was used to on Madison Avenue. He works publicists hard on book tours. In a "What I've Learned" video he recorded for the Literary Guild,

Patterson declared, "I know what I want in all my books. It's my way or the highway. I know who my readers are and how to engage them, how to scare them, how to get people to feel for the characters, how to make my readers laugh." Bill Robinson, co-president at James Patterson Entertainment, the company dedicated to promoting Patterson's efforts for film and television, recounted an exchange with his boss. "The other day we were discussing notes on a project, and I suggested something contrary to his impulse, and he said, 'I'm sorry, Bill, did you recently write an international best-seller that I'm not aware of?'"

Patterson's formula is brutally simple. His books have lots of periods in the paragraphs, lots of paragraphs per page, and very few pages per chapter—as few as three or four. Each chapter begins with a quick reminder of people and events in the prior one (to refresh the memory of any sleepy reader who put the book down the night before), and most books end with a bonus "free preview" chapter of another book in Patterson's voluminous oeuvre.

It is no insult to say that the prose is often bad, as in this example from *Unlucky 13*—the latest installment in Patterson's "Women's Murder Club" series, co-authored with Maxine Paetro—describing a terrorist who has hijacked a luxury cruise ship: "The sight of the man, the way he walked, his hardy-har attitude, and the random murders were so crazy-making, she felt this close to going bug-fuck." And here is the scene on the ship: "A gas lamp that had been placed on top of the piano threw a dim light over the formerly elegant room, which now looked debased, like a used-up exotic dancer turning tricks on the street."

The buzz in publishing circles is that success may have mellowed Patterson somewhat, that he is no longer so insistent and demanding. "I always thought he was a total dick," one non–Little, Brown executive told me. "I think that's not fair now." Pietsch, who is not only Patterson's ultimate boss but a friend and neighbor in Westchester, says diplomatically, "Having run a big corporation in a talent-based industry gave him a great deal of confidence in speaking with candor about things he doesn't like, which is a rarity for an author in the publishing business."

And Patterson is emphatically in business. A few years ago, he dropped his longtime agency, William Morris, in favor of the Washington superlawyer Robert Barnett. (Disclosure: Barnett also happens to be my agent.) His former agent, Jennifer Rudolph Walsh, maintains there are no hard feelings. "He didn't cost us tens of millions of dollars," she told me. "He made us tens of millions of dollars."

A DEVIL INSIDE HIM?

Patterson's self-presentation is remarkably sunny. His midday tipple of choice is a bottle of Stewart's Orange 'n Cream soda, and midway through our talk,

Patterson's wife brought in a plate of freshly baked chocolate-chip cookies, a signature gesture of Sue's hospitality that I have seen mentioned by others who have met with Patterson.

But Patterson's stories can be raw, with more than their share of sexual sadism—sliced breasts, sodomy by snake—and sociopathic killers. "I'm inside all of you!" the murderer in *Invisible,* one of Patterson's latest thrillers, declares. "The only difference is I don't hide behind some mask, driving my SUV and sipping Starbucks at my kid's soccer game."

Is there a devil inside James Patterson?, I asked. "Not a murderer!" he said with a laugh. "Or if there was, I'm not telling *Vanity Fair.*"

But there is darkness. James Brendan Patterson grew up in Newburgh, New York, just a few miles up the Hudson from his current home, the son of an emotionally withholding insurance agent, whose own father had abandoned his family, and who had grown up in the local poorhouse, where Patterson's grandmother was a charwoman. "The first time I think he ever hugged me was on his deathbed," Patterson says.

The Hudson Valley, with its dramatic palisades and twisting mountain roads, remains a frequent setting in Patterson's fiction. But when I suggested that he hadn't moved so far from where he began, he instantly demurred. "Oh, *very* far," he said. "*Very, very* far."

And he went on: "I think that I felt I needed to be this very bright, first-in-his-class kind of kid, for whatever reason, pretty serious. But underneath, it was just a million stories that I was already telling. You know, I grew up in the woods in Newburgh, and there weren't a lot of people around, and I would just wander in the woods out there and tell myself stories, one after the other. And I didn't really make anything of it. I never thought I was going to be a storyteller or a writer, but I was just in the habit."

At St. Patrick's High School, the Christian Brothers smacked him around a bit, but he worked hard, applying to Harvard, Yale, Colby, and Bates, only to learn that the school had never sent in his applications but had enrolled him on a scholarship at Manhattan College, in the Bronx, instead. By this point, his parents had moved to Massachusetts, where his father got a job with Prudential, and Patterson worked summers on the overnight shift at McLean Hospital, the renowned psychiatric institution in suburban Belmont, to help pay his bills. He began digging into highbrow literature—James Joyce, Jean Genet—to pass the long, quiet shift. A year in the Ph.D. English program at Vanderbilt ended when he got a high number in the draft lottery during the Vietnam War and didn't need to stay in school any longer to maintain a deferment. He took a job as a junior copywriter at Thompson, and in his first year there he wound up doing a dozen television commercials, including a smash hit for the Ford LTD that featured a side-by-side "quiet" test with a Jaguar.

As he rose to positions of power in the company, Patterson made it his policy never to hire anyone he wouldn't like working with. He especially enjoyed working on women's products, both because he had demonstrated a particular assurance in this area and because sessions with female copywriters were more collaborative ("In the male sessions everybody was 'I got it'"). Even today, women are Patterson's most faithful readers.

Patterson's characters reflect his own blend of light and dark. His protagonists are all a bit wounded and vulnerable—not just Alex Cross but also Michael Bennett, another widowed detective (this one an Irish-American in New York with 10 adopted children); Rafe Khatchadorian, a hapless discipline case, who is the hero of the "Middle School" series; and Jamie Grimm, a wheelchair-bound middle-schooler, who is the star of the "I Funny" series and who wants to be America's best young stand-up comic but can work only sitting down. Even Patterson's most villainous bad guys tend to have had a painful childhood or some other psychic heartbreak along the way.

"THE POWER TO DO THINGS"

In the 1960s, Stan Freberg, the satirical recording artist turned standout adman, promoted Sunsweet pitted prunes with the triumphant tag "Today the pits. Tomorrow the wrinkles." Patterson's forward march is just as determined. The one hill he feels he hasn't quite conquered is Hollywood (although there have been a couple of Alex Cross movies). "I think to some extent I've been stereotyped," he says. "I think that some of the people there think they're above mainstream fiction. I think they're kidding themselves, but, you know, that's fine." He has recently revved up his efforts with the help of Bill Robinson, a veteran producer, and Leopoldo Gout, a producer and artist and the other co-president at James Patterson Entertainment. Patterson now has a "first look" deal with CBS and has recently announced a raft of new projects, including a 13-episode series version of *Zoo* for the network next summer, and a partnership with Robert De Niro's Tribeca Productions for a pilot for another series based on his first novel, *The Thomas Berryman Number*. "I Funny" has been optioned to Nickelodeon. Out of his own pocket, Patterson has financed yet another pilot for a proposed children's variety series—with blackout sketches, pies in the face, and fake commercials in the manner of *Saturday Night Live* (for products like "Boys' Noise Canceling Headphones")—that Robinson described as a cross between *Zoom* and *The Electric Company*.

"Once they were educated on the power of his reach with kids, once they understood that he's got more people reading his books than some of these networks have people watching, people sit up and take notice," Robinson said. "And an interesting piece of this is that we're dealing with a billionaire, somebody who has more money than some of the studios. He has the power to do things that no other writer can do."

Patterson writes seven days a week, 365 days a year, typically rising with the sun, then walking the course for nine holes of golf at midmorning before having a simple lunch. In Palm Beach, a cook makes maybe two lunches and one dinner a week, but a lot of meals are eaten in restaurants with a small circle of close friends, many stretching back to grade school ("not a self-important blowhard among them," he says). Evenings are spent with a movie or a favorite TV show, including *The Good Wife* and *Justified*. Writer's block is never a problem. If he ever gets bored or stymied with one active project, there are a dozen others to turn to at any one time.

"Where do the stories come from?" Michael Pietsch repeated the question to himself when I posed it. "In his case, it's a drive like I've never seen. He's a very competitive person, but I think he's competitive with himself. Do I wake up at night wondering if it's going to stop? We had a meeting today in which I proposed that we might want to hold off a secondary format of a book for some point in the future when there might not be an abundance of them in future years, and he looked at me incredulously, as if 'When is that going to happen?'"

Patterson himself says his obituary would begin, "He was slowing down at 101, and had only finished four novels that year."

The Pattersons drive matching Mercedes sedans, but when he's in Westchester and has to go to Manhattan, he's apt to take the Metro-North commuter train, simply because it's most efficient. He confesses that he has lately started using private jets for the trip to Florida or for business. Increasingly, Patterson has devoted his time—and money—to promoting literacy and, paradoxically, to supporting independent bookstores, for whom his own books are arguably the least likely source of income. He gave $1 million in grants to bookstores in 2014 alone, which can be used for a variety of purposes. In November, he launched a national campaign to promote reading. He has contributed more than $26 million to his and Sue's alma maters, given another $5.8 million in scholarships at 22 colleges and universities, sent 650,000 of his books to U.S. troops at home and abroad, and provided a box of books to every public school in New York City, Los Angeles, Savannah, Georgia, and Palm Beach County, Florida. Patterson intends to arrange his estate so that about half of his wealth goes to charity, and he hopes that his son, Jack, might someday like to take charge of the giving. His philanthropy at this point is hands-on ("because I think institutions frequently are very sloppy"). He told me that he has no interest in having his name on buildings.

And he is philosophical about his critics, in particular critics of his craft. Patterson decided long ago that he'd rather be a successful popular novelist than a mediocre literary one. He says he thinks of himself above all as an entertainer. And he is keenly self-aware: he knows what he would likely be feeling about himself if he weren't already filling his own shoes. If he were not already James Patterson, he said, "I would be like, 'Well, what's this? He couldn't possibly do what he does.'" Indeed, if he were not James Patterson, "I'd probably be kind of irritated by the guy."

DONNA TARTT

IT'S TARTT—BUT IS IT ART?

by Evgenia Peretz

JULY 2014

"Have you read *The Goldfinch* yet?" Consider it the cocktail-party conversation starter of 2014, the new "Are you watching *Breaking Bad*?" Eleven years in the making, 784 pages long, the book has re-ignited the cult of Donna Tartt, which began in 1992 with her sensational debut novel, *The Secret History*. When *The Goldfinch* came out, last fall, recipients of advance copies promptly showed off their galleys on Instagram, as if announcing the birth of a child. Her readings sold out instantly. New York's Frick Collection, which in October began exhibiting the painting for which the book was named, hadn't seen so much traffic in years. The novel is already on its way to becoming a movie, or a TV series, made by the producers of *The Hunger Games*. It's been on the *New York Times* bestseller list for seven months, sold a million and a half print and digital copies, and drawn a cornucopia of rave reviews, including one in the daily *New York Times* and another in the Sunday *New York Times Book Review*. In April it won the Pulitzer Prize for fiction, the judges of which praised it as "a book that stimulates the mind and touches the heart."

It's also gotten some of the severest pans in memory from the country's most important critics and sparked a full-on debate in which the naysayers believe that nothing less is at stake than the future of reading itself.

For the few uninitiated, *The Goldfinch* is a sprawling bildungsroman centered on 13-year-old Theo Decker, whose world is violently turned upside down when, on a trip to the Metropolitan Museum of Art, a terrorist bomb goes off, killing his mother, among other bystanders. At the behest of a dying old man, he makes off with a painting—the 1654 Carel Fabritius masterpiece, *The Goldfinch*. For the next 14 years and 700 pages, the painting becomes both his burden and the only connection to his lost mother, while he's flung from New York to Las Vegas to Amsterdam, encountering an array of eccentric characters, from the hard-living but soulful Russian teenager Boris to the cultured and kindly furniture restorer Hobie, who becomes a stand-in father, to the mysterious, waif-like

Pippa, plus assorted lowlifes, con men, Park Avenue recluses, and dissolute preppies.

Michiko Kakutani, the chief *New York Times* book reviewer for 31 years (and herself a Pulitzer winner, in criticism), called it "a glorious Dickensian novel, a novel that pulls together all [Tartt's] remarkable storytelling talents into a rapturous, symphonic whole. . . . It's a work that shows us how many emotional octaves Ms. Tartt can now reach, how seamlessly she can combine the immediate and tactile with more wide-angled concerns." According to best-selling phenomenon Stephen King, who reviewed it for *The New York Times Book Review,* "'The Goldfinch' is a rarity that comes along perhaps half a dozen times per decade, a smartly written literary novel that connects with the heart as well as the mind."

READING LIKE A CRITIC

But, in the literary world, there are those who profess to be higher brows still than *The New York Times*—the secret rooms behind the first inner sanctum, consisting, in part, of *The New Yorker, The New York Review of Books,* and *The Paris Review,* three institutions that are considered, at least among their readers, the last bastions of true discernment in a world where book sales are king and real book reviewing has all but vanished. *The Goldfinch* a "rapturous" symphony? Not so fast, they say.

"Its tone, language, and story belong in children's literature," wrote critic James Wood, in *The New Yorker.* He found a book stuffed with relentless, far-fetched plotting; cloying stock characters; and an overwrought message tacked on at the end as a plea for seriousness. "Tartt's consoling message, blared in the book's final pages, is that what will survive of us is great art, but this seems an anxious compensation, as if Tartt were unconsciously acknowledging that the 2013 'Goldfinch' might not survive the way the 1654 'Goldfinch' has." Days after she was awarded the Pulitzer, Wood told *Vanity Fair,* "I think that the rapture with which this novel has been received is further proof of the infantilization of our literary culture: a world in which adults go around reading *Harry Potter.*"

In *The New York Review of Books,* novelist and critic Francine Prose wrote that, for all the frequent descriptions of the book as "Dickensian," Tartt demonstrates little of Dickens's remarkable powers of description and graceful language. She culled both what she considered lazy clichés ("Theo's high school friend Tom's cigarette is 'only the tip of the iceberg.' . . . The bomb site is a 'madhouse'") and passages that were "bombastic, overwritten, marred by baffling turns of phrase." "Reading *The Goldfinch,*" Prose concluded, "I found myself wondering, 'Doesn't anyone care how something is written anymore?'" Across the pond, the highly regarded *London Review of Books* likened it to a "children's book" for adults. London's *Sunday Times* concluded that "no amount of straining for high-flown uplift can disguise the fact that *The Goldfinch* is a turkey."

"A book like *The Goldfinch* doesn't undo any clichés—it deals in them," says Lorin Stein, editor of *The Paris Review,* perhaps the most prestigious literary journal in America. "It coats everything in a cozy patina of 'literary' gentility." Who cares that Kakutani or King gave it the stamp of approval: "Nowadays, even *The New York Times Book Review* is afraid to say when a popular book is crap," Stein says.

No novel gets uniformly enthusiastic reviews, but the polarized responses to *The Goldfinch* lead to the long-debated questions: What makes a work literature, and who gets to decide?

The questions are as old as fiction itself. The history of literature is filled with books now considered masterpieces that were thought hackwork in their time. Take Dickens, the greatest novelist of the Victorian period, whose mantle writers from John Irving to Tom Wolfe to Tartt have sought to inherit. Henry James called Dickens the greatest of superficial novelists . . . "We are aware that this definition confines him to an inferior rank in the department of letters which he adorns; but we accept this consequence of our proposition. It were, in our opinion, an offence against humanity to place Mr. Dickens among the greatest novelists. . . . He has added nothing to our understanding of human character." Many future offenses against humanity would follow:

"It isn't worth any adult reader's attention," *The New York Times* pronounced concerning Nabokov's *Lolita.*

"Kind of monotonous," the same paper said about Salinger's *The Catcher in the Rye.* "He should've cut out a lot about these jerks and all at that crumby school."

"An absurd story," announced *The Saturday Review* of F. Scott Fitzgerald's *The Great Gatsby,* while the *New York Herald Tribune* declared it "a book of the season only."

That said, for all the snooty pans of books now considered classics, there have been, conversely, plenty of authors who were once revered as literary miracles and are now relegated to the trash heap. Sir Walter Scott, for example, was considered perhaps the pre-eminent writer of his time. Now his work, reverential as it is to concepts of rank and chivalry, seems fairly ridiculous. Margaret Mitchell's Civil War blockbuster, *Gone with the Wind,* won the Pulitzer and inspired comparisons to Tolstoy, Dickens, and Thomas Hardy. Now it's considered a schmaltzy relic read by teenage girls, if anyone.

For many best-selling authors, it's not enough to sell millions of books; they want respectability too. Stephen King, despite his wild commercial success, has nursed a lifelong gripe that he's been overlooked by the literary-critical establishment. In 2003, King was given a medal by the National Book Foundation for his "distinguished contribution to American letters." In his acceptance speech, he took the opportunity to chide all the fancy pants in the room—"What do you think? You get social academic Brownie points for deliberately staying out of touch with your own culture?"—and to ask why they made it "a point of pride" never to have read anything by such best-selling authors as John Grisham, Tom Clancy, and Mary Higgins Clark. Harold Bloom, the most finicky of finicky literary critics, went into a tizzy, calling the foundation's decision to give the award to King "another low in the process of dumbing down our cultural life" and the recipient "an immensely inadequate writer on a sentence-by-sentence, paragraph-by-paragraph, book-by-book basis."

Bloom's fussing had little impact. King was already on his way to the modern canon—his essays and short stories had been published in *The New Yorker*—and thus he was now in the position to announce who *he* thought was garbage: James Patterson. "I don't like him," King said after accepting a lifetime-achievement award from the Canadian Booksellers Association in 2007. "I don't respect his books, because every one is the same." To which Patterson later replied, "Doesn't make too much sense. I'm a good dad, a nice husband. My only crime is I've sold millions of books."

WAR OF WORDS

In the long war over membership in the pantheon of literary greatness, no battle had quite the comical swagger of the ambush of Tom Wolfe after the publication of his 1998 novel, *A Man in Full,* which became a call to arms for three literary lions: Norman Mailer, John Updike, and John Irving. As the English newspaper *The Guardian* gleefully reported, they were adamant that Wolfe belonged not in the canon but on airport-bookstore shelves (between Danielle Steel and Susan Powter's *Stop the Insanity*). Updike, in his *New Yorker* review, concluded that *A Man in Full* "still amounts to entertainment, not literature, even literature in a modest aspirant form." Mailer, writing in *The New York Review of Books,* compared reading the novel to having sex with a 300-pound woman: "Once she gets on top it's all over. Fall in love or be asphyxiated." (Mailer and Wolfe had a history: Mailer had once remarked, "There is something silly about a man who wears a white suit all the time, especially in New York," to which Wolfe replied, "The lead dog is the one they always try to bite in the ass.") Irving said that reading *A Man in Full* "is like reading a bad newspaper or a bad piece in a magazine. It makes you wince." He added that on any given page out of Wolfe he could "read a sentence that would make me gag." Wolfe later struck back. "It's a wonderful tantrum," he said. "*A Man in Full* panicked [Irving] the same way it

frightened John Updike and Norman. Frightened them. Panicked them."
Updike and Mailer were "two old piles of bones." As for Irving, "Irving is a great
admirer of Dickens. But what writer does he see now constantly compared to
Dickens? Not John Irving, but Tom Wolfe . . . It must gnaw at him terribly."

> *The book of my enemy has been remaindered*
> *And I am pleased.*
> *In vast quantities it has been remaindered*
> *Like a van-load of counterfeit that has been seized*

So begins the Australian critic and essayist Clive James's poem about the
writer's best friends, Schadenfreude and his twin brother, Envy. Leon Wieseltier,
the longtime literary editor of *The New Republic* (where James Wood was a senior
editor before moving to *The New Yorker*), suggests there might just be a smidge
of this at work in the criticism leveled against Tartt. "Tartt has managed to do
something that almost never happens: she has created a serious novel—whether
you like the book or not, it is not frivolous, or tacky or cynical—and made it into
a cultural phenomenon. When a serious novel breaks out, some authors of other
serious novels have, shall we say, emotional difficulties." Curtis Sittenfeld, the
best-selling and acclaimed author of *Prep* and *American Wife*, similarly observes
that critics derive "a satisfaction in knocking a book off its pedestal."

It's a theory that holds appeal for authors who feel they've been unfairly ignored by critics, and it can lead to surprising, some might even say contorted,
rationales. Jennifer Weiner, the outspoken mega-selling author of such "women's
books" as *In Her Shoes, Good in Bed,* and *Best Friends Forever,* theorizes that
Wood's review may have been a response to the public's tepid reception of *The
Woman Upstairs,* by his wife, Claire Messud. "[Messud's] writing was gorgeous.
It was like beautiful carpentry. Everything fit. Everything worked. There wasn't
a single metaphor or simile or comparison you could pull out and say, 'This
doesn't work,' the way you can with *The Goldfinch.* But not many people read
that book. . . . The world doesn't think what she's doing is as worthy as what
Tartt is doing."

From the beginning, Tartt's work confused critics. When *The Secret History,*
about an erudite group of classics majors who turn to murder at a small New
England college, was published, in 1992, it was greeted with a kind of wonder
by writers, critics, and readers—not just because its author was a mysterious, tiny
package from Greenwood, Mississippi, who dressed in crisp tailored suits and
revealed little about herself, but because few could place it on the commercial-
literary continuum. Lev Grossman, the book reviewer for *Time* and author of the
best-selling fantasy series *The Magicians,* recalls, "You couldn't classify it easily

into high literature or genre fiction. It seemed to come from some other literary universe, where those categories didn't exist. And it made me want to go to that universe because it was so compelling." Jay McInerney, who'd had a splashy debut similar to Tartt's a few years earlier with *Bright Lights, Big City,* and became friends with her early on, recalls, "I loved it on many levels, not least because it's a literary murder mystery, but also because it initiates the reader from the outset into a secret club, which is probably what every good novel should do." In recent years it has been discovered by new readers such as Lena Dunham (creator of HBO's *Girls*), who found in Tartt not only this cool persona— "She reminded me, style-wise, of my mother's radical-feminist photographer friends in the 80s"—but a master of the tight-group-of-friends tradition.

It took 10 years for Tartt to come out with her next book, *The Little Friend,* but it was a disappointment to both critics and readers. Was she a one-hit wonder? To prove otherwise she spent the next 11 years, head down, spinning the adventures of Theo Decker, going down byways for as long as eight months that she would ultimately abandon. After the disappointment of her last book, everything was on the line.

The verdict among her fans? Perhaps too long in parts, but the story was as gripping as ever. She is "the consummate storyteller," says Grossman, who is a new voice leading the charge that certain works of genre fiction should be considered literature. "The narrative thread is one you just can't gather up fast enough," he explains.

HOW FICTION WORKS

"There seems to be universal agreement that the book is a 'good read,'" says Wood. "But you can be a good storyteller, which in some ways Tartt clearly is, and still not be a *serious* storyteller—where, of course, 'serious' does not mean the exclusion of the comic, or the joyful, or the exciting. Tartt's novel is not a serious one—it tells a fantastical, even ridiculous tale, based on absurd and improbable premises."

For Wood's crowd the measuring stick in determining what's serious literature is a sense of reality, of authenticity—and it's possible even in books that are experimental. In Lorin Stein's view, best-sellers such as Mary Gaitskill's *Two Girls, Fat and Thin* and Hilary Mantel's *Wolf Hall* may stand the test of time "not because a critic says they're good, but because . . . they're about real life. . . . I don't want stage-managing from a novel. I want fiction to deal in the truth."

It's a view he may have inherited from his former boss Jonathan Galassi, the president of Farrar, Straus and Giroux, which, along with Alfred A. Knopf, is arguably the most prestigious of publishing houses. (Galassi edits, among others,

Jonathan Franzen, Jeffrey Eugenides, Marilynne Robinson, Michael Cunningham, and Lydia Davis.) Determining what's serious literature isn't a science, says Galassi, who hasn't yet read *The Goldfinch*. The response isn't fully rationalized, but ultimately a book must be "convincing in some way. It can be emotionally convincing, it can be intellectually convincing, it can be politically convincing. Hopefully it's all those things. But with someone like Donna Tartt, not everyone is convinced on all levels."

To Grossman, this slavish devotion to reality is retrograde, and perhaps reviewers like Wood should not be reviewing people like Tartt in the first place. "A critic like Wood—whom I admire probably as much or more than any other book reviewer working—doesn't have the critical language you need to praise a book like *The Goldfinch*. The kinds of things that the book does particularly well don't lend themselves to literary analysis. . . . Her language is careless in places, and there's a fairy-tale quality to the book. There's very little context in the book—it's happening in some slightly simplified world. Which to me is fine. I find that intensely compelling in a novel. Every novel dispenses with something, and Tartt dispenses with that." As for Francine Prose's query "Doesn't anyone care how a book is written anymore?": Grossman admits that, with story now king for readers, the answer is no. Wood agrees that that's the state of things, but finds it sad and preposterous. "This is something peculiar to fiction: imagine a literary world in which most people didn't care how a poem was written!" (Tartt was not available to comment, but Jay McInerney says she doesn't read reviews, and isn't "losing any sleep" over the negative ones.)

Wieseltier has come to a rather more expansive definition of serious literature. "Tartt's novel, like all novels that purport to be serious, should of course pass before the bar of all the serious critics, and receive all the judgments that they bring forth," says Wieseltier, who has dipped into the book enough to put it in the serious category. "But if a serious book really catches on, it may be less important that its strictly literary quality is not as great as one might have hoped and more important that it's touched a nerve, that it is driven by some deep human subject and some true human need." Ultimately, he thinks, the success of *The Goldfinch* is a step in the right direction. "When I look at the fiction best-seller list, which is mainly an inventory of junk, and I see a book like this riding high, I think it's good news, even if it is not *The Ambassadors*."

Indeed, we might ask the snobs, What's the big deal? Can't we all just agree that it's great she spent all this time writing a big enjoyable book and move on? No, we cannot, say the stalwarts. Francine Prose, who took on the high-school canon—Maya Angelou, Harper Lee, Ray Bradbury—in a controversial *Harper's* essay, "I Know Why the Caged Bird Cannot Read," argued that holding up weak books as examples of excellence promotes mediocrity and turns young readers off forever. With *The Goldfinch* she felt duty-bound in the same way. "Everyone was saying this is such a great book and the language was so amazing. I felt I had to make quite a case against it," she says. It gave her some satisfaction, she reports, that after her *Goldfinch* review came out she received one e-mail telling her that the book was a masterpiece and she had missed the point, and about 200 from readers thanking her for telling them that they were not alone. Similarly, Stein, who struggles to keep strong literary voices alive and robust, sees a book like *The Goldfinch* standing in the way. "What worries me is that people who read only one or two books a year will plunk down their money for *The Gold-finch,* and read it, and tell themselves they like it, but deep down will be profoundly bored, because they *aren't* children, and will quietly give up on the whole enterprise when, in fact, fiction—realistic fiction, old or new—is as alive and gripping as it's ever been."

Is Donna Tartt the next Charles Dickens? In the end, the question will be answered not by *The New York Times, The New Yorker,* or *The New York Review of Books*—but by whether or not future generations read her. Just as a painter can be castigated by his contemporaries and still wind up the most prized painter at the Metropolitan Museum of Art, a writer can sell millions of books, win prizes, and be remembered as no more than a footnote or punch line. It's a fight that will be settled only on some new version of the Kindle, yet to be designed.

MEMOIR

· ·

BOSOM BUDDIES

....

by Laura Z. Hobson

NOVEMBER 1983

One of those storybook coincidences that make for such great anecdotes years later when all pain is spent tied Henry and Lila Luce's divorce to Thayer Hobson's and mine.

It was a Thursday night that Thayer told me about Isabelle, the third of January 1935. He had intended to tell me the night before, waiting only through the New Year's festivities, settling on the second night of the New Year to say, "I have something to tell you."

But on the morning of that second day, a Wednesday, Harry had called me on the office phone (I was writing promotion for *Time* magazine), asking if we were free that evening, and how about dinner and the opera with Lila and himself. I checked with Thayer and told Harry's secretary we'd love to. Thus my marriage lasted one day longer, courtesy of Harry Luce.

The Luces were living in a rather grand apartment on East Seventy-second Street, just off Fifth Avenue. Though we were just four at dinner, it was all very formal, with a couple of footmen in livery behind the dining-room chairs. (I'm sure this was Lila's doing, not Harry's.) We dined and went off to the old Metropolitan Opera House on Broadway, below Forty-second Street.

The opera was *Manon*, not anybody's favorite. During the intermission, going to the bar for drinks, we paired off, Lila with Thayer, Harry with me. Harry was bored with the music; he seemed nervous; he fidgeted and talked about the difficulties of launching *The March of Time* in the nation's movie houses next month.

"Harry," I said after a bit, "what with all the extra work on *The March of Time* and everything else, you look sort of bushed. Maybe you could do with a little vacation."

Lila, I later learned, was saying to Thayer, "You've been driving yourself too hard, Thayer, you sound tired out. Why don't you take off for a while, not on another publishing trip, just a vacation?"

The intermission ended and we all went back to our seats, two young couples in evening dress at the opera, living the fashionable life of New York. The next night I got the news from Thayer, and Lila got her news from Harry. He had fallen in love with somebody else and he was sorry to hurt her, but he wanted a divorce.

The someone else was Clare Boothe Brokaw, and he had met her a few months before, at a party at our house. We had known Clare for a couple of years; we'd met at a cocktail party at the Alfred Knopf's and had become friends. In those days she was not political at all. She was a wealthy woman because of the settlement her lawyers had won for her when she divorced the millionaire George T. Brokaw, whom she once described to me as a sadistic drunk who would force sex on her the very night she came home from the hospital after each of her several miscarriages. But "leading an alimony life" was not for her; she had recently become managing editor of *Vanity Fair*, one of the city's smart magazines. Her first book, *Stuffed Shirts*, was a success, full of barbed wit. She was amusing and clever to talk to, and one of the really beautiful women. She spoke with animation, and had an odd little trick of clipping off certain words and phrases. It gave her speech a staccato brightness, and today, when I hear her on television, I often catch that same little clipping off.

Many a hostess thinks an extra woman at dinner is a handicap, a load, a drag, but no hostess ever thought that about Clare. She had been at our house several times, and then came the night the Luces were there too. When I invited her, I told Clare who the other guests were to be, and I still remember her entrance. People were standing around in the living room, drinks in hand, chatting, waiting for whoever was missing to get there.

At last she came through the arch that led from the hall to the living room, and paused, waiting for Thayer or me to come and introduce her. She stood there with her blond head slightly tilted to one side; she was wearing a black evening dress with lovely jewels, but instead of the usual corsage at her shoulder, she was carrying a small nosegay of white flowers in both her hands. As she waited, she seemed to be looking demurely down at them.

Maybe she hadn't intended to make an entrance, but make it she certainly did. The only other thing I remember clearly about that night when the future Mr. and Mrs. Henry R. Luce first met is that after dinner they stood a little apart from everybody, talking by themselves, she leaning back into the curve of the piano, facing the room, and Harry, ignoring the room, turning his back on it, holding forth intensely and then listening intensely.

Clare was too clever to appear impressed with him; she would say something light and laugh, then change moods and seem totally absorbed by what he was saying. Some of our other guests told me she was baiting him about his beloved *Fortune* magazine, tossing out little mots about how bad it was and how easily it could be made better.

When Clare herself was a hostess, she never regarded an extra woman as a drag—if it was the right kind of extra woman. She invited so many men to her dinners and parties that she was delighted to meet women who would fit in.

"What I want," she told me once, "is a woman with brains who gets her clothes at Bergdorf Goodman."

It appears that I met her requirements; while Thayer was off on that second "publishing trip," she invited me to several dinners. She had an apartment high up in the Sherry-Netherland hotel on Fifth Avenue, across from the old Plaza, a large six-room affair on an annual lease, whose rent, her brother David told me, was $6,000 a year, which today would be more than $30,000. It was furnished with her own things, and each room could have been photographed in full color for any of the upper-bracket magazines.

Her dining room is the room I remember best. It had raspberry-colored walls, white carpet, draperies and chairs also in white, and the long roomy table was a gleaming oblong of blue mirror. My datebook tells me that on one of the nights I was there the other dinner guests were Bernard Baruch; Sir William Wiseman; Sam Behrman, the playwright; Raymond Moley, one of Roosevelt's "brain trust"; a Somebody Wiggin, first secretary of the British embassy; Mark Sullivan, the author; Marya Mannes, who would become an author; and Dorothy Hale, who was to become deeply involved with Harry Hopkins, another member of the brain trust.

But it was not anybody's brains that impressed me enough that evening for me to be writing about it now. It was something Clare said when we were alone after dinner. I had gone to her bathroom, and as she opened the door to it for me, I took one look and blurted out, "Ye gods."

It was twice the size of an ordinary bathroom, and the bath mat covering the large rectangle of floor was not your ordinary bath mat either. It was not terry-cloth or shag or carpeting; it was fur, white ermine, with the little blackish brown paws attached at intervals, as ermine was often done at that time.

But the bath mat was not the whole story. The same white ermine with the dangling dark paws had been made into a cover for the toilet seat.

Clare laughed at my astonishment.

"It used to be a coat," she said. "My mother-in-law, Mrs. Brokaw, gave it to me and I hated it. While I was married I had to wear it and wear it, but I always knew that once I was divorced, I'd find a perfect use for it."

Because of the odd juxtaposing of events in that one month of January 1935, and because I knew both Harry and Clare, I was to have a more concentrated friendship with Clare for a while than I would have for the rest of my days.

Like most of the world I still knew nothing about their plans to marry, but within three weeks Clare herself chose to let me in on the secret. Being Clare, she did it in her own special way.

At the end of the month she was leaving for a vacation at Hobcaw, Bernard Baruch's vast country estate in Georgetown, South Carolina. She gave herself a going-away party, and I was one of the people she invited.

My datebook for the entire month is blank except for three brief entries: the first about the Luces and the opera, the next night's "Thayer tells me about Isabelle," and a final one nine days later, "Thayer departed."

Clare knew about that, and when I declined her invitation, saying, "I just can't," she said, "You just *can*," and gave me a lecture about showing the world not only that you could take it, but that you were alive and free and available for something new and attractive.

I went, and it was one of her usual gatherings of the affluent and clever. Toward the end of dinner, she tapped her fork against a glass until she had everybody's attention. Then she said, "I have a big secret, but I'm only going to tell you a part of it."

"What secret?" The whole table said it in various forms, and after suitable suspense she said, "I'm going to be married."

"To whom?"

"When?"

"Why is it a secret?"

She obviously enjoyed the commotion. "I told you it has to stay a secret for a while, but I'll give you a clue." She looked mischievous and happy. "He's connected with the movies."

"Douglas Fairbanks?" somebody asked.

"Robert Taylor?"

"Clark Gable?"

Names of handsome movie stars tumbled about the table, with Clare shaking her head at each one. "He's not an *actor*—I never said he was an actor." Whereupon the name of every movie producer was mentioned, with the probable exception of Sam Goldwyn.

At last she put a stop to it; she was keeping us guessing just for fun, she said, but the marriage was no fabrication, and we'd all hear about it in due time.

But when we were alone, fixing our makeup in that ermined bathroom, she said, "You ought to know who it is—you know him."

"I *know* him? I don't know a soul in the movies."

"You know him quite well." I looked blank, and she added, "I'll give you one more clue—he's powerful and he's young and he's rich."

I still didn't catch on. Then she exclaimed, "Laura! It's Harry!"

"Harry Luce? But you said—"

"*The March of Time* is connected with the movies, isn't it?"

My gasp of comprehension made her laugh.

"I just had to tell somebody who knows Harry," she said, "or I'd go mad not being able to talk about him for the next few months."

She swore me to secrecy, and I gave her my pledge. Only later did I reflect on the order of those three adjectives she had used to describe her new love. Powerful and young and rich. And the greatest of these is . . .

It was only a few days before she showed that she really did need to talk about Harry with somebody who knew him. She called me from South Carolina and asked me to come down to Hobcaw for a week.

I couldn't possibly ask for a vacation seven weeks after I'd started at *Time*, I said, but she had already taken care of mundane details like that. She had told Harry she had confided in me, that she *needed* to see me; he had agreed; all I had to do was go through the motions of saying I would be grateful for a little time off.

That was the first time I ever felt that an invitation from Clare had something of command performance about it, and, heaven knows, the vision of a week away from that empty apartment was temptation enough.

I did see Harry, each of us deadpan, with no mention of Clare or where I was going. I had to put it off until the weekend to attend the gala black-tie party, celebrating first night of *The March of Time*, but the very next day I took the train for South Carolina—and ran into one more Clare-typical episode, the most bizarre in this period of our concentrated seeing of each other. At the time it shocked me out of my wits, though I see it differently now.

I was met at the railroad station by Mr. Baruch's car and chauffeur, driven to the dock where Mr. Baruch's yacht awaited me, and when we arrived at Hobcaw, though it was still very early in the morning, there stood Bernard Baruch himself to welcome me. Clare was nowhere in sight.

There had been a large house party in progress for several days, with various senators, generals, writers, all well known, but the guests were leaving that morning or afternoon—including Mr. Baruch. Clare and I were to be alone.

Thayer and I had, on occasion, been weekend guests at various large estates where fine tennis courts, swimming pools, croquet courts, and a stable full of splendid horses all awaited your pleasure, but this stay of mine at Hobcaw enlightened me further about some of the habits and foibles of the very rich.

In my bathroom every single morning, I found untouched bars of imported French soap still in their handsome wrappers and sealed—the new bars I had used the day before had vanished. I soon wondered what they did with all that expensive day-old soap. A new fire was laid in the fireplace every morning; my riding clothes and boots were brought back, the boots polished, the riding habit newly pressed; the underwear and evening dress I had worn the day before were collected while I was having my breakfast from a tray in bed. More impressive to me than any of this was the fact that in the bathroom exactly five sheets of toilet paper had been removed from the roll and then placed back ready to be plucked—presumably to save me the effort of yanking off the sheets myself.

I never saw Clare until we met for lunch. She was writing a play; I think the title was to be *Napoleon Slept Here*. (This was before her first smash hit, *The Women*.) We would part again after lunch, and she would go back to her play. I was also trying to write one, about newspaper reporters; mine was to be called *Thirty-Thirty*, because 30, or XXX, was the journalist's sign of the end of a story.

Then we would meet at five, dressed for a ride, our horses brought to us by grooms. She, I was sure, had had a productive afternoon—she looked happy and satisfied. I had spent most of the time weeping over my lost marriage, doing half a scene, trying to partake of my one anodyne, writing.

Each evening we dressed for dinner, the two of us, and then Clare would read me what she had written that day. I don't remember much of its plot, but I know that lines were witty, acidulous, and that many of them made me laugh. Then we would part and go to our firelit rooms—she to the happiness of new love and waiting for marriage and I to my nightly struggle for sleep.

One evening, just after dinner, we were in the living room, and Clare was talking about Harry and their plans. I was standing near the mantel, I remember, one arm propped up on the corner of it. Clare was telling me about some letters she had just received from Harry—she never read any of his letters aloud, but she would paraphrase and tell me bits that amused her and things she had written to him.

Quite suddenly, she said, "Do something for me, will you?"

"What? If I can."

She was looking at me speculatively.

"Take your dress off, Laura."

"My dress off?"

"Off." She made a sweeping gesture, indicating something tossed away. She was smiling. Nothing about her voice or expression had the slightest hint of sexual interest—the notion never even entered my head. She was up to something mysterious, and I couldn't imagine what, but it was instantly clear that sex or attraction had nothing whatever to do with it.

"Come on," she urged. "I'll say why in a minute."

I shrugged and dropped my dress to the floor. I wore no bra and stood there in my brief underpants, my dress making a silken circle around my ankles. I was still near the fireplace.

Clare was gazing at me, at my breasts. She cocked her head to one side and started for a moment. Then she said, equally calmly, "Would you lie down on the sofa? On your back?"

By now I was thoroughly intrigued myself. What was this crazy woman up to? What was behind all this? She was scheming something; I could almost feel her mind planning ahead. I lay down on the sofa. For a moment she didn't move.

She knelt about three feet away from me, her eyes now on a level with my own. It became clear she was interested not in my entire body but only in my breasts.

"Put your arms over your head, would you, just for one more minute?"

That I did too. I had never been particularly proud of my breasts, though in that day, long before the fashion for large, opulent bosoms, I had never needed to worry about them either. But as she continued to kneel there on the carpet motionless, gazing as if at a portrait in a museum, Clare managed a look of pure approval.

"Thanks a million," she said then, and turned away. I arose, slid into my forsaken evening dress in one swift movement. "Okay, let's have it—what the hell is all this about?"

She laughed, a laugh of self-congratulation and, I think, gratitude for a favor well done by me. Then she laid her hands over her own breasts and made a slight grimace.

"After five pregnancies," she began slowly, "and four miscarriages . . ."

She didn't finish the sentence; she was shaking her head in a kind of dismay. I remembered what she had told me about her marriage to George Brokaw; I knew that only one of her pregnancies had ended in the birth of a child, her daughter, Annie. I understood what she meant by that look of dismay.

"You've never gone through a lot of miscarriages and pregnancies," she said then, "so I wanted to see what virgin breasts looked like. I'm going to get myself fixed—I want to be perfect for Harry."

I never knew whether she ever actually did it or not, but at the time this little directional performance of Clare's left me speechless, especially the cool collectedness with which she brought it all off, sans apology, sans self-justification, except for that telltale gesture and little speech at the end. I kept the whole episode a secret for years and years, from everybody except my analyst.

But nowadays—and indeed for the past two decades or more—with half the movie and TV stars and countless other well-heeled women having their faces lifted, their buttocks tightened, bosoms raised, fat hips surgically shaved off, it merely shows me that fifty years ago, in 1935, I was useful to Clare the Pioneer.

Remembering that night now, finding myself smiling over it, I kind of admire the nerve and resolution she had then, and discover myself half wishing that she had never gone into politics, because it really used to be such fun knowing her before she did.

HIS JEWISH QUESTION

by Arthur Miller

OCTOBER 2001

Note: This essay was written to coincide with the release of Focus, *director Neal Slavin's cinematic adaptation of Arthur Miller's 1945 novel of the same name.*

Nothing in history really repeats itself. Which is not to say that the same types of people don't re-appear from era to era. Over time the cast of characters, indeed, is fairly changeless, and some of the underlying forces as well: greed is forever, public hysteria and the denial of what is happening, demagoguery, senseless cruelties, heroic resistance to these villainies—the ingredients, to be sure, are finite. But the details of the story and their unpredictability make the old seem brand-new when it crops up again.

I wrote the novel *Focus* at a particular moment. I wanted to expose to the light what I intimately knew about a topic that was largely unreported. The book went into many editions, and continues to do so more than half a century later, but initially the standard publishers would not touch it. A new house, New York's Reynal & Hitchcock, and a young and adventurous editor, Frank Taylor, brought it out and held their breaths when it first appeared, waiting for the explosion.

Focus deals with what were all but forbidden subjects at the time: American anti-Semitism and the threat of violence underlying it. This was the early 40s. Nazi forces were driving their way through Europe as its great armies, those of France and England, were fleeing or under siege. Fascism—what Anne Morrow Lindbergh, wife of the heroic flier and herself a pilot and best-selling author, called an expression of "the wave of the future"—had the magic touch that caused all resistance to evaporate. Soon, even its arch-enemy, the Soviet Union, would move into its camp. And the foundation of Fascism was race hate.

If Fascism had a political program, let alone a solution to the worldwide Depression, which none of the democracies had been able to cure, it was to militarize society and put millions in uniform. Its one idea (if it can be called that)—its veritable banner, which it unfurled everywhere—declared that the Jews were the cause of every imaginable misfortune. This ancient, magical formula was not too hard for even an idiot to grasp, and so the Jewish people, as they had been innumerable times since Christanity began, were up for sacrifice, their destruction required before the promise of social progress for non-Jews could take place. In medieval times, when plague had struck down whole populations, it was the Jews who were blamed, even as they were infected and died like everyone else. In short, the strength of anti-Semitism was its illogic, its supernatural nature.

Like most others in New York back then, I had run into anti-Semitism as a rather normal feature of everyday life, uncomfortable to be sure, since I was Jewish, but not pointedly dangerous except for one incident in 1939, a world away from the city, in the backwoods of North Carolina. I was there recording the rich variety of Carolina speech patterns for the folklore division of the Library of Congress, a unit devoted to preserving and documenting the nation's music, mythology, speech, and many aspects of popular life going back to the country's beginnings. My driver and I were looking down through the windshield of our government delivery van from the edge of a deep marble quarry where, far below us, men were working. I wanted to record the speech of those men, if I could only locate the road down to them. I happened to turn my head and looked into the octagonal barrel of an enormous shotgun a couple of feet from my eyes. It was wavering because, as I now noticed, a worried woman, beside the fat, middle-aged gunman, was pulling on his arm, apparently to dissuade him from killing me. "Get out of here right now, you Jew son of a bitch!" he growled. My driver, Johnny Langeneger, bless him, put the van in reverse, and we did probably 30 miles an hour going backward along a narrow, wooded road.

It might be asked how this citizen knew I was Jewish. The door of the green van was emblazoned in gold lettering with the seal of the Library of Congress, Washington, D.C., and the gunman, no doubt, was among the not inconsiderable number of Americans who believed that Jews ran Washington, and, indeed, that Roosevelt's real name was Rosenfeld. If frequent photos showed the president entering or leaving an Episcopal church, they only proved once again how wily the Jews were in camouflaging themselves. Even his so-called polio was a fake; it was really syphilis which had crippled him, as it had so many other Jews, who were famously irrepressible sexually. Witness the blatant exploitation of sex by Hollywood moguls, and by Sigmund Freud, whose writings on "infantile sexuality" contended that everyone, not excluding babies and their mothers, had sexual feelings.

I had lived the usual New York life on the subways, on the streets, on the job. I had driven a truck and pushed hand trucks on Seventh Avenue. I usually swam in Coney Island and in the early 1940s had worked as a shipfitter's helper in the Brooklyn Navy Yard. (Among its 60,000 workers were members of every ethnic group in the area, probably more Italians than any other.) Having been immersed in the New York mind-set, I would finally give up trying to argue rationally about how selfishly antisocial Jews were, on the one hand, and, conversely, how they generously stuck together to help one another in a kind of plot to secure their survival, unlike others who, unable to compete, were jumping out of windows or dying of drink. The twists and turns of the anti-Semitic fantasy were limitless. For me, finally, the problem came down to having to prove that one was not really and truly a form of walking poison gas. Difficult when, for example, the great universities—Yale, Harvard, and Columbia among them—were openly enforcing a *numerus clausus* (fixed ceiling) on Jewish admissions. One knew bright medical students who had had to go to Scotland to study, American medical schools being closed to them as Jews.

Things were beginning to get scary in the late 30s when one of the most popular radio shows in America was that of a Father Charles Coughlin, a Royal Oak, Michigan, priest. Every Sunday afternoon Coughlin preached the evils of the Jews and even used the texts, uncredited, of speeches by Joseph Goebbels, the Nazi propaganda minister, denouncing the Jews.

I had had to develop a hard shell to escape a certain kind of paranoid despair in the atmosphere of 30s New York. I had once answered a "Boy Wanted" ad in the Sunday *New York Times* for a shipping clerk's job at Chaddick-Delamater, a large auto-parts warehouse located where Lincoln Center now stands, which at that time was an industrial slum neighborhood. I was encouraged to apply not only by the $15-a-week salary, three times more than the usual "Boy" job paid, but also because unlike most other ads this one did not specify "Christian" or "Gentile firm," or simply "Chr." or "Cath." or "Prot."

Bright and early on Monday morning, I was interviewed by the manager of Chaddick-Delamater. I had often picked up parts there for Shapse Auto Supply in Long Island City, whose owner, my best friend's father, later had to let me go when business dwindled to nearly zero. I called Mr. Shapse to happily report that I had just been interviewed for this job at Chaddick's, and in a peculiarly somber tone he asked me to keep him informed about my progress. When no word came next day from Chaddick's manager, I called to tell Mr. Shapse, who said he would inquire; Chaddick's had never hired a Jew, he said, even though most of their local parts dealers were Jewish.

Next day, magically, I was called by the manager, who said I was hired. I worked there for a couple of years until I'd saved enough to go to college. Most of the workers in the place were Irish, with a few of German background, all of them Catholic. I can't say that I became close friends with them—their clan was too tight—but neither was there any open hostility. Dora Haggerty, one of the women in the front office, told me she admired Jews because they made good husbands, which she hoped her young nephew Carl would turn out to be. She was very sweet, very thin, and very unmarried, but I was grateful for her admiration.

I would emphasize that none of this was alarming in itself. Indeed, these impediments, if they can be called that, were more like challenges to be overcome than dire warnings of danger that might overwhelm. Jews expected obstacles and they were not alone in this regard. The Irish, well into the early decades of the century, had had a tough time entering any but the lowest levels of America's business and political circles; unlike the Jewish deity, their God was the same one the Protestant majority worshiped. As for black people at the time, most had simply been locked out, at the edges of the white working world.

In my two years on that job I kept trying to imagine myself as really no different than the others, but some membrane persisted between them and me. It was a mystery I could not solve. Most of the time, I thought of other things, such as how to get through the day cooped up in that warehouse, especially in good weather.

By 1938, the year I got my college degree, my habitual optimism (born, I suppose, of an awareness of an ability to write plays) was shaken by the news of Kristallnacht, the Nazis' Night of Broken Glass across Germany, Austria, and Sudetenland. Uniformed Germans, under government sponsorship, had burned synagogues, beaten and humiliated Jews, and this obviously signaled worse to come. Notwithstanding Hitler's having taken power several years before, my inherited view of Germany as a civilized nation had persisted, due, no doubt, to my grandfather's Eastern European respect for Germans in contrast to Russians and Poles. That a nation of such high cultural repute could embrace this kind of savagery opened up new and bloody prospects before me, and not in Germany but here in America. Now the everyday slights and threats against me—and against Jews in general—began to swell as portents.

Focus was possibly the first American novel about anti-Semitism, although *Gentleman's Agreement* (Laura Hobson's book on the same theme, which was later adapted for the screen by director Elia Kazan, winning best-picture honors in 1947) may have beaten it out by a few weeks. If *Focus* had grown out of my general experiences in Brooklyn and Manhattan, one incident in particular may have forced me to try to write it.

I had an acquaintance who actually owned a car, an unusual thing among my set, especially a car that ran. He had a steady girlfriend as well, also unusual, and they invited me for a drive in the country one Sunday afternoon. We crossed the then new George Washington Bridge and drove into New Jersey, and, as unshockable as I was at that time, I felt a blow inside my head on seeing a small sign at the driveway entrance to a country hotel that read: RESTRICTED CLIENTELE, CHRISTIAN. Personally, I wouldn't have even dreamed of renting a hotel room, but the idea of being forbidden to so much as enter the place somehow exploded something in my brain. It was like being shot at. The hatred in that little sign was indigestible. I suppose this indisposition was helped along by the fact that I was not always taken for a Jew. In short, there was an absurdity here that, like the pearl-seeding grain of sand in an oyster, started to accrete scenes around it, and the book began to form.

Could anything like this situation ever develop again in America? Certainly not in the same way, when the world today is so vastly different. Or is it? Not when one looks at ethnic cleansing in the Balkans, murderous hatred of gays in some American places, of blacks in others, and the undertow of persistent racist feelings in so many minds here and in other parts of the world. But, at the same time, more people than ever seem to be aware of the dissolution of civil societies that anti-Semitism has led to in Europe and elsewhere. Still, the world has been at odds with how to deal with the Jews for two millennia now, and one has to doubt that the dilemma has been resolved. In Europe one hears of a recrudescence of anti-Jewish feeling set off by the Israeli-Palestinian conflict, but the depth of this sentiment has yet to be measured. I may doubt or even dismiss the possibility of a repeat of the past, but I have to recognize that the answer is objectively unknowable. In the meantime, *Focus*—the story of two unlikely lovers caught in the swirling tides of that era, written not after the fact but in the midst of the period's turmoil—is the way we were, difficult to understand as some of our behavior may now appear. It is the raw evidence, unalloyed by any later wisdom or healing, at least as one young man saw it over half a century ago.

DARKNE// VI/IBLE

···

by William Styron

DECEMBER 1989

> For the thing which
> I greatly feared is come upon me,
> and that which I was afraid of
> Is come into me.
> I was not in safety, neither
> had I rest, neither was I quiet;
> Yet trouble came.
>   —JOB

To many of us who knew Abbie Hoffman even slightly, as I did, his death in the spring of 1989 was a sorrowful happening. Just past the age of fifty, he had been too young and apparently too vital for such an ending; a feeling of chagrin and dreadfulness attends the news of nearly anyone's suicide, and Abbie's death seemed for me especially cruel. I had first met him during the wild days and nights of the 1968 Democratic convention in Chicago, where I had gone to write a piece for *The New York Review of Books*, and I later was one of those who testified in behalf of him and his fellow defendants at the trial, also in Chicago, in 1970. Amid the pious follies and morbid perversions of American life, his antic style was exhilarating, and it was hard not to admire the hell-raising and the brio, the anarchic individualism. I wish I had seen more of him in recent years; his sudden death left me with a particular emptiness, as suicides usually do to everyone. But the event was given a further dimension of poignancy by what one must begin to regard as a predictable reaction from many: the denial, the refusal to accept the fact of the suicide itself, as if the voluntary act—as opposed to an accident, or death from natural causes—were tinged with a delinquency that somehow lessened the man and his character.

Abbie's brother appeared on television, grief-ravaged and distraught; one could not help feeling compassion as he sought to deflect the idea of suicide, insisting that Abbie, after all, had always been careless with pills and would never have left his family bereft. However, the coroner confirmed that Hoffman had taken the equivalent of 150 phenobarbitals. It's quite natural that the people closest to suicide victims so frequently and feverishly hasten to disclaim the truth; the sense of implication, of personal guilt—the idea that one might have prevented the act if one had taken certain precautions, had somehow behaved differently—is perhaps inevitable. Even so, the sufferer—whether he has actually killed himself or attempted to do so, or merely expressed threats—is often, through denial on the part of others, unjustly made to appear a wrongdoer.

A similar case is that of Randall Jarrell—one of the fine poets and critics of his generation—who one night in 1965, near Chapel Hill, North Carolina, was struck by a car and killed. Jarrell's presence on that particular stretch of road, at an odd hour of the evening, was puzzling, and since some of the indications were that he had deliberately let the car strike him, the early conclusion was that his death was suicide. *Newsweek*, among other publications, said as much, but Jarrell's widow protested in a letter to that magazine; there was a hue and cry from many of his friends and supporters, and a coroner's jury eventually ruled the death to be accidental. Jarrell had been suffering from extreme depression and had been hospitalized; only a few months before his misadventure on the highway and while in the hospital, he had slashed his wrists.

Anyone who is acquainted with some of the jagged contours of Jarrell's life— including his violent fluctuations of mood, his fits of black despondency—and who, in addition, has acquired a basic knowledge of the danger signals of depression would seriously question the verdict of the coroner's jury. But the stigma of self-inflicted death is for some people a hateful blot that demands erasure at all costs. (More than two decades after his death, in the summer-1986 issue of *The American Scholar*, a onetime student of Jarrell's reviewing a collection of the poet's letters, made the review less a literary or biographical appraisal than an occasion for continuing to try to exorcise the vile phantom of suicide.)

Randall Jarrell almost certainly killed himself. He did so not because he was a coward, nor out of any moral feebleness, but because he was afflicted with a depression that was so devastating that he could no longer endure the pain of it.

This general unawareness of what depression is really like was apparent most recently in the matter of Primo Levi, the remarkable Italian writer and survivor of Auschwitz who, at the age of sixty-seven, hurled himself down a stairwell in Turin in 1987 [*the subject of James Atlas's essay on page 173*]. Since I had survived a near-fatal siege of depression myself a year or so earlier, I had been more than ordinarily interested in Levi's death, and so, late last year, when I read an account in *The New York Times* about a symposium on the writer and his work held at New York University, I was fascinated but, finally, appalled. For, according to the article, many of the participants, worldly writers and scholars, seemed mystified by Levi's suicide, mystified and disappointed. It was as if this man whom they had all so greatly admired, and who had endured so much at the hands of the

Nazis—a man of exemplary resilience and courage—had by his suicide demonstrated a frailty, a crumbling of character they were loath to accept. In the face of a terrible absolute—self-destruction—their reaction was helplessness and (the reader could not avoid it) a touch of shame.

My annoyance over all this was so intense that I was prompted to write a short piece for the op-ed page of the *Times*. The argument I put forth was fairly straightforward: the pain of severe depression is quite unimaginable to those who have not suffered it, and it kills in many instances because its anguish can no longer be borne. The prevention of many suicides will continue to be hindered until there is a general awareness of the nature of this pain. Through the healing process of time—and through medical intervention or hospitalization in many cases—most people survive depression, which may be its only blessing; but to the tragic legion who are compelled to destroy themselves there should be no more reproof attached than to the victims of terminal cancer.

I had set down my thoughts in this *Times* piece rather hurriedly and spontaneously, but the response was equally spontaneous—and enormous. It had taken, I speculated, no particular originality or boldness on my part to speak out frankly about suicide, and the impulse toward it, but I had apparently underestimated the number of people for whom the subject had been taboo, a matter of secrecy and shame. The overwhelming reaction made me feel that inadvertently I had helped unlock a closet from which many souls were eager to come out and proclaim that they, too, had experienced the feelings I had described. It is the only time in my life I have felt it worthwhile to have invaded my own privacy, and to make that privacy public. And I thought that, given such momentum, it might be useful to try to briefly chronicle some of my own experiences with depression, and in the process perhaps establish a frame of reference out of which one or more valuable conclusions might be drawn. Such conclusions, it has to be emphasized, must still be based on the events that happened to one man. In setting these reflections down I don't intend my ordeal to stand as a representation of what happens, or might happen, to others. Although as an illness depression manifests certain unvarying characteristics, it also allows for many idiosyncrasies; I've been amazed at some of the freakish phenomena—not reported by other patients—that it has wrought amid the twistings of my mind's labyrinth.

Depression afflicts millions directly, and many millions more who are relatives or friends of victims. As assertively democratic as a Norman Rockwell poster, it strikes indiscriminately at all ages, races, creeds, and classes, though women are at considerably higher risk than men. The occupational list (dressmakers, barge captains, sushi chefs, Cabinet members) of its patients is too long and tedious; it is enough to say that very few people escape being a potential victim of the disease, at least in its milder form. Despite depression's eclectic reach, it has been demonstrated with fair convincingness that artistic types (especially poets) are particularly vulnerable to the disorder—which in its graver, clinical manifestation takes upward of 20 percent of its victims by way of suicide. Just a few of these fallen artists, all modern, make up a sad but scintillant roll call: Hart Crane, Vincent Van Gogh, Virginia Woolf, Arshile Gorky, Cesare Pavese, Romain Gary, Sylvia Plath, Mark Rothko, John Berryman, Jack London, Ernest Hemingway, Diane Arbus, Tadeusz Borowski, Paul Celan, Anne Sexton, Sergei Esenin, Vladimir Mayakovsky—the list goes on. (The Russian poet Mayakovsky was harshly critical of his great contemporary Esenin's suicide a few years before, which should stand as a caveat for all who are judgmental about self-destruction.) When one thinks of these doomed and splendidly creative men and women, one is drawn to contemplate their childhoods, where, to the best of anyone's knowledge, the seeds of the illness take strong root; could any of them have had a hint, then, of the psyche's perishability, its exquisite fragility? And why were they destroyed, while others—similarly stricken—struggled through?

When I was first aware that I had been laid low by the disease, I felt a need, among other things, to register a strong protest against the word "depression." Depression, most people know, used to be termed melancholia, a word which appears in English as early as the year 1303 and crops up more than once in Chaucer, who in his usage seemed to be aware of its pathological nuances. "Melancholia" would still appear to be a far more apt and evocative word for the blacker forms of the disorder, but it was usurped by a noun with a bland tonality and lacking any magisterial presence, used indifferently to describe an economic decline or a rut in the ground, a true wimp of a word for such a major illness. It may be that the scientist generally held responsible for its currency in modern times, a Johns Hopkins Medical School faculty member justly venerated—the Swiss-born psychiatrist Adolf Meyer—had a tin ear for the finer rhythms of English and therefore was unaware of the semantical damage he had inflicted by offering "depression" as a descriptive noun for such a dreadful and raging disease; nonetheless, for over seventy-five years the word has slithered innocuously through the language like a slug, leaving little trace of its intrinsic malevolence and preventing, by its very insipidity, a general awareness of the horrible intensity of the disease when out of control.

As one who has suffered from the malady *in extremis* yet returned to tell the tale, I would lobby for a truly arresting designation. "Brainstorm," for instance, has unfortunately been pre-empted to describe, somewhat jocularly, intellectual inspiration. But something along these lines is needed. Told that someone's mood disorder had evolved into a storm—a veritable howling tempest in the brain, which is indeed what a clinical depression resembles like nothing else— even the uninformed layman might display sympathy rather than the standard reaction that "depression" evokes, something akin to "So what?" Or "You'll pull out of it." Or "We all have bad days." The phrase "nervous breakdown" seems to be on its way out, certainly deservedly so, owing to its insinuation of a vague spinelessness, but we still seem destined to be saddled with "depression" until a better, sturdier name is created.

The depression that engulfed me was not of the manic type—the one accompanied by euphoric highs—which would have most probably presented itself earlier in my life. I was sixty when the illness struck for the first time, in the "unipolar" form, which leads straight down. I shall never learn what "caused" my depression, as no one will ever learn about their own. To be able to do so will likely forever prove to be an impossibility, so complex are the intermingled factors of abnormal chemistry, behavior, and genetics. Plainly, multiple components are involved—perhaps three or four, most probably more, in fathomless permutations. That is why the greatest fallacy about suicide lies in the belief that there is a single immediate answer—or perhaps combined answers—as to why the deed was done.

The inevitable question, "Why did he (or she) do it?" usually leads to odd speculations, for the most part fallacies themselves. Reasons were quickly advanced for Abbie Hoffman's death: his reaction to an auto accident he had suffered, the failure of his most recent book, his mother's serious illness. With Randall Jarrell it was a declining career, cruelly epitomized by a vicious book review and his consequent anguish. Primo Levi, it was rumored, had been burdened by caring for his paralytic mother, which was more onerous to his spirit than even his experience at Auschwitz. Any one of these factors may have lodged like a thorn in the sides of the three men, and been a torment. Such aggravations may be crucial and cannot be ignored. But most people quietly endure the equivalent of injuries, declining careers, nasty book reviews, family illnesses. A vast majority of the survivors of Auschwitz have borne up fairly well. Bloody and bowed by the outrages of life, most human beings still stagger on down the road, unscathed by real depression. To discover why some people plunge into the downward spiral of depression, one must search beyond the manifest crisis—and then still fail to come up with anything beyond wise conjecture.

The storm which swept me into a hospital in December of 1985 began as a cloud no bigger than a wine goblet the previous June. And the cloud—the manifest crisis—involved alcohol, a substance I had been abusing for forty years. Like a great many American writers, whose sometimes lethal addiction to alcohol has become so legendary as to provide in itself a stream of studies and books, I used alcohol as the magical conduit to fantasy and euphoria, and to the enhancement of the imagination. There is no need to either rue or apologize for my use of this soothing, often sublime agent which had contributed greatly to my writing; although I never set down a line while under its influence, I used it otherwise—often in conjunction with music—as a means to let my mind conceive visions that the unaltered, sober brain has no access to. Alcohol was an invaluable senior partner of my intellect, besides being a friend whose ministrations I sought daily—sought also, I now see, as a means to calm the anxiety and incipient dread that I had hidden away for so long somewhere in the dungeons of my spirit.

The trouble was, at the beginning of this particular summer, that I was betrayed. It struck me quite suddenly, almost overnight: I could no longer drink. It was as if my body had risen up in protest, along with my mind, and had conspired to reject this daily mood bath which it had so long welcomed and, who knows, perhaps even come to need. Many drinkers have experienced this intolerance as they have grown older. I suspect that the crisis was at least partly metabolic—the liver rebelling, as if to say, "No more, no more"—but at any rate I discovered that alcohol in minuscule amounts, even a mouthful of wine, caused me nausea, a desperate and unpleasant wooziness, a sinking sensation, and ultimately a distinct revulsion. The comforting friend had abandoned me not gradually and reluctantly, as a true friend might do, but like a shot—and I was left high and certainly dry, and unhelmed.

Neither by will nor by choice had I become an abstainer; the situation was puzzling to me, but it was also traumatic, and I date the onset of my depressive mood from the beginning of this deprivation. Logically, one would be overjoyed that the body had so summarily dismissed a substance that was undermining its health; it was as if my system had generated a form of Antabuse which should have allowed me to happily go my way, satisfied that a trick of nature had shut me off from a harmful dependence. But, instead, I began to experience a vaguely troubling malaise, a sense of something having gone cockeyed and awry in the domestic universe I'd dwelt in so long, so comfortably. While depression is by no means unknown when people stop drinking, it is usually on a scale that is not menacing. But it should be kept in mind how idiosyncratic the faces of depression can be.

It was not really alarming at first, since the change was subtle, but I did notice that my surroundings took on a different tone at certain times: the shadows of nightfall seemed more somber, my mornings were less buoyant, walks in the woods became less zestful, and there was a moment during my working hours in the late afternoon when a kind of panic and anxiety overtook me, just for a few minutes, accompanied by a visceral queasiness—such a seizure was at least slightly alarming, after all. As I set down these recollections, I realize that it should have been plain to me that I was already in the grip of the beginning of a mood disorder, but I was ignorant of such a condition at that time.

When I reflected on this curious alteration of my consciousness—and I was baffled enough from time to time to do so—I assumed that it all had to do somehow with my enforced withdrawal from alcohol. And, of course, to a certain extent this was true. But it is my conviction now that alcohol played a perverse trick on me when we said farewell to each other: although, as everyone should know, it is a major depressant, it had never truly depressed me during my drinking career, acting instead as a shield against anxiety. Suddenly vanished, the great ally which for so long had kept my demons at bay was no longer there to prevent those demons from beginning to swarm through the subconscious, and I was emotionally naked, vulnerable as I had never been before. Doubtless, depression had hovered near me for years, waiting to swoop down. Now I was in the first stage—premonitory, like a flicker of sheet lightning barely perceived—of depression's black tempest.

I was on Martha's Vineyard, where I've spent a good part of the year since the 1960s, during that exceptionally beautiful summer. But I had begun to respond indifferently to the island's pleasures. I felt a kind of numbness, an enervation, but more particularly an odd fragility—as if my body had actually become frail, hypersensitive, and somehow disjointed and clumsy, lacking normal coordination. And soon I was in the throes of a pervasive hypochondria. Nothing felt quite right with my corporeal self; there were twitches and pains, sometimes intermittent, often seemingly constant, that seemed to presage all sorts of dire infirmities. (Given these signs, one can understand how, as far back as the seventeenth century—in the notes of contemporary physicians, and in the perceptions of John Dryden and others—a connection is made between melancholia and hypochondria; the words are often interchangeable, and were so used until the nineteenth century, by writers as various as Sir Walter Scott and the Brontës, who also linked melancholy with a preoccupation with bodily ills.) It is easy to see how this condition is part of the psyche's apparatus of defense: unwilling to accept its own gathering deterioration, the mind announces to its indwelling consciousness that it is the body with its perhaps correctable defects—not the precious and irreplaceable mind—that is going haywire.

In my case, the overall effect was immensely disturbing, augmenting the anxiety that was by now never quite absent from my waking hours and fueling still another strange behavior pattern—a fidgety restlessness that kept me on the move, somewhat to the perplexity of my family and friends. Once, in late summer, on an airplane trip to New York, I made the reckless mistake of downing a scotch and soda—my first alcohol in months—which promptly sent me into a tailspin, causing me such a horrified sense of disease and interior doom that the very next day I rushed to a Manhattan internist, who inaugurated a long series of tests. Normally, I would have been satisfied, indeed elated, when, after three weeks of high-tech and extremely expensive evaluation, the doctor pronounced me totally fit; and I *was* happy, for a day or two, until there once again began the rhythmic daily erosion of my mood—anxiety, agitation, unfocused dread.

By now I had moved back to my house in Connecticut. It was October, and one of the unforgettable features of this stage of my disorder was the way in which my old farmhouse, my beloved home for thirty years, took on for me—especially in the late afternoon, when my spirits regularly sank to their nadir—an almost palpable quality of ominousness. The fading evening light—akin to that famous "slant of light" of Emily Dickinson's, which spoke to her of death, of chill extinction—had none of its familiar autumnal loveliness, but ensnared me in a suffocating gloom. I wondered how this friendly place, teeming with such memories of (again in her rhyme) "Lads and Girls," of "laughter and ability and Sighing, / And Frocks and Curls," could almost perceptibly seem so hostile and forbidding. Physically, I was not alone. My wife, Rose, was always present and listened with unflagging patience to my complaints. But I felt an immense and aching solitude. I could no longer concentrate during those afternoon hours, which for years had been my working time, and the act of writing itself, becoming more and more difficult and exhausting, stalled, then finally ceased.

There were also dreadful, pouncing seizures of anxiety. One bright day on a walk through the woods with my dog I heard a flock of Canada geese honking high above trees ablaze with foliage; ordinarily a sight and sound that would have exhilarated me, the flight of birds caused me to stop, riveted with fear, and I stood stranded there, helpless, shivering, aware for the first time that I had been stricken by no mere pangs of withdrawal but by a serious illness whose name and actuality I was able, for the first time, to acknowledge. Going home, I couldn't rid my mind of the line of Baudelaire's, dredged up from the distant past, that for several days had been skittering around at the edge of my consciousness: "I have felt the wind of the wing of madness."

Our perhaps understandable modern need to dull the sawtooth edges of so many of the afflictions we are heir to has led us to banish the harsh old-fashioned words: madhouse, asylum, insanity, melancholia, lunatic, madness. But never let it be doubted that depression, in its extreme form, is madness. The madness results from an aberrant biochemical process. It has been established with reasonable certainty (after strong resistance from many psychiatrists, and not all that long ago) that such madness is chemically induced amid the neurotransmitters of the brain, probably as the result of systemic stress, which for unknown reasons causes a depletion of the chemicals norepinephrine and serotonin, and the increase of a hormone, cortisol. With all of this upheaval in the brain tissues, the alternate drenching and deprivation, it is no wonder that the mind begins to feel aggrieved, stricken, and the muddied thought processes register the distress of an organ in convulsion. Sometimes, though not very often, such a disturbed mind will turn to violent thoughts regarding others. But with their minds turned agonizingly inward, people with depression are usually dangerous only to themselves. The madness of depression is, generally speaking, the antithesis of violence.

It is a storm indeed, but a storm of murk. Soon evident are the slowed-down responses, near paralysis, psychic energy throttled back close to zero. Ultimately, the body is affected and feels sapped, drained.

That fall, as the disorder gradually took full possession of my system, I began to conceive that my mind itself was like one of those outmoded small-town telephone exchanges, being gradually inundated by floodwaters: one by one, the normal circuits began to drown, causing some of the functions of the body and nearly all of those of instinct and intellect to slowly disconnect.

There is a well-known checklist of some of these functions and their failures. Mine conked out fairly close to schedule, many of them following the pattern of depressive seizures. I particularly remember the lamentable near disappearance of my voice. It underwent a strange transformation, becoming at times quite faint, wheezy, and spasmodic—a friend observed later that it was the voice of a ninety-year-old. The libido also made an early exit, as it does in most major illnesses—it is the superfluous need of a body in beleaguered emergency. Many people lose all appetite; mine was relatively normal, but I found myself eating only for subsistence: food, like everything else within the scope of sensation, was utterly without savor. Most distressing of all the instinctual disruptions was that of sleep, along with a complete absence of dreams.

Exhaustion combined with sleeplessness is a rare torture. The two or three hours of sleep I was able to get at night were always at the behest of the minor tranquilizer Halcion—a matter which deserves particular notice. For some time now many experts in psychopharmacology have warned that the benzodiazepine family of tranquilizers, of which Halcion is one (Valium and Ativan are others), is capable of depressing mood and even precipitating a major depression. Over two years before my siege, an insouciant doctor had prescribed Ativan as a bedtime aid, telling me airily that I could take it as casually as aspirin. The *Physicians' Desk Reference* manual, the pharmacological bible, reveals that the medicine I had been ingesting was (a) three times the normally prescribed strength, (b) not advisable as a medication for more than a month or so, and (c) to be used with special caution by people of my age. At the time of which I am speaking, I had become addicted to Halcion as a sleeping aid, and was consuming large doses. It seems reasonable to think that this was still another contributory factor to the trouble that had come upon me. Certainly, it should be a caution to others.

At any rate, my few hours of sleep were usually terminated at three or four in the morning, when I stared up into yawning darkness, wondering and writhing at the devastation taking place in my mind, and awaiting the dawn, which usually permitted me a feverish, dreamless nap. I'm fairly certain that it was during one of these insomniac trances that there came over me the knowledge—a weird and shocking revelation, like that of some long-beshrouded metaphysical truth—that this condition would cost me my life if it continued on such a course.

What I had begun to discover is that, mysteriously and in ways that are totally remote from normal experience, the gray drizzle of horror induced by depression takes on the quality of physical pain. But it is not an immediately identifiable pain, like that of a broken limb. It may be more accurate to say that despair, owing to some evil trick played upon the sick brain by the inhabiting psyche, comes to resemble the diabolical discomfort of being imprisoned in a fiercely overheated room. And because no breeze stirs this caldron, because there is no escape from this smothering confinement, it is entirely natural that the victim begins to think ceaselessly of oblivion.

One of the memorable moments in *Madame Bovary* is the scene where the heroine seeks help from the village priest. Guilt-ridden, distraught, miserably depressed, the adulterous Emma—heading toward eventual suicide—stumblingly tries to prod the abbé into helping her find a way out of her misery. But the priest, a simple soul and none too bright, can only pluck at his stained cassock, distractedly shout at his acolytes, and offer Christian platitudes. Emma goes on her quietly frantic way, beyond comfort of God or man.

I felt a bit like Emma Bovary in my relationship with the psychiatrist I shall call Dr. Gold, whom I began to visit as October became November, when the despair had commenced its merciless daily drumming. I had never before consulted a mental therapist for anything, and I felt awkward, also a bit defensive; my pain had become so intense that I considered it quite improbable that conversation with another mortal, even one with professional expertise in mood disorders, could alleviate the distress. Madame Bovary went to the priest with the same hesitant doubt. Yet our society is so structured that Dr. Gold, or someone like him, is the authority to whom one is forced to turn in one's crisis, and it is not entirely a bad idea, since Dr. Gold—Yale-trained, highly qualified—at least provides a focal point toward which one can direct one's dying energies, offers consolation if not much hope, and becomes a receptacle for one's outpouring of woes during fifty minutes that also provide relief for one's wife. Still, while I would never question the potential efficacy of psychotherapy in the beginning manifestations or milder forms of the illness—or possibly even in the aftermath of a serious onslaught—its usefulness at the advanced stage I was in has to be virtually nil. My more specific purpose in consulting Dr. Gold was to obtain help through pharmacology—though this too was, alas, a chimera for a bottomed-out victim such as I had become.

He asked me if I was suicidal, and I reluctantly told him yes. I did not particularize—since there seemed no need to—did not tell him that in truth many of the artifacts of my house had become potential devices for my own destruction: the attic rafters (and an outside maple or two) a means to hang myself, the garage a place to inhale carbon monoxide, the bathtub a vessel to receive the flow from my opened arteries. The kitchen knives in their drawers had but one purpose for me. Death by heart attack seemed particularly inviting, absolving me as it would of active responsibility, and I had toyed with the idea of self-induced pneumonia—a long, frigid, shirtsleeved hike through the rainy woods. Nor had I overlooked an ostensible accident, à la Randall Jarrell, by walking in front of a truck on the highway nearby. These thoughts may seem outlandishly macabre—a strained joke—but they are genuine. They are doubtless especially repugnant to healthy Americans, with their faith in self-improvement. Yet in truth such hideous fantasies, which cause well people to shudder, are to the deeply depressed mind what lascivious daydreams are to persons of robust sexuality. Dr. Gold and I began to chat twice weekly, but there was little I could tell him except to try, vainly, to describe my desolation.

Nor could he say much of value to me. His platitudes were not Christian but, almost as ineffective, dicta drawn straight from the pages of *The Diagnostic and Statistic Manual of the American Psychiatric Association* (much of which I'd already read), and the solace he offered me was an antidepressant medication called Ludiomil. The pill made me edgy, disagreeably hyperactive, and when the dosage was increased after ten days, it blocked my bladder for hours one night. Upon informing Dr. Gold of this problem, I was told that ten more days must pass for the drug to clear my system before starting anew with a different pill. Ten days to one stretched on such a torture rack is like ten centuries—and this does not begin to take into account the fact that when a new pill is inaugurated several weeks must pass before it becomes effective, a development which is far from guaranteed in any case.

This brings up the matter of medication in general. Psychiatry must be given due credit for its continuing struggle to treat depression pharmacologically. The use of lithium to stabilize moods in manic-depression is a great medical achievement; the same drug is also being employed effectively as a preventive in many instances of unipolar depression. There can be no doubt that in many moderate cases and some chronic forms of the disease (the so-called endogenous depressions) medications have proved invaluable, often altering the course of a serious disturbance dramatically. But until that day when a swiftly acting agent is developed, one's faith in a pharmacological cure for major depression must remain provisional. The failure of these pills to act positively and quickly—a defect which is now the general case—is somewhat analogous to the failure of nearly all drugs to stem massive bacterial infections in the years before antibiotics became a specific remedy. And it can be just as dangerous.

So I found little of worth to anticipate in my consultations with Dr. Gold. On my visits he and I continued to exchange platitudes, mine haltingly spoken now—since my speech, emulating my way of walking, had slowed to the vocal equivalent of a shuffle—and I'm sure as tiresome as his.

Despite the still-faltering methods of treatment, psychiatry has, on an analytical and philosophical level, contributed much to an understanding of the origins of depression. Much obviously remains to be learned (and a great deal will doubtless continue to be a mystery, owing to the disease's idiopathic nature, its constant interchangeability of factors), but certainly one psychological element has been established beyond reasonable doubt, and that is the concept of loss. Loss in all of its manifestations is the touchstone of depression—in the progress of the disease and, most likely, in its origin. At a later date I would gradually be persuaded that a devastating loss in childhood figured as a probable genesis of my own disorder; meanwhile, as I monitored my retrograde condition, I felt loss at every hand. The loss of self-esteem is a celebrated symptom, and my own sense of self had all but disappeared, along with any self-reliance. This loss can quickly degenerate into dependence, and from dependence into infantile dread. One dreads the loss of all things, all people close and dear.

Of the images of myself recollected from that time the most bizarre, and discomfiting, remains the one of me, age four and a half, tagging through a market after my long-suffering wife; not for an instant could I let out of my sight the endlessly patient soul who had become nanny, mommy, comforter, priestess, and, most important, confidante—a counselor of rocklike centrality to my existence whose wisdom far exceeded that of Dr. Gold. I would hazard the opinion that many disastrous sequels to depression might be averted if the victims received support like that which she gave me. But meanwhile my losses mounted and proliferated. There is no doubt that as one nears the penultimate depths of depression—which is to say just before the stage when one begins to act out one's suicide instead of being a mere contemplator of it—the acute sense of loss is connected with a knowledge of life slipping away at accelerated speed. One develops fierce attachments. Ludicrous things—my reading glasses, a handkerchief, a certain writing instrument—became the objects of my demented possessiveness. Each momentary misplacement filled me with a frenzied dismay, each item being the tactile reminder of a world soon to be obliterated.

November wore on, bleak, raw, and chill. One Sunday a photographer and his assistants came to take pictures for an article to be published in a national magazine. Of the session I can recall little except the first snowflakes of winter dotting the air outside. I thought I obeyed the photographer's request to smile often. A day or two later the magazine's editor telephoned my wife, asking if I would submit to another session. The reason he advanced was that the pictures of me, even the ones with smiles, were "too full of anguish."

I had now reached that phase of the disorder where all sense of hope had vanished, along with the idea of a futurity; my brain, in thrall to its outlaw hormones, had become less an organ of thought than an instrument registering, minute by minute, varying degrees of its own suffering. Mornings were bad enough, as I wandered about lethargic following my synthetic sleep, but afternoons were the worst, beginning at about three o'clock, when I'd feel the horror, like some poisonous fogbank, roll in upon my mind, forcing me into bed. There I would lie as long as six hours, stuporous and virtually paralyzed, gazing at the ceiling and waiting for that moment of evening when, mysteriously, the crucifixion would ease up just enough to allow me to force down some food and then, like an automaton, seek an hour or two of sleep again. Why wasn't I in a hospital? The answer is forthcoming.

For years I had kept a notebook—not strictly a diary, its entries were erratic and haphazardly written—whose contents I would not have particularly liked to be scrutinized by eyes other than my own. I had hidden it well out of sight in my house. I imply no scandalousness; the observations were far less raunchy, or wicked, or self-revealing, than my desire to keep the notebook private might indicate. Nonetheless, the small volume was one that I fully intended to make use of professionally and then destroy before the distant day when the specter of the nursing home came too near. So as my illness worsened I rather queasily realized that if I once decided to get rid of the notebook that moment would necessarily coincide with my decision to put an end to myself. And one evening during early December this moment came.

That afternoon I had been driven (I could no longer drive) to Dr. Gold's office, where he announced that he had decided to place me on the antidepressant Nardil, an older medication which had the advantage of not causing the urinary retention of the other two pills he had prescribed. However, there were drawbacks. Nardil would probably not take effect in less than four to six weeks—I could scarcely believe this—and I would have to carefully obey certain dietary restrictions, fortunately rather epicurean (no sausage, no cheese, no pâté de foie gras), in order to avoid a clash of incompatible enzymes that might cause a stroke. Further, Dr. Gold said with a straight face, the pill at optimum dosage was likely to have the side effect of impotence. Until that moment, although I'd had some trouble with his personality, I had not thought him totally lacking in perspicacity; now I was not at all sure. Putting myself in Dr. Gold's shoes, I wondered if he seriously thought that this juiceless and ravaged semi-invalid with the shuffle and the ancient wheeze woke up each morning from his Halcion sleep eager for carnal fun.

There was a quality so comfortless about that day's session that I went home in a particularly wretched state and prepared for the evening. A few guests were coming over for dinner—something which I neither dreaded nor welcomed and which in itself (that is, in my torpid indifference) reveals a fascinating aspect of depression's pathology. This concerns not the familiar threshold of pain but a parallel phenomenon, and that is the probable inability of the psyche to absorb pain beyond predictable limits of time. There is a region in the experience of pain where the certainty of alleviation often permits superhuman endurance. We learn to live with pain in varying degrees daily, or over longer periods of time, and we are more often than not mercifully free of it. When we endure severe discomfort of a physical nature our conditioning has taught us since childhood to make accommodations to the pain's demands—to accept it, whether pluckily or whimpering and complaining, according to our personal degree of stoicism, but in any case to accept it. Except in intractable terminal pain, there is almost always some form of relief; we look forward to that alleviation, whether it be through sleep or Tylenol or hypnosis or a change of posture or, most often, through the body's powers of self-healing, and we embrace this eventual respite as the natural reward we receive for having been, temporarily, such good sports and doughty sufferers, such optimistic cheerleaders for life at heart.

In depression this faith in deliverance, of ultimate restoration, is absent. The pain is unrelenting, and what makes the condition intolerable is the fore-knowledge that no remedy will come—not in a day, an hour, a month, or a minute. It is hopelessness even more than pain that crushes the soul. And so the decision-making of daily life involves not, as in normal affairs, shifting from one annoying situation to another less annoying—or from discomfort to relative comfort, or from boredom to activity—but moving from pain to pain. One does not abandon, even briefly, one's bed of nails, but lies upon it wherever one goes.

That December evening, for example, I could have remained in bed as usual during those worst hours, or agreed to the small dinner party my wife had arranged downstairs. But the very idea of a decision was academic. Either course was torture, and I chose the dinner not out of any particular merit but through indifference to what I knew would be indistinguishable ordeals of fogbound horror. At dinner I was barely able to speak, but the guests, who were all good friends, were aware of my condition and politely ignored my catatonic muteness. Then, after dinner, sitting in the living room, I experienced a curious inner convulsion that I can describe only as despair beyond despair. It came out of the cold air; I did not think such anguish possible.

While my friends quietly chatted in front of the fire I excused myself and went upstairs, where I retrieved my notebook from its special place. Then I went to the kitchen and with gleaming clarity—the clarity of one who knows he is engaged in a solemn rite—I noted all the trademarked legends on the well-advertised articles which I went about assembling for the volume's disposal: the new roll of Viva paper towels I opened to wrap up the book, the Scotch-brand tape I encircled it with, the empty Post Raisin Bran box I put the parcel into before taking it outside and stuffing it deep down into the garbage can, which would be emptied the next morning. Fire would have destroyed it faster, but in garbage there was an annihilation of self appropriate, as always, to melancholia's fecund self-humiliation. I felt my heart pounding wildly, like that of a man facing a firing squad, and knew I had made an irreversible decision.

A phenomenon that a number of people have noted while in deep depression is the sense of being accompanied by a second self—a wraithlike observer who, not sharing the dementia of his double, is able to watch with dispassionate curiosity as his companion struggles against the oncoming disaster, or decides to embrace it. There is a theatrical quality about all this, and during the next several days, as I went about stolidly preparing for extinction, I couldn't shake off a sense of melodrama—a melodrama in which I, the victim-to-be of self-murder, was both the solitary actor and lone member of the audience. I had not as yet chosen the mode of my departure, but I knew that that step would come next, and soon, as inescapable as nightfall.

I watched myself in mingled terror and fascination as I began to make the necessary preparation: going to see my lawyer in the nearby town—there rewriting my will—and spending part of a couple of afternoons in a muddled attempt to bestow upon posterity a letter of farewell. It turned out that putting together a suicide note, which I felt obsessed with a necessity to compose, was the most difficult task of writing that I had ever tackled. There were too many people to acknowledge, to thank, to bequeath final bouquets. And finally I couldn't manage the sheer dirgelike solemnity of it; there was something I found almost comically offensive in the pomposity of such a comment as "For some time now I have sensed in my work a growing psychosis that is doubtless a reflection of the psychotic strain tainting my life" (this is one of the few lines I recall verbatim), as well as something degrading in the prospect of a testament, which I wished to infuse with at least some dignity and eloquence, reduced to an exhausted stutter of inadequate apologies and self-serving explanations. I should have used as an example the mordant one-liner of the Italian writer Cesare Pavese, who in parting wrote simply, *Not too much gossip, please.*

But even a few words came to seem to me too long-winded, and I tore up all my efforts, resolving to go out in silence. Late one bitterly cold night, when I knew that I could not possibly get myself through the following day, I sat in the living room of the house bundled up against the chill; something had happened to the furnace. My wife had gone to bed, and I had forced myself to watch the tape of a movie in which a young actress, who had been in a play of mine, was cast in a small part. At one point in the film, which was set in late-nineteenth-century Boston, the characters moved down the hallway of a music conservatory, beyond the walls of which, from unseen musicians, came a contralto voice, a sudden soaring passage from the Brahms Alto Rhapsody.

This sound, which like all music—indeed, like all pleasure—I had been numbly unresponsive to for months, pierced my heart like a dagger, and in a flood of swift recollection I thought of all the joys the house had known: the children who had rushed through its rooms, the festivals, the love and work, the honestly earned slumber, the voices and the nimble commotion, the perennial tribe of cats and dogs and birds, "laughter and ability and Sighing, / And Frocks and Curls." All this I realized was more than I could ever abandon, even as what I had set out so deliberately to do was more than I could inflict on those memories, and upon those, so close to me, with whom the memories were bound. And just as powerfully I realized I could not commit this desecration on myself. I drew upon some last gleam of sanity to perceive the terrifying dimensions of the mortal predicament I had fallen into. I woke up my wife and soon telephone calls were made. The next day I was admitted to the hospital.

It was Dr. Gold, acting as my attending physician, who was called in to arrange for my hospital admission. Curiously enough, it was he who told me once or twice during our sessions (and after I had rather hesitantly broached the possibility of hospitalization) that I should try to avoid the hospital at all costs, owing to the stigma I might suffer. Such a comment seemed then, as it does now, extremely misguided; I had thought psychiatry had advanced long beyond the point where stigma was attached to any aspect of mental illness, including the hospital. This refuge, while hardly an enjoyable place, is a facility where patients still may go when pills fail, as they did in my case, and where one's treatment might be regarded as a prolonged extension, in a different setting, of the therapy that begins in offices such as Dr. Gold's.

It's impossible to say, of course, what another doctor's approach might have been, whether he too might have discouraged the hospital route. Many psychiatrists, who simply do not seem to be able to comprehend the nature and depth of the anguish their patients are undergoing, maintain their stubborn allegiance to pharmaceuticals in the belief that eventually the pills will kick in, the patient will respond, and the somber surroundings of the hospital will be avoided. Dr. Gold was such a type, it seems clear, but in my case he was wrong; I'm convinced I should have been in the hospital weeks before. For, in fact, the hospital was my salvation, and it is something of a paradox that in this austere place with its locked and wired doors and desolate green hallways—ambulances screeching night and day ten floors below—I found the repose, the assuagement of the tempest in my brain, that I was unable to find in my quiet farmhouse.

This is partly the result of sequestration, of safety, of being removed to a world in which the urge to pick up a knife and plunge it into one's own breast disappears in the newfound knowledge, quickly apparent even to the depressive's fuzzy brain, that the knife with which he is attempting to cut his dreadful Swiss steak is bendable plastic. But the hospital also offers the mild, oddly gratifying trauma of sudden stabilization—a transfer out of the too familiar surroundings of home, where all is anxiety and discord, into an orderly and benign detention where one's only duty is to try to get well. For me the real healers were seclusion and time.

The hospital was a way station, a purgatory. When I entered the place my depression appeared so profound that, in the opinion of some of the staff, I was a candidate for ECT, electroconvulsive therapy—shock treatment, as it is better known. In many cases this is an effective remedy—it has undergone improvement and has made a respectable comeback, generally shedding the medieval disrepute into which it was once cast—but it is plainly a drastic procedure one would want to avoid. I avoided it because I began to get well, gradually but steadily. I was amazed to discover that the fantasies of self-destruction all but disappeared within a few days after I checked in, and this again is testimony to the pacifying effect that the hospital can create, its immediate value as a sanctuary where peace can return to the mind.

I stayed in the hospital for nearly seven weeks. Not everyone might respond in the way I did; depression, one must constantly insist, presents so many variations and has so many subtle facets—depends, in short, so much on the individual's totality of causation and response—that one person's panacea might be another's trap. But certainly the hospital (and, of course, I am speaking of the many good ones) should be shorn of its menacing reputation, should not so often be considered the method of treatment of last resort. The hospital is hardly a vacation spot; the one in which I was lodged (I was privileged to be in one of the nation's best) possessed every hospital's stupefying dreariness. If in addition there are assembled on one floor, as on mine, fourteen or fifteen middle-aged males and females in the throes of melancholia of a suicidal complexion, then one can assume a fairly laughterless environment. This was not ameliorated for me by the sub-airline food or by the peek I had into the outside world: *Dynasty* and *Knots Landing* and the *CBS Evening News* unspooling nightly in the bare recreation room, sometimes making me at least aware that the place where I had found refuge was a kinder, gentler madhouse than the one I'd left.

As I got better I found distraction of sorts in the hospital's routine, with its own institutionalized sitcoms. Group Therapy, which I am told has value for some people, did nothing for me except make me seethe, possibly because it was supervised by an odiously smug young shrink, with a spade-shaped dark beard (*der junge Freud?*), who in attempting to get us to cough up the seeds of our misery was alternately condescending and bullying, and occasionally reduced one or two of the women patients, so forlorn in their kimonos and curlers, to what I'm certain he regarded as satisfactory tears. (I thought the rest of the psychiatric staff exemplary in their tact and compassion.) Time hangs heavy in the hospital, and the best I can say for Group Therapy is that it was a way to occupy the hours.

More or less the same can be said for Art Therapy, which is organized infantilism. Our class was run by a delirious young woman with a fixed, inde-fatigable smile who was plainly trained at a school offering courses in Teaching Art to the Mentally Ill; not even a teacher of very young retarded children could have been compelled to bestow, without deliberate instruction, such orchestrated chuckles and coos. Unwinding long rolls of slippery mural paper, she would tell us to take our crayons and make drawings illustrative of themes that we our-selves had chosen. For example: My House. In humiliated rage I obeyed, drawing a square, with a door and four cross-eyed windows, a chimney on top issuing forth a curlicue of smoke. She showered me with praise, and as the weeks ad-vanced and my health improved so did my sense of comedy. I began to dabble happily in colored modeling clay, sculpting at first a horrid little green skull with bared teeth which our teacher pronounced a splendid replica of my depression. I then proceeded through intermediate stages of recuperation to a rosy and che-rubic head with a Have a Nice Day smile. Coinciding as it did with the time of my release, this creation truly overjoyed my instructress (whom I'd become fond of in spite of myself), since, as she told me, it was emblematic of my recovery and therefore but one more example of the triumph over disease by Art Therapy.

By this time it was early February and although I was still shaky I knew I had emerged into light. I felt myself no longer a husk but a body with some of the body's sweet juices stirring again. I had my first dream in many months, confused but to this day imperishable, with a flute in it somewhere, and a wild goose, and a dancing girl.

By far the great majority of the people who go through even the severest de-pression survive it, and live ever afterward at least as happily as their unafflicted counterparts. Save for the awfulness of certain memories it leaves, acute de-pression inflicts few permanent wounds. There is a Sisyphean torment in the fact that a great number—as many as half—of those who are devastated once will be struck again; depression has the habit of recurrence. But most victims live through even these relapses, often coping better because they have become psy-chologically tuned by past experience to deal with the ogre. It is of great impor-tance that those who are suffering a siege, perhaps for the first time, be told—be convinced, rather—that the illness will run its course and that they will pull through. A tough job, this; calling "Chin up!" from the safety of the shore to a drowning person is tantamount to insult, but it has been shown over and over again that if the encouragement is dogged enough—and the support equally committed and passionate—the endangered one can nearly always be saved. Most people in the grip of depression at its ghastliest are, for whatever reason, in a state of unrealistic hopelessness, torn by exaggerated ills and fatal threats that bear no resemblance to actuality. It may require on the part of friends, lovers, family, admirers, an almost religious devotion to persuade the sufferers of life's worth, which is so often in conflict with a sense of their own worthlessness, but such devotion has prevented countless suicides.

After I began to recover in the hospital it occurred to me to wonder—for the first time with any really serious concern—why I had been visited by such a calamity. The psychiatric literature on depression is enormous, with theory after theory concerning the disease's etiology proliferating as richly as theories about the death of the dinosaurs or the origin of black holes. The very number of hypotheses is testimony to the malady's all but impenetrable mystery. As for that initial triggering mechanism—what I have called the manifest crisis—can I really be satisfied with the idea that abrupt withdrawal from alcohol started the plunge downward? What about other possibilities—the dour fact, for instance, that at about the same time I was smitten I turned sixty, that hulking milestone of mortality? Or could it be that a vague dissatisfaction with the way in which my work was going—the onset of inertia which has possessed me time and time again during my writing life, and made me crabbed and discontented—had also haunted me more fiercely during that period than ever, somehow magnifying the difficulty with alcohol? What part did the addiction to a tranquilizer play? Unresolvable questions, best left unresolved.

These matters in any case interest me less than the search for earlier origins of the disease. What are the forgotten or buried events that suggest an ultimate explanation for the evolution of depression and its later flowering into madness? Until the onslaught of my own illness and its dénouement, I never gave much thought to my work in terms of its connection with the subconscious—an area of investigation belonging to literary detectives. But after I had returned to health and was able to reflect on the past in the light of my ordeal, I began to see clearly how depression had clung close to the outer edges of my life for many years. The sovereign protection of alcohol always kept it at bay; I banished fear through self-medication. Suicide has been a persistent theme in my books— three of my major characters killed themselves. In rereading, for the first time in years, sequences from my novels—passages where my heroines have lurched down pathways toward doom—I was stunned to perceive how accurately I had created the landscape of depression in the minds of these young women, describing with what could only be instinct, out of a subconscious already roiled by disturbances of mood, the psychic imbalance that led them to destruction. Thus depression, when it finally came to me, was in fact no stranger, not even a visitor totally unannounced; it had been tapping at my door for decades.

The morbid condition proceeded, I have come to believe, from my beginning years—from my father, who battled the Gorgon for much of his lifetime, and had been hospitalized in my boyhood after a despondent spiraling downward that in retrospect I saw greatly resembled mine. The genetic roots of depression seem now to be beyond controversy. But I'm persuaded that an even more significant factor was the death of my mother when I was thirteen; this disorder and early sorrow—the death of a parent, before or during puberty—appears repeatedly in the literature on depression as a trauma sometimes likely to create nearly irreparable emotional havoc. The danger is especially apparent if the young person is affected by what has been termed "incomplete mourning"—has, in effect, been unable to achieve the catharsis of grief, and so carries within himself through later years an insufferable burden of which rage and guilt, and not only dammed-up sorrow, are a part, and become the potential seeds of self-destruction.

In an illuminating new book on suicide, *Self-Destruction in the Promised Land* (Rutgers), Howard I. Kushner, who is not a psychiatrist but a social historian, argues persuasively in favor of this theory of incomplete mourning and uses Abraham Lincoln as an example. While Lincoln's hectic moods of melancholy are legend, it is much less well known that in his youth he was often in a suicidal turmoil and came close more than once to making an attempt on his own life. This behavior seems directly linked to the death of Lincoln's mother, Nancy Hanks, when he was nine, and to unexpressed grief exacerbated by his sister's death ten years later. Drawing insights from the chronicle of Lincoln's painful success in avoiding suicide, Kushner makes a convincing case not only for the idea of early loss precipitating self-destructive conduct but also, auspiciously, for that same behavior becoming a strategy through which the person involved comes to grips with his guilt and rage and triumphs over self-willed death. Such reconciliation may be entwined with the quest for immortality—in Lincoln's case, no less than that of a writer of fiction, to vanquish death through work honored by posterity.

So if this theory of incomplete mourning has validity, and I think it does, and if it is also true that in the nethermost depths of one's suicidal behavior one is still subconsciously dealing with immense loss while trying to surmount all the effects of its devastation, then my own avoidance of death may have been belated homage to my mother. I do know that in those last hours before I rescued myself, when I listened to the passage from the Alto Rhapsody—which I'd heard her sing—she had been very much on my mind.

Near the end of an early film of Ingmar Bergman's, *Through a Glass Darkly*, a young woman who is experiencing the embrace of depression has a terrifying hallucination. Anticipating the arrival of some transcendental and saving glimpse of God, she sees instead the quivering shape of a monstrous spider. It is an instant of horror and scalding truth. Yet even in this vision of Bergman (who has suffered cruelly from depression) there is a sense that all of his accomplished artistry has somehow fallen short of a true rendition of the drowned mind's appalling phantasmagoria. Since antiquity—in the tortured lament of Job, in the choruses of

Sophocles and Aeschylus—chroniclers of the human spirit have been wrestling with a vocabulary that might give proper expression to the desolation of melancholia. Through the course of literature and art the theme of depression has run like a durable thread of woe—from Hamlet's soliloquy to the verses of Emily Dickinson and Gerard Manley Hopkins, from John Donne and Milton to Hawthorne and Poe, Camus and Conrad and Virginia Woolf. In many of Albrecht Dürer's engravings, there are harrowing depictions of his own melancholia; the manic wheeling stars of Van Gogh are the precursors of the artist's plunge into dementia and the extinction of self. It is a suffering that often tinges the music of Beethoven, of Schumann and Mahler, and permeates the darker cantatas of Bach. The vast metaphor which most faithfully represents this fathomless ordeal, however, is that of Dante, and his all too familiar lines still arrest the imagination with their augury of the unknowable, the black struggle to come:

> Nel mezzo del cammin di nostra vita
> Mi ritrovai per una selva oscura,
> Ché la diritta via era smarrita.

> In the middle of the journey of our life
> I found myself in a dark wood,
> For I had lost the right path.

One can be sure that these words have been more than once employed to conjure the ravages of melancholia, but their somber foreboding has often overshadowed the last lines of the best-known part of that poem, with their evocation of hope. To most of those who have experienced it, the horror of depression is so overwhelming as to be quite beyond expression, hence the frustrated sense of inadequacy found in the work of even the greatest artists. But in science and art the search will doubtless go on for a clear representation of its meaning, which sometimes, for those who have known it, is a simulacrum of all the evil of our world: of our everyday discord and chaos, our irrationality, warfare and crime, torture and violence, our impulse toward death and our flight from it held in the intolerable equipoise of history. If our lives had no other configuration but this, we should want, and perhaps deserve, to perish; if depression had no termination, then suicide would, indeed, be the only remedy. But one need not sound the false or inspirational note to stress the truth that depression is not the soul's annihilation; men and women who have recovered from the disease—and they are countless—bear witness to what is probably its only saving grace: it is conquerable.

For those who have dwelt in depression's dark wood, and known its inexplicable agony, their return from the abyss is not unlike the ascent of the poet, trudging upward and upward out of hell's black depths and at last emerging into what he saw as "the shining world." There, whoever has been restored to health has almost always been restored to the capacity for serenity and joy, and this may be indemnity enough for having endured the despair beyond despair.

E quindi uscimmo a riveder le stelle.

And so we came forth, and once again beheld the stars.

A Final Tale

KAY THOMPSON

....

KAY AND ELOISE

by Marie Brenner

DECEMBER 1996

In 1962, at the very height of her celebrity, Kay Thompson suddenly and myste-riously moved to Rome and took a splendid maisonette at the top of the Palazzo Torlonia, near the Spanish Steps. From her terrace she could see the Baroque domes of the city. Thompson seemed weary of her public persona, an identity so firmly established that one friend called it "the *Eloise* and *Funny Face* thing," as if it were a separate being. Thompson had just brought out a new edition of the third of the Eloise books, *Eloise at Christmastime*, and the quirky and poetic voice was unmistakable:

> *And when we awakened*
> *he'd come and gone*
> *and in all of this midnight and dark*
> *we could see these reindeers zimbering*
> *through the trees in Central Park*
> *We could even see this tail-light*
> *on Santa Claus' sleigh*
> *and Emily had a baby pigeon*
> *on absolutely Christmas day*

Eloise was more than a popular book; the dolls, toys, and wardrobe it pro-duced had been one of the first publishing saturation-marketing gambits. The author of *Eloise*, however, appeared to believe that her creations had overwhelmed her; she was in retreat. "The world is coming apart," she told her editor, Richard Grossman. "Why don't you move to Rome," he suggested casually. "There is nothing you can do here in New York that you can't do there." She picked up and left "with only a toothbrush," she later told a friend.

Thompson was a woman of certitude and imagination, known for her ex-acting standards on every aspect of her appearance and career. In Rome, there was the matter of a particular shade of beige she envisioned for a chiffon scarf. "It must be not quite bone, not pink, definitely not greige, perhaps the exact color of the sky one hour before sunset or just after twilight. It could even be red! You know what I mean?" she said to the fashion illustrator Joe Eula. The walls of her new apartment had to be "the exact hue of the water at Ostia." A jacket she required for an appearance on *The Garry Moore Show* had to be "burgundy and no other shade! A silk velvet—thin, thin, thin! Balenciaga and definitely not Chanel," she told the costume designer Robert Mackintosh.

Kay Thompson's Eloise had been published in 1955—Thompson insisted that her name be above the title, as on a marquee. By then Thompson had sung on the radio with Fred Waring and André Kostelanetz and had coached Judy Garland, Lena Horne, and Joan McCracken at MGM. Later, with Andy Williams and his three brothers, she had had a daring nightclub act. William Randolph Hearst and Maurice Chevalier had attended her opening at New York's elegant Le Directoire in 1948. But even after Thompson became a star, she was as restless as a six-year-old.

Eloise was a curious doppelgänger for Kay Thompson, a kindred spirit. Like her creator, Eloise was contradictory, both brazen and yearning. She was an imp of the perverse, a refreshing antidote to the coy and correct heroines of most children's literature. She "skibbled" through the Plaza hotel, ordering up room service and crayoning walls. She "sklonked" kneecaps and said "rawther" and "absolutely," but a genuine pathos neutralized her grandiose ways. The 1950s were Eloise's period, and she helped to define them; there was even a special room at the Plaza where one could pick up a telephone and hear the voice of Eloise herself. The voice was, of course, that of Kay Thompson, theatrical and breathy: *Hello, it's me, Eloise.* Her pronouncements were droll: "Getting bored is not allowed." "Sometimes I comb my hair with a fork." By 1963, more than a million copies of *Eloise* and its sequels had been sold.

Thompson always insisted that *Eloise* was not for children but for "precocious grownups," a phrase she approved for the book's jacket. She had a singular brio with words. "Boring" was a favorite Kay Thompson adjective; she pronounced it as if it were a musical phrase, extending the first syllable. So too with her other cherished descriptions—"too boring," "divine," "heaven." The absolute Thompson superlative was "pure heaven," which was conferred rarely.

Kay Thompson was tall and skinny, with blond hair, strong sharp features, and extraordinary agate eyes. She was handsome and offbeat, and possessed a kind of mannish look that was not in vogue at the time. Later she would grow to resemble the writer Isak Dinesen, but as a young woman there was an ebullience in her face, lightness around the edges. She was notorious for her style—the trailing scarves, the toreador pants. "She could take 10 yards of black jersey and wrap it around and make it look like a Schiaparelli," her friend the critic Rex Reed recalled. It was at times difficult to separate her from Maggie Prescott, the brittle and hilarious fashion editor she played in *Funny Face*, the 1957 Stanley Donen film starring Fred Astaire and Audrey Hepburn. Thompson might stride into a room gaily singing "Hello, hello!" as if she were eager to be noticed, but she was generally thought to be isolated from people. Over the years her friends have speculated about the zigzags of her life, the conflicts in her personality. She was prudish, even priggish about language and behavior, yet drawn to the uninhibited world of the theater. She lived in dazzling settings, but would often spend days alone. When she went out in public she pulled focus completely, but she was seldom intimate, and so wary of relationships that very few people had her telephone number. "I really don't know what made her tick," says Lena Horne. "Kay is a recluse hiding behind a pageant," another friend remarks.

In Rome she lived in a series of smallish rooms that she made into a "palace of crystal and tinkle," Joe Eula recalled. Thompson installed floor-to-ceiling mirrors, which had to be laboriously hauled through the garden of the palazzo and up an exterior elevator to the maisonette, which she called the *superattico*. Her drawing room had almost no furniture, except for zebra-skin rugs—"the zebes," she called them. Thompson shared the apartment with her pug, Fenice, who, like his mistress, often wore a scarf tied jauntily around his middle. Fenice went everywhere with her in Rome, seeming to exist on a diet of green Chuckles, which Thompson insisted he preferred. Her devotion to the pug was such that she reportedly sawed the legs off her grand piano in order to move it into her bedroom at the top of a spiral staircase, where she would play songs for him. But Thompson was restive in Rome, searching for a new project to utilize her prodigious energy. She turned down a featured role in *The Pink Panther*, as she had earlier turned down one in *Auntie Mame*, with a crisp wave of her arm and a single word: *No*.

The playwright Mart Crowley met her during these years. He had studied art, and Thompson discussed with him the idea of doing some sketches for a book she was working on called *The Fox and the Fig*. Crowley recalled that Thompson often resented it when people she met "expected her to be the Diana Vreeland parody she played in *Funny Face*." She seemed to believe that the caricature had come to define her, and her eccentricities were not too far from Maggie Prescott's in the movie. One day she announced to Crowley that she intended to have tiny Oriental lacquered tables for her bare living room. She was determined to paint them a shade of red she had seen in a Revlon ad.

"We went out and we bought 10 unpainted raw tables that were 12 inches high. 'No higher, no smaller,' she said. They needed priming, but did we do that? No. So we went out and bought nail varnish—cases and cases of it—and we sat around on the marble floor with the zebes and painted those tables for days, and we never got through." *The Fox and the Fig* was also left uncompleted. Crowley believed they were friends, but after Thompson became displeased with his work, he said, for some time he could no longer get her on the phone. However odd their relationship, it would have been inconceivable to Crowley at that time that the creator of Eloise would retreat from life completely and attempt to take America's most popular six-year-old with her. "Eloise is me. All me!" Thompson once told her friend Eleanor Lambert, the fashion publicist. "No, Kay. Eloise belongs to the world," Lambert recalled answering. She was surprised when Thompson did not reply.

"I think the story of our lives comes through these wonderful people we run into. You run into a stranger and: 'My God, the electricity!' And then you come into something terrible, and our lives are ruined by this," Kay Thompson recently told the writer Stephen Silverman in a telephone conversation. Since 1973, when Thompson and Eleanor Lambert staged an elaborate fashion show of American designers at Versailles, Thompson has slowly withdrawn from public and social life. She now lives quite purposefully as a recluse in a large apartment owned by her goddaughter, Liza Minnelli, on East 69th Street in New York. Thompson has narrowed her circle to a few friends, including Eleanor Lambert, Rex Reed, the film historian Hugh Fordin, and John Loring, a vice-president of Tiffany & Co. She is confined to a wheelchair, but often wears a favorite red Halston sweater and dancing shoes; her feet tap frequently to a beat that only she can hear. She routinely turns down interview requests. "Make them go away," she tells Allen Eichhorn, Liza Minnelli's publicist.

A theme of Thompson's life has been a relentless search for privacy. She returns calls, even from friends, haphazardly, if at all. When she does call back, however, she is vibrant and youthful. She will often stay on the telephone for an hour, then hang up and call right back to add a thought to the soliloquy that has gone before. She is part of a generation of women who speak in great, colorful dramatic arcs. "You have led me down the garden path, and I have followed!" she recently told a friend. News radio is often on in the background when she calls. She reads avidly and has strong opinions. Over the summer, she told me that she was convinced that O. J. Simpson was innocent. "You don't expect me to agree with Dominick, do you?" she asked testily, referring to the writer Dominick Dunne and his coverage of the Simpson trial [in the pages of *Vanity Fair*]. Often she will end conversations with a vibrant "Think pink!" "Think Pink" was the remarkable opening number in *Funny Face*, in which Thompson instructed her staff at *Quality Magazine* to "banish the black, bury the blue, burn the beige. Think pink! And that includes the kitchen sink!" At times she will close with another favorite phrase: "Be brilliant!"

Thompson's age is a subject of bemused speculation among her friends. Several believe she is close to 95, although she shrieks when that figure is mentioned: "Heavens, no!" An official biographical entry gives her birth date as November 9, 1912, although some references add "disputed." One music encyclopedia places her date of birth in 1902. Very little is known about Thompson's early life. She was born in St. Louis, where she was called Kitty Fink. She attended the same high school as Tennessee Williams and later went to Washington University. Thompson's father, a jeweler, encouraged his daughter's musical ability. According to a 1936 *Radio Guide*, Thompson had informed her family at the age of four that she would be an actress. She was not as pretty as her two sisters. UGLY DUCKLINGS CAN HAVE BEAUX, *Radio Guide* cruelly titled an early Thompson profile. The words below were equally mean: "When she looked into the mirror and a homely girl stared back, Kay Thompson went to work with a will—and made that homely girl a star!" By the time she was 16, she was a prodigy on the piano, performing Liszt with the St. Louis Symphony. She was close to her sister Marion, but she rarely talked about her childhood with friends. Like Eloise, she seemed to exist center stage with her family off in the wings.

At age 17 she moved to Los Angeles and took a job teaching diving at a summer camp. As a singer, she was talented but not appealing enough to be recognized as a natural radio star. She sang with the Mills Brothers before they were well known, and worked in San Francisco clubs. She had her nose straightened and lost her original name for the more euphonious "Thompson," but she was strong-willed, ferociously ambitious, and would not compromise her standards. According to a 1948 column in the New York *Daily News*, in 1934 she was fired from a radio show of hit songs. Soon after, she was hired to sing with Fred Waring, but he fired her too. She made two records for Victor, but the *News* columnist reported that the head of the company had hated them and refused to release them. She worked for André Kostelanetz, but he replaced her with Alice Faye.

The composer Hugh Martin met Thompson about 1935, when he became her rehearsal pianist. Later he was part of her group, Kay Thompson's Rhythm Singers, on CBS. "She was the cutting edge. The sophistication was in her singing and in her conversation," Martin recently recalled. "She was to vocal arrangements what Louis Armstrong was to jazz."

The Depression was raging, and the Shubert brothers controlled Broadway. Agnes de Mille worked for the Shuberts as a young choreographer and later described in a memoir the aura of "evil magic" about Lee Shubert. Without the protection of Equity, the dancers had no security and earned a pitiful salary: "thirty-five dollars a week, twenty dollars for rehearsal, and a little loving on the side," she reported. De Mille encountered Kay Thompson in 1937 in a Shubert production called *Hooray for What!*, a debacle that would prove traumatic for both of them. *Hooray for What!* could have made Thompson's name in the theater. Harold Arlen wrote the music, the book was by the venerable writing team of Howard Lindsay and Russel Crouse, and the lyrics were by E. Y. "Yip" Harburg.

In rehearsal, Arlen quickly realized that Thompson not only could act and sing but also was a gifted vocal arranger—an entirely new field at the time. Hugh Martin and his later collaborator Ralph Blane followed Thompson to *Hooray for What!* At CBS, Martin had observed her technique: "She did not come to the studio having made the arrangement. She would use us as her tools, the way a painter uses pigment. I would sit there and watch her fingers and try to soak up all the changes of key. At a certain point, when she felt the arrangement had reached its zenith, she would stand up and say, 'O.K., over to you!'" During *Hooray for What!*, Martin recalled, "Kay would be sitting in front of the footlights during rehearsal with a bandanna around her head, sweat pouring out, looking like the chic-est thing in the world while all of us were clapping and singing 'Down with Love' and 'Buds Won't Bud.'"

The Shuberts wanted to turn *Hooray for What!* into a bosomy-chorus-girl revue, and Lee Shubert felt that Thompson was not sexy enough. He and Vincente Minnelli, the director, battled over this and every other artistic decision. "Rehearsals were a horror," de Mille recalled. "The bosses . . . were prowling the aisles whispering. I developed a tic from snapping my head to see who was spying behind me." The Shuberts fired dancers and singers without warning. Thompson was "grim-lipped and sardonic," de Mille wrote, and Minnelli and Arlen took to their beds. De Mille was dismissed in the lobby, only hours before the leading man. One night, as Thompson was leaving the stage, she felt a tap on her back and heard the words "That will be your last performance."

Martin was in the basement of the theater when Thompson was fired. "I will never forget the cries, the sounds, and the sobs that came from her dressing room," he said. She was so devastated, Martin recalled, that in the end "she could not face thinking about it. It was banished from her life." *Hooray for What!* became one among many taboo subjects for Thompson, who resisted any unpleasant talk. Martin remains convinced that the humiliation kept Thompson from ever doing another Broadway show.

By then Thompson had married the trombone player Jack Jenney, who recorded "Star Dust" and later played with Artie Shaw. Jenney directed Thompson's recording sessions and appeared with her in a 1937 Republic movie, *Manhattan Merry-Go-Round*. By 1939 they had written a song called "What More Can I Give You?," but shortly after, Thompson left Jenney for CBS radio producer Bill Spier, who was among the first to broadcast music from Europe in a symphony hour. Thompson worked on Spier's show and reportedly traveled with the CBS crew abroad. Spier was married with three children, but he divorced his wife and married Thompson. Spier was "a boy genius," his third wife, the actress June Havoc, recently told me. Havoc had played vaudeville as "Baby June" with her sister, Gypsy Rose Lee. Spier was tall and dark, a concert-level pianist with a lethal sense of humor. He would later produce *Suspense* and introduce the Dashiell Hammett character Sam Spade to radio.

As Thompson became increasingly well known, Spier later told June Havoc, he felt on the periphery of her life. She was exuberant, but kept her distance. Spier seemed to understand the contradiction in her personality: bravado was her disguise.

There is a portrait of Kay Thompson leaning against a wardrobe rack with Lena Horne in the MGM days. She is all legs, in a sleek straight skirt with a wide belt and high sling-back pumps. Her face is radiant. Her friendship with Hugh Martin was responsible for propelling her in 1944 into a relatively new position as a vocal arranger at the elite unit of MGM run by Arthur Freed, the producer of *Singin' in the Rain, An American in Paris, Gigi,* and other major MGM musicals. Freed brought Cole Porter to Metro for *The Pirate* and promoted the careers of Judy Garland and Lena Horne. The Freed Unit, recalled Hugh Martin, was "the most intense concentration of talent I had ever seen."

Freed worked with Roger Edens, a gentle Texan who would later produce *Funny Face.* Like Thompson, Edens was a person with diverse abilities. He was Judy Garland's mentor as well as a composer. As a producer, Edens had signed Hugh Martin and his collaborator after the success of their show *Best Foot Forward. Meet Me in St. Louis* was Martin and Blane's first score for MGM; it was a triumph for Edens and Judy Garland, and "The Trolley Song" was nominated for an Oscar. One day Martin announced to Edens that he was leaving Metro to go off to the war. "Hugh, how are we going to replace you?" Edens asked. "There is someone much better than me: Kay Thompson," said Martin.

In the history of popular American music, Kay Thompson's role has been largely unreported. Her vocal arrangements helped bring jazz rhythms to MGM musicals; she taught Lena Horne to sing loud and gave Judy Garland a new sound. Horne says Thompson was "a major part of my time out there at MGM. Professionally she developed me as a singer completely. I had the groundwork there, but I did not know how to get it out. She is the best vocal coach in the world."

In Los Angeles, Kay Thompson and Bill Spier took a bungalow at the Garden of Allah, the hotel which had once been a haven for Sheilah Graham and F. Scott Fitzgerald. Later, she papered her apartment on Beverly Glen with tiny clusters of flowers; the walls and ceiling were completely covered. "The overall impression was like being inside a candy box," the writer Leonard Gershe recalled. Thompson and

Spier gave lavish parties for their musician friends. As Lena Horne recalled, she and Kay were homesick New Yorkers. Through her friendship with Thompson, Horne met her husband, the arranger Lennie Hayton. During Thompson's Hollywood years her urge to perform was subsumed into improvs she would do at parties, often with Judy Garland or Roger Edens. Much of this material was later recycled for her nightclub act. For Cyd Charisse, who starred in *The Band Wagon* and *Silk Stockings*, Kay was "a bundle of energy. I remember her flying by in the rehearsal hall with all this vivaciousness and energy—there was nobody more enthusiastic about everything than Kay." She wore pants that laced up the front like those worn by Jack Cole, whose sophisticated modern-dance company included Gwen Verdon and Carol Haney, Charisse said. Often Thompson would break into a jitterbug just for the sheer fun of it.

Roger Edens became a pivotal figure in Thompson's life. They shared the same birthday and were, according to Hugh Martin, "soul mates." Edens was married and by all accounts romantically unavailable to Thompson, but deeply connected to her emotionally. Each year on their birthday they threw an elaborate party. They would write songs for each other and rehearse their numbers for months. "Kay would have no clue what Roger was doing, and Roger would have no clue what Kay was doing," said Gershe. "People would die to get invited!" Ann Miller and Judy Garland would attend, as would Andy Williams, Cyd Charisse, and Lena Horne. One day Edens sat down at the piano and played a complex tribute he had written for Thompson, "The Passion of St. Kate." On the telephone 50 years later, Gershe sings it effortlessly: "There she was in St. Louis, / with no food and no heat and no money to pay the rent, / but she didn't care / little Katie, da-di-da . . ."

The satirical style of Edens and Thompson was on display in a song originally written as a vehicle for Greer Garson in the 1946 film *Ziegfeld Follies*. Garson had starred in *Madame Curie*, and the musical number "Madame Crematon" was a Thompson-Edens send-up of her great-lady character. It was high camp and witty, a set piece in which an imperious actress announces to reporters her plans for her next weighty part—Madame Crematon, the inventor of the safety pin. The night came when Vincente Minnelli and Arthur Freed were to hear it for the first time. "They all assembled at Arthur Freed's house," says Hugh Fordin. "Kay was playing the role, and Roger was playing the piano. The song ends with a big hurrah-hurrah, and there is silence from Garson.

Finally Garson's husband says, 'Your house is beautifully appointed, Arthur.' There was no way Greer was going to do this. Kay and Roger went out and sat in the backseat of Edens's car, speechless. Finally Roger said, 'Goddamn it. Judy is going to do it! She is the perfect mimic, and she will just mimic you.'" In the film, Garland, in a sleek satin dress, with a long chiffon scarf in her hand, vamped as Kay Thompson.

Judy Garland eventually came to rely more and more heavily on Thompson's coaching. Garland was a belter then, a ballad singer without subtlety in her interpretations. "Judy just had a big voice," said Rex Reed. "Kay softened the tones and made her hold certain notes longer. She is the one who put the sob in her voice. Judy was always running out of steam on notes and she would have to catch her breath. She'd say, 'Oh, God, I ruined it.' And Kay would say, 'You didn't ruin it—use it!'" Thompson coached her through *Ziegfeld Follies*, *The Harvey Girls*, and *The Pirate*, for which Thompson arranged the song "Mack the Black."

You could see Kay Thompson's style like a shadow print in a Garland performance. There was the hand on the hip—a gesture Liza Minnelli later adopted as well. Thompson had a distinct bow—one arm perpendicular, the other behind her back—which Garland used. Much has been written about the relationship between Judy Garland and Kay Thompson. Thompson could pull Garland out of her emotional funks in later years, when Garland's anxiety was so crippling that she would cancel concerts. Thompson was often contemptuous of Garland's lack of discipline and her reliance on pills. "I got so tired of taking care of her," she told a friend, but Garland became family for Thompson, who often traveled with her and her young children, Liza and Lorna. *The Pirate*, however, proved to be Thompson's nadir at MGM. Garland missed rehearsals and shoots. Years later, when *The Pirate* came up in a conversation, Thompson looked at a friend with an arched eyebrow. "Drugaroonies," she said.

By the end of Thompson's time at Metro, her style was fully recognizable: you could tell which singers had been trained by her. Lena Horne recalled, "Hazel Scott and I had to do a number called 'Joshua Fit the Battle of Jericho.' I had been going to Kay's for singing every day and doing her exercises. She said to me, 'All right, it's there. We just have to bring it out.' When Hazel came, she coached us both for the number. I began to sing with some kind of assertiveness through my training with her." Thompson instructed Horne specifically to use more breath. "Kay would play jazz, and I would sing. She took what little I had, and it just got bigger and bigger. We both liked jazz and jazz musicians, and musicians have a tendency to develop sounds you hear coming from an instrument."

Thompson was arguably at her best in the complex arrangement of the Harry Warren and Johnny Mercer standard "On the Atchison, Topeka, and the Santa Fe" in *The Harvey Girls*. She and Edens wrote a complicated series of lyrics introducing each Harvey girl ("We were schoolmarms from Grand Rapids, Mich / But reading, writing, 'rithmetic were not our dish!"). Ralph Blane assisted Thompson on the vocal arrangements. He later recalled to Hugh Fordin, "Kay would write twenty ideas while I threw out nineteen! They would just come to her like that, she was so fast! Kay could have been a great composer had she settled on one theme or one idea. She could never discipline herself to do the same thing twice."

*E*loise began as a vocal riff, a droll bit of shtick to pass the time between friends. Thompson was in her last days at MGM. Her marriage to Bill Spier was unraveling, and she was looking to escape. She later recalled, "I had a headache for two years, and I said, 'I have to get out of this place! It is just too much!'" Thompson attempted to blame MGM for her unhappiness: "I learned that in a big studio you are so categorized that you have to become what people think you are or get out. So I got out," she once said. "Everything was saying, 'You are going someplace else, and you are going to do something else.' So my contract was up on May 17. The choreographer Bob Alton said to me, 'You can always have an act,'" she told Stephen Silverman.

Andy Williams and his three brothers were also restless at the Freed Unit. Thompson had a daring idea, completely new for its time: a club act where she would be center stage with four men behind her, choreographed as a theater piece. Thompson called her new career "the saloon beat." For a time, the novelty of her idea commanded her imagination. Williams worried, he recently told me, about technical problems, such as what to do with a microphone. In 1947 the standard nightclub act was Hildegarde or Jean Sablon, just standing and singing in front of a band. Thompson enlisted the best talent at MGM for advice, and Bob Alton agreed to help her with the staging and movement. One day Thompson was late for a photo session at Alton's. "I drove the car across a golf course—Bob's house was right there. I got out of the car and I opened the door and went a few steps, and he said, 'Who do you think you are, coming here five minutes late?' I said, 'I am Eloise. I am six.'"

Eloise became an alternative persona for Kay Thompson, much as the dummy Charlie McCarthy was for Edgar Bergen. The noxious voice of the little girl allowed Thompson to express contrarian thoughts and ideas. Eloise took form as a lonely and whimsical child who created her own world. She became an immediate part of Thompson's daily conversation. "The boys loved Eloise! Andy gave himself two names, Junior and Melvin. They gave her names, too," Thompson recalled.

Thompson and the Williams Brothers opened their act at El Rancho in Las Vegas when Thompson was in residence in Nevada getting her divorce. A charged romantic atmosphere existed between Williams and Thompson, friends say. "She was madly in love with Andy," according to Leonard Gershe, but Williams denies this. However close they were, Thompson was determined that the act would be hers alone. Thompson, Williams remembers, exerted complete control. "At one time my brother Dick wanted to compose or arrange one of the songs. Very soon it was decided that that wasn't the way it was going to go."

There was no question but that the act was unique: "Now we are used to seeing a girl with four or eight guys, but at that time vocal groups had never done anything but stand around the microphone at the end of a number and put their arms up. It was that static!" Williams said. "We acted out scenes like a miniature Broadway show. When we got on the stage at El Rancho Vegas, we realized that no one could hear us. We hung microphones from a beam across the stage—this had never been done before. Kay got up there and hung the mikes herself!"

They received $2,500 a week at a time when Sophie Tucker, according to Williams, commanded $5,000. Eight weeks later, Thompson and the Williams Brothers moved to Ciro's in Los Angeles. "Walter Winchell began writing about us. Within a year we were making $15,000 a week," Williams said. When they opened in New York in April 1948 at Le Directoire, *Variety* headlined: KAY THOMPSON'S N.Y. CAFE WOW CUES ANSWER TO WAIL FOR 'SOMETHING NEW.' The review continued, "Miss Thompson is an atomic bomb of rhythm songapation with her equally supercharged vocal vitamins, the four Williams Brothers."

Thompson was taken up immediately in the New York of the postwar period. Her signature numbers—"Jubilee Time," "Pauvre Suzette," "Louisiana Purchase"—were fresh and sardonic. "She was really a throwback to Cole Porter and Noël Coward," Nina Bourne, who later worked on her books at Simon & Schuster, recalled.

Through Leonard Gershe, Thompson came to know D. D. Dixon, a young and deeply stylish editor at *Harper's Bazaar*. Dixon would later marry Johnny Ryan, a stage manager, and become a well-known social figure in New York, but as a young woman she often traveled with the photographer Richard Avedon and helped him organize shoots for the magazine. D. D. Ryan had a gift for understanding what was new, and she was fascinated by Thompson. "Kay would call me and do Eloise on the phone. She would say 'This is Eloise' in that funny little voice. I knew nothing about technology, but I finally said, 'Kay, you really ought to get a tape recorder and write this down!' This was the 1950s, and I did not even know what a tape recorder was. I said, 'There is a fellow across the hall, a great friend of mine, Hilary Knight.' He used to make little drawings and shove them under my door. One morning he made a drawing of a fat little prissy pretty girl with frizzy blond corkscrews. She had a satin ribbon in her hair and a bulging belly, and she was facing a little girl who looked just like Eloise. I said, 'I have a drawing of Eloise.' And Kay got enormously interested."

A black leather scrapbook rests on a shelf in Hilary Knight's apartment on East 51st Street in New York. In it is the entire publishing history of the phenomenon that became *Eloise*. Knight, a student of the painter Reginald Marsh, was 28 when he was introduced to Kay Thompson in 1954. He was starting his career as a magazine illustrator and was influenced by the work of the British artist Ronald

Searle. The son of two New York artists, Knight is modest and thoughtful. His small apartment is crammed with vintage theater recordings and his own sketches and paintings.

"I just *knew* this little girl," he said of Eloise. "D.D. took me to meet Kay—I believe it was her last performance at the Persian Room. We went to the lobby, and I remember sitting with her, and she told me about the book. We pretty much started working on it right away."

For Thompson, Knight was "Princetonian—shy, gentle, and soft-spoken." She had written, she recalled in a 1957 interview, "12 lines on a piece of paper and handed it to him. 'If you're interested, get in touch with me.' Then I spoke a few words of Eloisiana and left." That Christmas, Thompson received a card from Knight, a highly stylized picture of an angel and Santa Claus streaking through the sky. On the top of Santa's pack was Eloise. "It was immediate recognition on my part. There she was, in person. I knew at once Hilary Knight had to illustrate the book," she later recalled.

"I holed in at the Plaza and we went to work. I just knew I had to get this done. Eloise was trying to get out. I've never known such stimulation. This girl had complete control of me. Ideas came from everywhere. Hilary and I had immediate understanding. . . . We wrote, edited, laughed, outlined, cut, pasted, laughed again, read out loud, laughed and suddenly we had a book."

"I did a sketch of the little girl, and we worked together. It was a total collaboration," Knight recalled. "Kay talked about the way she looked, the little costume. The attitude was a combination of several different people. One was a woman, Eloise Davison, a food writer at the *New York Herald Tribune* and a friend of my family. All of these people—Nanny, Eloise—are really Kay," Knight said.

On the opening page, Eloise announces, "I am Eloise. I am six." Eloise's facial expression and pose invoked classical portraiture of great men—Ingres's wealthy noblemen, Jacques-Louis David's Napoleon. For the illustrator Joelle Shefts, Knight's perfect pitch for the body in motion "put him in a league with [Sir John] Tenniel, [Arthur] Rackham, and [Edmund] Dulac." Knight was able to alleviate the sardonic darkness of Thompson's text by spoofing Eloise's pomposity, splattering her across every page in a helter-skelter free-for-all. There was an ingenious quality to his drawings, an economy of line—almost as if they were preliminary sketches.

Soon after the text and drawings were completed, Thompson recalled, "we took Eloise to Jack Goodman at Simon & Schuster, and he recognized and understood Eloise immediately. We all became close friends, and the book went into print—only a thousand copies the first time, just to see how it went."

How it went was immediately: Jack Goodman, the editor of S. J. Perelman and Irwin Shaw, issued a memo dated November 18, 1955: "Thursday evening first copies came off press. Friday morning at 9:30 people in the office who had taken home copies came in making considerable noise. Friday morning at 11:30 we ordered a second printing. Friday afternoon, *Life* magazine told us they are running a story on *Eloise* (pictures and text in two colors) in their December 5th issue." Goodman then rounded up blurbs from a roster of distinguished authors. "To me *Eloise* is the most glorious book ever written about an endearingly frightful little girl. Completely enchanting, and you can quote me fulsomely," Cornelia Otis Skinner said. Noël Coward's appraisal was printed in the ads: "Frankly, I adore Eloise." Soon the book was selling 4,000 copies a week; it shared the best-seller lists that spring with John O'Hara's *Ten North Frederick* and *The Quiet American*, by Graham Greene.

At Simon & Schuster, Richard Grossman worked on the original promotion campaign with Jack Goodman. Later, he would edit Kay Thompson and become a close friend. "Kay had a clear idea of what she wanted—to get out of the 'saloon business,' as she referred to it, and be respected by classy people." With success, a whiff of myopia crept into her relationships. Barron Polan, Thompson's agent, who had helped make her career, took her to court over commissions on the *Eloise* books. He lost. She was often cranky, and used the expression "I'll cut them off at the knees" in rupturing relationships with longtime friends.

A few weeks before *Eloise* was published, Hilary Knight received a call from Thompson's secretary asking for a meeting. Knight was handed a one-page agreement to sign. Thompson had written an unusual addendum to her publishing contract. She would own the copyright to Knight's drawings, and any future Eloise books would be locked in at the same royalty split as the first—70 percent for Thompson and 30 percent for Knight. "I totally trusted her," Knight said. "I signed it without really looking at it. I totally signed my rights away." During the years of their collaboration, Knight would occasionally raise the subject with Thompson. Finally she agreed to discuss the onerous contract with Morris Ernst, a distinguished literary lawyer. "Ernst got nowhere with her. He was overwhelmed by her," Knight said. Nevertheless, Knight and Thompson soldiered on.

For a six-year-old, Eloise had a distinctly dark side, which resembled her creator's. She was isolated and self-involved. In an introduction to a special edition of *Madeline*, by Ludwig Bemelmans, the writer Anna Quindlen called Eloise pathetic. "When I think of Eloise grown up," she wrote, "I think of her with a drinking problem, knocking about from avocation to avocation, unhappily married or unhappily divorced, childless."

"I have experienced many bad moments from the beginning of Eloise's life," Thompson recently told Stephen Silverman, who was researching his biography of Stanley Donen, the director of *Funny Face*. Thompson became caught in the downdrafts of celebrity. She lived at the Plaza, purportedly rent-free, for many years, but she could not escape her creation. She staged tea parties at which she vamped as Eloise, and helped to mastermind the special Plaza menu for children with "Teeny Weenies" and "Eggs Eloise." Thompson traveled to Dallas to launch Eloise clothing at Neiman Marcus; Eloise dolls were sold at Lord & Taylor. At Simon & Schuster, Richard Grossman suggested to Robert Bernstein that he might enjoy working with Thompson manufacturing Eloise novelty items. Bernstein set up Eloise Ltd. and rewarded Grossman's generosity by taking Thompson with him to Random House, where Bernstein later became president. "Kay was such a perfectionist that getting something she was happy with was not easy," Bernstein recalled. Their only book project was Bernstein's idea, the poignant and sentimental *Eloise at Christmastime* in 1958:

> *So if no one remembers me*
> *and no presents can I find*
> *I'll know I don't deserve them*
> *It doesn't matter*
> *I don't mind*

Thompson turned down a chance to endorse caramels, but agreed to a disastrous production of *Eloise* on CBS. The cast was stellar—Ethel Barrymore, Louis Jourdan, Charles Ruggles, Monty Woolley—but the script departed wildly from the book. In it, Eloise was caught in the middle of her parents' threatened divorce in a hotel filled with intrigue. John Frankenheimer directed, and called the experience "a nightmare." The reviews were savage. TURKEY WAS THE SPECIAL, one headline said of the Thanksgiving production. Just as she had done after *Hooray for What!*, Thompson, acutely sensitive to criticism, burrowed in and closed another chapter of her life. She resolved, she told friends, that she would never allow Eloise to be dramatized again.

The success of *Eloise* was followed swiftly by Thompson's role in *Funny Face* as the redoubtable Maggie Prescott, who storms her way to Europe and lands in France singing the enduring "Bonjour, Paris!" "I never considered anyone else for the part," Stanley Donen said. If the publication of *Eloise* placed the nightclub performer in the public mind as a hypersophisticated and world-weary woman, Thompson's image was italicized by her staccato interpretation of a fashion editor inspired by Diana Vreeland. Like Vreeland, Thompson was brassy and shrewd: "She's got to have bizzazz!" she declaimed about one model, and "bizzazz"— a Vreeland word used in *Funny Face* by Gershe—instantly entered glossy fashion copy.

Funny Face had originally been inspired by Leonard Gershe's friendship with Richard Avedon and his wife, Doe. Gershe was impressed by Doe's beauty and her ambivalence about her profession, and he talked about the Avedons with the English writer Clemence Dane. "What a glorious idea for a musical—the fashion world, a fashion photographer, and a model who doesn't want to be a model," Dane told him. "Why don't you write it?" For years, Gershe's *Wedding Day*, as the script was first called, languished. Robert Alton wanted to direct it, under one condition—if Kay Thompson would play the fashion editor. Thompson, Gershe recalled, "had never got over *Hooray for What!* She turned it down flat. She was afraid to go on the stage."

Two years later, Gershe met Roger Edens, who was looking for a movie to produce on his own. Edens had several suggestions for Gershe's script: move the wedding to the end of the story and borrow several songs from George and Ira Gershwin's 1927 stage musical, *Funny Face*. By then D. D. Dixon had regaled Gershe with stories of her fabulous boss, Diana Vreeland, and her famous aphorisms, such as "Pink is the navy blue of India." *Funny Face* went into production in the summer of 1956. Throughout production, there was an undercurrent of tension on the set. Fred Astaire, who played the photographer, seemed to take an instant dislike to Kay Thompson. "He liked willowy women," Gershe said. "There was no reason for it. She never did anything to him. She found him a prima donna and mean to Audrey." Thompson told Stephen Silverman, "Stanley never yelled at anyone, except Fred, sort of, at the end." During the filming of Thompson and Astaire's duet, "Clap Yo' Hands," Thompson was playing the piano. "Fred said, 'Stanley? Come over here.' Stanley said, 'O.K., stop the camera.' And Fred said to him, 'What is she doing on the piano?'" Moments after Thompson and Astaire finished dancing up the stairs, Thompson told Silverman, "Fred grabbed me out of the blue and said, 'Where did you learn balance?'"

In Paris, Thompson and Hilary Knight went to work on a sequel. Thompson was determined to put Eloise in a small Left Bank hotel, the Relais Bisson. Knight dutifully sketched Paris scenery—the Pont Neuf, pigeons at Fouquet's. Thompson's eccentricities became more evident. "When we were in Paris," Knight said, "Kay was going to come back to New York to do a song called 'Bizzazz' on *The Ed Sullivan Show*. We went to Balmain, and they gave her a fabulous beige chiffon dress and jewelry for her appearance. I forget what the reason was, but she decided that she did not like it. She threw it in the tub and washed it! She just ruined it."

Like the original *Eloise, Eloise in Paris* was fresh and inventive. Thompson's text was enchantingly fey:

> *When you are in your chambre which is your room*
> *you are allowed to fall on the bed and sort of sklathe*
> *yourself into these large pillows for a while*
> *because here's what you are*
> *absolutely fatiguée*

which is tired tired tired
The absolutely first thing you have to do
is put on your bedroom slippers
which is pantoufles

Simon & Schuster planned a record ad campaign for *Eloise in Paris*. Thompson was photographed at book-and-author lunches with Dean Acheson; Eloise endorsed Renaults and Kalistron luggage; and Thompson recorded the song "Eloise" with Archie Bleyer.

Soon after, Richard Grossman had the idea of sending Thompson and Hillary Knight to Moscow. "I took her out to the airport with Hilary in what was the only rentable Rolls-Royce in New York, owned and driven by a wonderful man named Roosevelt Zanders," Grossman recalled. Thompson and Knight set up at the National Hotel. Many nights they went to the Bolshoi, Knight later recalled. Thompson wore three cashmere sweaters, special wool fezzes, and a red coat made of guanaco, a thick camel-like fur. In Moscow she deliberately wore a dress "inside out" to a wedding, Knight remembered. She was so famous then that when she came back she made an album, *Kay Thompson Party: Let's Talk About Russia*, on which she held forth in a daffy monologue: "The plumbing was divine—I had my own stopper for my own bathtub! . . . I said to Hilary, 'Can you stand it? Here we are in Moscow!' It was heaven." Thompson and Grossman composed a song called "The Moscow ChaChaCha," which Thompson recorded.

However celebrated Thompson had become, she was unable to reconcile her public and private lives. The mania for Eloise seemed to have taken over her life, but she played her public role with gusto and little noticeable ambivalence. On the day she met the American designer Norman Norell, Thompson painted two red dots on her eyelids. "Norell was intrigued by the subliminal flash-of-red effect," Hilary Knight said. When Robert Bernstein walked into his office on his first day at Random House, he was greeted by a half-dozen pigeons flying around and the sign WELCOME TO RANDOM HOUSE, FROM ME, ELOISE. Thompson jumped out of a closet.

In the summer of 1966, Hilary Knight returned to Rome to work with Kay Thompson on their fifth Eloise collaboration. Knight had drawn hundreds of sketches for a new idea—Eloise lolling in an overflowing bathtub and deluging movie stars in fox coats and the Plaza hotel's long-suffering manager, Mr. Salomone. Knight recalled the atmosphere between them as odd and frenetic. Thompson hung his drawings all over the studio and snapped, "Think of this as a movie." They worked all day long and into the night. Thompson would compliment Knight's sketches—"That's great, Hil"—but the next morning, he recalled, "that drawing that was so glorious would have a big clot of rubber cement on it, and there would be a piece of paper over the drawing." She refused to accept any of his suggestions. In the end, the idea was too thin to sustain. Even the working title seemed false and affected: *Eloise Takes a Bawth*.

Often artistic collaboration is not entirely congenial. It was said that Gilbert and Sullivan communicated through letters because they could not stand to be in the same room. The union of Lorenz Hart and Richard Rodgers ultimately collapsed, and Bertolt Brecht and Kurt Weill became fed up with each other. Thompson's alliance with Hilary Knight resembled most closely the partnership of Lewis Carroll and John Tenniel. As with Tenniel's drawings for *Alice in Wonderland*, the charm of *Eloise* was greatly enhanced by Knight's vision, but Thompson insisted on complete control. At times, the writer and the artist were so exasperated with each other that their editor had to write to Knight urging him to stay calm. They would become strained, imagining slights and betrayals where once there had been a productive, even joyous exchange of ideas.

By the time Thompson moved to Rome in 1962, she clearly had lost any detachment in her relationship with her six-year-old alter ego. Thompson later told Stephen Silverman, "People make Eloise what they want her to be. So why should I come in with a Mexican hat and a dish of spaghetti? The book was out one day when Elsa Maxwell left a note that said, 'Dear Miss Thompson, How did you know I lived at the Plaza?' And that is exactly what has taken place . . . the idea of these people playing child!" She ultimately refused to allow *Eloise in Paris, Eloise in Moscow*, and *Eloise at Christmastime* to remain in print. She called the books "rotten" and said, "Eloise is all of us. She is not the girl with the hat on in Mexico."

In Rome, Thompson seemed ready to escape from her creation. "The story of why Eloise is under wraps is also the story of Kay Thompson," Rex Reed said. "Eloise is hiding because Kay is hiding." Just as *Eloise Takes a Bawth* was ready to go to press, Thompson pulled it from the publisher.

On the telephone now, without too much prompting, Thompson will still drop into the Eloise baby voice. She speaks to very few people. Hugh Martin is baffled that she does not return his calls. Liza Minnelli has hired a companion to live in the apartment with her godmother. When Minnelli is in New York, she usually stays elsewhere, according to a friend. Minnelli continues to be influenced by Thompson's recordings, and in 1970 they appeared together in Otto Preminger's film *Tell Me That You Love Me, Junie Moon*. Last year Eloise turned 40, but Thompson continues to freeze out Hilary Knight. "She is totally turned off by me. And I honestly can't tell you why," he says. Thompson is consumed by rage and tells friends that Knight continues to draw Eloise. "All he is entitled to is a share of the royalties," she told Rex Reed. "Eloise has another life, and I am planning it right now." It was to Rex Reed that Thompson gave her last formal interview, in 1972. She told Reed then that she was on the verge of publishing her fifth book, *Eloise's Wit and Observations*, but she never did. "My life has been *sic transit*, and now I'm sick of transit. No point in saving memorabilia— somebody always steals it. I own an orange tree here, a rattan chair there, and the rest is in storage in Rome."

All over America, *Eloise* continues to sell briskly. Last year almost 45,000 copies were sold. First-edition copies are rare, and cost almost $300. "They leave the store usually the day they come in," says Schuyler Hooke, the manager of Books of Wonder on West 18th Street in New York. Thompson continues to turn down all book and film offers, including one from Knopf for her memoirs and another from Francis Ford Coppola. Coppola talked to her on the telephone for hours about Eloise and finally realized, a friend said, that Thompson was hopelessly tangled with her creation. "Well, good-bye to both of you," he reportedly told her. Some years ago, Hilary Knight was swimming in the pool at a midtown New York Y.M.C.A. Suddenly he recognized his former publisher, Bob Bernstein. "You know, Hilary, you and Kay could have been millionaires," Bernstein told him.

For the 40th anniversary, there were special Eloise promotions, including an elaborate display in the windows of Books of Wonder. One night Schuyler Hooke was working late when the telephone rang. "A voice said, 'This is Kay Thompson.'" Miss Thompson was crisp: "'What is the title of the book in the window?' And I said, 'Well, it's *Eloise*.' And she shouted, 'That is incorrect! The title of the book is *Kay Thompson's Eloise*,'" Hooke remembered. Recently, my telephone rang as well. The voice on the other end was theatrical and enthusiastic, immediately recognizable as that of Kay Thompson. "I don't want my story to be told. I am too busy working. I have so many projects. I keep them all here in a trunk. But do call again. . . . Maybe someday I will talk."

ACKNOWLEDGMENTS

EDITOR	·	GRAYDON CARTER
V.F. BOOKS EDITOR	·	DAVID FRIEND
MANAGING EDITOR	·	CHRIS GARRETT
ASSISTANT EDITOR	·	ISABEL ASHTON, BECCA SOBEL

Editorial guidance was provided by Ella Banka, John Banta, Aimée Bell, Pat Craven, David Georgi, Dana Leshem, Mary Alice Miller, Cullen Murphy, Louisa Strauss, Julia Vitale, and Leora Yashari.

We gratefully acknowledge our partners at Penguin Books, including Kathryn Court, Patrick Nolan, Emily Murdock Baker, and Victoria Savanh; Louise Braverman and Chris Smith; Matt Giarratano, Norina Frabotta, Marlene De Jesus, and Katie Hurley; Roseanne Serra, Colin Webber, and Elke Sigal; and John Fagan.

And we sincerely thank Sarah Schmidt and Camille Zumwalt Coppola (*Vanity Fair* Business Office); Christopher P. Donnellan, Matthew Barad, and Lindsay Herron (Condé Nast Contracts and Rights Department); Vincent LaSpisa and our colleagues at Sabin, Bermant & Gould; and Andrew Wylie and Jeffrey Posternak of the Wylie Agency.

THE WRITERS

MARTIN AMIS (1949–), the British novelist and essayist, is known for his darkly satiric take on contemporary society. His most prominent works include *Money*; *Time's Arrow* (which was shortlisted for the Booker Prize); and the memoir *Experience* (for which he won the James Tait Black Memorial Prize).

LILI ANOLIK (1978–) is a contributing editor at *Vanity Fair*, whose journalism and essays have been featured in *Harper's*, *Esquire*, and *The Believer*. In 2015, she published her debut novel, *Dark Rooms*.

JAMES ATLAS (1949–) has been a *Vanity Fair* columnist, biographer (Delmore Schwartz, Saul Bellow), editor (*The New York Times Magazine*, HarperCollins, Penguin, Norton, Amazon), and book publisher. *My Life in the Middle Ages: A Survivor's Tale* is an adaptation of pieces he wrote for *The New Yorker* in the 1990s.

W. H. AUDEN (1907–1973), the Anglo-American poet, is considered one of the masters of twentieth-century verse. Although he would later excel as an essayist, playwright, and editor, Auden made his mark with his 1930 collection, *Poems*, which established his reputation as a distinguished voice in British letters. His eclogue, *The Age of Anxiety*, earned him the Pulitzer Prize for Poetry.

JAMES BALDWIN (1924–1987), the Harlem-born novelist, was also an essayist, playwright, poet, teacher, and civil rights activist. Baldwin produced groundbreaking works on race, sexuality, and the African-American experience, including *Go Tell It on the Mountain*, *Notes of a Native Son*, *Giovanni's Room* (the subject of Jacqueline Woodson's contribution, herein), *Another Country*, *The Fire Next Time*, and *If Beale Street Could Talk*.

ISHMAEL BEAH (1980–) was a child soldier during the civil war in Sierra Leone until his rescue by UNICEF in 1997. He is the author of a best-selling memoir, *A Long Way Gone*, as well as the novel *Radiance of Tomorrow*. Beah serves as a human-rights spokesperson and UNICEF ambassador.

SAUL BELLOW (1915–2005), the celebrated Canadian-born American novelist, used his fiction to address the complex intellectual and moral challenges of modern life. He was honored with three National Book Awards (for *The Adventures of Augie March*, *Herzog*, and *Mr. Sammler's Planet*), the Pulitzer Prize (for *Humboldt's Gift*), and, in 1976, the Nobel Prize in Literature.

A. SCOTT BERG (1949–), the esteemed biographer and *Vanity Fair* contributor, is the recipient of a National Book Award (*Max Perkins: Editor of Genius*), a Pulitzer Prize (*Lindbergh*), and a Guggenheim Fellowship. His most recent book, *Wilson*, examines the life of President Woodrow Wilson.

ELIZABETH BISHOP (1911–1979) was an acclaimed American poet whose precise, detailed verse was framed with a cool, remote objectivity. She served as America's Poet Laureate (at that time called "Consultant in Poetry to the Library of Congress"), receiving a Pulitzer Prize (for *Poems: North & South/A Cold Spring*) and a National Book Award (for *The Complete Poems*).

JUDY BLUME (1938–), noted for her young adult novels, including *Are You There God? It's Me, Margaret*, has been the recipient of numerous honors in the field of young people's literature. Blume, who also has four adult titles to her credit, is active with the National Coalition Against Censorship, defending her own books against sporadic bans and standing up for the freedom to read.

PATRICIA BOSWORTH (1933–) is a journalist and a contributing editor at *Vanity Fair*. A winner of the Front Page Award, she has taught at Columbia and Barnard. She is the author of biographies of Montgomery Clift, Diane Arbus, Marlon Brando, and Jane Fonda, as well as a book about her attorney father's defense of film directors and writers caught up in the Hollywood-blacklist purge during the Cold War.

PAUL BOWLES (1910–1999) gained renown as a composer for film and the theater. In 1947 he relocated from New York to Morocco, where he wrote his semi-autobiographical first novel, *The Sheltering Sky,* and continued his career as a travel writer, novelist, poet, folklorist, and translator.

MARIE BRENNER (1949–), a writer-at-large for *Vanity Fair* and a contributor since 1985, has written for *New York*, *The New Yorker*, *Vogue*, and *The New York Times Magazine*. Her *V.F.* article on tobacco-industry whistleblower Jeffrey Wigand was adapted into the Oscar-nominated movie *The Insider*. She is the author of a memoir, *Apples and Oranges*, along with other works.

JOSEPH BRODSKY (1940–1996), the Russian-American poet, was exiled from the Soviet Union in 1972, following internment in a labor camp. The author of nine volumes of verse, Brodsky was awarded the 1987 Nobel Prize in Literature and served as U.S. Poet Laureate in the 1990s.

MICHAEL CALLAHAN (1963–), a contributing editor at *Vanity Fair*, has been an editor at *Philadelphia* magazine, *Marie Claire,* and *Town & Country*. He is the author of the novel *Searching for Grace Kelly* and is finishing his second, *The Night She Won Miss America*.

TRUMAN CAPOTE (1924–1984) earned distinction for his fiction (*Other Voices, Other Rooms*; *Breakfast at Tiffany's*) and for helping develop the narrative nonfiction genre (*In Cold Blood*). An outsize presence on the New York social circuit, the Louisiana-born Capote fell out of favor after publishing a scathing, unfinished social satire in a series of pieces in *Esquire*—published posthumously as *Answered Prayers* (the subject of Sam Kashner's essay in this volume).

WILLA CATHER (1873–1947) was a novelist whose portrayals of the Nebraska plains secured her place as a canonical American writer. She published a dozen literary works during her lifetime, among them *Alexander's Bridge, O Pioneers!, My Ántonia*, and *Death Comes for the Archbishop*.

SUSAN CHEEVER (1943–) is a memoirist, biographer, and novelist. She has written fifteen books, including *E.E. Cummings: A Life,* a portion of which is adapted in these pages. For many years a member of the Yaddo artists' community, Cheever is the recipient of a Guggenheim Fellowship for Creative Arts and a Laurence L. & Thomas Winship/PEN New England Award.

AMY FINE COLLINS, a *Vanity Fair* special correspondent since 1993 (covering fashion, society, art, and design), is on the committee that selects the annual International Best-Dressed List. Collins is the author of the memoir *The God of Driving*.

E. E. CUMMINGS (1894–1962) was a *Vanity Fair* correspondent during the Jazz Age, often writing dispatches from Europe. In time, he would become one of America's best-known and revered poets, distinguished by his innovative use of grammar, punctuation, and typography.

CHRISTOPHER DICKEY (1951–), formerly of *The Washington Post* and *Newsweek*, is the foreign editor of *The Daily Beast*. A prolific journalist who has reported on politics, crime, and terrorism, Dickey is the author of *Expats* (about Westerners in the Muslim world), which has been described by the *Los Angeles Times* as one of the best travel books of all time.

JOAN DIDION (1934–), the essayist and novelist, has been widely celebrated for her collections *Slouching Towards Bethlehem* and *The White Album*, and for her memoirs, *The Year of Magical Thinking* and *Blue Nights*. *The New York Times*, acknowledging Didion's ability to translate nostalgia and loss into incisive prose—as well as her unsparing powers of observation—has called her "one of America's most distinctive and acute literary voices."

DOMINICK DUNNE (1925–2009) was a *Vanity Fair* special correspondent; a television and film producer (*The Boys in the Band, The Panic in Needle Park*); and a best-selling novelist who built his narratives around real-life scandals (*The Two Mrs. Grenvilles, A Season in Purgatory*). In 1984, in writing an account of the trial of his daughter Dominique's killer, he began a twenty-five-year tenure at *V.F.*, during which he specialized in coverage of crime and high-profile court cases.

JOHN GREGORY DUNNE (1932–2003), the journalist, novelist, screenwriter, and critic, contributed frequently to *The New York Review of Books*. He was an insightful observer of Hollywood and was known for his works of satire and analysis, his reflections on Irish-American life, and his collaborations with his wife, writer Joan Didion.

DAVE EGGERS (1970–) achieved acclaim for his best-selling memoir, *A Heartbreaking Work of Staggering Genius*, and as the founder and publisher of *McSweeney's* literary journal and publishing house. A prize-winning novelist, he is the author of *What is the What*, *Zeitoun*, and *The Circle*, among other works.

PAUL ELIE (1965–), formerly a senior editor at Farrar, Straus & Giroux, is a Wilbur Award–winning *Vanity Fair* contributor and a senior fellow at Georgetown's Berkley Center for Religion, Peace, and World Affairs. His book *The Life You Save May Be Your Own: An American Pilgrimage* examines the lives of four American Catholic writers—Flannery O'Connor, Walker Percy, Thomas Merton, and Dorothy Day.

NADINE GORDIMER (1923–2014), the South African author and member of the African National Congress, was recognized for her active opposition to apartheid. Her novels and short stories emphasized the destructive effects of racial segregation, and won her the Nobel Prize in Literature.

DAVID HALBERSTAM (1934–2007), who joined *Vanity Fair* as a contributor in 1994, conceived the magazine's New Establishment rankings, with *V.F.* editor Graydon Carter, and reported on his local firehouse in the aftermath of the 9/11 attacks. Halberstam's exceptional coverage of the Vietnam War, as a reporter at *The New York Times,* earned him a Pulitzer Prize. His books *The Best and the Brightest* and *The Powers That Be* are considered seminal works on American authority, power, and influence.

ROBERT HARRIS (1957–), the British journalist, columnist, and author of best-selling historical fiction, has written about subjects as diverse as the Roman Empire, World War II, and the global financial markets. Many of his works have been adapted for television and cinema.

ERNEST HEMINGWAY (1899–1961), the novelist, short-story writer, and correspondent, emerged from Paris's expatriate community in the 1920s to become one of the giants of twentieth-century prose, earning the Nobel Prize in Literature. Among his most enduring works are *The Sun Also Rises*, *A Farewell to Arms, For Whom the Bell Tolls*, and *The Old Man and the Sea.*

CHRISTOPHER HITCHENS (1949–2011), the British-American journalist, critic, essayist, and self-described contrarian, was a *Vanity Fair* columnist for two decades. His books include *God Is Not Great,* the memoir *Hitch-22*, and a shelf of essay collections featuring memorable pieces from publications such as *The Atlantic, Harper's, New Statesman*, *Slate*, and *Vanity Fair.*

LAURA Z. HOBSON (1900–1986) received widespread acclaim for her novel *Gentleman's Agreement*, a scathing depiction of anti-Semitism in America, which became the basis for the film that won the 1947 Best Picture Oscar. The essay in this volume was adapted from her memoir, *Laura Z: A Life.*

MIKE HOGAN (1975–), who got his start as the assistant to Dominick Dunne's editor, is *Vanity Fair*'s digital director, overseeing web properties, social media, and video. In between, he served as executive entertainment editor for the *Huffington Post* and editor in chief of *Moviefone*. Hogan writes regularly about entertainment and politics for VF.com and cohosts *Little Gold Men*, a podcast dedicated to obsessively analyzing Hollywood's awards season.

NICK HORNBY (1957–), the British novelist, essayist, and Oscar-nominated screenwriter (*An Education, Brooklyn*) has gained prominence through his comedic and semi-autobiographical fiction (*High Fidelity, About A Boy)*, which draw richly from the spheres of pop culture, music, and sports.

LAURA JACOBS (1956–) has been a *Vanity Fair* contributing editor for twenty-one years, focusing on fashion, the arts, and all aspects of American culture. The former editor of *Stagebill*, she writes dance criticism for *The New Criterion*, books on dance and couture, and is the author of the novels *Women About Town* and *The Bird Catcher*.

WARD JUST (1935–), who, as a journalist, covered conflicts in Southeast Asia, is best known as a novelist and short-story writer. His most well-regarded books include *A Family Trust*, *Echo House*, *An Unfinished Season*, *Exiles in the Garden*, and *American Romantic*.

SAM KASHNER (1954–) is among *Vanity Fair*'s most versatile and prolific contributors. His stories have explored both celebrated and lesser-known figures in popular culture. A chronicler of the Beat scene (described in his book *When I Was Cool*), Kashner has authored or co-authored biographies of Oscar Levant, Elizabeth Taylor, and Richard Burton, along with the novel *Sinatraland*.

JACK KEROUAC (1922–1969) was the vagabond voice of rebellious America in the 1950s. His most widely praised work, the semi-autobiographical *On the Road*, captured the outlaw essence of the Beat generation.

STIEG LARSSON (1954–2004) was a Swedish novelist and crusading political reporter, who gained global renown for his dark, posthumously published Millennium trilogy, beginning with *The Girl with the Dragon Tattoo*.

JOHN LEONARD (1939–2008), a cultural and literary critic for *The New York Times*, *Life*, *New York*, *Harper's*, and other publications, also served as an editor at *The New York Times Book Review* and *The Nation*. Leonard championed aspiring authors, among them Gabriel García Márquez and Toni Morrison, both of whom are the subjects of essays in this volume.

PRIMO LEVI (1919–1987) was an Italian chemist-cum-writer who, in memoir and fiction, bore witness to the horrors of the Holocaust and his time at the Auschwitz death camp. The Royal Institution of Great Britain named Levi's *The Periodic Table* the best science book ever written.

MICHAEL LEWIS (1960–) is a writer and contributor to *Vanity Fair*, whose work humanizes the worlds of power and finance. His *V.F.* articles have covered topics as diverse as the European economic crisis and President Barack Obama's decision-making process. Lewis's books include *Liar's Poker*, *The New New*

Thing, and *Flash Boys*; three of his titles—*Moneyball*, *The Blind Side*, and *The Big Short*—became Oscar-nominated films.

CLARE BOOTHE LUCE (1903–1987), a *Vanity Fair* editor in the 1930s, helped recast *Life* as a weekly picture magazine, wrote the Broadway hit *The Women* and the script for *Come to the Stable*, which earned her an Oscar nomination for Best Screenplay. A force in Republican Party politics and American diplomacy, Luce served in the U.S. Congress and as ambassador to Italy, advising presidents Eisenhower, Kennedy, Nixon, Ford, and Reagan.

NAGUIB MAHFOUZ (1911–2006), the Egyptian civil servant turned author, critiqued contemporary Egyptian society in his novels, short stories, plays, and screenplays. Mahfouz was the first writer from the Arab world to be awarded the Nobel Prize in Literature.

NORMAN MAILER (1923–2007), a towering, bellicose presence in twentieth-century fiction and journalism, made his literary debut with *The Naked and the Dead*, and twice won the Pulitzer Prize (*The Armies of the Night*, *The Executioner's Song*) along with two National Book Awards. Mailer helped launch *The Village Voice*; directed films; wrote for *Vanity Fair* and other magazines, reporting on everything from civil unrest to the moon landing; and ran, unsuccessfully, to be mayor of New York City.

GABRIEL GARCÍA MÁRQUEZ (1927–2014), the Colombian journalist and screenwriter, became Latin America's most influential novelist. He pioneered magical realism in tour de force works such as *One Hundred Years of Solitude* and *Love in the Time of Cholera*, earning the Nobel Prize in Literature.

CORMAC McCARTHY (1933–) has won the National Book Award for Fiction (*All the Pretty Horses*), a Pulitzer Prize (*The Road*), a Rockefeller grant, a Guggenheim Fellowship, and a MacArthur "genius grant." Four of his works—*The Road*, *All the Pretty Horses*, *Child of God*, and *No Country for Old Men*—have been adapted for the screen, the latter receiving the 2007 Academy Award for Best Picture.

MARY McCARTHY (1912–1989) was an author, critic, and outspoken political activist. Her novel *The Group* became a national sensation, using the intersecting lives of eight Vassar graduates to illustrate the social, familial, and sexual issues affecting many American women.

JAY McINERNEY (1955–), the writer and essayist, first gained prominence for his novel *Bright Lights, Big City*. He would go on to write, among other works,

Brightness Falls, Model Behavior, and *The Good Life*. A sometime contributor to *Vanity Fair*, McInerney is the wine critic at *Town & Country*.

SONNY MEHTA (1942–), the India-born, British-educated American publishing eminence—known for his keen literary and commercial instincts—is the chairman of the Knopf Doubleday Publishing Group and the editor-in-chief of Alfred A. Knopf, which recently celebrated its 100th anniversary.

GRACE METALIOUS (1924–1964), a housewife who tried her hand at fiction, riveted America with her scandalous bestseller, *Peyton Place* (later a film and TV's first prime-time soap opera), which explored the gossip, sex, avarice, and hypocrisy in small-town New England.

ARTHUR MILLER (1915–2005) started his literary career with the novel *Focus* (the subject of his essay republished in this collection) and went on to become a playwright without peer. Miller, whose works include *The Crucible, A View From the Bridge,* and *After the Fall,* won a Pulitzer Prize for *Death of a Salesman.* An occasional director, he also wrote short stories, essays, and the screenplay for *The Misfits,* which starred his then wife, Marilyn Monroe.

MARIANNE MOORE (1887–1972) emerged as a Modernist poet on the eve of the 1920s and was eventually honored with a National Book Award, a Pulitzer Prize, and poetry's prestigious Bollingen Prize. Among her closest confidantes was poet Elizabeth Bishop, who profiles Moore, her mentor, in this anthology.

WILLIE MORRIS (1934–1999), at age thirty-two, became the youngest editor to run *Harper's* magazine. A novelist, essayist, and memoirist (*North Toward Home*), Morris would resettle in his native Mississippi, focusing his attention on themes of the American South.

TONI MORRISON (1931–) has transformed American perceptions about race and gender through her novels, criticism, commentary, and her years as an educator. The recipient of the Nobel Prize in Literature, Morrison is renowned for classics such as *Song of Solomon* (winner of the National Book Critics Circle Award) and *Beloved* (which won the Pulitzer Prize and, in 2011, was named the best work of American fiction of the last twenty-five years by *The New York Times Book Review*).

DOROTHY PARKER (1893–1967) was an American poet, essayist, and humorist. Her first published work—a poem she sent to *Vanity Fair* in 1914, when she was twenty-one—would lead to positions as a lowly caption writer at *Vogue* and as a *V.F.* columnist, house poet, and drama critic. A founding member of the Algonquin Round Table and one of the great wits of the Jazz Age, she also turned her talents to journalism, fiction, and screenwriting.

JAMES PATTERSON (1947–) is among the most prolific of all contemporary novelists, relying, in part, on the marketing savvy he acquired during his days heading up the J. Walter Thompson advertising firm. With a prodigious output of detective thrillers, mysteries, romance novels, and works of nonfiction (many of them co-authored), he is the first writer to place simultaneous titles atop the adult *and* children's *New York Times* best-seller list.

EVGENIA PERETZ (1969–), a *Vanity Fair* contributing editor, has covered politics, media, and the arts; written major profiles on celebrated figures; and delved into eccentric subcultures. Also a screenwriter, Peretz co-wrote the film *Our Idiot Brother.*

REYNOLDS PRICE (1933–2011), one of the most important literary voices of the American South, lived nearly all of his life in North Carolina. Price, who taught writing at Duke University for more than half a century, captured the regional culture and dialect in his novels, stories, and poems, winning the National Book Critics Circle Award for his novel *Kate Vaiden.*

TODD S. PURDUM (1959–) joined *Vanity Fair* as its national editor in 2006, after twenty-three years at *The New York Times.* The author of *An Idea Whose Time Has Come: Two Presidents, Two Parties, and the Battle for the Civil Rights Act of 1964,* he is completing a biography of Rogers and Hammerstein, the musical-theater writing team. Purdum now serves as a contributing editor at *V.F.* and a senior writer at *Politico.*

SALMAN RUSHDIE (1947–) is a British-Indian novelist whose works include *Midnight's Children* (which earned him the Booker Prize) and *The Satanic Verses,* which prompted worldwide geopolitical and religious reaction (a subject explored in these pages by Martin Amis). Rushdie was knighted by Queen Elizabeth for his services to literature.

WOLE SOYINKA (1934–) is a Nigerian playwright, poet, and political activist whose works range from lighthearted satire to philosophical analyses of the African experience. Winner of the Nobel Prize in Literature, Soyinka is the first sub-Saharan African to be so honored.

ROGER STRAUS (1917–2004) co-founded the fabled Farrar, Straus & Giroux publishing house. Under Straus's leadership, FSG developed an international roster of award-winning writers of fiction, nonfiction, and poetry, who, all told, have accounted for twenty-two Nobel Prizes in Literature.

WILLIAM STYRON (1925–2006) was an American novelist whose books probe subjects ranging from family dynamics (*Lie Down in Darkness*), to slavery (*The Confessions of Nat Turner*, which earned a Pulitzer Prize), to the Holocaust (*Sophie's Choice*, which earned a National Book Award). Styron addressed his own struggles with depression in *Darkness Visible*, a book that grew out of a National Magazine Award–winning *Vanity Fair* essay, reproduced here.

JACQUELINE SUSANN (1918–1974) abandoned acting to write popular, sin-soaked fiction that served as a send-up of American celebrity and excess. She would become the first novelist to publish three No. 1 *New York Times* best-sellers: *The Valley of the Dolls*, *The Love Machine*, and *Once Is Not Enough*.

DONNA TARTT (1963–), the novelist and short-story writer, is the author of *The Secret History*, *The Little Friend*, and *The Goldfinch*, which was awarded the Pulitzer Prize for fiction.

JOSEPHINE TEY (1896–1952) was the pen name of the Scottish-born mystery writer and playwright Elizabeth MacKintosh, who also went by the pseudonym Gordon Daviot. Tey, especially beloved for her Miss Pym and Alan Grant novels, achieved distinction for breaking away from the customary standards of the crime and mystery genres.

KAY THOMPSON (1909–1998), who began her career as a singer-songwriter, arranger, and actress (appearing most notably in the screen adaptation of the musical *Funny Face*), would partner with illustrator Hilary Knight to create the iconic children's book series that followed the escapades of Eloise, a girl living in Manhattan's Plaza Hotel.

ANNE TYLER (1941–) is an American novelist (*Celestial Navigation, Dinner at the Homesick Restaurant*), whose work—often oriented around everyday existence, familial life, and her city of residence, Baltimore—has earned her a National Book Critics Circle Award (*The Accidental Tourist*) and a Pulitzer Prize (*Breathing Lessons*).

EUDORA WELTY (1909–2001), a Depression-era photographer for the Works Progress Administration, gained fame as a Pulitzer Prize–winning novelist (*The*

Optimist's Daughter) and master of the short story, known for her depictions of the American South. Three years before her death, Welty became the first living writer to be inducted into the Library of America series of collected works.

FRANCIS WHEEN (1957–) is a British journalist, columnist, biographer (*Karl Marx: A Life*), and broadcaster, who has written for—or served as editor at—the *New Statesman*, the *Guardian*, the *Evening Standard,* and *Private Eye*. Wheen is the author of the celebrated collection *Hoo-hahs and Passing Frenzies: Collected Journalism, 1991–2001*, winner of the George Orwell Prize.

JAMES WOLCOTT (1952–) is one of America's foremost culture critics and columnists, having written for *Vanity Fair* since 1983. Among other honors, he has received a National Magazine Award for reviews and criticism as well as a PEN Award for the art of the essay. Wolcott is the author of *The Catsitters,* a novel; the political critique *Attack Poodles and Other Media Mutants*; and the much-heralded memoir *Lucking Out*.

TOM WOLFE (1931–) helped shape the New Journalism movement in the 1960s, bringing a novelistic perspective to nonfiction. His groundbreaking essays for *New York* and *Esquire* became best-selling collections, along with his books *The Electric Kool-Aid Acid Test* and *Radical Chic & Mau-Mauing the Flak Catchers*. Wolfe's classic study of astronauts and test pilots, *The Right Stuff,* won the National Book Award; his dispatches on '80s greed, serialized in *Rolling Stone*, became the basis of *The Bonfire of the Vanities*.

MEG WOLITZER (1959–) is a short-story writer and author of novels for young adults (*Belzhar*); middle schoolers (*The Fingertips of Duncan Dorfman*); and adults (*The Interestings, The Uncoupling, The Ten-Year Nap, The Position,* and *The Wife*).

JACQUELINE WOODSON (1963–), recently won the National Book Award for *Brown Girl Dreaming*, a memoir in verse. She is the recipient of numerous citations for her children's and young adult works, including the Coretta Scott King Book Award for *Miracle's Boys*, the Jane Addams Children's Book Award for *Each Kindness*, and four Newbery Honors. Woodson, the author of the adult title *Another Brooklyn*, was also named the Young People's Poet Laureate by the Poetry Foundation.

RICHARD B. WOODWARD (1953–), a journalist and critic specializing in photography and art, writes frequently for *The New York Times* and *The Wall Street Journal*, among other publications. His essays have appeared in some twenty exhibition catalogues and scholarly monographs.